THE LIFE AND WORK OF SIGMUND FREUD

VOLUME III

1919–1939

THE LAST PHASE

Books by Ernest Jones

DAS PROBLEM DES HAMLET

HAMLET AND OEDIPUS

PAPERS ON PSYCHO-ANALYSIS
(5 volumes)

TREATMENT OF THE NEUROSES

DER ALPTRAUM

PSYCHO-ANALYSIS AND THE WAR NEUROSES
(with Abraham, Ferenczi and Simmel)

ESSAYS IN APPLIED PSYCHO-ANALYSIS
(2 volumes)

HOW THE MIND WORKS
(with Cyril Burt)

ZUR PSYCHOANALYSE DER CHRISTLICHEN RELIGION

ON THE NIGHTMARE

WHAT IS PSYCHO-ANALYSIS

THE LIFE AND WORK OF SIGMUND FREUD
(Volumes I and II)

SIGMUND FREUD: FOUR CENTENARY ADDRESSES

Translations

CONTRIBUTIONS TO PSYCHO-ANALYSIS
by Sandor Ferenczi, M.D.

The Life and Work of

SIGMUND

FREUD

By Ernest Jones, M.D.

VOLUME

3

The Last Phase

1919-1939

New York

BASIC BOOKS, INC.

Publishers

To Anna Freud,

TRUE DAUGHTER OF AN IMMORTAL SIRE

Contents

Illustrations

following page 238

Sigmund Freud, 1922, age 66

Freud with the Committee, Berlin, 1922

Freud with grandsons Heinerle and Ernstl, Hamburg, 1922

Freud with grandson Stephen Gabriel, Berlin, 1922

Freud with his daughter Anna, Tegelsee, 1929

Freud in Berchtesgaden, 1929

Roof garden in Paris, June 5, 1938. Freud, his wife, and son Ernst

Driving through London, June 6, 1938

Arrival at Elsworthy Road, June 6, 1938

Reading manuscript of *An Outline of Psychoanalysis*, July, 1938

Garden at 20 Maresfield Gardens

Study at 20 Maresfield Gardens

Freud with his wife, 1939

Preface

THIS VOLUME COMPLETES THE TRILOGY OF MY ACCOUNT OF FREUD'S life and work.

Freud retained his stature to the end. Two features in particular exemplified it during this last phase of his life. One was the truly astonishing fresh outburst of original ideas he produced in those years, just when it was thought he had rounded off his life's work. These ideas effected a revolution in both the theory and the practice of psychoanalysis, and they furnished stimuli which are still bringing about fruitful results. The other was the dauntless fortitude with which he endured the political and financial dangers that threatened to engulf both him and his work, the loss of several of those dear to him, and above all the cruel tortures of the many years of suffering from the devouring cancer that ultimately killed him.

I cannot agree with those biographers who write as if their subject had no body or only one that functioned so perfectly as not to be worth mentioning. On the contrary, I am sure that the relation between body and mind constitute an important part of the whole personality, and I have therefore not pandered to the squeamishness of any readers by omitting some account, however brief, of Freud's bodily misfortunes. The extract from the surgical notes of an unusual clinical case, in Appendix B is, of course, intended only for medical readers.

It would be invidious to select any period when Freud's mental powers could be said to be at their highest level, but one might perhaps suggest that different aspects of those powers were more prominent at one time, and others at another. There was the tireless concentration of the patient investigator in the first period; then the astounding courage of the pioneer that broke through barriers that had for centuries baulked the best thinkers; the critical judgment and wide range of his most prolific period in the years of maturity; followed by the bold imaginative visions of the final period—the one we are as yet least in a position truly to evaluate.

I have related at some length the episode of Otto Rank's leaving Freud because it furnishes the most complete refutation of the myth, still current, of Freud's being a dictatorial person who would not tolerate on the part of his followers the least departure from his own ideas, and who at once drove them out from his circle. In that chapter it is recorded how pleased Freud was on hearing of Rank's original and startling ideas, how he was even prepared to consider remodeling his own theories in the light of them, and what astonishing efforts he made to retain Rank's cooperation. The whole picture is the reverse of that often portrayed. I could have demonstrated the same thesis from my own experience. I differed completely from Freud in many matters, some of which he regarded as fundamental: on Lamarckism, telepathy, child analysis, lay analysis, the "death instinct," the origin of anxiety, not to mention the identity of Shakespeare. They led to many arguments, and to his expressing regret that we differed, but never to any marring of our personal friendship.

In addition to the material mentioned in earlier Prefaces, I have had sent me from all over the world much information and an enormous number of Freud's letters; as is well-known, he was a prolific and punctilious correspondent. The largest collections of these are the letters (for the most part on both sides) between Freud and Franz Alexander, Lou Andreas-Salomé, Marie Bonaparte (Princess George of Greece), Joan Riviere, Eduardo Weiss, Arnold Zweig and Stefan Zweig. To those who have placed them at my disposal (including two executors) I owe most grateful thanks. All the members of the Freud family, in Europe and America, have been uniformly cooperative and helpful. Among the many others who have helped me in various ways I would specially mention Kurt Eissler, Eduard Hitschmann, Joan Riviere, James Strachey and Alfred Winterstein. Mrs. Wittels sent me Freud's long letter, only part of which had been published, on her husband's biography of him, with all the corrections of misstatements it contains.

Max Schur deserves my very special thanks. He not only procured the Pichler notes of the surgical treatment of Freud's case over sixteen years, supervising moreover the laborious translation of them which Lajos Levy so very kindly made, but he also composed for my use an essay of forty pages describing in detail the course of Freud's illnesses and his heroic behavior during those periods.

Mrs. Vacey, whose services grants from the Bollingen Foundation and the Foundations Fund for Research in Psychiatry enabled me to enlist, has not only carried out admirable research work, but also made a number of useful suggestions.

What I cannot express in words is the debt I owe to my dear wife's precious devotion and cooperation in my work, and her ceaseless encouragement. I would also mention that my daughter Nesta has mended my deficiencies in style and grammar.

Chronology

January 1919—*Internationaler Psycho-analytischer Verlag* founded.

Spring 1919—*Beyond the Pleasure Principle* begun.

May 1919—*Group Psychology* drafted.

September 1919—Ferenczi and Ernest Jones visit Freud.

September 1919—Eitingon joins "Committee."

January 1920—Death of Anton von Freund.

January 1920—Death of Freud's daughter Sophie.

January 1920—*International Journal of Psycho-Analysis* founded.

February 1920—Berlin Policlinic founded.

February 1920—Wagner-Jauregg investigation.

May 1920—*Beyond the Pleasure Principle* finished.

September 1920—Freud attends Hague Congress.

December 1920—*Group Psychology* finished.

July 1921—Brill visits Freud.

September 1921—Harz tour with "Committee."

May 1922—Vienna Clinic founded.

June 1922—Schnitzler visits Freud.

September 1922—Freud attends Berlin Congress.

April 1923—First operation for cancer.

April 1923—*Ego and Id* published.

June 1923—Death of Freud's grandson Heinz.

October 1923—Radical operation.

Summer 1924—*Gesammelte Schriften* begun.

August 1924—Rank breaks with Freud.

June 1925—Death of Breuer.

July 1925—Anna Freud joins "Committee."

July 1925—*Inhibition, Symptom and Anxiety* written.

September 1925—*Autobiography* written.

December 1925—Death of Karl Abraham.

May 1926—Seventieth birthday.

June 1926—Reik persecution. *Lay Analysis* written.

September 1926—London Clinic founded.

December 1926—Einstein visits Freud in Berlin.

August 1927—*The Future of an Illusion* written.

September 1927—Dissolution of "Committee."

August 1928—Freud consults Schroeder in Berlin.

July 1929—*Civilization and its Discontents* written.

Autumn 1929—Ferenczi withdraws from Freud.

Summer 1930—Last holiday from Vienna.

August 1930—Goethe prize.

September 1930—Death of Freud's mother.

September 1930—Book on President Wilson written.

May 1931—Seventy-fifth birthday.

June 1931—Threat of cancerous recurrence.

October 1931—Ceremony at birthplace in Freiberg.

July 1932—*New Introductory Lectures* written.

September 1932—*Why War?* written with Einstein.

September 1932—International Association assumes responsibility for *Verlag*.

October 1932—Hanns Sachs leaves Europe.

May 1933—Death of Sandor Ferenczi

May 1933—Freud's books burned in Berlin.

December 1933—Max Eitingon leaves Europe.

Summer 1934—*Moses and Monotheism* written.

March 1936—*Verlag* stock of books confiscated in Leipzig.

May 1936—Eightieth birthday. Thomas Mann's address. Fellowship of Royal Society and other honors.

July 1936—First recurrence of cancer.

September 1936—Golden wedding.

January 1937—Fliess correspondence discovered.

March 1938—Nazi invasion. Decision to leave Vienna.

June 1938—Journey to London.

August 1938—*Moses and Monotheism* published.

September 1938—Last operation.

February 1939—Inoperable recurrence of cancer.

September 23, 1939—Death.

He wakes or sleeps with the enduring dead.

ADONAIS

1

PART

LIFE

1

Reunion
(1919-1920)

THE YEARS SUCCEEDING THE WORLD WAR WERE EXTREMELY HARD. EVERY-thing had come to a standstill in Vienna and life there was scarcely bearable. The monotonous diet of thin vegetable soup was far from being adequately nourishing and the pangs of hunger were continuous. The winters of 1918-19 and 1919-20 were the worst of all, with their completely unheated rooms and feeble illumination. It needed a tough spirit to endure sitting still and treating patients for hour after hour in that deadly cold, even if equipped with an overcoat and thick gloves. Then in the evening Freud had his correspondence to answer with his half-frozen fingers, numerous proofs to correct of new editions of his books and of the periodicals for which he felt responsible. Yet somehow there was energy left to contemplate new ideas and produce further works.

To the inevitable hardships there were added many sources of anxiety. It was months before any news could be had of Freud's eldest son who was a prisoner of war in Italy. For a couple of years he was concerned about his sons' chances of finding work—one was still a student—and he had to help not only them but also his son-in-law in Hamburg besides other members of his family and various friends. The economic situation in Austria was as bleak as it could be, and the future prospects just as dark. Freud's own financial position was very serious and its future still more precarious. His earnings could not keep pace with the steady rise in prices, and he was forced to live on his savings. In October, 1919, he estimated that these would last another eighteen months, but that was on the optimistic assumption that the inflation would not increase.[1] Actually he lost all his savings, amounting to 150,000 Crowns (then worth $29,000.00) and so had nothing left for his old age.[2] But his chief anxiety concerned his wife's future, on the expectation that she would survive him—as she did. He had insured his life on her behalf for 100,000 Crowns ($19,500.00). He had felt satisfied on that score, but through the inflation this was soon not enough to pay a cab fare.[3]

It soon became plain that the only hope of keeping his head above water lay in the possibility of acquiring American or English patients who would pay in their relatively unimpaired currency. Early in October, 1919, a London physician, Dr. David Forsyth, came for seven weeks to learn something of psychoanalysis. Freud welcomed him, not only as the first swallow, but also for his distinguished personality which made a considerable impression on him. Then in that November I induced an American dentist who had sought my help to brave the rigors of life in Vienna. He was to pay the low fee of $5.00 but Freud commented it was right he should pay only half fees since he was only half American; the other half was a Hungarian Jew.[4] In the following March I was able to send him an Englishman who paid a guinea fee. Freud told me that without these two patients he could not make ends meet.[5] And he asked Ferenczi: "What would happen to me if Jones were not able to send me any more patients?"[6] At the end of that year, however, the flow became continuous. Budding analysts from England, and later from America, came to learn his technique, and he had more than enough to do. But this led to another trouble. Freud did not find it easy to follow the differing accents and he complained bitterly that English was not spoken with the clear enunciation to which he was accustomed with Continentals. After six hours' effort to follow such patients he was completely exhausted.[7]

Having as yet no foreign currency at his disposal, Freud had to borrow 2,000 Marks ($476.00) from Max Eitingon to pay the expenses of his stay at Badersee and of the journey to Berlin and Hamburg in September, 1919; six months later, however, he was able to repay it.[8] Then three months later he was surprised by a letter announcing that Eitingon had sent 3,000 Swedish Crowns ($780.00) to his bank in the event of his being short of money. Freud read the letter at the dinner table and there was an interesting response from the family. The two sons present found the news very satisfactory, but his wife and daughter were furious at the implied slight cast on his capacity to provide for them. The latter even declared she would punish Eitingon by relinquishing her plan of visiting him in Berlin that Christmas; as it turned out the visit proved impossible because of the absence of trains. So Freud telegraphed to Eitingon that he should cancel the order at the bank. In thanking him he assured him that he would not hesitate to call on him were he in need and that he was grateful to have such a friend.[9] He took the precaution, however, of converting into Marks the Austrian Crowns he still possessed, confident that German Marks would be as little likely to collapse as Germany itself.[10] A few months later he was sure that their value would go up,[11] an expectation doomed before long to bitter disappointment.

Freud was concerned to help not only his immediate family and friends but also, as far as he could, his compatriots in their suffering. A group of American physicians had donated the equivalent of 3,000,000 Crowns ($608,000.) to establish a convalescent home for children in Vienna and had, as he put it, enough confidence in him to ask him by cable to serve on the committee of administration; the other members were the Bürgermeister of Vienna; the Dean of the Medical Faculty; Tandler, the Under-Secretary of the Ministry of Health; and the pediatrist Professor von Pirquet.[12] It was a long time since he had had anything to do with such high officials. Then a few weeks later his brother-in-law, Eli Bernays, sent from New York in his wife's name another million Crowns to the same fund.[13]

In spite of several offers he would not for a moment think seriously of emigrating. To my urging him to come to England he gave the answer, as he was to later in 1938: "I will stay at my post as long as I reasonably can." [14] Just before that, however, he had evidently been toying with the idea of England as a last resort, since he wrote to Eitingon as follows: "I have engaged a teacher today so as to get my English polished up. The situation here is hopeless and will doubtless remain so. I believe that England will be willing to allow former enemies to enter by the time I have spent the last of my savings, in about 18 months from now. My two brothers already rest in English soil; perhaps I shall also find room there." [15] In the end he did.

His faith in England's generosity proved to be justified. But had he been wise to stay in Vienna at the very beginning of his medical career? He raised that question in a letter to Sandor Ferenczi: "Thirty-three years ago today I was facing as a newly-qualified physician an unknown future with the resolve to go to America if the three months for which my reserves could last did not produce something very hopeful. Would it not have been better on the whole had fate not smiled so friendlily on me at that time? Whatever else I may have attained since then I have not attained security. Still I shall not be able to carry out much more than another third of a century's hard work with human beings and demons." [16]

A little later an ex-patient of Freud's announced that her brother was emigrating from The Hague to Palestine and that his house could be transferred to Freud if he wished to settle in Holland.[17] This offer also was declined with thanks. Nor did he accept an invitation to give a course of lectures in Holland that autumn.[18]

The cataclysmic events that had passed over Europe in those two years, and most of all over Austria, evoked in Freud a mood of helpless but cheerful resignation. The following passages are from letters written within a couple of weeks of each other. In one of the first letters I got after the war he wrote: "You shall hear no complaints. I am still upright and hold myself not responsible for any part of the world's nonsense." [19] To Ferenczi, who was counting on some official recognition in Budapest, he wrote at the same time: "Keep a reserved attitude. We are not suited to any kind of official existence, and we need independence in all respects. Perhaps we have reason to say: God protect us from our friends. So far we have dealt successfully with our enemies. Moreover, there is such a thing as a future, in which we shall again find some place. We are and must remain far from any tendentiousness except for the one aim of investigating and helping." [20] Eitingon, in congratulating him on his birthday, had expressed the hope of better times. Freud echoed this, but added: "I cannot deny that in the cheerful pessimism that was always characteristic of me the second element occasionally becomes the more prominent one. Of one's cares the easiest to mention is renunciation of any summer holiday; this year there will no longer be any Hungary for us. I expect the next few months will be full of dramatic movement. We are no onlookers, however, nor actors or really even a chorus, but merely victims." [21]

In that same month I suggested that if I could not get permission to enter Austria we might perhaps meet somewhere else. He correctly inferred from my making such a suggestion that I could not imagine the conditions in Vienna and the utter impossibility of traveling abroad. He then gave me news of his wife's serious illness, of Anton von Freund's days being numbered and so on, and he continued: "I can't remember a time of my life when my horizon was so dark or if so I was younger then and not vexed by the ailments of beginning old age. I know you had a bad time and bitter experiences yourself and feel extremely sorry that I have nothing better to report and no consolation to offer. When we meet, as I trust we shall in this year, you will find I am still unshaken and up to every emergency, but it is so only in sentiment, my judgement is on the side of pessimism. . . . We are living through a bad time, but science is a mighty power to stiffen one's neck. Take my best love and send your better news to your old friend Freud." [22]

The last consideration, the consolation of scientific work, was well expressed by Ferenczi in a letter to Freud written in the month after the collapse of the Central Powers, and I feel sure the sentiments in it would also have been Freud's. "The only thing that has kept up my spirits in these days, and will continue to do so, is the optimism I owe to the circumstance of being a collaborator in psychoanalysis, a school of thought [a] which undoubtedly has a future. Regarded *sub specie* psychoanalysis, the recent frightful events fall into place as merely episodes in a still very primitive social organization. And even if our hopes deceive us and mankind remain the victim of their unconscious to the very end, still we have been vouchsafed a glimpse behind the scenes, and knowledge of the truth can compensate us for much we are deprived of and also for much suffering." [23]

In 1917 Freud had reached the nadir of his expectations about the future of his life's work. After the defection of Alfred Adler, Wilhelm Stekel and the Swiss he felt he could almost count on the fingers of one hand the number of adherents in the whole world whom he could trust to further his work in the way he would wish. But the events of 1918—the Hungarian von Freund's magnificent donation toward the founding of the private publishing house, the *Internationaler Psychoanalytischer Verlag*, which began its existence the following year, and the enthusiastic official reception of his work at the Budapest Congress in the September of that year—had revived his spirits. In that autumn Freud considered it certain that Budapest would be the main center for psychoanalytic work. The Hungarian Government had promised to organize a Psychoanalytical Institute there and to arrange for lectures on the subject to be given at a special Department in the University. The fund that von Freund was donating was in Budapest, and Rank spent some months there organizing with him and Ferenczi the establishment of the new

[a] *Geistesrichtung.*

publishing house. Indeed, it looked as if Rank would have to reside there permanently, although Freud was averse to that plan which would have meant dispensing with Rank's valuable editorial and secretarial help in Vienna.

But two events changed all these plans. The political changes at the end of the war, whereby Hungary became quite independent of Austria and soon after came under a Bolshevist regime, cut off that country from its previous close contact, and there would be months when no letter could pass between Budapest and Vienna. The availability of the fund thus became more than doubtful. Then there was von Freund's fatal illness, of which some account will be given presently.

After depicting the background of Freud's life in Vienna in the years immediately after the great World War, and before considering it in more detail, it will be well to mention at the outset the main matters in which his interest and emotions were concerned in those years.

First of all there naturally came his concern with his family. Here there were three happy events to record. On the first day of 1919 Freud announced that his daughter Sophie had given birth to a second grandchild, Heinz Rudolf[24]—the boy who was to bring Freud some of the greatest happiness and the greatest pain in his life. At the end of the year, on December 7, Freud's eldest son, Martin, married Esti Drucker in Vienna, and a few months later, on May 18, 1920, his youngest son, Ernst, married Lucie Brasch in Berlin. Anna and her mother attended the wedding in Berlin. Ernst, who had the family name of "the lucky child," was lucky here also, and his marriage proved to be as happy as his parents'. Five of Freud's children were now married and out in the world.

In March, 1919, Martha Freud was struck down with a severe influenzal pneumonia from which she took some months to recover. Then in the early days of the following year came the hardest blow Freud had yet suffered in his life, the death, from the same disease, of his second daughter, Sophie. Only a few days before he had been at the death bed of his young friend, Anton von Freund, to whom he had been greatly attached.

Next in importance to these personal experiences would come Freud's interest in the novel conception of the mind with which he was to startle the world of psychologists. It must have occupied his deepest thoughts.

A more mundane interest, one which was to concern Freud extensively for many years, was the founding of a private publishing house, which I shall simply call the *Verlag*, in January, 1919. These two last topics will be discussed at some length later.

Finally, there were the happenings that gave this chapter its title, the reunion with his friends and colleagues. Of the "Committee," Otto Rank was the first to return to Vienna at the close of the war, and he was of the greatest assistance to Freud's literary enterprises in these years. Eitingon, who was not yet a member of the Committee, visited Freud during his holiday in August, 1919, and Freud met him and Karl Abraham in Berlin a couple of weeks later. Ferenczi and I visited Freud in Vienna together in September. Hanns Sachs was in Switzerland, and he did not meet Freud until April of the following year. At that Congress Freud met many new and old friends from different countries.

After this introduction we may proceed in a somewhat more chronological order.

Eli Bernays' son, Edward, did his best in these years to further Freud's interests in America. When in Paris at the beginning of 1919 he had managed to get a box of Havana cigars taken to Vienna by the head of a mission investigating the conditions there; he knew that no present could have been more welcome to his uncle who had not tasted a good cigar for years. In return Freud sent him a copy of his *Introductory Lectures on Psychoanalysis*, and Edward promptly offered to arrange for a translation, to which Freud at once agreed. When I saw Freud the following October I told him of our plan to produce an English translation of the book and of the difficulty of finding an English publisher if the American rights had already been disposed of; this was a recurrent source of misunderstanding between us. He at once cabled to New York to stop the translation there, but it was too late. Edward Bernays had lost no time in securing a number of Columbia graduates to work on a mixed translation and had arranged a contract with Boni and Liveright to produce the book, which appeared in the following spring under the title of *A General Introduction to Psychoanalysis*. Freud was displeased with the numerous errors and other imperfections in the translation and later on expressed his regret at having sanctioned it in spite of the welcome royalties it brought him during a time of stringency. Edward Bernays had certainly done his best for his uncle, and Freud gratefully acknowledged it; unfortunately one's best is not always good enough.

In the meantime Joan Riviere made a careful translation which appeared in 1922 with the more correct title of *Introductory Lectures on Psycho-Analysis*. A still further translation by James Strachey will soon appear in his *Standard Edition of the Complete Psychological Works of Sigmund Freud*. The book played a considerable part in the "boom" of interest in Freud's work that followed the First World War—a not unmixed blessing.

To further the sales of their book Boni and Liveright offered Freud $10,000.00 in December, 1919 if he would give a course of lectures in New York. They had to be in English, and that together with his unsatisfactory state of health decided him to decline.

It took more than financial stringency to prevent Freud from leaving Vienna in the summer when there was the apparent need to do so. On July 15, 1919, he left for Bad Gastein (Villa Wassing) with Minna Bernays, both of them being in need of the refreshment provided by the "cure" there.[25] His wife was unable to accompany him, since she was convalescing in a sanatorium near Salzburg from the aftereffects of the pneumonia she had contracted two months before.[26] Freud expected both Ferenczi and me to join him there, but neither of us could obtain the necessary permits for entering Austria. On August 12 he left for Badersee, a beautiful spot in the Bavarian Alps a few miles from Partenkirchen. Here Eitingon paid him a visit. On September 9 he set out on the uncomfortable journey to Hamburg, via Munich, to see his daughter Sophie—as it turned out, for the last time; she died only four months later. On the return journey Abraham and Eitingon met Freud and his wife in Berlin, and they spent six hours at the former's temporary flat. Vienna was reached on September 24, where I soon joined him—our first meeting for nearly five years.

The excuse Freud gave for his apparent heedlessness in spending money on holidays in such times was that since the Austrian currency was steadily depreciating it was wise to make use of it as long as one could. It was certainly pointless to save it.

Events at the end of the war turned Freud's thoughts in the direction of the outer world from which he had been for years almost completely isolated. The dismal situation in Vienna, together with the separation from Hungary where only recently he had perceived the most promising center of psychoanalysis and the extreme difficulty even of communicating with Ferenczi there, made him very eager to learn authentic news of what progress his work had made in more distant countries; his appetite was further whetted by the favorable accounts I was able to send him from abroad. James Putnam had recently died, and we could get no news from A. A. Brill, so naturally I was the chief source of information.[b]

I remember cheering Freud about this time by quoting to him Arthur Clough's verse.

> *And not by eastern windows only,*
> *When daylight comes, comes in the light;*
> *In front the sun climbs slow, how slowly!*
> *But westward, look, the land is bright!*

Freud certainly needed cheering up, since the professional attitude toward his work was as antagonistic as ever in Austria and Germany. Alfred E. Hoche, at the meetings of the South-West German Neurologists and Alienists in 1919, 1920 and 1921, ceaselessly belabored Freud and his theories. They were "impermissible mystical efforts in a scientific veil." [28] Ernst Kretschmer used similar language. To use the word "unconscious" as a noun was to create "a kind of mystic underworld for specters of scientific fancy"; it was "a conception chimera," "a hellish spook from a brain mythology." [29]

In the years just after the World War there was a great deal of talk about Freud and his theories among intellectual circles in England. There was, in fact, a considerable cult or vogue which was by no means welcome to serious students, and we did our best to confine ourselves to our scientific work—even at the cost of being labeled sectarians or hermits. The British Psycho-Analytical Society was reorganized in February, 1919, with twenty members; the change of name from "London" to "British" was part of a decision I had proposed for all Societies, so that "Berlin" became "German," "Budapest" became "Hungarian" and so on. The British Psychological Society also was undergoing an extensive transformation; J. C. Flugel was Secretary and I was Chairman of the Council that was carrying it out. One outcome was the founding of a special Medical Section, which proved an invaluable forum for the discussion of

[b] A prominent American journalist, Viereck, had the very week after the Armistice sent him books and newspaper cuttings, as did the Bernays family in New York. Freud had gladly accepted Viereck's offer of food, remarking that any meat that could be sent would certainly increase his productivity.[27]

our ideas with other medical psychologists. To heighten its prestige we got W.H.R. Rivers, the distinguished anthropologist, to act as its first President, but the next seven were all psychoanalysts, as have been many since.

Although Freud and I were equally anxious to resume contact by a personal meeting, the difficulties in the way were almost insuperable. The authorities behaved as if the danger of Germany renewing the war was imminent, instead of being twenty years ahead, and were extremely suspicious of the motives of anyone who wished to travel abroad. For four months I haunted in vain various Ministries—of War, Health, Trade, etc., and only then succeeded in getting the Ministry of Education to vouch for my *bona fides* at least so far as Switzerland. The French authorities were even more difficult to persuade, and I have retained undying memories of what bureaucracy can accomplish when working at full pressure. Nevertheless, I reached Berne on March 15, 1919, and met Otto Rank there. Hanns Sachs arrived two days later. Rank had been there for a week already, negotiating with a Swiss publisher; our efforts in that direction, however, came to nothing. He was accompanied by Tola, his recently married wife, who was to prove her worth in years to come.

In the previous month Sachs had written from Davos to Freud, announcing his decision to change his profession from that of a lawyer to that of a practicing psychoanalyst.[30] The prospects of any success in his former position in Vienna were, in view of the general state of collapse there, exceedingly dim; Sachs compared the notion of resuming it to the situation of Nestroy's shopkeeper who said "In order to earn something to buy food I am in a trade where I have to starve."

I was very astonished at the remarkable change the war years had wrought in Rank. I had last seen him a weedy youth, timid and deferential, much given to clicking of heels and bowing. Now in stalked a wiry, tough man with a masterful air whose first act was to deposit on the table a huge revolver. I asked him what he wanted with it, and he nonchalantly replied: *"Für alle Fälle"* (for any eventuality). How had he got it through the frontier examination? When the official pointed to his bulging pocket Rank had calmly answered "bread." The change had coincided with his resuming his work in Vienna after the war years spent in Krakow. At the time his Viennese friends connected it with some response to his recent marriage, but later on it became plain that it must have been a hypomanic reaction to the three severe attacks of melancholia he had suffered while in Krakow.

A Budapest friend of Ferenczi's and Freud's, Ignotus, was head of the Hungarian delegation in Berne that was vainly seeking contact with the Entente authorities, and he could not be persuaded that the first British civilian to get abroad after the war had not great influence which could be used to obtain better terms for Hungary. His hopes were sadly dashed, and the day before I parted from him we got the news of Bela Kun's Bolshevist revolution in Hungary, which at once abolished his delegation. This political change affected Freud in two ways. For five months it was barely possible for him to get a word of news from Ferenczi, which was a source of considerable anxiety. Then the Bolshevists, who had not yet discovered that psychoanalysis was a bourgeois deviation, and that the capitalists had suborned Freud in opposition to Marx, favored it somewhat, and they installed Ferenczi as the first University Professor of Psychoanalysis. Sandor Rado had some influence with the new masters, and it was he who maneuvered this;[31] Róheim had been made Professor of Anthropology a couple of weeks before.

Ferenczi was to pay dearly enough for his incautious acceptance of the honor. After the Roumanians entered Budapest in August the reactionary regime they supported was violently anti-Semitic, and for a long time Ferenczi was afraid to show himself in the street. To his great chagrin he was even expelled from the Medical Society of Budapest,[32] and the fact that only he could negotiate with the authorities over the von Freund fund proved a fatal obstacle. Freud was deeply disappointed over this outcome.

On March 22, after a couple of days in Lucerne, the three of us left for Zurich and on March 24, 1919, addressed the newly constituted Swiss Psychoanalytical Society which had replaced the prewar one headed by Jung. We spent a couple of days at Neuchâtel and I parted from my friends on March 28. The Council of the new Swiss Society consisted of Ludwig Binswanger, F. Morel, Emil Oberholzer, Oskar Pfister and Hermann Rorschach. We naturally advised them to apply for admission to the International Association as soon as contact could be established with Ferenczi, then President. But on May 20 Pfister wrote Freud a letter of seven huge sheets, complaining bitterly that Sachs had intervened and was now pressing them to withdraw their application. Sachs had also sent Freud his side of the case, so Freud was forced into the role of Solomon, one which he disliked but could fill very well. Here is his reply to Pfister.

"Lieber Herr Doktor,

"There you have set me a disagreeable task! The *simplest thing,* in a matter concerning two friends who are seeking sincerity through psychoanalysis, *would be* to send on each one's letter to the other and let each find out for himself the erroneous accusations of the other. However, I have never been allowed to evade vexatious tasks. So I will tell each of you what displeases me, but neither of you what I censure in the other.

"Your concrete question may be answered first and definitely. You have applied for admission to the International Association and have to regard yourselves as provisionally accepted. Your getting no reply from the Central Executive comes merely from its being cut off through the postal service being suspended. You will find the acceptance of your group registered in the next number of the *Zeitschrift.* . . .

"That being so, it is plain that until the next Congress no one has the authority to expel you. When Sachs advised you to withdraw he was speaking for himself only, and there is not the slightest need for you to take his advice. If you had a clear conscience, and felt sure that your scientific convictions warranted your joining the Association, you could have quite calmly told him so.

"On the other hand, no one has the power to keep you in the International Association, nor would anyone try to do so, if you do not wish to stay in it. And much in your letter rather looks like that. Even in that event, however, it does not seem to me imperative for you to decide immediately on withdrawal. You can wait till the Congress (probably in 1920) to see if the antagonisms in question get enhanced or clear up, and whether it is possible to work with the other members of the Association; in that way you would avoid the harm you fear for your Society.°

"I have, however, not only to orient you concerning a matter of fact, but if possible tell you that you are in the right. Gladly, if I had not something to reproach you with (here I mean chiefly you, Dr. O. Pf. and not the Zurich Society). In your letter there is not a single word of what in Sachs's letter is the main point. Sachs got the impression from the discussion, from the response to the remarks

° I.e. public discredit at withdrawal or expulsion.

he made, from the subsequent talk with you and probably from various other hints, that in the Society there was the intention so far as possible not to mention the theme of sexuality. I hope he was wrong in this, since the Society when it joins us must know that that is our shibboleth. Perhaps he distrusts the 'Psychology of the Swiss,' and fears that Jung's influence has penetrated more deeply among you than you are willing to admit either to yourselves or to others. I should therefore willingly think him in the wrong if—that little word in question had occurred in your letter even only once. That would have cleared up and eased so much. As it is, it gives the impression of a symptomatic act, which supports Sachs's suspicion.

"I cannot believe that Sachs based his obtruding advice on the fact that the International Association consists only of fully qualified analysts. There must be some misunderstanding there. Sachs knows, in the first place, that is not true of the Intern. Assoc., and, in the second place, that no new Society can consist of fully qualified analysts.

"The other thing I do not like is the attitude you describe as having taken shape toward our friend. When the members are prepared straightaway to see in him an emissary of the High Inquisition who has to keep watch over your orthodoxy, I find this political conception highly unsuited to a *scientific* relationship. The republican struggle for Independence might just as well rebel against the compulsion of the Table of Logarithms. In scientific work it would be more opportune to reflect that there might be something to be learned from an experienced expert when he exhorts or criticizes. I must say I should take the whole affair very lightly did it not show also that aspect.

"That Sachs in his remarks ignored his own interests so completely should be for you one more witness for his honesty and his aversion to any opportunism.

"With that I conclude my answer in the official role I was placed in. Privately I still hope that you and Sachs will withstand this 'storm' and profit by this experience to strengthen your common interests.

> "With cordial greetings
> "Your
> "Freud"

It is pleasing to record that the hope Freud expressed in his final sentence was soon fulfilled.

I managed to get to Switzerland again in August. It was not easy, for the authorities were very suspicious of this sinister wish to go abroad twice in the same year. But in my capacity as a publisher I succeeded in procuring a permit from the Board of Trade for myself and my assistant Eric Hiller. It was strictly forbidden, however, to enter either Austria or Germany, which were still "enemy occupied countries." We met Sachs in Basle on August 25 and, after passing a few days with van Emden in Lucerne, we spent a well-earned holiday at Locarno. It was out of the question to obtain a permit to travel to Garmisch in Germany, near which place Freud was on holiday, but I had more success with the Austrian Ambassador in Berne. In his nonchalant aristocratic manner he expressed surprise that anyone should wish to go to such an unhappy and dismal place as Vienna, but, adding, "It's a matter of taste," raised no objection, nor did the Swiss authorities. So Hiller and I set out. The provinces of Austria had declared themselves temporarily autonomous, and exacted a toll from anyone wishing to pass through. It did not take long to confirm Freud's hints of the desolate situation of his country. The starved and ragged officials were evidence enough, nor shall I forget the vain efforts of the emaciated dogs to stagger to the food I threw to them. We were the first foreign civilians to reach Vienna and were joyfully received at the Hotel Regina, where visiting analysts always stayed.

I found Freud somewhat greyer and a good deal thinner than before the war; he never regained his former plump figure. But his mind had lost nothing of its alertness. He was as cheerful and warmly friendly as ever, so it was hard to think we had not seen each other for nearly six years. We had not been together long before Ferenczi burst into the room and to my astonishment effusively kissed us both on the cheeks. He had not seen Freud for more than a year. We all had endless news to exchange about what had been happening to us in all those years, and this was the first of many talks. There were, of course, comments on the vast changes in the European situation, and Freud surprised me by saying he had recently had an interview with an ardent Communist and had been half converted to Bolshevism, as it was then called. He had been informed that the advent of Bolshevism would result in some years of misery and chaos, and that these would be followed by universal peace, prosperity and happiness. Freud added: "I told him I believed the first half."

He had hard things to say about President Wilson, whose vision of a friendly Europe based on justice was rapidly becoming illusory.

When I pointed out how complex were the forces at work in arranging the peace settlement and that it could not be dictated by any one man, he replied: "Then he should not have made all those promises." It was evidently one of those numerous cases in Freud's life where his optimism, or credulity, led him to build high hopes about someone, followed by resentment at the almost inevitable disappointment later. His poor opinion of Wilson persisted. In 1930 he collaborated with Ambassador Bullitt in composing a book consisting of an analytic study of Wilson's personality.[*]

The next day, September 28, I invited the Freud family, with Rank and his wife, to a luncheon at the beautiful Hotel Cobenzl outside Vienna, and it was moving to see what an experience a proper meal seemed to mean to them. That evening I shared in the celebration of Martin's engagement—a full family party; the wedding followed in a couple of months.

During the week I spent in Vienna every minute was occupied with talks, chiefly with Rank, about the manifold details of our publishing plans, both in Vienna and in London. I got some insight into the enormous technical difficulties with which he was strenuously coping.

The severance of Hungary from Austria after the war had brought with it such a dislocation of railway, postal and, above all, political communications that it had become almost as difficult to reach Vienna from Budapest as it was from London; even from Berlin trains to Vienna ran only twice a week.[33]

It was immediately evident to Freud that what he called "the center of gravity of psychoanalysis" would have to be moved westward.[34] So he proposed to Ferenczi that he transfer to me the acting presidency of the International Association to which the Budapest Congress had voted him during the war. Ferenczi agreed with a good grace, but in years to come it was a source of keen regret to him that he was never called upon to function in that position and I had good reason later for thinking that he bore me an irrational grudge for having had to supplant him. Freud remarked on that occasion: "It is to be hoped we have found the right man this time," evidently expecting that my position would be a lasting one. Unfortunately, from my point of view, there were times later on when he no longer held that opinion.

It was during that conference in Vienna that Freud suggested to us that Eitingon be invited to join our private "Committee." We at

[*] See pp. 150-51.

once agreed to this, and Abraham was commissioned to procure Eitingon's consent; the necessary insignia of a ring followed a few months later. In May, 1920, Freud gave his daughter Anna a similar ring; the only other women to receive this honor were Lou Salomé, Marie Bonaparte and my wife.

On November 19, 1919, Rank left Vienna together with Pfister and Forsyth. He got to Holland, but it took some time before he could procure a permit to come to England. He ultimately did so, however, in the company of van Emden and Johann van Ophuijsen. We had of course again much to discuss in connection with our plans for a London branch of the *Verlag* which will presently be described. He got back to Vienna on December 31.

In October, 1919, Freud was given the title of full Professor of the University. He described it as an "empty title," [35] since it brought with it no seat on the Board of the Faculty. But, fortunately, neither did it bring any special teaching responsibilities. So Freud never taught any students of the University, only those who wished to attend his private lectures; these were not official lectures, but were delivered in his capacity as Docent, i.e. permissively. Freud had a great number of congratulations on this occasion, and he commented that the establishing of a Republic had made no difference to the Austrians' respect for titles.[36]

1920

In the first month of 1920 fate dealt Freud two grievous blows: one for which he was prepared, though not resigned, the other a startlingly unexpected blow. The former was the death of Toni von Freund. Following an operation for sarcoma at the age of thirty-nine, von Freund had developed a severe neurosis for which Freud successfully treated him in the years of 1918-19. But in March of the latter year suspicious signs of an abdominal recurrence of the sarcoma appeared, and for months his friends wavered between hopes and fears. In October Freud was cheered by Forsyth, then in Vienna, who expressed the opinion that the tumor in question was not malignant, and as late as the middle of November Freud himself discovered a floating kidney which for a moment he hoped was the tumor about which the Hungarian physicians were so concerned.[37] A further exploratory operation, however, put the sinister diagnosis beyond doubt, and the patient's state rapidly worsened. In December Abraham, who had come to know von Freund at the time of the Budapest Congress, asked Freud whether he was aware of his approaching end, so as to know in what terms to write to him. Freud answered that von Freund knew everything, and had even ordered the ring Freud had given him to be restored after his death so that it could be passed over to Eitingon. Von Freund was to have been a member of the private "Committee," but Eitingon took his place. After von Freund's death, however, his widow claimed the ring, so Freud gave Eitingon the one he had himself worn. Freud had visited the dying man every day and done all he could to comfort him. The end came on January 20, 1920, and Freud remarked that von Freund had died heroically without disgracing psychoanalysis.[38] Freud had been specially fond of him, and his death was a severe personal blow; he said it was an important factor in his aging.[39]

Then only three days later, on the very evening of the day von Freund was buried, came news announcing the serious illness of Freud's beautiful daughter Sophie, the one they called their "Sunday child," at her home in Hamburg; it was the influenzal pneumonia so rife in that year. There were no trains leaving Vienna for Germany and so no possibility of reaching her. Two of her brothers, Oliver and Ernst, who were in Berlin, traveled to Hamburg together with Eitingon, arriving there, however, only after her death. Two days later, on January 25, a telegram announced her death. She was only twenty-six, had been in perfect health and happiness, and left behind her two children, one of whom was only thirteen months old. The news was a thunderbolt from a clear sky. On the day after receiving it Freud wrote to me: "Poor or happy Toni Freund was buried last Thursday, 22nd of this month. Sorry to hear your father is on the list now,[e] but we all must and I wonder when my turn will come. Yesterday I lived through an experience which makes me wish it should not last a long time." A day later he wrote to Pfister: "She was blown away as if she had never been." Telling Ferenczi of the news, he added: "As for us? My wife is quite overwhelmed. I think: *La séance continue.* But it was a little much for one week." [40] Freud's stoicism could conceal deep, though controlled, emotion. Writing a little later to Eitingon, who as usual had been as helpful as possible, he described his reaction: "I do not know what more there is to say. It is such a paralyzing event, which can stir no afterthoughts when one is not a believer and so is spared all the conflicts that go with that. Blunt necessity, mute submission." [41]

• I had just told him my father was dying.

Ferenczi had been deeply concerned about the effect of this terrible blow on Freud's spirits. Freud reassured him in these pathetic lines:

"Lieber Freund:

"Do not be concerned about me. I am just the same but for a little more tiredness. The fatal event, however painful, has not been able to overthrow my attitude toward life. For years I was prepared for the loss of my sons; [t] now comes that of my daughter. Since I am profoundly irreligious there is no one I can accuse, and I know there is nowhere to which any complaint could be addressed. *'Des Dienstes ewig gleichgestellte Uhr'* [g] and the *'Daseins süsse Gewohnheit'* [h] will see to it that things go on as before. Quite deep down I can trace the feeling of a deep narcissistic hurt that is not to be healed. My wife and Annerl are terribly shaken in a more human way." [44]

If Freud had ever been asked to submit gladly to the decrees of Providence he would certainly have made some vehement criticisms of that high authority.

When a couple of weeks later I told Freud of my father's death he replied: "So your father has not to hold out until he got devoured piecemeal by his cancer as poor Freund was. What a happy chance. Yet you will soon find out what it means to you. I was about your age when my father died (43) and it revolutionised my soul." [45] Actually we were each of us forty-one when we lost our fathers, but Freud was forty-three when he wrote *The Interpretation of Dreams,* so this slip of memory is one more confirmation of how closely linked in his mind the two events were.

Still life had to go on. Freud's next interest was the opening of the Berlin Policlinic on February 14, 1920. This in his opinion made Berlin the chief psychoanalytical center. It was Eitingon's generosity that made it possible to establish it, and Ernst Freud had designed the arrangement of the building in a manner that evoked general praise. There was, of course, a library for research, and plans were being laid for a Training Institute; it was the first, and for long the most famous, of its kind. In the summer Hanns Sachs came from Switzerland to Berlin to assist in the teaching, and he was joined there not long after by Theodor Reik from Vienna.

[t] In battle.
[g] "The unvarying circle of a soldier's duties." [46]
[h] "Sweet habit of existence." [46]

Naturally the members of the Vienna Society wished to follow suit, and it was proposed to establish a similar clinic as a department of the General Hospital. Freud was very much against the idea. The reasons he gave Abraham were that he could give no time to it himself, and he would not know to whom in the Society he could entrust the directing of it.[46] To Ferenczi, however, he confessed that in his opinion Vienna was not a suitable center for psychoanalysis, so it was not a proper place to have such a clinic. "A raven should not don a white shirt." [47] Nevertheless, the need was undeniable, and the clinic, given the name of *Ambulatorium*, was opened on May 22, 1922.

From time to time Freud exchanged letters with Havelock Ellis, and he often sent him copies of his books. But he was not pleased with a paper Ellis had written during the war,[48] which just now came to his notice. In it Ellis maintained that Freud was an artist, not a scientist; Freud called that "a highly sublimated form of resistance." [49] Writing to me, he described Ellis's essay as "the most refined and amiable form of resistance, calling me a great artist in order to injure the validity of our scientific claims." He added: "This is all wrong. I am sure in a few decades my name will be wiped away and our results will last." [50] Havelock Ellis, at one time the leading pioneer in the world on the subject of sexuality, had at first been enthusiastic about Freud's contributions, but, then finding himself quite displaced by Freud, his jealous nature led him to write about Freud's work in an increasingly carping spirit which ended in a completely negative attitude.

At the end of the war there were many bitter complaints about the harsh, or even cruel, way in which Austrian military doctors had treated the war neurotics, notably in the Psychiatric Division of the Vienna General Hospital of which Professor Julius Wagner-Jauregg was the Director. At the beginning of 1920 the Austrian military authorities instituted a special Commission to investigate the matter, and they invited Freud and Emil Raimann (Wagner-Jauregg's assistant) to submit memoranda on it. Incidentally, this is evidence of the scientific standing Freud held at that time in the eyes of the authorities in Vienna. The memorandum he wrote reposes in the State Archives in Vienna, from which it has with much trouble been extracted. It was entitled "Memorandum on the Electrical Treatment of War Neurotics," and was dated by Freud February 23, 1920. It was first published in 1955 in the *Standard Edition*.[51]

Freud began by remarking on the division of opinion that had subsisted in the medical profession about the nature of traumatic neuroses following on railway and other accidents, some maintaining that they were due to minute injuries to the nervous system, even when these could not be demonstrated, and others that they were purely disturbances of function with an intact nervous system. The experiences of the war, particularly of the war neuroses that occurred far from the front without any physical trauma such as the bursting of bombs, had decided the question in favor of the second view.

Psychoanalysis had traced all neuroses to emotional conflicts, and it was easy to attribute at least the immediate cause of war neuroses to the conflict between the instinct of self-preservation, with the need to get away from military dangers, and the various motives that would not allow this to be fully avowed—the sense of duty, the training to obedience and so on. The therapy that had been evolved to meet this situation, first of all in the German Army, was to apply electrical treatment in such doses as to be even more disagreeble than the thought of returning to the front. "As to its use in the Vienna Clinics I am personally convinced that Professor Wagner-Jauregg would never have allowed it to be intensified to a cruel pitch. I cannot vouch for other doctors whom I do not know. The psychological education of doctors is in general pretty deficient, and many of them may well have forgotten that the patient he was seeking to treat as a malingerer was not really one. . . .

"The brilliant initial successes of the treatment with strong electric currents afterwards proved not to be lasting. A patient who had been restored and sent back to the front could repeat the story afresh and relapse, whereby he at least gained time and avoided the immediate dangers. When he was once more under fire his dread of the electric current receded, just as during the treatment his fear of active service had faded. Furthermore, the rapidly increasing weariness in the popular spirit and the growing disinclination to continue the war made itself felt more and more, so that the treatment began to fail in its effect. In these circumstances some gave way to the characteristically German inclination to achieve their aims quite ruthlessly. Something happened which never should have: the strength of the currents, as well as the severity of the treatment otherwise, were increased to an unbearable point in order to deprive war neurotics of the advantage they gained from their illness. The fact has never been contradicted that in German hospitals there were cases of death during the treatment and suicides as the result of it. I have no idea at all, however, whether the Vienna Clinics also passed through this phase of the therapy."

It will be observed that in Freud's opinion examples of pure malingering were in a small minority. That he was right in this judgment has been amply borne out by further experiences. The very detailed investigations of Kurt Eissler, for instance, result in profound scepticism about the very existence of such a condition.[52] But most army doctors certainly thought otherwise. Even Wagner-Jauregg, who administered relatively mild electric currents when the war neurotic showed physical symptoms, such as tremors, admitted in his autobiography: "If all the malingerers I cured at the Clinic, often by harsh enough measures, had appeared as my accusers it would have made an impressive trial." [53] Fortunately for him, as he remarked, most of them were scattered over the former Austro-Hungarian Empire and were not available, so the Commission ultimately decided in his favor.

On his return to Vienna from the Hague Congress in September Freud was faced with the disagreeable task of giving evidence before the Commission that was investigating these complaints about the treatment of war neuroses. They centered on Professor Wagner-Jauregg, the man who was ultimately responsible. Freud said he intended to be as friendly as possible to Wagner-Jauregg, since the latter was not personally responsible for anything that had happened.[54] At the meeting on October 15 Professor Alexander Löffler, the Chairman of the Commission, presided. All the Viennese neurologists and psychiatrists were present, and the press was also invited. Freud first read aloud the Memorandum he had sent in eight months before and then expounded his views in a calm and objective fashion. Wagner-Jauregg maintained that all the patients with war neuroses were simply malingerers and that he had had a far richer experience of them than Freud, to whom such patients never came. Freud said he could agree with that opinion insofar as all neurotics were in a certain sense malingerers, but only unconsciously so; that was the essential difference in the two views. He also agreed that it was difficult to apply psychoanalysis in such cases in war time—the multiple languages in the Austro-Hungarian Army were in themselves an obstacle—but he maintained that a knowledge of psychoanalytical principles would have been more useful than the electrical therapy adopted. He also pointed to the conflict between a doctor's duty to put his patient's interests always first and the demand of the military authorities that the doctor should be chiefly concerned with restoring patients to military duty. This was followed by a sharp debate, with the entire Commission siding violently against Freud. In the course of it very hard things were said to the discredit of psychoanalysis, so once again Freud was no prophet in his own country. Afterward he said the meeting had only confirmed his opinion of the insincerity and hatefulness of the Viennese psychiatrists.[55]

Freud had always been personally friendly toward Wagner-Jauregg since their student days; they addressed each other with the intimate Du. The letter of congratulations Freud received from him on his sixtieth birthday was an agreeable surprise, since, as he frankly told his friend, the violent attacks proceeding from Wagner's assistants had made him uncertain about the latter's personal attitude. Freud wrote to him on his seventy-fifth birthday in 1932, and also got the Vienna Psycho-Analytical Society to send him a warm letter in which he was addressed as the *"Weltmeister der Psychiatrie"* (world master of psychiatry). The two men also congratulated each other on their eightieth birthdays, in 1936 and 1937 respectively.

Freud's friendliness was by no means reciprocated. One would have thought that he had been generous enough in his Memorandum, more so than a stranger would have been, but Wagner-Jauregg was not satisfied. When he wrote his autobiography, published posthumously but written between 1928 and 1935, he not only accused Freud of intolerance, but maintained that out of revenge for the criticisms emanating from the Psychiatric Clinic he instituted in the Memorandum he composed for the Commission a personal attack on Wagner-Jauregg; fortunately, as mentioned previously, this Memorandum is now published, so that readers can see for themselves on which side lay the intolerance. Not content with that, Wagner-Jauregg perpetuated the legend, which had long been thoroughly disproved, that Janet was the true father of psychoanalysis, that Freud had met him at Charcot's Clinic and that the *Studies in Hysteria* were founded on Janet's work.[56] Such statements do not redound to Wagner-Jauregg's credit.

We hoped very much to hold the first full meeting of the Committee that Easter, but neither Abraham nor Eitingon were able to obtain the necessary complicated permits to travel from Germany to Austria. Ferenczi had managed to get to Vienna, and I myself was there from March 30 to April 9; so together with Rank and Sachs, who came from Zurich, we were able to have prolonged discussions on various administrative and scientific problems.

About this time Freud heard of the rumor that had been current in America during the war, to the effect that the hard conditions in Vienna had driven him to suicide.[57] He said he could not regard it as a kind thought.

In July, 1920, Eitingon got a Viennese sculptor, Paul König-berger, to make a bust of Freud. Freud was badly overworked at the time, but he could refuse Eitingon nothing. Like so many busy people he much disliked such "sittings." He felt like being annoyed with the sculptor, but instead he took a liking to him and thought him very skillful. "So I will sacrifice myself for posterity." [58] He certainly could not have foreseen how prophetic this joke was to prove, since it was a copy of that bust that I gave later to the University of Vienna where it was unveiled on February 4, 1955. Freud himself and his family were pleased at the result: "it gives the impression of a head of Brutus, with a rather overwhelming effect." [59] The members of the Committee subscribed to buy the original as a presentation gift on Freud's sixty-fifth birthday, and Eitingon unveiled the finished product on the anniversary in the following year. It then had to find a place in Freud's domicile as "a ghostly, threatening, bronze double of himself." [60] But he complained he had been taken in. "I really believed Eitingon wanted it for himself; otherwise I should not have sat for it last year." [61]

On July 20, 1920, later than his usual date, Freud and his sister-in-law again went to Gastein for the "cure," his wife spending the time near Ischl with her eldest daughter who was in poor health. After a month at Gastein Freud, together with his daughter Anna, went to Hamburg to visit his bereaved son-in-law, Max Halberstadt, and his two grandchildren. Eitingon joined them there and they traveled together to the Congress at the Hague, reaching it on the morning of September 7.

As soon as the war was over we had begun speculating about the feasibility of holding the next International Congress. A neutral country seemed the obvious place, and Holland was preferable to Switzerland because of the complicated restrictions about traveling across France. In the spring of 1919 I hoped we might hold one that autumn, but a little investigation of the conditions showed the impossibility of doing so. Abraham had suggested that we hold at least a "private Congress" of the Committee members in either London or Constance.[62] In the following winter Abraham kept raising objections against the plan of a Congress in Holland. The fall in German and Austrian currency would mean that no Austrian, German or

Hungarian analysts could attend, and that would reduce the Congress to a farce. He was also eager to have Freud and others give a series of public lectures after a Congress in Berlin for which he hoped. This request led to some animated arguments between the two men. Freud gave details of how his short holiday was already almost fully occupied with work, so that he had only a week to rest before beginning the year's practice in Vienna, but Abraham obstinately insisted on his coming to Berlin; furthermore, that the Committee was there only to assist Freud, not gradually to replace him in the way Freud thought. Finally there had to be a firm statement: "When you come to be 64 years old, with ten months behind you of such work, you will no longer regard a demand for an undisturbed pause in one's work as unjustifiable stubbornness, and any effect on the Berlin medical circle will seem a matter of indifference in comparison. So leave me out. I shall not lecture in Berlin either *before* or *after* the Congress. . . . You say that your arrangements have no prospect unless I cooperate. That is just the attitude I am opposing. Only try, and you will see it will succeed. Tomorrow or after tomorrow you will have to, so you had better begin today." [63]

Freud then pointed out that it was as difficult for Viennese to travel to Berlin as to Holland, and that Abraham was underestimating the "prejudices" of Anglo-Saxon members against visiting Germany. That was true enough. The bitter feelings against Germany were, strangely enough, incomparably stronger after the First World War than after the Second. Abraham told me later he could not at all understand that, and that he could not have had the slightest objection to attending a Congress in Paris; I asked him if he knew what would happen to anyone overheard speaking German in a Paris restaurant, and my question astonished him. The currency problem itself was solved through the generosity of our Dutch colleagues, who subscribed 50,000 Crowns ($10,130.00) to pay the traveling expenses of analysts from Central Europe, and, moreover, offered to house twenty of them during their stay in Holland: seven from Austria, seven from Germany and six from Hungary.

The sixth International Psycho-Analytical Congress opened on September 8, 1920, and lasted four days. It was held in the Louis XV salon of the building known as the "Pulchri Studio" belonging to the Society of Artists at The Hague. Of the sixty-two members present two came from America (Dorian Feigenbaum and William Stern), seven from Austria, fifteen from England, eleven from Germany (including Georg Groddeck), sixteen from Holland (including G.

Jelgersma and van Renterghem), three from Hungary (including Melanie Klein), one from Poland and seven from Switzerland. Among the fifty-seven guests who also attended were Anna Freud, James Glover and John Rickman.

Freud gave a paper, entitled "Supplements to the Theory of Dreams." He made three points. One was the expansion of his wish-fulfillment theory to include those where the wish proceeded not from the pleasure-seeking side of the unconscious, but from the self-punishing tendencies of the conscience. A more disturbing observation to subsume under his theory was the simple repetition in a dream of a traumatic experience; this was one of the considerations that at that time was leading him to postulate a "repetition compulsion" in addition to the familiar pleasure principle. The third point was his rejection of various recent attempts to discern a "prospective tendency" in dreams, attempts which he maintained betokened a confusion between the manifest and latent content of dreams. The paper was never published as such in German, only in English,[64] but its contents were later incorporated in parts of Freud's writings.

Other outstanding papers were by Abraham: "Manifestations of the Female Castration Complex," [65] and Ferenczi: "Further Development of an Active Therapy in Psycho-Analysis." [66] Róheim gave an astonishing extempore address in English on Australian totemism.[1]

Ferenczi wanted a rule made that no member should be elected anywhere until all the various Societies had been consulted, but it was easy to convince him of the impractibility of the suggestion.

The British group of those attending the Congress entertained Freud and his daughter at a luncheon, and she pleased her father and us by making a graceful little speech in very good English.

The Congress closed with a superb banquet which gave the starved Central Europeans the impression of having been transported into the Land of Cockayne.

Freud and his daughter had arrived on the morning of September 7 and stayed at the Hotel Paulez in The Hague. They intended paying a visit to England after the Congress, and I did my best to procure permits for them from the British Consul in Rotterdam. Freud received his, but his daughter's was so delayed—possibly because of the suspicious circumstance of her having been in England at the outbreak of the war!—that they had to renounce the plan. Instead van Emden and van Ophuijsen accompanied them on a tour

[1] Nearly twenty years later Mrs. Riviere's memory erroneously ascribed this performance to Freud himself.[67]

around Holland. It was a complicated tour, and various forms of transport were used: steamer, motor car, horse carriage, canoes, and even walking. Freud had twice been in Holland before: once when he broke his journey on the way to England in September, 1908, and then when the family spent their summer holiday there in 1910. He was therefore already familiar with the main towns of Amsterdam, Haarlem, Leyden, Utrecht and The Hague, but now his expert guides escorted him through the lesser known parts of the country, including a voyage by canoe along the waterways of Zeeland. The pair left Holland on September 28, but separated in Osnabruck. Anna went to spend some weeks with her little orphaned nephews in Hamburg, while Freud proceeded via Berlin to Vienna, getting home on September 30.

It was in every way a successful Congress, with the happy reunion of workers who had been for years out of mutual contact. Freud wrote afterward that "he was proud of the Congress," [68] and it was a matter of general congratulation that it was the first occasion when any workers from hostile countries had come together for scientific cooperation.

Nevertheless, when the excitement had died down, Freud's feelings of satisfaction gave way to a more critical attitude towards the outer world. When Pfister wrote congratulating him on the progress psychoanalysis was making in the world, he replied: "It is true that our cause[j] is everywhere progressing, but you seem to overestimate my enjoyment of it. What personal gratification is to be drawn from psychoanalysis I had already enjoyed in the time when I was alone, and have been more annoyed than pleased since others have joined me. The way in which people accept and digest it has brought me no other opinion of them than their previous behavior when they uncomprehendingly rejected it. An unbridgeable gulf between me and them must have come about in that time." [69]

We took steps on the occasion of the Hague Congress to consolidate further the internal structure of the private Committee, which now met together in full for the first time. We decided to replace, in part at least, the irregular correspondence passing among its various members by a regular *Rundbrief* (circular letter), which every member would receive and which would keep us all *au courant* with the changing events and plans. The first of this series began on October 7, 1920. It was at first weekly, but was changed at various times to intervals of ten days or even a fortnight. This time-saving

[j] *die Sache.*

device, however, was not intended to abrogate the more personal correspondence, particularly with Freud himself, which might still be desirable.

In October, 1920, Freud, cheered by the appearance of American royalties, wrote to his nephew offering to write four articles for a good magazine in New York. They would be of a popular nature, and he proposed that the first should bear the title of "Don't use Psychoanalysis in Polemics." [70] Bernays at once took up the suggestion with *Cosmopolitan Magazine.* They offered Freud $1,000.00 for the first article; if that proved a success they would take further ones. They countered Freud's suggestion of a topic by offering several of their own, such as "The Wife's Mental Place in the Home," "The Husband's Mental Place in the Home," and so on. Freud was outraged. That the acceptance of articles by "an author of good esteem" should have to depend on the taste of the general public, and that his themes should be dictated for him, hurt his pride or dignity. "Had I taken into account the considerations that influence your editor from the beginning of my career I am sure I should not have become known at all in either America or Europe." [71] He sent a stinging letter of refusal to Edward Bernays, but I cannot help thinking that some of his indignation emanated from feeling a little ashamed himself at having descended from his usual standards by proposing to earn money through writing popular articles. It was the only time in his life that he contemplated doing such a thing.

A month later Bernays cabled to him that a group in New York would guarantee from $10,000.00 if he would spend six months there treating patients in the morning and lecturing in the afternoons. The reply cabled was simply "Not convenient," and it was followed by a long letter that was a masterpiece of business acumen. Freud calculated in detail his expenses, which he would have to pay himself, with the accruing income taxes, etc., and concluded that he would return to Vienna exhausted and poorer than when he started; the point about lecturing in English was also decisive.

Later in 1920 Freud's financial situation began to show signs of rehabilitation. By November he was already earning two thirds of his income before the war.[72] He even began to accumulate a little foreign currency. For this purpose he got me that summer to open an account in my name in a Dutch bank to which he could remit some of the fees from foreign patients. Many people in Austria were adopting similar devices, and Freud was one of the realists; his head was never in the clouds when it came to practical affairs.

Toward the end of the year a plan was set on foot to organize a jubilee volume to commemorate the twenty-fifth anniversary of the publication of the *Studies in Hysteria* in 1895, from which the inception of psychoanalysis was generally dated. But Freud got to hear of it in time and squashed the idea;[73] he was always averse to such formalities or anything resembling a ceremony.

About the same time Freud was very interested to hear of an account Dr. Chaim Weizmann had given me of the great interest in psychoanalysis in Palestine. He had told me that immigrants from Galicia arrived there with no clothes, but with copies of *Das Kapital* and *Die Traumdeutung* (*The Interpretation of Dreams*) under their arms.[74]

The publishing house which was to play a large part in Freud's life from then on, the *Internationaler Psychoanalytischer Verlag*, was founded in Vienna in the middle of January, 1919. It was in many ways a very successful undertaking, though it gave us years of financial worry and also caused personal difficulties. The Directors were Freud, Ferenczi, von Freund and Rank. In September I took the place of von Freund, who was slowly dying, and in 1921 Eitingon also became a Director. It was the only occasion when I met von Freund, and I shall never forget the mournful expression of the doomed man as he gazed at his successor. Rank was installed as the Managing Director, presently with Reik as his assistant. At the end of 1920 Eric Hiller went to Vienna to work in the English Department. In July, 1921, when Reik moved to Berlin, A. J. Storfer took his place. The first book the new undertaking issued was that on *Psycho-Analysis and the War Neuroses*, by Abraham, Ferenczi, Ernst Simmel and myself, in May, 1919. Freud wrote the Preface for it, but he said later he regretted doing so and had only written it because of Ferenczi and myself.[75]

Freud's interest in the fortunes of the *Verlag* was mainly an expression of his strong desire for independence. The idea of being completely free of the conditions imposed by publishers, which had always irked him, and of being able to publish just what books he liked and when he liked, made a forcible appeal to this side of his nature. Then with his own *Verlag* the continued existence of the psychoanalytical periodicals, which had been gravely threatened during the war, should be more secure. Lastly, penurious authors could be sure of having a good work published which commercial publishers might not accept. From the point of view of the outside public there would be some guarantee that books published by such a *Verlag*, although inevitably varying in value, belonged to the corpus of psychoanalytical literature, and could thus be distinguished from many other publications masquerading under that name.

Most of these aims were achieved, though at considerable cost, both financial and in much energy diverted from scientific work. There were occasions later on when I was not sure whether the effort we put into the scheme had been worth while, but on balance perhaps it was. In the twenty years of its existence the *Verlag* published some hundred and fifty books, including five set series and also Freud's *Collected Works*, besides maintaining five psychoanalytical periodicals. What started as its branch in England has also published more than fifty volumes, many of them being translations of the more valuable of the *Verlag* books. The outstanding difficulty throughout, however, was finance. The *Verlag* was only solvent at rare moments, and recourse had constantly to be had to periodical appeals for contributions from psychoanalysts themselves; throughout Freud accepted no royalties for his books and also sank a good deal of his own money in the *Verlag*. This gave me in particular a good deal of trouble, since analysts in non-German speaking countries were not always easy to convince of the value of the project. A crisis, for example, arose soon after its inception, at the end of 1920, when the parlous state of our finances forced us to consider an offer from another Austrian firm to take over the *Verlag* as a special department of their own. Since my main argument in appealing for subscriptions had been the independent nature of the *Verlag*, the news that it was to be commercialized made some subscribers feel that they had not been treated fairly. Fortunately for my peace of mind, however, the head of the other firm died at an appropriate moment, and the idea of amalgamation fell through. The financial stringency had the further effect of defeating one object we had in mind, namely of assisting penurious authors. On the contrary, we were compelled to ask them to pay some of the cost of producing their books, so they were often worse off than if they had approached a commercial firm. Still, weighing everything, the *Verlag* must be counted as a laudable undertaking. To Freud himself it brought much anxiety, enormous personal labor, but profound satisfaction.

What is certain is that the *Verlag* could not have come into existence at all, or survived for a day, without the truly astounding capacity and energy, both editorial and managerial, with which Rank threw himself into the task. It was four years before he ever got away from Vienna on any sort of holiday, taking with him even then a mass of material to deal with. The five years in which Rank continued at this furious tempo must have been a factor in his subsequent mental breakdown.

One might ask whether in these circumstances Freud had been wise in embarking on this arduous project on an amateur basis, since publishing is without doubt a highly technical occupation. He did so only because at the outset he seemed assured of a very substantial capital, which would have enabled him to employ the necessary technical help on any desired scale. As we shall presently note, the prospects of securing the fortune von Freund was donating to the cause faded only by degrees, and after having made a promising start with the Verlag it became ever harder to relinquish the efforts to continue. Such matters of judgment looked different at the time from the appearance they may present in retrospect. But of the considerable cost in nervous energy to Freud, Rank and myself there can be no question.

Von Freund had left a large sum as a special fund to support the Verlag and other undertakings Freud had in mind. It was the equivalent of $500,000.00. It had, however, a very checkered career. It was only possible to transfer less than a quarter of it, half a million Crowns, to Vienna. It was decided to keep half of this in Vienna and transfer the other half to London. Over the former half Rank made the only financial miscalculation I ever knew him to make. At that time, when the Austro-Hungarian Monarchy was dissolving, one had the option of keeping Crowns in the Austrian currency or converting it into the Crowns of the new Czechoslovak Republic. Rank judged, as a good many people did, that the new State would not prove to be viable and so kept the money in Austrian notes. Within a couple of years the inflation made these worthless, whereas the Czech notes actually increased in value. It was doubly unfortunate, since the printers we employed were in Czechoslovakia and so had to be paid in their currency. I was in Vienna that September (1919), together with Eric Hiller, who was to assist in the fresh publishing schemes we were embarking on, and we undertook to smuggle the other quarter of a million Crowns out of the country and into England. On crossing the Austrian frontier we were stripped naked by the Custom officials, so the maneuver needed some finesse. My suitcase was examined first, so I then calmly fetched the roll of notes from Hiller's case and placed it in my own, which had now passed through the Customs. Both cases were, however, to be re-examined on the following day when the train left for Switzerland, so I hired a cab the next morning and drove over the Rhine bridge separating the two countries. At its boundary we could justly claim that our luggage had been already examined and stamped. This feat, however, met with no reward, since in another year or two the notes were hardly worth the paper they were printed on. Rank had not allowed us to change them into the few English pounds that at first we could have got for them; no one could believe at that time that a national currency could entirely disappear.

The Bolshevist regime in Hungary, followed by the Roumanian occupation in August, 1919, made for the time being all efforts vain to transfer any more of the main body of the fund to Vienna. The Red Terror there was followed by a White Terror with a strong wave of anti-Semitism that, as mentioned previously, seriously affected Ferenczi's situation. Nevertheless, he, Rank and von Freund continued to struggle, and at the end of 1919 there seemed some slight prospect of saving at least some of the money from confiscation. The municipal authorities held that a charitable bequest should be devoted to local philanthropical purposes and that in any case the money should not leave the country. Ferenczi then suggested that half of it should remain with the municipality and the other half be devoted to psychoanalytical purposes, an Institute, etc. in Budapest. Before agreeing to this the Mayor asked the Professor of Medicine for a report on the scientific standing of psychoanalysis. The one sent to him consisted, however, merely of a long quotation from one of Hoche's denunciatory outbursts,[76] which did not make things any easier. Ferenczi was asked to send in a counter-report, and he took Freud's advice on how to proceed. Freud's manly reply deserves to be quoted at length.

"1.1. 1920.

"Dear Friend:

"*Prosit* New Year and may you, being so much younger than I, live to see some emergence from this sea of misery.

"I regret very much the impression I have that you did not get far with Bódy and think he must be a cowardly and deceitful animal. I believe one must deal with him in another and more peremptory fashion. You seem to have behaved toward him like a humble applicant at Court to whom he denies the time to state his proposals, whereas you could have dealt with him as a party with equal rights. Furthermore, your idea of getting support from a Hofrat strikes me as utterly mistaken; it is a good thing he refused your request. . . .

"So I suggest that instead of begging B. again to grant you the favor of an audience you get Lévy Béla to send him a formal letter written in a firm decided style somewhat as follows:

'You, the person to whom the donor has entrusted plenary powers, are in no doubt that the representatives of the city have adopted an inimical negative attitude toward the use of the fund which the donor intended and which had been approved by the former Mayor.

'Unmistakable evidence of this was the obtaining of a verdict from someone without the slightest expert knowledge that might guard him from common prejudices. This attitude on the part of the city is very regrettable, since an Institute for the treatment of impecunious nervous patients would have been an eminently humanitarian and scientifically very valuable undertaking which would place Budapest ahead of other great centers.

'If Budapest rejects this plan you will not press the matter any further. Moreover, you feel sure that the suggested adoption of a number of strangers to the Board of Trustees, men unfamiliar with the work and whose interests lie in other directions, could only be a source of constant disagreement, and would inevitably jeopardize the whole undertaking.

'On the other hand, you can give the absolute assurance in the name of the donor that no other employment of the fund will be considered other than the one intended. In the event of his demise he will see to it that his heirs and executors will carry out his wishes just as inflexibly. The only consequence of this mutual intransigeance would be that the fund would find no way of being used, and that neither the city nor science would have any of it. The representatives of the city should be quite clear that any attempt on their part to dispose of the fund according to their own views must both now and later be doomed to failure.

'In the light of this disagreeable possibility you propose—again in the name of the donor—the following solution, which can dispel all the difficulties. You are prepared to transfer two-sevenths of the fund to the city for its free use provided that the rest is placed immediately, and with no further control or restriction, at your disposal as the donor's representative for the fulfilment of his scientific aims. If the representatives of the city do not accept this division and sharp separation you will have to make them responsible for the nullifying of the donor's humanitarian aims.'

"So much for the letter. You can make it ruder if you like, but in no case milder. Reject decisively any idea of frittering away the money or any sort of compromise. As an ultimatum you might (though unwillingly) agree to letting the city have three sevenths of the amount.

"Your decisiveness will in the end make an impression. Any further 'reports' or 'opinions' are quite superfluous. The premise of such an attitude on your part would be your agreeing to Toni's[k] original intention not being fully carried out. That can't be done in Budapest now. Retain something through autonomy. . . .

"Swift and energetic action on your part is indicated.

"*Herzlich*

"*Ihr* Freud"

Sad to relate, this energetic action which so deserved success met with none. The obstruction of the anti-Semitic and anti-psychological forces was too strong, and it was only after three years that a small amount of that valuable fund was rescued. It placed Freud and the Verlag in an awkward position, since they had in the meantime undertaken rather extensive financial commitments. Eitingon, however, the ever-dependable stand-by, saved the situation a few months later by inducing a sympathetic brother-in-law in New York to make to the Verlag the handsome donation of $5,000.00.

From the beginning there was present the obvious desirability of extending our publishing activities beyond the German language. A week after the Verlag was founded a publishing firm in Berne offered to combine with it by issuing French translations of the works published in Vienna. Even before that, during the war, an American, Samuel Tannenbaum, had suggested to me that we start an Anglo-American periodical devoted to psychoanalysis. I was unwilling to contemplate action of this sort independently of my Viennese colleagues, and begged him to postpone the idea until after the war. Then, when the *International Journal of Psycho-Analysis* was being planned, he claimed the right to share the editorial work with me.

[k] Von Freund.

Naturally I wanted a broader basis of an international order, and it then turned out that no American analyst was willing to be associated with Tannenbaum. He was understandably, though inevitably, offended at not being accepted as co-Editor, and not long afterward joined Stekel and Herbert Silberer in issuing a separate periodical entitled *Eros-Psyche* which had a very short life.

When I met Rank in Switzerland in March, 1919, we concocted a plan that seemed most promising, though it had the defect of trying to kill too many birds with the same stone. A branch of the *Verlag* should be founded in London that would publish a periodical and English translations of the books appearing in Vienna. All our publications, however, would be printed in Austria, or rather in the new Czechoslovakia, where paper and labor were many times cheaper than in England. So we should fulfill the capitalist's dream of producing in a cheap currency and selling in a dear one. The expected profits would of course be used to support the parent *Verlag*, which was now being thrown on its own slender resources. We were very pleased with ourselves for devising such a brilliant scheme, one which two such good friends as we were could not fail to put into operation harmoniously and successfully. The final outcome of our plan was that it fulfilled the aim of providing the English-speaking public with much needed psychoanalytical literature, but hardly at all that of supporting the *Verlag* from our sales. This was a disappointment to Freud whose chief interest for some years was in the progress of the *Verlag*; early on he had expressed the opinion that "the German *Verlag* cannot exist without the English one." [77]

The firms of "ex-enemy" countries were at that time not allowed to have branches in England, or only under impossible restrictions, so I had to become an independent publisher by establishing what we called the International Psycho-Analytical Press. Its independence was of course only nominal. It had three main activities. It began with a shop in Weymouth Street, where mainly German books, otherwise unobtainable, were sold; Eric Hiller was in charge of it. This undertaking hardly lasted a year, when we sold the stock for £100 ($280.00) and closed the shop. Then came the International Psycho-Analytical Library Series, of which I have just finished editing the fiftieth volume; the first two volumes appeared in 1921. Seven of them were printed abroad according to our plan. After that, in 1924, the London Institute came to a satisfactory arrangement with the Hogarth Press, and their joint publication has continued ever since.

Of the enormous labor of translating Freud's works the chief matter that concerns us here is the constant detailed cooperation he himself afforded us. We sent him question after question about slight ambiguities in his expositions, and made various suggestions concerning inner contradictions and the like. This process has continued ever since under James Strachey's able leadership, with the noteworthy result that the English translation of Freud's works under the name of the *Standard Edition* will from an editorial point of view be considerably more trustworthy than any German version.

To help me in editing the *International Journal of Psycho-Analysis*, the third and most important of our undertakings, I enlisted the names of Douglas Bryan and Flugel in England. The delicate matter of choosing the American editors proved more complicated. Legally speaking, the choice was the Director's, i.e., Freud's. Both of us began by writing to Brill for his advice, but could get no answer. Then the Hague Congress in September, 1920, passed a resolution asking for the opinion of the New York Psychoanalytical Society. This was erroneously construed there as giving the Society the choice, and difficulties arose when they suggested names that seemed to us undesirable. Freud thought very highly of H. W. Frink, of New York, who was at the time studying psychoanalysis with him, and Frink also did some choosing. After some tactful maneuvering, however, the final choice fell on the names of Brill, Frink and Clarence Oberndorf; the last of these continued in this position until his recent death (1954). Freud was for a time dubious about including Brill, because of the difficulty of getting letters from him, but I gave my vote for him and Freud then consented.[78]

An arrangement, one which illustrates the value of friendly cooperation, was made between the *Journal* and the *Internationale Zeitschrift für Psychoanalyse*, of which incidentally I was also co-Editor, whereby either could freely use any material, papers, reviews and other communications, published in the other. The plan looked most promising, and yet it was the difficulties arising in connection with the *Journal* that loosened the publishing bonds between London and Vienna. Only three volumes were published in Austria. After that we employed a London agent, Jonathan Cape, and finally the famous medical firm of Bailliere, Tindall & Cox.

I had, of course, at the outset communicated our plans to Brill, and he at once promised me his cordial support.[79] He made at the same time the curious suggestion that we form an Anglo-American Psycho-Analytical Association in contrast to the International Association, which was at that time essentially German or at least German-speaking. Brill had been strongly pro-German in the early part of the war, but later events seemed to have over-Americanized him. Being among other things a good European as well as being always internationally minded, I frowned on the suggestion and heard nothing further of it.

Apart from that friendly letter there was a dead silence for a long time. I should have liked to open the *Journal* with a paper from Brill, but repeated requests, including three cables, failed to elicit any response. Freud had not heard from him since the beginning of the war, and as time went on after it was over he became more and more concerned about him. Then there was a sign of life. "From Brill I got the translation of Leonardo, Wit, and Totem. No letter." [80] In the meantime, however, Brill had nobly collected $1,000.00 to help the *Verlag*, and told Rank so. It was no news to me when Freud wrote saying that "Brill is really all right." [81]

He had not attended The Hague Congress in September, 1920, but then came the explanation of his prolonged silence. "I have received a letter from Brill, a long, tender, crazy letter not mentioning a word about the money but explaining away the mystery of his behaviour. It was all jealousy, hurt sensibility and the like. I will do my best to soothe him." [82] Brill had evidently been going through a very bad time, but it was the only one in his life of that kind. Forever after he was his old loyal and friendly self. The trouble had been Brill's belief, quite unfounded in fact, that Freud was displeased with him because of the severe criticisms that had been made of his translations. Freud had never taken them at all amiss, but from that time Brill wisely decided to leave such work to others.

We now come to the matter of Freud's works in these two years, and it might be of interest to preface it by a more general remark. Freud was seldom satisfied with any of his productions: they always fell so far short of what he really had to say, and the topics were so incredibly rich that only a part of them could be expounded in the very little time he had at his disposal for literary work; in the circumstances of his life it is truly amazing that he managed to produce as much as he actually did. It is easy to state the parts of his work to which Freud attached the highest importance: those by which he would have wished to be remembered if he ever cherished such an irrelevant wish, but certainly those which he considered to be his most valuable contributions to human knowledge. They were (1) the seventh chapter of *The Interpretation of Dreams* (1900),[88] (2) the last chapter of *Totem and Taboo* (1913),[84] and (3) the essay on "The Unconscious" in his metapsychological series (1915).[85] They amount altogether to only 220 pages!

By 1916, in the middle of the war, Freud must have felt that he had given to the world all that was in his power, so that little remained beyond living out what was left of life—indeed, only the two years that at that time he believed were allotted to him. In the amazing, and almost incredible, burst of energy in the spring of 1915 he had poured his deepest thought and his most far-reaching ideas into the theoretical series of essays on metapsychology, and in the following year he had brought his years of lecturing and exposition to an end by writing and publishing the *Introductory Lectures on Psycho-Analysis*.

In the winter of 1918-19 the students of the Budapest University were petitioning for lectures on psychoanalysis to be given, and Ferenczi had hopes of being given an official position at it. Freud supported this by writing a paper for a Hungarian medical periodical entitled "Should Psycho-Analysis be taught at the University?" [86] No German version of it has as yet appeared, but a Spanish translation was published in 1955.[87]

For the next couple of years there seemed to be nothing to look forward to, either in further development or in the spread of his doctrines. Then with the stimulation at the end of 1918 of the successful Budapest Congress, the foundation of the *Verlag* and the good news coming in from beyond the seas, Freud's spirits revived. At the beginning of the New Year he had told Ferenczi he was still quite held up with respect to scientific ideas,[1] but only a couple of weeks later we hear of some new ideas on the theme of masochism, of the truth of which he felt assured.[89] In March there came a longer account of the fermenting that was evidently going on in that spring. "I have just finished a paper, 26 pages long, on the genesis of masochism, the title of which will be 'A Child is Being Beaten.' [90] I am beginning a second one with the mysterious caption 'Beyond the Pleasure Principle.' [91] I don't know whether it is the cold spring or the vegetarian diet that has suddenly made me so productive." [92] Then, a fortnight later, he wrote: "I am writing the new essay on 'Beyond the Pleasure Principle,' and count on your understanding,

[1] *Wissenschaftlich noch vernagelt.*[88]

which has never yet failed me. Much of what I am saying in it is pretty obscure, and the reader must make what he can of it. Sometimes one cannot do otherwise. Still I hope you will find much in it that is interesting." [93]

In a couple of months the first draft was done,[94] but he planned to rewrite it during his treatment at Bad Gastein.[95] In the meantime, however, he filled in his few spare hours before leaving by rewriting an old paper of his which he found in his drawer.[96] It was an interesting one, entitled "The Uncanny," which he published in *Imago* toward the end of the year.[97]

The progress during the holiday was slow, and he told me he could not get on because he felt too well.[98] Evidently he was not satisfied with the effort, and he seems to have dropped it till the following summer. In the interval he wrote one of his great case histories, the one on female homosexuality.[99] This was finished in January, 1920, and published in March[100] in the *Zeitschrift*.[101]

In that May he told Eitingon: "I am now correcting and completing the 'Beyond the Pleasure Principle,' and find myself in a productive phase." [102] On June 16 he gave an abstract of it before the Vienna Society. In the same month he wrote to Ferenczi that "curious continuations" had turned up in it, presumably the part about the potential immortality of protozoa. He finished it before leaving for his summer holiday, and asked Eitingon to bear witness that it had been half-ready at a time when his daughter Sophie was in the best of health; he added: "Many people will shake their heads over it." [103] It was a rather curious request, and one might have wondered if it did not betoken an inner denial of his novel thoughts about death having been influenced by his depression over losing his daughter were it not that in another letter written only two weeks after that unhappy event he had casually referred to what he had been writing about the "death instinct." [104] The book appeared at the beginning of December, 1920.[105] Freud told Eitingon he had an "unruffled conscience" [m] over it.[106]

Freud seemed to have expected people to draw the inference that his thoughts about a death instinct had been evoked by the mourning over Sophie, and in fact Wittels, in his biography of Freud, did so.[107] The list of corrections Freud sent him in a letter of December 18, 1923, contained the following passage on this erroneous conclusion of Wittels'. "That always seemed interesting to me. I cer-

[m] *ein ruhiges Gewissen.*

tainly would have stressed the connection between the death of the daughter and the Concepts of the Hereafter in any analytic study on someone else. Yet still it is wrong. The Hereafter[n] was written in 1919, when my daughter was young and blooming, she died in 1920. In September of 1919 I left the manuscript of the little book with some friends in Berlin[o] for their perusal, it lacked then only the part on mortality or immortality of the protozoa. *Probability is not always the truth.*" [p]

Incidentally, the child whose behavior played such a significant part in stimulating Freud's theory of the repetition-compulsion was his eldest grandson, Ernst.[108]

Freud was right. Many people, including many analysts, did shake their heads over the new ideas and are still doing so. Consideration of them will be reserved for a later chapter.

The startling ideas Freud here put forward on the relation of life to death, with his introduction of the conception of the "death instinct," were not only profoundly philosophic, but in the nature of things highly speculative. Freud himself put them forward as such and in a quite tentative fashion, though later he came to accept them entirely. He had never written anything of the sort in his life before, and this itself is a matter of the highest interest to any student of his personality. He had, it is true, often admitted having a speculative or even phantastic side to his nature, one which he had for many years strenuously checked. The restraint he had put on his imagination in his early neurological years had twice caused him to miss fame,[109] and it was the release of it under the encouragement of his friend Fliess that had enabled him to apprehend the unknown in the years of his greatest discoveries. Now he was surrendering the old control and allowing his thoughts to soar to far distant regions. What had happened?

It is interesting in this connection to recall a passage from a letter Freud wrote to his betrothed thirty-seven years before when he was in his mid-twenties: "Philosophy, which I have always pictured as my goal and refuge in my old age, gains every day in attraction, as do human affairs altogether or any cause to which I could give my devotion at all costs, but the fear of the supreme uncertainty of all political and local matters keeps me from that sphere." [110]

[n] I.e. *Jenseits* (*des Lustprinzips*).
[o] Eitingon and Abraham.
[p] Not underlined in the original.

I would correlate this remarkable and unexpected change in the mode of Freud's working with two considerations. As was expounded above, he felt he had contributed all in his power to strictly scientific knowledge, and after completing that mighty task had allowed his mind to lie fallow for a couple of years or even resigned himself to having come to the final end of his labors. This feeling, that he had fulfilled his task on earth, had done his duty with a completeness that would save him from any possible reproach, must have lifted a burden from Freud's mind. He was at last free, and need no longer restrain the flight of his own personal thoughts.

Then, secondly, he had come closer than ever to the dread phenomenon of death. There was the massacre of the terrible war in which he had feared, or even expected, his dearly loved sons to be killed, and had been doubtful if he himself would survive its privations. He had been increasingly looking forward to the promised date of his own death in February, 1918,[111] with mingled feelings of dread and longing. Furthermore, we should not forget that the theme of death, the dread of it and the wish for it, had always been a continual preoccupation of Freud's mind as far back as we know anything about it. We can even trace the beginnings of it all to the sinful destruction of his little brother in his earliest infancy.

The second book dating from this period, *Group Psychology and Analysis of the Ego*,[112] was conceived in the same outburst of productivity that created *Beyond the Pleasure Principle*. Over two months after announcing the inception of the latter, and while he was still engaged in writing it, Freud wrote to say that he had just thought of a "simple idea that will serve as a psychoanalytic foundation for group psychology." [113] Then in the winter of 1919-20, when he was being held up over the difficulties inherent in the earlier book, he turned to the second one, on which he was "meditating in a slow and hesitating way." [114] But he had already started to write it.[115] In May he said that his essay on group psychology was turning into a book, and that, being so overworked at present, he intended writing it in Gastein.[116] There he was at first too tired "to reflect on these deep problems," [117] but in a few weeks he was able to report progress in the writing.[118] The draft was finished in September.[119] At the end of the holidays he sent it to Berlin for Abraham and Eitingon to read; he would take it up again and finish it when Anna brought it back from Berlin.[120] In the New Year he started rewriting it, and by the middle of February had written eight pages.[121] He then finished it rapidly and sent it to the printers on March 28;[122] It was published at the beginning of August, 1921.[123]

In these first two years after the war, therefore, we see that Freud had hopefully resumed his active life, was full of new productive ideas and of practical plans for extending the knowledge of his work in the world at large. After this time things never went so well with him again. Disappointments with friends and terrible physical suffering were sorely to test his fortitude.

2

Disunion
(1921-1926)

THERE WAS SOMETHING IN FREUD'S ATTITUDE TO THE COMMITTEE THAT transcended his cordiality toward its individual members, and it is important to bear it in mind when the following story is being unfolded. More than individual friendships Freud had come to treasure the value of his discoveries and all that ensued from them. He had been lucky enough to make them, but that did not necessarily constitute him a great man. It was as if he had been entrusted with a valuable accession to our knowledge, and it was his function above everything else to cherish and to further it, rather as a conscientious hereditary landowner might feel about his estate. Now Freud never expected to live long, so inevitably he was deeply concerned with the transmission of his main function in life, the care of psychoanalysis, to what might—to continue the analogy—be called his heirs. During their voyage to America in 1909 Freud used to relate his dreams to his companions, Jung and Ferenczi, as they did to him, and they told me shortly after that the predominant theme running through them was care and anxiety about the future of his children and of psychoanalysis. These two ideas must have been closely associated, since there is much reason to suppose that in his unconscious his work in psychoanalysis ultimately represented some product of his body, i.e. a child. We were trustees for that child.

It would be a mistake to think that Freud felt any personal dependence on any member of the Committee, even on the one nearest to him, Ferenczi. All traces of such dependence had vanished for good after the break with Wilhelm Fliess. In the nature of things his attitude toward us was more that of a father than of a colleague of our own age. He was interested in our well-being and in our family life, particularly our children, but he had no occasion to enter into our intimacies except in the case of Ferenczi, who constantly demanded personal help in his private difficulties.

It follows from these considerations that the preservation of harmony in the Committee was to Freud a matter of prime concern, and that any difficulty that might arise between any two members made him anxious about its preservation. How long could such harmony continue in a group composed of men of very different temperaments, coming from five different nationalities, who had only rare opportunities of coming together to exchange their views and consolidate their friendship? Besides that friendship there was of course the great common bond of devotion to a cause, the pursuit of psychoanalytical knowledge. The most likely source of dissension would be manifested in any faltering in that pursuit, and so it turned out. But, as is often so, the signs of this were at first indirect and masqueraded under other guises.

Adherence to what psychoanalysis had revealed signifies the same as retaining one's insight into the workings of the unconscious, and the ability to do so presupposes a high degree of mental stability. My hope when founding the Committee naturally was that the six of us were suitably endowed for that purpose. It turned out, alas, that only four of us were. Two of the members, Rank and Ferenczi, were not able to hold out to the end. Rank in a dramatic fashion presently to be described, and Ferenczi more gradually toward the end of his life, developed psychotic manifestations that revealed themselves in, among other ways, a turning away from Freud and his doctrines. The seeds of a destructive psychosis, invisible for so long, at last germinated.

The harmony that had prevailed for some ten years was now to be disturbed, and seriously so. The evil spirit of dissension arose, and by 1923 the Committee so important to Freud's peace of mind looked like disintegrating. It did in fact cease functioning for a space of several months. It is not surprising that this calamity caused Freud deep distress, especially as it coincided with the onset of what he knew to be a fatal affliction in his own body. His philosophic powers of resignation, which had already withstood so many blows from fate, came to the rescue, and he bore it all with his customary fortitude. But he would not have been human had he failed to reproach those of us whom he took to be responsible for what had happened. The blame fell on Abraham and to a lesser extent myself. It was only after a lapse of a few years that the true source of the trouble became manifest: namely, in the failing mental integration on the part of Rank and Ferenczi.

The first sign of anything going wrong was a gradually mounting tension between Rank and myself over the business of publication. The circumstances of the time, and a certain incompatibility in our temperaments, were responsible. I had always been very fond of Rank and continued to be so up to the very time of the rupture. We always saw eye to eye whenever we had to confer together personally. Operating at a distance, however, was another matter, and it led to difficulties that could possibly have been smoothed out had we lived in the same town. In our joint plan of founding the English Press in 1919, which was to sustain the Verlag, we had made fatal miscalculations. The fall in the Austrian currency had given us the idea, of which we were very proud, that it would pay handsomely to produce goods in that currency and sell them in a better one. It all sounded so simple. Two things, however, we did not know, and they were then unknown to most people. One was that however low a currency falls the rise in costs and prices would sooner or later keep pace with world prices, so before long it was hardly cheaper to produce in Austria than in England. Then, no one living had had the experience of a national currency not merely falling in value, but dissolving into nothingness as the Austrian, and soon afterward the German, currency did. Our joint work soon became a race against time. We were also, for different reasons, both working under strains and against obstacles that were hardly to be borne.

The general machinery of life had so run down in Austria after the war that there were indescribable difficulties in getting anything done. Paper and type had to be scrounged from odd corners, labor disputes were frequent and communications exasperatingly slow. Rank struggled heroically with the endless problems and accomplished superhuman feats in coping with them almost single-handed: as a single example, he had to buy his own string, make up the parcels of books to be despatched and carry them himself to the post office. But the strain told on his sensitive nature.

On the personal side our relationship was hampered by a tendency of mine that often caused me difficulties in life, a rather obsessive insistence on doing things in what I conceived to be the best way, with an impatience for sloppiness, at the risk of provoking the sensibilities of other people concerned. Rank on his side was working with an almost maniacal fury in the aim of achieving and producing at all costs, so my occasional protests irritated him beyond measure. He responded—or was it that he began?—by displaying toward me an overbearing and hectoring tone which I found extremely strange when coming from an old friend. This proceeded by degrees into an overruling or ignoring of decisions I had to make in the conduct of the Press which made cooperation difficult, to say the least. What had aroused this harsh dictatorial, and hitherto unseen, vein in Rank's nature I could not guess; it took a couple of years before it became plain that a manic phase of his cyclothymia was gradually intensifying.

I had known that Rank had suffered much in childhood from a strongly repressed hostility to his brother, and that this usually covered a similar attitude toward a father. This was now being unloaded on to me, and my dominant concern was how to protect Freud from the consequences. I sensed, truly enough, how much harmony in the Committee meant to Freud, so I strove to conceal the Rank-Jones difficulties from him. My partner, however, was at his side and had not the same scruples. He constantly poured into Freud's ears stories of how impossible I was as a colleague, and Freud's native scepticism commonly left him in the lurch in such personal situations. I kept reassuring him that he should not trouble himself about us, that we two could surely arrange matters between ourselves, but as his opinion of me deteriorated this outlet did not avail long.

For three years I lived with the fear lest Rank's "brother-hostility" regress to the deeper "father-hostility," and I hoped against hope that this would not happen in Freud's lifetime. My fear was unfortunately justified, since at the end of that time Rank openly expressed an ungovernable hostility against Freud, and I shall relate presently how Freud coped with this totally unexpected blow. It was in a manner that throws a vivid light on his noble character, but also on the way in which personal influences could deflect his judgment.

The actual nature of the differences between Rank and myself are no longer of much interest, but since they greatly concerned Freud at that time a short description of them seems necessary. The background was the intense opposition to psychoanalysis with which I had to struggle in England. The hatred felt in Germany in the war against England who had spoiled her chances of victory was increasingly reciprocated. After the First World War the strong dislike in England of everything German was incomparably stronger than it was after the Second World War, although one might have thought it was more justified on the latter occasion. Our opponents exploited this to the full, and psychoanalysis, with the stress it had to lay on the less seemly aspects of human nature, was vilified as a typical product of German decadence and general beastliness. My protests that Freud was more Jewish than German had little effect—it was enough that he wrote in German—but it is understandable that I was eager not to emphasize the German associations of our work. It was bad enough that the *International Journal* had unavoidably to be printed in obviously foreign type, there being no English type available in Austria. The foreign printers, having no knowledge of English, interlarded the text with germanisms, which I was at pains to eliminate. This meant sending proofs more than once from Vienna to London with the considerable delay involved. Despite all efforts the January number of the first volume did not make its appearance until July, 1920, with the April number following in November. Then Rank, who at that time knew very little English, took to correcting the proofs himself without informing me. I recollect that the straw that broke the camel's back was finding Mrs. Riviere's name printed in the membership list as Frau Riviere! So we had to install someone in Vienna who could correct proofs there and save the time spent in posting them to London. Eric Hiller, who had been assisting the press in the bookseller's shop we started in London, was sent to Vienna in December 1920, and that much improved matters. An invaluable, though at the time apparently incidental, gain was the enlisting of Anna Freud's help in the English department in Vienna, work which brought her closer to psychoanalysis than ever before and which foreshadowed her future career.

The anti-German prejudice was of course only part of the general opposition to psychoanalysis, and the years 1921-22, with which we are here concerned, were particularly difficult ones for us in London. There were scores of "wild analysts," * and all their misdemeanors were ascribed to the iniquities of psychoanalysis. The press revelled in stories of raped patients who were then blackmailed, and so on. When an American teacher was sent to prison, and then deported, for indecent behavior with "patients," that again was an ex- ample of our perfidy, and *The Times* refused to publish a letter we sent them disclaiming any connection with him. Newspaper placards

---

* An "English Psycho-Analytical Publishing Company" published the following advertisement: "Would you like to earn £1,000 a year as a psycho-analyst? We can show you how to do it. Take eight postal lessons from us at four guineas a course!" [1]

blared such news and shrieked about the supposed dangers of psycho-analysis, and the *Daily Graphic* appointed a committee of lawyers and doctors to inquire into our practices; it published daily reports on their progress. The Archbishop of Canterbury appointed a Committee to study the ethics of masturbation in response to a little book on the subject written by a clerical ex-patient of mine, and I had an interesting time giving evidence before it.

There was a clamor for some official body, particularly the General Medical Council, to investigate our work. The Royal College of Physicians were approached, but refused to act; a little later, however, the British Medical Association did so, with results entirely favorable to us. The Lord Mayor ordered a somewhat erotic autobiography published by Kegan, Paul & Co. to be burned by "the Common Hangman," and Sir Stanley Unwin narrowly escaped a police prosecution for publishing the translation of a book issued by the *Verlag, A Young Girl's Diary*, which I had luckily refused to incorporate in our Library Series. It was not all grim, however, and some light relief was afforded by an Oxford undergraduate who, under the pseudonym of Professor Busch, allegedly an intimate colleague of Freud's, gave a nonsensical disquisition in a lecture which appears to have deceived even the College Dons.

Then there were American pirates to cope with, a theme on which Rank and I assuredly saw eye to eye. This meant endless correspondence and interviews with lawyers. One medley from Freud's writings had been edited by somebody whose preface was nothing but a panegyric of Adler and Jung. The London publishers who had acquired the British rights wanted to compromise by accepting a monetary payment from the pirate, but Freud stood firm, on my advice, and insisted on the piracy being entirely withdrawn. The American editor then sought an injunction to prevent the *Journal* being admitted into the United States in revenge for a scathing exposé I had written of the book; fate willed it, however, that he died a month later.

Although it was not really his concern, Rank kept sending me sharp criticisms on the way I edited the *Journal*. He would even reject a paper I sent him to print if he was not satisfied with it. What he specially objected to was what he called "transatlantic rubbish," and that was the first sign of the conflict between Vienna and New York in which I was to spend the next twenty years. I had wanted the *Journal* to be not simply a duplicate of the German *Zeitschrift*, but to serve also as an opportunity for the budding analysts in England and America to publish their contributions even if their first efforts were undeniably not of a classic nature. Being eager to enlist American cooperation I would invite the then President of the New York Psychoanalytic Society to send a contribution to the *Journal*, and then when it proved to be mediocre it was impolitic to refuse it. Freud also expressed dissatisfaction with the contents of the first two years of the *Journal*.[2]

The troubles over the *Journal*, however, were mild in comparison with those in connection with the translation of Freud's works, and here he was more directly concerned. For a long time he was curiously indifferent to this matter, and he was opposed to my "wasting my time" in even revising the translations that were being made in England. Then when he observed the ambitious plans I was making his attitude changed. Always obsessed with the idea that he had not long to live, he became very eager to see some of the promised volumes appear in his lifetime, and he got increasingly censorious over the delays. Freud fully accepted Rank's views that I was solely to blame for them, as well as for the delays in issuing the *Journal*; it was my meddling interference. Apart from the printing itself there were enormous difficulties in agreeing about the arrangement of the items making up the four volumes of the *Collected Papers*. Freud himself, Rank, the translator and I all had different views on the matter, and, what was worse, the views kept changing. At one moment I received final instructions from Rank that the order of the papers was to be "the same as in the enclosed list just like that of the publication in German, i.e. chronological." I had to point out that the two lists did not correspond and that neither of them were chronological, so we had to start over again. It took months to get this simple matter straight, but fortunately it did not interfere with the translating work which was proceeding.

Securing the copyright for the *Collected Papers* was also a complicated problem. Freud was distinctly cavalier about the copyright of his translations, and it has taken his son Ernst some years of legal work to clear the way for Strachey's *Standard Edition*. Freud would give us the full copyright in English, then hand over the American rights to his nephew Edward Bernays, restore them to us for a limited period, then get Rank to dispose of them during his visit to America, and so on. All this led to appalling difficulties in concluding contracts with publishers who were not accustomed to such vagaries.

In the fourteen years I had known Freud our personal relations had always been excellent and had never been marred by any trace of disagreement; over and again he had paid me the highest compliments, both personally and in respect of my work. It was therefore a shock to find that his opinion of me had deteriorated. Early in 1922 I was startled, and of course pained, to receive the following letter from him:[b] [3]

"Dear Jones: *

"I am sorry you should still be suffering and as I felt rather ill myself these two weeks I am full of sympathy for you.

"This last year brought a disappointment not easy to bear. I had to find out that you had less control of your moods and passions, were less consistent, sincere and reliable than I had a right to expect of you and than was required by your conspicuous position. And although you had yourself proposed the Committee you did not refrain from endangering its intimacy by unjust susceptibilities. You know it is not my habit to suppress my true judgement in relations of friendship and I am always prepared to run the risk attaching to that behaviour.

"You are quite right in asking that friends should treat each other as unrelentingly as fate does, but just imagine how much more satisfactory it is to a friend to acknowledge, or praise or to admire the other man than to forgive him. . . .

"Wishing for a complete restoration of faith and friendship in 1923 [*sic*].

"affectionately yours
"Freud"

As Massinger said centuries ago, "No man's a faithful judge in his own cause," and I must leave it to others to decide whether Freud was here presenting a true bill or giving an example of his suggestibility. The allusions to my "passions," which could hardly have emanated from Rank, particularly puzzled me, especially as it was followed in later letters by mysterious allusions to "adventures" (which could only mean erotic ones) and how they distract one from work. The explanation came months later. Among the many patients I was sending to Freud in those years was a woman I had partly analyzed myself, so I sent Freud a short account of the case. She had taken a couple of kindnesses I had shown her as proofs of personal affection on my part and, as I put it in my letter, "it came to a declaration of

> * Throughout this volume, an asterisk has been used to enable the reader to identify that correspondence which Freud wrote in English.

love" on her part. Freud had misread this as meaning that it was my declaration and even assumed I had sexual relations with her; when she came to him for analysis he was pleased to find his mistake.

Presently Freud came to more concrete criticisms of my behavior, and they were much easier to cope with. The essential problem was the source of the inordinate delay in the publishing of Freud's books in English. He became more and more impatient and doubted if he would live to see any of them. Three months after the letter just quoted he wrote:

"Dear Jones: *

"Another wheel in the machinery seems to be wrong and I imagine it is your position in the middle of it and the ceremonial, that prescribes your personal interference in every step of the process. So I hear that every *Korrektur*^c has to go to you and as there are three to five men who do the correcting I understand why I get one sheet of the *Mssenps.*^d in two weeks see no chance to live up to the finishing of these two poor pamphlets (*Jenseits* and *Mass.*),* let alone bigger things like my *Sammlung.* I don't see why you want to do it all alone and suffer yourself to be crushed by the common drudgery of the routine work. . . . It would do if you got a glimpse of the last *Korrektur,* make it the final one and leave the intermediate phases to others. . . . Many months could be spared if you could be moved to throw down part of the burden. . . .

"Pardon my meddling with your affairs but they are ours and mine too and Rank is too meek to oppose you in these quarters. My broad shoulders are as you say better to lift this weight. . . .

"With best love to you, wife and children
"affectionately yours
"Freud"

The innocent allusion to Rank, which evoked what novelists term a mirthless laugh, showed me that Freud never saw the overbearing letters I was constantly receiving from him. In my reply I said ". . . As you say, we must also see what can be done to hasten matters at the London end, and there I shall be very grateful for any definite suggestions. The only one you make, of leaving all but the final proof corrections to Vienna, I have already put into force some eighteen months ago. Not since the first two numbers of the *Journal*

* Proof.
ᵈ *Group Psychology.*
* *Beyond the Pleasure Principle* and *Group Psychology.*

have I seen any proofs except the last final 'printing off' ones, and the same is true of all the Press books, from the first to the ones now being printed. Hiller, with occasional help from visitors, has done all this on the spot. Of course I could give up seeing even the final proofs and should like your opinion on the point. I don't think Rank would feel happy if he never saw a single proof of the *Zeitschrift* unless he had more trustworthy workers under him than I have. On this matter of proofs, therefore, his information seems very out-of-date, and probably relates to the beginning of the *Journal* when there was no English person in Vienna and the printers were quite unused to the work. At that period, it is true, Hiller and I had to see all the proofs in London, and when we omitted to do so the results were deplorable. But now, and for a long time, I do exactly what you suggest, rapidly look through the final proofs, the first I have seen, and return them on the day of their arrival.

"I have no love at all for detailed work of this sort, on the contrary, and have feared I have been too complaining in expressing my strong desire to be relieved of routine work wherever possible. . . . What trouble I have got into is due rather to my deputing too much (i.e., translations for the *Journal*). . . . So you see my anxiety coincided with your advice to relieve myself of burdens and is not at all, as Rank mistakenly thinks, the desire to keep control of details. I had better write fully to him describing the procedure of what happens from the reception of work to its appearance and ask him to suggest some modifications, of which I should be only too glad.

". . . You know how sorry I am that your translations are not more advanced, but they constitute a good case in point. You rightly complain about the two brochures, *Jenseits* and the *Massenpsychologie*. Well, judge from them. I revised the translation of the former a year ago and sent it to Vienna to be printed last *May*. Since then I have had nothing to do with its existence except to receive last December the first two *Bogen*,[1] and to make repeated inquiries about its fate. So much for my interfering with details. The only information I can get from Hiller during these eleven months is the repeated message that he has been held up for lack of type or of paper but that he hopes things will soon be better. I am quite helpless except to keep writing to him and to Rank about it. Similarly with the *Massenpsychologie*. I finished the revision last August, and Strachey took it with him to Vienna. This week I get the first of the proofs.

[1] Folios.

"I am sorry to trouble you at such length, but the matter concerns us all, and I wanted to put the true situation before you since you have been so good as to take deep interest in it all. You know that it is essentially for you that we are all working, which is why your inspiration and approval mean so much to us all. If I can produce a Collected Edition of your works in my lifetime and leave the *Journal* on a soundly organised basis I shall feel that my life has been worth living, though I hope to do more for psycho-analysis even than that." [4]

This matter-of-fact reply brought a postcard: "Thank you so much for your kind letter. Afraid I am growing old and moody. You spared me all criticism." [5] In the next letter he wrote: "This letter I might have written you some weeks before, but. . . . Also I had cleared my mind by that card which confessed my being wrong on your account. . . . My first suspicion that the fault lay with you I had to take back and to apologise to you. . . . Now I am getting sick of this translation business. I was deeply stirred by your saying that you considered the bringing out of my English books as one of the foremost tasks of your work and hope you will see this in the light of a tender exaggeration produced by some sudden impulse, while your substantial work is sure to aim higher and lose sight of my personal interests. I still appreciate your words as an expression of an unfailing kindness towards me which as you know I always intend to return." [6]

After that Freud's criticisms, though they continued from time to time, became milder, but my relations with Rank kept on worsening. He now took to censoring my conduct of the International Association affairs, usually on grounds that could be easily refuted. This brought Abraham into the situation, since Rank interfered with the arrangements for the Berlin Congress of 1922 for which Abraham was largely responsible. Presently, when Abraham had become Secretary of the International Association, Rank, without letting either of us know, circularized the various Societies on matters that solely concerned the Central Executive. Abraham's response to Rank was much sharper than any of mine,[7] and Freud composed a personal letter to both of us in which he defended Rank against our supposedly neurotic susceptibilities.[8] We both of course disputed Freud's version.[9]

The affairs of the Press and *Verlag* were fully discussed on the occasion of the last amicable Committee meeting we held, immediately after the Berlin Congress at the end of September, 1922. Hiller refused to work any longer with Rank and had resigned; he finally left Vienna in March, 1923. Without an English representative there it was out of the question to continue on the old lines, and after trying various compromises it was ultimately agreed that the Press should, with the support of the Institute of Psycho-Analysis that was just then being founded in London, lead an independent existence. Freud did not think it possible for us to survive for more than a year, which was one reason why he withdrew the American sales of his books from us, but we conquered all difficulties, as the continued success of the *International Journal* and the *International Psycho-Analytical Library Series* bear witness.

I had hoped that the separation in our business relations would lead to a *détente* on the personal side, but I was surprised to find that Rank's hostility to me became increasingly manifest. This came to a head at the last Committee meeting we ever held together, toward the end of August, 1923. Ferenczi and Rank had spent the previous month together at Klobenstein in the Tyrol, where they worked together finishing a book, *The Development of Psychoanalysis*,[10] on which they had been engaged for a couple of years. Freud had commented a year before on this literary cooperation of the two men that it was very promising for the future;[11] events were to show that "sinister" would have been a more appropriate term.

We all met at San Cristoforo, on Lake Caldanozzo in the Dolomites, so as to be near Freud who was spending his holiday at Lavarone, 2,000 feet higher. This was four months after Freud's first operation for cancer, and two months before the more radical one that was to follow. At the time neither Freud nor anyone else had been told of the malignant nature of the disease, with the sole exception of Rank who had heard of it from the medical attendants. Freud always maintained later that this news had had a fateful effect on Rank, who was entirely dependent on him for a living, and that it had stimulated Rank to strike out on an independent path. The chronology, however, shows that this could only have been a partial determining factor in the development of Rank's ideas and behavior.

Freud had proposed that we should try the experiment of meeting together to learn to achieve harmony without him; if we succeeded he would be pleased to greet us afterward. It appears that I had made some critical remarks about Rank—I cannot remember now to whom—and he at once brought up this unfriendliness on my part. I apologized for having hurt his feelings, but he refused to accept this and demanded that I be expelled from the Committee. This the others naturally would not allow, Abraham in particular defending me, but there was a very painful scene with Rank in uncontrollable anger and myself in a puzzled silence.

Although harmony had not been restored, Freud agreed to receive us, and I shall never forget the kindly forbearance with which he made every effort to bring about some degree of reconciliation.

After that painful event I fade out of the Rank picture and my place as a "disturber of the peace" is taken by Abraham. Ferenczi and Rank published *The Development of Psychoanalysis* toward the end of that year, 1923. This remarkable book, which was to play a fateful part in the story, appeared suddenly without anyone else in the Committee except Freud knowing about it, and that alone surprised the other members of the Committee, who could not help regarding it as an inauspicious circumstance so much at variance with our customs and, indeed, mutual promises. It was a valuable book inasmuch as it gave a brilliant account of many aspects of psychoanalytic technique, but it had inconsistent and self-contradictory passages, and it sounded a strange note as if heralding a completely new era for psychoanalysis. The main theme it dealt with was the propensity of patients to live out their unconscious impulses in action. Freud had devoted a special paper to this topic[12] and had stressed the struggle between this propensity and the more analytic aim of reviving the original and now repressed impulses of childhood. This book very properly showed how the analysis of the acting-out tendency could itself be of great value, and Freud accepted this conclusion as a correction of his former attitude and technique. Actually in the seven years since writing that paper Freud had advanced further in his technique and was making a more active use of the "living out" tendencies than he had earlier.[13]

But there were many passages in the book which suggested, if not quite explicitly, that analysis of such tendencies might be sufficient without penetrating their historical sources in childhood. To me this was reminiscent of the charge I had brought against Jung at the Munich Congress of 1913 that he was replacing analysis of childhood by discussions of current situations only, and indeed that ambitious or reactionary analysts might exploit it in this sense. I hinted at this when I opened a symposium at the Innsbruck Congress four months later. Freud also had this doubt, although he felt sure it would not apply to the authors of the book.[14] The analysts in Berlin, particularly Abraham and Rado, were less happy on this point, and time was to justify their fears.

Freud had read the book before it was published and had made a number of suggestions, to which perhaps may be ascribed many of its merits.[15] He told Ferenczi later that he had at first been captured by it, especially because of the stress it laid on the advance in technique he had himself been making. But that as time went on he had come to think less and less of the book. He found it "not honest." Concealed behind it were Rank's ideas about birth trauma and Ferenczi's technical method of "activity," both of which were aimed at shortening an analysis, and yet neither of these was mentioned in the book. He had told Rank and Ferenczi that the paths opened here promised to be suitable for "commercial travelers," [g] but a warning should be enough to prevent this abuse.[16]

On January 2, 1924, Ferenczi read a paper from the book before the Vienna Society in Freud's presence. When he asked for Freud's opinion on it later Freud wrote him that it had left a curious impression on the audience, since Ferenczi did not touch on the main theme of the book—the tendency to live out memories instead of recalling them—and had dealt only with his new technique of "active therapy," which Freud guessed was being stressed in opposition to Rank's birth theory. Freud also made a mild remark in this letter that he did not entirely agree with all that the book contained.[17] Ferenczi in a letter ten pages long said he had been "shattered" by this remark, and excitedly protested that he could never dream of departing by a hair's breadth from Freud's teaching. This overemphasis did not arouse the slightest suspicion in Freud, but he disapproved of the unscientific attitude it implied. In his answer he wrote: "As for your endeavor to remain completely in agreement with me, I treasure it as an expression of your friendship, but find this aim neither necessary nor easily attainable. I know that I am not very accessible and find it hard to assimilate alien thoughts that do not quite lie in my path. It takes quite a time before I can form a judgment about them, so that in the interval I have to suspend judgment. If you were to wait so long each time there would be an end of your productivity. So that won't do at all. That you or Rank should in your independent flights ever leave the ground [h] of psychoanalysis seems to me out of the question. Why shouldn't you therefore have the right to try if things won't work in another way from that I had thought? If you go astray in so doing you will find that out yourself

[g] *Handlungsreisende.*
[h] *Boden.*

some time or other, or I will take the liberty of pointing it out to you as soon as I am myself sure about it." [18]

This whole matter was greatly complicated by the appearance about the same time, December, 1923, of a far more disturbing book by Rank entitled *The Trauma of Birth*.[19] Neither Freud nor Ferenczi had read this beforehand, though they knew Rank was writing it, and it came as a great surprise to the rest of us. Freud had long thought that the painful experience of being born, when suffocation inevitably brings the infant into mortal peril, was a prototype of all later attacks of fear.[1] Rank, now applying the word "trauma" to this event, maintained that the rest of life consisted of complicated endeavors to surmount or undo it; incidentally, it was the failure of this endeavor that was responsible for neurosis. The book, badly and obscurely composed, was written in a hyperbolical vein more suitable for the announcement of a new religious gospel. It accorded with the hypomanic phase through which Rank was then passing. No data were given which could be tested, and most of the book consisted of extravagant speculations in the fields of art, philosophy and religion. Clinically it followed that all mental conflicts concerned the relation of the child to its mother, and that what might appear to be conflicts with the father, including the Oedipus complex, were but a mask for the essential ones concerning birth. Psychoanalytic treatment, therefore, should consist solely in concentrating from the outset in compelling the patient to repeat in the transference situation the drama of birth, and the resulting re-birth would constitute the cure.

These ideas of Rank had germinated slowly. It stayed in my mind that in March, 1919, when I met him with his pregnant wife in Switzerland, he had astonished me by remarking in a dismal tone that men were of no importance in life; the essence of life was the relation between mother and child. On March 16, 1921, he had read a curious paper before the Vienna Society on the relation between married partners; they, he maintained, always repeated in essence those between mother and child (on both sides alternately).[20] It was a paper that attracted no attention at the time. Freud had on a few rare occasions used the device of putting a term to a patient's analysis, a date before which he had to finish it. Rank now took to doing this in every case without exception, thus greatly reducing the length of an analysis. It gave him the idea that an analysis should consist in one gigantic "living-out" experience, and before long this assumed the form of re-birth.

[1] *Angst.*

Rank told Freud of his theoretical ideas, not the practical clinical ones, in the summer of 1922, and Freud repeated them to Ferenczi on the occasion of the Berlin Congress in September, 1922. When he heard them from Rank his first remark was: "Anyone else would have used such a discovery to make himself independent." It looked like an uncanny prevision—although, if so, a completely unconscious one—of what actually happened three years later. His comment to Ferenczi was: "I don't know whether 66 or 33 per cent of it is true, but in any case it is the most important progress since the discovery of psychoanalysis." [21]

Freud's varying responses to Rank's theory throw an interesting light on his personality, so I propose to relate them in some detail. The initial one was of mistrust,[22] and four months after the book appeared he said that his first shock of alarm—lest the whole of his life's work on the etiology of the neuroses be dissolved by the importance attached to the trauma of birth—had not entirely vanished.[23] Very soon, however, this gave way to the pleasure he felt that Rank had made a discovery of fundamental importance, and his interest turned to the problem of how it was to be woven into the previous fabric of psychoanalysis. Nevertheless, as time went on, probably influenced by the criticisms coming from Berlin, which voiced the very misgivings he was trying to stifle, he became more and more doubtful about the value of Rank's work. This oscillation, with at times his contradictory comments on the theory, naturally made it hard for others to know what was really his opinion. It is plain now that the part of his response that calls for explanation was the exaggerated praise he bestowed in certain moods, and this has a bearing on his curious reaction to the criticisms that kept coming in.

At Christmas, 1923, Sachs was in Vienna and Freud expressed to him the doubts he felt about Rank's theory. Sachs wrote this to Berlin, where it reinforced the critical attitude already prevailing there. Then Freud heard from Eitingon about what he called the "storm" in Berlin, and he felt he should do something to assuage it. He therefore dictated the following circular letter to all members of the Committee.

"*Wien*   "15 Februar. 1924
"*Liebe Freunde,*
    "I have heard from various sides, not without some astonishment, that the recent publications of our Ferenczi and Rank—I refer to

their joint work and that on birth trauma—have evoked considerable disagreeable and agitated discussion.[j] One of our friends[k] has begged me to ventilate among ourselves the as yet undetermined matter, in which he perceives a germ of dissension. When I accede to this request please do not think I am obtruding. I should myself prefer to keep as much as possible in the background and let each of you follow his own way.

"When Sachs was here recently I exchanged some comments on the birth trauma with him; hence perhaps the impression that I discern an antagonistic tendency in the publication of that work or that I absolutely disagree with its contents. I should have thought, however, that the very circumstance of my accepting the dedication should invalidate this idea.

"The fact of the matter is this: neither the harmony among us nor the respect you have often shown me should hinder any of you in the free employment of his productivity. I do not expect you to work in a direction to please me, but in whatever way accords with your observations and ideas. Complete agreement in all scientific details and on all fresh themes is quite impossible among half a dozen men with different temperaments, and is not even desirable. The sole condition for our working together fruitfully is that none of us abandons the common ground of psychoanalytical premises. Then there is another consideration with which you must be familiar and which makes me specially unfitted for the function of a despotic censor always on the watch. I do not find it easy to feel my way into alien modes of thought, and I have as a rule to wait until I have found some connection with my meandering ways. So if you wanted to wait with every new idea until I can endorse it you would run the risk of getting pretty old.

"My attitude toward the two books in question is as follows. The joint work I value as a correction of my conception of the part played by repetition or acting-out in the analysis. I used to be apprehensive of them, and used to regard these happenings—'experiences' you call them nowadays—as undesired mishaps. Rank and Ferenczi have called attention to the fact that these 'experiences' cannot be avoided and can be made good use of. In my opinion their description has the shortcoming of not being complete; i.e. they give no account of the changes in technique with which they are so concerned, but only hint at them. There are certainly many dangers

[j] *unliebsame Erregung.*
[k] Eitingon.

attaching to this departure from our 'classical technique,' as Ferenczi called it in Vienna, but that doesn't mean that they cannot be avoided. Insofar as it is a question of technique, of whether for practical purposes we could carry out our work in another way, I find the experiment of the two authors entirely justified. We shall see what comes of it. In any event we must guard against condemning at the outset such an undertaking as heretical. All the same, we need not suppress certain misgivings. Ferenczi's 'active therapy' is a risky temptation for ambitious beginners, and there is hardly any way of preventing them from making such experiments. Nor will I conceal another impression or prejudice I have. In my recent illness I learned that a shaved beard takes six weeks to grow again. Three months have passed since my last operation, and I am still suffering from the changes in the scar tissue. So I find it hard to believe that in only a slightly longer time, four to five months, one can penetrate to the deepest layers of the unconscious and bring about lasting changes in the mind. Naturally, however, I shall bow to experience. Personally I shall continue to make 'classical' analyses, since in the first place, I scarcely take any patients, only pupils for whom it is important that they live through as many as possible of their inner processes—one cannot deal with training analyses in quite the same way as therapeutic analyses—and, in the second place, I am of the opinion that we still have very much to investigate and cannot yet, as is necessary with shortened analyses, rely solely on our premises.

"Now for the second, and incomparably more interesting, book, the Birth Trauma by Rank. I do not hesitate to say that I regard this work as highly significant, that it has given me much to think about, and that I have not yet come to a definitive judgment about it. We have long been familiar with womb phantasies and recognized their importance, but in the prominence Rank has given them they achieve a far higher significance and reveal in a flash the biological background of the Oedipus complex. To repeat it in my own language: some instinct must be associated with the birth trauma which aims at restoring the previous existence. One might call it the instinctual need for happiness,[1] understanding there that the concept 'happiness' is mostly used in an erotic sense. Rank now goes further than psychopathology and shows how men alter the outer world in the service of this instinct, whereas neurotics save themselves this trouble by taking the short cut of phantasying a return to the

[1] *Glückstrieb.*

womb. If one adds to Rank's conception the one of Ferenczi, that a
man can be represented by his genital, then for the first time we get
a derivation of the normal sexual instinct which falls into place with
our conception of the world.

"Now comes the point where I find the difficulties begin. Obstacles, which evoke anxiety, the barriers against incest, are opposed to
the phantastic return to the womb: now where do these come from?
Their representative is evidently the father, reality, the authority
which does not permit incest. Why have these set up the barrier
against incest? My explanation was an historical and social one,
phylogenetic. I derived the barrier against incest from the primordial
history of the human family, and thus saw in the actual father the
real obstacle, which erects the barrier against incest anew. Here
Rank diverges from me. He refuses to consider the phylogenesis,
and regards the anxiety opposing incest as simply a repetition of the
anxiety at birth, so that the neurotic repression is inherently checked
by the nature of the birth process. This birth anxiety is, it is true,
transferred to the father, but according to Rank he is only a pretext
for it. Basically the attitude toward the womb or female genital is
supposed to be ambivalent from the start. Here is the contradiction. I find it very hard to decide here, nor do I see how experience
can help us, since in analysis we always come across the father as
the representative of the prohibition. But naturally that is not an argument. For the time being I must leave the matter open. As a
counter-argument I might also point out that it is not in the nature
of an instinct to be associatively inhibited, as is the instinct to return
to the mother through the association with the birth terror. Actually
every instinct in its urge to restore a former condition presupposes a
trauma as the cause of the change, and thus there cannot be any
ambivalent instincts, i.e. any accompanied by anxiety. Naturally a
good deal more could be said about this in detail, and I hope that
the thoughts Rank has conjured up will become the subject of many
fruitful discussions. We have to do here not with a revolt, a revolution, a contradiction of our assured knowledge, but with an interesting addition the value of which we and other analysts ought to recognize.

"When I add that it is not clear to me how the premature interpreting of the transference as an attachment to the mother can
contribute to shortening the analysis, I have given you a faithful
picture of my attitude to the two works in question. I value them
highly, already accept them in part, have my doubt and misgiving

about several sections of their content, look forward to a clarification from further reflection and experience, and would recommend all analysts not to form too quickly a judgment, least of all a disapproving one, about the questions that have been stirred.

"Forgive my discursiveness. Perhaps it will keep you from provoking me to express opinions over matters which you can just as well judge for yourselves.

"Freud"

This perhaps over-tolerant letter failed to allay Abraham's misgivings. He did not like to reply in a circular letter lest it irritate the two people concerned, so he wrote a private letter to Freud saying that he saw signs of a fateful development which concerned vital questions of psychoanalysis. They compelled him to issue a warning to Freud, and he said that finding himself robbed of his customary optimism was a measure of his perturbation.[24] Freud asked him to specify the danger he saw threatening, since he himself could see none. He added: "I should be sorry to believe that your fraternity will collapse as soon as I die, but I am egotistic enough to want to prevent that as long as I am still here." [25] Abraham then composed what must have been a very difficult letter for him to send, particularly since he knew Freud to be in a state of great physical misery as the result of his recent radical operation. Encouraged on hearing that Freud was open to listen to criticism, even of his near friends, he said outright that he saw in the two books in question signs of a scientific regression which closely resembled that of Jung's twelve years before. The only hope lay in a frank discussion among the Committee members before the next Congress (in April).

Sachs was more sympathetic to Rank's innovation than Abraham, but he put his finger on a fatal weakness in Rank's exposition of it. "The trauma of birth can be proved from ethnological material, and from the psychology of religion as little as can the Oedipus complex. The interpretation of dreams and the theory of neuroses are the presupposition without which Totem and Taboo would not be thinkable. Without such a basis the whole exposition remains not a proof, but an analogy. . . . So the book can only be called a torso." [26] "I will support with my whole heart your endeavors to achieve an accommodation and a mutual adherence for both material and personal reasons. I have tried, with some success, to soften Abraham's opinion, but Rank and Ferenczi will also have to show themselves more amenable to his criticisms." [27] But he was by no means an apostle of "appeasement." A few days later he answered a letter of Freud's: "There is one point where I do not entirely agree with you. It is this. If a tendency were to develop (I am almost certain that the Rank-Ferenczi will not prove to be of this order) which neglected our causal-psychological point of view, which at the same time gave up our previous technique, replacing it by explaining the trauma of birth to the patient with an outside limit of a few months of treatment, then I should feel sure that to cooperate with such a tendency would be just as little fruitful as that with the Jungian or Adlerian school." [28]

Freud was a little piqued that Abraham should for a moment have doubted his willingness to listen to a painful criticism, and he admitted that the possibilities Abraham had envisaged were not so remote from his own mind. But, he declared, the two men in question differed fundamentally from Jung and were moved by nothing more than a desire to find something new. So the only danger they ran was that of being in error, "which is hard to avoid in scientific work. Let us take the most extreme case, that Ferenczi and Rank made a direct assertion that we have been wrong in pausing at the Oedipus complex. The real decision is to be found in the birth trauma, and whoever had not overcome that would come to shipwreck in the Oedipus situation. Then instead of our actual etiology of the neuroses we should have one conditioned by physiological accidents, since those who became neurotic would be either the children who had suffered a specially severe birth trauma or had brought to the world an organization specially sensitive to trauma. Further: on the basis of this theory a number of analysts would introduce certain modifications in technique. What further harm would ensue? One could stay under the same roof with the utmost calm, and after a few years' work it would become plain whether some had overestimated a valuable find or whether others had underestimated it. So it seems to me. Naturally I cannot beforehand invalidate the thoughts and arguments you intend to bring forward and for that reason I am fully in favor of the discussion you propose." [29]

These two letters of Freud's—to which a number of others could be added—constitute in themselves a decisive rebuttal of the legend that some writers have invented about him: that he was averse to allowing any of his adherents to have ideas of their own or ideas that diverged from his. Naturally he never disputed the right of anyone to leave psychoanalysis altogether, and some did; then he had no more concern with them. But on the broad basis of psychoanalysis he often welcomed original ideas, even when they differed from his own; as we shall see presently, they stimulated his interest. Here is one instance out of many. He gave later as the reason why he had at the beginning overestimated the importance of Rank's own views the fact that, as he said, "I was so delighted that he had mounted to a thoroughly original achievement in the analytical field that I was prepared to make the friendliest judgment about it. Naturally that did not mean that I had given up the right to acquire an opinion of it through my own experience, one independent of that attitude." [30]

Freud had evidently not reckoned with the reactions of the two authors. Two days after writing to Abraham he, not very wisely, told Rank of Abraham's suspicions and his analogy with Jung, and Rank of course passed on the news to Ferenczi. It is hard to say which of the two got angrier. Ferenczi wrote denouncing the "limitless ambition and jealousy" that lay behind Abraham's "mask of politeness," declared that by his action he had sealed the fate of the Committee, and claimed that he had forfeited the right to be elected President of the International Association which it had been arranged would take place at the coming Congress.[31] The fat was fairly in the fire.

Freud reproved Ferenczi about this re-emergence of his "brother complex," which he had hoped was done with. As to the presidency he would play no part in the matter, but leave it to us to decide among ourselves. He remarked, however, that it would be a painful slight to Abraham to deny it to him, "in spite of the wrong he has done," after it had long been understood that he, being the Secretary, was the next to succeed me.[32]

Freud had been too optimistic in supposing that the four of us, Abraham, Ferenczi, Rank and myself, would find it easy to thrash matters out calmly, and he was evidently badly shaken by the turmoil he had unwittingly provoked. He hastened to assure Ferenczi of his absolute confidence in his and Rank's loyalty, adding: "It would be sad if one could find oneself deceived after living together for fifteen to seventeen years." But he could not conceal his distress at what had happened. "I do not doubt that the other members of the former Committee feel considerateness and good will toward me, and yet it has come to pass that I shall be left in the lurch just when I have become an invalid with diminished powers of working and in an enfeebled frame of mind which turns away from any increased burden and no longer feel equal to any carking care. I am not trying to move you by this complaint to take any step to retain the lost

Committee. I know: gone is gone, and lost is lost.[m] I have survived
the Committee that was to have been my successor. Perhaps I shall
survive the International Association. It is to be hoped that psychoanalysis will survive me. But it all gives a somber end to one's
life." [33]

In this mood of resigned despair Freud even turned against the
faithful Abraham whom he now blamed for all the trouble just as in
the old days a ruler would pour his wrath on the messenger of bad
tidings. According to him Abraham should not have replied to
Freud's circular letter, but should have discussed the issues with
Ferenczi and Rank directly—an action that would have had little
if any prospect of success. He wrote a hard and not at all friendly
letter to Abraham in which he said: "However justified your reaction
to Ferenczi and Rank may be, your behavior was certainly not
friendly. And that is what has made it quite clear that the Committee no longer exists; because the sentiments are not there that would
make a Committee out of this handful of people. In my opinion it is
up to you now to stop any further disintegration and I hope that Eitingon will help you in that. It surely cannot be your object to allow
your uneasiness to rupture the International Association and all
that depends on it." [34] Freud could on rare occasions be distinctly unfair, and this was one of them. His rather irrational blame of Abraham persisted, as such attitudes were apt to with Freud. But writing
in reference to Abraham's supposed bad behavior (and perhaps also
mine) he concluded: "A little more or less injustice when one lets
oneself be driven by passions is not a reason for condemning people
of whom one is otherwise fond." [35] In the same letter he expressed
the hope that Ferenczi would be able to come to terms with Abraham, with Eitingon's help, since he had to confess that these constant squabbles were most abhorrent to him and would probably
result in his not concerning himself with them, whatever the consequences.

Abraham did not take this lying down. In a friendly and manly letter he disputed such accusations, and was bold enough to attribute
Freud's changed attitude—quite correctly—to his resentment at being told a painful truth.

An attack of influenza made it impossible for Freud to attend the
Salzburg Congress at Easter, 1924. Ferenczi and Rank had absolutely refused to take part in any discussion of their work, so the

[m] *hin ist hin, verloren ist verloren.* A quotation from "Lenore," a poem
by Bürger.

Committee meeting that had been arranged for the day before the Congress did not take place. In fact, ten days before that Rank sent us a circular letter in which he announced the dissolution of the Committee, a decision in which Ferenczi had angrily and Freud sorrowfully acquiesced. So, though fortunately only for the time being, were buried Freud's and our hopes.

Neither the indefatigable Abraham nor myself, however, were content to leave matters in that state. Together we tackled Ferenczi at the first opportunity during the Congress, and Abraham quite frankly told him he was starting on a path that would take him away from psychoanalysis altogether. His manner was so absolutely sincere and impersonal that Ferenczi could only respond with a smile and protests such as: "You can't really mean that." A calm and increasingly amicable conversation followed. Presently Sachs joined us, and a fair degree of harmony was restored. It could then be said that five of the six members of the Committee were once more in a working comradeship.

Rank, however, proved quite inaccessible, and he left the Congress on the second day for his journey to America. He told Freud later that he had left the Congress hurriedly before the Business Meeting because he could not bear to witness Abraham being made President.[36] At the banquet the evening before, Edward Hitschmann, in one of his witty after-dinner speeches, apostrophized him as the author of "The Myth of the Trauma of Birth," a play on the title of Rank's best known book *The Myth of the Birth of the Hero.* Freud's fears about an acrimonious rupture at the Congress proved to be unfounded. In the symposium at which the topic of birth trauma had to be mentioned the three Berlin analysts who conducted it spoke with restraint and objectivity. We could all be pleased with the success of the Congress, in spite of the unfavorable auspices under which it was held.

When it came to the point it was Ferenczi himself who proposed Abraham's election to the presidency. When writing to congratulate Abraham on his new position, Freud said: "In the judgment on the facts I am very near your point of view, or rather I keep approaching it more and more, but in the matter of personalities I still cannot side with you. I am convinced of the correctness of your behavior, but nevertheless think you should have done things differently." [37] His affection for Abraham had fully returned. In the next letter he called him his "rock of bronze" and explained his former mood. "To avoid being cross with me you have to feel yourself (intensively)

into my condition. Though I am supposed to be on the way to recovery there is deep inside a pessimistic conviction that the end of
my life is near. That feeds on the torments from my scar which
never cease. There is a sort of senile depression which centers in a
conflict between an irrational love of life and more sensible resignation. . . . If I am deceived and this proves to be only a passing
phase I shall be the first to note it and then once more put my shoul-
der to the plough." [38]

His earlier enthusiasm for Rank's work was rapidly diminishing. In
that same letter he wrote: "I am getting further and further away
from the birth trauma. I believe it will 'fall flat' if one does not
criticize it too sharply, and then Rank, whom I value for his gifts and
the great service he has rendered, will have learned a useful lesson."

This was the only occasion I have ever known Freud to speak
favorably of statistics in connection with psychoanalysis; usually he
regarded them as irrelevant or inapplicable. Now he told Ferenczi
that, had he been in Rank's position, he would never have thought of
publishing such a revolutionary theory without at first collecting
some statistical data comparing the mentality of first-born children,
those who had specially difficult births and those born by means of
Caesarean section.[39] For some weeks he had tried to apply Rank's
theory in his daily work by interpreting the associations wherever possible in terms of birth, but he got no response from his patients,
nor had the interpretations any other effect on them.[40] Ferenczi, on
the other hand, had had wonderful results by applying the same
method and could not do without it in a single case.[41]

Thaddeus H. Ames, then President of the New York Society, had
invited Rank to come there for six months. Being regarded as Freud's
right-hand man he was well received, and he gave lectures before
several of the leading neurological societies in New York. After some
three months disturbing accounts of his activities began to reach
Europe.[42] The teaching that the "old" psychoanalysis had been quite
superseded by his new discoveries and that an analysis could now
be completed in three or four months caused a considerable stir.
Many of the younger men were captivated by the wonderful
improvement, but the more tough-minded, notably Brill, were
merely puzzled and naturally wanted to know what Freud had to
say about it all. Freud himself hoped at first that the accounts were
exaggerated, though he thought it wrong of Rank to propagate ideas
that had not yet been properly tested. He began to talk of Rank's

psychoneurosis, though he did not agree with Ferenczi that this was evoked by success going to his head. It was rather due to his having not been analyzed.[43] Yet only eighteen months before he had remarked that in the fifteen years he had known Rank he had scarcely ever had the idea of Rank needing any analysis. The conclusion he had now come to strengthened the natural impulse to treat Rank affectionately[n] on his return. A few weeks later, however, an extremely unpleasant letter from Rank arrived.[o] Freud found it hard to believe what he read, it seemed so unlike the Rank he had known. He was completely bewildered. "I simply don't understand Rank any longer. Can you do anything to enlighten me? For fifteen years I have known him as someone who was affectionately concerned, always ready to do any service, discreet, completely trustworthy, just as ready to receive new suggestions as he was uninhibited in the working out of his own ideas, who always took my side in a quarrel and, as I believed, without any inner compulsion to make him do so. . . . Which is the real Rank, the one I have known for fifteen years or the one Jones has been showing me in the past few years?" [44]

He sent a copy to Eitingon. "Naturally Abraham is not to learn anything about the content of Rank's letter. The sentiments he expresses in it are too ugly. There is in it a tone of malice and hostility that makes me doubt any good issue." [45] Rank had evidently reproached Freud for his bad treatment of him in not fully accepting all the new ideas that had been offered him. In a letter to Ferenczi Freud protested: "I too claim the right to form my own judgment and am not bound to agree unconditionally with a beginner's innovations when I am myself prepared to let everyone have his opinion within the natural boundaries of common work." [46] Rank also explained his feelings of hostility as the result of Freud's listening to Abraham's criticisms; Freud appositely commented that he was indulging in a queer kind of revenge on Abraham in following along the very path the latter had suspected him of taking. In a letter to Rank Freud had rather incautiously suggested that he would not have written the book if he had been analyzed, because of the danger of importing his own complexes into his theory, whereupon Rank angrily replied that from what he had seen of the analysts Freud had trained he thought he was lucky never to have been

[n] *liebevoll.*
[o] Jessie Taft is publishing some of the correspondence between Freud and Rank in these years.

analyzed. Freud commented on this: "That passes everything, just as does his description of Abraham as an absolute ignoramus and a precocious child who doesn't know when to hold his tongue." [p]

In spite of still nourishing some hope of the prodigal's return Freud was prepared for all contingencies. "Rank is carried away by his discovery, just as Adler was, but if he becomes independent on the strength of it he will not have the same luck, since his theory contravenes the common sense of the laity who had been flattered by Adler's striving for power. . . . When he comes to his senses it will of course be the time to recollect his extraordinary services and his irreplaceability and to forgive him all his divagations. I dare not hope for that, however; experience shows that once the devil is loose he goes his way to the very end. I feel very mortified to think that Jones should prove to have been right." [47] Freud's judgment of the matter then showed for the moment a somewhat harsher note. "It looks now as if from the very beginning he had the intention of establishing himself on the basis of his patent procedure, which he kept secret, and wanted you to join him. I am astonished that you let yourself in so far with this secret business. In my innocence I had no idea of how much he was concealing. . . . He seems to me now to resemble the employee in Victor Hugo's *Les Travailleurs de la Mer* who achieved great confidence through years of correct behavior so as to be able to embezzle an enormous sum. . . . I see that I am in angry ebullition. I still find it hard to believe that Jones's suspicions should have been so right. But it is also hard to take another view from all the indications we have. . . . If that is really so it is neither dignified nor hopeful to try to keep him." [48] A month later he again reproached Ferenczi: "It vexes me to think how deeply you let yourself get involved with him." [49]

The talk Abraham and I had had with Ferenczi at the Salzburg Congress had probably had some effect on him. He had been on the edge of a precipice, and he now drew himself back in an unmistakable fashion. He announced to Freud after reading Rank's rude letter that he had definitely turned his back on him.[50]

At the end of September Freud got another letter from Rank, this time written in a cooler but even more final tone. After getting it Freud regarded him as definitely lost.[51] The whole episode of Rank's curious behavior in America had been very reminiscent of Jung's visit there in 1912, and the final issue proved to be the same.

When Rank came back to Vienna in the next month he had a

[p] *ein vorlauter Schreier.*

three hours' talk with Freud. He made a confused impression, and attributed all his behavior to his resentment at Abraham's provocation. This had given him the idea that Freud wanted to drop him, so he had to think of making a living elsewhere. The interview was unsatisfactory and led nowhere.[52] The main note in it was of evasive denials. At the end of the talk Rank announced his intention of returning to America for at least six months, at which Freud commented to Ferenczi that an Editor and *Verlag* Director who spent only six months in the upper regions belonged rather to the sphere of mythology[q] than to that of an analytical organization.[53] Rank and he agreed, however, to discuss the whole situation at the end of the week together with Eitingon and Ferenczi who came to Vienna for the purpose. Freud sent me an account of that interview, which took place on November 1 and which proved even more unsatisfactory.[54] On November 19 Rank called on Freud to say good-by. It must have been a painful and embarrassing interview. Freud said he felt dreadfully sorry for him because he could see he had something heavy on his heart which he was quite unable to express. He had not much hope of ever seeing him again. On the same day Freud got a letter from Brill which made a deep impression. Brill reported in lurid terms the extraordinary doctrines which Rank had been inculcating in New York and the confusion he had thereby created;[55] Rank's pupils had gleefully related that it was no longer necessary to analyze dreams, nor to make any interpretations beyond that of birth trauma, and they were relieved also from going into the unpleasant topic of sexuality. Freud circulated the letter, and its contents certainly seemed to render our opinion about Rank final.

Against Rank he felt no resentment at all, much as he deplored his loss. Nor did I. When Freud thought Rank had left Vienna for good, he had written to me about the situation. "As you see, an open break has been averted. Rank himself had not intended one, and a scandal would not be in our interest either. But all intimate relations with him are at an end. . . . Not only I, but the two others present at the interview,[r] found it very hard to regard him as honest and to believe his statements. I am very sorry that you, dear Jones, have proved to be so entirely right." [56] In my letter acknowledging this I said: "Although his loss bears most of all on you I can genuinely say that I am as sorry I was right as you are yourself. Your words were, it is true, no surprise to me, for bearing the brunt

[q] An allusion to Persephone.
[r] Eitingon and Ferenczi.

of his neurotic behaviour in these last years forced me to think deeply about him and to recognize the situation. My one hope was that you should never know, and my endeavour to prevent this cost me dearly in many ways. But I was throughout very fond of Rank, so that I too suffer an intense regret at the course fate has chosen." [57] Freud then wrote as follows: "The Rank affair is now meeting its end. . . . You must not think that the matter has greatly discomposed me or will have any aftereffect. That is perhaps rather queer when one reflects on what a part Rank has played in my life for a decade and a half. But I know of three explanations for the coolness in my feelings. First it may be a result of age which does not take losses so heavily. In the second place I tell myself that the relationship has so to speak been amortized in these fifteen years; it is not the same if someone is disloyal after two or three years or only after he has for years performed superlative work. In the third place, and last but not least, perhaps I am so calm because I can trace absolutely no part of the responsibility for the whole process." [58]

Sixteen months later, after having just read his book *Inhibition, Symptoms and Anxiety* in which he plumbed further depths of the problem of anxiety, I wrote to him: "My last comment on the book is that you provide a fourth, and perhaps the most important, reason in addition to the three you related to me at the time of why you were not more disturbed by the difficulty with Rank. It is now clear that you were wise enough to do what none of us others could do: namely, to learn something from it all by allowing Rank's views to work on you in a stimulating and fruitful way. What a splendid reaction to a depressing difficulty—*alle Ehre!*" [59]

Then a miracle happened. Rank got as far as Paris on his way and was seized there with a severe attack of depression; his last one had been five years before. He returned to Vienna and came to see Freud in the second week of December. He was once more a changed man. Apart from the depression he seemed to have clear insight into his condition. As Freud put it, he had emerged from a psychiatric condition. [60] He discussed the whole matter with Freud as if in a confessional. It had been a really sad episode which had nearly ended in an actual tragedy. Freud was deeply moved by it and overjoyed at finding again his old friend and adherent. Writing to Eitingon he said that Rank had acted out his neurosis on the very lines he and Ferenczi had described in their joint book, and that the content of it was closely similar to the theories Rank had put forward in his book on birth trauma.[61] Rank was now overwhelmed at the thought of what had happened and had only one wish, to undo the harm he had caused. His intention was to return to America for this purpose, which Freud said would not be very easy to carry out. Freud remarked that he could understand our reserving a certain mistrust, but that for his own part, with his fuller knowledge of the condition, he had completely overcome it.[62] He told Abraham he was quite sure Rank had been cured of his neurosis through his experience* just as if he had gone through a regular analysis.

Freud's optimism and relief were both expressed in a letter to Joan Riviere of the same date: "You will have heard that there has been a disagreeable intermezzo with Dr. Rank, but still it was only a passing feature. He has come back to us completely and has accounted for his behavior in a fashion that calls for tolerance and forgiveness. He has passed through a severe neurotic state, has now come to himself, and sees through and understands everything that happened; he has not yet overcome the depression which is an understandable result of his experience. I may say that I was quite blameless in this disunion unless you count my illness in the sense of *Erewhon*. But I am very happy that it proved to be only a temporary one." [63] How mistaken these optimistic judgments were we shall presently see.

A year later he told Marie Bonaparte that in that semi-analytic interview Rank had explained that his theory about the trauma of birth was derived from an unconscious wish he had detected in himself to be born from his father's head like Athene. Then the shock of hearing that his "father" Freud was suffering from an incurable disease had been more than he could bear. It also aroused fears about not being able to support himself if Freud died, so he determined to carve a new career for himself. He also told her that no "heresies" ever disturbed him so much as feeble concessions to opposition, such as Bleuler's substitution of "autistic" for "auto-erotic" so as to avoid the idea of sexuality; it would have been all right, he added jokingly, if Bleuler had inserted a footnote: "by autistic is meant auto-erotic."

There are two remarkable features about Freud's optimism which can only be explained by his intense relief at the thought of not having lost a friend who for so many years had been invaluable to him. One was his knowledge that Rank suffered from cyclothymia,† a fact

---

* *Erlebnis.*
† I.e. manic-depressive psychosis.

he had commented on years before.[64] Freud had been trained in psychiatry and was thoroughly familiar with the feature of almost inevitable recurrence in this complaint, yet he was able to repress this obvious consideration; actually Rank's present melancholic phase was again replaced by another manic one only six months later, with the usual oscillation in later years. The other curious feature was Freud's apparent acceptance of just the heresy we had been combatting in the theory that study of a repeating experience could supersede the need for a deeper genetic analysis: that *Erlebnis* therapy could replace psychoanalysis.

On December 20, 1924, Rank sent a circular letter to us explaining what had happened to him and asking for our forgiveness. He humbly apologized to Abraham and myself for the wrongs he had done us, and hoped we could resume our friendly relations. His hostility to Freud, so he told us, was part of a neurosis that had become manifest in association with Freud's dangerous illness from cancer. Naturally we all replied reassuring him of our understanding and sympathy. He did not, however, acknowledge my very friendly letter, nor one I wrote in February, 1925, condoling with him on the death of his brother—incidentally, the brother who had unconsciously been the source of much distress to me through Rank's neurotic transference from him.

Freud wrote to me saying he felt sure I would be prepared to overlook the past, adding: "It is a cheering issue that we don't have once more to leave by the wayside one of our group who has fallen or become a *Maraudeur*,[*] but may hope that after a time of convalescence he will again fight bravely in our ranks." [65]

We had not, however, waited for this dénouement before taking steps to repair the impaired links in the Committee. Indeed before that happened Freud had already suggested to Ferenczi that, there now being a harmonious Committee again, we resume our former custom of sending regular circular letters to one another. The first one, emanating from Ferenczi, ran as follows:

"Nov. 16, 1924.

"*Liebe Freunde,*

"I cannot deny our friend Ernest the sad satisfaction of having in his judgment of Rank's personality been nearer the truth than I was. After the experience of the past months I find myself compelled to

[*] *Maraudeur auf der Strecke.* Compare the Austrian Army expression "Maroder," a soldier who has fallen out on the march.

renounce any endeavor at reconciling Rank with Herr Professor, and indeed to take action against certain tendencies of Rank's which are not free from danger. To be able to do so in an advantageous manner I wish to support the suggestion Herr Professor has made to reconstitute the Committee correspondence. Will the members of the old Committee please express their opinions on this."

Naturally we had all gladly responded to this invitation, and we also previously accepted Abraham's earlier proposal that Anna Freud, who had started her analytic work the year before, take the place in the Committee then vacated by Rank.[66] The names of Brill and August Stärcke had also been suggested, but rejected.

Rank left for America again on January 7, 1925, and Freud wrote at length to Brill explaining the situation and asking him to help Rank in the difficult task that lay in front of him. Such appeals to Brill's generosity were never made in vain. He informed us that Rank was doing what he could, but was in a poor state. Rank only stayed a few weeks in New York this time, and came back to Vienna before the end of February in a miserable and depressed condition. He had, however, managed to deliver a lecture at the Sorbonne on his way home. He was still full of good intentions, but was too apathetic to attempt any sort of work.[67]

In June Freud reported that Rank had emerged from his depression and that they were having fruitful analytic talks together.[68] Rank read a paper at the Homburg Congress in September, 1925. It was very obscure and was gabbled at such a pace that even Ferenczi, who knew his thoughts so well, could not follow it.[69] He was very excited and talked about his vast plans for the future, but he did not display any personal friendliness to any of us. After the Congress he departed on his third visit to America. Freud approved of his doing so and was still sure there would be no recurrence of his former outbursts.[70]

From America Rank wrote friendly letters to Freud, announcing his return at Christmas, 1925, when he hoped to regain his former position.[71]

On his return to Vienna, however, he kept himself quite aloof, and on April 12, 1926—significantly enough three weeks *before* the celebration of Freud's seventieth birthday—he came for the last time to say good-by. "Rank has left Vienna for Paris to begin with, but probably that is merely a halt on his way to America. He may have had several motives . . . but the main thing is that now he has carried out in a so to speak sober cold fashion the intention he first tried to achieve in a stormy pathological attack: the separation from me and from all of us. Two facts were unambiguous: that he was unwilling to renounce any part of the theory in which he had deposited his neurosis; and that he took not the slightest step to approach the Society here. I do not belong to those who demand that anyone should be chained and sell themselves forever out of 'gratitude.' He has been given a great deal and accomplished much in return. So quits! On his final visit I saw no occasion for expressing my special tenderness; I was honest and hard. But we have certainly lost him for good.▼ Abraham has proved right." [72]

To Eitingon Freud had written: "The demon in him has now carried him along a slow tranquil path to the goal he tried to reach at first in a pathological attack. The secondary gain of the illness in the form of material independence was very considerable. I confess I was very deceived in my prognosis of the case—a repetition of fate. On the other hand Abraham's premature diagnosis certainly hastened and favored the course of events." [73] One sees that even now Freud had not quite forgiven Abraham, and probably also myself, for venturing to warn him of coming disaster.

When Freud thought he had really finished with Rank there was still another episode. A month or two after Rank's final departure in 1926 he published a pretentious book on technique[74] with Deuticke, not the *Verlag* (!). In it he maintained that a well-known childhood dream Freud had extensively analyzed before the war[75] must have really been dreamed late in the patient's analysis; the patient had simply taken Freud in. The six or seven wolves on a walnut tree in the dream were taken from the six photographs of the members of the Committee which were hung up in Freud's consulting room. Freud found this stupid as well as impudent. It was so easy to disprove. The photographs of the six Committee members appeared only after 1919; at the time of this patient's treatment, before the World War, there were only three, of Ferenczi, Rank and myself. But the conscientious Freud, sure as he was of all the facts, took the trouble to write to the patient, the "Wolfman," and ask him, without giving any reason, for his memories of the dream. The answer was unequivocal. There was not the slightest doubt in the patient's mind about the early date of that terrifying dream; the memory of it had tormented him all through his childhood. He had related it to Freud in the first year of his analysis, in 1911, three years before Freud

▼ *Also wir können das Kreuz über ihn machen.*

was able to analyze it fully. Freud got Ferenczi to comment on these facts when he reviewed Rank's book.[76] Freud's mild comment on the episode to Eitingon was "I can't get indignant about Rank. Let him err and be original." [77]

One of the rare allusions to Rank that Freud made later was written in 1937, the year before he died. It was on the topic of short analyses and the difficulty of making them efficient. Referring to Rank's attempt to carry out analyses in a few months by concentrating on the theme of trauma at birth, Freud said: "It cannot be denied that Rank's train of thought was bold and ingenious, but it did not stand the test of critical examination. It was conceived under the stress of the contrast between the post-war misery of Europe and the "prosperity" of America, and it was designed to accelerate the tempo of analytic therapy to suit the rush of American life. We have heard little of the results of Rank's plan. Probably it has not accomplished more than would be done if the men of a fire-brigade, summoned to deal with a fire from an upset oil lamp, contented themselves with merely removing the lamp from the room in which the conflagration had broken out. Much less time would certainly be spent in so doing than in extinguishing the whole fire." [78]

We are not concerned here with Rank's further career, any more than with those of the earlier dissidents, Adler, Stekel and Jung. All that mattered to Freud was that their work should be clearly differentiated from psychoanalysis. There are certain analogies between Rank's defection and Jung's which are perhaps worth commenting on. Both began with great secrecy, followed by considerable obscurity in the presentation of the divergences. Both were first manifested during visits to America, then with a rude personal letter. Then came a profound, but temporary, apology. The divergencies were perceived by others long before Freud would admit the possibility of them. When he did so he made every effort toward reconciliation, and when that failed he dismissed the events into oblivion. The outstanding difference in the two cases is of course that Jung was not afflicted by any of the mental trouble that wrecked Rank and so was able to pursue an unusually fruitful and productive life.

3

Progress and Misfortune (1921-1925)

1921

CONTRARY TO FREUD'S FOREBODINGS DURING THE WAR, HIS WORK AND his name were by now becoming more widely known than ever. His books were eagerly sought and were being translated into various languages. Even from France there was a request from André Gide, one of the Directors of the *Nouvelle Revue Française*, for permission to publish his writings. In Germany new Societies were being founded in Dresden, Leipzig and Munich.[1] The British Association for the Advancement of Science had decided to found a branch devoted to psychology, and invited Freud to inaugurate it with an address, but he declined.[2] He always disliked playing a prominent part in public; the lectures in America in 1909 had been an almost unique exception.

Professionally he was fully occupied. From this time onward he took fewer patients, there being so many pupils, mainly from America and England, who wished to learn his technique. In July he said he had promised to analyze twice as many people as he could actually take on resuming work in October.[3] As things turned out, he accepted ten.[4]

Early in the year the *Verlag* published a book by Groddeck entitled *Der Seelensucher* (The Seeker of the Soul). It was a racy book, with some bawdy passages. Several analysts, particularly Pfister, felt it was not the type of book for an avowedly scientific firm to publish, and the Swiss Society held a special meeting of protest. Freud had found the book very entertaining, and all he said in reply to the indignant letters that kept pouring in from Switzerland was: "I am defending Groddeck energetically against your respectability.

What would you have said had you been a contemporary of Rabe-
lais?" [5]

On April 3 a third grandson was born, Anton Walter, the son of
Martin Freud, and on July 31 yet another, Stephen Gabriel, Ernst
Freud's first son. Freud complained at having four grandsons, but no
granddaughter.[6]

Eitingon, who seldom missed being present on Freud's birthday,
attended for the celebration of his sixty-fifth, on May 6, and presented
him with the Königsberger bust in the name of the Committee, none
of whose other members were able to get to Vienna at that time of
year.

About this time Freud's constant complaints about getting old
took a sudden turn: "On March 13 of this year I quite suddenly
took a step into real old age. Since then the thought of death has
not left me, and sometimes I have the impression that seven of my
internal organs are fighting to have the honor of bringing my life
to an end. There was no proper occasion for it, except that Oliver
said good-by on that day when leaving for Roumania. Still I have not
succumbed to this hypochondria, but view it quite coolly, rather as
I do the speculations in *Beyond the Pleasure Principle*." [7]

In May I sent Freud a copy of the *Burlington Magazine* which
contained a description of a bronze statue of Moses made by Nicho-
las of Verdun in the twelfth century. It was cast in the intermediate
posture that Freud had assumed must have preceded the final one
depicted by Michelangelo. Freud was highly gratified at this confirmation of his interpretation, though his only comment in a letter
was: "Should I be right after all?" Four years later he published an
account of this find.[8]

In July the *Verlag* bought from Heller for 65,000 Marks ($15,-
470.00) the rights of all the books he had published for Freud, and
this greatly strengthened its position.

On July 15 Freud went to Bad Gastein, as usual to the Villa Wassing, with his sister-in-law Minna, who also needed treatment there.
His wife and daughter were in the meantime spending a holiday at
Aussee in the Salzkammergut. On August 14 they all met at Seefeld, a village nearly 4,000 feet high in the North Tyrol close to the
Bavarian frontier; they stayed there at the Pension Kurheim.[9] He was
still complaining of a tired heart, with palpitation and other cardiac
symptoms,[10] but he soon recovered in the mountain air; it was an
ideal spot, and he could walk for hours.[11]

There he had several visitors. Van Emden, who was staying at Salzburg, came twice to see him, and Ferenczi also spent a day with him. Most important was a visit from Brill, whom he had not seen since the war, after which it had been almost impossible to get another letter out of him. Freud always minded very much not getting an answer to his letters, and he began to lose his patience. At the end of January he sent Brill a very strong letter, which was tantamount to an ultimatum; he threatened to break off all relations with him and withdraw all further translation rights.[12] It was six months, however, before even this brought any reply. Freud was more and more incensed and began to feel the case was hopeless: "Brill is behaving shamefully. He has to be dropped." [13] Then at last Brill did the sensible thing, which I had been urging on him for some time, and came to Europe to talk it all out with Freud. As was to be expected, the result was entirely satisfactory: "Brill has been with me these last few days. He is all right, quite willing to assist us, thoroughly reliable, confessing his neurotic faults. It is a great gain." [14] This was a very considerable relief to me, since apart from personal feelings many practical issues turned on his accessibility. Brill tried to see me in England, but I had already left for the Continent, so we missed each other. It was another three years before we managed to meet.

Yet another visitor was Hans Kelsen, the distinguished Viennese economist. During one of their walks together Kelsen told Freud that a friend of his, who happened to be staying in a near-by village, would be grateful for his advice. This friend was dreaming regularly about the death of his children; although the memory of these dreams troubled him in the daytime they caused him no disquiet at all when they were happening. Only the previous night he had dreamed that someone came and told him the children had died, whereupon with the utmost equanimity he replied: "Well, put them in the ice box." Freud said it was hardly fair to expect him to interpret a stranger's dreams at a distance, but he could not help surmising that the man was unhappily married and regarded the existence of the children as an obstacle to a divorce. Kelsen felt this interpretation must be correct, since he knew the friend was maintaining a relationship with his secretary who was actually staying with the family at the time.[15]

Freud left Seefeld for Berlin on September 14, and from there went to Hamburg to see his two grandsons. We, all the members of the Committee, met him in Berlin on September 20 and traveled together to Hildesheim. We had planned making a ten days' tour of the Harz region, Abraham, who knew it well, acting as guide. We stayed first at Hildesheim and then in the charming old town of Goslar. From here we climbed to the top of the Brocken, a spot of particular interest to me because of its association with witches, and even caught a glimpse of the famous Brocken specter. Another memory that comes back to me was being on top of a tower that had around the platform an iron rail about the level of one's hips. Freud got us all to lean forward against the rail with our hands behind our backs and our feet well back, and then suddenly to imagine that it was not there—a quite good test for the fear of heights. We all came out of the test quite well, and I naturally asked Freud if he had ever suffered from that particular fear. He said he had as a young man, but had conquered it by will power. I remarked it was not a very analytic way of dealing with it, but it was of course long before the days of psychoanalysis. Every day there were walking expeditions, and we were all impressed with Freud's swift and tireless capacities in this pursuit.

It was one of the rare occasions when the whole Committee had the opportunity of meeting together, and the only one when we all spent a holiday together with Freud. It was thus a momentous event. At the end of the tour Freud said to us: "We have lived through some experiences together, and that always binds men." Few experiences, however, are perfect, and this one was slightly marred by our all having severe colds. Freud's was particularly bad, but he assured me it did not affect him: "It is only the outer man." I envied him this, since the toxic effects of a cold seldom left me unaffected.

During those days there was of course ample time for extensive discussions among us on various scientific topics of common interest. Freud read to us two papers he had specially written for the occasion, the only time he ever did this. One was on telepathy, which he had begun to write at the end of July[16] and had finished in three weeks.[17] It was found in Freud's papers after his death and subsequently published,[18] though with the incorrect statement that it had been read before the Central Executive Committee of the International Association. We received it with mixed feelings, Ferenczi being at the one extreme of enthusiasm and I at the other.

Freud, however, evidently felt the need to express himself publicly on this topic, so he composed a more noncommittal paper, "Dreams and Telepathy," which was published in *Imago* in the following January (1922).[19]

The other paper he read to us is better known, since it was published in the following year.[20] Freud had announced in the previous January that he had suddenly obtained a deep insight, "as to the hewn rock," into the mechanism of paranoic jealousy.[21] This came from the study of an American patient I had sent him, his first foreign patient since the war. I should suppose he wrote it at that time, in January, 1921, since he told us then he was going to read it to us during the holiday.

Freud also related to us the contents of a paper on dreams which was published eighteen months later.[a]

After the tour Freud got back to Vienna on September 29,[22] and it was not long before he was "regretting Hildesheim and Schiercke like a distant dream." [23]

In October Pfister was concerned about a resolution passed by a Congress in Breslau severely condemning any psychoanalysis of adolescents, which constituted his main work.[24]

At the beginning of November Freud reported having had an interesting talk with Hans Prinzhorn, a Swiss who came with an introduction from Binswanger.[25]

In December Freud was gratified at being made an Honorary Member of the Dutch Society of Psychiatrists and Neurologists, all the more so because his name had been approved by Professor Winckler, a man who had often opposed psychoanalysis. The resolution was not unanimous, but was carried by fifty votes to twenty. It was the first time Freud had been honored in this fashion, and it marked the beginning of a change in the professional estimate of his work. From now on it was common to recognize that some of it, in spite of its many supposed "errors," was of outstanding importance, and that Freud himself was a man of scientific eminence.

Freud did not accomplish much original work in 1921; the difficult environment was too unfavorable. He wrote a Preface, couched in warm terms, for the collection of his old friend Putnam's writings, *Addresses on Psycho-Analysis*, which appeared in May as the first volume of the *International Psycho-Analytical Library* series. And he rewrote and published his well-known book on *Group Psychology and the Analysis of the Ego*.[b]

1922

The year began with the visit of several members of the Committee to Vienna. There were at that time a number of American and English students studying psychoanalysis with Freud, and he con-

[a] See p. 100.
[b] See pp. 338-39.

ceived the idea of adding to what they learned in their own analyses by getting several Viennese analysts to lecture to them on the theoretical aspects of the subject. Then, at their request, Abraham, Ferenczi, Róheim and Sachs came to Vienna in the first week of January and delivered a couple of lectures each. The plan proved very successful.

Freud's name was becoming a household word in London at this time. In January his photograph appeared in the fashionable weekly magazine, *The Sphere*. But publishers had to beware of the police. Kegan, Paul & Co. who had been prosecuted for publishing an allegedly obscene autobiography—and in those days sexuality and psychoanalysis were interchangeable concepts—decided that the sale of a translation of Freud's *Leonardo* they were publishing was to be restricted to members of the medical profession,[26] so artists were preserved from contamination. Freud was very concerned at the risk I was running of contravening our blasphemy laws by publishing my essay on the Madonna,[27] so I took the precaution of consulting an eminent counsel who reassured me on the matter.[28]

But Freud found his increasing popularity only a burden: "I am sorry I did not answer your last but one. Sometimes my pen gets weary. I have so much business correspondence to do, warning patients not to come as I have not the time to treat them and declining flattering offers to write a paper on such a subject for such a periodical. These are the drawbacks of popularity. I see not much of its blessings." [29]

Freud does not seem to have been in a very cheerful mood in these early months of the year. Comparing his situation with that of the time when he first met Eitingon he wrote: "My situation has greatly changed in those fifteen years. I find myself relieved of material cares, with the hubbub on all sides[c] of a popularity that I find repellent,[d] and involved in undertakings that take away time and energy from tranquil scientific work." [30] And this is how he described his mood to Ferenczi in the same week: "Naturally it pleases me when you write enthusiastically, as in your last letter, about my youthfulness and activity, but when I turn toward the reality principle I know it is not true and am not astonished it is not. My capacity for interest is so soon exhausted: that is to say, it turns away so willingly from the present in other directions. Something in me rebels against the compulsion to go on earning money which is

[c] *umrauscht.*
[d] *widerlich.*

never enough, and to continue with the same psychological devices that for thirty years have kept me upright in the face of my contempt of people and the detestable world. Strange secret yearnings rise in me—perhaps from my ancestral heritage—for the East and the Mediterranean and for a life of quite another kind: wishes from late childhood never to be fulfilled, which do not conform to reality as if to hint at a loosening of one's relationship to it. Instead of which—we shall meet on the soil of sober Berlin." [31]

In April there was the death of Rorschach, a man whose name has since become famous. Freud rated his intelligence very highly, but did not consider he had any deep knowledge of psychoanalysis.[32] He wrote at once some lines of condolence to his widow.

The University of London, in combination with the Jewish Historical Society, arranged a series of lectures on five Jewish philosophers: Philo, Maimonides, Spinoza, Freud and Einstein. That on Freud was given by Israel Levine (with my assistance). In the following year Levine published a book entitled The Unconscious; he was the first philosopher to show a full appreciation of Freud's conceptions. When Freud read it he wrote to me: "Who is Israel Levine? I never was so much pleased by a book on psycho-analytical matter as by his Unconscious. A rare bird if he is a philosopher. I want to know the man better." [33]

Freud had, from 1906 onward, occasionally corresponded with the famous writer Arthur Schnitzler. Strangely enough they had never met, although they moved in similar circles and Freud was well acquainted with Schnitzler's brother, the distinguished surgeon. Arthur Schnitzler, in his own medical days, had reviewed Freud's translation of Charcot's Leçons du Mardi in 1893, a fact he recorded in his diary.[34] Despite his remarkable psychological intuition and also his admiration for Freud's writings, with which he had early been familiar, Schnitzler would never admit to agreeing with Freud's main conclusions. He had many arguments about them with Reik, Alfred von Winterstein, myself and other analysts, but he could not overcome his objection to the ideas of incest and infantile sexuality. Ten of Freud's letters to him have been preserved, and Henry Schnitzler, who recently published them in German,[35] has kindly given me permission to reproduce a translation of the most interesting one, which provides a remarkable explanation of Freud's dilatoriness in seeking an obvious contact.[e]

In New York this year there had been considerable agitation over

[e] See Appendix A, No. 3.

an incident with Frink. He had studied with Freud from March, 1920 to June, 1921, and Freud always spoke in the highest terms of his intelligence and promise. He had now fallen in love with one of his patients, both of them being unhappily married, and proposed to secure a divorce and marry her. The patient's husband was furious and threatened to provoke a scandal that would ruin Frink. Frink himself had not made himself popular after his return from Europe and many analysts, Brill and Smith Ely Jelliffe being prominent among them, took a very serious view of the situation. Actually Freud approved of the step Frink was contemplating; the falling in love was a mistake, but it now had to be accepted. In New York the wildest rumors were current, one being that Freud himself was proposing to marry the lady! The end of it all was that the husband in question died at the critical moment.[36]

Another trouble in New York at this time, which also concerned Freud nearly, was the piracy mentioned earlier.[f] The editor of the book, a not very reputable person, had written a highly unsuitable preface to it which annoyed Freud and was one of the reasons for his insistence that the book be withdrawn. The man had taken legal action. Not content with seeking an injunction to prohibit the *International Journal* from being admitted into the United States, he instituted a libel action against Brill for alleged slander.[37] Fortunately he also died in time.[38]

Anna Freud, who had read a paper before the Vienna Society on "Beating Phantasies and Day Dreams" on May 31, was made a member of the Society on June 13, 1922, to her father's gratification.

As was mentioned earlier, Freud had been lukewarm at first about the idea of having a psychoanalytical clinic in Vienna. [39] Nevertheless, the other analysts in Vienna, notably Hitschmann, Helene Deutsch and Paul Federn, persisted, and in June, 1921, the Ministry of Education offered them quarters in the *Garnisonsspital* (military hospital).[g] Freud himself decided to play no part in the undertaking; he certainly had enough to do otherwise. Finally, after the overcoming of many difficulties and obstructions, a clinic, called the *Ambulatorium*, was opened in the Pelikangasse on May 22, 1922, Hitschmann being the Director.[40] It contained a large room in which the Society meetings were then held. Even so, after six months the Municipal Medical authorities abruptly ordered it to be closed, and

[f] See Chapter 2, p. 49.
[g] See Chapter 1, p. 21.

it took another three months of argumentation before they allowed it to be re-opened. In a report written ten years later Hitschmann gave a painful account of the obstacles that had to be overcome, particularly from the side of the official psychiatrists, before this plan at last came to fruition.[41]

Freud left Vienna for Bad Gastein on June 30.[42] On August 1 he started his holiday proper by going to Obersalzburg, near Berchtesgaden, where Eitingon had procured him rooms in the Hochgebirgskurheim (formerly Pension Moritz). It was near the spot where he had written the most important part of the *Interpretation of Dreams* twenty-three years before, and "he found the accommodation and outlook beautiful enough for him to write another one." [43] Only the hill to the town was three times as high and steep as it had been on a visit seven years before.

Three days later Freud's wife and daughter joined him, and his son Oliver a few days afterward. Later on his other daughter Mathilde, with her husband, and Ernst, with his wife, came too, so they were a happy family party. But their enjoyable holiday was soon disturbed by the news of the death at the age of twenty-three of his niece Caecilie (Mausi), of whom he was specially fond. Finding herself pregnant, she took an overdose of veronal; she died of pneumonia on August 18. She was the remaining child of Freud's favorite sister Rosa, whose only son had been killed in the war. Freud was "deeply shaken" by this unexpected tragedy.[44]

Ferenczi was staying at Seefeld that August together with Rank, and Abraham and Sachs both visited them there. It was on that occasion that the rather belated decision was taken for the members of the Committee to consolidate their intimacy by addressing each other as *Du* and using our first names. This certainly saved much embarrassment, since previously the custom had varied among the differerent members; thus, for example, I had been accustomed to addressing Ferenczi, Rank and Sachs with the familiar *Du*, but not Abraham or Eitingon, and so on.

Freud addressed us all with the more formal *Sie*. The only persons outside his family I know of addressing him as *Du* were the psychiatrist, Professor Julius Wagner-Jauregg and the archaeologist, Professor Löwy, both of them friends from student days. Other old friends, such as Professor Königstein, Rosenberg and the Rie brothers did so as well, but it is curious that Josef Breuer retained the old-fashioned mode of address as "*Verehrter Herr Professor*." The only people I know of addressing Freud by his surname without any title were the famous French diseuse and family friend, Yvette Guilbert, the American Ambassador W. C. Bullitt, and the English novelist H. G. Wells. Freud naturally addressed the members of the Committee by their surnames, both in conversation and in letters, with the exception that letters to Eitingon began after June 1920, at the latter's request, as *Lieber* Max. It is a little strange that he never used Ferenczi's first name; in letters he and Abraham were always *Lieber Freund*.

Freud spent six weeks at Obersalzburg. From there he went to Hamburg to see his grandsons, and then on to the Congress in Berlin, where he was Eitingon's guest. The Committee spent the day of Saturday, September 23, with Freud discussing the arrangements for the Congress and trying to bring some order into the vexing question of the relations between the *Press* and the *Verlag;* we also spent a day together after the Congress, but by then our difficulties had been enhanced by Hiller's announcing his forthcoming retirement, a consideration which in itself made it impossible to continue publishing the English periodical and books from Vienna. The next day, Sunday, was devoted to a long meeting of the various officials of the constituent Societies.

This was the last Congress Freud was destined to attend, although he made serious efforts to come to the next two. The paper he delivered on this occasion was entitled "Some Remarks on the Unconscious"; it was never published. The new ideas he here promulgated were taken from a book, *The Ego and the Id*,[45] which appeared soon afterward. They overthrew his original identification of the unconscious proper with the mental processes in a state of repression, and he now discussed the unconscious aspects of the non-repressed ego. It was the beginning of the new psychology of the ego, a fundamental advance in the theory of psychoanalysis.

Among the many other papers those by Franz Alexander, Abraham, Ferenczi, István Hollós, Karen Horney, Melanie Klein, Hermann Nunberg, Pfeiffer, Rado, Róheim and myself have subsequently proved to have had stimulating effects. Abraham's on melancholia[46] and Ferenczi's on genital theory[47] were outstanding. The general scientific level of the Congress was as high as any yet reached. It occupied three very full days, September 25-27.

Two hundred and fifty-six persons attended the Congress, of whom one hundred and twelve were members of the International Association. Ninety-one came from Berlin, and twenty-nine from the rest of Germany; thirty-one from England; twenty-eight from Vienna;

twenty from Switzerland, and eleven from America. Rivers of Cambridge had intended to come, but he died suddenly three months before. In my Report I mentioned that the membership of the Association had risen in the past two years from 191 to 239.

Freud was very satisfied with the success of the Congress, and he complimented me particularly on my after-dinner speech. I can recollect the passage in it which most amused him, and it may serve to show that analysts are not so destitute of humor as is often alleged. It concerned the rumor going round that the anonymous donor of the Berlin Policlinic had in fact been Eitingon. So I said: "In English we have two notable proverbs: 'Charity begins at home' and 'Murder will out.' If now we apply the mechanisms of condensation and displacement to these we reach the conclusions that 'Murder begins at home,' a fundamental tenet of psychoanalysis, and 'Charity will out,' which is illustrated by the difficulty of keeping secret the name of the generous donor of the Berlin Policlinic."

Even in Vienna interest in psychoanalysis was at last reaching wider circles, and Freud had been asked to give lectures by the *Doktoren-Kollegium* (Medical College), by the Society of Freethinkers and even by the highest police authorities (!).[48] Needless to say, he did not accede to any of these requests. His professional work, added to the difficulty of conducting most of it in a foreign language, was proving very tiring, and he told Eitingon he was reducing it to eight hours a day.[49] To Pfister, who had long been urging him to reduce his work, he promised never to take nine patients again.[50]

In November the son of an old servant of Freud's shot his father, though not fatally, while the latter was in the act of raping the youth's half-sister. Freud did not know the youth personally, but his humanitarian nature was always moved by sympathy with juvenile delinquents. So, paying all the legal expenses himself, he engaged Dr. Valentin Teirich, the leading authority in that sphere and founder of an institution for the reform of judicial procedures in such cases, to defend the youth. He also wrote a memorandum saying that any attempt to seek for deeper motives would only obscure the plain facts. Professor Sträussler wrote a similar one, maintaining that the excitement of the moment caused a "short circuit" in the boy's mind which was tantamount to temporary insanity. This plea was accepted and the youth discharged. Dr. Teirich, to whom I am indebted for the information, tells me that Freud wrote a newspaper article on the case,[51] but I have the best of reasons for thinking that he was mistaken in this.

On December 8 a fifth grandson (still no granddaughter!) arrived, Ernst's son Lucian Michael, now a distinguished painter.

Freud did not write much in 1922, but his thoughts were already occupied with the important book *The Ego and the Id*, which was to appear in the following year. In the month he spent in Gastein (July) he wrote a paper entitled "Remarks on the Theory and Practice of Dream-Interpretation," [52] the contents of which he had communicated to us in the Harz the year before.[53] It appeared in the following January number of the *Zeitschrift*, 1923. It was also in this year that he wrote for the *Zeitschrift* the short postscript to the Little Hans case.[54]

1923

This was one of the critical years in Freud's life, the last of them. It was one in which the friction between Rank and myself made him very unhappy because it threatened the harmony of the Committee on which was based his main hope for the continuance of his work after his death. Much grimmer, however, were the first signs of the mortal disease that was to cause untold suffering before it attained its final goal. He had often imagined that his days were numbered, but now at last the dread reality came in sight.

The first sign of trouble appeared in February, but Freud did nothing about it for a couple of months. Nor did he mention it to anyone, family or friends. The first I heard about it was in a letter dated April 25:[h] "I detected two months ago a leucoplastic growth on my jaw and palate right side, which I had removed on the 20th. I am still out of work and cannot swallow. I was assured of the benignity of the matter but as you know, nobody can guarantee its behaviour when it be permitted to grow further. My own diagnosis had been epithelioma but was not accepted. Smoking is accused as the etiology of this tissue-rebellion." Leucoplakia is not such a sinister occurrence at the age of sixty-seven as it is at fifty-seven, and still more so at forty-seven, so I took it that this was only a local trouble that had now been got rid of. The only aspect that gave me a little misgiving was Freud's mentioning it to me at all. It was not his custom to discuss his health with anyone except Ferenczi—

[h] Written in English.

even this I did not know in those days—so I half wondered whether Freud was making light of something serious.

What had happened was this.[1] In the third week of April Freud consulted a leading rhinologist, Marcus Hajek, an old acquaintance of his; he was a brother-in-law of Schnitzler. Hajek said the trouble was a leucoplakia due to smoking, but in reply to a question made the ominous remark: "No one can expect to live forever." He advised, however, that the little growth be removed—"a very slight operation"—and asked Freud to come to his out-patient clinic one morning. A few days before Felix Deutsch had been visiting Freud over some private matters and at the end of their talk he was asked to look at "something unpleasant" in Freud's mouth which a dermatologist had called leucoplakia, advising its excision. He at once recognized the cancer and was further discomposed to hear Freud ask him for help to "disappear from the world with decency" if he was doomed to die in suffering. Then Freud spoke of his old mother, who would find the news of his death very hard to bear. Deutsch seems to have taken these remarks as a more direct threat of suicide than they probably were; we shall see that Freud held out well past the eleventh hour. So Deutsch contented himself by saying there was a simple leucoplakia which it was advisable to remove.

After a few days of reflection Freud quietly turned up at Hajek's clinic without saying a word to anyone at home; it should be said that the clinic was part of a general teaching hospital that had no private wards. Presently the family were surprised by getting a telephone message from the clinic requesting them to bring a few necessities for him to stay the night. Wife and daughter hurried there to find Freud sitting on a kitchen chair in the out-patient department with blood all over his clothes. The operation had not gone as had been expected, and the loss of blood had been so considerable that it was not advisable for the patient to return home. There was no free room or even a bed in the clinic, but a bed was rigged up in a small room already occupied by a cretinous dwarf who was under treatment. The ward sister sent the two ladies home at lunch time, when visitors were not allowed, and assured them the patient would be all right. When they returned an hour or two later they learned that he had had an attack of profuse bleeding, and to get help had

[1] In writing the account that follows I have been assisted by Freud's medical attendant at the time, Felix Deutsch, who has unreservedly put at my disposal his full notes and also the relevant correspondence between him and Freud.

rung the bell, which was, however, out of order; he himself could neither speak nor call out. The friendly dwarf, however, had rushed for help, and after some difficulty the bleeding was stopped; perhaps his action saved Freud's life. Anna then refused to leave again and spent the night sitting by her father's side. He was weak from loss of blood, was half-drugged from the medicines, and was in great pain. During the night she and the nurse became alarmed at his condition and sent for the house surgeon, who, however, refused to get out of bed. The next morning Hajek demonstrated the case to a crowd of students, and later in the day Freud was allowed to go home.

So ended the first of the thirty-three operations Freud underwent before he ultimately found release.

The excised growth was examined and found to be cancerous, but Freud was not told of this. Nor had the surgeon taken the various precautions against the shrinking of the scar that were always taken later. So considerable contraction took place, which reduced the opening of the mouth greatly and thereby caused great hardship ever after.

It is not easy to understand Hajek's cavalier attitude throughout. It may be that he was under the impression that he had accomplished everything possible, and that the growth would probably not recur, or on the other hand it may be that he regarded the case from the start as so hopeless that any special concern would be superfluous. But two x-ray treatments followed, carried out by Guido Holzknecht, which did not accord with the supposed harmlessness of the condition. This was followed by a series of drastic treatments with radium capsules administered by an assistant of Hajek's called Feuchtinger. The doses must have been very large, for Freud suffered greatly from the toxic effects. Even four months later he wrote saying he had not had an hour free from pain since the treatment ceased. He added: "a comprehensible indifference to most of the trivialities of life shows me that the working through the mourning¹ is going on in the depths. Among these trivialities I count science itself. I have no fresh ideas and have not written a line." [55]

In the same month something happened that had a profound effect on Freud's spirits for the rest of his life. His grandchild, Heinerle (Heinz Rudolf), Sophie's second child, had been spending several months in Vienna with his aunt Mathilde. Freud was extremely fond of the boy, whom he called the most intelligent child he had ever encountered. He had had his tonsils removed about the time of

¹ For his grandson. See p. 92.

Freud's first operation on his mouth, and when the two patients first met after their experiences he asked his grandfather with great interest: "I can already eat crusts. Can you too?" Unfortunately the child was very delicate, "a bag of skin and bones," having contracted tuberculosis in the country in the previous year. He died of miliary tuberculosis, aged four and a half, on June 19.[56] It was the only occasion in his life when Freud was known to shed tears.[57] He told me afterward that this loss had affected him in a different way from any of the others he had suffered. They had brought about sheer pain, but this one had killed something in him for good. The loss must have struck something peculiarly deep in his heart, possibly reaching even so far back as the little Julius of his childhood. A couple of years later he told Marie Bonaparte that he had never been able to get fond of anyone since that misfortune, merely retaining his old attachments; he had found the blow quite unbearable, much more so than his own cancer.[58] In the following month he wrote saying he was suffering from the first depression in his life,[59] and there is little doubt that this may be ascribed to that loss, coming so soon as it did after the first intimations of his own lethal affliction. Three years later, on condoling with Binswanger whose eldest son had died, he said that Heinerle had stood to him for all children and grandchildren. Since his death he had not been able to enjoy life; he added: "It is the secret of my indifference—people call it courage—toward the danger to my own life." [60]

Freud saw Hajek several times in the next couple of months, and the latter raised no objection to his going away for his usual three months' holiday. But at the last moment he startled Freud by asking him to send a report of his condition every fortnight and to come to see him at the end of July. In the middle of July Freud wrote from Gastein to ask if he really need come to Vienna, whereupon Hajek, after a fortnight's delay, answered that it was not necessary and that he could stay away for the whole summer. This ambiguity, or ambivalence, was one of the things that made Freud increasingly mistrustful of his surgeon. A doctor in Gastein who inspected the scar gave a good report, but the general discomfort was so great that, on his daughter's insistence, Freud asked Deutsch to visit him at Lavarone where he was spending most of the holiday with his family. Deutsch at once perceived a recurrence of the growth and the necessity for a further and more radical operation. Several motives, however, acted in preventing him from putting the situation frankly before Freud. There was the uncertainty whether Freud would consent to such a major operation and would not prefer to die, there was the deep mourning over his grandson, and finally a reluctance to cast such a shadow over the projected visit to Rome with his daughter on which Freud had greatly counted. So he and Anna came down to San Cristoforo where the members of the Committee had gathered to hold a meeting. Rank had already been informed of the seriousness of the situation and now to our consternation the rest of us learned of it. We then joined Anna and went in to supper. During the meal Freud's name was of course mentioned, whereupon to our amazement Rank broke out in a fit of uncontrollable hysterical laughter. It was only a couple of years later that the events related in the preceding chapter made this outburst intelligible.

Afterward Deutsch and Anna walked back up to Lavarone. On the way, so as to find out his real opinion, she remarked that if they liked being in Rome they might make a more prolonged stay there. At this Deutsch got excited and made her promise faithfully not to do so. It was a broad hint, quite enough for Anna's perception.

In the meantime at the Committee meeting a discussion arose about the most potent motive that would persuade Freud to agree to the operation. Sachs suggested that this would be the thought of Anna, and Rank, striking to a deeper level, suggested Freud's old mother. I protested that we had no right to take such a decision out of Freud's hands, and the other medical men present, Abraham, Eitingon and Ferenczi supported me. Many years later, when Freud was living in London, I told him that we had discussed whether or not to inform him, and with blazing eyes he asked: "*Mit welchem Recht?*" [k] But he told Ferenczi later that from the beginning he was sure the growth was cancerous.[61]

Even then Freud was not told the truth. On the contrary, Hajek, in spite of having seen the pathologist's report, assured Freud that the growth had not been malignant and that the operation had been a purely prophylactic measure.[62] But the necessary arrangements were made for a big operation to be carried out on his return to Vienna. Thinking to himself, however, that it might be his last opportunity he decided to carry out a long cherished plan of showing Rome to his daughter. He had made this decision the very week of his first operation in April.[63] They spent a night and the following day in Verona, taking the night express from there to Rome. On the journey a couple from Cincinnati got into conversation with them, explaining that they always liked to talk to the "natives." A grim episode in

[k] "With what right?"

the train, however, took place during breakfast. Suddenly a stream of blood spurted from Freud's mouth, a hard crust having evidently loosened a piece of tissue. There was no doubt of its significance in either of their minds. Nevertheless the visit to Rome was highly enjoyable, and Freud, who was an admirable guide, took great delight in his daughter's enthusiastic responses to what he had to show her. "Rome was very lovely, especially the first two weeks before the sirocco came and increased my pain. Anna was splendid. She understood and enjoyed everything, and I was very proud of her." [64]

Only twice more in his life, in 1929 and 1930, was Freud to spend a holiday away from Vienna or the near-by Semmering.

While he was in Rome he got a newspaper cutting from Chicago announcing that he was "slowly dying," had given up work and transferred his pupils to Otto Rank. Freud's comment was "It is very instructive for the origin of rumors and for what coverings can be developed around a real kernel. It is not entirely invented. The article consoles me that there is no such thing as death, only for wicked people; the writer is a Christian Scientist." [65]

During Freud's absence in Rome Deutsch went ahead. He persuaded Professor Hans Pichler, the distinguished oral surgeon, to take charge of the case, and in this he made a most excellent choice for which Freud was always grateful to him. He also made all the necessary arrangements for the probable operation, and then patiently awaited Freud's return.

On September 26 Pichler and Hajek together examined Freud and found an unmistakably malignant ulcer in the hard palate which invaded the neighboring tissues, including the upper part of the lower jaw and even the cheek. Pichler decided at once that a radical operation was necessary. Freud wrote the same day to Abraham, Eitingon and me, adding: "You know what it all means." [66] Pichler began the usual preparations (teeth, etc.) on the very next day. He performed the major operation on October 4 and 11 in two stages. In the first operation the external carotid artery was ligatured and the submaxillary glands, some of which were already suspiciously enlarged, removed. In the second operation, after slitting the lip and cheek wide open the surgeon removed the whole upper jaw and palate on the affected side, a very extensive operation which of course threw the nasal cavity and mouth into one. These frightful operations were performed under local anesthesia. (!) After the second one the patient was unable to talk for some days, during which time he also had to be fed through a nasal tube. He made a good recovery, however, and went home on October 28. Freud wrote twice while still in the hospital (Auersperger Sanatorium). One was a telegram to me, which did not mention the operation. The other was a letter written only a week after the operation to Abraham, who had sent him one of his most cheerful letters:

"19. X. 23

"Lieber unverbesserlicher[1] Optimist

"Tampon renewed today. Out of bed. What is left of me put into clothes. Thanks for all the news, letters, greetings and newspaper cuttings. As soon as I can sleep without an injection I shall go home.

"*Herzlich*

"*Ihr*

"Freud"

Then began sixteen years of discomfort, distress and pain, interrupted only by recurrence of the trouble and further operations. The huge prosthesis, a sort of magnified denture or obturator, designed to shut off the mouth from the nasal cavity, was a horror; it was labeled "the monster." In the first place it was very difficult to take out or replace because it was impossible for him to open his mouth at all widely. On one occasion, for instance, the combined efforts of Freud and his daughter failed to insert it after struggling for half an hour, and the surgeon had to be fetched for the purpose.[m] Then for the instrument to fulfill its purpose of shutting off the yawning cavity above, and so making speaking and eating possible, it had to fit fairly tightly. This, however, produced constant irritation and sore places until its presence was unbearable. But if it were left out for more than a few hours the tissues would shrink, and the denture could no longer be replaced without being altered.

From now on Freud's speech was very defective, though it varied a good deal from time to time according to the fit of the denture. It was nasal and thick, rather like that of someone with a cleft palate. Eating also was a trial, and he seldom cared to do so in company. Furthermore the damage done to the Eustachian tube, together with constant infection in the neighborhood, greatly impaired his hearing on the right side until he became almost entirely deaf on that side. It was the side next to his patients, so the position of his couch and chair had to be reversed.

[1] Incorrigible.
[m] See p. 196.

From the onset of this illness to the end of his life Freud refused to have any other nurse than his daughter Anna. He made a pact with her at the beginning that no sentiment was to be displayed; all that was necessary had to be performed in a cool matter-of-fact fashion with the absence of emotion characteristic of a surgeon. This attitude, her courage and firmness, enabled her to adhere to the pact even in the most agonizing situations.

Freud was very fortunate in his second choice of surgeon. Pichler's reputation as an oral surgeon was unsurpassed, and he gave of his best. He had only a vague idea of Freud's standing in the world, but he could not have served him more faithfully had he been an emperor. He belonged to the best type of German-Austrian, and was a man of the highest integrity. No trouble was too great for his keen professional conscience. That was just the kind of doctor Freud wanted, a man he could trust absolutely, and their relations were excellent throughout.

There is no doubt whatever that Felix Deutsch had throughout acted from the best motives and in all good faith. Some years later he assured Freud that he did not regret what he had done and in similar circumstances would act in the same way again, but he could not get Freud to agree. Freud, who was always very sensitive to the possibility of being deceived by his doctors, found it hard to forgive the way the full truth had been kept from him, although it never made any difference to his friendly feelings toward Deutsch or his gratitude to him. What he seems to have specially minded was the implication that he might be unwilling to face courageously a painful truth, since his ability to do so was one of his outstanding virtues. Deutsch of course sensed this, so some months after the operations, when Freud had resumed a more or less normal existence, he boldly told him that what had happened precluded in the future the complete confidence so essential in a doctor-patient relationship. Freud regretfully agreed, but he reserved the right to ask Deutsch at any time for further help. A full reconciliation took place in January, 1925.[67]

After this introduction to the epic story of Freud's suffering we have to return to the day-to-day chronology of the time.

In February Count Kayserling, the well-known essayist and philosopher, paid Freud a visit. It was the first of several.[68]

In the same month L'Encéphale, the leading French neurological periodical, requested Freud's photograph to print with a full exposition of his work. On the other hand an excellent book by Raymond de Saussure, *La Méthode psychoanalytique,* had been forbidden in France under the pretext that a dream analysis by Odier contained in it offended against professional discretion.[69] In that spring a French journalist, Raymond Recouly, interviewed Freud and then published an account in a French newspaper.[70] He thought Freud looked like an old Rabbi straight from Palestine who played with his ideas just as an Oriental plays with the amber beads of his rosary!

The *Verlag* was by now having to negotiate an immense number of translations of Freud's works into various languages. Two thousand copies of the Russian translation of the *Introductory Lectures* were sold in Moscow in a single month.[71] There was widespread interest in psychoanalysis in Russia in those days: another psychoanalytical society had just been started in Kazan.[72] When it came to Chinese Freud expressed a doubt whether psychoanalysis would prove to be more intelligible in that language than in the original.[73] The *Verlag* was having great difficulties this year in publishing in Germany, because of the unstable currency there. In the autumn there was even a question of amalgamating the *Zeitschrift* and *Imago,* but it took a second world war to bring this about.

On February 22, 1923, Romain Rolland wrote to Freud thanking him for some laudation Freud had written about him to their common friend Edouard Monod-Herzen; it was probably about Rolland's book *Au dessus de la Mêlée* which had not long before created a sensation. It was the first of an interesting correspondence between them, from which one sees that Freud thought very highly of him. He told Freud he had been following his work for twenty years, which seems very remarkable if correct.

It was at this time that the decision was made to issue Freud's collected works under the title of *Gesammelte Schriften.* The first volume to appear was Volume IV, and three volumes were ready to be displayed at the Salzburg Congress in April, 1924.

The next event was the wedding of Freud's son, Oliver, to Henny Fuchs, which took place in Berlin on April 10, 1923. His mother and his brother Martin went to the wedding.[74] It was Oliver's second marriage; the first had not lasted long.

In June Freud was interested to hear that *Hamlet* was being played in New York on the basis of the psychoanalytical interpretation; the title role was taken by Barrymore.[75]

Freud and Minna Bernays left Vienna on June 30 for their usual "cure" at Bad Gastein. While there he received a letter from a young Jew called Leyens, an enthusiastic German Nationalist who had fought in the First World War and was a follower of Hans Blüher. He wanted Freud to disperse his bewilderment over the paradox that Blüher, a rabid nationalist and anti-Semite, was an admirer of Freud. In his reply, dated July 4, 1923, which contained some depreciatory words about Blüher, Freud wrote: "I would advise you against wasting your energies in the fruitless struggle against the current political movement. Mass psychoses are proof against arguments. It is just the Germans who had occasion to learn this in the World War, but they seem unable to do so. Let them alone. . . . Devote yourself to the things that can raise the Jews above all this foolishness, and do not take amiss my advice which is the product of a long life. Do not be too eager to join up with the Germans." In the Nazi time Leyens got away to America; and from there wrote to Freud telling him how right he had been. Here is Freud's modest reply, dated July 25, 1936. "You surely don't think I am proud at having been right? I was right as a pessimist against the enthusiasts, as an old man against a young one. I wish I had been wrong." [a]

On August 1 they joined the rest of the family at the Hotel du Lac, Lavarone, an old favorite haunt. The members of the Committee met at Castel Toblino on August 26 and went on to stay at San Cristoforo. After our discussion there, described in the previous chapter, we visited Freud in Lavarone a couple of days later and then dispersed. In the first days of September Martha Freud and her sister went to Meran, Freud and Anna to Rome where they stayed at the Hotel Eden. They got back to Vienna a couple of days before the consultation with Pichler.

As mentioned earlier, Freud was allowed to go home on October 28 after his big operation. He was due to resume work on November 1, but complications arose in connection with the scar of the original operation. In the septic and necrotic tissue traces of cancerous material were found on examination, so Pichler immediately performed a further operation, his third, on November 12. This time a wide excision was made of the soft palate, together with the old scar tissue and the pterygoid process of bone; this was carried out under a combination of pantopon and local anesthesia in the Auersperg Sanatorium. There was severe bleeding during the operation, and particularly distressing aftereffects.

On November 17 Freud underwent a Steinach operation at his

[a] For the opportunity to read these letters I am indebted to Dr. Niederland and Mr. Leyens.

own request—ligature of the vas deferens on both sides. This was in the hope that the rejuvenation such an operation promised might delay the return of the cancer. The idea had come from von Urban, who had worked with Steinach and was enthusiastic about the results he had seen. He got Federn to urge it on Freud, who then asked von Urban about his experiences. Freud told Ferenczi two years later, however, that he had not perceived any benefit from it.[76]

The rest of the year was taken up with almost daily visits to Pichler and constant changes being made in the "monster" in the hope of attaining enough comfort to make talking possible. He also had several x-ray treatments in those months. Freud could not see any patients until the new year. He had earned nothing for six months, and his expenses had been considerable. He insisted on paying Pichler full fees, as he did with all his doctors.

The most important literary production of this year was a book that broke quite new ground, *The Ego and the Id*. It appeared in the third week of April.[77] Its inception dated from the previous July, one of Freud's most productive spells. He had written to Ferenczi: "I am occupied with something speculative, a continuation of *Beyond the Pleasure Principle*; it will result in either a small book or else nothing at all. I will not yet [78] reveal to you the title, only that it has to do with Groddeck." It was written between that July and the end of the year, 1922. At the Berlin Congress in September he had already propounded some of the new ideas in the book, notably the concept of an unconscious ego.

In an appraisal of the book Ferenczi suggested, among other things, that the reason why the super-ego could in large part remain unconscious was because of theoretical components in its original structure.[79] Freud in replying regretted it was too late to incorporate the suggestions in the proofs, and added: "Now I am in the well-known depression after correcting the proofs, and I am swearing to myself never again to let myself get on to such slippery ice. It seems to me that since the *Jenseits* the curve has descended steeply. That was still rich in ideas and well written, the *Group Psychology* is close to banality, and the present book is decidedly obscure, composed in an artificial fashion and badly written. . . . Except for the basic idea of the 'Id' and the *aperçu* about the origin of morality I am displeased with really everything in the book."

Dorothy Thompson had written a severe criticism of the book which had so angered Edward Bernays, Freud's nephew, that he wrote to Freud asking what steps should be taken to defend him. In reply he received a terse cablegram consisting only of two words "Never mind."

Freud wrote in this year several odd articles, prefaces and the like, and two more ambitious papers. The two papers published in January, 1923, had both been written in the previous year: the "Remarks on the Theory and Practice of Dream-Interpretation" in July while in Gastein; and "A Seventeenth Century Demonological Neurosis" [80] in the last months of 1922.[81]

In those months he wrote also two expository articles, "Psycho-Analysis" and "Libido Theory," for an encyclopedia entitled *Handwörterbuch der Sexualwissenschaften*, (Cyclopedia of Sexology) edited by Max Marcuse. It was cast in dictionary form with paragraphs under forty headings, and it constitutes one of the most lucid introductions to the various topics to be found anywhere in Freud's writings. It was published in 1923 and reprinted in the *Gesammelte Schriften* two years later.[82]

Although Freud was never interested in questions of priority, which he found merely boring, he was fond of exploring the source of what appeared to be original ideas, particularly his own. I mentioned earlier his paper on the "Prehistory of the Technique of Psycho-Analysis," [83] in which he traced his idea of free association to a stimulus he had read, and then forgotten, while a youth in his teens. Now he wrote a short paper, entitled "Josef Popper-Lynkeus and the Theory of Dreams," on having discovered that a Viennese engineer and amateur philosopher, who wrote under the name of Popper-Lynkeus, had expressed in the same year as *The Interpretation of Dreams* Freud's essential theory of the nature of the censorship and consequent distortion in dreams.[84]

On the occasion of Ferenczi's fiftieth birthday a special number of the *Zeitschrift* was dedicated to him, and Freud wrote a couple of pages introducing it. Naturally he generously acknowledged Ferenczi's oustanding talents and contributions; incidentally, he complimented him, prematurely as it turned out, on having overcome a severe brother complex in his personal life.

The most important paper Freud wrote in 1923, composed in February, was published in the April number of the *Zeitschrift*. It was entitled "The Infantile Genital Organization of the Libido," [85] and, like other papers, will be commented on in the appropriate chapter.

1924

This year was mainly taken up with the distressing complications arising from Abraham's criticisms of Ferenczi and Rank, and the remarkable changes in the latter's personality, which were related in the previous chapter. In the first couple of months Freud had looked forward to a personal discussion at the Salzburg Congress with all the members of the Committee, which he hoped would re-establish a better relationship and also throw more light on the new ideas that had been propounded. But both Ferenczi and Rank refused to agree to any such discussion and insisted on dissolving the Committee. Nevertheless Freud had fully intended coming to the Congress in April, though to Abraham he expressed the fear that listening to fifteen papers would be too great a strain for him.[86] Freud had made a point of listening to every single paper read at all the Congresses he had hitherto attended, an example followed in later years by his daughter. However, in March he had an attack of influenza which left unpleasant aftereffects in the nasal mucous membrane and sinuses—an old trouble of Freud's—so he was compelled to take a rest. Instead of going to Salzburg he spent the Easter weekend at the Kurhaus Semmering. It was the first time in thirty-eight years that he had taken a weekend holiday.[87] Anna accompanied him, so was not able to attend the Salzburg Congress.

Freud had resumed his professional work with six patients on January 2,[88] but the difficulty he had in talking made this effort very tiring. "You belong to those who refuse to believe that I am no longer the same man. In reality, however, I am very tired and in need of rest, can scarcely get through my six hours of analytic work, and cannot think of doing anything else. The right thing to do would be to give up all work and obligations, and wait in a quiet corner for the natural end. But the temptation—nay the necessity—to go on earning something as long as one spends so much is strong." [89] There was constant trouble with the "monster," which had to be modified every few days. A second prosthesis was made in February and a third in October, but without much success. Smoking was allowed, but to get a cigar between his teeth he had to force the bite open with the help of a clothes peg.[90]

The news of Freud's serious operation seems to have got known in Vienna, and signs of friendliness appeared. The *Neue Freie Presse* published a laudatory article on him on February 8; it was written by

Alfred von Winterstein. Then the City Council, now with a Social Democratic majority, bestowed on him on his birthday the *Bürgerrecht* of Vienna, a title akin to the British "Freedom of the City." "The idea that my coming 68th birthday may be the last must have occurred to other people too, since the City of Vienna has hastened to bestow on me on that day the honor of its *Bürgerrecht*, which usually waits for one's 70th birthday." [91] Freud did not mention this to Ferenczi, and when the latter inquired about it this was the reply: "There is little to be said about the Vienna *Bürgerrecht* you mention. It seems to be essentially a ritual performance, just enough for one Sabbath." o [92]

Stekel also, probably moved by the same considerations, as well as by a revival of his old personal attachment to Freud, made an appeal for reconciliation. In a letter of January 22, 1924, he proposed that the group he had formed around him should cooperate with the Vienna Society in the fight against their common enemies. Past differences were to be forgotten and not mentioned. Things would have been different if only Freud had recognized in time that the pre-war dissensions had arisen from mutual jealousy in demands for his love rather than pretensions to his intellect. If Freud agreed he would like to call on him and discuss the situation. I do not know if Freud ever answered this letter of Stekel's—probably not; he certainly did not see him.

On April 24 Freud's sixth and last grandson was born, Clemens Raphael. His mother, Ernst's wife, had been so confident that she would bear three sons that from the beginning she decided to give them each the name of an archangel in addition to a more mundane one.

The Eighth International Psycho-Analytical Congress took place from April 21-23 at Salzburg, the site of the first Congress sixteen years before. Eight members had been present on both occasions: two of these still survive, Hitschmann and myself. Immediately after the Congress I went to Vienna to visit Freud and report; I was there for three days. It was of course a considerable shock to observe his altered appearance and the great change in his voice and one had to get used to his habit of keeping his prosthesis in its place with his thumb; this, however, after a time produced rather the impression of philosophical concentration. It was plain that Freud was as alert and keen mentally as he had ever been. Abraham also tried to come, but his short visa to visit Austria had already expired. He and

o *Man kann Schabbes davon machen.*

Ferenczi sent Freud full accounts of the Congress, and Freud was very relieved to know that it had passed off with no untoward happenings; he had been anxious lest the Berlin criticisms of Ferenczi and Rank provoke some wider dissension.[p]

Romain Rolland visited Freud on May 14.[93] It was Stefan Zweig who brought him to Freud's home and they spent the evening together, Zweig acting as interpreter; with his defective speech Freud at times found it not easy to make himself understood in German, so to do so in French was beyond him.[94] The same thing happened a couple of years later when Freud was visiting Yvette Guilbert at the Bristol Hotel. He turned to her husband with the pathetic remark "My prosthesis doesn't speak French." [q] [95]

Georges Seldes has kindly sent me details of the following incident belonging to that time. Two youths, Leopold and Loeb, had carried out in Chicago what they described as "the perfect murder." They were nevertheless detected, and the long trial that ensued provided a first class sensation in America. Their wealthy relatives and friends made every effort to save them from capital punishment, an aim they ultimately achieved. Seldes, on the staff of the *Chicago Tribune*, was instructed by Colonel McCormick to approach Freud with the following telegram: "Offer Freud 25,000 dollars or anything he name come Chicago psychoanalyze (i.e. the murderers)." Freud replied to Seldes in a letter dated June 29, 1924:

"Your telegram reached me belatedly because of being wrongly addressed. In reply I would say that I cannot be supposed to be prepared to provide an expert opinion about persons and a deed when I have only newspaper reports to go on and have no opportunity to make a personal examination. An invitation from the Hearst Press to come to New York for the duration of the trial I have had to decline for reasons of health."

The last sentence refers to an invitation from Hearst of Chicago for Freud to come to America to "psychoanalyze" the two murderers, and presumably demonstrate that they should not be executed. He offered Freud any sum he cared to name and, having heard that he was ill, was prepared to charter a special liner so that Freud could travel quite undisturbed by other company.

For the past four years discussions, which just now came to a head,

[p] See Chapter 2, p. 67.
[q] *Meine Prothese spricht nicht französisch.*

had been going on between Freud and Rudolf von Urbantschitsch over a project to found a psychoanalytical sanatorium on the lines of Simmel's Tegelsee in Berlin. Von Urbantschitsch, who had founded the immense Cottage Sanatorium in Vienna in 1908, sold it in 1922, and was toying with the idea of starting a new one on psychoanalytical lines. Field Marshal Archduke Friedrich, who owned a magnificent castle in a huge park, the Weilburg in Baden near Vienna, had learned of this plan from one of his daughters, who had been a volunteer nurse in the Cottage Sanatorium during the war, and, no doubt affected by the downfall of the Monarchy in Austria, offered to let it for the purpose. The necessary alterations, however, would cost more than was available, or than could be borrowed from any bank in the prevailing financial stringency. But two years later the President of the *Bodencreditanstalt*, Excellenz Rudolf Sieghard, who had been a patient of von Urbantschitsch's, expressed his gratitude by telling him confidentially that drilling operations in Galicia had struck a rich flow of first-class oil. All the money accruing from the sale of the Cottage Sanatorium was immediately invested in the Fanto Oil Company in June, 1924, and sure enough two days later trebled in value when the news leaked out. The plans of the excited speculator at once soared, and he discussed them at length with Freud. Freud was to be the nominal director, of course free from all administrative cares, and would continue his training analyses; a commodious house would be specially built for him. Freud was delighted. The idea of living in spacious surroundings in the green of the country and far from the turmoil of the city greatly appealed to him. His daughter, on the other hand, was more cautious and regarded the scheme as too speculative. And indeed, only two days later the oil ceased to flow, the shares tumbled and the speculator was broke. So the plan dissolved. Some time later the same bank approached von Urbantschitsch with a different offer. They would carry out the building and he would be a paid official. It was not so good as the first plan, but nevertheless Freud again entertained it favorably. This time it was the gradual failing of the *Bodencreditanstalt* itself that put an end to the whole scheme.[96]

In June Freud hopefully booked rooms for July at the Waldhaus, Flims, in the canton Grisons.[97] He had often wished to spend a holiday in Switzerland, but somehow never managed to. Now, again he was to be disappointed, since the local discomfort in his mouth made it imperative to remain within easy reach of his surgeon. So he rented the Villa Schüler on the Semmering, from where he paid regular visits to Vienna. He went there on July 8[98] and returned on September 27.[99] He took with him an American patient,[100] whom he referred to as his "negro." [101] He had told us of this old joke, dating back to 1886,[r] but curiously enough none of his children were familiar with it.

Abraham, who had been spending a holiday at Sils Maria in his beloved Engadine, visited Freud on August 10 for a couple of days. It was the last time the two men were to meet. Incidentally, they had been conducting an interesting discussion by correspondence on the symbolism of the number seven. Freud suggested that it went back to the era when the number six was the basis of the numeral system, so that there would be a taboo on the number that began a new series. This seemed confirmed by the superstitious feeling about the beginning of the third system, thirteen, and he quoted a similar belief from ancient Assyria concerning nineteen, the start of the fourth of such series. He then remarked on how curious it was that there were so many prime numbers in the series: 1, 7, 13, 19, (25), 31, 37, 43, and then 49 (7 × 7), but added, "One can make the queerest play with number: so be careful." [102] Abraham was not entirely satisfied with this explanation, and finally came to the solution that the number must be a compound of the male three and the female four.[103] I find it odd that neither thought of the tendency to strengthen male symbolism by intensifying it (3 plus 3 with 1 on top, as in the fleur de lys, etc.).

Of the news I had to give Freud at this time there was the report of Sachs's success in a course of lectures he gave in London that summer, and the more surprising fact that at the National Eisteddfod in Wales the chief bard received his prize for a poem that dealt with psychoanalysis.[104]

Oliver Freud's daughter, Eva Mathilde, was born on September 3. She was Freud's second granddaughter, Martin's daughter, Miriam Sophie, having been born on August 6, 1924.

This year brought Freud a keen personal disappointment, second only to that concerning Rank. Frink of New York had resumed his analysis in Vienna in April, 1922, continuing until February, 1923, and Freud had formed the very highest opinion of him. He was, so Freud maintained, by far the ablest American he had come across,

---

[r] At that time Freud's consultation hour was at noon, and for some time patients were referred to as "negroes." This strange appellation came from a cartoon in the *Fliegende Blätter* depicting a yawning lion muttering "Twelve o'clock and no negro."

the only one from whose gifts he expected something.[105] Frink had passed through a psychotic phase during his analysis—he had indeed to have a male nurse with him for a time[106]—but Freud considered he had quite overcome it, and he counted on his being the leading analyst in America. Unfortunately, on returning to New York Frink behaved very arrogantly to the older analysts, particularly Brill, telling everyone how out of date they were. Frink's second marriage, which had caused so much scandal and on which high hopes of happiness had been set, had proved a failure, and his wife was suing for a divorce. That, together with the quarrels just mentioned, must have precipitated another attack. Frink wrote to me in November, 1923, that for reasons of ill health he had to give up his work for the *Journal* and also his private practice.[107] In the following summer he was a patient in the Phipps Psychiatric Institute, and he never recovered his sanity. He died in the Chapel Hill Mental Hospital in North Carolina some ten years later.

Brill stayed with me in September, 1924. It was our first meeting in eleven years, and there were endless matters of common interest to talk over. He had by now completely recovered his temporarily lost equilibrium, and for the rest of his life was a rock of reliability.

In that autumn the first edition of Wittels's book on Freud appeared. When I reviewed it Freud wrote to me: "I need not say that I enjoyed greatly your criticism of the bad, unreliable and misleading biographical pamphlet of Wittels.[*] Perhaps I could have wished it to be more severe in its tone and his dependence on Stekel might have been more conspicuously exposed. But it is a nice and dignified production." [108] However, when Wittels applied for readmittance to the Vienna Society in the following year Freud supported his application.[109]

Freud had been impatient and critical about the translation of his collected papers into English, not realizing the immense labor entailed if the work was to be done at all thoroughly. But at last they began to appear. "The news Mrs. Riviere sends me about the first volume of the collection was a pleasure and a surprise. I confess I was wrong. I underestimated either my length of life or your energy. The prospects outlined in your letter concerning the following volumes seem splendid." [110] He was also complimentary about the survival of the *Press*, about which he had had the gravest doubts. "The final success of the *Press* is a matter you may be proud of, I had given up all hope of such an issue. I know what your sacrifices were

* See p. 40.

and feared they would prove a barren expense. I am particularly glad of the praise you give to your helpmates." [111] Then when the first volume of the *Collected Papers* actually arrived: "The first volume of the 'Collection' has arrived. Very fine. Impressive. My only misgiving, that these old writings do not make a good introduction to the English public, is compensated by the news that the second volume will follow in a few weeks. It is to be hoped that the Case Histories will soon come also; they are what I attach the greatest importance to. I see that you have achieved your aim of securing a place in England for the psychoanalytical literature, and I congratulate you on this result for which I had almost given up hope." [112]

Freud knew that he could no longer fulfill his duties as President of the Vienna Society, and he intended to be succeeded by Rank, who was then Vice-President. By the autumn Rank's behavior made this plan no longer feasible. Freud's solution of the quandary was to retain his position, but with leave of absence, Federn, who had been made Vice-President, functioning in his stead;[113] in the meantime Siegfried Bernfeld and Rank were to be Secretaries.[114] In October, 1925 Nunberg replaced Rank in the latter position.[115]

Only once after his operation did Freud ever attend a meeting of the Vienna Society. That was in January, 1926, at a meeting specially held on the occasion of Abraham's death.

At the end of the year Helene Deutsch proposed that a Training Institute be established, on the same lines as that in Berlin. She was made the Director, Bernfeld Vice-Director, and Anna Freud Secretary.[116]

Both Freud and Ferenczi were very eager for the latter to settle in Vienna. There he would become Director of the Clinic, probably of the new Institute also, and would replace Freud as President of the Vienna Society instead of Rank. Vienna, however, was so overcrowded after the war that it was practically impossible to secure living accommodation. A lady, Frau Kraus, offered to build a proper clinic and see to it that it contained suitable living rooms for the Director. She got offended over something, however, and at the last moment withdrew her offer—another keen disappointment for Freud.[117] He said that with that vanished his last hope of seeing Vienna made into an important psychoanalytical center.[118] He added that he had set all his hopes on Ferenczi's coming.

Toward the end of the year Freud underwent several further x-ray treatments as a precaution, although there had been no signs as yet of a recurrence of the cancer.

Freud published, besides a few prefaces and the like, five papers in 1924. Two of them, "Neurosis and Psychosis," [119] and "The Loss of Reality in Neurosis and Psychosis," [120] concerned ideas that were extensions of those expounded in his book *The Ego and the Id*. The former was written during his convalescence in the last months of 1923, and it appeared in January, 1924. The latter, which appeared in October, 1924, was written in the spring of this year, since Abraham had read it in May.[121]

A very important paper, "The Economic Problem of Masochism," [122] appeared in April. It had been written in the winter, and finished by January 21.[123] The stimulus for writing it came from some puzzling problems which were the consequence of the ideas put forward in the book *Beyond the Pleasure Principle*. A paper with the surprising title "The Dissolution of the Oedipus Complex," [124] was published in July. It was written about February, and contained at first a slight criticism of Rank's theory about birth trauma (later omitted). Freud delayed publishing it lest he should give the impression, which at that time he wished to avoid, that in his opinion Rank's work represented a serious divergence.[125] Ferenczi assumed from the strong word *Untergang* in the title that Freud was combatting Rank's tendency to replace the Oedipus complex by the birth trauma as the essential etiological factor in the neuroses and elsewhere, so he begged Freud to keep the manuscript secret and not to publish it for some time to come.[126] Freud admitted that the word in the title might have been emotionally influenced by his feelings about Rank's new ideas, but said that the paper itself was quite independent of the latter.[127]

In October and November of 1923, while still convalescing from his radical operation, Freud had written by request a short account of psychoanalysis, partly autobiographical, for the American publishers of the *Encyclopaedia Britannica*.[128] It appeared there in the summer of 1924 under the rather sensational title of "Psychoanalysis: Exploring the Hidden Recesses of the Mind" as Chapter LXXIII of a volume: *These Eventful Years. The Twentieth Century in the Making, as Told by Many of its Makers*. It was published four years later in the *Gesammelte Schriften* under the title "*Kurzer Abriss der Psychoanalyse*" ("A Brief Sketch of Psycho-Analysis").[129]

Incidentally, Freud had used the occasion of Ferenczi's fiftieth birthday (on July 16th) to present him with a complete set of the *Encyclopaedia Britannica*.[130]

Freud's writings in the latter part of 1924 were published in 1925 and will be mentioned in the account of that year.

1925

In January I notified Freud that, following the example of Berlin and Vienna, an Institute of Psycho-Analysis had been established in London.

At the Salzburg Congress it had been proposed to hold the next in Lucerne; nine years later a Congress was really held there. The Swiss, however, preferred Geneva. They also made a proviso that there should be general discussions after each paper, free discussion befitting a meeting in *"die freie Schweiz."* There were all manner of practical reasons against this, so, after two months of argumentation, Abraham had to change the plan and decide to hold the next Congress in Germany. He wrote to Landauer, in Frankfort, asking if he could make arrangements for a Congress in Bad Homburg, and the next day the matter was settled.[131] Freud fully intended to come to that Congress—it was the last he even tried to attend—and he actually promised to take part in a symposium on technique that was being mooted.[132] The Directors of the spa placed at his disposal a quiet villa with all comforts.[133] When the time came, however, his physical condition made the journey quite out of the question.

In February Freud reported that he had had no new ideas for the past four months, the longest such period he could remember.[134] This state of affairs, however, did not last long.

Abraham and his wife planned a visit to Vienna at Easter, and Freud was as eager as he for their meeting. But Pichler was just then undertaking a reorganization of the prosthesis, which practically deprived Freud of the powers of speech and caused him great discomfort. So, to his intense regret, he had to put Abraham off, but with the hope of seeing him in the summer.[135] It was their last chance of meeting, since in the summer Abraham was convalescing from the first spell of what proved to be a fatal illness; he died in December.

On Freud's birthday, May 6, the only members of the Committee present were Ferenczi and ever faithful Eitingon, who seldom missed that occasion.[136]

About that time I sent the following news to Freud: "You may have seen that Lord Balfour in his speech in Jerusalem† referred in a personally friendly way to the three men who he considered have

† At the opening of the Hebrew University.

most influenced modern thought, all Jews—Bergson, Einstein and Freud. At a recent dinner of the Anglo-Austrian Society at which I was present, Lord Haldane, the guest of the evening, dealt in his speech with the contributions made to culture throughout the ages by Vienna. The four names he singled out to illustrate this were Mozart, Beethoven, Mach and Freud." [137] Freud had just got reprints of his *Autobiography*,[138] and he sent me a couple to forward to the gentlemen in question; Balfour formally acknowledged his, but Haldane did not.[139]

On May 29 Sante de Sanctis, the distinguished Italian psychologist, visited Freud, who related that they spent an enjoyable evening together.[140]

In June Freud was pleased to hear that one of the Society's members, Schilder, was given the title of Professor on the recommendation of his chief, Wagner-Jauregg. Freud commented that it was the first time anyone associated with psychoanalysis had received promotion in the University of Vienna, and he suspected that Wagner-Jauregg did not know how closely Schilder was thus associated.[141]

Freud left for the Semmering, where he had again rented the Villa Schüler, on June 30. He had that day had a telangiectasis* in the gum destroyed by an electric cautery. A fortnight before that there was a curetting of some pockets in the wound, of course under local anesthesia. Before that the pulp had to be killed in four teeth and fillings inserted. A week after leaving Vienna in June Freud had to return to have a papilloma and the surrounding mucous membrane cauterized. All these minor operations were interludes in the constant struggle to improve the prosthesis by one modification after another, so one understands how Freud was tied to being within reach of his surgeon.

On June 20 Josef Breuer died, at the age of eighty-four. Freud sent his family warm condolences,[142] and he wrote an obituary for the *Zeitschrift*.[143]

Presently there was a brighter note: "For your amusement I will mention that today there arrived a number of *Le Matin* which contained a leading article on psychoanalysis. There does not seem anything special in that, but this *Matin* is published in Port-au-Prince in Haiti, a place one does not correspond with every day." [144]

In August Freud's nephew, Edward Bernays of New York, visited him and unfolded an ambitious plan of collecting a large fund which would be used to further the opportunities of psychoanalytical train-

* A tumorlike dilation of pre-capillary vessels.

ing in America and Europe. Freud, who was to be the nominal chairman, chose as European members of the organizing committee Abraham, Eitingon, Ferenczi and Storfer (who had by now replaced Rank as Managing Director of the *Verlag*); the American members were to be A. A. Brill, Edward Bernays and C. P. Oberndorf. Freud in a letter to Bernays defined the purposes of the fund in a statement which was issued to the press.[145] The plan, however, though painted in glowing terms in the New York press,[146] did not achieve all the objects it set out to.

Still better news came from New York, which was that Brill had resumed the presidency of the Society there. After serving for only two years at its founding he had transferred it to Frink for the next two years, since which time there had been no real leader. Brill now occupied the position for the next eleven critical years, during six of which he was also President of the American Psychoanalytic Association. By the time he retired from these two positions he had successfully regulated the relationship between them and also with the International Association. In the forty years of his active life, by his unwavering conviction of the truths of psychoanalysis, his friendly but uncompromising way of coping with opponents, and his unfailing readiness to help younger analysts he rendered far more service to psychoanalysis in America than anyone else. At the time we are now considering the struggle in America for recognition was particularly severe, and it was not easy to win new adherents; in 1925, for instance, there was only one analyst west of New York, Lionel Blitzsten in Chicago.

August was a much better month, and Freud said he had enjoyed a week of better health than at any time since the first operations.[147] Ferenczi had paid him a visit and found him in excellent condition.[148] He furnished just then one more example of his proneness to superstitious beliefs, which were always concerned—as such beliefs usually are—with thoughts of death. His daughter Anna had been to Ischl to congratulate her grandmother on her ninetieth birthday, and was returning via Vienna where Freud was to fetch her. "In the night there was a railway accident on the part of the line she was to travel on. So—as a protection—I lost my pince-nez and case when bending down in the woods." [149] It reminds one of a similar hostage to fortune Freud had many years before performed in the hope of fending off a fatal outcome to an illness of his eldest daughter.[150] In both cases success was achieved.

Freud resumed work in Vienna on October 1.[151]

At Whitsun Abraham had given some lectures in Holland and returned with a bronchial cough. The story we were told at the time was that he had inadvertently swallowed a fishbone that lodged in a bronchus; the condition refused to heal, and it was thought that it had led to a chronic bronchiectasis. In July he went first to Wengen and then to Sils Maria to recuperate, with some slight beneficial result. At the Homburg Congress, however, at which he had to preside, he was a sick man and evidently under the influence of the morphia with which he was trying to control his chronic cough. Back in Berlin he was treated for his throat by Fliess, Freud's old friend, and he reported his astonishment at finding how closely the phases of his mysterious illness corresponded with Fliess's numerical calculations. Since Abraham had always been very sceptical of Fliess's ideas one would attribute his conversion to his bewilderment, which everyone else shared, at the impossibility of making a reasonable diagnosis of his condition.

The Homburg Congress, which took place September 2-5, had been a success, though its scientific level was not quite so high as at the previous one. Many Americans were present, and it was becoming plain that serious differences were arising between them and the European groups over the vexed question of lay analysis. I suggested to Eitingon that the Congress institute an International Training Commission whose function should be to correlate as much as possible the methods and standards of training candidates for psychoanalysis in the various Societies, and to provide opportunities for the common discussion of the technical problems concerned. He was enthusiastic about the idea and got Rado to make the necessary proposal before the Business Meeting, where it was at once accepted. Unfortunately this gave rise to future trouble when the next President, Eitingon, who was also President of this Commission, took the view, and was to some extent supported therein by Freud and Ferenczi, that the Commission had the right to impose the same standards and rules of admission everywhere, a view that many of us, especially the Americans, resisted.

The event of the Congress, however, was the news that Freud had entrusted his daughter Anna to read a paper he had specially written for it. This mark of attention on his part, the content of the paper, and the way in which it was read, all equally gave general pleasure. The paper, entitled "Some Psychological Consequences of the Anatomical Distinction between the Sexes," [152] was published in the *Zeitschrift* a month later. Freud had read it to Ferenczi on the latter's visit in August.[153]

In the autumn Professor Tansley (afterwards Sir Arthur Tansley), a distinguished pupil of Freud's, who had just written for *The Nation* a favorable review of the volume of Freud's case histories, was attacked in that periodical. It led to a heated polemical discussion between him and three very bitter opponents, Miss E. C. Allmond, Sir Bryan Donkin and Dr. A. Wohlgemuth. Some of the language used by the latter rivaled the German outbursts before the war, and have for that reason a certain historical interest. Then a distinguished physiologist, Dr. Ivor Tuckett, gave a short anonymous account from the point of view of a successfully treated patient. After the correspondence had been stopped the Editor got James Glover to write an article for the science section on "Freud and his Critics," in an excellently objective piece of writing which poured oil on the troubled waters.

In October Freud said he had read Alexander's paper on Ferenczi's genital theory[154] with special enjoyment. "The young man is extraordinarily good. It is long since I have read such a beautiful piece of work. It does him credit." [155]

In November Freud was considerably disturbed about the financial situation of the *Verlag*. He had himself ploughed back into its accounts all the royalties he should have received, and in addition had given his personal surety for an overdraft of £2,000 ($5,600.00). There was, however, a limit to what he could do, and he begged Eitingon for advice.[156] Both Eitingon and Rank's wife lent 5,000 Marks ($1,190.00),[157] but the situation remained serious. Freud blamed Rank's extravagant production, in costly leather, of the *Gesammelte Schriften*. This was an edition of 3,000 copies, and by now only a hundred had been sold.[158]

For a little time Freud had been unable to sleep for pain in the lower jaw on the left side. It was discovered that a retained tooth, united to the bone of the jaw, had become badly infected, with the formation of an abscess. On November 19 this was chiseled out, and a granuloma and cyst in the neighborhood also removed. The operation sounds distinctly unpleasant, but all that Freud had to say about it was that it had been very elegently performed.[159] A sequestrum of bone came away a week later.

Freud was already becoming somewhat of a lion, on whom visitors to Vienna felt impelled to call. In later years this became at times a considerable plague, and Freud was not always very discriminating in the choice of the interviews he granted. Among the visitors in the present year we may mention the following.

The first was the famous French writer Lenormand who wished to discuss with Freud his Don Juan play. He made a very serious and sympathetic impression on Freud, and they agreed that writers who made use of psychoanalysis by simply taking over its data were to be condemned as dangerous and undignified.[160]

At Easter there were several analytical visitors: Alexander, Landauer and Pfister. And Freud reported that a two hours' talk with the famous Danish essayist Brandes was exceptionally interesting.[161] About the same time Count Kayserling paid Freud two more visits, but their talk seems to have turned into a consultation, for Freud recommended him to put himself in Abraham's hands.[162]

In December there were visits from two other well-known writers, Emil Ludwig and Stefan Zweig. Freud said he had no special impression of the former,[163] and Ludwig, to judge from the extraordinary book on Freud he wrote more than twenty years later, evidently returned the compliment.[164]

It is sad to relate that Abraham's relations with Freud in the last months of his life were more clouded than at any other time, though without doubt this would have been a very temporary phase. It all began with Samuel Goldwyn, the well-known film director, approaching Freud with an offer of $100,000.00 if he would cooperate in making a film depicting scenes from the famous love stories of history, beginning with Antony and Cleopatra. Freud was amused at this ingenious way of exploiting the association between psychoanalysis and love, but of course he refused the offer and even declined to see Goldwyn. Hanns Sachs reported that Freud's telegram of refusal created a greater sensation in New York than his magnum opus, *The Interpretation of Dreams*.[165] In June, Neumann, on behalf of the Ufa Film Company, suggested that the film be made illustrating some of the mechanisms of psychoanalysis. Abraham, who had been approached, asked Freud for his opinion, and thought himself it would be better to have one produced under authentic supervision than assisted by some "wild" analyst.[166] Freud refused to give his own authorization, but did not actively discourage Abraham's making the attempt. His main objection was his disbelief in the possibility of his abstract theories being presented in the plastic manner of a film. If, against all his expectations, it proved to be feasible, he would reconsider giving his own authorization, in which event he would give the *Verlag* any money he was paid.[167]

The film was made, and I saw it in the following January in Berlin. The news of it caused a good deal of consternation, particularly the fact that such a film should be authorized by the President of the International Association. The newspapers in England, where at the time a periodic wave of abuse was under way, took full advantage of the story. They said that Freud, having failed in securing support for his theories among professional circles, had in despair fallen back on the theatrical proceeding of advertising his ideas among the populace through a film. This accusation was typical of the bad feeling which was attacking psychoanalysis in every possible manner.

In August Freud complained that the film company were announcing, without his consent, that the film was being made and presented "with Freud's co-operation." [168] In New York it was stated that "every foot of the film, *The Mystery of the Soul*, will be planned and scrutinized by Dr. Freud." [169] On the other side Sachs, who was mainly responsible for the film because of Abraham's continued illness, complained about Storfer, then Director of the *Verlag*, distributing copies of a newspaper article he had written which deprecated the value of the film. Siegfried Bernfeld then composed a film script of his own, and together with Storfer offered it to various other companies. They even tried to enlist Abraham's cooperation in their enterprise, but Abraham pointed out the important clause in his own contract promising that no other psychoanalytical film should be officially supported, least of all by the *Internationaler Verlag*, for a period of three years. This led to an agitated controversy in the course of which Abraham came to form a poor opinion of the trustworthiness of the two Viennese. Freud thought his view an exaggerated one, but Abraham sent him an elaborate statement of his criticisms, and reminded Freud how right his judgment had proved in the earlier cases of Jung and Rank. This rather piqued Freud, who told him there was no reason why he should be *always* right, but if he proved to be so he would be willing to agree with him again.[170] The correspondence ended on this note, but with Freud expressing the warmest wishes for Abraham's recovery.

Abraham had continued hopeful about his own illness, but it went on and on and the doctors were unable to find out why. Freud found this uncanny and became more and more anxious about the outcome. In October Abraham reported a complication in the form of a painful and swollen liver. He took this to be some gall bladder trouble, and insisted on an operation,[171] the date to be chosen according to Fliess's calculations. This was carried out without more light being thrown on the condition, and the operation did more harm than good. In the same letter Abraham conveyed a message of sympathy from Fliess to Freud. Freud's comment was that "this expression of sympathy after twenty years leaves me rather cold." [172] That sounds as if he were still hurt over Fliess's separation from him.

The anxious time continued, and a few weeks later Freud had almost given up hope of Abraham's recovery.[173] In the light of later medical knowledge we are agreed that the undiagnosed complaint must have been a cancer of the lung, which ran its inevitable course in a little over six months. On December 18 I was terribly shocked to get a telegram from Sachs: "Abraham's condition hopeless." A week later, on Christmas Day, the end came. The news reached Freud that day, and on the same day he composed the short obituary notice which was to be complemented later by the fuller biographical one I wrote. Referring to the line in it he quoted from Horace: *Integer vitae, scelerisque purus*[v] he wrote to me: "Exaggerations on the occasion of a death I have always found specially distasteful. I was careful to avoid them, but I feel this citation to be really truthful." [174] Many years before, when he was present at the unveiling of a memorial tablet to Fleischl-Marxow in 1898, he had heard Professor Exner, Brücke's successor, apply the same words to his dead friend. Freud could never have known two men who deserved them better than Fleischl and Abraham.

He continued in the same letter: "Who would have thought when we were all together in the Harz that he would be the first to leave this senseless life! We must work on and hold together. No one can replace the personal loss, but for the work no one must be irreplaceable. I shall soon fall out—it is to be hoped that the others will do so only much later—but the work must be continued, in comparison with whose dimensions we are all equally small."

The most notable production in 1925 was Freud's *Autobiography*, the fullest of the sketches of this kind he had had to write on various occasions. It was written in August and September, 1924, and Abraham had read the first draft on his visit to the Semmering in the former month.[175] When Eitingon read it in October he begged Freud, who was just then correcting the proofs,[176] to omit the allusion to German barbarism, but Freud refused;[177] it was not many years before Eitingon's own Germanophilism was thoroughly cured. In De-

[v] "A man of upright life and free of stain."

cember Freud told Pfister he was expecting copies of the *Auto-biography* "shortly," but it was the month of February 1925 before they arrived.[178]

Bleuler was piqued at the passage about him in the *Autobiography* and he protested at length to Freud that the difference between their views was minimal. He closed by saying: "Anyone who would try to understand neurology or psychiatry without possessing a knowledge of psychoanalysis would seem to me like a dinosaur—I say 'would seem' not 'seems,' for there no longer are such people, even among those who enjoy depreciating psychoanalysis! " [179]

The essay was written as No. 4 of a collective work edited by Professor Grote and entitled *Die Medizin der Gegenwart in Selbst-darstellungen* (Present-day Medicine as Reflected in Autobiographies). It was reprinted in Volume XI of the *Gesammelte Schriften* in 1929, and as a separate book in 1934; the second edition of the latter, in 1936, was revised and enlarged.

This *Autobiography* is one of the most important source books for the student of Freud. As was to be expected in the context in which it was written, it gives an account of his scientific career, with the development of his ideas, rather than of his personal life.

Another essay, also written by request, was composed in the same holiday, probably in September. Freud had given his name as one of the editorial committee of a periodical, the *Revue Juive*, which was published in Geneva. The Editor, Albert Cohen, now pressed him for a contribution, using as a flattering bait the statement that Einstein and Freud were the two most distinguished living Jews.[180] The contribution, called "The Resistances to Psycho-Analysis." [181] appeared in that periodical in March, 1925, the German version being published in the July number of *Imago*. After an interesting disquisition on the ambivalent attitude toward anything new, the dread of it and the eager search for it, Freud gave reasons for attributing the opposition to psychoanalysis to affective motives, principally those based on repression of sexuality. Since civilization depended on control of our primitive instincts the revelations of psychoanalysis seemed to be a threat that might undermine that control. Finally Freud suggested that anti-Semitic prejudices concerning his person might be a contributory reason for there being so much opposition and for the unpleasant form it so often took.

A little paper with the curious title of "A Note upon the 'Mystic Writing-Pad' " [182] appeared in the January number of the *Zeitschrift*, 1925. It was probably written in Vienna in the autumn of 1924, since Freud spoke of revising it in November.[183] The other two clinical papers published in 1925, "Negation" [184] and "Some Psychological Consequences of the Anatomical Distinction between the Sexes," referred to earlier, were both written in July of that year, as was also the more important *Inhibition, Symptoms and Anxiety*,[185] a book which appeared in the following year; according to Freud, they had "no serious intentions," [186] a typical self-depreciation. He read the two former papers to Ferenczi on his visit in August.[187]

Thus, 1925 proved to be quite as productive a year as the previous one; after this Freud's literary activity began to diminish.

4

CHAPTER

Fame and Suffering
(1926-1933)

1926

AS WELL AS AN IRREPARABLE GAP, ABRAHAM'S DEATH LEFT MANY IM-
portant problems. There was, to begin with, the question of replacing him on the Committee. Brill being at too great a distance for
frequent communications, I suggested the names of James Glover,
van Ophuijsen, Rado and Joan Riviere, but it was decided to continue as we were.[1] Then there were two presidential vacancies. Since
Eitingon was on holiday in Sicily, Ferenczi, Sachs and I were the
only members present at the funeral in Berlin, and we had several
discussions about the situation. Ferenczi put in a claim to be the next
President of the International Association, but Freud, when we informed him, thought this would be a serious slight on Eitingon who
as Secretary had been intended in due course to be Abraham's successor. We were not sure whether he would accept the onerous position, which would among things interfere with his custom of taking
long holidays abroad at various times of the year. However, on his
return from Sicily he not only expressed his willingness to accept the
position but from then on developed a high sense of responsibility
which was to many somewhat of a surprise. He firmly refused, on the
other hand, to succeed Abraham as President of the German Society,
and after much discussion our choice fell on Simmel, who also
fully lived up to our expectations. Anna Freud replaced Eitingon as
Secretary of the International Association.

Freud had given up attending the Vienna Society since his big
operation, but he made a point of being present at the Abraham
memorial meeting held on January 6. His short obituary notice ap-

peared in the first number of the 1926 *Zeitschrift*. The following number was to have been devoted to a commemoration of Freud's seventieth birthday, but Freud instructed Rado, the active Editor, to postpone this and devote the next number to the memorial notices of Abraham which Rado had wished to publish at the end of the year. "One cannot celebrate any festival until one has performed the duty of mourning." [2] So the second number contained the full obituary of Abraham, written by myself, together with the speeches made at various Societies from Moscow to New York.

In February Freud was made an Honorary Fellow of the British Psychological Society. It was my third attempt at getting this done; on the previous occasions there had been too much opposition.[3]

On February 17 and 19 Freud suffered in the street mild attacks of angina pectoris (stenocardia); the pain was not accompanied by any dyspnoea or anxiety. On the second occasion he found himself only a few steps from the house of a friend, Dr. Ludwig Braun, a well-known physician, so he managed to get there.[4] Braun made the diagnosis of myocarditis and advised a fortnight's treatment in a sanatorium. Freud resisted the advice and was for once optimistic about his condition, which, doubtless correctly, he attributed to an intolerance of tobacco. He had been smoking some de-nicotined cigars, but even these had produced on each occasion some cardiac discomfort; he regarded it as an ominous sign that he was not finding abstinence at all hard.[5] Ferenczi was convinced that the condition was psychological and offered to come to Vienna for some months to analyze him.[6] Freud was touched by the offer and in thanking him added: "There may well be a psychological root and it is extremely doubtful if that can be controlled through analysis; then when one is three score and ten has one not a right to every kind of rest?" [7]

For a while Freud contented himself with leading a quiet life and treating only three patients a day. But Braun's insistence, reinforced by a consultation with Dr. Lajos Levy of Budapest, ended in Freud's moving to the Cottage Sanatorium on March 5, where he continued to treat his three patients.[8] His daughter Anna slept in the adjoining room and acted as nurse for half the day, his wife and sister-in-law taking turns for the other half. He jokingly announced to us that he was spending a holiday on the Riviera. He returned home on Good Friday, April 2.[9]

By now Freud had taken his condition more seriously, and he wrote about it to Eitingon as follows: "Yes, I will assuredly receive the Committee, you, Ferenczi, Jones and Sachs, at the beginning of May. I intend to give up my work from May 6 to May 10 in order to devote myself exclusively to my guests. An idea contributing to that decision is that it may easily be the last meeting with my friends. I say that without any railing against fate, without making any effort at resignation, but as a calm matter of fact, though I know how hard it is to persuade other people of that outlook. When one is not an optimist, as our Abraham was, one is naturally put down as a pessimist or hypochondriac. No one is willing to believe that I can expect something unfavorable simply because it is the most likely.

"It is pretty certain that I show signs of a myocardial affection which cannot be dealt with simply by abstaining from smoking. My doctors' talk of finding only something slight and that there will soon be a great improvement, etc. is naturally only professional cloaking with the calculation that I am not a spoil-sport, and I shall behave properly and not offend against the conventions. I do not feel at all well here, and even if it were the Riviera I should long ago have returned home.

". . . The number of my various bodily troubles makes me wonder how long I shall be able to continue my professional work, especially since renouncing the sweet habit[a] of smoking has resulted in a great diminution of my intellectual interests. All that casts a threatening shadow over the near future. The only real dread I have is of a long invalidism with no possibility of working: to put it more plainly, with no possibility of earning. And just that is the most likely thing to happen. I do not possess enough to continue without earning afresh to live as I have, or to fulfill my ceaseless obligations. It is those serious and personal considerations that matter in the last resort.

"You will understand that in this conjunction—threatening incapacity for work through impaired speech and hearing with intellectual weariness—I cannot be out of humor with my heart, since the affection of the heart opens up a prospect of a not too delayed and not too miserable exit. . . . Naturally I know that the diagnostic uncertainty in such matters has two sides to it, that it may be only a momentary warning, that the catarrh may get better, and so on. But why should everything happen so pleasantly about the age of seventy? Besides, I have always been dissatisfied with remnants; I have not even been able to put up with having only a couple of cigars in my cigar-case.

[a] Probably a play on a phrase from *Egmont*. See Chapter 1, p. 20.

"Why am I telling you all this? Probably so as to avoid doing so when you are here. Besides that, in order to enlist your help in relieving me as much as possible of the formalities and festivities to come. . . . Do not make the mistake of thinking I am depressed. I regard it as a triumph to retain a clear judgment in all circumstances, not like poor Abraham to let oneself be deceived by a euphoria. I know too that were it not for the one trouble of possibly not being able to work I should deem myself a man to be envied. To grow so old; to find so much warm love in family and friends; so much expectation of success in such a venturesome undertaking, if not the success itself: who else has attained so much?" [10]

The main reason why Freud had at first been reluctant to accept his doctor's advice was that he wished to continue his work so long as Marie Bonaparte could stay in Vienna. Incidentally, it was on her return to Paris that she induced her old groom to admit that he used to have intercourse with her nurse in her presence when she was just under a year old.[11] Freud had to her great astonishment divined this episode from analytic material, and they were both excited at the confirmation. He wrote: "Now you understand how contradiction and recognition can be completely indifferent when one knows oneself to possess a real certainty. That was my case, and it was why I have held out against scorn and disbelief without even getting bitter." [12]

Freud continued a semi-invalid existence after returning to Vienna, and he used to take a drive in the morning to the green suburbs before beginning work. That gave him the opportunity of discovering how beautiful the early spring can be—lilac time in Vienna! "What a pity that one had to grow old and ill before being able to make this discovery." [13] He added that nothing rendered the feeling of spring so vividly as Uhland's lyric *"Die Welt wird schöner mit jedem Tag,"* [b] which he quoted in full from memory.

Early in the year the shadow of the seventieth anniversary of his birthday began to fall on Freud's mood. It was by no means simply his advancing age that troubled him, but the thought of the diverse celebrations that were sure to accompany the occasion itself. Previous birthday celebrations had been bad enough, but this was bound to be worse. At one moment he considered escaping by immuring himself in a sanatorium for a week, but concluded that would be too cowardly and too unkind to his well-wishers. At the time he had reduced his working hours because of his heart affection he told us: "I

[b] Everyday the world becomes more beautiful.

can report some external successes from my restricted activity. Thus, for example, I have managed to suppress a Special Number of the *Wiener Medizinische Zeitschrift* [*sic*] which was being planned." [14]

The Editor announced that Freud had gratefully declined his offer of a Festival Number, and published instead a laudatory article written by Rudolf von Urbantschitsch. [15]

For several days it rained telegrams and letters of congratulations from all parts of the world. Of the latter those that pleased Freud most were from Georg Brandes, Einstein, Yvette Guilbert, Romain Rolland and the Hebrew University of Jerusalem of which he was one of the Directors. [16] He was evidently moved by a letter of congratulation from Breuer's widow, which he answered as follows:

"May 13, 1926

"*Verehrteste Frau:*

"The lines in which you congratulate me on my seventieth birthday moved me most deeply. Your black-edged letter brought back like a flash of lightning everything from the moment when, glancing through the door of the consulting room, I first saw you sitting at the table with your barely two-year-old daughter, through all the years when I could almost count myself as one of your family, and then all the changing events of my life since. Take my most deferential thanks, also in remembrance of the past.

"*Ihr ergebenster*
"Freud"

All the Vienna newspapers and many German ones published special articles, mostly full of recognition. The best were those by Bleuler and Stefan Zweig. [17] The Bürgermeister of Vienna, Herr Seitz, accompanied by a Councillor, Professor Tandler, presented personally the diploma of the *Bürgerrecht* of the city, referred to earlier, which had been bestowed on him two years before.

The official academic world in Vienna, however, the University, the Academy, the *Gesellschaft der Aerzte* (Society of Physicians), etc., completely ignored the occasion. Freud found this was only honest of them. "I should not have regarded any congratulations from them as honest." [18]

The following incident in the University shows how right Freud's estimate was. Sir Charles Webster, the distinguished historian, was lecturing before the Historical Department of the University, having been made a Professor Extraordinary for the occasion. On the day of Freud's birthday he used the occasion to make some laudatory reference to him as one of the greatest men of the epoch, and to express the great debt historians owed to his work, which enabled them to see deeper into the character of many great men of action. It was received in a chilling silence.[19]

The Jewish *Humanitätsverein* (B'nai B'rith Lodge), to which Freud belonged, published a commemoration number of their periodical containing a number of friendly essays. "They were pretty harmless on the whole. I regard myself as one of the most dangerous enemies of religion, but they don't seem to have any suspicion of that." [20] They also held a festival meeting at which Professor Ludwig Braun, the doctor who treated Freud for myocarditis, made a specially brilliant speech. The family were present, but Freud stayed away: "It would have been embarrassing and tasteless to attend. When someone abuses me I can defend myself, but against praise I am defenseless. . . . Altogether the Jews are treating me like a national hero, although my service to the Jewish cause is confined to the single point that I have never disowned my Jewishness." [21]

In addition Hitschman gave an address before the B'nai B'rith, since published,[22] and also wrote articles for the *Arbeiter-Zeitung* and the *Volkszeitung*.

On the day itself, May 6, some eight or ten of his pupils assembled in Freud's drawing room and presented him with a sum of 30,000 Marks ($4,200.00) collected from the members of the Association. He gave four-fifths of it to the *Verlag* and one-fifth to the Vienna Clinic. In thanking us Freud made a speech of farewell. I recollect the three main points in it. One was that we must now regard him as having retired from active participation in the psychoanalytical movement, and that in future we must rely on ourselves. Another was an appeal to us to bear witness to posterity about what good friends he had. The most emphatic part, however, was his appeal to us not to be deceived by apparent successes into underestimating the strength of the opposition yet to be overcome. As he rightly said, it is hardly possible to exaggerate the power of inner resistances against acceptance of unconscious tendencies. Besides the members of the Committee there were a few analysts present from various Societies, particularly the Vienna one. The only one I now recall was Federn, since he stood next to me and I observed him taking shorthand notes of the speech. Not long before his death I asked him whether he still had these, but unfortunately they had got lost during his escape from Vienna in 1938.

There were many other more personal presents. Of these I recall a valuable antique from Marie Bonaparte, a complete set of Anatole France's works from the French Society, and from Ferenczi a beautiful malacca cane with an ivory handle and with S.F. engraved on a gold band; I gave him a similar one with a tortoise shell handle. After Freud's death Mrs. Freud gave me that cane, but it was unfortunately stolen the year after during the London blitz.

On the following day Freud held his last meeting with the whole Committee. It lasted seven and a half hours, though not of course continuously, but he showed no signs of fatigue.

The third number of that year's *Zeitschrift* was a Commemoration number, and it contained a copy of an etching made for the occasion by the well-known Viennese artist, Professor Schmutzer. On hearing that Ferenczi had been deputed to write the introductory address of greeting Freud wrote to him: "Had I been compelled to write three such articles instead of the one I wrote for your fiftieth birthday[e] I should have ended by becoming aggressive against you. I don't want that to happen to you, so take into account a piece of emotional hygiene you may need." [23]

Among the events which that date marked was also the opening of a Training Institute in London, so there were now three in Europe.

On May 12, 1926, Pilsudski effected his *coup d'état* in Warsaw. In a book written many years later an American writer, Drawbell, published the following story about the well-known journalist, Dorothy Thompson. "One night at a concert someone told her that trouble would break out in Warsaw. Pulling on a wrap she rushed to her office and there the news tapes were already ticking out the news that revolution had broken out in Poland and that Pilsudski was marching on Warsaw. She had an hour to catch the train. She packed quickly, borrowed one hundred pounds from her companion at the concert—none other than Dr. Sigmund Freud, the great psychologist—and dashed to the station." [24] Not having heard that Freud had ever in his life attended a musical concert, least of all in 1926, I asked Dorothy Thompson what core of truth there might be in this astonishing story. She kindly informed me that it was correct, except that it was at the opera, not at a concert, and that Freud was not her companion. In her emergency she conjectured that Freud was the most likely person in Vienna to have foreign currency in his possession, so was bold enough to call at his house and put her situation before him. He willingly helped her.

[e] See p. 100.

An American journalist, George Sylvester Viereck, who had known Freud slightly for a few years, paid him a visit late in June. He has recorded their conversation at considerable length.[25] One cannot of course rely on the memory of such a long talk, but the following passages seem characteristic of Freud's outlook at that time. "Seventy years have taught me to accept life with a cheerful humility. . . . I detest my mechanical jaw because the struggle with the mechanism consumes so much precious strength. Yet I prefer a mechanical jaw to no jaw at all. I still prefer existence to extinction. . . . Perhaps the gods are kind to us in making life more disagreeable as we grow older. In the end death seems less intolerable than the manifold burdens we carry. . . . I do not rebel against the universal order. . . . Fame comes to us only after we are dead, and frankly what comes afterwards does not concern me. I have no aspirations to posthumous glory. My modesty is no virtue." Asked whether it meant nothing to him that his name should live, he replied: "Nothing whatsoever, even if it should live, which is by no means certain. . . . I am far more interested in this blossom than in anything that may happen to me after I am dead. . . . I am not a pessimist. I permit no philosophic reflection to spoil my enjoyment of the simple things of life."

On June 17 Freud took up residence in the Villa Schüler at the Semmering,[26] where he stayed until the end of September. From there he paid frequent visits to his surgeon in Vienna in the endeavor to get more comfort from modifications of his terrible prosthesis. There was much suffering that summer, and it was a couple of months before Freud's heart condition improved. The last month or two of the holidays, however, were better, and Freud was treating two patients daily in these months.

After the birthday jubilations there was a wave of reaction and Freud attributed to it the legal suit that was brought against Theodor Reik for "quackery," [27] the first open attack on lay analysis. Freud responded by hurriedly writing his booklet *Lay Analysis*, which he described as being "very outspoken." [d]

Eitingon visited Freud on June 28 for a couple of days and Ferenczi came on August 22 to spend a week before sailing for America on September 22. On his way to embark at Cherbourg he met Rank in a travel bureau in Paris; it must have been a curious *rencontre* between the two coadjutors of only two years before. It had been a very happy week at the Semmering, and it was the last occasion on which

[d] *recht scharf.*

Freud felt really happy in Ferenczi's company. For we are now at the beginning of a sad story in their relationship. Ferenczi had for some time been feeling dissatisfied and isolated in Budapest, and in the spring had again been wanting to move to Vienna, a plan his wife did not favor. In April he had received an invitation from Frankwood Williams to give a course of lectures in the autumn at the New School of Social Research in New York, and with Freud's approbation he accepted it. He gave the first of the series on October 5, 1926, with Brill in the chair. Some intuitive foreboding, probably based on the unfortunate sequels to Jung's and Rank's similar visits, made me advise him to decline, but he ignored this and planned to spend six months in New York where he would analyze as many people as possible in the time. Eitingon had also felt unhappy about Ferenczi's acceptance of the invitation, though on other grounds.[28] The outcome was to justify my foreboding. Ferenczi was never the same man again after that visit, although it was another four or five years before his mental deterioration became manifest to Freud.

On returning from his long holiday Freud decided to take only five patients instead of his previous six, but since he then raised his fees from $20.00 to $25.00 he did not lose financially by the reduction in his work.[29] Another change in his arrangements was that, still feeling unable to conduct the meetings of the Vienna Society, he consented to have a small number of selected members come to his home on every second Friday in the month for an evening's scientific discussion.[30] About this time he expressed the opinion that H. Meng and Alexander were the most promising of the younger generation of analysts.[31]

Max Marcuse of Berlin had invited Freud and myself to serve on the Council of the International Congress for Sexual Research that was being organized. After consultation we agreed to accept, but then Freud heard that the proposed President, Albert Moll, had been using abusive language at a press conference about psychoanalysis. So Freud wrote to Marcuse giving this as his reason for withdrawing his name,[32] and asked me to do the same.[33]

In England this was a year of heavy weather, and Freud took a sympathetic interest in our troubles. The first sign of the renewed wave of opposition concerned a patient who consulted one of our members, Dr. Millais Culpin. He was advised against undertaking an analysis, but when he committed suicide not long after it was widely hailed as one more proof of the dangers of psychoanalysis; it either drove people mad or sent them to their death. Both *The*

Times and the *British Medical Journal* declined to publish a letter of disclaimer, but we managed to get one into *The Lancet*.[34] The storm continued, and Sir Bryan Donkin, Sir Robert Armstrong-Jones, Charles S. Myers, then the President of the International Congress of Psychology—all high authorities—made themselves notorious by the strength of their invective. Incidentally, in the midst of it all I was startled to read an anonymous advertisement in the "agony" column of *The Times* which ran "Homage to Copernicus, Darwin and Freud." Four doctors were expelled from the profession that year for communicating with the press, so we were specially indignant that the appearance of the German psychoanalytical film[e] in London should provide an occasion for the leveling of similar accusations of publicity against us. *The Times* and other newspapers were clamoring for a medical investigation of psychoanalysis; The Royal College of Physicians and the Commissioners in Lunacy discussed the matter but decided to do nothing about it; and the International Council of Mental Hygiene appointed a committee of which nothing came. On the other hand the *British Medical Association* appointed a special committee which sat continuously for three years and resulted in our being issued a document which more closely resembles a charter than any other we have ever obtained for our work.[35] On September 28 the London Clinic of Psycho-Analysis opened, this being made possible by a munificent donation from an ex-patient, Pryns Hopkins.

In the previous month I had to report the sad news of James Glover's premature death. Freud replied: "Very sad. I scarcely knew him, but the general opinion about him leaves no doubt that he was your best man." [36]

In October, years after he had given up all hope, Freud received a sum of money for the *Verlag* from the Anton von Freund fund.[37] It was, it is true, only $10,000 Swiss Francs ($1,930.00), a far smaller amount than had originally been promised, but in those bad times it was welcome enough.

On October 25 Freud called on Rabindranath Tagore in Vienna on the latter's request. He did not seem to have made much of an impression on Freud, since when another Indian, Gupta, a Professor Philosophy in Calcutta, visited him a little later Freud commented: "My need of Indians is for the present fully satisfied." [38] He only allowed visitors from abroad at that time. The sole European exception was Meng, of whom he had the highest opinion.[39]

* See pp. 114-15.

Then a psychiatrist from Rio de Janeiro[t] appeared and presented him with a book on psychiatry with forty pages of it devoted to psychoanalysis.[40] There was reputed to be great interest in the subject at that time in Brazil, both in Rio and Sao Paulo.

In November came the interesting news that Simmel had opened near Berlin a psychoanalytical sanatorium called Tegelsee, designed to take patients—dipsomaniacs, etc.—who needed to be under observation. Freud took a keen interest in the scheme, and in later years when he had to go to Berlin to see a surgeon he several times stayed at Tegel. Although Freud naturally kept up his interests in the various undertakings connected with psychoanalysis, he had a way of concentrating on the latest one with particular interest. They were in order: the Vienna Society, the International Association, his psychoanalytical periodicals, the *Verlag*, the Training Institutes, and now—the last of all—Tegel.

I have described the various phases of Freud's personal relations with the members of the Committee, which meant so much to him, and I therefore cannot omit reference to myself in the same connection. For ten years, from 1922 onward, these were not so undisturbed as they had been before and were to be again later. In this period while his affection for me continued, and from time to time expressed itself warmly, he was more critical of me and not so intimate. The trouble had begun with Rank's prejudicing him against me, and it was a long while before he overcame his annoyance with Abraham and me for unmasking his illusions about Rank and his ideas. Then Ferenczi was to play a precisely similar role. From now on he kept expressing to Freud his antagonism to me, of which I knew nothing whatever at the time nor, indeed, until I recently read his correspondence; just as with Rank, this was the precursor of the hostility he was to manifest later against Freud himself. Then there were matters on which I had to disagree with Freud: on the subject of telepathy, on the precise attitude towards lay analysts, and in my support of Melanie Klein's work; these are topics that will be discussed later.

I will quote here a letter that has more than a personal interest.

"20. XI. 1926
"Dear Jones:
"Is it really twenty years since you have been in the cause?[s] It has really become altogether your own, since you have achieved every-

[t] Professor Porto-Carrero.
[s] *bei der Sache.*

thing there was to be got from it: a Society, a Journal and an Institute. What you have meant to it we will leave the historians to establish. That you can mean still more is my sure expectation, when the many business matters of which you have to complain are changed into a smooth routine. Then you will find the leisure to give more from your experience to your colleagues and to posterity.

"We may be well satisfied with each other. I have myself the impression that you sometimes overestimate the significance of the dissensions that have occurred between us. It is, it is true, hard to succeed in completely satisfying one another; one misses something in everyone and criticizes a little. You have yourself remarked that even between Abraham and myself there were certain differences of opinion; with one's wife and children the same things happen. Only the speeches at the grave side deny these indications of reality; the living have the right to maintain that such impairments of an ideal picture do not spoil the enjoyment of reality.

"You will be astonished when I disclose the reason that hinders my correspondence with you. It is a classical example of the petty restrictions to which our nature is subject. It is that I find it very hard to substitute Latin characters for Gothic handwriting, as I am now doing. All fluency—inspiration one would say on a higher plane —at once leaves me. You have often told me that you cannot read Gothic handwriting, so only two ways of contact have remained, both of which disturbed the sense of intimacy: either to dictate to Anna on the machine or to employ my clumsy English.

. . . [comments on my paper on the super-ego]

"My state of mind is turning away from work—I believe forever. It is better not to deceive oneself. I feel I shall be allowed to live a little longer on bounty [*Gnadenbrot*]. Your wife, whom I greet warmly, can translate that word for you.

"cordially yours
"Freud"

After this I got him to write to me in Gothic characters, which he then nearly always did.

It is evident that the mere physical act of writing, which he performed at an unusually swift speed, had for Freud some special emotional significance. Both his ideas and his feelings flowed best when he had a pen in his hand.

In the same month as he wrote this letter, Freud, on the supposition that trouble in the frontal sinus might be responsible for the continued catarrh, consulted a rhinologist, Dr. Sibanek, but with negative results. Pichler then made him his fourth prosthesis in the hope, also vain, that it might alleviate his discomfort.

At the beginning of December Binswanger, then the President of the Swiss Psychiatric Society, notified Freud that they had unanimously elected him to the honorary membership vacant since the death of Emil Kraepelin. He remarked that the honor should have been bestowed on him long before, that it would have given him pleasure twenty years ago, but that now it probably would not make much impression on him. Freud replied: "I thank you. You are right: the honor as such leaves me cold, but I am sensible of its value as a sign of the steady diminution of resistance among psychiatrists. Twenty or thirty years ago such a recognition of the still baby-like[h] analysis would scarcely have any meaning. At that time I had not expected anything of the sort, so I did not miss it." [41]

Freud and his wife traveled to Berlin at Christmas, returning on January 2.[42] It was his first journey since his operation more than three years ago, and was the last one to Berlin which he took for pleasure. Its object was to see his two sons there, one of whom was about to leave to execute some work in Palestine, and the four grandchildren who were there: of these he had previously seen only one, and that when he was only a year old.

This was the occasion of Freud's first contact with Albert Einstein. He was staying with his son Ernst, and Einstein and his wife paid him a visit there. They chatted for two hours together, after which Freud wrote: "He is cheerful, sure of himself and agreeable. He understands as much about psychology as I do about physics, so we had a very pleasant talk." [43] "The lucky fellow has had a much easier time than I have. He has had the support of a long series of predecessors from Newton onward, while I have had to hack every step of my way through a tangled jungle alone. No wonder that my path is not a very broad one, and that I have not got far on it." [44]

The book entitled *Inhibitions, Symptoms and Anxiety*,[45] which Freud had written in the previous July and revised in December, appeared in the third week of February, 1926. Freud's judgment of it was that "it contains several new and important things, takes back and corrects many former conclusions, and in general is not good." [46] Then came the only too frequent annoyance over the translation

[h] *babyhaft.*

rights. We had hoped that after publishing the *Collected Papers* and other books in the Library Series we should be able to continue producing presentable translations. But Freud lightheartedly gave the American rights to Pierce Clark, a man who had left the Society and whose English was as defective as his knowledge of German. I had to explain patiently all over again to Freud that without those rights no English publisher would think of issuing this type of book, and indeed it was not until 1936 that a proper translation by Alix Strachey could appear in the Library Series; even then, just when it was ready, we learned that Freud had also given the translation rights to H. A. Bunker in New York without informing either translator of the other. Finally, however, two good translations exist, one American and one British. I quoted to Freud the comment Joan Riviere had made when I told her the news: "And this is how we are treated after all our work." All he could say was "I meant no harm," [1] whereupon I had to continue enlightening him about the legal aspects of the publishing world.

About this time the new American owners of the *Encyclopaedia Britannica* decided to issue a new edition, the thirteenth, and invited Freud to write a short account of psychoanalysis for it;[47] it appeared in the third of three supplementary volumes called *These Eventful Years*. The Editors changed his simple title to the more tendentious one of "Psycho-Analysis: Freudian School," which has been retained in the subsequent editions. They also omitted a passage about Adler and Jung.[48]

In June Freud began to write another book,[49] *The Question of Lay Analysis.*[50] As mentioned previously, the occasion of his doing so was the prosecution that had been undertaken against Theodor Reik on the ground of quackery, an action which in the end failed. Freud described the book as "bitter," since he was in a bad mood when he wrote it.[51] He began it in the last week of June,[52] it was actually printed before the end of July[53] and it appeared in September.[54] Exactly the same trouble arose over the translation rights as with the former book. Freud disposed of the rights to an American publisher who insisted on publishing the book in the same volume as the *Autobiography*.[55] It was only in 1935 that we managed to secure the latter for the Library Series, but we were never able to publish the other book. After the failure of all our negotiations I wrote to Freud: "You may imagine how loth we are to see one after another

[1] An English phrase interpolated in a German letter, a frequent habit of Freud's.

of your books slipping through our fingers. To change the metaphor: it seems to be always a question of salvaging something out of the wreckage. Our beautiful plan of a worthy English translation of your collected works recedes farther and farther away in the light of one complication after another." [56] Fortunately, however, after another thirty years of struggle that plan, thanks to the efforts of Ernst Freud and James Strachey, is at last approaching fulfillment.

1927

The chief events of this year were the first signs of the changes in Ferenczi's personality that were to lead to his estrangement from Freud; the dispute with the Americans and Dutch at the Innsbruck Congress; and the disagreement between Freud and myself on the matters of lay analysis and child analysis.

Things were quiet at the beginning of the year. There was little local news, but "much international post: on one day a pupil from India who wishes to come, the offer of translations from a Norwegian publisher, Archives from Lima (Peru) which dedicates to me an essay and a magnificent caricature. The times of splendid isolation have been thoroughly overcome." [57]

Freud had for some years known and corresponded with Stefan Zweig, and this spring he began a much more extensive correspondence with Arnold Zweig. The two men, who were not even remotely related to one another, were very unlike. Stefan, the son of wealthy parents, moved in the most cultivated and artistic circles in Vienna. He glided easily through life. A fluent and gifted writer, he composed a number of attractive and fascinating books, particularly historical biographies, which displayed considerable psychological insight. But he left little to his readers' imagination, and fully instructed them about what they ought to feel at every passage of his stories. Arnold, on the other hand, had had a hard life and was also constitutionally less happy. His Prussian style was heavier, but more thorough and profound. Freud's attitude toward the two men was indicated by his mode of address. Stefan was *Lieber Herr Doktor*, Arnold was *Lieber Meister* Arnold. He had of course been familiar with Arnold Zweig's writings earlier, but it was the famous war novel *Sergeant Grischa* that brought the two men together.

Although the New York analysts had been somewhat offended at Ferenczi's not communicating with them about his approaching visit they received him in a friendly fashion and invited him to address the winter meeting of the American Psychoanalytic Association, which he did on December 26, 1926. Brill was cordial to his old and respected friend, invited him to dinner, etc., and presided at Ferenczi's opening lecture before the New School of Social Research; incidentally, Rank was at the same time giving a course of lectures to the Old School of Social Research. Then came a period of American lionizing and hospitality which stimulated Ferenczi to an excited outburst of energy; every day there was a new engagement for him to speak at both private and public gatherings. He was at the same time engaged in training analytically eight or nine people, mostly lay. They were necessarily short analyses, but the total number was enough for a special group of lay analysts to be formed, which he hoped would be accepted as a separate Society by the International Association. These and other activities brought him into conflict with the New York analysts, who had on January 25, 1927, passed strong resolutions condemning all therapeutic practice by non-medical people. Relations became more and more strained as the months went on until he was almost completely ostracized by his colleagues. When Ferenczi gave a farewell dinner party on the eve of his leaving for Europe on June 2, even the friendly Brill declined to attend it, as did also Oberndorf.

Ferenczi traveled first to England, where he gave addresses to the British Psychological and Psycho-Analytical Societies. We received him warmly, which must have been a welcome change after his recent experiences in New York. I gave a garden party and several dinner parties for him, and he spent a couple of days at my country home. I was under the impression that nothing had disturbed our old friendship, and in fact remained under that impression until, as mentioned earlier, I recently read his correspondence with Freud. Yet on that occasion when he asked me if I had been in Italy to meet Brill and I answered in the negative, he wrote to Freud saying he was convinced I was lying and that Brill and I had certainly been together in Italy apparently conspiring on the topic of lay analysis.[58] Such a remark in itself betokens a serious state of mind, and it was followed in the next couple of years by a series of similar remarks expressing both suspicion and derogation of my activities. There is evidence in the letters that Freud was thereby influenced unfavorably against me, of course without my knowledge.

From London Ferenczi went to Baden-Baden to visit Groddeck, then to Berlin to see Eitingon, then back to Baden-Baden, and it was only after the Innsbruck Congress in September that he went to visit

Freud. Freud was piqued that he had not come sooner instead of spending three months in Europe first. He suspected it betokened some tendency to emancipate himself (from Freud or from psychoanalysis or, as the event showed, from both); "when one gets old enough one has at the end everyone against one." [59] He found Ferenczi distinctly reserved since his visit to America. [60] It was the first indication of his gradual withdrawal from Freud. At that time Freud could not have known how far this would go, nevertheless for some reason they found it necessary to reassure each other of the permanence of their old friendship. In his first letter after returning to Budapest Ferenczi wrote that "neither time nor the many storms that rage about us can ever change in any way the steadfast personal and scientific bond between us." [61] And Freud replied: "We have come a long way together since 1909, always hand in hand, and it will not be otherwise for the little distance that is left." [62]

Freud's main administrative preoccupation in this year was the problem of lay analysis, which will be discussed later. As will be related then, the controversy concerning it came to a head at the Innsbruck Congress, which took place in the first week of September. Eitingon, who had been acting as temporary President of the International Association since Abraham's death, did not wish to carry the burden any longer. He asked Freud whom he would recommend, and Freud told him he would much prefer that Eitingon himself would continue; should he decline he would suggest Ferenczi. [63] Freud was determined that I should not succeed Eitingon—not that anyone had put forward my name—and hoped up to the last minute that Ferenczi would be elected. [64] This, as Ferenczi himself soon came to see, [65] would have been intolerable to the Americans and Dutch, and would have led to a split in the Association. So I prevailed on Eitingon to continue in his position, [66] and it was Ferenczi who proposed him at the Business Meeting.

After the Innsbruck Congress we changed the structure of the Committee by converting it into a group, no longer private, of the officials of the International Association. They were Eitingon, the President; Ferenczi and myself, Vice-Presidents; Anna Freud, Secretary and van Ophuijsen, Treasurer. Sachs, who had for years been rather a silent partner, dropped out; Freud had long thought he didn't really belong in the Committee. [67] By now, therefore, Ferenczi and I were all that was left of the original Committee. The regular circular letters were continued, the first of the new series starting in October.

The most urgent problem we had to discuss was the ever parlous state of the Verlag finances. Storfer, the Managing Director, a clever and energetic but erratic person, had unfortunately little idea of strict bookkeeping, so that it was always hard to know exactly how we stood. He gave notice of his resignation in March,[68] but after much discussion Eitingon persuaded him to stay on until the end of 1928. Things were so bad that serious negotiations were going on to sell the stock and good will to a commercial firm (Springer),[69] as we had been compelled to with the British branch some time before—fortunately in our case with very beneficial results. Freud was very loath to relinquish control of a project that had always been very near to his heart, so Eitingon nobly struggled on with the difficulties; as he put it, "once we give it away we shall never get it back again." [70] A donation of $5,000.00 from Miss Grace Potter stayed off the immediate crisis.[71]

Freud's health had been if anything worse this year than in the last. In March his doctors had advised him to undergo another course of heart therapy. He resisted for a while, saying to Eitingon: "I will wait till I really need it. I find living for one's health unbearable." [72] But in April he spent a week in the Cottage Sanatorium as in the previous year, and from then on took only three patients instead of five. As the time of his birthday approached he gave orders that no further birthday was to be celebrated until he was seventy-five; the seventieth had been strain enough. A new prosthesis had been made for him that spring, but the results were disappointing and he began to wonder if he should not consult another surgeon.[73]

The summer was again spent in the Villa Schüler, at the Semmering, from June 16 until the end of September. In August he was complaining of being "eternally ill and plagued with discomfort," [74] and there were abdominal troubles "to make a change." [75] In September after the Congress he had to put up with the strain of receiving many visitors: Binswanger, Rene Laforgue, Joan Riviere and others in addition to the usual visits from Eitingon, Ferenczi and myself.

In August he was very pleased at receiving from Yvette Guilbert, the famous diseuse, a copy of her Mémoires.[76] The year before she had sent him through her niece Eva Rosenfeld her photograph inscribed "A un grand savant d'une artiste," [1] and he had immedi-

[1] To a great scholar from an artist.

ately returned the compliment. He had become an enthusiastic admirer of hers since, on Mme. Charcot's advice, he had attended her little concerts in the few days he spent in Paris in 1889.[k] From 1927 on he never missed attending her annual performances in Vienna, and they became good friends.

In the same month Freud heard of an agitation Groddeck was setting on foot to procure him a Nobel Prize. As on former occasions, he begged that it cease; such an honor would not suit him.[1]

In September Freud sent me a long letter complaining strongly about a public campaign I was supposed to be conducting in England against his daughter Anna, and perhaps therefore against himself. The only basis for this outburst was my having published in the *Journal* a long report of a discussion on child analysis.[78] It was a topic that had for years interested our Society, which contained so many women analysts, and it had been further stimulated by Melanie Klein's coming to England the year before. I wrote a comprehensive account of the whole matter to Freud, and he replied: "I am naturally very happy that you answered my letter so calmly and fully instead of being very offended by it." [79] But he remained sceptical, and possibly prejudiced, about Melanie Klein's methods and conclusions. I had later several talks with him on the subject of early analysis, but I never succeeded in making any impression on him beyond his admitting that he had no personal experience to guide him.

In November the Vienna Municipality offered Freud a plot of ground in the Tandlmarkt at the lower end of the Berggasse for him to build an institute of psychoanalysis there.[80] There was, however, no money for the purpose, and Freud ruefully remarked, alluding to the costume worn by mountaineers in Austria, "all we have for the tour is the bare knees."

There were three literary productions in 1927. The first was a supplement to the essay on Michelangelo's Moses that Freud had published anonymously thirteen years before.[81] It was written in June,[82] and was published in *Imago* at the end of the year[83] after having

---

[k] In this respect also I seem to have followed Freud, and at the time of the Paris Congress in 1938 I reminded her of a piquant song I remembered from the days of her private concerts thirty-five years before; with her usual charm she sang it again for me on the spot.

[1] *Der passt nicht zu mir.*[77]

first appeared that summer in the first number of the new *Revue Française de Psychanalyse*. Then he wrote, "suddenly" as he said, a little paper on "Fetishism," [84] which was despatched at the end of the first week in August.[85] He remarked dolefully: "probably nothing will follow this." [86] It was published in the last number of the *Zeitschrift*, 1927. Freud had delayed the publication until he could find out whether Stekel had touched on the solution he was now propounding in a book Stekel had recently devoted to the topic.[87] He could not bring himself to read that book himself, so he commissioned Wittels to examine it.[88]

The day that paper was sent off he announced he was writing a paper on "Humour," [89] being in a good mood because the bankruptcy of the *Verlag* had once more been staved off.[90] His interest in the subject dated from his book on jokes, *Der Witz und seine Beziehung zum Unbewussten*, written more than twenty years before, but it had remained an unsolved problem until now. The paper took him only five days to write.[91] Anna Freud read it before the Innsbruck Congress in September.

He also published a book in that year, *The Future of an Illusion*.[92] It started many acrimonious controversies which still continue; even as I write these lines I note the appearance of another book and two long essays dealing with some of its implications.[93] Freud must have been contemplating writing it as early as that spring, since in May Eitingon inquired how it was progressing.[94] He read it out to Eitingon during his visit in September and sent him the proofs in the third week of October.[95] He told him it had very little value but would be useful in bringing in some money for the *Verlag*.[96] To Ferenczi he was still more outspoken in his derogation of the book: "Now it already seems to me childish; fundamentally I think otherwise; I regard it as weak analytically and inadequate as a self-confession." [97] This sentence will cause many people to scratch their heads; it is evidently open to many interpretations. There was at the time a good deal of religious controversy in England, starting from the Bishop of Birmingham's exposition of the anthropological origin of the belief in transubstantiation, so Freud was very eager that we publish a translation of the book with the minimum of delay and that it should be done by James Strachey.[98] I remarked that there was a certain incompatibility between his two wishes, and to Strachey's relief the work was undertaken by another literary person, W. D. Robson-Scott.

1928

This was a year of increased physical suffering and a desperate attempt to alleviate it. As usual, however, I will describe the events chronologically.

At the beginning of the year there was great excitement over Geza Róheim's expedition to the Pacific and Australia which had been made possible through Marie Bonaparte's generosity and foresight. These were Freud's suggestions for the enterprise: "Róheim is burning with eagerness to 'analyze' his primitive natives. I think it would be more urgent to make observations concerning the sexual freedom and the latency period of the children, on any signs of the Oedipus complex, and on any indications of a masculine complex among the primitive women. But we agreed that the program would in the end follow the opportunities that presented themselves." [99]

Róheim planned to settle in Berlin after his return, which he then did. Ferenczi complained that so many Hungarians were doing this, and felt very inclined to follow them; he asked Freud's opinion about how he would be received there,[100] but Freud advised him to stay at his post as long as it was possible in the face of the bitter anti-Semitism of the Horthy regime. Freud was more urgently concerned with Reik's situation. Although the legal action against him had failed he was finding it very hard to make a living in Vienna. He paid a visit to Paris, but Laforgue discouraged him against settling there[101] and later he moved for a while to Berlin.[102]

I had arranged a meeting of the Committee in Paris at the end of February. The fatal illness of my daughter prevented me from going, and Ferenczi found the distance too great, so the meeting was confined to Anna Freud and Eitingon.

In February I asked Freud if he knew of the renewed efforts that were being made to procure him a Nobel Prize. He answered: "No, I know nothing of efforts to secure me the Nobel prize and I do not appreciate them. Who is fool enough to meddle in this affair?" [103]

In that month he suffered from a severe conjunctivitis in one eye which lasted for six weeks and made reading extremely difficult, but at the end of March he acted as witness at the wedding of Ruth Mack with Mark Brunswick. It was the third wedding he had attended apart from his own.

On the first day of April he had to mourn the sudden loss of an old medical friend, Ludwig Rosenberg, one of the three who played the weekly game of cards with him; (the others were Dr. Oskar Rie and Prof. Königstein). He died early in the morning after having parted from Freud half an hour after midnight; on leaving he had remarked: "Anyhow we have got the better of this month." [104]

About that time Eitingon sent him a small book by the Russian philosopher Chestov, of whom Eitingon was a friend and admirer. Freud said he got through it in one reading, but without being able to discover the author's attitude. "Probably you cannot imagine how alien all these philosophical convolutions[m] seem to me. The only feeling of satisfaction they give me is that I take no part in this pitiable waste of intellectual powers. Philosophers no doubt believe that in such studies they are contributing to the development of human thought, but every time there is a psychological or even a psychopathological problem behind them." [105]

When Freud heard of the death of my first child he wrote suggesting a piece of Shakespeare research in the hope of its distracting me. When I answered that I should have preferred to receive some words of consolatory wisdom he replied: "When I did not write to you what you had expected I had good reasons for it. I know of only two consolations in such a case. The one is bad, since it robs life of all its value, and the other, more effective one, is suitable only for old people, not for young ones like you and your poor wife. What this second is you may easily guess. . . . As an unbelieving fatalist I can only let my arms sink before the terrors of death." [106]

Freud's seventy-second birthday that year was kept very quietly in accord with his wishes, the ever-faithful Eitingon being the only one of us who came to it. Ferenczi had visited Freud in Vienna in April; he again visited him on the Semmering in July and in Berlin in September. I did not see Freud in 1928, the only year I had missed since the war.

That spring Dr. Gilbert Robin, former chief of the Paris Psychiatric Clinic, visited Freud and published an account of his impressions,[107] a translation of which appeared also in a Vienna newspaper.[108] Robin summed up his character well by describing him as "the most incorruptible *savant* in a time of corruption." Psychoanalysis must have been a vogue in Paris at that time, for Robin asked rhetorically "Have we ever known a psychologist, a philosopher or a physician attain such a height of fame in his life time? Has so much noise ever emerged from so much silence? Psychology, pathological medicine, literature can no longer dispense with him; the salons know

[m] *Verkrampfungen.*

no other conversation; there is no dinner party at which his name does not turn up during the dessert."

Freud left for his summer vacation on June 16, but this time he had not at first been able to rent the villa he had found so comfortable and for a fortnight had to be content with quarters in the Südbahn Hotel. The piece of news he had to report was that "the enormous talent for laziness, which I have always suspected in myself and which has no chance of developing in my fully occupied life, is now coming to expression." [109] He had the company of his first chow, with which Dorothy Burlingham, who was becoming intimate with the family, presented him. Like most Jews of his generation Freud had had little contact with animals, but a couple of years before an Alsatian dog, Wolf, had been procured to accompany his daughter Anna on her walks through the forests of the Semmering. Freud had taken a considerable interest in observing canine ways, and from now on he became more and more fond of one dog after another—evidently a sublimation of his very great fondness for young children which could no longer be gratified. This first chow, called Lun Yu, unfortunately survived only fifteen months. In August of the following year Eva Rosenfeld was escorting her from Berchtesgaden to Vienna when she broke loose in the station at Salzburg and after three days was found run over on the line. Freud remarked that the pain they all felt resembled in quality, though not in intensity, that experienced after the loss of a child." [110] Before long, however, she was replaced by another, Jo-fi, who was a constant companion for seven years.

Freud had been through an exceptionally distressing time that spring, and by March he reported that his tiredness had reached an unusual degree.[111] The discomfort and pain in his mouth had been almost unbearable, and despite Pichler's constant endeavors he was losing hope of finding alleviation. If only he could afford it he would give up working.[112] His son Ernst had for a year been begging him to consult a famous oral surgeon in Berlin, Professor Schroeder, but Freud's disinclination to leave his own surgeon made him put off this plan until Pichler himself confessed he was at the end of his tether and could do no more.[n] A joint consultation was then arranged, and Schroeder came to see Freud on June 24. The result was so promising that Freud agreed to spend some time in Berlin as soon as Schroeder should be free. He asked us to keep this news as quiet as possible,[113] not wishing anyone to think that it betokened

[n] Pichler notes, May 8, 1928.

any reflection on his Viennese surgeon. It was given out that he was paying another visit to his children and grandchildren in Berlin. He left on August 30 with Anna as his companion, and they stayed, for the first time, at the Tegel sanatorium. Marie Bonaparte and Ferenczi visited him there that month, but Freud was in poor shape, hardly able to talk and plagued by uncertainty about the success of the undertaking. However, when he returned to Vienna at the beginning of November the new prosthesis, though by no means perfect, was proving a distinct advance on the previous one, so that life was once more tolerable. It was 70 per cent better than before.[114]

For the next two and a half years Freud's surgeon was Dr. Joseph Weinmann, a Viennese who spent some time with Schroeder in Berlin in 1929 so as to become familiar with the details of Freud's case. It was Weinmann who suggested the use of orthoform, a member of the novocain group and therefore a benefit derived from Freud's early work on cocaine. This proved a great boon for some years, but unfortunately it later caused irritations leading to a local hyperkeratosis, a precancerous condition. After that its use had to be considerably restricted.

That summer Freud had been told that the French translation of his *Autobiography* was to be accompanied by his photograph, and here is his comment: "Adding pictures of an author seems to me a bad habit, 'a nuisance,' a concession to the bad taste of the public. What the author looks like has nothing to do with the reader. If the reader feels like doing so he can equip him in his phantasy with ideal beauty without being contradicted." [115]

It is not surprising that in a year so full of bodily suffering there is hardly any literary production to note. Freud seems to have written nothing at all in this year; it was a quarter of a century since such a statement could have been made.

Two short papers which he had written in the previous year were published in January, 1928, both in *Imago*. One was the little essay on "Humour" which his daughter had read at the Innsbruck Congress the previous September; at the Lucerne Congress in 1934 Ernst Kris read a paper expanding Freud's views and correlating them with his earlier work on jokes twenty-three years before.[116] The other, written at the end of 1927, was a short account of a simple case of religious conversion which an American doctor had related to him.[117]

A more extensive essay, "Dostoevsky and Parricide," also appeared in this year.[118] Freud had been invited a couple of years before to write a psychological introduction to a scholarly volume on *The Brothers Karamasov* which F. Eckstein and F. Fülöp-Miller were editing. He started working on it in the spring of 1926. There was a great deal to read and cogitate over, but in the holiday he began writing his essay and read the beginning of it to Eitingon when the latter visited him on the Semmering at the end of June, 1926. He turned aside, however, to write the urgently needed booklet on lay analysis, and when he came back from the freedom of the holiday to the yoke of Vienna his energy and interest had both waned.[119] Then he confessed that what made him disinclined ever to write the essay was his discovery that most of what he had to say from the point of view of psychoanalysis was already contained in a little book by Neufeld which the *Verlag* had published not long before.[120] Eitingon, however, kept pressing him to finish the work and sent him book after book, including a complete set of Dostoevsky's correspondence, so ultimately the essay got written, presumably early in 1927.

1929

Freud's chief preoccupation in this year was the continued tension with the Americans over the matter of lay analysis, a theme that has so many ramifications that it will deserve a chapter to itself. It was also in this year that Ferenczi's estrangement from Freud began to become more evident.

In January the Professor of Philosophy at Harvard University invited me to edit a source book of Freud's writings, i.e., to select one-ninth of them, arrange these and write an introduction. I asked Freud for his advice, and his answer was so typical of him that I will reproduce it here:

"4. 1. 1929

"Dear Jones

"I do not find it easy to answer your question, and shall not be able to get beyond a for and against. Fortunately I don't have to decide.

"Fundamentally the whole idea is very repellent to me, typically American. One can be sure that when such a 'source book' exists no American will ever touch the original writings. But perhaps he will not do so anyhow, and will go on getting his information from the muddy popular sources. So that speaks in favor of your doing it. On

the other hand, if you undertake it, it would be a tedious and laborious task, one not quite worthy of you. Now that you are fifty you
should employ your working powers for more original work. Speaking as your friend I can only advise you not to undertake it.

"Against this, however, is the fact that when the publisher fancies
he has found something that will pay him he will not desist because
of your refusal. He will hand over the task to someone else, and
heaven knows what he will make of it. Most certainly he would not
do it as well as you.

"That is how the considerations balance each other. Beyond them
all an inner voice tells me that the world will go on very much the
same whether the Americans get a good or a bad source book for
my writings.

"I believe I have been sincere. And I shall not be offended at
hearing that you have refused the offer.

> "Herzlichst
> "Ihr
> "Freud"

I told him his amusing letter was so exactly what I had expected
that I did not know why I bothered him to write it.

In that winter the *Verlag* was passing through one of its periodic
crises, and Freud was greatly relieved when Marie Bonaparte volunteered to save it from bankruptcy.[121] In March other donations also
came in: the Budapest Society subscribed $1,857, Ruth Brunswick
induced her father to send $4,000, and $1,500 came from Brill, $500
from himself and $1,000 from an anonymous patient.

On March 11 Freud and Anna went to Berlin for a further consultation with Schroeder. They stayed in Tegelsee, returning to Vienna after a fortnight. After that an assistant of Schroeder's, Karolyi,
continued with the necessary manipulations.

Marie Bonaparte had been pressing Freud to engage a regular
medical attendant who could watch daily over his general health
and also be in contact with the surgeons, and she recommended Dr.
Max Schur, an excellent internist who had the advantage of being
analytically trained as well. Freud gladly agreed.[122] At their first interview Freud laid down the basic rule that Schur should never keep
the truth from him, however painful it might be, and the sincerity of
his tone showed that he meant it literally. They shook hands on it.
He added, "I can stand a great deal of pain and I hate sedatives, but
I trust you will not let me suffer unnecessarily." The time was to

come when Freud had to call on Schur to fulfill this request. Except for a few weeks in 1939 Schur was close to Freud throughout the last ten years of his life.

Schur was a perfect choice for a doctor. He established excellent relations with his patient, and his considerateness, his untiring patience and his resourcefulness were unsurpassable. He and Anna made an ideal pair of guardians to watch over the suffering man and to alleviate his manifold discomforts. Moreover, the two became in time highly competent experts at evaluating the slightest change in the local condition. Their watchful care and their skill in detecting the earliest signs of danger undoubtedly prolonged Freud's life by years. Anna had to play with her characteristic unostentation many parts: nurse, a truly "personal" physician, companion, assistant secretary, co-worker and altogether a shield against the intrusions of the outer world.

On his side Freud's behavior deserved this high degree of attentiveness. He was throughout a model patient, touchingly grateful for any relief and in all the years completely uncomplaining. There was never a sign of irritability or annoyance, whatever the distress. There was no grumbling at what he had to endure. A favorite expression was "it is no use quarreling with fate." ° His gracious politeness, considerateness and gratitude toward his doctor never wavered.

That spring a book appeared by Maylan, *Freud's Tragic Complex,* [123] which purported to give a psychoanalysis of Freud's personality. The author was eager to have Freud's opinion of it, but Freud contented himself with sending him a message through Eitingon to the effect that his opinion of the book could best be conveyed by Caliban's retort in Shakespeare's *Tempest*: "You taught me language; and my profit on't is, I know how to curse." [124]

We left Freud in peace again at his birthday this year, Eitingon and Lou Salomé being the only visitors. Freud gave as a reason for keeping it particularly quiet that it was the oddest number possible, seventy-three being a prime number.[125]

In that same month of May I was able to report the accomplishment of my most difficult achievement on behalf of psychoanalysis, the satisfactory report of the special committee of the British Medical Association which has sometimes been called the Psycho-Analytical Charter.ᵖ [126] Edward Glover and myself had for over three years

° *man darf nicht mit dem Schicksal hadern.*
ᵖ See p. 128.

fought at heavy odds against our twenty-five bitter opponents, but when a sub-committee of three, of which I was one, was instructed to draw up the final report, my chances improved. One of the clauses officially defined psychoanalysis as work employing Freud's technique, thus excluding all the other pretenders to the name. I do not think it made any special impression on Freud, because it was after all a medical pronouncement, whereas his aim was to make psychoanalysis independent of medicine.

Freud stopped work on June 16, and on June 18 the family moved to Schneewinkel, Berchtesgaden, for the summer, where I visited him on June 23; Ferenczi came a week later. Brill also visited him there in July, and later on Laforgue and Joan Riviere arrived. After five summers spent at the Semmering this resort made a delightful change, and Freud particularly enjoyed being there. He said he had never been so pleased with any holiday resort as with this one.[127] Very likely the old association of having written *The Interpretation of Dreams* there played a part in this mood.[q] However, he had to break the holiday to go to Berlin for further treatment. He and Anna stayed again at Tegel sanatorium, the bankruptcy of which had been postponed for a while—from September 15 to October 20.

At the end of May the newly organized Committee met in Paris to discuss the difficult problem of dealing with the Americans at the coming Congress. There were warm arguments between Anna and Ferenczi on the one side and van Ophuijsen and myself on the other, Eitingon being the peacemaker, but we hoped for the best. We agreed to propose that Eitingon be re-elected as President.

Eitingon begged Freud to write a paper to be read at the Oxford Congress at the end of July, but this is the answer he got. "You persist in picturing things as very simple. I write down one of my discoveries I have kept back, Anna types the small but important paper on her machine, she then reads it before the Congress, who have nothing to do but to applaud. Unfortunately I have nothing to communicate. Even I am surprised at that state of affairs, but it is so. Let us be resigned!" [128] Nevertheless in the next month Freud started writing a new book.

Ferenczi had throughout this year continued making highly critical remarks about me to Freud, and not without effect. He was convinced that I was using the problem of lay analysis as a pretext for my ambition, based on financial motives, to "unite the

�q See Volume I, p. 335.

Anglo-Saxon world under my sceptre" (!).[129] I was "an unscrupulous and dangerous person who should be treated more severely. The British group should be freed from my tyranny." [130] Neither I nor anyone else heard anything about these feelings of suspicion and hostility, which were reserved for Freud alone. It was not long, however, before their true source, antagonism to Freud himself, began to betray itself. The story of Rank was being repeated.

The Oxford Congress passed off both peaceably and enjoyably. As Freud acknowledged, the avoidance of a split in the Association over the matter of lay analysis was due to the efforts Brill and I made to prevent it, and he thanked us both warmly for this.[131] The foreigners were amused at the restrictions imposed on them as residents of the old colleges, and we did everything to interest them in our monuments by having conducted tours to Windsor Castle, Stonehenge, the Tower of London, and so on. Ferenczi, however, was disappointed at not being made President, and from that time on he withdrew from the concerns of the Association into his scientific researches. The success Abraham and I had had five years before in dissociating him from Rank's errors in technique and theory was probably not so complete as we had thought, and from about this time he began to develop lines of his own which seriously diverged from those generally accepted in psychoanalytical circles. In the paper he read at Oxford he denounced what he called the one-sidedness of paying so much attention to the phantasies of childhood and maintained that Freud's first view of etiology had been the correct one: namely, that the origin of neuroses was to be found in definite traumas, particularly the unkindness or cruelty of parents. This had to be remedied by the analyst's showing more affection toward his patient than Freud, for instance, thought wise.

After visiting Freud in June Ferenczi only wrote to him once before Christmas, a great contrast with former years when a week seldom went by without a long letter. He himself gave as the main reason for this silence his acute fear lest Freud might not agree with his new ideas (a situation he would not be able to tolerate), and also the necessity of formulating them on a firm basis before enunciating them.[132] Freud in his reply said: "You have without doubt withdrawn yourself outwardly from me in the past few years. But not so far, I hope, that a move toward creating a new oppositional analysis is to be expected from my Paladin and secret Grand Vizier." [133]

As may be seen from the balance of this letter, Freud's health was troubling him a great deal at this time. "The greatest part of my activity has to be devoted to maintaining that amount of health needed to carry on my daily work. A real mosaic of therapeutic measures to compel various organs to serve this purpose. Recently my heart has joined in with extra-systolic arhythmia and attacks of palpitation. My wise physician, Professor Braun, says that all that has no serious significance. He ought to know. Is he already beginning to swindle? One cannot avoid one's fate: perhaps medical deception is also part of that."

In November Freud returned to Pichler for a single consultation. Weinmann, who accompanied him, had found a suspicious area in his mouth. It was, however, a false alarm.

In December I reported on my visit to New York where I had given an address at the opening of the Psychiatric Institute of Columbia University. I was there only three days, returning on the same ship. I was able to reinforce Brill's efforts to induce the New York members to cooperate more closely with their European colleagues.

In 1929 Freud resumed his literary activity by writing another book. He started doing this in July,[134] and had finished the first draft in a month or so.[135] The title he first proposed for it was "Das Unglück in der Kultur" which was later altered to "Das Unbehagen in der Kultur." Unbehagen was a hard word for us to translate, since the most suitable word in English "Dis-Ease" was too obsolete to use. Freud himself suggested "Man's Discomfort in Civilization," [136] but it was finally entitled Civilization and its Discontents.[137]

The book was sent to press at the beginning of November,[138] and it must have appeared before the end of the year, since I see I was thanking Freud for my copy, inscribed "Meinem lieben Ernest Jones," on January 1, 1930. In a year's time the edition of 12,000 was sold out, and a new one had to be issued.[139] Freud himself, however, was very dissatisfied with the book.[r]

1930

The two outstanding events of this year were the death of Freud's mother and the award of the Goethe prize.

To proceed chronologically, in the first two months of the year Ferenczi's mental health was seriously disturbing, and his state of sensitiveness resulted in some plain speaking between the two men which had very beneficial results. Freud said he sympathized with

[r] Letter to Lou Salomé. Appendix A, No. 13.

his friend's bitterness over the way he had been treated by the Americans, and also with his disappointment at not being proposed as President, which, as Freud pointed out, would have resulted in a split in the International Association; but he could not understand why Ferenczi should be feeling hostile to him.[140] Ferenczi went into the past: why had Freud not been kinder to him when he sulked on the Sicily journey twenty years ago, and why had he not analyzed Ferenczi's repressed hostility in the three weeks' analysis fifteen years ago? [141] Without mentioning Ferenczi's name Freud gave a short description of this aspect of his case in a paper he wrote in 1937.[142]

For some years Ferenczi had concealed from Freud his growing scientific divergencies and his view of Freud's "one-sidedness," partly because of Freud's state of health and partly because he feared Freud's response were he to know of them. Freud's friendly letters reassured him, and when Ferenczi paid him a visit on April 21 they had a long and satisfactory talk which convinced him that his fears about being disapproved of were greatly exaggerated.[143] For the rest of the year they remained on amicable terms, and there was no further talk of any differences. Ferenczi admitted that his feelings about Freud and his colleagues (particularly Brill and myself) were bound up with his childhood difficulties with his father and brothers.[144] But the sensitiveness remained. When later in the year Freud praised Ferenczi's last paper as being "very clever," [*] Ferenczi regretted that instead of that word Freud had not written "correct, probable, or even plausible." [145]

In May Ferenczi bought a charming villa in Buda, and he reminded Freud of the latter's prophecy when they were gazing at a famous surgeon's villa in Budapest twenty-two years before that Ferenczi would have a similar one in ten or twelve years' time. After congratulating him Freud added: "So I was not wrong. The miscalculation over the date came from my not taking into account the coming war. My prophetic talent is, like that of all prophets, very one-sided; while we apprehend one element of the future another one escapes us." [146] He doubted if he would ever see the villa, but what he hoped was that through excavations in the garden Ferenczi would discover that it had once been the site of a Roman villa whose owner had spent some time in Egypt and brought back many souvenirs from there.

Freud knew that further manipulations of his prosthesis would soon be necessary, but Trebitsch, another assistant of Schroeder's,

[*] *sehr geistreich.*

happened to be in Vienna and his attentions postponed for a time the inevitable journey to Berlin.[147] Freud had arranged to go to Berlin in the third week of April for a new prosthesis to be made, but, just as had happened about that time three years before, he had to obey medical orders and retire to the Cottage Sanatorium for treatment of both his cardiac and his abdominal conditions. He went there on April 24 and stayed until he left for Berlin on May 4. He had made a rapid recovery, "not through any therapeutic miracle but by an act of autotomy." [148] He had suddenly developed an intolerance for cigars, and on ceasing to smoke felt much better than he had done for a long time.[149] But this abstinence lasted only twenty-three days. Then he allowed himself one daily cigar, which after some months increased to two. At the end of the year he could report smoking three or four a day "to the applause of my physician, Braun." [150]

In April Freud was surprised at receiving the seventh volume of a projected set of forty volumes of his translated works in Japanese. There was also a long visit to Europe by an enterprising Japanese, Yabe, who made an excellent impression on us; he had an astonishingly thorough knowledge of psychoanalysis.

In the same month a Viennese graphologist, Robert Saudek, ventured on a study of Freud's handwriting, and his report on it, dated April 29, 1930, has been preserved. From it one would surmise that he knew who the writer was. That was also Freud's opinion, and he stigmatized it as a bad joke. In Freud's posthumously published essay on telepathy, written in 1921, he mentioned a similar effort by another graphologist, Raphael Schermann. He made two points, the obvious one that the handwriting was that of an old man and the curious statement that he must be an unbearable tyrant at home. Freud mildly commented that his family would scarcely confirm this.[151]

Freud had expected that six weeks in Berlin would suffice, but he had to stay there, or rather in Tegelsee, for more than twice that time. At the end of May an expedition of three days was made to a fisherman's cottage Ernst had acquired on the island of Hiddensee, near Rügen on the Baltic. Freud greatly liked the spot, but the traveling tired him badly. He also had the experience of a short pleasure flight in an airplane, the only one in his life.

It was during this stay in Berlin that the American Ambassador, W. C. Bullitt, persuaded Freud to cooperate with him in writing a psychoanalytic study of President Wilson. They completed the book, which will be published at a suitable time, and I have been the only person privileged to read it. It is a full study of Wilson's life and contains some astonishing revelations. Although a joint work, it is not hard to distinguish the analytical contributions of the one author from the political contributions of the other.

I may add that a few years before Freud had read with gusto a semi-analytical book on Wilson, a detailed study of the peculiarities of his style of writing which was very revealing.[152]

Ambassador Bullitt tells me of a remark Freud made to him during this stay which shows how hopeful he then was of the Germans being able to contain the Nazi movement: "A nation that produced Goethe could not possibly go to the bad." It was not long before he was forced to revise this judgment radically.

Eva Rosenfeld and Mrs. Freud had procured him accommodations at Rebenburg, Grundlsee, in the Salzkammergut, a wonderfully beautiful spot in spite of the constant rain. It was the last holiday Freud was to have away from the environs of Vienna. He arrived there on July 28, and only a couple of days later he received "a quite charming letter" announcing that the Goethe prize for that year had been awarded to him. The letter was from Paquet, a well-known lyric poet and essayist, who was the Secretary of the Committee that administered the Foundation in question. The amount of the prize was 10,000 Marks ($2,380.00), which just covered the expenses of Freud's long stay in Berlin.[153] In Freud's opinion, the association with Goethe made it a specially worthy honor, and it gave him great pleasure. Freud had to compose an address, which he did in the next few days,[154] and in it depicted in masterly lines the relation of psychoanalysis to the study of Goethe.[155] He made a convincing plea justifying his having made intimate psychological studies of great men such as Leonardo and Goethe, "so that if his spirit reproaches me in the next world for adopting the same attitude toward him likewise I shall simply quote his own words in my defense." Anna Freud read this at the very dignified ceremony that took place at the Goethe House in Frankfort on August 28.

The idea itself had come from Paquet. He was supported at the meeting held to discuss it by an analytically oriented psychiatrist, Dr. Alfred Döblin, who represented the Section on Poetry of the Prussian Academy of Arts. The majority of the Committee, which comprised several clergymen, was, after much discussion, against the proposal, but no vote was taken. It did not look very hopeful, but Paquet was determined to overcome the opposition, and after some weeks of private propaganda he succeeded.[156]

A few days before the ceremony, on August 24, Dr. Michel, a City Councillor of Frankfort, came to Grundlsee to confer the diploma and prize on Freud. He was accompanied by his wife and, to Freud's astonishment, also by the wife of his famous patient "Little Hans." [157]

Freud immediately discounted my hope that Frankfort would prove a step on the way to Stockholm. On the contrary, from the beginning he guessed he would have to pay dearly for the honor.[158] He was right. The opposition to psychoanalysis and to his person showed itself very soon in a flood of alarming articles in the newspapers "regretting" that Freud was on the point of death. This naturally had a very deleterious effect on his practice, his sole means of livelihood. On the other hand he was somewhat amused to hear from all over the world what an enormous number of cures for cancer existed.

In the same momentous month Freud's mother was in a dangerous state. She was suffering from gangrene of the leg, the pain of which necessitated the constant use of morphia. Federn managed to escort her from Ischl to Vienna,[159] where she died on September 12, aged ninety-five. The number of people who wrote to Freud on that occasion from the most distant parts of the world made him remark that people seem in general more willing to condole than to congratulate.[160] Freud described to two of us his response to the event as follows. "I will not disguise the fact that my reaction to this event has because of special circumstances been a curious one. Assuredly, there is no saying,* what effects such an experience may produce in deeper layers, but on the surface I can detect only two things: an increase in personal freedom, since it was always a terrifying thought that she might come to hear of my death; and secondly, the satisfaction that at last she has achieved the deliverance for which she had earned a right after such a long life. No grief otherwise, such as my ten years younger brother is painfully experiencing. I was not at the funeral; again Anna represented me as at Frankfort. Her value to me can hardly be heightened." [161] "This great event has affected me in a curious manner. No pain, no grief, which is probably to be explained by the circumstances, the great age and the end of the pity we had felt at her helplessness. With

* These words in English.

that a feeling of liberation, of release, which I think I can understand. I was not allowed to die as long as she was alive, and now I may. Somehow the values of life have notably changed in the deeper layers." [162]

Eva Rosenfeld has told me two stories of incidents during their stay in Grundlsee and I shall relate them in her own words. "At the end of the summer Professor Freud was far from well, and Ruth Brunswick, evidently forgetting that I was at that time in analysis with him, confided to me her anxiety lest his symptoms were of a serious nature. I was much perturbed and tried not to disclose this during my next interview. Freud of course sensed my hesitation, and after he had wrested my unhappy secret from me he said something which has ever since remained my most significant 'lesson' in analytic technique. It was this: 'We have only one aim and only one loyalty, to psychoanalysis. If you break this rule you injure something much more important than any consideration you owe to me.'"

The other story was this, also in her words. "I once had occasion to remind Freud of an aunt of mine who had consulted him with her daughter thirty years before; I told him her name and several details about the family. He commented: 'Yes, I remember. A beautiful woman of great mental capacity and distinguished features, but she had "no eye." ' [a] What he meant was revealed to me in a flash as the reason why the woman could not really be called beautiful. One could not say anything more characteristic about her than that her eyes were cold and expressionless. But how was it possible for Freud to recall this after thirty years, or for that matter to have taken notice of it in the mother of a patient whom he saw only once?"

Freud got back to Vienna at the end of September. Eitingon then wanted him to allow Professor Orlik, a distinguished artist, to make an etching of him, one to be better than Struck's, but Freud refused, saying that the one Schmutzer had made a few years before could not be surpassed and anyhow he had promised Max Pollak the "final visage." [163] A more urgent reason was that he was at the moment suffering badly. A few days later, on October 10, he underwent another operation. It was on a part of his scar that Schroeder had thoroughly burned in June, but which had to be watched carefully. Now Pichler excised four inches and, as he several times did, grafted the exposed part with skin taken from the patient's arm. The operation lasted an hour and a half and was "thoroughly unpleasant, although as an operation it does not rank very high." [164] Pichler's

[a] *Aber kein Auge.*

notes give a much grimmer account. A week later, on October 17, he went down with a broncho-pneumonia and was in bed for ten days, but he made a good recovery and was back at work with four patients by November 1.[165]

Later in the month Ferenczi visited him and was glad to think his new ideas were not so revolutionary as he had supposed.[166] One piece of news from Budapest was that the reactionary and anti-Semitic government there had forbidden the opening of any psychoanalytical clinic.

About this time Eitingon asked Freud for permission to read the letters he had exchanged with Einstein. This he declined, giving his reason as follows: "I was in Berlin just at the time of his fiftieth birthday and wrote him a card in which I called him 'a lucky one.' In his reply he asked me how I knew that, since I had not investigated the inside of his mind. Whereupon I wrote him a long letter explaining why I regarded him as lucky: namely, because he could work at mathematical physics and not at psychology where everyone thinks they can have a say. But I could not admit my envy of him in this respect without breaking a lance for my science and claiming for it the preference over all others. Since I had expressly begged him not to trouble to answer me, our correspondence came to an end. But my letter was after all a piece of nonsense, first as an unnecessary intimacy with a stranger, and secondly, unsuitable since later on his complete lack of understanding for psychoanalysis became evident. The only interest I have in your getting hold of the letter is if you are empowered to destroy it." [167]

I met Eitingon in Paris on December 14, and we had a most satisfactory talk about all the vexing administrative problems of the International Association, in which we mostly saw eye to eye. We agreed that Ferenczi be nominated to succeed Eitingon as President at the next Congress.

Toward the end of the year Freud was for a few days in much better health, and even went so far as to contemplate enjoying life once again.[168] That was the time when he was smoking his three or four cigars daily. In the last few months he had put on more than fourteen pounds in weight.[169]

Besides a couple of short notices, a Preface to the *Report of the Berlin Institute* and to the Hebrew translation of his totem book, and a greeting to the *Medical Review of Reviews*, all that Freud wrote in 1930 was the Goethe address already mentioned.

1931

In this year, the seventy-fifth anniversary of Freud's birth, there were several matters of note: increased physical suffering in the first half of the year; a revival of literary activity; the honors paid him by the *Gesellschaft der Aerzte* and by his birthplace, Freiberg; and, at the end of the year, the coming to a head of Ferenczi's differences with him.

In January Freud was highly gratified at being invited by the University of London to deliver the annual Huxley lecture. These were given at Charing Cross Hospital, Huxley's old medical school, to which David Forsyth was attached as physician, and it was he who had procured the invitation.[170] No German had received such an invitation since Virchow in 1898.[v] Freud had been a great admirer of T. H. Huxley,[171] and he intensely regretted not being able to accept the honor; how he wished it had been offered earlier in his life. Nothing, he said, would give him greater pleasure than to hear of its some day coming my way, but he was right when he added he did not expect to live long enough for that.[172]

Freud used often to express in a half-jocular tone his intense dislike of ceremonies. His seventy-fifth birthday was already casting its shadow ahead. After discussing with Eitingon the difficulties with Storfer in the *Verlag* he continued: "Last week there also began the threat of another calamity,[w] fortunately a less troublesome one. The *Gesellschaft der Aerzte* have nominated me and Landsteiner (the Nobel Prize man) for the Honorary Membership of the Society, and it will soon be ratified. A cowardly gesture at the appearance of success, very disgusting and repulsive. It won't do to refuse; that would only mean creating a sensation. I shall cope with the affair by a cool letter of thanks." [173] It was certainly not easy to know how to respond to such a gesture made by people who for years had done nothing but jeer contemptuously at him.

The exodus of analysts to America was by now beginning. Alexander was already in Chicago, and in March Rado accepted an invitation from Brill to work at an Institute of Psychoanalysis which a fund of $40,000.00 he had collected made possible. Naturally there was some regret that no such sums ever reached the European Institutes. But there was the good news that after all it had been possible to open a psychoanalytical clinic in Budapest.[174]

[v] I well remember listening to Virchow's lecture.
[w] *Unheil.*

That spring there was a deal of trouble with Storfer, the Manager of the *Verlag*, who was again threatening to resign. Eitingon persuaded him to postpone his departure until July, 1932, and he suggested that he might be succeeded by Martin Freud.[175] This would mean Martin's giving up his position at a bank in exchange for the management of a most precarious concern, but since he seemed willing to contemplate it Freud said that he was old enough to decide for himself.[176] He told Eitingon that Martin had proved to be thorough and trustworthy in everything he undertook,[177] and in October Martin began his work in the *Verlag*, where he replaced Storfer in the next year.

Then came the matter of the birthday celebration, always a problem for Freud. He had unwillingly consented to a fund being collected for the occasion, his motive being the acute need of the *Verlag* for money which would then be devoted to it. But he instructed Eitingon that no analyst or patient be asked to subscribe. After writing this the obvious reflection occurred to him, "one that ought to have occurred to me earlier," that there could be no other source for such a collection, so now he regretted having agreed to the whole idea." [178]

In this connection he described his attitude towards gifts in a way that illustrates his penetrating and unsparing realism. "It evidently won't do for one to accept a gift and decline to be present when it is bestowed. Thus, for instance: 'You have brought something for me. Just put it down. I'll fetch it sometime.' The aggression bound up with the tenderness of the donor demands its gratification. The recipient has to get worked up, annoyed, embarrassed, and so on. Feeble old people who on such occasions learn to their surprise how highly their young contemporaries esteem them are often overcome by their excess of emotion, and a little later succumb to the aftereffects. You get nothing for nothing,[x] and you have to pay heavily for living too long." [179] Eitingon naturally promised to do what he could not to overtax Freud's strength.

What remained of this strength, however, was being taxed more than enough by agencies other than human ones. The misery from the last operation in October had lasted into the present spring,[180] and in February another suspicious spot showed itself which was dealt with by electro-coagulation.[181] This healed badly, however, and two months later he reported that he had not had since then a single bearable day.[182] Moreover, a few days after that operation yet

[x] *Umsonst ist bekanntlich nichts.*

another suspicious place developed which the surgeon, Pichler, wished to remove before it became malignant. Freud and his two physicians argued that a similar state of affairs might follow the next operation, or indeed result from it, whereas the operation would certainly mean more months of misery. As a possible way of avoiding it one of the latter, Dr. Schur, suggested consulting a specialist in radium treatment. Since there was no one in Vienna with much experience of this Marie Bonaparte wrote to the greatest authority in Paris, G. V. Rigaud, who was a friend of hers, but he was of opinion that radium should not be used in such a case if it might be an early cancerous growth. As a last resort they consulted Guido Holzknecht, the radiologist, who agreed with his colleague, and the upshot was that on April 24 another operation was carried out and a pretty large piece excised. Examination of it revealed that it was removed "at the twelfth hour," on the point of becoming definitely malignant.

For eight years the hope had been entertained that the first radical jaw operation had led to a permanent cure. Now that hope had vanished,[183] and Freud had to face a future that could only consist of watching for further recurrences[y] and combatting them as early as possible. This future was to endure still another eight years.

Holzknecht, who had been a former patient of Freud's, was the leading radiologist in Vienna and one of the pioneers of that science. Like so many of those pioneers he was also a victim and was now in hospital dying of cancer, which an amputation of his right arm had failed to arrest; he died a few months later. Freud and Schur visited him, none of them being under any illusion, and when they parted Freud said, "You are to be admired for the way you bear your fate." Holzknecht replied, "You know I have only you to thank for that."

Freud returned home from the sanatorium on May 4, so to the family's relief he was able to spend his birthday at home. But he was quite exhausted from the experience, the pain, the effects of drugs, lung complications (a slight pneumonia), and, above all, starvation from being unable to swallow any food. There was plainly no question of any celebrations. Even Eitingon was not allowed to come—the first time he missed. Ferenczi was in Vienna, but Freud saw him for only two minutes.[184] Of the congratulatory messages the

[y] Strictly speaking, these were not recurrences of the original cancer, but fresh outbreaks in degenerating tissue. The order of events were: leucoplakia; proliferation; precancerous papillomata; carcinoma.

one he most enjoyed receiving was that from Romain Rolland. Stekel wrote a very friendly letter, with some sad reflections on the good old days when as Freud's oldest pupil he had helped him to build the edifice of psychoanalysis.

We had collected a fund of 50,000 Marks ($12,000.00), and there was now the question of its disposal. Storfer had advanced various monies to cover loans from the bank, and he would soon be leaving, so Eitingon, who was the ultimate authority on the *Verlag* finances, sent Freud a check for 20,000 Marks to repay Storfer for a loan that would fall due on May 15, just in time. The rest he proposed to give to Freud himself as part payment for the royalties long due to him. From the beginning Freud had refused to accept any royalties whatever from the *Verlag* for the sale of his books, and by now they had amounted to 76,500 Marks ($18,360.00).[185] Freud, however, sternly refused to touch a penny of this sum, and in fact he never received anything of those royalties. His reasons were that were he to do so it would leave the *Verlag* in the same precarious situation as before, and what would people (and he himself) think were he to pocket money subscribed for the *Verlag!* The latter argument was not really valid; we had collected the money as a personal gift.

Kretschmer, presiding over the Sixth International Medical Congress of Psychotherapy in Dresden on May 14, paid a graceful tribute to Freud's work in connection with his seventy-fifth birthday.[186] Most of the papers at the Congress were devoted to the theme of dream psychology.

In New York a committee arranged a banquet for two hundred guests at the Ritz-Carlton Hotel. William A. White made the main speech; other speeches were made by A. A. Brill, Mrs. Jessica Cosgrave, Clarence Darrow, Theodore Dreiser, Jerome Frank and Alvin Johnson. They sent this cablegram to Freud: "Men and women recruited from the ranks of psychoanalysis, medicine and sociology are assembling in New York to honor themselves by honoring on his 75th birthday the intrepid explorer who discovered the submerged continents of the ego and gave a new orientation to science and life."

Naturally there was a mass of congratulatory letters and telegrams, including one from Einstein. Not to mention "a forest of splendid flowers and at least one Grecian vase so that Calchas should prove right." [187] Thanking Marie Bonaparte for the one she had sent he added, "it is a pity one cannot take it into one's grave";[188] a wish that was strangely fulfilled, since his ashes now repose in that vase. A belated present came at the end of the year from India, which the news of his birthday had just reached. It was an ivory statue of Vishnu, eight inches high, modeled after an old stone one in Travancore. It was accompanied by a letter, a protocol of the celebration in the Indian Society, and a poem in Sanskrit with an English translation.[189]

Jacob Erdheim had written a masterly report on the pathology of the material removed from Freud's jaw at the April operation; he accused nicotine of being a causative agent. Freud merely shrugged his shoulders at what he called "Erdheim's nicotine sentence." It is noteworthy that he would never renounce smoking on account of his cancerous jaw, nor for his abdominal troubles which seemed also to be affected by smoking, but only for cardiac complications. These he took seriously.

By the end of the month Freud was able to smoke again, and on June 1 he moved away for the summer, taking with him five patients. This time, alas, he could not go further than a suburb, and indeed he never left Vienna again until his flight from the Nazis in 1938. But he had found a very pleasant spot in Pötzleinsdorf (Khevenhüllerstrasse 6, Wien XVIII), with a very agreeable small park. His surgeon came out to see him every day. Eitingon visited him there on June 13. In July Freud told him that in his leisure time he had composed what he called a "hate list" of seven or eight people.[190] One would dearly like to know what names were on it, but the only one he mentioned was that of a certain Theodor Lessing who had recently dedicated "a repulsive book" called *Jewish Self-Hatred* to Freud with the words "In Devotion from an Opponent."

Some years later light was shed on this last hatred. In 1936 Kurt Hiller wrote a biographical essay on Theodor Lessing which he later incorporated into a book.[191] He sent the essay to Freud, who replied at length. Here is an extract from Freud's letter of February 9, 1936.

"I have read your essay on Th. Lessing with great interest and, I believe, understanding. I was able to divine why you treated him so indulgently. To me he was to the depths of my being antipathetic. Many years ago, long before the War, I had a curious experience with him. It was the time when every day, or at least every week, brought me an abusive article about my psychoanalysis. One day a newspaper article reached me which ridiculed it in the most hateful manner as a lucubration of the Jewish spirit. It was signed by a Theodor Lessing who was then quite unknown to me. In my innocence I assumed he must belong to the family of the great classic, so, although I never otherwise reacted to such attacks, I wrote him a letter recalling the memory of his revered ancestor. To my astonishment he told me he was himself a Jew and mentioned the Old Testament name of his daughter. You know that many Jewish families have out of respect for Lessing, Schiller and others adopted their names. I turned away from him in disgust."

At the end of the letter Freud discussed in general terms the occurrence of self-hatred. "It may come about through someone hating his father intensely and nevertheless identifying himself with him; that results in the self-hatred and the splitting of the personality." He added "Don't you think that the self-hatred as shown by Th. L. is an exquisitely Jewish phenomenon? I really think it is." [192] Ironically enough Lessing later met his death at the hands of the Nazis.

It was in this year that H. G. Wells first made Freud's acquaintance. Together with his friend Baroness Budberg he paid him a visit in the summer, one that they were to repeat several times after Freud came to London. Wells was a great admirer of Freud's work and he averred that Freud's name was as important in the history of thought as that of Charles Darwin.

After the bad time Freud had been through he felt like indulging himself. He maintained that "abstinence (from tobacco) was not justified at his age." [193] Further, in the same connection, after the age of seventy-five he ought not to be refused anything.[194] Since he couldn't smoke anything obtainable in Austria he depended on Eitingon's efforts to find him something suitable in Germany. In the latter part of the year, however, the economic crisis led to a law forbidding the export of any goods from Germany to Austria, so a complicated system of smuggling had to be invented and carried out by any friend traveling from the one country to the other. Then Eitingon went away for a winter holiday, and that was a real crisis, since by then Freud was smoking pretty heavily and it was already hard to maintain the supply.

Freud was often shy of expressing the warmth of affection he felt for people, but on the occasion of Eitingon's fiftieth birthday he felt impelled to express at some length his gratitude to him. "We are all so built that criticisms and reproaches commonly clamor for expression, while feelings of contentedness and tenderness think they have to hide themselves in embarrassment. I do not often tell you, but I never forget, what you have done for us in these years." [195]

We come now to a period when external events began to press on Freud's life and on the psychoanalytical movement in general. The world economic crisis initiated by the failure of the Vienna *Creditanstalt* was in full swing in 1931, and its political consequences were soon to prove disastrous for both Germany and Austria. In every country analysts were feeling the pinch badly in their practice, and it became very doubtful if more than a handful could afford to attend the Congress that was due to take place that autumn. By the end of July we decided it was necessary to postpone it for another year.

The infernal prosthesis was as ever unsatisfactory, and in August another desperate attempt was made to improve it. Ruth Brunswick had heard that Professor Kazanijan of Harvard, a man reputed to possess magical talents, was attending a dental congress in Berlin, and every day she telephoned to him begging him to come to see Freud. He finally refused, but then Ruth Brunswick and Marie Bonaparte, who was also in Vienna, put their heads together. The former got her father, Judge Mack, who was on the Board of Harvard University, to use his influence by cable, and the latter took a train for Paris, caught the unwilling magician on his way home, and brought him back with her, "so to speak on a lead," accompanied by Dr. Weinmann who had also been to the Congress. For this journey he would charge Freud the fee of $6,000.00.[196] He worked on Freud's prosthesis for twenty days, but the result was very far from satisfactory.[197] The ladies had had the best possible intentions, but the consequences proved to be unfortunate for the *Verlag's* finances.

This was the month when, all efforts to save it having failed, it was decided, to Freud's keen regret, to close the sanatorium at Tegelsee. It was not long before the Director, Simmel, emigrated to Los Angeles where, after founding a Society and Institute, he died in 1947.

In October, however, a really cheering event took place. The Town Council of Freiberg, now Příbor, decided to honor Freud (and themselves) by placing a bronze tablet on the house in which he had been born. The streets were beflagged for the ceremony that took place on October 25, and many speeches were made. Anna

Freud read a letter of thanks Freud had written to the Mayor.[198] The only other analysts present were Federn and Eitingon; the latter made a speech about the spread of Freud's work. This was the fourth honor paid to Freud in this year in which he attained the age of seventy-five. It is hard to say which of them gave him the most pleasure, probably the first and the last (the Huxley invitation and the Freiberg ceremony). But he was getting rather old for the enjoyment of such experiences. "Since the Goethe prize last year the world has changed its treatment of me into an unwilling recognition, but only to show me how little that really matters. What a contrast a bearable prosthesis would be, one that didn't clamor to be the main object of one's existence." [199]

In November Freud suffered a "rebellious" attack in the abdomen, with some hours of painful cramp in the colon; a spastic colon was the source of much of his abdominal trouble. Freud had to break off an analytic treatment in the hour, something that had only happened to him once before in his life.[200]

Ambassador Bullitt spent some time in Vienna that autumn completing the book on Wilson he was writing with Freud. Freud evidently expected it to be published soon, since he told Eitingon that he hoped the sale of it would help the Verlag.[201]

Freud was a great admirer of the philanthropic Count Richard Coudenhove-Kalergi, and he gave his name as a supporter of the Pan-European movement to which the Count devoted his life. Among the many other well known personages who did the same was Winston Churchill—he wrote a Preface to the English translation of Coudenhove's book, An Idea Conquers the World, 1953—so perhaps Coudenhove's ideas furnished one of the sources of inspiration for Churchill's famous Zurich speech in 1946. In 1931 Freud was one of those who proposed Coudenhove's name for the Nobel Peace Prize, but as unsuccessfully as his own name was often proposed.[202] One may also mention here that toward the end of his life Freud praised a book by Coudenhove's father, Count Dr. Heinrich Coudenhove, Das Wesen des Antisemitismus (The Essence of Anti-Semitism), as being one of the best books ever written on the subject.[203]

In May Ferenczi had sent Freud a copy of the paper he intended to read before the Congress, in which he claimed to have found a second function of dreams—dealing with traumatic experiences. Freud drily answered that this was also their first function, as he had expounded years before.[204]

After three months' interval there came another letter in which Ferenczi described how bewildered he felt over the various new methods he was attempting. Freud, in his reply, said: "There is no doubt that by this interruption in our contact you are becoming more distant from me. I do not say more estranged, and hope not. I accept it as my fate, like so much else. . . . I am sorry to note that you are proceeding in all sorts of directions which do not seem to me to lead to any desirable goal. But I have, as you know well, always respected your independence, and am content to wait till you yourself retrace your steps." [205] In October Ferenczi spent a holiday in Capri, and Freud hoped he would find rest from his analytic work beneficial. On the way back Ferenczi spent a couple of days in Vienna, from October 27 on, and the two men had a heart to heart talk over their differences. Ferenczi thought it all over, but after five weeks wrote to say it had not changed any of his opinions.[206]

The essence of these differences lay in the matter of technique. In connection with his recent ideas about the central importance of infantile traumas, particularly parental unkindness, Ferenczi had been changing his technique by acting the part of a loving parent so as to neutralize the early unhappiness of his patients. This also entailed allowing the patients to analyze him as they went along, with the risk of the mutual analysis depriving the situation of its necessary objectivity. The part played by the father, and the dread of him, was kept in the background, so that, as Freud put it later, the analytic situation was being reduced to a playful game between mother and child, with interchangeable roles.[207]

Freud now sent Ferenczi an important letter, which, incidentally, illustrates his unconventional outlook in sexual matters.

"13. XII. 1931

"Lieber Freund:

"I enjoyed getting your letter, as I always do, but not so much its content. If by now you cannot bring yourself to change your attitude at all it is very unlikely that you will do so later. But that is essentially your affair; my opinion that you have not chosen a promising direction is a private matter which need not disturb you.

"I see that the differences between us come to a head in a technical detail which is well worth discussing. You have not made a secret of the fact that you kiss your patients and let them kiss you; I had also heard that from a patient of my own. Now when you decide to give a full account of your technique and its results you will have to chose between two ways: either you relate this or you conceal it. The latter, as you may well think, is dishonorable. What one does in one's technique one has to defend openly. Besides, both ways soon come together. Even if you don't say so yourself it will soon get known, just as I knew it before you told me.

"Now I am assuredly not one of those who from prudishness or from consideration of bourgeois convention would condemn little erotic gratifications of this kind. And I am also aware that in the time of the Nibelungs a kiss was a harmless greeting granted to every guest. I am further of the opinion that analysis is possible even in Soviet Russia where so far as the State is concerned there is full sexual freedom. But that does not alter the facts that we are not living in Russia and that with us a kiss signifies a certain erotic intimacy. We have hitherto in our technique held to the conclusion that patients are to be refused erotic gratifications. You know too that where more extensive gratifications are not to be had milder caresses very easily take over their role, in love affairs, on the stage, etc.

"Now picture what will be the result of publishing your technique. There is no revolutionary who is not driven out of the field by a still more radical one. A number of independent thinkers in matters of technique will say to themselves: why stop at a kiss? Certainly one gets further when one adopts 'pawing' as well, which after all doesn't make a baby. And then bolder ones will come along who will go further to peeping and showing—and soon we shall have accepted in the technique of analysis the whole repertoire of demiviergerie and petting parties, resulting in an enormous increase of interest in psychoanalysis among both analysts and patients. The new adherent, however, will easily claim too much of this interest for himself, the younger of our colleagues will find it hard to stop at the point they originally intended, and God the Father Ferenczi gazing at the lively scene he has created will perhaps say to himself: may be after all I should have halted in my technique of motherly affection *before* the kiss.

"Sentences like 'about the dangers of neocatharsis' don't get very far. One should obviously not let oneself get into the danger. I have purposely not mentioned the increase of calumnious resistances against analysis the kissing technique would bring, although it seems to me a wanton act to provoke them.

"In this warning I do not think I have said anything you do not know yourself. But since you like playing a tender mother role with others, then perhaps you may do so with yourself. And then you are to hear from the brutal fatherly side an admonition. That is why I spoke in my last letter of a new puberty, a Johannis impulse, and now you have compelled me to be quite blunt.

"I do not expect to make any impression on you. The necessary basis for that is absent in our relations. The need for definite independence seems to me to be stronger in you than you recognize. But at least I have done what I could in my father role. Now you must go on.

> "With cordial greetings
> "Your
> "Freud"

Ferenczi did not take this letter well. As he said, it was the first time that he and Freud really disagreed.[208] But it would have been asking too much to expect Freud to agree with him on such fundamental questions of technique, which were after all the basis of all Freud's work.

The family business from which Eitingon drew his income was in America, and the disastrous economic situation there had proved catastrophic for it. Before long Eitingon was for the first time in his life a poor man. One consequence was that he now found himself unable to finance the Berlin Institute, as he had done from the beginning, and there was nothing left but to appeal to the members of the Society to contribute what they could, despite their own poor circumstances, and to see how much of the institution could be salvaged.[209] They did what they could, but it remained in a crippled condition. It was probably this situation of Eitingon's that impelled Freud to make a similar appeal in the following year when he found himself unable to sustain any longer the financial burden of the *Verlag*.

Two papers by Freud appeared together in the October number of the *Zeitschrift*. They must have been written early in 1931, since he showed the first drafts of them both to Eitingon when he visited Vienna on February 28.[210] They were finished during the summer holidays and appeared in October.[211] The first one, "Libidinal Types," [212] distinguished three main types of people, which Freud termed the erotic, the obsessive and the narcissistic respectively; there are also three composite forms of them. The paper, short as it was, constituted an important addition to the subject of characterology. The other one, "On Female Sexuality," [213] studied a theme Freud always confessed to find difficult, and there were only a couple of outstanding conclusions of which he felt sure. The stimulus to writing it just then doubtless came from the interest that the British Society had of late been devoting to it; it was a topic on which I differed from Freud's views in some rather important respects.

Dr. Josef Hupka, the Professor of Jurisprudence in the University of Vienna, asked Freud to write a memorandum for him on the conclusions of the Innsbruck Medical Faculty about the case of Philipp Halsmann, who had been accused of killing his father. Hupka was engaged in defending the youth. Freud's comments concerned the risk of taking too literally the concept of the Oedipus complex in adult life without unmistakable evidence of its operation.[214]

In the last month of the year Freud was engaged in writing a paper on "The Acquisition and Control of Fire,"[215] which was published in the following year.

1932

No honors came this year, but anxiety in full measure to add to the continual physical distress. Its two main sources were deep concern over the Verlag and the progressive deterioration in Ferenczi's mental condition.

The first little trouble was an editorial question. Wilhelm Reich had sent in a paper for publication in the Zeitschrift, the theme of which was the amalgamation of Marxism and psychoanalysis, and which, according to Freud, "culminated in the nonsensical statement that what we have called the death instinct is a product of the capitalistic system."[216] This was certainly very different from Freud's view that it constituted an inherent tendency of all living beings, animal and vegetable. He naturally wanted to add an editorial comment disclaiming any political interests on the part of psychoanalysis, which, speaking as an editor myself, I should have had no hesitation in doing. Reich himself agreed to this, but Eitingon, Ludwig Jekels and Bernfeld, whom Freud consulted, were against it, and Bernfeld said it would be equivalent to a declaration of war on the Soviets! Whereupon Freud became uncertain, nor would he accept Ferenczi's suggestion that the International Executive should request him formally to insist that every contributor to the Zeitschrift should mention his adherence to any non-scientific body.[217] The matter was finally settled by Reich's paper being published,[218] but followed by a full criticism by Bernfeld.[219]

Far more serious was the real crisis in the affairs of the *Verlag*, the most alarming of the many it had survived. The economic situation all over the world, especially in Germany, had reduced to a minimum the sale of Freud's books, on which the *Verlag* mainly subsisted. Freud's earnings had similarly shrunk, and there were sons out of work. Eitingon's American income, which was always the last resource, was fast disappearing and in fact came to an end in February. He now had the novel experience of being faced with the need to earn a livelihood; he had one solitary patient and no prospect of seeing any others.

Freud telegraphed to Eitingon immediately on the latter's return from a holiday, begging him to come to Vienna without delay.[220] In a letter of the following day he confessed that the situation was disturbing his sleep, and it took a good deal for this to happen to Freud. If only he had had the $7,000.00 (sic) the American dentist's visit had cost him he would have been able to save the *Verlag*.[221] This was heavily in debt, the creditors were pressing hard, and there was no current money to carry on with.

Eitingon came to Vienna on January 15, and they agreed that the only course was for Martin, who had begun his duties as Manager, to call a meeting of creditors, ask for a moratorium, and if possible come to a compromise settlement with them on condition that the *Verlag* incurred no further debts and paid cash for everything. Soon after that Freud had two further ideas. It would save postal costs to concentrate the editorships of the two periodicals in Vienna instead of Berlin. He was eager to retain Rado as chief Editor of the *Zeitschrift*, but it became more and more doubtful whether Rado would ever return from New York where Brill was desirous of keeping him. So after much deliberation Freud chose Federn and Hitschmann to be the Editors of the *Zeitschrift*, with Kris and Wälder for *Imago*. They proved to be excellent choices.

By February Freud decided that it was impossible to maintain the *Verlag* any longer on such a slender personal basis, and he announced his intention to issue an appeal to the International Psycho-Analytical Association to take responsibility for it in future.[222] That meant that a Congress must at all costs be held that year in spite of the unfavorable auspices. It had been planned to hold it at Interlaken, but it was impossible for the Germans to obtain funds to travel out of their country, so Wiesbaden was chosen.

In April Freud wrote out a full statement, several pages long, describing the situation of the *Verlag*, and making an appeal for help from the International Psycho-Analytical Association. He sent copies to the Presidents of the various Societies, and we made further copies of the translation and distributed them among all the members.

Just at that moment Eitingon suffered from a slight cerebral thrombosis with a paresis of the left arm. He had already resolved not to seek re-election as President of the International Association, and this indication of the state of his cerebral circulation made the decision absolute. In the meantime he had to spend several weeks in bed. Freud, surmising he might be in financial need, offered to lend him $1,000.00.[223]

Freud was very pessimistic about the probable effect of his appeal. "I do not expect any result from it. It will have been an amusing exercise in style." [224] In the face of the catastrophic economic situation the prospect seemed grim enough. "It is superfluous to say anything about the general situation of the world. Perhaps we are only repeating the ridiculous act of saving a birdcage while the whole house is burning." [225] In this, however, he was completely wrong, for the appeal met with an immediate and gratifying response. He was also wrong, as I was myself, in expecting the criticism that the *Internationaler Verlag* had been too exclusively German in its outlook. I wrote: "You are right in assuming in your circular that some prejudice may be voiced on the score of the *Verlag* having in the past been too exclusively German in its outlook and insufficiently international. As you know, I have endeavoured in English-speaking countries to further the same object that you describe as being the Verlag's: namely, to stamp a body of literature as being entirely distinct from the medley of rubbish all around. In pursuit of this aim we have been considerably hampered by the encouragement repeatedly given in the most official way to rival and inefficient undertakings, publishers, translators, other journals, etc. It has been an uphill fight against the difficulties from within and without, but we have accomplished something. As you will remember my own wish has always been for a closer cooperation, so that all the undertakings should be entirely and jointly international." [226]

The implied criticism in this paragraph received another illustration only a month later. A small group in New York decided to found a new periodical, *The Psychoanalytic Quarterly*. There was the possibility that it might seek to become recognized as the official organ in America, in which case the *International Journal* might cease to be so. The *Journal* had recently become self-supporting, with no help any longer from my pocket, but without the American subscriptions it certainly could not survive. That seemed a pity, since the level of the work it was producing was beginning to be really satisfactory. I was never in favor of private ventures, and I took it amiss that my friend Eitingon, the President of the Association, should have officially supported a rival to its official organ without consulting with its Editor, and might in that way have even dealt it a death blow. Freud also had given the *Quarterly* permission to translate a paper he had recently published in the *Zeitschrift*, ignoring the contract we had that gave us the first claim on all papers published in it. My protests met with no understanding, and I offered to resign my editorship. What saved the situation was the generosity of our American colleagues, for which they deserve all praise. Neither then nor later did they withdraw their official support of the *Journal*; the future of the *Quarterly* proved to be far more satisfactory than I had at first expected. Before long the editorship of it fell into more responsible and competent hands, and the standard it has since attained has placed it in the first rank.

There were two tasks in front of us in our endeavor to save the *Verlag*: to meet the immediate crushing debts, and then to provide a regular annual support for its continuation. Martin Freud had obtained from the creditors a moratorium until the summer, but when he disclosed to us the total sum of the debts accumulated during Storfer's extravagant regime we were appalled, and despaired of being able to raise anything like that amount. However, most of the Societies did their best. The British one, for instance, unanimously and enthusiastically voted a resolution of support, and in the first week subscribed the amount of $1,400.00.[227] In addition to the contributions from the New York Society Brill sent $2,500.00 and Edith Jackson sent $2,000.00.[228] There was no criticism of the purely German nature of the *Verlag*, it being recognized, as Freud had hoped, that its productions were of international value, but Eitingon was censured for retaining the Storfer regime so long. Freud recognized the justice of this, and applied it also to himself.[229]

I visited Eitingon in Berlin on May 21. He had recovered far enough to be able to have a thorough discussion of the difficult *Verlag* problems and also to plan the arrangements for the coming Congress. As usual, we reached complete agreement.

It cost Martin Freud all his efforts to come to a compromise with one creditor after the other, but by the end of the year he had accomplished this difficult task, and the *Verlag* was for the time being cleared. At the Wiesbaden Congress in September we imposed by general consent an obligation on all members to subscribe three dollars monthly for the next two years at least. An international committee was formed to assume responsibility for the future conduct of the *Verlag*. It consisted of Marie Bonaparte, A. A. Brill, Ernest Jones, Clarence Oberndorf, J. H. W. van Ophuijsen, R. A. Spitz, and P. Sarasin. The working sub-committee consisted of Sarasin, van Ophuijsen and myself.

It had been the rule that only past Presidents of the International Association could become Vice-Presidents, but at this Congress we passed a special resolution admitting Brill to this position, taking advantage of his being the President of the American Psychoanalytic Association. Brill had been in his best form in recent years, actively helpful and loyal in all kinds of collaboration with his European colleagues. Indeed he sometimes went too far in this for his peace of mind after returning to New York, where he was disappointed in the lack of support he found there for such collaboration.

In March of this year Thomas Mann paid his first visit to Freud. Freud at once got on to intimate terms with him: "what he had to say was very understanding; it gave the impression of a background." [230] His wife and her sister, who were enthusiastic readers of Mann, were still more delighted. Mann's association with the Hanse Towns was an additional link.

In April Eduardo Weiss proudly announced to Freud that he had founded a psychoanalytical Society in Italy and also a periodical, the *Rivista di Psicanalisi*.[231]

In the same month, April 22, Ludwig Binswanger, accompanied by his daughter, visited Freud. There had been a close affinity between the two men ever since Freud had witnessed his heroic attitude on his visit to Kreuzlingen when Binswanger's life was in danger.[232] The friendship was never impaired, despite a very considerable difference in their scientific and philosophic views.

This spring Freud's analytical practice showed for the first time signs of diminishing spontaneously. "In the summer I must write something, since I shall have few analyses. At the moment there are four, at the beginning of May there will be only three, and there are no fresh applications whatever. They are of course quite right; I am too old, and working with me is too precarious. I should not need to work any longer. On the other hand it is pleasant to think that my 'supply' has lasted longer than the 'demand.' " [233] This was certainly the remark of an optimist, not a pessimist.

In May Freud was amused to hear that, according to good reports, it was the Archbishop of York who had got my name taken off the black list of the British Broadcasting Corporation, where I had had the honor of being bracketed with Bertrand Russell as a dangerously immoral person, and that I had been invited to broadcast a series of talks on psychoanalysis.[234] The four talks in question were given in the following autumn, of course without my name being mentioned.

That summer Henri Barbusse called on the medical profession in all countries to attend a World Congress in Geneva, July 28, 1932, to protest against the possibility of another World War. An appeal was widely distributed, its closing sentence being as follows: "As guardians of the peoples' health we raise our voice in a warning against a new interminable carnage into which the nations are being driven, the consequences of which are unforeseeable." I possess the copy signed by Freud, and also that signed by Jung.

Freud moved to the same house as before in Pötzleinsdorf on May 14, and was there until the middle of September. He was especially glad to go, since in March he had had a slight attack of "what other people might call depression." [235] His birthday that year passed off quietly. For the first time no member of the Committee was present, Eitingon being just convalescing from his stroke. Eitingon's absence gave Freud the opportunity of spending the day in the way he "had always wanted to, just like any other week day. In the morning a visit to Kagran with the dogs. In the afternoon the usual visit to Pichler, then four hours' analytic work, and a harmless game of cards in the evening. Some doubt whether one should be glad to have lived to this date, and then resignation." [236]

The emigration to America was continuing. Alexander was exchanging his temporary position in Boston for a permanent one in Chicago, Sachs had agreed to replace him in Boston in the autumn, and Karen Horney was going to New York.[237]

We had all taken it for granted that Ferenczi would succeed Eitingon as President. Freud was entirely in favor of this, although he was unhappy about Ferenczi's withdrawal from him. In April he complained to Eitingon: "Isn't Ferenczi a tribulation? Again there is no news from him for months. He is offended because one is not delighted to hear how he plays mother and child with his female patients." [238]

It was Ferenczi himself who raised doubts about his suitability for the position. Being so concentrated on his therapeutic investigations, he wondered if he had enough energy for the heavy work attaching to the presidency.[239] Freud brightly suggested that accepting the position would act as a "forcible cure" to take him out of his isolation,[240] but this rather offended Ferenczi who denied there was anything pathological in his isolation: it was simply concentration.[241] Late in August, ten days before the Congress was to begin, he announced his decision not to stand for the presidency on the grounds that his latest ideas were so in conflict with the accepted principles of psychoanalysis that it would not be honorable for him to represent the latter in an official position.[242] Freud, however, still pressed him to accept, and refused to accept the reason he gave. He could certainly be President unless he was contemplating creating a new variety of psychoanalysis.[243]

Ferenczi now shifted his ground. He maintained he was not thinking of founding a new school, but was still not sure that Freud really wanted him to be President.[244] He would visit Freud on his way from Budapest to Wiesbaden and then decide. In the meantime he sent a last minute telegram to Eitingon, on August 30, asking him not to begin negotiations with me until after his visit to Freud. After this had taken place Freud telegraphed to Eitingon: "Ferenczi inaccessible. Impression unsatisfactory." Eitingon, who had for some time been of the opinion that in the circumstances Ferenczi would be an unsuitable candidate, was relieved and at once asked me if I would stand. According to Eitingon, I was too healthy-minded for there to be any danger of my starting a different direction.[245] I could not well refuse, although I had hoped I should not have to assume such a burden again for some time, until I could more easily delegate a few of my posts in London. It was many years before there was any opportunity of laying down the burden, so that my two spells of work in that office amounted to nearly twenty-three years—an experience I am glad to think no one will ever be called upon to repeat.

Something should be said about the critical interview, which was the last time the two old friends ever met. Some days before it took place Brill had visited Freud, on August 24. He had been to see Ferenczi in Budapest and had received an unhappy impression of his attitude. He was especially astonished to hear Ferenczi say that he couldn't credit Freud with any more insight than a small boy; this happened to be the very phrase that Rank had used in his time—a memory that could but heighten Freud's forebodings. Without a word of greeting Ferenczi announced on entering the room "I want you to read my Congress paper." Half way through Brill came in and, since Ferenczi and he had recently talked over the theme, Freud let him stay, though he took no part in the talk.[246] Freud evidently tried his best to bring about some degree of insight, but in vain. A month later Ferenczi wrote to Freud accusing him of having smuggled Brill into the interview to act as judge between them, and also expressing anger at having been asked not to publish his paper for a year.[247] In his reply Freud said the latter suggestion was made solely in Ferenczi's own interest in the hope, which Freud had still clung to, that further reflection might show him the incorrectness of his technique and conclusions. He added: "For a couple of years you have systematically turned away from me and have probably developed a personal animosity which goes further than you have been able to express. Each of those who were once near me and then fell away might have found more to reproach me with than you of all people. (No, Rank just as little.) It has no traumatic effect on me; I am prepared and am accustomed to such happenings. Objectively I think I could point out to you the technical errors in your conclusions, but why do so? I am convinced you would not be accessible to any doubts. So there is nothing left but to wish you the best." [248]

At the Congress itself a delicate question arose. Freud thought the paper Ferenczi had prepared could do his reputation no good and had begged him not to read it. Brill, Eitingon and van Ophuijsen went further and thought it would be scandalous to read such a paper before a psychoanalytical congress. Eitingon therefore decided to forbid it firmly. On the other hand I thought the paper too vague to leave any clear impression, for good or bad—which it turned out to be—and that it would be so offensive to tell the most distinguished member of the Association, and its actual founder, that what he had to say was not worth listening to that he might well withdraw altogether in dudgeon. My advice was taken, and Ferenczi responded warmly to the welcome he received when he read his paper; moreover, he took part in the business discussions and showed he was still one of us. He was very friendly to me and revealed, somewhat to my surprise, how deeply disappointed he had been at never having been elected as President by a full Congress—the Budapest Congress being only a rump. He also told me he was suffering from pernicious anaemia, but hoped to benefit from liver therapy. After the Congress he went on a journey to the South of France, but spent so much of his time there in bed that he decided to shorten the holiday and return home as directly as possible without even pausing in Vienna. There is no doubt he was already a very sick man.

Writing to Marie Bonaparte about his satisfaction at the success of the Congress, Freud added: "Ferenczi is a bitter drop in the cup. His wise wife has told me I should think of him as a sick child! You are right: psychical and intellectual decay is far worse than the unavoidable bodily one." [249]

In November another of Freud's Tarock companions died, Alfred Rie. Jekels took his place in the card parties.[250]

In the same month Freud had an exceptionally severe attack of influenza with an otitis media.[251] The resulting catarrh, which was one of the chief sources of discomfort in the wound, lasted for more than a month. It had been altogether a bad year, with five operations, one of which, in October, was pretty extensive.

In December Hans Halbe, a Hungarian journalist, asked Freud, or rather his daughter, for an interview, something that was becoming increasingly hard to obtain. The news had got about that Freud was writing something on the sensational topic of occultism (the chapter "Dreams and Occultism" [252] in his New Introductory Lectures), and there was a widespread wish to procure a firsthand account of his views. Maintaining that hitherto no journalist had ever reported correctly what he may have had to say in an interview, Freud offered to submit a written statement on the topic in question. This document, four pages long, was an abstract of the opening sections of his chapter and contains nothing that is not to be found there. It was published on Christmas Day.[253]

The journalist, however, was not going to miss a chance of an incorrect statement; in this case it was that a German University had recently bestowed an honorary doctorate on Freud.

In March, when the Verlag affairs were so desperate, Freud conceived the idea of helping them by writing a new series of his Introductory Lectures in which he would say something about the progress that had taken place in his ideas in the fifteen years since the first series had appeared.[254] "Certainly this work comes more from a need of the Verlag than any need on my part, but one should always be doing something in which one might be interrupted—better than going down in a state of laziness." [255] He began by writing the chapters on dreams and on Weltanschauung.[256] In July he gave Eitingon a description of the first four he had written,[257] and a month later said that he had finished all seven of them.[258] The publication was dated 1933, but they actually appeared on December 6, 1932.[259]

In August Freud announced that he was conducting a discussion with Einstein for a League of Nations publication.[260] He added drily that he did not expect to get a Nobel Peace Prize for it.[261] Three weeks later he reported that he had finished writing "the tedious and sterile so-called discussion with Einstein." [262] He evidently did not think much of it and said he was lowering his pretensions about his work just as he had had to do about his prosthesis.

1933

The previous year had been unpleasant enough, but 1933 brought still more serious crises. Freud had feared that the destruction and enmity of the First World War might reduce interest in psychoanalysis to a minimum or even bring it to an end.[263] Now the Hitler persecutions constituted a renewal of the same threat, and indeed they successfully carried it out so far as the homelands of psychoanalysis—Austria, Germany and Hungary—were concerned.

To Freud the situation was already beginning to look serious. He wrote to Marie Bonaparte: "How fortunate you are to be immersed in your work without having to take notice of all the horrible things around. In our circles there is already a great deal of trepidation. People fear that the nationalistic extravagances in Germany may extend to our little country. I have even been advised to flee already to Switzerland or France. That is nonsense; I don't believe there is any danger here and if it should come I am firmly resolved to await it here. If they kill me—good. It is one kind of death like another. But probably that is only cheap boasting." [264]

Then ten days later: "These are times when one is not inclined to write, but I should not like not to be in contact with you.

"Thank you for your invitation to St. Cloud. I have decided to make no use of it; it will hardly be necessary. The brutalities in Germany seem to be diminishing. The way France and America has reacted to them has not failed to make an impression, but the torments, small but none the less painful on that account, will not cease, and the systematic suppression of the Jews, depriving them of all positions, has as yet scarcely begun. One cannot avoid seeing that persecution of the Jews and restriction of intellectual freedom are the only features of the Hitler program that can be carried out. All the rest is weakness and utopianism. . . .

"I have looked into Celine's book,[265] and am half way through it. I have no taste for this depicting of misery, for the description of the senselessness and emptiness of our present-day life, without any artistic or philosophical background. I demand something other from art than realism. I am reading it because you wished me to." [266]

In the following month there was a further comment: "I am glad, and it makes me proud to hear, how much sympathy and help you are showing the victims of the persecution in Germany. And France in general is behaving well and sees how justified was her war-time abuse of the Boches. The movement will come to us too, perhaps very soon, but we think it cannot lead to such excesses. Our people are not quite so brutal; minority laws* are forbidden by the peace treaty, and the great Powers will never allow union with Germany. So now many of the things about which we used to complain are in our favor." [267]

After their meeting in the previous September Freud and Ferenczi did not again discuss their differences. Freud's feeling for him never changed, and Ferenczi remained on at least outwardly friendly terms. They continued to exchange letters, the burden of which was mainly Ferenczi's increasingly serious state of health. The medical treatment was successful in holding the anaemia itself at bay, but in March the disease, as it sometimes does, attacked the spinal cord and brain, and for the last couple of months of his life he was unable to stand or walk; this undoubtedly exacerbated his latent psychotic trends.

In America some former pupils of Ferenczi's, notably Izette de Forest and Clara Thompson, have sustained a myth of Freud's ill-treatment of Ferenczi.[268] Phrases such as Freud's "enmity," "harsh and bitter criticism," have been used, and he is said to have pursued Ferenczi with hostility. Freud's correspondence, and also my personal memories, leave no doubt that there is no truth whatever in this story, although it is highly probable that Ferenczi himself in his final delusional state believed in and propagated elements of it. Freud's only feelings at his friend's self-absorbed withdrawal were of sadness and regret, while his attitude toward what he and all the rest of us regarded as Ferenczi's errors of regression was that of a friend who, until it was plainly hopeless, did what he could in the endeavor to save him from them.

In replying to New Year's greetings from Ferenczi, Freud wrote:

* E.g. against the Jews.

"11. 1. 1933

"Lieber Freund:

"I thank you and your dear wife warmly for the New Year's greetings which arrived today. I need not say that we all fully reciprocate your good wishes. You speak of the many years of good understanding between us. I should say it was more than that, rather a close sharing of our life, emotions and interests. When today I have to conjure all this only from my memory the sole consolation I have is the certainty that I contributed remarkably little to the transformation. Some psychological fate has brought it about in you. At all events we are glad to hear of the restoration of your health, a precious piece of the more beautiful past.

"Always your
"Freud"

The next letter was written three weeks after the Reichstag fire in Berlin, the signal for widespread Nazi persecution. Ferenczi in a somewhat panicky letter urgently entreated Freud to flee from Austria while there was yet time to escape the Nazi danger. He advised him to leave for England at once with his daughter Anna and perhaps a few patients. For his part, if the danger approached Hungary he intended to leave for Switzerland. His doctor assured him that his pessimism came from his pathological state, but with our hindsight one must admit there was some method in his madness. Here is Freud's answer, the last letter he ever wrote to his old friend.

"2. 4. 1933

"Lieber Freund:

"I was very distressed to hear that your convalescence, which began so well, suffered an interruption, but am all the more glad to hear of the latest improvement. I would beg you to refrain from heavy work; your handwriting shows clearly how tired you still are. Any discussions between us about your technical and theoretical novelties can wait; they will only profit from being put aside for the present. What is more important to me is that you should recover your health.

"As to the immediate reason for your writing, the flight motif, I am glad to be able to tell you that I am not thinking of leaving Vienna. I am not mobile enough, and am too dependent on my treatment, on various ameliorations and comforts; furthermore, I do not want to leave my possessions here. Probably, however, 1 should stay even if I were in full health and youth. There is naturally an emotional attitude behind this, but there are also various rationalizations. It is not certain that the Hitler regime will master Austria too. That is possible, it is true, but everybody believes it will not attain the crudeness of brutality here that it has in Germany. There is no personal danger for me, and when you picture life with the suppression of us Jews as extremely unpleasant do not forget what an uncomfortable life settling abroad, whether in Switzerland or England, promises for refugees. In my opinion flight would only be justified by direct danger to life; besides, if they were to slay one it is simply one kind of death like another.

"Only a few hours ago Ernstl[aa] arrived from Berlin after disagreeable experiences in Dresden and on the frontier. He is German and so cannot go back; after today no German Jew will be allowed to leave the country. I hear that Simmel has got out to Zurich. I hope you will remain undisturbed in Budapest and soon send me good news of your condition. With cordial greetings to you and Frau Gisela,

"Your

"Freud"

The last letter from Ferenczi, written in bed on May 4, was a few lines for Freud's birthday. The mental disturbance had been making rapid progress in the last few months. He related how one of his American patients, to whom he used to devote four or five hours a day, had analyzed him and so cured him of all his troubles. Messages came to him from her across the Atlantic—Ferenczi had always been a staunch believer in telepathy. Then there were the delusions about Freud's supposed hostility. Toward the end came violent paranoic and even homicidal outbursts, which were followed by a sudden death on May 24. That was the tragic end of a brilliant, lovable and distinguished personality, someone who had for a quarter of a century been Freud's closest friend. The lurking demons within, against whom Ferenczi had for years struggled with great distress and much success, conquered him at the end, and we learned from this painful experience once more how terrible their power can be.

I of course wrote to condole with Freud over the loss of our [aa] Freud's grandson.

friend, "of that inspiring figure we all loved so much. I am more glad than ever that I succeeded at the last Congress in keeping him within our circle." [269] Freud replied: "Yes, we have every reason to condole with each other. Our loss is great and painful; it is part of the change that overthrows everything that exists and thus makes room for the new. Ferenczi takes with him a part of the old time; then with my departure another will begin which you will still see. Fate. Resignation. That is all." [270]

Thanks to Martin Freud's strenuous efforts the situation of the *Verlag* had by now somewhat eased. He had persuaded six of the main creditors to consent to a compromise arrangement, and he settled with the remaining, and most difficult, ones by the end of the year. The loss of the German sales, however, was ominous for the future.

About this time Dr. Roy Winn, of Sydney, proposed to Freud that he write a more intimate autobiography. He could hardly have made a less welcome suggestion. But Freud, in a charming letter, quietly replied: "Your wish that I should write an intimate autobiography is not likely to be fulfilled. Even the amount of autobiography (exhibitionism) needed for writing *The Interpretation of Dreams* I found trying[bb] enough, and I do not think anyone would learn much from such a publication. Personally I ask nothing more from the world than that it should leave me in peace and devote its interest to psychoanalysis instead." [271]

In April I heard that Freud was very concerned about Abraham's widow and children in Berlin, whom the political changes had deprived of all means of a livelihood. He thought of various possibilities of helping them, adding: "As for myself, it is true, I can do nothing except contribute money." [272]

On Freud's birthday Schur as usual examined his condition. Schur's wife was expecting a baby which was some days overdue. Freud urged him to hasten back to his wife, and on parting said in a meditative tone "You are going from a man who doesn't want to leave the world to a child who doesn't want to come into it."

With his great fondness for children Freud always took a special interest in the news of a fresh arrival. When I told him we were expecting another baby before long he wrote: "The lovely news of your expectation in May deserves a hearty congratulation without any delay in the name of us all. If it prove to be the youngest child,

[bb] *beschwerlich.*

you may see from my own family that the last is far from being the least." [273] When I notified him of the event, about the time of his own birthday, these were his reflections:

"7. 5. 1933

"Dear Jones:

"The first answer after the flood of receptions has subsided naturally belongs to you, because there is nothing so lovely and important in the other letters and because there is the opportunity of replying to one congratulation with another, better grounded one. In all the familiar uncertainty of life one may envy parents the joy and hopes which soon center round the new human creature, whereas with old people one must be glad when the scales are nearly balanced between the inevitable need of final rest and the wish to enjoy a while longer the love and friendship of those near to one. I believe I have discovered that the longing for ultimate rest is not something elementary and primary, but an expression of the need to be rid of the feeling of inadequacy which affects age, especially in the smallest details of life.

"You are right in saying that in comparison with the time of my seventieth birthday I no longer feel anxious about the future of psychoanalysis. It is assured, and I know it to be in good hands. But the future of my children and grandchildren is endangered and my own helplessness is distressing.

"With warm greetings to both parents and all the children

"Your

"Freud"

A consultation Freud gave in this month had interesting consequences a few years later. Weiss brought to him from Rome a difficult patient he was treating. They were accompanied by her father, who happened to be a close friend of Mussolini's. The father asked Freud to make Mussolini a present of one of his books, and further begged him to write an inscription in it; for Weiss's sake Freud consented to do so. The book he chose was *Why War?*, which he had written together with Einstein, and he wrote on the fly-leaf, in allusion to the archaeological excavations Mussolini was just then encouraging, the words: "From an old man who greets in the Ruler the Hero of Culture." [274]

This year Freud was not able to rent the house in Pötzleinsdorf he had enjoyed so much in the three last summers, but he found a pleasant enough substitute in Döbling (XIX. Hohe Warte. 46).

The tide of Jewish emigration from Germany was now in full flood, and the prospects for those analysts who remained there was dark enough. Some emigrants found temporary resting-place, for a year or two, in Copenhagen, Oslo, Stockholm, Strasbourg and Zurich, but the majority ultimately reached America. I had, with great difficulty, obtained permission for four of them to practice in England, where two more were shortly expected.[275] Oliver Freud, who had lost his position in Berlin a year before and was dependent on his father, got to Vienna early in April,[276] and Freud's other son in Berlin, Ernst, settled in London shortly after. Ernst's youngest son, Clemens, who had recently been staying in Vienna and whom Freud called "a charming youth," had remarked: "What a different situation I should be in today if I were an Englishman." Freud expressed a warm hope that this wish could be fulfilled, which before long it was.

Freud was by no means pessimistic about Austria, as indeed few people were at that time before Mussolini gave up defending it. In April he reported: "Vienna is despite all the riots, processions, etc., reported in the newspapers calm, and life is undisturbed. One can be sure that the Hitler movement will extend to Austria—indeed it is already here—but it is very improbable that it signifies the same kind of danger as in Germany. It is more likely to be contained through joining the other parties of the Right. We are passing over to a dictatorship of the Right, which means the suppression of social democracy. That will not be a pretty state of affairs and will not be pleasant for us Jews, but we all think that special laws against Jews are out of the question in Austria because of the clauses in our peace treaty which expressly guarantee the rights of minorities —a clause that was not inserted in the Treaty of Versailles (with Germany). Legal persecution of the Jews here would lead to immediate action on the part of the League of Nations. And as for Austria joining Germany, in which case the Jews would lose all their rights, France and her Allies would never allow that. Furthermore, Austria is not given to German brutality. In such ways we buoy ourselves up in relative security. I am in any event determined not to move from the spot." [277] That was before the campaign in England and France for peace at all cost!

Two months later he commented to Marie Bonaparte: "The political situation you have yourself described exhaustively. It seems to me that not even in the War did lies and empty phrases dominate the scene as they do now. The world is turning into an enormous prison. Germany is the worst cell. What will happen in the Austrian cell is quite uncertain. I predict a paradoxical surprise in Germany. They began with Bolshevism as their deadly enemy, and they will end with something indistinguishable from it—except perhaps that Bolshevism after all adopted revolutionary ideals, whereas those of Hitlerism are purely medieval and reactionary. This world seems to me to have lost its vitality and to be doomed to perdition. I am happy to think that you still dwell as on an island of the blessed." [278]

Then in another fortnight: "We pass the time here in a state of tension wondering whether the historical event of 1683, when the waves of the Turkish onslaught broke against the walls of Vienna, will be repeated with the repulse of these barbarians who this time come from another quarter. That time, however, a friendly army came to the rescue, while today the world around seems to be shortsighted enough to leave us to our own resources." [279]

As soon as Hitler rose to power Eitingon went to Vienna, on January 27, to discuss the situation with Freud. His chief concern was of course the future of the Berlin Institute for which he had done so much. His visit was followed by a lengthy correspondence with Freud over the various eventualities that might occur, and Freud encouraged him to hold out as long as possible—not that Eitingon needed encouragement. In one letter Freud wrote: "There is no lack of attempts here to create panic, but just like you I shall leave my place only at the very last moment and probably not even then." [280] Nor did the Nazi bonfire of his books in Berlin, which took place at the end of May, much perturb him. His smiling comment was: "What progress we are making. In the Middle Ages they would have burnt me; nowadays they are content with burning my books." He was never to know that even that was only an illusory progress, that ten years later they would have burned his body as well.

On April 11 Eitingon and his wife left for a fortnight's holiday in Mentone. About that time a decree was passed that no foreigner was to function in the central executive committee of any medical society in Germany. Eitingon had Polish nationality, having chosen it when there was an option at the break up of the Austro-Hungarian Empire in 1919. Instead of letting sleeping dogs lie, Boehm, who would succeed Eitingon were he displaced from his position at the head of the Institute, immediately rushed to the authorities and enquired whether the decree applied to psychoanalytical societies also; naturally they said yes. Then Boehm went to Vienna to seek Freud's approval for what he had done. To avoid any subsequent misunderstanding of anything he might say Freud took the precaution of getting Federn to be present at the interview; I made the same use of van Ophuijsen when I went to Holland in the September for my interview with Boehm. Freud was rather non-committal, but he made it clear that any concessions made to other forms of psychotherapy would be followed by exclusion of the Berlin Society from the International Association[281]—something that actually happened some years later.

On Eitingon's return to Berlin a general meeting was held and he had to resign. His affairs were so pressing that he was unable to visit Freud on the latter's birthday, so that no member of the Committee except his daughter was present. It was, incidentally, an occasion on which Freud suffered a severe attack of vertigo, which had disagreeable aftereffects.[282] Eitingon visited Freud on August 5, and on September 8 left on a preliminary visit to Palestine. He had already decided to settle there, and in the two months he now spent there he organized a Palestinian Psycho-Analytical Society which still flourishes. On the last day of the year he left Berlin forever.

That autumn Freud had one of his many unfortunate experiences with journalism. On October 4, 1933, he had a talk with a well-known Austrian journalist, Ludwig Bauer, the son of a medical friend of Schnitzler's. Freud took a liking to him and—"fool that I was," as he said later—spoke freely about the political situation in Europe. In a widely publicized article on Austria Bauer described his visit to Freud. He was pictured as a helpless old man trembling with fear who could say little except repeat the anxious questions "Do you think they will chase me away? Do you think they will take away my books?" The Zurich psychiatrist Hanns Maier on reading it wrote to relieve Freud's supposed depressed state by offering him an asylum in Burghölzli. A similar response came from the Argentine, where the Spanish poet Xavier Bóveda in the name of a group of writers invited Freud to settle in Buenos Aires. Here is Freud's reply.

"Hochgeehrter Herr:

"6 Dez. 1933

"I read and understand the beautiful language in which you compose, but I cannot trust myself to use it myself. So I take the liberty of answering you in German; you will surely be able to find a translator in the Argentine.

"I should have been loth to miss your charming, though perhaps overenthusiastic, letter. I only regret that Dr. Ludwig Bauer's article was the occasion for your writing it, since from this you could only have got a completely wrong idea of myself and my present situation.

"Dr. Bauer, with the well-known unscrupulousness of journalists who are always ready to sacrifice the truth for sensational effect, has made me say things I never said, put questions which I never asked, make gestures I never made. So I appear in his description an old fool trembling with fear, and all that only to heighten the sympathy he is trying to arouse in his readers. In reality I by no means underestimate the danger threatening myself and others if Hitlerism conquers Austria. But I envisage it calmly, prepared to bear what has to be borne and resolved to hold out as long as it is at all possible. At the moment it looks as if we in Austria should be spared the German ignominy.

"With cordial thanks for the expression of your sympathy which surely concerns the cause of humanity more than my person, I am
"*Ihr ergebener*
"Sigm. Freud"

Freud bitterly reproached Bauer for turning him into a journalistic sensation. When Bauer said he had expected gratitude for expounding Freud's importance "to millions of readers," Freud could only retort that he had vastly overestimated his importance.[283]

In the letter to Arnold Zweig in which he stigmatized Bauer's account as "impudent inventions" he continued: "I am afraid you have under the influence of our personal relation talked too much about me in your book.[284] That is harmful to yourself and useless to me, since it is plain that this era rejects me and what I have had to offer, and it will not be willing to change its opinion for anything you may say. Probably my time will still come, but it is not now."

At the end of the year I was left as the only remaining member in Europe of the original Committee. Abraham and Ferenczi were dead, Rank had left us, Sachs was in Boston, and now Eitingon almost as far, in Palestine. Many exciting things, both happy and unhappy, had happened to us since I founded it in 1912. It had carried out an immense amount of useful work and on the whole had been successful in its original aim of creating a bodyguard around Freud which dispelled the last traces of his loneliness and isolation.

5

CHAPTER

Last Years in Vienna
(1934-1938)

1934

THIS YEAR SAW THE FLIGHT OF THE REMAINING JEWISH ANALYSTS from Germany and the "liquidation" of psychoanalysis in Germany. It was one of Hitler's few successful achievements. Looking back it is remarkable how thoroughly the knowledge of Freud and his work, once so widely spread throughout Germany, could be almost completely obliterated, so that twenty years afterward it is still at a lower level than, for instance, in Brazil or Japan. Naturally it caused Freud great distress and confirmed his pessimistic views about the ubiquitous presence of anti-Semitism.

The first signal of what was to happen had been the bonfire of Freud's and other psychoanalytical books in Berlin at the end of May, 1933, shortly after Hitler had come to power. On April 17, 1933, Boehm visited Freud in Vienna to ask his advice about the situation. The immediate question was the new order that no Jews were to serve on any scientific council. Freud was of the opinion that merely to change the personnel in this way would not prevent the government from forbidding psychoanalysis in Germany. Yet it would be wise not to give them that pretext by refraining from making the change, and he agreed that Boehm replace Eitingon on the Council. Some physicians of the Charité Hospital composed an indictment against the Psychoanalytical Society, and there were many other rumors of the worsening situation. So on October 1, 1933, I met Boehm and Carl Müller-Braunschweig in The Hague and discussed it with them, reporting afterward to Vienna. At a general meeting of the Society on November 18 Eitingon proposed that the

Council be restricted to two members, those just mentioned, and this was unanimously agreed.

In June, 1933, the German Society for Psychotherapy had come under Nazi control and masqueraded under the aegis of an "International General Medical Society for Psychotherapy," which in its turn was "readjusted" in terms of the "German National Revolution."[1] Reichsführer Dr. Göring explained that all members were expected to make a thorough study of Hitler's *Mein Kampf*, which was to serve as the basis for their work. Kretschmer promptly resigned as President and his place was as promptly taken by C. G. Jung. Jung also became Editor of the official organ, the *Zentralblatt für Psychotherapie*, and in 1936 was joined by Göring as co-Editor; he resigned in 1940. Jung's chief function was to discriminate between Aryan psychology and Jewish psychology, and to emphasize the value of the former. A Swiss psychiatrist immediately protested against this departure from the neutrality of science,[2] and since then Jung has been severely criticized in many quarters for his conduct.[3]

In November, 1933, two official Nazi psychotherapists met Boehm and Müller-Braunschweig and told them that the only chance of psychoanalysis being allowed to continue lay in the exclusion of all Jewish members from the Society. Pressure in this direction increased, not unaccompanied by threats. The matter was coming to a head, and I remember receiving on one day telephone calls from Berlin, Paris, Prague and Vienna. In response I went to Berlin and presided at a meeting of the Society on December 1, 1933, where the few remaining Jews volunteered to resign so as to save the Society from being dissolved. Opinions have since differed about this step, and some have thought it would have been more dignified for all the members to resign in protest, as the Dutch colleagues did later on a similar occasion. But there was still a little hope that something could be saved.

The leveling process (*Gleichschaltung*), however, continued, and the various branches of science were being "nationalized" and brought under a central control. Dr. M. H. Göring, a cousin of the Deputy Führer, was made President of the "General German Medical Society for Psychotherapy" the function of which was to unify as far as possible all forms of psychotherapy and to provide them with National-Socialistic aims. The German Psycho-Analytical Society would not be allowed to lead an independent existence, but it could function as a special branch of the general organization. At a meeting of the Society it was decided to accept this offer, and

Boehm had a long interview with Anna Freud on March 8, 1936 in Brünn, it being already forbidden for Germans to travel to Austria. He went back under the impression that he had obtained her and her father's assent to the decision, but they certainly could not have been very enthusiastic about it. The Nazi authorities then demanded that what was left of the German Society should withdraw from membership of the International Psycho-Analytical Association, and at a general meeting on May 13, 1936, this was agreed to. The fact was noted in the Bulletin of the Association,[4] but subsequently the authorities rescinded their decision. I thought it wise, however, to allow their membership to continue silently without making any public announcement of it.

It took some time to bring about the new organization, and on July 19, 1936, I had a meeting in Basle with Göring, Boehm and Müller-Braunschweig. Brill was also present. I found Göring a fairly amiable and amenable person, but it turned out later that he was not in a position to fulfill the promises he made me about the degree of freedom that was to be allowed the psychoanalytical group. No doubt in the meantime the Jewish origin of psychoanalysis had been fully explained to him. Training analyses were forbidden, but lectures still allowed. Göring or his wife, however, made a point of attending the latter to ensure that no psychoanalytical technical terms were used, so the Oedipus complex had to figure under a synonym. In January, 1937, Boehm managed to get once more to Vienna. At an interview Freud proposed that he describe the situation to a larger group, which he did on the following day; there were present among others Anna and Martin Freud, Federn and Jeanne Lampl-de Groot. Boehm talked for three hours until Freud's patience gave out. He broke into the exposition with the words: "Quite enough! The Jews have suffered for their convictions for centuries. Now the time has come for our Christian colleagues to suffer in their turn for theirs. I attach no importance to my name being mentioned in Germany so long as my work is presented correctly there." So saying he left the room.

I toiled hard in those years arranging for the escape of our colleagues who were more than ostracized in Berlin and in obtaining with the utmost difficulty permits for them to enter other countries, particularly England. I shuddered to think what would happen if the same situation ever arose in Austria. It meant among other things spending hours in our Home Office and using what influence I could muster. But I got my reward in receiving one of the two or three compliments I have treasured in my life. The President of the Jewish Board of Trustees remarked to a friend that the name Ernest Jones must cover a pretty large committee, for it was impossible for one man to have accomplished what had been done under that name.

Freud was deeply concerned, not only about the effect on his work of the Nazi persecution in Germany, and not only about the sufferings inflicted on his followers there, but also with the resulting fate of his *Verlag*. This depended in the main on the sale of its books and periodicals in Germany, all of which had now come to an end. Leipzig was the central depot for Germany and Austria where all the stocks of books, including those of the *Verlag*, were stored. On March 28, 1936, Martin Freud telephoned to me the disastrous news that the Gestapo had seized all the *Verlag's* property there. I immediately cabled to the Chief of Police in Leipzig explaining that it belonged to an international body, but of course this did not deter their action. So for the next two years the *Verlag* had to continue its existence in Vienna as a gravely mutilated torso. It was especially sad inasmuch as just then it was arranging to occupy part of a building, appropriately enough in the Berggasse itself—at number 7, a few doors from Freud's dwelling—that was to be devoted entirely to psychoanalysis. The Society meetings were to be held there, and its library was housed there as well as the Vienna Psychoanalytical Institute and Clinic. It was my duty to inaugurate the opening of that promising undertaking on May 5, 1936, the eve of Freud's eightieth birthday. So, thanks to Martin Freud's energy, the *Verlag* managed to function until the Nazis confiscated it in March, 1938.

After completing this general account we may return to a more chronological narration of the year's happenings. In January Freud approved of our nominating van Ophuijsen as Vice-President of the International Association to replace Ferenczi. The rule that only previous Presidents could hold this position had already been abrogated in Brill's favor.[a]

That spring Freud had a deal of trouble with the local condition in his jaw. In February Roentgen rays were applied several times with little effect, so in March radium was used. This was done many times in the following months, with the result that a whole precious year was gained without any operation. The pain and distressing reactions, however, were often very great, though these were less after Dr. Ludwig Schloss, who had been trained at the Curie In-

* See p. 170.

stitute in Paris, discovered that the metal in the prosthesis was producing secondary radiation; another apparatus was built to obviate this.

In March Freud was distressed to hear of a motor accident in England in which his daughter-in-law, Ernst's wife, sustained a fracture of the skull. She made a good recovery, but suffered for some time from delayed shock. Freud sent me much sage advice for the management of the case which showed that his medical knowledge was still available.

At the beginning of May Freud was happy to exchange his cloistered life in the city for more rural surroundings. For this summer he had been luckier than the year before and had found a house with extensive grounds in Grinzing, not far from Cobenzl (Strassergasse 47 in the nineteenth Bezirk). Freud described it as "beautiful as fairy land." [5] Part of the garden, however, was only accessible to him in a bath chair.

Eitingon, who by then had settled in Palestine, could not come for Freud's birthday as he usually did, but he came to see him in the following August. Freud wrote to him "Nearly all those who have congratulated me on my birthday this year will wait in vain for thanks or acknowledgement. I will educate them by this technique not to do it again next time. But I must make an exception for you and for the warm cable our youngest group sent me." [6]

In June there was the death of Groddeck, a man who had always attracted Freud in spite of, or perhaps partly because of, his vagaries. In the letter telling me of this news he asked if I thought Mussolini was selling Austria to Hitler; his suspicions about the future were beginning to be aroused.

He made a very original comment on the "Roehm purges" in June when the Nazis murdered a number of their own leaders. It illustrates how unexpectedly Freud's imagination could work. He told Arnold Zweig that his impression of the event afforded a striking contrast to an experience he had had at the Hague Congress in 1920. There the hospitable Dutch had invited their half-starved colleagues from central Europe to a sumptuous banquet. Being used to so little food they found the hors d'oeuvres a sufficient meal and could eat no more. "Now the hors d'oeuvres in Germany leave one hungry for more." [7]

In April Arnold Zweig had told him he was planning to write a book on Nietzsche's mental collapse and he sent Freud the first draft of it. Freud was inclined to advise him to abandon the whole plan, though he admitted to not being clear about his reasons for doing so. These, however, are given in a subsequent letter printed elsewhere.[b]

Zweig nevertheless continued with his writing and sent Freud a full exposition of his aims—essentially to express his hatred for the Germans. He asked Freud for any suggestions about Nietzsche's life. In his reply Freud said: "You overrate my knowledge concerning Nietzsche, so I cannot tell you anything of much use for your purpose. For me two things bar the approach to the Nietzsche problem. In the first place one cannot see through anyone unless one knows something about his sexual constitution, and with Nietzsche this is a complete enigma. There is even a legend that he was a passive homosexual and had acquired his syphilis in a male brothel in Italy. Whether that is true: quien sabe? In the second place he had a serious illness and after a long period of warning symptoms a general paralysis became manifest. Everyone has conflicts. With a general paralysis the conflicts fade into the background of the etiology. Whether writers are allowed to change around the gross facts of pathology I do not know. They are not usually very amenable people." [8]

Zweig had also just written a play about Napoleon in Jaffa in which he severely criticized the episode about the shooting of prisoners. In the letter just quoted Freud remarked: "So you have just dashed off a new piece, an episode from the life of that terrible scamp Napoleon who, fixated as he was on his puberty phantasies, favored by incredible luck and uninhibited by any bonds except to his family, roved through the world like a somnambulist only to founder at the end in megalomania. There has hardly ever been a genius to whom every trace of nobility was so alien, such a classical anti-gentleman. But he was built on a grandiose scale." In a subsequent letter he said more about Napoleon. "I have one criticism of your play. It seems to me too cruel, unjustifiably so, inasmuch as you pick out a situation in which the revolting and inhumane nature of war becomes manifest far beyond the misdeed of a given individual. In one of Caesar's battles in Gaul it happened that the besieged (was it Alesta, and Vercingetorix?) had nothing more to eat. They drove out their women and children into the no man's land between the fortress and the besieging Roman army where the poor wretches starved between their own people who could give them nothing and their enemies who would give them nothing—or perhaps did not

[b] Appendix A, No. 28.

have much either. It would have been more merciful to have slain them in the town. At the thought of such decisions one recoils with horror and without passing any verdict. It is like shipwrecked mariners slaughtering one of their comrades.

"Have I ever given you the analytic explanation of his phantastic expedition to Egypt? Napoleon had a great Joseph complex. His elder brother was called that, and he had to marry a woman named Josephine. His gigantic jealousy of the older brother had been transformed into warm love under the influence of a father identification, and the obsession then extended to his wife. Incorrigible dreamer that he was, he had to play the part of Joseph in Egypt, and later on provided for his brothers in Europe just as if he had been successful in his conquest of Egypt." [9]

Actually the importance of Joseph in Napoleon's life was a suggestion I had made to Freud more than twenty years before, though his own identification with the name, of which he was fully aware,[10] made him attach more significance to it than I should probably have done. I had before the First World War spent two years in collecting material for a book to be called *Napoleon's Orient Complex*, and had talked over its contents several times with Freud. He passed on some of the ideas to Ludwig Jekels, who was then in analysis with him and who happened to be a rival of mine with a certain lady. Jekels seized on them avidly and wrote an excellent essay on the subject.[11] The cream was gone, the war and other interests supervened, and my book never got written.

The International Congress that year was held at Lucerne on August 26. It was the first without Ferenczi's presence. New Societies were accepted from Boston, Holland, Japan and Palestine. My original plan of all American Societies being united under the aegis of the American Psychoanalytical Association was at last, after twenty-three years, being acted upon, although there was still considerable opposition to it from the strong local groups. It was on this occasion that Wilhelm Reich resigned from the Association. Freud had thought highly of him in his early days, but Reich's political fanaticism had led to both personal and scientific estrangement.

After the Congress I flew to Vienna for three days to visit Freud in Grinzing. I had not seen him for five years, the longest interval except for the war years, and naturally found him rather older and somewhat altered by all the suffering he had gone through. But there was not the slightest sign of weakening in his mental grasp and quick intuitions. The *Verlag* and the German situation occupied most of our talk. Eitingon, coming from Palestine, had visited Freud shortly before the Congress.

In November Freud reported two adverse actions that had been taken. One was that the *Rivista Italiana di Psicanalisi* had been suspended by order of the Vatican and, as Freud suspected, at the instance of his Viennese Catholic opponent, Pater Schmidt. Mussolini promised to rescind the ban, but even his authority was not great enough for the purpose. Then a book of collected papers Berkeley-Hill had published had been banned from circulation in Bengal. This act of the British authorities was not so much directed against psychoanalysis as dictated by fear that the sexual interpretations of the Hindu religion the book contained might lead to popular disturbances.

The following little incident illustrates Freud's punctiliousness in replying to unknown correspondents. J. G. Green, who was attached to the Tufts College School of Religion in Boston, wrote a letter to Freud expressing his admiration for his work and saying he was sending him a reprint of an article on the Emmanuel Movement. Here is Freud's reply:

"Nov. 16, 1934
"*Sehr geehrter Herr:*
"Naturally I was very surprised at the high estimation in which you hold me, and in order to accept it I reflect on the many invectives to which I have been exposed and still am. At all events what you say is a striking proof that theology has not damaged your capacity for free thought. . . . I shall read attentively your article on the Emmanuel Movement. Perhaps one may express regret that so much energy has been expended in America in these religious movements. But America is over-rich in energy.

"With best wishes
"*Ihr Freud*"

The only thing Freud seems to have published in this year was a Preface to the Hebrew edition of his *Introductory Lectures*.[12] But it was the year in which he conceived, and for the most part wrote, his ideas on Moses and religion, ideas that were to engross him for the rest of his life. That happened in the summer, since he mentioned them to Eitingon and myself in August. The first full account comes in a letter to Arnold Zweig: "Not knowing what to do with my leisure time I have been writing something, and against my original intention it so took hold of me that everything else was put aside. Now do not start rejoicing at the thought of reading it, for I wager you will never do so. But let me explain how it goes.

"The starting-point of my essay you are familiar with; it is the same as that of your *Bilanz*.ᵉ In view of the recent ordinances one asks oneself again how Jews have become what they are, and why they have drawn on to themselves such undying hatred. I soon discovered a formula for it: Moses created the Jews. So my essay got the title: *The Man Moses, an historical novel* (more fittingly than your Nietzsche novel). It is divided into three sections: the first romantically interesting; the second laborious and tedious; the third full of content and pretentions. The undertaking breaks down on the third one, which brings something new and fundamental for strangers— though nothing new for me after *Totem and Taboo*. It is the thought of those strangers that makes me keep the finished essay secret. For we live here in an atmosphere of strict Catholic beliefs. It is said that the politics of our country are made by a P. Schmidt who is the confidant of the Pope and unfortunately carries out himself researches into ethnology and religion; in his books he makes no secret of his abhorrence of psychoanalysis and particularly of my Totem theory. . . . Now one may very well expect that a publication from me will attract a certain attention and not escape the inimical Pater's. In that way one would be risking the banning of analysis in Vienna and the cessation of all our publications. If the danger concerned only myself it would make little impression on me, but to deprive our members in Vienna of their livelihood is too great a responsibility. Then there is also the consideration that my contribution does not seem to me well founded enough nor does it please me much. So it is not the right occasion for a martyrdom. Finis for the time being."¹³

Zweig related the contents of this letter to Eitingon (they were both at the time in Palestine) and told him he had suggested to Freud that the book might be printed privately in Palestine. Eitingon pointed out that there would be no protection in this, since the style would infallibly betray the identity of the author. But he asked Freud if the book contained anything stronger than *The Future of an Illusion*, about which Schmidt had raised no official complaint.¹⁴ Freud replied that it only differed from the earlier book in admitting that religion was not based entirely on illusion but also had an his-

ᵉ I. e. the persecution of the Jews in Germany.

torical kernel of truth, to which it owed its great effectiveness. He added that he would not be afraid of the outer danger were he only surer of his thesis about Moses. "Experts would find it easy to discredit me as an outsider," [15] which is in fact what they did when the time came. He added that the book was now finished. Incidentally, he had remarked to Eitingon in August that he was afraid it would offend Jews to be told that their great Moses was really an Egyptian, but for some reason this consideration did not seem to have weighed very much with him.

It was with the historical part that Freud was dissatisfied. "It won't stand up to my own criticism. I need more certainty and I should not like to endanger the final formula of the whole book, which I regard as valuable, by appearing to found the motivation on a basis of clay. So we will put it aside." [16] At the same time he said to Eitingon: "I am no good at historical romances. Let us leave them to Thomas Mann." [17] But, as we shall see, this was by no means the end of the Moses story.[d]

1935

There was no outstanding event in this year. Disease and age were making their steady attack on Freud's vitality, but he was displaying his customary resilience.

In January he wrote to Lou Salomé a full account, several pages long, of his ideas about Moses and religion. They culminated in a formula to the effect that religion owes its strength not to any real literal truth, but to an historical truth it contains. He concluded: "And now you see, Lou, one cannot publish this formula, which has quite fascinated me, in Austria today without running the risk of the Catholic authorities officially forbidding the practice of analysis. And only this Catholicism protects us against Naziism. Moreover, the historical basis of the Moses story is not solid enough to serve as a basis for my invaluable piece of insight. So I remain silent. It is enough that I myself can believe in the solution of the problem. It has pursued me through my whole life." [18] And a little later he told Arnold Zweig, with whom he was having a considerable correspondence on the topic, that Moses entirely engrossed his thoughts.[e]

On February 6 the famous French archaeologist Levy-Bruhl paid Freud a visit at which they exchanged books. Freud commented: "He is a real *savant*, especially in comparison with myself." [20] In the

---

[d] See Chapter 13.
[e] *Moses giebt meine Phantasie nicht frei.*[19]

same month he wrote to Arnold Zweig in Palestine: "Your description of the spring makes me sad and envious. I have still so much capacity for enjoyment that I am dissatisfied with the resignation forced on me. The one bright spot in my life is the success of Anna's work." [21]

In April a despairing mother in America wrote to Freud for advice. A photostat of Freud's reply has been published,[22] but with permission I am repeating his letter here as an example of his kindness in doing what he could to help a stranger even when he was preoccupied with his own suffering. She herself had sent the letter anonymously to Dr. Kinsey with this note: "Herewith I enclose a letter from a great and good man which you may retain. From a Grateful Mother."

"April 9, 1935

"Dear Mrs. . . .

"I gather from your letter that your son is a homosexual. I am most impressed by the fact that you do not mention this term yourself in your information about him. May I question you, why you avoid it? Homosexuality is assuredly no advantage, but it is nothing to be ashamed of, no vice, no degradation, it cannot be classified as an illness; we consider it to be a variation of the sexual function produced by a certain arrest of sexual development. Many highly respectable individuals of ancient and modern times have been homosexuals, several of the greatest men among them (Plato, Michelangelo, Leonardo da Vinci, etc.). It is a great injustice to persecute homosexuality as a crime, and cruelty too. If you do not believe me, read the books of Havelock Ellis.

"By asking me if I can help, you mean, I suppose, if I can abolish homosexuality and make normal heterosexuality take its place. The answer is, in a general way, we cannot promise to achieve it. In a certain number of cases we succeed in developing the blighted germs of heterosexual tendencies which are present in every homosexual, in the majority of cases it is no more possible. It is a question of the quality and the age of the individual. The result of treatment cannot be predicted.

"What analysis can do for your son runs in a different line. If he is unhappy, neurotic, torn by conflicts, inhibited in his social life, analysis may bring him harmony, peace of mind, full efficiency, whether he remains a homosexual or gets changed. If you make up your mind he should have analysis with me!! I don't expect you will!! he has to come over to Vienna. I have no intention of leaving here. However, don't neglect to give me your answer.

"Sincerely yours with kind wishes,
"Freud"

"P.S. I did not find it difficult to read your handwriting. Hope you will not find my writing and my English a harder task."

Easter fell late that year, so Freud took advantage of the holiday to move to his summer quarters earlier than usual, in the third week of April. He had fortunately been able to rent the same house as before in Grinzing. I spent a week in Vienna at that time, together with my wife and two elder children, and on Easter Sunday paid him our first visit. He surprised my little girl, aged five, by taking hold of her nose between two fingers; but ignoring this castrating symbolism, she won his heart by immediately offering him her doll. To the boy then aged thirteen, he presented some antiquities from his collection with the recommendation that archaeology would be an interesting career to choose, advice to which my son's literary bent did not respond. The proud father must record that Freud in his next letter said he had seldom met such delightful children; he always inquired about them afterward. I have not often known a man so fond of children as he was.

His birthday this year passed off fairly quietly with few visitors but very many letters to answer. Freud commented that seventy-nine was "a quite irrational number." [23] But it had been a miserable time personally. There had been operations in March and April, and on his birthday Freud tried till he was quite exhausted to insert the horrible "monster" into his mouth. Nor could Schur or Anna succeed, so it meant calling on Pichler for help.

About this time some differences had developed between some of the London analysts, including myself, and the Viennese. The latter, who adhered closely to Freud's teaching, had had the advantage of close contact and discussions with him. It seemed desirable to clarify the differences by more personal contact, and that was one of my objects of this visit. My own differences were partly doubt about Freud's theory of a "death instinct" and partly a somewhat varying conception of the phallic stage in development, particularly in the female. So I read a paper on the latter topic before the Vienna Society on April 24, 1935. Freud never agreed with my views, and perhaps they were wrong; I do not think the matter has been entirely cleared up even yet. More troublesome were the views Melanie

Klein had been expounding in contradistinction to Anna Freud's, not always in a tactful manner. In a long discussion with Freud I defended Melanie Klein's work, but it was not to be expected that at a time when he was so dependent on his daughter's ministrations and affections he could be quite open-minded in the matter. Shortly after my visit he wrote: "I do not estimate our theoretical differences of opinion as slight, but so long as there is no bad feeling behind them they can have no troublesome results. I can say definitely that we in Vienna have not infused any ill will into the contradiction, and your amiableness[f] has repaired the way in which Melanie Klein and her daughter erred in this respect toward Anna. It is true I am of opinion that your Society has followed Frau Klein on a wrong path, but the sphere from which she has drawn her observations is foreign to me so that I have no right to any fixed conviction." [24]

I then suggested a return visit of a Viennese to London. Robert Wälder was chosen, and he addressed the British Society on November 21, 1935. Joan Riviere returned the compliment in the following year, addressing the Vienna Society on the occasion of Freud's eightieth birthday.

In his correspondence this year Freud made many allusions to his Moses book, the thought of which would not leave him. He kept reading all the books he could find on Jewish history. In May he was excited at reading of some excavations in Tell el-Amarna because the name of a certain Prince Thothmes was mentioned. He wondered if that was "his Moses" and wished he had the money to further the researches there.[25]

In May Freud was made an Honorary Fellow of the Royal Society of Medicine and was told that the resolution was passed unanimously. He boyishly asked me if it meant that he could now put a row of letters after his name, such as H.F.R.S.M.[26]

At the same time there was a less pleasing episode which is described in a letter of the same date to Marie Bonaparte. "You will also have got a book by a M. Vigné d'Octon[27] which contains an assessment of psychoanalysis. You have contributed something yourself to it. I assume you will see that it is reviewed in your *Revue*. In the first chapter V. d'O. relates personal reminiscences about meeting me in the years 1885-1886 in the Salpêtrière. They are very flattering to me, but unfortunately there is not a word of truth in them. He must have confounded me with someone else he got to know there. I have never seen him or spoken to him; the episode about

[f] *Liebenswürdigkeit.*

an article in *Figaro* in which I am supposed to have made certain remarks about Charcot is completely strange to me; Brissaud, whom he
makes figure as an Interne of the Clinic, was not there in my time,
so that I never got to know him. When M. V. d'O. sent me the
proofs of his book I did not conceal my objections, but he did not
let them disturb him."

This is only one example of the many erroneous statements that
have been made concerning Freud's work at the Salpêtrière. One,
still current in Paris,[28] is that he acquired his ideas there from Janet
and never admitted it. The fact that he never met Janet, who at
that time had not yet come to Paris from Le Havre, is disregarded
by these lovers of rumors.

That summer a cruel story was going round about a supposed pro-
cession of Jews in Berlin carrying banners with the device "Throw us
out." [g] Naturally it was nothing but one of those savage jokes Jews
seem to like making about themselves, but Freud believed it was true
and wrote a bitter letter about it to Arnold Zweig in which he said he
had never heard anything so revolting, but that the lack of dignity
it displayed was a characteristic feature of the Jews. The only consolation he could find was that the people in question were half
German.[29] His indignation at any possible self-abasement on the part
of Jews reminds one of his early reaction to his father's story about
picking up his cap from the gutter.[30]

On August 1 Anna Freud met Eitingon and me in Paris to discuss
training matters, so at that time Freud was evidently well enough
to get on without her ministrations for a couple of days—a rare
possibility.

Arnold Zweig had just finished his book *Erziehung vor Verdun*,
which dealt with his experiences of German brutality in the World
War. Freud was feeling extremely indignant about German behavior
at this time toward the Jews, and this is what he wrote after pe-
rusing the book. "It is like a long yearned-for liberation. At last the
truth, the grim, final truth, which one has to have. One cannot understand the Germany of today if one does not know about 'Verdun'
(and for what that stands). The dispelling of illusions comes late, it
is true, also with you. Hence the striking anachronism that the idyll
of Grischa, a book in which there is so little to be seen of the
fading of all illusions, followed your education at Verdun. That fits
in with the fact that after the war you settled in Berlin and even
built a house there. Today one would say 'Had I drawn the right

[g] *Hinaus mit uns.*

conclusions from my experience at Verdun I should have known that one cannot live with such a people.' We all thought it was the war and not the people, but the other countries also had war and behaved quite differently. Then we would not believe it, but it was true what the others told about the Boches." [31]

In the following month he mentioned the conflict between Britain and Italy over Abyssinia and foretold quite correctly that Germany would play the part of a tertium gaudens, so that the Jews of Austria would have to pay the price.[32]

On October 13 there was a pleasant visit from Thornton Wilder of Chicago, the well-known author of *The Bridge of San Luis Rey*. The autumn of 1935 was very beautiful, so Freud stayed in his delightful summer house in Grinzing until the middle of October. He thus had six full months there, the longest spell he had ever spent away from his home.

Another example, one of many that could be quoted, of Freud's easy tolerance toward his followers' criticism or correction of his conclusions may be mentioned here. In his book *The Psychopathology of Everyday Life* he had described how repressed trends could interfere with what he called the "harmless" conscious intentions. Ludwig Eidelberg had now written a paper pointing out that the conscious intentions were often not "harmless," and that the slip of the tongue or pen could be determined by ego-syntonic reactions against them—in other words, the reverse mechanism to that described by Freud. When this paper was for some reason not accepted by the *Zeitschrift* he sent it to Anna Freud, who showed it to her father. She then replied to Eidelberg, quoting her father's opinion. "Your criticism of the word 'harmless' for the trend that is disturbed is thoroughly justified, and further investigation of the apparently 'harmless' is undoubtedly important. He suggested that the relation of the two tendencies is probably a variable one. Further investigation along these lines would probably be very rewarding." [33]

In June of this year the Fischer Verlag asked Freud to write a letter that could be published commemorating Thomas Mann's sixtieth birthday. From the heights of his eightieth year he must have smiled at the idea of this juvenile feat. The letter was re-printed in the following year in the *Almanach der Psychoanalyse*.[34]

The American publishers of his *Autobiographical Study*, Brentano, asked him that summer to write a supplement to it, which he did at once.[35] In it he expressed his regret at having ever published details of his private life and advised his friends never to do the same.

1936

Two events dominated this year: Freud's eightieth birthday, and his election as a Corresponding Member of the Royal Society. That the former would involve the strain of celebrations had given him many anxious thoughts for months beforehand, and he did all he could to reduce them to a minimum. A year before I had planned a Commemoration volume of essays as an appropriate gift for his adherents, one that would take some time to organize. He somehow got to hear of it and wrote to me: "Now a word from behind the scenes. It has come to my ears that you are preparing a special celebration for my eightieth birthday. Apart from the possibility that it may never happen and from my conviction that a telegram of condolence would be the only suitable response to its happening, I am of the opinion that neither the situation within analytical circles nor the state of the world justifies any celebration. If the need for some expression cannot be altogether restrained you should turn it into some direction that necessitates the minimum of trouble, stir and work, such as an album with the photographs of the members." [36] I shuddered at this astonishing proposal, which struck me as most impracticable to carry out. But anything to give pleasure. So I wrote back: "I am reluctantly inclined to think you are right about my proposal of a *Gedenkbuch*. It would be useless to think of any proposal that would not give you pleasure, and I daresay you can guess that the risks of invidiousness in the choice of contributors might result in considerable jealousy and ill feeling. We shall probably fall back on the photograph suggestion, which strikes me as a very interesting one with many possibilities in it. Fortunately for you Eitingon will not be President at the time of your birthday.[h] I think you know that I share more fully your quiet attitude about ceremonial occasions." [37]

Then came a fuller exposition of his views. "I agree that I have reasons to be glad that you are at the helm of the psychoanalytical bark, and not only because of the *Gedenkbuch*. You meet my misgivings with such understanding that I have the courage to go a step further.

"So let us bury the *Gedenkbuch* or *Sammelband*, etc. I turn to my own suggestion of an album and confess that now it pleases me

[h] Eitingon was apt to make the most of such occasions.

just as little; indeed it fundamentally displeases me. Leaving aside the two objections that it would mean a deal of trouble and bring me no guarantee that I live to the date, now I am taking umbrage at the aesthetic monstrosity of 400 pictures of mostly ugly people of whom I don't at all know the half and of whom a good number do not want to know anything of me. No, the times are not suited to a festival, '*intra Iliacos muros nec extra.*'[1] The only possible thing seems to me to renounce any action in common. Whoever feels that he must congratulate me let him do so, and who does not need not fear my vengeance.

"There is still another argument. What is the secret meaning of this celebrating the big round numbers of one's life? Surely a measure of triumph over the transitoriness of life, which, as we never forget, is ready to devour us. Then one rejoices with a sort of communal feeling that we are not made of such frail stuff as to prevent one of us victoriously resisting the hostile effects of life for 60, 70 or even 80 years. That one can understand and agree with, but the celebration evidently has sense only when the survivor can in spite of all wounds and scars join in as a hale fellow; it loses this sense when he is an invalid with whom there is no question of conviviality. And since the latter is my case and I bear my fate by myself I should prefer my 80th birthday to be treated as my private affair—by my friends."[38]

To which I could only reply: "I was very interested in your human document and find the arguments in it very convincing. I should like to add to them the desire to express one's pleasure at the co-existence of someone one loves, which one can do more decidedly on a selected occasion than in everyday life. A birthday seems a natural occasion for this, it being a celebration of one's gladness at their birth, and there are obvious reasons why the desire comes to the forefront specially in reference to childhood and old age. In any event, however over-determined the desire may be, there is no doubt it loses all sense if it gives no pleasure to the recipient. So you may be sure we shall respect your definite wishes in the matter."[39]

There the matter rested for the time being, but as the dreaded date drew nearer Freud's anxieties about the strain to be imposed on him kept increasing. A number of adherents and strangers announced their intention of paying him a visit, among them Eitingon, Landauer, Laforgue and myself. Marie Bonaparte offered to come, but then thoughtfully postponed her visit till later and con-

[1] Let us keep it among ourselves.

tented herself with delivering an eulogy of Freud at the Sorbonne. In March he had written to her: "My birthday is naturally a burdensome threat for me and for others. I am in favor of our disposing of it as briefly and informally as possible, in fact denying it as far as I am concerned. That should succeed with friends, but of course one has no influence on strangers. Fortunately we have avoided any participation from official bodies." [40] Then, a little later: "The rumors that reach me about preparations for my birthday annoy me as much as the newspaper gossip about a Nobel Prize. I am not easily deceived, and I know that the attitude of the world toward me and my work is really no friendlier than twenty years ago. Nor do I any longer wish for any change in it, no 'happy end' as in the cinema." [41] Even earlier he had written to Arnold Zweig about the intentions of the press in various countries and remarked: "What nonsense to think of making good at such a questionable date the ill-treatment of a long life. No; rather let us stay enemies." [42] He consoled himself with the thought that the celebration would last only a few days and that it could happen only once in a lifetime; "afterward there will be a wonderful rest when no crowing of a cock will be able to disturb me." [43]

In April Freud had added to his other troubles a disturbed action of the heart, which any excitement or strain would increase to the point of distress. It was evidently exacerbated by nicotine, since it was relieved as soon as he stopped smoking. So he had to change his usual tune when Heinrich Meng visited him shortly afterwards. His custom had been to offer him a cigar, and when Meng, who was a non-smoker, declined Freud would remark: "You unlucky fellow, missing the pleasure of smoking." This time, however, when the same thing happened Freud commented: "You lucky fellow, not missing the privation of not smoking."

About this time Freud's brother, Alexander, commissioned a Viennese artist, Wilhelm Victor Krausz, to paint a portrait of him. This disappeared during the war and was afterward discovered in the Vienna Art Museum under the caption "Portrait of an Unknown Gentleman" and with the painter's name erased. It is now in the possession of Alexander's son Harry.

The birthday itself passed off quietly enough, with Freud's rooms turned into a flower shop of bouquets. He was in excellent form, having recovered well from a painful operation in March. On the evening before I had had the privilege as President of the International Association of opening the new premises the Institute had acquired.[j] In my address on "The Future of Psychoanalysis," at which Freud was of course not present, I remarked on the taboo he had placed on celebrating his birthday and on the awful consequences that follow the breaking of taboos. So the Viennese left him in peace. But six weeks later Freud was still struggling to cope with the congratulations from all over the world he had to answer.

The occasion led to a charming exchange of letters between the two great men of the twentieth century which should be quoted in full.

"Princeton. 21. 4. 1936

"*Verehrter Herr* Freud:

"I am happy that this generation has the good fortune to have the opportunity of expressing their respect and gratitude to you as one of its greatest teachers. You have undoubtedly not made it easy for the sceptical laity to come to an independent judgment. Until recently I could only apprehend the speculative power of your train of thought, together with its enormous influence on the *Weltanschaung* of the present era, without being in a position to form a definite opinion about the amount of truth it contains. Not long ago, however, I had the opportunity of hearing about a few instances, not very important in themselves, which in my judgment exclude any other interpretation than that provided by the theory of repression. I was delighted to come across them; since it is always delightful when a great and beautiful conception proves to be consonant with reality.

"With most cordial wishes and deep respects

"Your

"A. Einstein"

"P.S. Please do not answer this. My pleasure at the occasion for this letter is quite enough."

"Wien. 3. 5. 1936

"*Verehrter Herr* Einstein:

"You object in vain to my answering your very kind letter. I really must tell you how glad I was to hear of the change in your judgment—or at least the beginning of one. Of course I always knew that you 'admired' me only out of politeness and believed very little of any of my doctrines, although I have often asked myself what indeed there is to be admired in them if they are not true, i.e. if they do not contain a large measure of truth. By the way, don't you think that I should have been better treated if my doctrines had con-

[j] See p. 188.

tained a greater percentage of error and craziness? You are so much younger than I am that I may hope to count you among my 'followers' by the time you reach my age. Since I shall not know of it then I am anticipating now the gratification of it. (You know what is crossing my mind: *ein Vorgefühl von solchem Glück geniesse ich, etc.*) :ᵏ

"*In herzlicher Ergebenheit und unwandelbarer Verehrung*
"*Ihr*
"Freud"

On May 7 Ludwig Binswanger and his wife paid a visit to Freud in his Grinzing house. That evening Binswanger gave an address before the *Akademischer Verein für Medizinische Psychologie* (Academy of Medical Psychology). While praising Freud's achievements, he maintained that they needed to be supplemented by contributions from philosophy and religion. His address was printed, and in October he sent Freud a copy. Here is the reply he received, written on October 8, 1936.

"*Lieber Freund:*
"Your address was a delightful surprise. Those who listened to it and told me of it were evidently unaffected: it must have been too difficult for them. On reading it I enjoy your beautiful diction, your erudition, the scope of your horizon, your tact when contradicting me. You know one can tolerate endless amounts of praise.

"Naturally I still don't believe you. I have always dwelt only in the ground floor and basement of the building. You assert that, when one changes one's viewpoint, one can also see upper stories in which such distinguished guests as religion, art, etc., reside. You are not the only one in that; most cultivated types of homo natura think the same. In that you are the conservative, I am the revolutionary. Had I only another life of work in front of me I should dare to offer even those highly born people a home in my lowly dwelling. I have already found one for religion after I came across the category 'neurosis of mankind.' Probably, however, we are 'talking past each other,' [1] and our dispute will take centuries to settle.

"In cordial friendship and with greetings to your dear wife,
"Your
"Freud"

ᵏ That lofty moment I foreknow is this
And now enjoy the highest moment's bliss. (*Faust*, Act V)
[1] *Vorbeireden.*

The feature of the occasion Freud most enjoyed, or least minded, was Thomas Mann's visit to him.[44] On May 8 Mann gave an impressive address before the *Akademische Verein für Medizinische Psychologie*.[45] In that month he delivered it five or six times in different places, and then six weeks later, on Sunday, June 14, he read the address to Freud, who commented that it was even better than he had gathered from hearsay.[46] But Freud was not beguiled by other demonstrations: "Viennese colleagues also celebrated the occasion, and betrayed by all sorts of indications how hard they found it to do so. The Minister of Education ceremoniously congratulated me in a polite fashion, but the Austrian newspapers were forbidden under pain of confiscation to mention this sympathetic action. Numerous articles here and abroad expressed plainly enough their rejection and hatred. So I had the satisfaction of observing that honesty has not quite vanished from the world." [47]

Among the many presents that reached Freud was an Address signed by Thomas Mann, Romain Rolland, Jules Romains, H. G. Wells, Virginia Woolf, Stefan Zweig and 191 other writers and artists. Mann delivered it to him personally on his birthday. Two people refused to sign it: one surprisingly was T. G. Masaryk (who was probably ill); the other, whose name Freud would not have regretted, Emil Ludwig. Since the Address has not to my knowledge ever been published I will reproduce a translation of it. The style is unmistakably Thomas Mann's.

"The eightieth birthday of Sigmund Freud gives us a welcome opportunity to convey to the pioneer of a new and deeper knowledge of man our congratulation and our veneration. In every important sphere of his activity, as physician and psychologist, as philosopher and artist, this courageous seer and healer has for two generations been a guide to hitherto undreamed-of regions of the human soul. An independent spirit, 'a man and knight, grim and stern of visage' as Nietzsche said of Schopenhauer,[48] a thinker and investigator who knew how to stand alone and then drew many to him and with him, he went his way and penetrated to truths which seemed dangerous because they revealed what had been anxiously hidden, and illumined dark places. Far and wide he disclosed new problems and changed the old standards; in his seeking and perceiving he extended many times the field of mental research, and made even his opponents indebted to him through the creative stimulus they derived from him. Even should the future remould and modify one result or another of his researches, never again will the questions be stilled which Sigmund Freud put to mankind; his gains for knowledge cannot permanently be denied or obscured. The conceptions he built, the words he chose for them, have already entered the living language and are taken for granted. In all spheres of humane science, in the study of literature and art, in the evolution of religion and prehistory, mythology, folklore and pedagogics, and last not least in poetry itself his achievement has left a deep mark; and, we feel sure, if any deed of our race remains unforgotten it will be his deed of penetrating into the depths of the human mind.

"We, the undersigned, who cannot imagine our mental world without Freud's bold lifework, are happy to know that this great man with his unflagging energy is still among us and still working with undiminished strength. May our grateful feelings long accompany the man we venerate."

Among the many tributes in foreign periodicals was a striking one by Selma Lagerlöf, the distinguished Swedish writer. There were of course many personal callers. One of them, Elisabeth Rotten, asked Freud how he felt and received the answer "How a man of eighty feels is not a topic for conversation." [m]

At the same time Freud was made an Honorary Member of the American Psychiatric Association, the American Psychoanalytic Association, the French Psychoanalytical Society, the New York Neurological Society and the Royal Medico-Psychological Association. Above all there was the highest recognition he ever received and therefore the one he most treasured, the Corresponding Membership of the Royal Society. His name had been put forward by a distinguished physicist, an ex-patient of mine, and I remember Wilfred Trotter, who was then on the Council of the Society, telling me of the surprise it caused. They had all heard vaguely of Freud, though none of them were familiar with any of his work. But Trotter had a way of convincing any Committee.

No university, however, bestowed an honorary degree on Freud; the only one he received in his life had been awarded by Clark University, Massachusetts, nearly thirty years before.[49]

Having disposed of this troublesome but memorable birthday we may resume our narration of earlier minor events. At the turn of the year Arnold Zweig related an exciting story Professor Smith, an Ameri-

[m] *Das Befinden eines 80 jährigen ist kein Gesprächsthema.*

can working at the University of Chicago Oriental Institute in Luxor, had told a friend of Zweig's, Dr. Jizschaki: in the correspondence they had found in the excavations at Tell el-Amarna—the center of the Aten cult—there were tablets giving a list of the pupils of the Re-Aten temple in Heliopolis, and that among these were two names which could only be interpreted as Moses and Aaron; the tablets had been presented to the Vatican. All this seemed an astonishing confirmation of Freud's thory that Moses had acquired the monotheistic Aten religion in Egypt and then passed it on to the Jews. Freud, however, was more cautious. He pointed out that cuneiform tablets were used in ancient Egypt only for foreign correspondence and that a temple list should be on papyrus.[50] So they decided to await further information.

In January Nemon, the Jugoslav sculptor who had made a bust of Freud some five years previously, now made a new and better full length statue. It now stands in the New York Institute. In the same month Freud sent a telegram to Romain Rolland congratulating him on his seventieth birthday, and contributed in his honor a fascinating little analysis of a curious experience he had had in Athens in 1904.[51] Freud remarked that Rolland was exactly the same age as his brother Alexander, with whom he had had the experience in Athens, so perhaps it was this association that gave him the idea of describing it for Rolland's benefit.[52]

Marie Bonaparte on a recent visit to Stockholm had tried in vain to interest the authorities there in procuring a Nobel Prize for Freud, and on returning home incited Thomas Mann and Romain Rolland in the same cause. Freud reproved her for wasting time in such a hopeless endeavor.[53] A couple of months later an ambiguous passage in a newspaper article by Stefan Zweig produced many rumors about the same topic which considerably annoyed Freud.[54]

Stefan Zweig had in the same article referred to a work Freud was writing on religion, so, not having heard about it, I inquired if there was any truth in the story. Here is Freud's reply. "What he said about my preparing a work on the history of religion has some truth in it. Last year I wrote a book "The man Moses, an historical novel," and the last time (Stefan) Zweig visited me I told him about it. But the title itself shows why I have not published it and shall not do so. The necessary historical evidence for my theory is lacking, and since my results, which contain a refutation of the Jewish national mythology, seem to me to be very important, I am not inclined to submit it to the easy criticism of opponents. The book would create a considerable sensation and I am not in a position to guarantee the trustworthiness of its pre-suppositions. Only a few people, Anna, Martin, Kris, have read the thing." [55]

In May Freud and Lou Salomé exchanged letters for the last time, thus closing a correspondence that had continued for twenty-four years. She died in the following February.

Freud was shocked and somewhat alarmed to hear that Arnold Zweig was proposing to write his biography. He firmly forbade him to, telling him he had far more useful things to write. Freud's views on biographical writing were certainly extreme, since he added: "Whoever undertakes to write a biography binds himself to lying, to concealment, to hypocrisy, to flummery and even to hiding his own lack of understanding, since biographical material is not to be had and if it were it could not be used. Truth is not accessible; mankind does not deserve it, and wasn't Prince Hamlet right when he asked who would escape a whipping if he had his deserts?" [56] And yet I continue with my task in the face of these terrible dicta; I feel sure that Freud would have been surprised to find that one could get nearer to the truth about himself than he imagined possible.

Hearing that Arnold Zweig was making a collection of coins, Freud sent him some rare gold ones from Cyprus out of his own collection, which was not a systematic one.[57]

Freud's sister-in-law, Minna Bernays, was operated on for glaucoma in both eyes about this time.[58] She was devoted to doing fine and beautiful needle work, so that the effect was specially distressing. The trouble continued for the rest of her life.

Alfred Adler had died suddenly in Aberdeen at the end of May, and Arnold Zweig had said he was very much moved at the news. Freud replied: "I don't understand your sympathy for Adler. For a Jew boy out of a Viennese suburb a death in Aberdeen is an unheard-of career in itself and a proof of how far he had got on. The world really rewarded him richly for his service in having contradicted psychoanalysis." [59]

In the same month Freud mentioned some local Viennese news. "That my chief enemy P. Schmidt has just been given the Austrian Award of Honor for Art and Science for his pious lies in ethnology I claim as *my* credit. Evidently he had to be consoled for Providence having let me reach the age of eighty. Fate has its own ways of making one altruistic. When my Master Ernst Brücke received this Award I became aware of the wish that I myself might sometime attain it. Today I contentedly resign myself to having indirectly helped someone else to do so." [60]

Freud was by now becoming surer that the future of Austria lay with the Nazis, though the people he specially had in mind were the Austrian Nazis whom he (wrongly) expected to be milder. So he commented "I am waiting with less and less regret for the curtain to fall for me." [61]

In July Freud underwent two exceptionally painful operations, and for the first time since the original one in 1923 unmistakable cancer was found to be present.[n] For the last five years the doctors had been warding it off by removing precancerous tissue, but from now on they knew they were face to face with the enemy itself and must expect constant recurrences of the malignancy.

The next event was the Marienbad Congress on August 2. The place was chosen so that Anna Freud should not be too far away from her father in case she was urgently needed. In my presidential address I described Czechoslovakia as an island of freedom surrounded by totalitarian states and made some remarks about the latter that got me on to the Nazi black list of those to be "liquidated" as soon as they invaded England. Eitingon visited Freud before the Congress—he had not been able to be present for his eightieth birthday—and I did so shortly after it; it was the last time I saw Freud until the emigration crisis eighteen months later. Arnold Zweig and Viktor Kraus were among the other visitors that summer, the former in August. On that occasion Freud presented Zweig with a seal ring, the only man to whom he gave one with the exception of his son Ernst and the members of the Committee. In July one of the latter, Hanns Sachs, had come from Boston to visit Freud in his garden in Grinzing, near to one in which Sachs had spent much of his youth. He presented Freud with a little Mayan household god carved in black stone, which he had brought himself from Guatemala.[62]

On September 13 Freud's golden wedding was quietly celebrated. Four of his surviving children were present, all except Oliver. To Marie Bonaparte he commented in a characteristically succinct understatement: "It was really not a bad solution of the marriage problem, and she is still today tender, healthy and active." [63] Freud stayed this summer in the same house in Grinzing as before, though not for so long a period.

[n] Pichler notes, July 17, 1936.

On December 20 Otto Loewi, Professor of physiological chemistry in Graz, visited Freud and gave him an account of the ceremony in Stockholm at which he had just received a Nobel Prize.

The turn of the year was another hard time for Freud, after Anna detected another suspicious spot which Pichler thought, wrongly as it turned out, to be carcinomatous. "On Saturday, Dec. 12, Pichler told me he was obliged to burn a new spot that seemed to him suspicious.[o] He did so and this time the microscopic examination showed only harmless tissue, but the reaction was frightful. Severe pain above all, then in the following days a badly locked mouth so that I could not eat anything and had great difficulty in drinking. I carry on with my analyses by changing a hot water bottle every half hour to hold by my cheek. I get slight relief from short wave therapy, but it does not last long. I am told I have to put up with this existence for another week.[p] I wish you could have seen what sympathy Jo-fi [q] shows me in my suffering, just as if she understood everything.

"Our Minister of Education has issued a formal announcement that the days of any scientific work without presuppositions, as in the Liberal era, are over; from now on science must work in unison with the Christian-German *Weltanschauung*. That promises me a good time! Just like in dear Germany!" [64]

The operation just mentioned was the only occasion in the long travail of those years when Freud, somewhat to Pichler's surprise, cried out "I can't go on any longer." But the surgeon's iron nerve enabled him to complete the operation, and that was the only protest.

Besides the congratulatory letters to Thomas Mann and Romain Rolland and the autobiographical supplement already mentioned, Freud published in this year only a short paper, "The Subtleties of a Faulty Action," [65] a delicate self-analysis concerning the present of a gem he was giving to Lou Andreas-Salomé. The letter to Romain Rolland, referred to above, turned into an interesting little essay, which was finished at the end of January, 1936. The title, "A Disturbance of Memory on the Acropolis," referred to a piece of self-analysis which illuminated some aspects of Freud's personality.

[o] This was only one of many such experiences at that time.
[p] It lasted, however, a good deal longer.
[q] The chow.

1937

This year was dominated by the waves of political unrest that increasingly threatened to engulf Austria and in the following spring did so.

In January Freud had another visit from Thomas Mann.

In that month he suffered a novel loss, that of the female dog to which he had been very attached for the past seven years. He used often to exchange confidences with Marie Bonaparte, another animal lover. Only a month ago, on December 6, he had written:

"*Meine liebe* Mane:

"Your card from Athens and the manuscript of the Topsy book[66] have just arrived. I love it; it is so movingly real and true. It is, of course, not an analytic work, but the analyst's search for truth and knowledge can be perceived behind this creation. It really gives the real reasons for the remarkable fact that one can love an animal like Topsy (or my Jo-fi) so deeply: affection without any ambivalence, the simplicity of life free from the conflicts of civilization that are so hard to endure, the beauty of an existence complete in itself. And in spite of the remoteness in the organic development there is nevertheless a feeling of close relationship, of undeniably belonging together. Often when I stroke Jo-fi I find myself humming a melody which, unmusical though I am, I can recognize as the (Octavio) aria from Don Juan:

> A bond of friendship
> binds us both, etc.

"When you at a youthful 54 cannot avoid often thinking of death you cannot be astonished that at the age of 80½ I fret whether I shall reach the age of my father and brother or further still into my mother's age, tormented on the one hand by the conflict between the wish for rest and the dread of fresh suffering that further life brings and on the other anticipation of the pain of separation from which I am still attached.

> "Warm greetings to you (and Topsy)
> "from your
> "Freud"

Jo-fi, however, had to be operated on because of two large ovarian cysts. It seemed successful, but two days later she suddenly died.

Freud then, feeling he could not get on without a dog, took back from Dorothy Burlingham another chow called Lün which he had had to transfer to her four years before on account of Jo-fi's jealousy.[67] During her absence on a holiday Dorothy Burlingham had asked Felix Deutsch to care for the dog, and he has related a curious episode on that occasion.[68] I quote his account: "This dog is a psychosomatic case, indeed! She supposedly had too narrow a pelvis for ever having puppies without danger to her life. For this reason, she had to be watched carefully whenever she was in heat. At those times Helene and I alternated in the anti-baby-sitting service. Once, on a Sunday, sitting in our garden with the dog, I fell asleep, and when I awakened the dog had disappeared. Frantically searching for her, I found her finally in the neighbor's garden with a beautiful male poodle. The chow looked very sheepish, but no real evidence of a love act could be established. Nothing could be done at the moment more than to wait and see. Several weeks went by without any change in her behavior. At the end of the second month, however, the teats began to swell and colostrum appeared. She began to get fat rapidly. When on the street, she scratched and dug holes in the ground, altogether unmistakable signs of pregnancy. I resigned myself to the inevitable, but nothing happened.

"On the contrary, in the fourth month, instead of increasing, these signs started to decrease. I rushed with the dog to the veterinarian. Diagnosis: Pseudocyesis. Have you ever heard of a dog with a false pregnancy? I am almost inclined to say: 'That can only happen to the dog of an analyst!' "

Freud also must have been amused at this example of the power of wish-fulfillment combined with the phenomenon of somatic compliancy.

Yet another event occurred in this same month which had important consequences later for our knowledge of Freud's personality and work. Marie Bonaparte had notified him that she had acquired his letters to Fliess. He replied immediately: "The affair of the Fliess correspondence has staggered me. After his death his widow asked me for his letters to me. I assented unconditionally, but could not find them. Whether I destroyed them or cleverly hid them away I still do not know. . . . Our correspondence was the most intimate you could imagine. It would have been most distressing had they fallen into strange hands. So it was extraordinarily kind of you to acquire them and guard them from all danger. I am only sorry about the expense it put you to. May I offer to pay half the cost of it? I should have had to buy them myself if the man had come to me directly. I should not like any of it to come to the knowledge of so-called posterity." [69] The subsequent fate of these important letters has already been described. [70]

Then there came Lou Andreas-Salomé's death. Freud had admired her greatly and been very fond of her, "curiously enough without a trace of sexual attraction." He described her as the only real bond between Nietzsche and himself. [71]

In March Freud was getting more concerned about the approach of Nazidom. "The political situation seems to be becoming ever more sombre. There is probably no holding up the Nazi invasion, with its baleful consequences for psycho-analysis as well as the rest. My only hope is that I shall not live to see it. It is a similar situation to that in 1681 when the Turks were besieging Vienna. That time a rescuing army came over the Kahlenberg, but today there is nothing of the sort to be expected. An Englishman[r] has already discovered that the frontier they have to defend is the Rhine. He should have said: at Vienna. If our town falls the Prussian barbarians will flood over Europe. Unfortunately the only protector we have had hitherto, Mussolini, seems now to be giving Germany a free hand. I should like to live in England like Ernst and to travel to Rome as you are doing." [72]

Arnold Zweig was planning to come to Europe again in the summer, and Freud warned him not to put off his visit any longer because his "hereditary claim to life would run out in November." By then Freud would be eighty and a half, the age at which both his father and his brother Emmanuel had died. It was the third date Freud had superstitiously imagined for his death. [73] (When it passed, however, he began to fear he would have to live as long as his mother —to the age of ninety-five!)

In the same letter Freud commented on the writer Schönherr having been given the Award for Art and Science, "the only honor I have ever really wished for." He added that Schönherr must be a clever writer since he had coined the word *"Dauerkältung"* [s] which exactly described his own condition. [74]

Edouard Pichon, a French analyst who happened to be Janet's son-in-law, wrote to Freud asking if Janet might call on him. This is Freud's comment to Marie Bonaparte: "No, I will not see Janet. I could not refrain from reproaching him with having behaved un-

[r] Stanley Baldwin in July, 1934.
[s] A condensation of the words for "continuous catarrh."

fairly to psychoanalysis and also to me personally and having never corrected it. He was stupid enough to say that the idea of a sexual etiology for the neuroses could only arise in the atmosphere of a town like Vienna. Then when the libel was spread by French writers that I had listened to his lectures and stolen his ideas he could with a word have put an end to such talk, since actually I never saw him or heard his name in the Charcot time: he has never spoken this word. You can get an idea of his scientific level from his utterance that the unconscious is *une façon de parler.*[t] No, I will not see him. I thought at first of sparing him the impoliteness by the excuse that I am not well or that I can no longer talk French and he certainly can't understand a word of German. But I have decided against that. There is no reason for making any sacrifice for him. Honesty the only possible thing; rudeness quite in order." [75]

Freud left Vienna for the same house in Grinzing on April 30, though on that day he was suffering from a bad attack of otitis. At the end of the month he was once more in the Sanatorium Auersperg for another of his numerous operations, this time with an intravenous injection of evipan.

May 6 passed off more quietly than usual. Freud told me he had decided he would have no more birthdays after the age of eighty.[76]

In August he had for three days a disagreeable attack of haematuria without any ascertainable cause. Freud was under the impression, ever since his visit to America in 1909, that he was afflicted with prostatitis,[77] but his medical reports do not confirm this. On the whole, however, both the summer and autumn passed off very tolerably and Freud got a good deal of enjoyment from his pleasant surroundings.

Freud had written to Otto Pötzl, then Professor of Psychiatry in Prague, on his sixtieth birthday, and here is the latter's reply, dated November 15.

"Hochverehrter Meister:

"On my sixtieth birthday the post brought me a letter of good wishes written by your own hand, a most kind remembrance. It was for me a joyful happening which moved me to the depths. It was the only thing that gave some value to an occurrence I had previously regarded as merely something unwished for: namely, the publishing of that date against my will, probably through an indiscretion of

[t] A form of speaking.

Kronfeld's (October calendar of the *Wiener Medizinische Wochenschrift*). Now that I possess your lines, however, I am happy at what this day has brought me.

"I cannot thank you without expressing my deep, unflagging and absolute respect for your personality and admiration for your work, feelings that always move me. I can only give expression to them in my lectures to students; even then not adequately, since to do so would need your mastery. My own researches, which I cannot boast of being more than an honest investigation of pathological data in the brain—the results of which are perhaps not worth the effort—have only brought me constantly to the borderland of psychoanalysis. The teaching I do, however, I cannot imagine without psychoanalysis; in it I and my audience are your enthusiastic followers!

"*In Verehrung und Ergebenheit*
"Otto Pötzl"

Then we have a letter, written in the same month, to Stefan Zweig.

"Wien. 17. XI. 1937

"*Lieber Herr Doktor:*
"It is hard for me to say whether your kind letter gave me more pleasure or pain. I suffer from the times we live in just as you do. The only consolation I find is in the feeling of belonging together with a few others, in the certainty that the same things remain precious to us, the same values incontestable. But I may in a friendly fashion envy you in that you can spring to the defense through your lovely work. May that succeed more and more! I am enjoying your *Magellan* in advance.

"My work lies behind me, as you say. No one can predict how later epochs will assess it. I myself am not so sure; doubt can never be divorced from research, and I have assuredly not dug up more than a fragment of truth. The immediate future seems dark, also for my psychoanalysis. In any event I shall not experience anything agreeable in the weeks or months I may still have to live.

"Quite against my intention I have got as far as complaining. What I wanted was to come nearer to you in a human manner, not to be admired as a rock in the sea against which the stormy waves break in vain. But even if my defiance remains silent, it is still defiance and *impavidum ferient ruinae.*[a]

* "The falling ruins will leave him undismayed." (Horace)

"I hope you will not keep me too long from the reading of your next, beautiful and courageous books.

"*Mit herzlichen Grüssen*

"*Ihr alter*

"Sig. Freud"

The preliminary essays on Moses had produced the wildest rumors in the press, such as that he had written two large books on the Bible.[78] At the end of the year he told Marie Bonaparte and Arnold Zweig that several American, "and even English," publishers had offered him terms for a psychoanalysis of the Bible, which caused him much amusement.[79] An echo of this odd rumor has recently been extended in a book on Freud and religion by Dr. Philp. There one may read that "For many years he had planned a vast work which would apply psychoanalytical theories to the whole of the Bible. *Moses and Monotheism* was the only part of it which he was able to complete." [80] This of course is pure fancy.

Freud managed to get some writing published in 1937 in spite of his distressing condition. There was a short obituary notice of Lou Andreas-Salomé,[81] and the essay for Romain Rolland's birthday mentioned above. There were two short but important clinical papers which will be discussed later. At the beginning of February he had told Eitingon that he was writing a technical paper, evidently the one published in June under the title "Analysis Terminable and Interminable." [82] The other appeared in December: "Constructions in Analysis." [83]

Freud in this year also made several attempts at rewriting the third part of what became his book on Moses. In August he said he had finished Moses II two days ago and had put it aside;[84] it was, however, published at the end of the year. A couple of weeks later he announced that he was rewriting Moses III, but only very slowly. He found it too difficult, would probably not finish it and in any event would not publish it.[85] The rewriting made . . . little progress, and the reason Freud gave for this throws an interesting light on his need for complete freedom and independence. "I am so little used to concealing my ideas and taking into account various foreign considerations (e.g. political ones) that I do not seem to get over the conflict. The grandiose nature of the perception that religion contains an *historical* truth continues to fascinate me, but the impetus to present it to others is paralyzed." [86] The first two sections, "Moses an Egyptian" and "If Moses was an Egyptian," [87] appeared in this year in the first and fourth number respectively of *Imago*. They will be reviewed in connection with the book as a whole.

1938

The first couple of months of this year were filled with the apprehension of a Nazi invasion of Austria, which indeed came about in March. Like so many Austrian Jews Freud had hoped against hope till the last minute that Schuschnigg might conjure up some device for warding off the danger.[88] As late as February he wrote to Eitingon: "Our brave, and in its way honest, Government is at present more energetic in defending us against the Nazis than ever, although in view of the newest events in Germany no one can be sure what the outcome will be. . . . One cannot avoid occasionally thinking of Meister Anton's closing words in one of Hebbel's dramas: 'I no longer understand this world.' [89] Have you read that Jews in Germany are forbidden to give their children German names? They can only reply with the demand that the Nazis renounce the use of the popular names Johann, Josef and Marie." [90]

In January Freud underwent one of the operations that had now become almost regular, and this time the microscopic findings were more than suspicious. But twelve days later he had resumed his analytic work.

Writing of the Nazi attacks towards the end of February he said: "It undeniably looks like the beginning of the end for me. But we have no other choice than to hold out here. Will it still be possible to find safety in the shelter of the Catholic Church? Quien sabe?" [91]

6

London—The End

1938

THE NAZI INVASION OF AUSTRIA, WHICH TOOK PLACE ON MARCH 11, 1938, was the signal for Freud's leaving his home for a foreign land, thus following the road his ancestors had so often wearily trod. But this time it was to a land where he was more welcome than in any other. On many occasions in his life he had debated taking such a step, and on many others he had been invited to do so. But something deep in his nature had always striven against such a decision and even at this final and critical moment he was still most unwilling to contemplate it.

Knowing how strong was this reluctance, and how often in the last few years he had expressed his determination to stay in Vienna to the end, I was not very hopeful about the outcome. But a couple of days after the invasion I had a telephone talk with Dorothy Burlingham, who was by now almost one of the Freud family, and three with Marie Bonaparte in Paris, so I decided to make a final effort to persuade Freud to change his mind. There were no airplanes flying to Vienna just then, but I got one on March 15 as far as Prague and there found a small monoplane that completed the journey. The sight on arriving was depressing enough. The airfield was stacked with German military planes and the air was full of them assiduously intimidating the Viennese. The streets were full of roaring tanks and also of roaring people with their shouts of "Heil Hitler," but it was easy to see that most of these were imported Germans from the trainloads Hitler had sent in for the purpose. After calling at my sister-in-law's where Anna Freud got into touch with me I went first, on her advice, to the premises of the *Verlag* where we hoped that my asserting its international character might be of use. The stairs and rooms were occupied by villainous-looking youths armed with daggers and pistols, Martin Freud was sitting in a corner under arrest, and the Nazi "authorities" were engaged in counting the petty cash in a drawer. As soon as I spoke I was also put under arrest, and the remarks made when I asked to be allowed to communicate with the British Embassy (to which I had special introductions) showed me how low my country's prestige had fallen after Hitler's successes. After an hour, however, I was released and then made my way down the street to Freud's residence.

In the meantime a curious scene had been taking place there. It had been invaded by a similar gang of the S.A., and two or three of them had forced their way into the dining room. Mrs. Freud, as people do in an emergency, had responded to the occasion with the essence of her personality. In her most hospitable manner she invited the sentry at the door to be seated; as she said afterward, she found it unpleasant to see a stranger standing up in her home. This caused some embarrassment which was heightened by her next move. Fetching the household money she placed it on the table with the words, so familiar to her at the dinner table, "Won't the gentlemen help themselves?" Anna Freud then escorted them to the safe in another room and opened it. The loot amounted to 6,000 Austrian Schillings (about $840.00), and Freud ruefully commented on hearing of it later that *he* had never been paid so much for a single visit. They were debating their prospects of continuing their career of petty burglary when a frail and gaunt figure appeared in the doorway. It was Freud, aroused by the disturbance. He had a way of frowning with blazing eyes that any old Testament prophet might have envied, and the effect produced by his lowering mien completed the visitors' discomfiture. Saying they would call another day, they hastily took their departure. (On their return to headquarters, however, they were reprimanded for their pusillanimity and a week later the Gestapo came and made a thorough search of the rooms, allegedly seeking for political anti-Nazi documents; significantly enough, however, they did not enter Freud's own rooms. When they departed they took Anna Freud away with them.)

Immediately after this I had a heart to heart talk with Freud. As I had feared, he was bent on staying in Vienna. To my first plea, that he was not alone in the world and that his life was dear to many people, he replied with a sigh: "Alone. Ah, if I were only alone I should long ago have done with life." But he had to admit the force of what I had said and then proceeded to argue that he was too weak to travel anywhere; he could not even climb up to a compartment, as one has to with Continental trains. This not being accepted, he pointed out that no country would allow him to enter. There was certainly force in this argument; it is hardly possible nowadays for people to understand how ferociously inhospitable every country was to would-be immigrants, so strong was the feeling about unemployment. France was the only country that would admit foreigners with any measure of freedom, but on condition that they did not earn a living there; they were welcome to starve in France if they wished. I could only ask Freud to allow me on my return to England to see if an exception could not possibly be made in his case. Then came his last declaration. He could not leave his native land; it would be like a soldier deserting his post. I have already related how I successfully countered this attitude by quoting the analogy of Lightoller, the second officer of the Titanic who never left his ship but whom his ship left; and this won his final acceptance.[1]

That was the first hurdle, and possibly the hardest. The second one, that of obtaining permission to live in England, I felt pretty hopeful about, and, as events proved, rightly so. The third one, persuading the Nazis to release Freud, I could do nothing about, but great men often have more friends, even in high places, than they know of. W. C. Bullitt, then American Ambassador in France, was a personal friend of President Roosevelt, and he immediately cabled to him asking him to intervene. The President of the United States, with his responsible position in the world, has to think twice before interfering in the internal affairs of another country, but Roosevelt got his Secretary of State to send instructions to his Chargé d'Affaires in Vienna, Mr. Wiley, to do all he could in the matter, and this Wiley within the limits of his powers conscientiously did. M. Schabad has stated that Roosevelt also asked the German Ambassador in Washington to call on him and explained the importance of treating Freud well.[2] It is possible, however, that this story may have been derived from Bullitt's similar action in Paris. For Bullitt was not content. He called on Graf von Welczeck, the German Ambassador to France, and let him know in no uncertain terms what a world scandal would ensue if the Nazis ill-treated Freud. Welczeck, being an Austrian man of culture and a humanitarian, needed no persuading, and at once took steps to bring the matter before the highest Nazi authorities.

Then Edoardo Weiss, who was at the time in near contact with the

Duce, tells me that Mussolini also made a *démarche*, either directly to Hitler or to his Ambassador in Vienna. Probably he remembered the compliment Freud had paid him four years before.[a] This was at the moment when Hitler was feeling genuine gratitude towards Mussolini for the free hand he had been given in the seizure of Austria.

So between one thing and another the Nazis felt they dared not risk refusing Freud an exit permit, though they were determined to exact their pound of flesh first.

The few days I could spend in Vienna were hectic ones. I was constantly besieged with applications for help in getting from Austria to England, and naturally I was in no position to make any definite commitments of the kind. Apart from the problem of obtaining permits from the government I felt I should consult my own colleagues on their attitude toward admitting large numbers of Viennese analysts toward whom some British ones did not feel entirely friendly. Then Müller-Braunschweig, accompanied by a Nazi Commissar, arrived from Berlin with the purpose of liquidating the psychoanalytical situation. A meeting of the Board of the Vienna Society had, however, been held on March 13 at which it was decided that everyone should flee the country if possible, and that the seat of the Society should be wherever Freud would settle. Freud commented: "After the destruction of the Temple in Jerusalem by Titus, Rabbi Jochanan ben Sakkai asked for permission to open a school at Jabneh for the study of the Torah.[b] We are going to do the same. We are, after all, used to persecution by our history, tradition and some of us by personal experience," adding laughingly and pointing at Richard Sterba, "with one exception." Sterba, however, decided to share the fate of his Jewish colleagues and left for Switzerland [c] two days later; he sternly refused the blandishments of the German analysts to return and become Director of the Vienna Institute and Clinic. So there was not even a rump for the Germans to take over and they had to be content with seizing the library of the Society, not to mention the whole property of the *Verlag*. The thin excuse for the latter theft, by the way, was that it supported an anti-Nazi political party; on my inquiring what this could have meant, if anything, Martin Freud told me he had been in the habit of transmitting Freud annual subscription to the B'nai B'Brith Jewish lodge.

On March 17 Marie Bonaparte arrived from Paris and I felt

[a] See p. 180.
[b] This remark may also be found in Freud's *Moses and Monotheism*.[*]
[c] Not Italy, as I had written in a previous allusion.[*]

easier about leaving Vienna for the urgent task of seeking permits in England. The Home Secretary at that time was Sir Samuel Hoare (now Lord Templewood), whom I knew slightly through belonging to the same private skating club; that was why I referred to him in my letters to Vienna, which had to be disguised, as "my skating friend." But in such a critical matter it was desirable to procure all support available, and the weightiest seemed to be that of the Royal Society, which had honored Freud only two years before; on the rare occasions when they intervene in social or political affairs they are listened to with peculiar respect. So my first act on reaching London on March 22 was to obtain from Wilfred Trotter, who was on the Council of the Society, a letter of introduction to Sir William Bragg, the famous physicist who was then the President of the Royal Society. I saw him the next day and he at once gave me a letter to the Home Secretary. I was taken aback at discovering, though not for the first time, how naïve in worldly matters a distinguished scientist can be. He asked me: "Do you really think the Germans are unkind to the Jews?" He was shocked when I described to him the bodily marks I had seen on friends who had got away from concentration camps, but I daresay the impression I made was soon blotted out.

Then came the Home Office. To my great relief, but not to my surprise, Sir Samuel Hoare without any hesitation displayed his usual philanthropic qualities and gave me carte blanche to fill in permits, including permission to work, for Freud, his family, servants, his personal doctors, and a certain number of his pupils with their families. Refugees at that time were otherwise less lucky; they had to find someone willing to guarantee their support, and they were seldom granted permission to work for a living.

Thus one of the difficulties was easily overcome, though there remained the greater one—obtaining permission from the Nazis to leave. There followed nearly three months of anxious waiting, even more anxious of course for those waiting in Vienna. Freud employed a friendly lawyer, Dr. Indra, who did everything possible. By good luck the Commissar, Dr. Sauerwald, a fervent anti-Semitic Nazi appointed by the Nazis to supervise the arrangements, including the complicated financial ones, proved also to be helpful, and for a curious reason. He had studied chemistry at the University under Professor Herzig, one of Freud's lifelong Jewish friends,[5] and had conceived a great respect and affection for him. This, so he said, he had now extended to Freud. Thus, when Martin Freud was at the last moment prevented from tearing up Freud's will, it was discovered that it contained a reference to money Freud kept abroad. Sauerwald, at great risk to himself, suppressed this fact until Freud was out of the country and his belongings despatched; after that Freud could safely refuse the Nazis' request for the money to be handed over to them.

Marie Bonaparte had come to Vienna on March 17 and stayed until April 10; she returned on April 29, leaving again for Paris on May 4. She and Anna Freud went through all Freud's papers and correspondence, burning masses of what they considered not worth taking to London. Before they would grant the necessary *Unbedenklichkeitserklärung* (!) the Nazi authorities demanded large sums of money under imaginary captions of income tax, *Reichsfluchtsteuer,*[a] and so on, which it was difficult for Freud to pay. But they threatened, if he did not, to confiscate his library and collection. So Marie Bonaparte advanced some Austrian Schillings for the purpose. He repaid this to her in the following summer after arriving in England —the sum of which amounted to 12,000 Dutch Gulden ($4,824.00)— and she then devoted it to the cost of reproducing the *Gesammelte Werke* in London to replace those destroyed by the Nazis.

The inquisition proceeded in great detail. When, for instance, the Nazis found that Martin Freud had for safety been keeping a store of the *Gesammelte Schriften* in a neutral country, Switzerland, they insisted that he and his father issue instructions for them to be brought back to Vienna, where they were more or less ceremoniously burned. Of course Freud's bank account was confiscated.

The American Chargé d'Affaires, Mr. Wiley, kept a watchful eye on what was happening. He called on Freud on the evening of the first Nazi raid described above, and on the occasion of Anna Freud's arrest he intervened by telephone with some success. A member of the American Legation traveled with Freud on his journey from Vienna to Paris. Again we do not know whether this was accidental or official, but he did all he could to secure their comfort on the journey.

Martin Freud was frequently called to the Gestapo headquarters for questioning, but was never detained overnight. More serious was the dreadful day when Anna Freud was arrested by the Gestapo and detained for the whole day. It was certainly the blackest day in Freud's life. The thought that the most precious being in the world, and also the one on whom he so depended, might be in danger of being tortured and deported to a concentration camp, as so

[a] Fugitive tax.

commonly happened, was hardly to be borne. Freud spent the whole day pacing up and down and smoking an endless series of cigars to deaden his emotions. When she returned at seven o'clock that evening they were no longer to be restrained. In his diary for that day, however, March 22, there is only the laconic entry "Anna bei Gestapo."

There had grown up in these years a quite peculiarly intimate relationship between father and daughter. Both were very averse to anything at all resembling sentimentality and were equally undemonstrative in matters of affection. It was a deep silent understanding and sympathy that reigned between them. The mutual understanding must have been something extraordinary, a silent communication almost telepathic in quality where the deepest thoughts and feelings could be conveyed by a faint gesture. The daughter's devotion was as absolute as the father's appreciation of it and the gratitude it evoked.

There were many ways of killing the weary time of waiting. Freud went through his books, selected those he wished to take to London and disposed of the ones he no longer wanted. The latter were found a few years ago in a bookshop and the New York Society acquired them to add to their library. Freud carefully studied the map of London and read guide books about it. He and Anna completed the translation of Marie Bonaparte's book, Topsy, which Anna had begun some eighteen months before; it was finished on April 9. Freud entered fully into the spirit of the book—a fondness for chows was one of the many links between him and the author—and liked it greatly. Then Anna Freud translated a book called The Unconscious by Israel Berlin, and Freud himself translated the chapter on Samuel Butler. This was the first work of the kind Freud had done since his translations of Charcot and Bernheim so long ago. Then there was still correspondence. The day after my departure he wrote to Arnold Zweig about his uncertain future. The necessary conditions did not exist for moving to another country, it was unlikely he could rent the house in Grinzing again, and where should he spend the summer? There was also the news about his sister-in-law having just undergone an operation for cataract.[6] To me he wrote:

"Two letters from you, to Anna and myself, arrived today. They are so refreshingly kind [e] that I am moved to write to you at once without any external occasion but from an inner impulse.

[e] liebenswürdig.

"I am sometimes perturbed by the idea that you might think we believe you are simply wishing to do your duty, without our appreciating the deep and sincere feelings expressed in your actions. I assure you this is not so, that we recognize your friendliness, count on it and fully reciprocate it. This is a solitary expression of my feelings, for between beloved friends much should be obvious and remain unexpressed.

. . . "I also work for an hour a day at my Moses, which torments me like a 'ghost not laid.' I wonder if I shall ever complete this third part despite all the outer and inner difficulties. At present I cannot believe it. But quien sabe?" [7]

In May, when the chances of obtaining an exit permit were getting more hopeful, Freud wrote to his son Ernst in London:

"In these dark days there are two prospects to cheer us: to rejoin you all and—to die in freedom.[f] I sometimes compare myself with the old Jacob whom in his old age his children brought to Egypt. It is to be hoped that the result will not be the same, an exodus from Egypt. It is time for Ahasverus [g] to come to rest somewhere.

"How far we old people will succeed in coping with the difficulties of the new home remains to be seen. You will help us in that. Nothing counts compared with the deliverance. Anna will assuredly find it easy, and that is decisive, for the whole undertaking would have had no sense for the three of us between 73 and 82.

"If I were to come as a rich man I should start making a new collection. As it is I shall have to be content with the two little pieces the Princess rescued on her first visit, together with those she bought during her stay in Athens and is keeping for me in Paris. How much of my own collection I can get sent on is quite uncertain. It rather reminds one of the story about saving a birdcage from a house on fire." [8]

The first member of the family to be allowed to travel was Minna Bernays, whom Dorothy Burlingham fetched from the sanatorium and escorted to London; they left Vienna on May 5. Freud's eldest son, Martin (whose wife and children were already in Paris) and daughter, Mathilde Hollitscher (with her husband), both managed

[f] These last words were written in English.
[g] The wandering Jew.

to get away before their parents. The former reached London on May 16 and the latter on May 26. Mathilde did the housekeeping in the first house Freud occupied in London, after which she and her husband rented a flat for themselves.

Freud retained his ironic attitude toward the complicated formalities that had to be gone through. One of the conditions for being granted an exit visa was that he sign a document that ran as follows: "I Prof. Freud, hereby confirm that after the Anschluss of Austria to the German Reich I have been treated by the German authorities and particularly by the Gestapo with all the respect and consideration due to my scientific reputation, that I could live and work in full freedom, that I could continue to pursue my activities in every way I desired, that I found full support from all concerned in this respect, and that I have not the slightest reason for any complaint." [9] When the Nazi Commissar brought it along Freud had of course no compunction in signing it, but he asked if he might be allowed to add a sentence, which was: "I can heartily recommend the Gestapo to anyone."

Again when Indra took a photograph of him Freud's comment was: "It is one of my best likenesses. The Nazis will be very much obliged to you, for now they will be sure it is me when they hang it in the Hall dedicated in honor of their scholars."

Even in these anxious times Freud's thoughtfulness for other people did not desert him. When Hanna Breuer, the widow of Robert Breuer, Josef Breuer's eldest son, approached him with a request for help in emigrating he at once asked her daughter, Marie, to come to see him. He was extremely kind to her and he got Brill to issue to the family the necessary American affidavits. They spent five months in England on their way, and when Freud heard this he again asked them to visit him (in October, 1938), although at that time he could speak only with the greatest difficulty.[10] He inquired with the greatest solicitude, however, about the other members of the family and spoke of his early memories of them.

The anxious waiting came to an end at last and on June 4, armed with all the necessary documents and exit permits, Freud, with his wife and daughter, took a final leave of the city where he had dwelt for seventy-nine years and to which he had felt so bound. With them were two maid servants. One was Paula Fichtl, a remarkable personality who has sustained the family economy ever since.

Here the story of Freud's long years in Vienna comes to a close. But it is worth recording that on May 6, 1954, the World Organization for Mental Health affixed a tablet on the door at 19 Berggasse bearing the inscription:

HERE LIVED AND WORKED PROFESSOR SIGMUND FREUD
IN THE YEARS 1891-1938. THE CREATOR AND
FOUNDER OF PSYCHO-ANALYSIS.

During the Vienna Festival week in 1955 the tenants of the Sigmund Freud Hof, the block which the Municipality had named after him in 1949, held a special commemorative festivity in his honor on June 4. So his memory was not entirely forgotten in Vienna.

The Königsberger bust I had presented to the University of Vienna was unveiled on February 4, 1955, thus fulfilling an eighty-year-old dream of Freud's.[11]

On May 6, 1931, in Freud's lifetime, therefore, a tablet had been affixed to the house in Freiberg where he was born, and on May 6, 1956, I unveiled one, provided by the London County Council, on the house where he died in Maresfield Gardens. Thus tablets now exist on the three chief houses in which Freud had resided. The one where he spent his early married years, the *Sühnhaus* in Vienna, was destroyed during the second World War.

At three o'clock the next morning they crossed the frontier into France at Kehl on the Orient Express and breathed a sigh of relief at the thought that they should never have to see another Nazi. Dr. Schur, Freud's physician, had been prevented from accompanying them by an untoward attack of appendicitis, but Dr. Josephine Stross, a friend of Anna's, made an excellent substitute for him on the tiring journey. They were met in Paris by Marie Bonaparte, Ambassador Bullitt, Harry Freud who was staying in Paris, and Ernst Freud who had crossed over to Paris so as to accompany them on the last stage of their journey. They spent twelve wonderful hours in Marie Bonaparte's beautiful and hospitable home, and she informed Freud that his gold was safe. Having passed through the miserable experience of a total inflation in which the value of a currency entirely vanished, Freud had wisely preserved an amount of gold money as a guard against any future disaster. Marie Bonaparte could not safely take it out of the country, so she got the Greek Embassy in Vienna to despatch it by courier to the King of Greece, who a little later transferred it to the Greek Embassy in London. Freud wrote to her soon after his Paris visit: "The one day in your house in Paris restored our good mood and sense of dignity; after being surrounded by love for twelve hours we left proud and rich under the protection of Athene." [12] (Athene was a statuette on Freud's desk which Marie Bonaparte had smuggled to Paris and restored to him there.)

They crossed by night on the ferryboat to Dover, and since Lord De La Warr, then Lord Privy Seal, had arranged that they be accorded diplomatic privileges none of their luggage was examined there or in London. He also arranged with the railway authorities that the train to Victoria should arrive at an unusual platform so as to circumvent the battery of cameras and the huge crowd of welcoming or curious visitors. They were greeted and bade welcome by the Superintendent of the Southern Railway and the Station Master of Victoria. Freud's eldest children Mathilde and Martin, and of course my wife and myself, were waiting, and the reunion was a moving scene. We made a quick get-away in my car, and it was some time before the newspaper reporters caught up with us; Ernst and Anna remained behind to collect the extensive luggage. I drove past Buckingham Palace and Burlington House to Piccadilly Circus and up Regent Street, Freud eagerly identifying each landmark and pointing it out to his wife. The first stop was at 39, Elsworthy Road, where Ernst Freud had rented a house while he was searching for a permanent home.

The mythopoeic faculty of the surrounding world, always so busy with Freud's personality—it has certainly not ceased with his death—pursued him to London. There is a story that a visitor to Elsworthy Road was distressed at witnessing a scene between him and his wife. It was a Friday evening and Mrs. Freud was supposed therefore to be lighting the ritual candle. Freud blew it out every time she lit it until at last she cried. This is one of the myths without even a nucleus of truth; there never were such candles, and Freud's unsurpassable tenderness towards his wife was never marred in the fifty-three years of their married life.

Freud's heart had stood the journey better than he expected, though it had needed several doses of nitroglycerine and strychnine to carry him through.

During the night journey from Paris to London he dreamed that he was landing at Pevensey. When he related this to his son he had to explain that Pevensey was where William the Conqueror had landed in 1066. That does not sound like a depressed refugee, and indeed it foreshadowed the almost royal honors with which he was greeted in England.

Freud rallied well from the strain of the journey and was soon able to stroll in the garden for short spells. This garden abutted on Primrose Hill with Regent's Park beyond and a distant view of the City. On his first stroll into the garden on arriving Freud threw up his arms and made the famous remark to me: "I am almost tempted to cry out 'Heil Hitler.' " The change to this pleasant prospect from his confinement to his flat in Vienna during the long winter and spring cheered him enormously, and he had moments of great happiness. This was added to by the truly remarkable evidences of the welcome with which he was received in England, no doubt somewhat to his surprise. This is what he wrote two days after his arrival: "Here there is enough to write about, most of it pleasant, some very pleasant. The reception in Victoria Station and then in the newspapers of these first two days was most kind, indeed enthusiastic. We are buried in flowers. Interesting letters came: only three collectors of autographs, a painter who wants to make a portrait when I have rested, etc. . . . Then greetings from most of the members of the English group, some scientists and Jewish societies; the *piece de resistance* was a lengthy telegram of four pages from Cleveland signed by 'the citizens of all faiths and professions,' a highly respectful invitation, with all kinds of promises, for us to make our home there. (We shall have to answer that we have already unpacked!) Finally, and this is something special for England, numerous letters from strangers who only wish to say how happy they are that we have come to England and that we are in safety and peace. Really as if our concern were theirs as well. I could write like this for hours without exhausting what there is to say." [13]

The newspapers were for a few days full of photographs and friendly accounts of Freud's arrival, and the medical journals published short leading articles expressing welcome. The *Lancet* wrote: "His teachings have in their time aroused controversy more acute and antagonism more bitter than any since the days of Darwin. Now, in his old age, there are few psychologists of any school who do not admit their debt to him. Some of the conceptions he formulated clearly for the first time have crept into current philosophy against the stream of wilful incredulity which he himself recognised as man's natural reaction to unbearable truth." [14] *The British Medical Journal* said: "The medical profession of Great Britain will feel proud that their country has offered an asylum to Professor Freud, and that he has chosen it as his new home." [15]

There were even gifts of valuable antiques from people who

evidently shared Freud's uncertainty about getting his collection sent from Vienna. Taxi drivers knew where he lived, and the bank manager greeted him with the remark "I know all about you."

And yet it was not entirely unmixed happiness. Apart from his concern at Minna's grave condition and at the state of his own heart, there were other emotions to move him. On the very day he arrived in London he wrote to Eitingon: "The feeling of triumph at being freed is too strongly mingled with grief, since I always greatly loved the prison from which I have been released." [16] But his son Ernst was really "what we have always called him—a tower of strength."

That the conflicting emotions about Vienna persisted was shown by a curious occurrence a year later. In May, 1939, Indra called on Freud on his way home from America to Austria. On saying good-by Freud said: "So you are going back to—I can't recall the name of the city!" [17] Indra, not being familiar with Freud's special type of humor, took this literally as an act of forgetfulness, but I have no doubt that Freud deliberately intended the pretended amnesia to convey his struggle to forget Vienna. It was probably an allusion to the Jewish curse "let him be forgotten" [h] so terribly described by Heine.

The remark to Eitingon about loving Vienna is very noteworthy, since it is, as far as I know, the only occasion in his life when he admitted this sentiment. There are, on the contrary, endless allusions to his intense dislike of Vienna.[18] The deep love which was kept so hidden must be the explanation for his persistent refusal to contemplate leaving. It was the kind of emotion that Freud was most shy of displaying, and doubtless there were profound motives for his attitude deriving from his childhood.

Marie Bonaparte paid several visits to Freud in this year. She was in London, from June 23 to June 26, August 6-7, and again from October 29 to November 2.

Minna Bernays had already arrived in London, but she was seriously ill and was confined to bed on the first floor where Freud was unable to visit her because of the stairs. Not long after she was taken to a nursing home.

Freud also greatly missed the constant companionship of his chow, Lün. Because of the strict British regulations against rabies she was placed in quarantine for six months in Ladbroke Grove in the west of London. Freud visited her there four days after his arrival in

[h] *Nicht gedacht soll seiner werden.*

London and on several other occasions. As a substitute during this time of privation Freud was given a little Pekinese called Jumbo, but Jumbo, following the habits of his species, attached himself almost exclusively to Paula, the provider of nourishment.

Not having any prospect of maintaining them in London, Freud had had to leave his four old sisters, Rosa Graf, Dolfi Freud, Marie Freud and Paula Winternitz, in Vienna, but when the Nazi danger drew near he and his brother Alexander gave them the sum of 160,000 Austrian Schillings (about $22,400.00) which would suffice for their old age, provided that the Nazis did not confiscate it. Toward the end of the year Marie Bonaparte endeavored to bring them into France, but she failed to get permission from the French authorities. Freud had no special reason to be anxious about their welfare, since the persecution of the Jews was still in an early stage. So fortunately he never knew of their fate; they were incinerated some five years later.

The family, which included also the two Hollitschers, could not stay long in the house they had rented temporarily, so they had to disperse to other quarters. Freud with his wife and daughter went to the Esplanade Hotel in Warrington Crescent on September 3, intending to stay until their home was ready. But a serious complication had arisen in the meantime. In the middle of August a new suspicious spot was discovered in the scar, and Schur suggested fetching Pichler from Vienna. Freud was against this, and they consulted George G. Exner, a former assistant of Pichler's now in London, and a radiologist, Gotthold Schwarz, who advised the painful treatment of diathermy. For a while, however, Freud felt better, and he even allowed himself to be modeled by Ivelli Levy, and photographed by Steinberger at Stefan Zweig's special request. He also continued to treat a few patients. His brother Alexander with his son Harry arrived in London on September 4, but they soon left for Canada.

A few days before leaving Elsworthy Road Freud was told that although the suspicious spot in question had dissolved another had taken its place. Schur, Exner and a radium specialist, Carter Braine, agreed that a new operation was necessary and only four days after he had moved to the hotel Freud was transferred to a surgical Clinic. I visited him there that evening and for the first time saw him clean shaven, since they had decided to slit open the cheek to give better access to the trouble. Pichler had after all been fetched from Vienna and he performed the operation, which lasted two and a quarter hours, on the following morning, September 8; he returned to Vienna the next day. In a letter a month later Freud said it was the most severe operation since the original radical one in 1923. He said he was frightfully weak and tired still and found it hard to write or talk.[19] The doctors told him he should recover within six weeks, as soon as a sequestrum of bone came away. Three months later, however, this had not yet happened, and Freud began to think it was a fiction of the doctors invented to pacify him. Even by the end of November he had not been able to resume his favorite occupation of writing, except for a few letters.[20] He never really fully recovered from the effects of this severe operation and became more and more frail.

Mrs. Freud and the maid (Paula) were installed in the permanent home at 20, Maresfield Gardens on September 16. Freud and Anna joined them on September 27, and he was highly pleased with it. He said it was too good for someone who would not tenant it for long, but that it was really beautiful. He greatly enjoyed the pretty garden there although it had no distant prospect. It was a roomy garden behind the house, its beds and borders well stocked with flowers and shrubs; rows of high trees secluded it from neighboring houses. Freud spent as much time as possible in this garden, and he was provided with a comfortable swing lounge couch shaded by a canopy. His consulting room, filled with his loved possessions, opened through French windows directly into the garden—the very spot where a year later he died. His son Ernst had arranged all pictures and the cabinets of antiquities to the best possible advantage in a more spacious way than had been feasible in Vienna, and Paula's memory enabled her to replace the various objects on Freud's desk in their precise order, so that he felt at home the moment he sat at it on his arrival. The front of the house also had a small garden, visible from the other end of his room, and Freud was particularly fond of a superb almond tree which in the following April was covered with blossom. All his furniture, books and antiquities had arrived safely in London on August 15, and in his large consulting room, or study, everything was excellently arranged to display his beloved possessions to their best advantage: the house was more commodious than their apartment in Vienna, and Ernst had even managed to insert a lift in the most unlikely space.

There were of course a number of strange English customs to learn, which foreigners often find bewildering. Freud used to comment on these with interest, and he remarked that of his three women it was his wife who proved quickest at adaptation. Mrs.

Freud never looked back to Vienna, only forward to her new mode of life as if she were twenty-seven years old instead of seventy-seven. She insisted on continuing her Vienna custom of doing all the shopping herself, a habit she kept up till the very end of her long life, and she soon got on to friendly terms with the various shopkeepers. She evidently considered it one of her chief functions to provide a smooth and comfortable background for her distinguished husband, and she admirably succeeded in this throughout. She was at once a capable and considerate mistress of the house, a charming companion, and a most gracious hostess.

We may retrace our steps a little at this point. In May Hanns Sachs suggested that he found a periodical in America to be devoted to the non-medical applications of psychoanalysis, thus continuing the life of the *Imago* of which he had long been co-Editor; a sympathetic friend to psychoanalysis, Milton Starr, had guaranteed the financial basis of the undertaking. Freud favored the plan, but he had not yet become reconciled to the disappearance of his own periodicals in the German language. Indeed for a time a combined *Zeitschrift* and *Imago* was published in London, though it did not survive the opening of the next World War. So Freud was a little unwilling to part with the title *Imago*. He soon gave in on the point, however, and the *American Imago* was born and has proved to be one of the most valuable of the psychoanalytical periodicals.

The Nazi destruction of his beloved *Verlag* had been a blow to Freud, and as soon as he got to England he sought for means to restore it. Fortunately he came across a friendly, intelligent and enterprising publisher, John Rodker, who at once founded the Imago Publishing Company. It began operations by issuing the periodicals just mentioned and planned a new edition of Freud's collected works, the *Gesammelte Werke* to replace the *Gesammelte Schriften* destroyed by the Nazis; when complete they will run to eighteen volumes instead of the twelve of the latter. The title of this firm was another reason why Freud hesitated to let Sachs use the same word.

In his first month in England Freud occupied himself with correcting a series of lectures by Simmel, to the latter's great delight.[21] Later in the year Simmel was able to report the founding of a Sigmund Freud Clinic in Los Angeles.

Arnold Zweig had been making another of the vain attempts— the last of how many!—to procure a Nobel Prize for Freud, a proceeding the latter always deprecated as a waste of time. His reproof this time took the following form: "Don't let yourself get worked up over the Nobel chimera. It is only too certain that I shall not get any Nobel Prize. Psychoanalysis has several very good enemies among the authorities on whom the bestowal depends, and no one can expect of me that I hold out until they have changed their opinions or have died out. Therefore, although the money would be welcome after the way the Nazis bled me in Vienna and because of the poverty of my son and son-in-law, Anna and I have agreed that one is not bound to have everything, and have decided, I to renounce the prize and she the journey to Stockholm to fetch it. . . . To come back to the Nobel Prize: it can hardly be expected that the official circles could bring themselves to make such a provocative challenge to Nazi Germany as bestowing the honor on me would be." [22]

In the same letter Freud gave a little news about the Moses book. "I am at present enjoying writing the third part of the Moses. Just half an hour ago the post brought me a letter from a young American Jew imploring me not to deprive our poor unhappy people of the only consolation remaining to them in their misery. The letter was very well-meaning, but what an overestimation! Is it really credible that my dry essay, even were it to reach him, should disturb the belief of a single believer conditioned by heredity and upbringing?"

Among the callers in the early days may be mentioned Freud's nephew, Sam Freud, from Manchester (June 9), H. G. Wells (June 19), Professor Yahuda, the learned Jewish historian, who begged Freud not to publish his Moses book, Prince Loewenstein, Arnold Höllriegel, R. Bermann, Stefan Zweig, Professor Malinowski, the well-known anthropologist, and a specially welcome visitor, Chaim Weizmann, the famous Zionist leader, whom Freud held in the highest esteem. Malinowski informed Freud of a resolution of the Sociological Institute expressing a welcome to him that had been passed at a meeting on June 17.

Then on June 23 there was a very special visit, one previously only paid to the King himself. Three secretaries of the Royal Society, Sir Albert Seward, Professor A. V. Hill and Mr. Griffith Davies brought the official Charter Book of the Society for Freud to sign. It was a meeting he much enjoyed. They presented him with a copy of the great book which contains among others the signatures of Isaac Newton and Charles Darwin.

Then we may note a letter of welcome in September from a former friend, Wilhelm Stekel, who had just found refuge in England, where he later died. On July 19 Stefan Zweig brought

Salvador Dali to visit Freud, and the famous painter made a sketch
of him on the spot, maintaining that surrealistically Freud's cranium
was reminiscent of a snail! He described the visit later in his autobiography[23] and printed two pictures he had made of him. On the
following day Freud wrote to Stefan Zweig:

"20. 7. 1938

"*Lieber Herr Doktor.*

"I really owe you thanks for bringing yesterday's visitor. For until
now I have been inclined to regard the surrealists, who apparently
have adopted me as their patron saint, as complete fools (let us say
95%, as with alcohol). That young Spaniard, with his candid
fanatical eyes and his undeniable technical mastery, has changed
my estimate. It would indeed be very interesting to investigate
analytically how he came to create that picture.

"As to your other visitor, the candidate,[1] I feel like making it not
easy for him, so as to test the strength of his desire and to achieve a
greater measure of willing sacrifice. Psychoanalyis is like a woman
who wants to be won but knows that she is little valued if she offers
no resistance. If your J. spends too much time in reflecting he can
go to someone else later, to Jones or to my daughter.

"I am told you left some things behind on your departure, gloves,
etc. You know that signifies a promise to come again.

"*herzlich*

"*Ihr*

"Freud"

On November 19 Mrs. Knopf interviewed Freud about the arrangements for publishing his Moses book in America, but he refused to
accept various suggestions she made about modifying his conclusions.

One great wish of Freud's was destined never to be gratified: to
die a naturalized British subject. Commander Locker-Lampson raised
the question in the House of Commons, but the Government refused to shorten the normal waiting period, presumably lest it set a
troublesome precedent.

On August 1 the International Psychoanalytical Congress was held
in Paris; it was the last to be held for some years. It was on this
occasion that a sharp difference of opinion arose, essentially over
the question of lay analysis,[j] between the European and American

---

[1] The poet, Edward James.
[j] See pp. 295-96.

colleagues. A committee of each was formed to find a suitable solution of it. The European Committee met in Freud's presence at his house on December 4 when he stated his well-known views. It met again, also in Freud's presence, on July 20, 1939, though this time he was too ill to contribute much. Fortunately the whole problem was shelved by the coming war, since when the relations between the two continents have been excellent. This was the last Congress at which Eitingon was present; he crossed over to London to pay what was to prove his last visit to Freud, and then returned to Palestine. Anna Freud managed to leave her father to attend part of the Congress.

There is a noteworthy passage in a letter of August 20 to Marie Bonaparte. "Perhaps it will interest you to learn (and to see) that my handwriting has come back to what it used to be. For weeks it has been disturbed as the result of my last attack of urinary trouble which is now subsiding. There is an inner connection between urinating and writing, and assuredly not only with me. When I noticed the first signs of prostatic hypertrophy in the functioning of the bladder, in 1909 in New York, I suffered at the same time from writer's cramp, a condition foreign to me until then." [k]

In the autumn Freud had a visit from Arthur Koestler. Koestler has since published two accounts of this interview which contain some curious statements.[25] He described his acute feeling of bewilderment and apprehension on approaching the great man, and this no doubt accounts in part for the mistakes in what he thought he observed. Besides saying that Freud's study was upstairs instead of on the ground floor, he maintained that Freud apologized for his imperfect speech "because of this thing on my lip." There had never been anything wrong with his lip and Freud must have pointed toward his prosthesis which hampered him so much in talking. From this simple fact Koestler drew the far-fetched conclusion that Freud, the writer on taboos, had erected a strict taboo of his own according to which the word "cancer" was never to be uttered in his presence nor to be written in any letter. He even added the surprising remark: "The man who knew more than any other mortal about the ruses of self-deception had chosen to enter the darkness with a transparent veil over his eyes." This quite baseless conclusion is easy to refute with endless examples, of which I can even quote an amusing one. Freud once remarked jokingly to Marie Bonaparte that it was odd he

[k] Not quite accurate. In his letters of the eighteen-eighties Freud had mentioned similar attacks.[24]

should suffer from cancer since he was so fond of crabs.[1] The German word *Krebs* is used for both, and Freud was not always averse to punning.

Freud preserved his interest in the doings of the outer world. After the Munich crisis had subsided he commented: "The behavior everywhere during the days when war seemed imminent was masterly, and it is good to see how, now that they have got over the intoxication of peace, the people and Parliament have come to their senses and are willing to face painful truths. Naturally we too are grateful for the little bit of peace, but we cannot feel happy about it." [26] He evidently had no illusions about how long it would last.

On Freud's arrival in London the Committee of the Yiddish Scientific Institute, commonly known by the initials Y.I.V.O., expressed a wish to pay their respects to him;[m] he answered at once:

"June 8, 1938

"Dear Sirs:

"I was very glad to receive your greeting. You no doubt know that I gladly and proudly acknowledge my Jewishness though my attitude toward any religion, including ours, is critically negative.

"As soon as I recuperate to some extent from the recent events in Vienna and from tiredness after my strenuous journey I shall be glad to see you.

"devotedly yours
"Freud"

He made several attempts to arrange this interview, but it was not until November 7, 1938, that his health permitted it. Jacob Meitlis has published a full account of the meeting.[27] Freud spoke at length of his views on Moses and Monotheism and the warnings he had received from Jewish sources not to publish them. But to him the truth was sacred and he could not renounce his rights as a scientist to voice it. Soon after this he sent Dr. Meitlis a letter of recommendation to America. In another letter he wrote: "We Jews have always known how to respect spiritual values. We preserved our unity through ideas, and because of them we have survived to this day."

In the following August, a month before Freud died, he was invited to replace Dr. Moses Gaster, who had died, as President of

[1] On Feb. 1, 1926.

[m] He had been an Honorary President of the Vienna branch since

the London Y.I.V.O. This is his reply (in English), the only letter of the series not written in his own hand.

"August 19, 1939

"Dear Dr. Meitlis,

"The delay in answering your letter of the fifth of this month was occasioned by a serious cause. Even now I cannot say that I feel sufficiently better to be in a position to be utilized for any kind of work. The project discussed in the second part of your letter thus becomes impractical.

"Because of the active opposition which my book *Moses and Monotheism* evoked in Jewish circles I doubt whether it would be in the interests of Y.I.V.O. to bring my name before the public eye in such a capacity. I leave the decision to you.

"With highest regards
"your devoted
"Freud"

In the first week of December William Brown, the psychologist and psychotherapist, visited Freud, but on my advice Freud declined to do any analytic work with him.

Freud was still able to take an interest in reading. About this time he was strongly recommending some books to Marie Bonaparte. One was *Refugees: Anarchy or Organization*, 1938, by Dorothy Thompson.[28] Another was *Der Kaiser, die Weisen und der Tod* (The Kaiser, the Wisemen and Death), 1937, by Rachel Bardach Bardi.[29] The author was a refugee in London who had recently called on Freud and told him she was writing a second book. The book in question dealt with life at the Court of the Hohenstaufen Friedrich II, and Freud called it "a remarkably beautiful book steeped in analytical wisdom and of course with a true Jewish background."

By the end of the year Freud had so far recovered as to be able to conduct four analyses daily, and he continued to do so, with a few interruptions, until he was not far from the end. Even the English weather did not live up to its bad reputation that autumn and added to the warm welcome Freud had received. In November there was a June temperature of 68°, and I remember Freud in his garden saying with delight "it is just like May." In late December, however, it fell to 23°, and there was an old-fashioned "white" Christmas.

Sigmund Freud, *1922, age 66.*

Freud with Committee, Berlin, 1922. Back row, left to right: Otto Rank, Karl Abraham, Max Eitingon, Ernest Jones. Front row: Freud, Sandor Ferenczi, Hanns Sachs.

Photograph by Max Halberstadt

Freud with grandsons Heinerle and Ernstl, Hamburg, *1922*.

Freud with his grandson Stephen Gabriel, Berlin, 1922.

Freud with his daughter Anna, Tegelsee, 1929.

Freud in Berchtesgaden, 1929.

Photograph by Marie Bonaparte

Roof garden in Paris, June 5, 1938. Freud, his wife, and son Ernst.

Driving through London, June 6, 1938.

Arrival at Elsworthy Road, June 6, 1938.
Mathilde Hollitscher, Freud, Ernest Jones, Lucie Freud.

Reading manuscript of An Outline of Psychoanalysis, July, 1938.

Garden, 20 Maresfield Gardens.

Study, 20 Maresfield Gardens.

Freud with his wife, 1939.

Freud had managed to add the finishing touches to the third part of his Moses book before his operation, and it was printed in Amsterdam by August;[30] that German edition sold some 2,000 copies by the following summer.

The other production of those last years, *An Outline of Psycho-Analysis*,[31] was never completed. Freud had had the intention years ago of writing a short presentation of this kind, but when my little booklet, *Psycho-Analysis*, appeared in 1928 he was so pleased with it that he thanked me for saving him the trouble of writing a similar one. Now, however, he revived his intention, but principally for the purpose of occupying his spare time; there was always the itch to write. He began the book during the waiting time in Vienna, and by September had written sixty-three pages.[32] He kept saying how ashamed he felt in writing nothing but repetition without any new idea, and he hoped it would prove a still birth. It was in fact published in the *Zeitschrift* the year after his death. It consists of a valuable series of essays, of a quality far better than Freud had indicated.

There was another paper that also appeared the year after Freud's death: "Splitting of the Ego in the Process of Defence," [33] which had been written at Christmas, 1937. It is short but important. Freud maintained it was an error to regard the ego as a unitary synthesis; there were ways in which in early childhood a splitting of it could take place in regard to the attitude toward reality, and this splitting could deepen with the years. He related the fragment of a case history to illustrate how this can come about. I do not know why Freud never completed the little paper and never published it, but I surmise it was because some details of the case might reveal the identity of the patient, a well-known public figure.

Finally we may mention a little article Freud wrote in the autumn of 1938 entitled "A Word on Anti-Semitism." [34] Arthur Koestler says it was written at his request,[35] but I could find no confirmation of this. The essence of it was a long quotation from a Gentile writer who suggested that the typical attitude of those who protest against anti-Semitism is as follows: the Jews are an objectionable and inferior people, but our religion of love or our belief in humanism should prevent us from ill-treating them. The writer protested that this depreciatory judgment was very unfair and indeed one that itself originated in anti-Semitic feeling. Freud said he had been very impressed by the article and tried in vain to remember where he had read it; he had cut it out to keep some time before. Nor have our own researches succeeded in tracing the source. It has been suggested that Freud invented it for the occasion; he would put into words what some Gentile should have, his remark about not being able to find the original constituting an oblique reproach.

1939

We approach the end. The anxious feature now was that in the last two years suspicious areas no longer proved to be precancerous leucoplakias, but definitely malignant recurrences of the cancer itself. At Christmas time Schur removed a sequestrum of bone, the one about whose existence Freud had become doubtful, and this gave considerable relief. But at the same time a swelling appeared and gradually took on an increasingly ominous look. Early in February Schur was certain it meant a recurrence, although he could not persuade Exner of the diagnosis. It was decided to call in Wilfred Trotter, the greatest authority of his time on cancer. I brought him along to introduce him to Freud, who had last met him at the Salzburg Congress forty-one years before. He made an examination on February 10 and again on February 21 and 24, but was also doubtful of the diagnosis and recommended further observation. Schur and Anna were desperate. Daily observation over years had made them equally expert in a way no stranger could be. Schur wrote urgently to Pichler who answered on February 15 with the advice to apply electro-coagulation followed by radium treatment. Professor Lacassagne, the Director of the Curie Institute in Paris, was fetched and made an examination on February 26. He could not advocate radium treatment, however. A biopsy had disclosed an unmistakable malignant recurrence, but the surgeons decided it was inaccessible and that no further operation was feasible. So the case bore now the fatal title "inoperable, incurable cancer." The end was in sight. Only palliative treatment remained, and for this purpose recourse was had to daily administration of Roentgen rays. Lacassagne came again from Paris on March 12 to superintend the special arrangements for this. The journeys for the treatment in Dr. Neville Samuel Finzi's house in Harley Street proved extremely exhausting, but the treatment had some success in keeping the trouble at bay.

Freud notified Eitingon of his situation, and that the treatment would give him a few more weeks of life during which he could continue his analytic sessions.[36] His last letter to him was on April 20, a few lines only.

On March 19 Heinz Hartmann, one of Freud's favorite pupils, paid him a visit, a final one. Marie Bonaparte was also in London from February 5 to February 18, from February 25 to March 1, and from March 13 to March 19. Freud wrote to her after these visits: "I want to say again how sorry I am not to have been able to give you more of myself when you stayed with us. Perhaps things will be easier next time you come—if there is no war—for my pain has been better of late. Dr. Harmer, who has just been, finds that the treatment has had an unmistakable influence on the appearance of the sore place." [37]

She was again in London from March 31 to April 1, and this visit was followed by a much less cheerful letter.

"April 28, 1939

"Meine liebe Marie:

"I have not written to you for a long time, and no doubt you know why; you can tell by my handwriting. I am not getting on well; my complaint and the effects of the treatment share the responsibility in a proportion I cannot determine. The people around have tried to wrap me in an atmosphere of optimism: the cancer is shrinking; the reactions to the treatment are temporary. I don't believe any of it, and don't like being deceived.

"You know that Anna will not be coming to the Paris Congress because she cannot leave me.[n] I get more and more dependent on her and less on myself. Some intercurrent illness that would cut short the cruel proceeding would be very welcome. So should I look forward to seeing you in May? . . .

"With that I greet you warmly; my thoughts are much with you.

"Yours

"Freud"

She came for his last birthday and stayed three days, which seem to have been more enjoyable. Freud wrote after it: "We all specially enjoyed your visit, and the prospect of seeing you again soon is splendid, even if you don't bring anything from S.[o]

"Just think, Finzi is so satisfied that he has given me a whole week's holiday from the treatment. All the same I have not noticed the great improvement and I daresay the growth will increase again in the interval, as it did in a previous one." [38]

[n] The Congress of French-speaking analysis.
[o] Segredakei used to sell Greek antiquities in Paris.

Marie Bonaparte came again to London on June 2 for a couple of days, and after that got the last letter she was ever to receive from Freud: "The day before yesterday I was about to write you a long letter condoling with you about the death of our old Tatoun^p and to tell you that on your next visit I should eagerly listen to what you may have to relate about your new writings, and add a word wherever I feel I can. The two next nights have again cruelly destroyed my expectations. The radium has once more begun to eat in, with pain and toxic effects, and my world is again what it was before—a little island of pain floating on a sea of indifference.

"Finzi continues to assure me of his satisfaction. My last complaint he answered with the words: 'At the end you will be satisfied too.' So he lures me, half against my will, to go on hoping and in the meantime to go on suffering." [39]

Marie Bonaparte came to see Freud twice more, on June 29 for a couple of days, and, for the last time, from July 31 to August 6.

Freud was very eager to see his Moses book appear in English in his lifetime, so my wife, who was translating it, worked hard and the book was published in March, to Freud's gratification. He wrote to Hanns Sachs: "The Moses is not an unworthy leavetaking." He of course received a number of letters about it. Here is one from H. G. Wells.

"March, 1939

"My dear Freud:

"Your book was waiting in the hall when I came home from the Royal Society Conversazione at half past eleven and I found it so fascinating that I did not get to bed until one. I am rather exercised about one point, about Aaron. The Bible makes it clear that Moses could not talk to the Israelites. He needed a spokesman. Now if Moses was not simply tongue-tied but ignorant of Hebrew and without any desire to learn Hebrew Aaron becomes his interpreter, which seems to me to strengthen your case enormously. But for some reason you do not stress this. All the rest of your suggestions I find immensely probable.

"My warmest salutations
"Yours ever
"H. G. Wells"

And here is a translation of one from Einstein.

^p A favorite chow.

"May 4, 1939

"*Sehr geehrter Herr* Freud:

"I thank you warmly for sending me your new work, which has naturally interested me greatly. I had already read your two essays in *Imago*, which Dr. Klopstock, a physician friend, had brought me. Your idea that Moses was a distinguished Egyptian and a member of the priestly caste has much to be said for it, also what you say about the ritual of circumcision.

"I quite specially admire your achievement, as I do with all your writings, from a literary point of view. I do not know any contemporary who has presented his subject in the German language in such a masterly fashion. I have always regretted that for a non-expert, who has no experience with patients, it is hardly possible to form a judgment about the finality of the conclusions in your writings. But after all this is so with all scientific achievements. One must be glad when one is able to grasp the structure of the thoughts expressed.

"With sincere admiration and with cordial wishes

"Yours

"A. Einstein"

The British Psycho-Analytical Society celebrated the twenty-fifth year of their existence by holding a banquet in March, and it was the occasion of my receiving the last letter I ever did from Freud.

"March 7, 1939

"Dear Jones:

"I still find it curious with what little presentiment we humans look to the future. When shortly before the war you told me about founding a psychoanalytical society in London I could not foresee that a quarter of a century later I should be living so near to it and to you, and still less could I have imagined it possible that in spite of being so near I should not be taking part in your gathering.

"But in our helplessness we have to accept what fate brings. So I must content myself with sending your celebrating Society a cordial greeting and the warmest wishes from afar and yet so near. The events of the past years have brought it about that London has become the main site and center of the psychoanalytical movement. May the Society which discharges this function fulfill it in the most brilliant fashion.

"*Ihr alter*

"Sigm. Freud"

The reason why he here added his first name to his signature was because he had learned that in England only peers of the realm signed with a single word; it was one of the peculiarities of England that much amused him.

He had written on February 20 to Arnold Zweig, giving him an account of the uncertain progress of his condition, and on March 5 he wrote his last letter to him. In it he advised him to emigrate to America rather than England. "England is in most respects better, but it is very hard to adapt oneself to it, and you would not have my presence near you for long. America seems to me an Anti-Paradise, but it has so much room and so many possibilities, and in the end one does come to belong to it. Einstein told a friend recently that at first America looked to him like a caricature of a country, but now he feels himself quite at home there. . . . There is no longer any doubt that I have a new recurrence of my dear old cancer with which I have been sharing my existence for sixteen years. Which of us would prove to be the stronger we could not at that time predict."

In April a blow fell that Freud found hard to bear. He was very dependent on the day to day ministrations of his personal doctor, Schur, in whose judgment he had supreme confidence and to whom he was devoted. Yet Schur himself was now faced with a painful dilemma. His quota number for the United States had been called up, and if he did not accept it he would imperil his and his children's future. He decided to take it, and to pay a visit to America where he would take out his first naturalization papers. He left on April 21 and got back on July 8. Dr. Samet took his place temporarily, and then Dr. Harmer, with Exner in charge. During his absence he received regular reports which showed no serious worsening until the end of the time.

On his return he found a great change in Freud's condition. He looked much worse in general, had lost weight and was showing some signs of apathy. There was a cancerous ulceration attacking the cheek and the base of the orbit. Even his best friend, his sound sleep which had sustained him so long, was now deserting him. Anna had to continue her practice of applying orthoform locally several times in the night.

One of the very last visitors was one of Freud's earliest analytical friends, Hanns Sachs, who came in July to take what he knew would be his last leave of the man he called his "master and friend." Sachs was particularly struck by two observations. One was that with all the distress of his painful condition Freud showed no sign of complaint or irritability—nothing but full acceptance of his fate and resignation to it. The other was that even then he could take interest in the situation in America and showed himself fully informed about the personalities and recent events in analytical circles there. As Freud would have wished, their final parting was made in a friendly but unemotional fashion.

Freud, like all good doctors, was averse to taking drugs. As he put it once to Stefan Zweig, "I prefer to think in torment than not to be able to think clearly." Now, however, he consented to take an occasional dose of aspirin, the only drug he accepted before the very end. And he managed somehow to continue with his analytic work until the end of July. On September 1, his granddaughter Eva, Oliver's child, paid him a last visit; he was specially fond of that charming girl, who was to die in France five years later.

In August everything went downhill rapidly. A distressing symptom was an unpleasant odor from the wound, so that when his favorite chow was brought to visit him she shrank into a far corner of the room, a heart-rending experience which revealed to the sick man the pass he had reached. He was getting very weak and spent his time in a sick bay in his study from which he could gaze at his beloved flowers in the garden. He read the newspapers and followed world events to the end. As the Second World War approached he was confident it would mean the end of Hitler. The day it broke out there was an air raid warning—a false alarm, as it turned out—when Freud was lying on his couch in the garden; he was quite unperturbed. He watched with considerable interest the steps taken to safeguard his manuscripts and collection of antiquities. But when a broadcast announced that this was to be the last war, and Schur asked him if he believed that, he could only reply: "Anyhow it is my last war." He found it hardly possible to eat anything. The last book he was able to read was Balzac's *La Peau de Chagrin*, on which he commented wryly: "That is just the book for me. It deals with starvation." He meant rather the gradual shrinking, the becoming less and less, described so poignantly in the book.

But with all this agony there was never the slightest sign of impatience or irritability. The philosophy of resignation and the acceptance of unalterable reality triumphed throughout.

The cancer ate its way through the cheek to the outside and the septic condition was heightened. The exhaustion was extreme and the misery indescribable. On September 19 I was sent for to say good-by to him and called him by name as he dozed. He opened his eyes, recognized me and waved his hand, then dropped it with a highly expressive gesture that conveyed a wealth of meaning: greetings, farewell, resignation. It said as plainly as possible "The rest is silence." There was no need to exchange a word. In a second he fell asleep again. On September 21 Freud said to his doctor: "My dear Schur, you remember our first talk. You promised me then you would help me when I could no longer carry on. It is only torture now and it has no longer any sense." Schur pressed his hand and promised he would give him adequate sedation; Freud thanked him, adding after a moment of hesitation: "Tell Anna about our talk." There was no emotionalism or self-pity, only reality—an impressive and unforgettable scene.

The next morning Schur gave Freud a third of a grain of morphia. For someone at such a point of exhaustion as Freud then was, and so complete a stranger to opiates, that small dose sufficed. He sighed with relief and sank into a peaceful sleep; he was evidently close to the end of his reserves. He died just before midnight the next day, September 23, 1939. His long and arduous life was at an end and his sufferings over. Freud died as he had lived—a realist.

Freud's body was cremated at Golder's Green on the morning of September 26 in the presence of a large number of mourners, including Marie Bonaparte and the Lampls from abroad, and his ashes repose there in one of his favorite Grecian urns. The family asked me to deliver the funeral oration. Stefan Zweig then made a long speech in German which was doubtless more eloquent than mine but which could not have been more deeply felt. Having preserved the private notes I prepared for that poignant occasion I will reproduce them here.

As a close friend of Prof. Freud and his family for more than thirty years it is my privilege to voice our last respects to him. I speak for his family and his friends gathered here, and I also think of friends far away, of Brill, Eitingon, Hanns Sachs and others and of the shades of Abraham and Ferenczi. Our first thought must surely be for the dead man himself. Those who know the horrors of suffering he has passed through, sufferings which reached an unspeakable intensity in the last few months, must be possessed with a sense of relief for his sake. He will suffer no more. It was hard to wish that he would live a day longer when his life was reduced to a pin point of personal agony. Nor did he in any way dread death, and that although what in others expresses itself as religious feeling did so in him as a transcendent belief in the value of life and in the value of love. Thus one can say of him that as never man loved life more, so never man feared death less. He had lived a full life, had experienced and felt its heights as well as its depths; he had warmed both hands at the fire of life, and life had nothing left to offer. He died surrounded by every loving care, in a land that had shown him more courtesy, more esteem and more honor than his own or any other land, a land which I think he himself esteemed beyond all others. He is being buried today in the atmosphere he would have wished, one of stark truth and realism; in sheer simplicity, without a note of pomp or ceremony.

He has lost nothing through death, so we cannot truly mourn for his sake. But what of ourselves? A world without Freud! A world without that vivid personality, without that entrancing and benign smile; without those wise and trenchant comments on the great and small things of life, that *Grosszügigkeit* [q] in instant readiness to help. It is not long since he wrote to me about a sad case of misfortune: *"Leider kann ich hier nur mit Geld helfen."* [r] How small this kind of help seemed when compared with his wont. At my first meeting with him so long ago three qualities in particular produced an impression on me that only deepened as the years passed. In the first place his nobility of character, his *Erhabenheit*.[s] It was impossible to imagine his ever doing a petty thing or thinking a petty thought. Many years ago he conducted a private correspondence with Putnam on the subject of ethics. Putnam showed it to me and I remember these two sentences: *"Ich betrachte das Moralische als etwas Selbstverstaendliches. . . . Ich habe eigentlich nie etwas Gemeines getan."* [t] How many of us, if we search our hearts, could truthfully say that? Those of us who have special knowledge concerning the imperfections of mankind are sometimes depressed when we consider ourselves and our fellow men. In those moments we recall the rare spirits that transcend the smallness of life, give life its glory and show us the picture of true greatness. It is they who give life its full value. There are not many of those rare spirits and Freud was among the highest of them.

Then his direct and instinctive love of truth, his hatred of all de

[q] Generosity.
[r] Unfortunately in this case I can only help with money.
[s] Loftiness.
[t] I consider ethics to be taken for granted. Actually I have never done a mean thing.

ception, ambiguousness and prevarication. One feels that no one could ever have lied to him. Not only that it would have been useless, but any wish to do so would have melted in his presence. With his love of truth went that of justice and fair dealing. "Fairness" was one of the English words he was fondest of. Lastly, his courage and inflexible determination. That concerns more his scientific life, of which we are not here thinking in the first place; but when one recollects his detractors in that field, and his imperviousness to their attacks, many of us are reminded of the lines in Shelley's "Adonais"

> *He wakes or sleeps with the enduring dead;*
> *Thou canst not soar where he is sitting now.*

A great spirit has passed from the world. How can life keep its meaning for those to whom he was the center of life? Yet we do not feel it as a real parting in the full sense, for Freud has so inspired us with his personality, his character and his ideas that we can never truly part from him until we finally part from ourselves in whom he still lives. His creative spirit was so strong that he infused himself into others. If ever man can be said to have conquered death itself, to live on in spite of the King of Terrors, who held no terror for him, that man was Freud.

And so we take leave of a man whose like we shall not know again. From our hearts we thank him for having lived; for having done; and for having loved.

2

PART

HISTORICAL REVIEWS OF CERTAIN TOPICS

7

Clinical Contributions (1919-1939)

IN THE LAST TWENTY YEARS OF HIS LIFE FREUD, ALTHOUGH HIS INTERESTS had mainly passed over to metapsychological and sociological problems, continued to make a number of clinical contributions. There are some twenty papers as well as two books that come essentially under this heading. Some of these are concerned with matters of technique, others with theoretical problems, and a still larger number with specific aspects of libido development. We may consider them in that order.

Technique

The first of these was a paper written in 1922, though published in 1923, called "Remarks on the Theory and Practice of Dream Interpretation." [1] It was a useful comment on the important matter of how to deal with dream interpretation in day to day work. The contents were described in a former volume of this biography.[2]

The other three papers were written in the last years of Freud's life. One was a note, only a couple of pages long, analyzing a slip of the pen when writing instructions to a jeweler to make up a ring Freud intended to give as a birthday present to Lou Andreas-Salomé.[3] It was a most trivial slip, but the lesson of the analysis is that one should not be content with the first superficial interpretation, because even such slight material may be connected with surprisingly complicated trains of thought interwoven in the most delicate fashion.

In 1937 there were two weighty papers. In April "Analysis Terminable and Interminable" appeared.[4] It is for the practicing psychoanalyst possibly the most valuable contribution Freud ever wrote. The deep wisdom and close thinking it displays are truly remarkable, and show how Freud at the age of eighty-one had retained his mental powers without the slightest impairment. He began with a few remarks on the frequent attempts that have been made to shorten an analysis, the optimism of which he traced to the earlier underestimation of the significance of neurotic disturbances, of the deep and powerful forces concerned. In this connection he described some of his experiences with the device of setting a term to the analysis in the endeavor to stimulate the wish for a cure, and pointed out the strict limitations in the way of a general use of the method.

But Freud's main theme was the problem of how complete a psychoanalysis could ever be, and what precisely are the forces that hinder the achievement of such an ideal result. The three main factors on which the result depends are: (1) the relative importance of traumatic agencies in the etiology of a particular case; (2) the relative strength of the primitive impulses, either congenitally or through physiological reinforcement, e.g. puberty; and (3) the changes brought about in the ego in the course of development, essentially the various defense mechanisms employed. Success in analysis is unquestionably greater when the first of these factors has been the most prominent in the particular case; altogether analysis is much more potent in dealing with older factors than with current acute crises.

Freud raised the question as to whether it was possible to forestall future neurotic disturbance by dealing with an instinctual conflict the presence of which could be divined even when it was not causing active trouble. He answered the question on the whole in the negative. After discussing various possible measures of deliberately treating a patient in a hostile fashion so as to provoke the latent complex he concluded they would only have the effect of impairing the positive transference necessary for curative results; and merely to point intellectually to its existence would have no more dynamic effect than much of the sexual enlightenment of children has, a procedure the value of which is often exaggerated.

Perhaps the most important part of this essay is the section on changes in the ego, where there are many stimulating thoughts that have by no means all been fully exploited even yet. Freud stressed that the possibility of a successful cure can become a challenge to the defenses on which the ego has depended for safety since early life, and which therefore oppose the therapeutic aim. He then pointed to deep constitutional factors, such as the peculiar quality he termed "adhesiveness of the libido," which in spite of their fundamental importance are extremely hard to define precisely.

In October of the same year, 1937, there appeared another useful practical paper, "Constructions in Analysis." [5] It seems to have been provoked by the criticism that analysts think their interpretation correct whether the patient agrees with it or denies it. Freud showed how very complex the situation really is, and then discussed at some length what precisely the analyst should infer from the patient's response to his interpretations. He was concerned here not with single interpretations but with reconstructions of various parts of the patient's early life. A very definite point he made was that when the patient denies the truth of a given reconstruction it always means that it is, if not necessarily incorrect, certainly incomplete. A sign that such a construction is probably correct is that a patient in a negative stage of transference nearly always responds with a worsening of his symptoms. An interpretation or reconstruction in an analysis is not a dogmative assertion, but a supposition, more or less probable, designed to provoke various responses from the patient, and it is the nature of those responses that is significant.

Theory of the Neuroses

We have five papers to consider here besides various chapters in the two clinical books Freud wrote in this period. The first one, "Some Neurotic Mechanisms in Jealousy, Paranoia and Homosexuality," [6] was written in 1921 and published in the following year.[a] It gave an analysis of the three main varieties of jealousy, which Freud termed "normal," "projection" and "paranoid" respectively. The first one he connected partly with the sense of loss and partly with the wound to narcissism. The second variety, as the name implies, signifies a projection of a subjective infidelity that has been repressed. The third variety Freud associated specifically with repressed homosexuality. Insight into the meaning of this last one had, so he said, come to him quite suddenly when analyzing a case notably in the Schreber case.[7] There are several examples of Freud of the sort in the first foreign patient he treated after the war, but there were plain evidences of the same idea already in other writings,

[a] See p. 82.

obtaining a clear insight which he subsequently forgot, and then later suddenly coming across it again as a new revelation.

In 1924 Freud published two short papers on the essential differences between neuroses and psychoses. The first one, which appeared in the January number of the *Zeitschrift*, was entitled "Neurosis and Psychosis." [8] It was an attempt to reformulate earlier conclusions on the subject in the light of those he had recently expounded in his book *The Ego and the Id*. He now summed them up as follows: Psychoneuroses represent the outcome of a conflict between the ego and the id; narcissistic neuroses, such as melancholia, one between the ego and the super-ego; the psychoses one between the ego and the outer world. The second paper, which appeared in the October number of the *Zeitschrift*, dealt with "The Loss of Reality in Neurosis and Psychosis." [9] It is a deeper and more closely reasoned paper than the former one. As he had pointed out in the first paper, what is decisive in the difference between neuroses and psychoses is the superior strength in the former of the influence of the outer world, in the latter of the impulses in the id. Impairment of the sense of reality is therefore inherent with the psychoses, but it also takes place with the neuroses in a different and more secondary manner. Two stages can be distinguished in both conditions: a primary flight followed by subsequent efforts at reconstruction or compromise; and in both the happenings can be depicted ultimately in terms of conflict between the demands of the outer world (or its inner representative) and those of the id.

With the neuroses the initial flight is from the demands of the id, so that those of outer reality may be said to be victorious. At a certain cost of energy this may succeed, as it often does in mental health. But neuroses come about when the id impulses rebel, a compromise is reached and impairment of a certain section of reality takes place. With the psychoses, on the other hand, it is the id impulses that are victorious, and there is a flight from a piece of reality which is denied. In the second phase of psychotic development a false reality is invented (delusions, etc.) as a substitute for the true one. So one may say that neurosis does not deny the existence of reality, it merely tries to ignore it; psychosis denies it and tries to substitute something else for it.

A paper may be mentioned in the present connection, "The Resistances to Psycho-Analysis," [10] which was written for a French periodical, *La Revue Juive*, and then also published in *Imago*, July, 1925. It was the fifth paper Freud wrote for a French periodical in his long career. Here Freud compared the attitude of the outside world to that of his patients when first brought into contact with psychoanalysis. In both cases the reaction is primarily that of fear, fear lest the barriers that hold forbidden sexual impulses in check be broken down through the investigation of them. The opposition is far more emotional than intellectual.

In the same number of *Imago* there appeared a short paper entitled "Negation." [11] It begins by considering the important part played by negative responses during psychoanalytic practice. After an interpretation the patient may deny the existence of a repressed idea which he has just admitted into consciousness. By means of the negation one aim of repression has been defeated, the keeping of an idea from consciousness, but not the main one—of minimizing its significance. Further work may then enable the patient to change his negative attitude into an affirmative one, and so to accept the truth of the particular interpretation. Still, even then the acceptance may remain purely intellectual, with no emotional appreciation of the idea.

From this starting point Freud developed some highly ingenious conceptions about the nature and origin of the faculty of judgment, and also of the thinking process itself. He traced the former to the original distinction the newborn infant makes between what is pleasant, and therefore part of its "pleasure-self," and that which is unpleasant and therefore belongs to the outer world. A later problem is one of deciding whether an imagined idea is purely subjective or corresponds with something in the outer world, a distinction which did not exist in the earliest phases of life. Since all knowledge of the outer world comes through the sensorium, recognizing whether an idea corresponds with something in the outer world is a sort of finding something *again*, though of course often in an altered shape. The condition is that some object must have been lost which at one time afforded gratification. The process of thought Freud suggested is an abbreviated motor action at little cost of energy, and its function is to decide whether such action is desirable. This "tasting" procedure was originally acquired in the sensorial area of the mind. Freud regarded perception not as a passive process but as an active investigation of the outer world, a way of "tasting" it which originally was literally a tasting with the mouth.

The most valuable clinical contribution Freud made in the period after the war years was undoubtedly his book *Inhibition, Symptoms and Anxiety*.[12] It is essentially a comprehensive study of the various problems concerning anxiety, and it owes its inception to the thoughts Rank's theory of the importance of birth trauma[13] had induced. Much of its interest indeed lies in watching Freud's efforts to get a clearer view of the problems Rank's theory had stimulated, a theory which at the time had overimpressed Freud. After all it was a sentence of his own, written in 1910, which must have been the starting point of Rank's speculations. "Birth is in fact the first of all dangers to life, as well as the prototype of all the later ones we fear; and this experience has left its mark behind it on that expression of emotion which we call anxiety." [14]

Freud's thoughts concerning the relation of anxiety to birth had had a rather curious history. In later life he told the story of a midwife having directed his attention to it when he was a resident in hospital, perhaps in 1884.[15] But after that the idea of there being such a connection slumbered entirely for fifteen years. On the contrary, in those years he always associated the genesis of anxiety with frustrated coitus.[16] In 1908 he wrote a preface to a book of Stekel's[17] which dealt very extensively with the theme of anxiety in connection with womb phantasies, although the phrase *Geburtangst* itself was not mentioned. In the following year Freud when writing about womb phantasies added a footnote to the second edition of *The Interpretation of Dreams* saying simply that "the act of birth is the first experience of anxiety, and thus the source and prototype of the affect of anxiety"; [18] this seems to be his first allusion to the idea. And the year after he amplified the point in his first essay on the psychology of love.[19]

Then there is another long gap until the full exposition in the *Introductory Lectures*[20] in 1917. After another interval the idea re-emerged in *The Ego and the Id*[21] in 1923, and a little while later came the fullest discussion of all in *Inhibition, Symptoms and Anxiety*.[22]

It is a rather discursive book, with little of the incisiveness we expect from Freud, and it was evidently written for himself, to try to clarify his own ideas rather than as an exposition of them. Freud was far from satisfied with the result, but the way in which he indicated the complexity of many problems that had been overlooked has proved very stimulating to serious workers. Some of these problems are by no means solved even yet.

Freud's cautious way of working, with its absence of dogmatism, is well illustrated in the following quotations. "Whence does neurosis come—what is its ultimate, its own peculiar meaning? After whole decades of psychoanalytic work we are as much in the dark about this problem as ever." [23] "It is almost humiliating that, after working so long, we should still be experiencing difficulty in understanding the most fundamental facts. But we are determined to simplify nothing and to hide nothing. If we cannot see things clearly we will at least see clearly what the obscurities are." [24]

The book is so rich in suggestive ideas and tentative conclusions that it is only possible here to select a few of the more striking ones. Freud reverted to one of his earliest conceptions, that of "defense," which for over twenty years he had replaced by that of "repression"; he now regarded the latter as simply one of the several defenses employed by the ego. He contrasted the central part repression plays in hysteria with the more characteristic defenses of "reaction-formation," "isolation" and "undoing" (a form of restitution) in the obsessional neurosis. Altogether the contrasts he pointed out between these two psychoneuroses are very illuminating. Thus he remarked on the way the defense in the former (repression) belongs typically to the genital level of development, those of the latter to the pregenital level.

Freud admitted his former error in maintaining that morbid anxiety is simply transformed libido, and explained how he came to make it.[25] As early as 1910 I had criticized this unbiological view and maintained that anxiety must proceed from the ego itself, but Freud would not listen and only changed his opinion when he approached the subject in his own way sixteen years later. Even now he still clung to the possibility of this transformation occurring in the "actual neuroses," [26] conditions which are now generally regarded as syndromes rather than independent neurotic affections. This belief, however, he also discarded seven years later.[27]

Freud then pursued the question of the nature of the danger with which anxiety is concerned. The situation of "real anxiety" differs from that of morbid anxiety in that the nature of the danger is evident in the former, whereas in the latter it is unknown. In morbid anxiety the danger may emanate from dread of impulses in the id, from threats from the super-ego or from fear of punishment from without, but with males it is always ultimately a fear of castration, with females more characteristically the fear of not being loved. However, Freud was able to penetrate more deeply into the problem by distinguishing between the vague sense of danger and the ultimate catastrophe itself, which he termed the trauma. The latter is a situation of helplessness in which the subject is unable without assistance to master some excessive excitation. The act of birth itself is the prototype of this, but Freud did not agree with Rank that subsequent attacks of anxiety were merely repetitions of this and constant endeavors to abreact it. In the traumatic situation all the protective barriers are overrun, and a panicky helplessness results, a response which Freud called inevitable but inexpedient. Most clinical instances of anxiety, however, may be called expedient, because they are essentially signals of approaching danger which for the most part may then be avoided in various ways. Among these is the action of repression itself, which Freud now regarded as being set in action by the anxiety instead of, as he had previously thought, being the cause of the anxiety.

The precise relation of neurotic symptoms to anxiety provides another difficult problem. On the whole Freud would consider them as partial defenses destined to obviate anxiety by affording substitutive outlets for the feared impulses. But the most obscure question is under what conditions is the original danger situation retained in full strength in the unconscious? There may, for example, occur in adult life a lively reaction to the infantile dread of castration as if it were an imminent contingency. With this fixation is bound up the riddle of the neurosis. Doubtless the economic element of quantity is the decisive one, but Freud pointed out three factors which greatly influence it. The first or biological one is the remarkable and prolonged immaturity of human infants in contrast to other animals; this heightens the significance of dependence on the helping mother, whose absence so commonly evokes alarming anxiety. The second, historical or phylogenetic, factor Freud inferred from the curious occurrence of two stages in man's libidinal development separated by the years of the latency period. The third, psychological, factor has to do with the peculiar organization of the human mind with its differentiation into id and ego. Because of external dangers (castration) the ego has to treat certain instinctual impulses as leading to danger, but it can deal with them only at the expense of undergoing various deformities, by restricting its own organization and acquiescing in the formation of neurotic symptoms as partial substitutes for the impulses in question.

Finally Freud opened up the problems of the relation of anxiety to mourning and to pain,[b] since the loss of a loved object may lead to any of these three responses. Mourning Freud had already fully dealt with on a previous occasion,[28] and he now offered an explana-

[b] *Schmerz.*

tion of physical pain in terms of narcissistic hyper-cathexis of the damaged area.[29]

In a book he wrote seven years later, the *New Introductory Lectures*,[30] Freud devoted a part of a chapter to the topic of anxiety, but it contributed little more to the more detailed discussion he had already provided.

Finally there is the remarkable and comprehensive essay entitled "An Outline of Psychoanalysis" which Freud wrote in the last year of his life and which was published posthumously.[31] It is perhaps the best general account of the theory of psychoanalysis that exists, and it embodied Freud's latest ideas, e.g. those on splitting of the ego. It was not intended as a popular exposition, but as one suitable for serious thinkers in any sphere of life and it was written with a nervous firmness and lucidity unsurpassed in any of Freud's writings. At the age of eighty-two there was not the slightest weakening in his powers of thought and exposition.

Libido Theory

As soon as he rallied from the depressing war years Freud wrote two important papers which have already been reviewed in Volume II of this biography: "A Child is being Beaten" [32] and "The Psychogenesis of a Case of Female Homosexuality." [33]

A short contribution in 1920 may be mentioned, entitled "An Association by a Four-Year-Old Child." [34] It related a spontaneous symbolism that showed how a child was solving the riddle of birth.

In the summer of 1922 Freud wrote two expository articles in dictionary form for a German encyclopaedia which were published in the following year;[35] one was entitled "Psycho-Analysis," the other "Libido Theory." They both constitute valuable summaries for reference purposes, but they added little new material to Freud's previous publications.

In the same year there appeared a short but important paper called "The Infantile Genital Organization of the Libido." [36] It was an addition to his book on sexual theory which rectified a statement there contrasting the imperfect genital organization of the child with that of the adult. Freud now maintained that the resemblance between the two was greater than he had thought earlier. In fact, apart of course from the physical change of seminal production, he could perceive only one difference between the libidinal development of a five-year-old and that of an adult; namely, that with the former there is only one genital organ in the world, the penis. Freud termed this the phallic stage of development,[c] and was of the opinion that it was as true for girls as for boys. He discussed the effect on the boy's mentality of discovering the absence of this organ in the opposite sex, its association with the fear of castration, repulsion toward the female, and so on. In his opinion neither sex believed at this age that there were two genital organs, a male and a female; people were simply divided into those with and those without a penis, the latter having presumably lost theirs. He maintained stoutly that at the age in question nobody had ever discovered the existence of a female organ. In spite of the truth of Freud's clinical observations on which these conclusions were based it is doubtful whether his generalizations here were not too absolute; further research has in some respects modified them. Although he pointed out that the most characteristic feature of this age (especially in boys) was the extent to which interest in the penis stimulates sexual curiosity, Freud does not seem to have taken sufficiently into account the thrusting tendency of the organ and its almost physical search for a corresponding counterpart.

In the following year, 1924, Freud published a penetrating study of masochism, which was also rich in theoretical conclusions: "The Economic Problem of Masochism." [38] It reversed a good many of his previous ideas.[d] Thus, whereas he had always regarded the pleasure-unpleasure principle as a manifestation of Fechner's "tendency to stability," i.e. that the heightened tension signifies unpleasure and release of tension pleasure, he now admitted that, as the experience of sexual excitement alone shows, this correlation could only be a very partial one. Some other unknown factor, perhaps rhythm, must also play an essential part. The stability principle must be closely connected with the death instinct he had recently postulated,[e] and the pleasure-unpleasure principle must arise from the interaction of the life instinct, Eros or libido.

Freud then distinguished three forms of masochism: erotogenic, feminine and moral. The first two have a similar explanation. Freud had previously regarded them as secondary to sadism, a turning inward of this upon the self. He still thought this mechanism held

[c] Freud had given a plain indication of this conception nearly ten years before.[37]
[d] E.g., those expressed in 1915.[39]
[e] See p. 272.

good, but used the term "secondary masochism" to distinguish it from a primary masochism. This he suggested was the direct action on the self of the death instinct, which had not all been directed outward in an aggressive or destructive form. This idea of a quite primary masochism was new, and it has not yet been fully accepted by psychoanalysts.

The third kind, moral masochism, differs in being not obviously erotic and also in having no special relation to significant persons. It is the suffering or self-injury itself that matters, no matter who inflicts it, whether some person or fate. Freud traced this to an unconscious sense of guilt,[f] and he thought a better name for it was "the need for punishment." It plays an extensive part in social life, and in analysis it represents perhaps the most difficult problem to solve.

In the same year Freud astonished us by again revising one of his fundamental ideas in a paper entitled "The Dissolution of the Oedipus Complex." [41] He first discussed the various factors leading to the resolution of the Oedipus complex in the latency period—frustration and disappointment, predestined evolution and so on—and he concluded that the most important one for boys was the fear of castration; with girls the original wish for a penis is transformed into that for a baby and it is the disappointment of the father's refusal to gratify this that leads to the change in the Oedipus complex. The substitute for it is the super-ego, derived from various identifications with the parents. All this represents a process of repression, but whereas Freud had previously maintained that repression merely holds the repressed impulses in check in the unconscious, and does not prevent them from exercising various activities there, he now spoke of further steps in the process. He maintained that the Oedipus wishes are not merely repressed, but are actually destroyed and annuled. It is true he termed this the "ideal" solution of the complex, implying that it was seldom complete, but it was news to hear that in his opinion any unconscious impulses could undergo such a fate, one surely never encountered in analytic practice.

A year later, in 1925, Freud put forward in a tentative fashion some conclusions which he thought would prove to be important if their truth were confirmed by further observation. They were contained in a paper entitled "Some Psychological Consequences of the Anatomical Distinction between the Sexes." [42] Concerning the boy's discovery of the anatomical difference, Freud had little to say which was new, though he stressed the fact that its significance be-

[f] Freud had recognized this as early as 1907.[40]

comes apparent at the time when castration fears arise in connection with the Oedipus complex. The main part of the paper is taken up with the girl's reactions to the discovery. At first she either denies it, maintaining the illusion that she also really has a penis, or else she builds hopes of acquiring one later. Freud suggested that this early envy of the penis explains why women are more prone to jealousy than men. Two other important differences in her development from that of the boy's are these. She has a stronger aversion to masturbation than he, and the relation of her discovery of the anatomical difference to the Oedipus complex is exactly the reverse of his. With the boy the fear of castration puts an end to the Oedipus complex, whereas with the girl the idea of being castrated is what turns her from her mother to her father. But her attraction to her father is not a simple one like that of the boy's toward his mother. It is secondary to the wish to obtain a baby in place of the missing penis. In consequence the failure of the Oedipus wishes to obtain gratification has not such a catastrophic end with girls as it has with the boys. Their conversion into a super-ego does not therefore proceed so far as it does with a boy as a rule, and that is the reason why in general the super-ego of a woman is less harsh and inexorable than that of a man! Women are often thought to be more personal and emotional in making decisions than men, whose moral principles are more binding, and are also thought to find it harder to accept the inevitable frustrations imposed by nature.

Freud confessed that these conclusions were derived from studying a handful of cases, but he thought they might prove to be important if more extensively confirmed. At the same time one should allow for enormous individual differences irrespective of sex, and also for the mingling of male and female elements in everyone.

Two years later, in 1927, there was a short, but very useful paper on "Fetishism." [43] Freud described here more fully a conclusion he had briefly mentioned seventeen years before in his book on Leonardo,[44] that every sexual fetish represents a penis substitute. But it is not any kind of penis, only the one the young boy had attributed to the mother. The fetishism is, therefore, a reaction to the fear of castration so often associated with the discovery of the organ's absence in the female, and it is always accompanied by an attitude of alienation toward the female genital region. We do not know why this early situation, probably an invariable one, leads in one case to fetishism, in another to homosexuality, and in still another to a more normal development. The choice of the particular fetish itself is of course determined by individual experiences, and Freud quoted several interesting examples of this.

The topic gave rise to a further point of theoretical interest. Freud had recently put forward a conclusion, which he said he had reached along purely speculative lines, about the essential difference between neuroses and psychoses.[g] He now quoted two examples from recent clinical practice in cases of fetishism which seemed definitely to contradict his conclusion that denial of reality was the hallmark of psychoses. In both these cases of neurosis the patient had refused to believe that his father had died; one patient was nine years old at the time. Analysis showed, however, that this denial was only partial; one part of the mind had accepted the news while another part was denying it. With a psychosis the acceptance would be lacking.

The same ambivalence often occurs in the structure of a fetish, which may contain at the same time the idea that the mother still had a penis and also the idea that the father had castrated her. Finally Freud threw out the interesting suggestion that what corresponds to a fetish in a normal man is his own penis.

In 1931 two important papers appeared; they were both published in the October number of the *Zeitschrift*. The first was called "Libidinal Types."[45] The manifold variety of human beings may be grouped in different ways by either physical or mental classifications. Freud here attempted a classification based on libidinal characteristics. He distinguished three main types: erotic, narcissistic and obsessional. The first of these are people whose love life is their main interest; usually the desire to be loved is the most prominent feature. In the second, narcissistic type, the desire to love is stronger than the need to be loved, but both are subordinate to self-preservation and self-assertion. Such subjects display little tension between ego and super-ego, and indeed the latter may not be at all highly developed. They are usually confident people and often play the part of leaders. They are capable of considerable aggressivity, and so may either benefit their social surroundings through stimulation or injure it through their ruthlessness. Obsessional types, on the contrary, display a domination of the super-ego, so that they fear their conscience more than they do the risk of not being loved. They are independent, and they represent the conservative aspects of society.

Most often we meet with mixed types, and in analytic practice they are very familiar. There is the erotic-obsessional type in whom

[g] See p. 252.

the influence of the super-ego restricts the free exercise of the erotic tendencies; such people have been subject more strongly than others to the influence of their parents and teachers, also of authorities in later life. The erotic-narcissistic type seems to be the most frequent of all. In it one sees that activity and aggressivity is closely connected with the dominance of narcissism. The narcissistic-obsessional type Freud regarded as the most valuable culturally; independence of the outer world combined with respect for the demands of conscience give scope for free activity, and the strong ego is not dominated by the super-ego.

As to the nature of a possible erotic-obsessional-narcissistic type Freud said it would represent the ideal harmony of the so-called normal, a non-existent type.

The second paper, on "Female Sexuality," [46] was a more extensive production, twenty pages long. It was written in great part as a response to the special interest that several analysts in England and Germany had recently been taking in this subject. Although, according to Freud, it contained no ideas that had not already been expressed in the psychoanalytical literature, he summarized his experiences and conclusions in his own clear and characteristic fashion. Perhaps the main novelty was the stress he laid here on the duration and intensity of the girl's early attachment to her mother, which he thought had been previously underestimated. This plays a part in psychopathology, e.g. in female paranoia, as well as in normal psychology. An example of the latter in married life is its transference to the husband, who may thus inherit both the special demands the girl had made on her mother (being "mothered") and the hostility of this early phase.

Freud maintained that in this phase of attachment to her mother the girl's attitude is predominantly active. Even her fondness for playing with dolls later on shows traces derived from it in the active behavior toward the doll, who may represent not only a child but the mother herself. The later change of love object from mother to father, one which the boy does not have to make, betokens, therefore, more than a simple exchange; it signifies also a change of attitude, from active to passive.

The idea of castration, i.e. the discovery of the anatomical differences between the sexes, may lead to three characteristic lines of development. The shock and accompanying sense of inferiority may lead to an extensive renunciation of all sexuality, with fatal consequences for adult life. On the other hand the belief in the possession of a penis, or the wish for it, may be obstinately retained, leading to a permanent "masculinity complex" or even homosexuality; this is usually accompanied by a defiant masturbation. The third path open is the normal one of turning to the father and developing an Oedipus complex.

Freud then discussed the many sources of hostility toward the mother in this early phase. It is invariable and is only strengthened by the subsequent rivalry during the true Oedipus phase, which is far from being the only cause of this hostility. There are the unavoidable frustrations of infantile life, and also the ambivalence which seems to be a normal accompaniment of that stage of development. Most important appears to be the girl's resentment that her mother brought her into the world less well equipped than the boy. When another child is born the girl may have the phantasy that she had created it with the mother before her discovery of the part played by the father.

I did not wholly agree with some of these conclusions, and this led to considerable discussion between Freud and myself, both in correspondence and in publications.[47] Several of the disputed questions are still not satisfactorily solved.

Two years later, in 1933, Freud devoted a chapter of his *New Introductory Lectures* to the subject of femininity.[48] It makes enjoyable reading, being couched in Freud's attractive, friendly and candid style, but there was little really new in its content. Freud was rather sceptical about the vaginal sensations in infancy reported by some analysts, remarking that they must be hard to distinguish from other sensations arising in the neighborhood, and in any case could not be very important. In the controversy over the phallic phase in girls he decidedly favored the view that its early pre-oedipal source was more important than any regression occasioned by the disappointments of the Oedipus stage itself.

Freud made a contribution of historical interest to the story of his early difficulties with the seduction phantasies of his female hysterical patients.[49] It will be remembered that the analytic technique had unfailingly led back to accounts of paternal seduction of the patients in their childhood, and that it was some time before Freud recognized these to be typical phantasies belonging to the Oedipus phase.[h] Now he pointed out that the ultimate source of these phan-

[h] Incidentally, a French writer recently made the scurrilous accusation that Freud had dishonestly concealed the fact (!) that it was he who had suggested these stories to his patients.[50]

tasies was the girl's relation to her mother, and that they have so much connection with reality as to relate to the excitations induced by the mother's bodily care in cleansing the genital area.

Freud raised the question as to whether there might be different kinds of libido, such as male and female, possibly with a chemical difference, but answered it definitely in the negative. He found, therefore, no justification at all for such expressions as "female libido."

8

CHAPTER

Metapsychology

IT WILL BE RECALLED THAT FREUD USED THE TERM "METAPSYCHOLOGY"
to denote any account of mental processes that comprised a description of them from a dynamic, topographical and economic point
of view; he had first used the word in 1896.[1] When Freud wrote his
important metapsychological essays in the spring of 1915[2] he felt he
had completed his life work, and that any further contributions he
might make would be of a subordinate and merely complementary
order. His followers would doubtless have taken a similar view at
that time. Had his work come to an end then we should have possessed a well-rounded account of psychoanalysis in what might be
called its classical form, and it would not have been easy to predict
its future development at the hands of his successors. There was not
the slightest reason to expect that in another few years Freud would
have produced some revolutionary conceptions which necessarily
had the effect of extensively remodeling both the theory and the
practice of psychoanalysis.

For the succeeding three or four darkest years of the war Freud's
mind was relatively fallow; the miserable day-to-day life was a full
occupation. The new ideas appeared in 1919-21. There were two
main themes, and the essence of them may be stated thus: the importance of a biological tendency in the organism to restore earlier
states of being, and the threefold differentiation of mental processes.
Reflection on the non-libidinal components of the ego serves as a link
between the two. The former, which preceded the other in time,
was of an avowedly speculative nature, the latter more directly

based on clinical investigation. These ideas have not only their scientific value; they are of special interest also to the study of Freud's personality.

Repetition-Compulsion and Death Instinct

The circumstances in which Freud wrote his fascinating *Beyond the Pleasure Principle*[3] in 1919-20 have been mentioned earlier.[a] It is many respects a remarkable book. In dealing with such ultimate problems as the origin of life and the nature of death Freud displayed a boldness of speculation which was unique in all his writings; nothing that he wrote elsewhere can be compared with it. Then it is very evident that while writing it Freud had no audience in mind beyond himself; it was written in the hope of clarifying some problems that had long puzzled him. It is somewhat discursively written, almost as if by free associations, and there are therefore occasional gaps in the reasoning. Sunk in thought, Freud revived many ideas dating from his neurological period or even earlier, passing swiftly from these to the impressions of his years of analytical experience. This mode of writing in itself indicates that the ideas propounded must be transmuted from some personal and profound source, a consideration which greatly adds to their interest. The book is further noteworthy in being the only one of Freud's which has received little acceptance on the part of his followers. Thus of the fifty or so papers they have since devoted to the topic one observes that in the first decade only half supported Freud's theory, in the second decade only a third, and in the last decade none at all. But whatever may be the final judgment of the startling theory Freud put forward in this book there is no doubt about the hard and close thinking it contains. Many of the ideas thrown out in it—that on man's striving for perfectibility, to mention only one—will stimulate other thinkers for years to come.

The problem that was the starting point of Freud's cogitations was the dualism of the mind. He was in all his psychological work, as the result of his extensive experience, seized with the conception of a profound conflict within the mind, and he was very naturally concerned to apprehend the nature of the opposing forces. Never for a moment did he think of adopting a monistic conception, as Jung, and later Fenichel, did. Nor did he contemplate a pluralist view of the instincts, as most biologists do. Freud was an obstinate

* See pp. 40-41.

dualist, and we might pause to wonder why. Conflict itself could not be the whole reason, since this is by no means confined to two simple opponents. The dualism must have sprung from some depths in Freud's mentality, from some offshoot of his Oedipus complex, perhaps the opposition between the masculine and the feminine sides of his nature.

For the first twenty years or so of his work Freud was content to state the terms of mental conflict as being erotic impulses, derived from what biologists call the reproductive instinct, on the one hand, and ego impulses, including notably the instinct of self-preservation, on the other. This formulation was radically disturbed in 1914 when convincing reasons forced him to postulate the concept of narcissism, and in this self-love he felt the instinct of self-preservation must be included. So the only conflict then visible was between the narcissistic and the allo-erotic impulses, i.e. between two forms of the sexual instinct. This was profoundly unsatisfying, since Freud always felt sure that there must be some instinct in the mind, presumably in the ego, besides the sexual one; he had temporarily labeled it "self-interest." In the following year, 1915, two things happened. In "Instincts and Their Vicissitudes," an essay that formed part of Freud's extraordinary outburst of productivity in that spring he formed the conclusion that *hate*, later to be called the aggressive instinct, was distinct from the sexual instinct and was a primary constituent of the ego.[4] This was the beginning of the concept of a non-libidinal part of the ego which could be contrasted with the sexual instincts. The other event was his repeated observation of a game played by his eldest grandson, who kept carrying out over and over again actions which could only have an unpleasant meaning for him—actions relating to his mother's absence. The precise date of these observations can be ascertained: it was September, 1915, when he spent some weeks at his daughter's home in Hamburg. The incident seems to have made a deep impression on Freud, and he made it the starting point of his arguments in his *Beyond the Pleasure Principle* four years later.

During these next war years, which I have called relatively fallow ones, Freud seems to have relegated this train of thought to the back of his mind, but we may be sure that it never entirely disappeared. Associations must have been forming in his unconscious mind long before the creative ideas emerged. Even as late as the beginning of 1919 he reported being destitute of new ideas, but in March the ferment began at last to stir him to action. The flow of writing, however, was not so easy as it often was with him, and after reaching a certain point he postponed the work until the summer holidays. Then also the ideas refused to flow; the struggle for expression was proving exceptionally severe. It was only in the following spring that he succeeded in getting them on to paper, but by no means in the lucid and direct style he usually compassed. In reading the book one almost feels the struggle of the hard intellectual work going on in Freud's mind.

He began by re-stating his opinion of the importance of the pleasure-unpleasure principle, which in agreement with Fechner he had regarded as following the stability principle the latter had laid down. According to this the essential function of mental activity consists in reducing to as low a level as possible the tensions induced by either instinctual or external excitation. Freud used a term suggested by Barbara Low, the "Nirvana principle," to apply to both, whether the goal was to abolish or merely to reduce the excitation.[5] The common term used nowadays, with a very similar meaning, is Cannon's "homeostasis," which, incidentally, seems also nearly equivalent to Alcmaeon of Crotona's "isonomy." The whole train of thought is a remarkable anticipation of the modern science of cybernetics. It is interesting that Fechner was the only psychologist from whom Freud ever borrowed any ideas, and there is reason to think that he did so at Breuer's instance. The principle seemed to accord well with Freud's experience of abreaction, and indeed with his whole theory of wish-fulfillment where impulses seek satisfaction and then come to rest. But by now he had come to see that the correlation between increased excitation and unpleasantness, and between relief and pleasure, could not be so close as he had hitherto assumed; the pleasure obtained by the increase of sexual tension would seem to be a flagrant contradiction of the rule, and now the experience of "war dreams" seemed an equally striking one. There must be other factors besides the mere amount of tension, perhaps some relation to time or to rhythm. Four years later Freud clarified all these conceptions by stating that the stability or constancy principle had to do only with quantitative variations, whereas the pleasure-unpleasure principle was affected by qualitative ones also.[6]

Freud then related the story of the child's game alluded to above, and commented on the fondness of children for repeating games, stories and so on quite irrespective of whether they are pleasurable or not. It was this observation that made him wonder if there was some principle independent of the pleasure-unpleasure principle, and he suggested there was one to which he gave the name *repeti-tion-compulsion*. A number of apparently similar phenomena then came to his mind which seemed to fit in with this conception: the recurrent dreams of war neurotics in which the original trauma is revived again and again; the pattern of self-injuring behavior that can be traced through the lives of certain people; the tendency of many patients during psychoanalysis to act out over and again un-pleasant experiences of their childhood. It would not be hard in all these cases to discover some other motive for these repetitions, and indeed Freud himself suggested some. Thus with the war dreams, where the shock had broken through the defensive barrier in the ab-sence of any preparation, he remarked that the repetition during sleep, accompanied by intense anxiety, might represent an endeavor to supply the warning "anxiety signal," the absence of which had accounted for the traumatic effect of the shock. Nevertheless, Freud thought that such dreams proved an exception to his general theory of dreams representing a wish-fulfillment. It may be pointed out, however, that none of these dreams were quite confined to an accurate presentation of the traumatic experience. One always found in them some other irrelevant feature which called for analy-sis, and which may well have signified a tendency to manipulate the traumatic memory in the direction of a wish-fulfillment, even if the patient waked in terror before this could be accomplished. Indeed it would seem possible to bring all the examples mentioned above un-der the broad tendency of abreaction. But Freud was searching for some more general principle that would cover all these cases. He reverted to his and Breuer's distinction between free and bound en-ergy,[b] one which he had made a fundamental basis of his own psy-chology, and he now correlated this with the endeavor to "master" or "bind" unpleasant experiences which to him was the meaning of the repetitions in question.

The conception was not entirely new to Freud, although this was the first time he expounded it. In preparing a second edition of the *Studies in Hysteria*, in 1924, he related a story of having in-quired about an old patient of his, Frau Emmy von N., from a doc-tor he met at a *Naturforscher* congress. This was in all probabil-ity in 1894, the only year in which he was likely to have attended a medical congress.[8] On hearing how the patient had kept on repeat-ing the same behavior Freud was so struck by this perseverating fea-

[b] Penrose has pointed out that the sense in which Breuer and Freud used these terms is the precise opposite of that in which physicists use them.[7]

ture, often pronounced in the neuroses, that it stayed in his memory and thirty years later he termed it "a genuine instance of the repetition-compulsion." [9] Then there is a noteworthy passage in the first edition of *Three Essays on the Theory of Sexuality*, 1905.[10] Dealing with the fixations and lack of plasticity characteristic of neuroses he said that the early sexual impressions "tend in a compulsive manner towards repetition." [c]

Freud had now found the second principle he was looking for. It was this necessity to bind or master primitive impressions, to transform them from the "primary system" into the "secondary system"— to use his characteristic language. This he now regarded as more fundamental than the pleasure principle; it was indeed a necessary preliminary before the latter could be allowed to operate.

We may mention here an interesting thought Freud threw out casually in the present connection, and I will quote in full the sentence in question: "It is also well known, although the libido theory has not yet made sufficient use of the fact, that such severe disorders in the distribution of the libido as are present in melancholia are temporarily brought to an end by intercurrent organic illness, and indeed that even a fully developed condition of dementia praecox is capable of a temporary remission in the same circumstances." [11] This thought may well have been influenced also by the experiments Wagner-Jauregg was conducting about that time of infecting certain patients with malaria, knowledge of which Freud would surely have had; it will be remembered that it was these experiments in actively interfering with the mental economy which in time led to the convulsion treatment with insulin and later to the present vogue for electric shock therapy.

Three ideas, of equal importance in Freud's way of thinking, now came together in his mind. The primary processes that had to be bound before the pleasure principle could operate emanated from internal stimulation and so belonged to the instincts. The tendency to repetition was also pretty evidently of an instinctual nature. It also was more fundamental than the pleasure principle and contrasted with it in its "demonic" character; the former was often refined into a "reality principle." The tendency toward stability, also called the "constancy principle," was a fundamental attribute of the mind. It is perhaps the most hypothetical of the three, and Dorer has plausibly suggested that it derives from the quietistic teaching of Buddhism which is known to have greatly influenced

[c] *zwangsartig auf Wiederholung hinwirken.*

Fechner.[12] From the three ideas just mentioned two further ones began to emerge in Freud's train of thought, and they constituted his final theory of the mind.

It was the tendency to repetition that most occupied Freud's mind at this point; the other two ideas mentioned above had been familiar to him for many years. He rightly perceived that this tendency was a typical feature of instinctual life, which was therefore in its nature essentially conservative. Human instincts, it is true, are notable for their extraordinary plasticity, but the lower we go in the animal scale the more stereotyped does instinctual behavior appear; as is well known, it may in some creatures be so stupid as to threaten the very existence of the species when it is faced with a changing environment. So far, therefore, we are still within a biological compass, but Freud's imagination began to give the repetition-compulsion a more transcendental significance. We might even wonder how far he was influenced here by the memory of Fliess's law of inevitable periodicity, which was to account for all the happenings of life, and by Nietzsche's doctrine of the "eternal recurrence of the same"—a phrase Freud actually quoted in the book. At any rate there appears here a step in the reasoning which is not easy to follow and which has given rise to much misgiving.

The step in question was to equate the tendency to repetition with that of restoring a *previous* state of affairs, an equation which is far from obvious. On the contrary, as Lichtenstein has very trenchantly expounded, so far from their being identical they are in their very nature diametrically opposed.[13] The repetition-compulsion has the effect of not changing anything; the same thing happens over and over again. Restoring an *earlier* state of affairs, however, is a movement, one of a regressive kind, which changes the present state of affairs into one of a previous period in time. It implies an acceptance of the notion of time, whereas, as Lichtenstein interestingly showed, the repetition-compulsion implies rather a denial of time or change and perhaps even has this meaning.

Be all that as it may, Freud came to the conclusion that the fundamental aim of all instincts is to revert to an earlier state, a regression. It is a conclusion that, as Brun has fully shown, can receive no support from biology.[14] The main illustration Freud chose is open to quite a different interpretation; it was that of the recapitulation phenomena of embryology. When a human germ cell on its forward progress to develop into a metazoic creature displays en route rudiments of gills, then an amphibian heart, and finally a mammalian structure, that cell is not for a moment going backward; it is going forward all the time. It is influenced by its past history, it is true, but as a guide to develop further, not as a call to revert to the past.

Freud, however, now preoccupied with his conception of instinctual aims constantly moving backward toward the past, saw no reason to halt at what looked like a logical conclusion. If instincts aimed at the past why should they stop before reducing a living organism to a pre-vital state, that of inorganic matter? So the ultimate aim of life must be death. In this way arose Freud's celebrated concept of the *Death Instinct*. There would seem to be here some confusion between *telos* and *finis*. We are in psychoanalytic work justified in treating these two conceptions as extensively interchangeable. When we find that a patient's behavior has in fact led to a certain result we are very apt to suspect that his behavior had that intention, whether consciously or unconsciously, from the beginning, and often enough we find our suspicion to be well founded. But we should be very chary indeed of applying this method of reasoning to non-mental processes. If streptococci invading a human body kill the patient, with incidentally the death of the streptococci, we have no grounds for supposing that this unfortunate accident was in any respect the original aim of the whole proceeding; still less could we ascribe the fatality to an invisibly acting death instinct. And Freud's death instinct was not at all limited to mental aims; it was supposed to operate throughout the whole of living nature, and indeed perhaps in inorganic nature as well[15] (radium!). With such a cosmic principle in his mind one may imagine Freud's scorn when a communist announced that the death instinct was merely a by-product of the capitalistic system!

Freud remarked that while consideration of the repetition-compulsion was the first motive for his postulating a death instinct it is the stability principle that affords the strongest argument for it.[16]

Contemplating an all-pervading "instinct" with a range of this order now brought Freud into the danger of having to recognize a monistic view of life, the danger he had narrowly escaped in 1914 when the concept of narcissism extended the scope of the sexual instinct over a huge field. In his opinion the sexual instinct was the most conservative of all,[17] while the instinct of self-preservation, which one might have hoped would be opposed to the death instinct, turned out to be its servant; its only function was to ensure as far as possible that the organism died in its own way according to its inner law and at the time ordained by this, not through any avoidable accident or disease. Even the famous pleasure principle itself, which had done such yeoman service, was now stated to be the handmaid of the death instinct.[18] The impasse appeared absolute this time, and Freud seemed to have landed in the position of Schopenhauer, who taught that "death is the goal of life." Incidentally, Goethe himself had expressed in one of his conversations a very similar idea. "The moment of death, which is thus most appropriately called *dissolution,* is that in which the chief or ruling monad[d] dismisses all those subordinate monads which have hitherto been faithful vassals in her service. I therefore regard the quitting life, as well as the entering it, as a spontaneous act of this chief monad, whose very constitution is utterly unknown to us." [19] But Freud dexterously extricated himself once more, this time by pointing out that although the sexual instincts were conservative and obeyed both the repetition-compulsion and the constancy-nirvana principle they did so in a way peculiar to themselves. It was true that they tended to reinstate earlier forms of being and must therefore form part of the death instinct, but at least their mode of action had the merit of indefinitely postponing the final goal of the latter. One could even say that by doing so through creating ever new life they were thwarting the aim of the death instinct, and so could be viewed in contradistinction to it. So Freud succeeded after all in establishing two opposing forces in the mind: he termed them Life Instincts and Death Instincts respectively, the former being entitled *Eros.* They were of equal validity and status[20] and in constant struggle with each other, although the latter inevitably won in the end.

It is a little odd that Freud himself never, except in conversation, used for the death instinct the term *Thanatos,* one which has become so popular since. At first he used the terms "death instinct" and "destructive instinct" indiscriminately, alternating between them, but in his discussion with Einstein about war he made the distinction that the former is directed against the self and the latter, derived from it, is directed outward.[21] Stekel had in 1909 used the word Thanatos to signify a death-wish,[22] but it was Federn who introduced it in the present context.[23]

Then came a further problem. That mute force, operative in both the mind and in every single cell of the body, intent on ultimate destruction of the living being, performed its work silently. Was there any way of detecting signs of its existence? Freud thought he

[d] A Leibnitzian term.

could discover two such signs, or at least indications, that might proceed from the hypothetical death instinct. It was the cruelty in life that afforded the clue; the Great War itself had recently afforded a massive spectacle of aggression, brutality and cruelty. Not long before Freud had admitted the existence of a *primary* aggressive or destructive instinct, one which when fused with sexual impulses becomes the familiar perversion called sadism. When he first did so (in 1915) he counted it as part of the ego instincts, but later he gave it a more fundamental status, one independent of the ego and antedating its formation. Masochism he had always hitherto regarded as secondary to sadism, a sadistic impulse that had been turned inward against the self. Now he reversed the order, and suggested that there could be a primary masochism, a self-injuring tendency which would be an indication of the death instinct. Destructive and sadistic impulses would be derived from this, and no longer its source. Freud's idea was that the sexual or life instincts—responsible for the "clamor" of life—in their struggle against their opponent endeavor to save life a little longer by diverting the self-destructive tendency outward against other people, much as a ruler may deflect rebellious or revolutionary impulses against the foreign world by instigating a war—the very motive with which his country, Austria, had brought about the great World War. It was a highly ingenious conception, and with it Freud had to his satisfaction rounded his dynamic conceptions of mental functioning.

It is plain that here Freud was thinking essentially in human, and indeed in clinical, terms. He made no allusion to the vegetarian animals such as sheep and rabbits whose aggressive impulses are less evident than in man; when a farmer calls rabbits destructive creatures he does not imply that they have a passion for destroying their enemies.

Although Freud had of course from early on been familiar with the savage aspects of human nature, with its cruel and murderous impulses, he does not appear, except for the slight hint in 1915,[e] to have reflected closely on their nosological status until now, when he postulated an "aggressive instinct" derived from a self-destructive "death instinct." It has been claimed by Adlerians that Freud was here adopting a suggestion Adler had made in 1908 of a primary aggressive instinct, but there is a world of difference between the two conceptions. Adler's was more sociological than psychological, a striving for power and superiority, while Freud's was not only

* See Volume II, p. 319.

biological but even reached beyond this into the realm of chemistry and physics.

Freud admitted later to having felt a personal aversion to accepting the independent existence of an aggressive instinct. In *Civilization and its Discontents*, 1930, he confessed: "I can no longer understand how we could have overlooked the universality of non-erotic aggression and destruction, and could have omitted to give it its due significance in our interpretation of life." [24] And he continued: "I can remember my own defensive attitude when the idea of an instinct of destruction first made its appearance in psychoanalytical literature,[25] and how long it took before I became accessible to it."

Somewhat on the analogy of the physiological processes of anabolism and catabolism Freud regarded the operation of Eros as essentially a binding one, as the cells of a metazoon are bound together; union was its supreme aim, as that of the death instinct was disintegration or separation. These principles, or instincts, were by now assuming something of a transcendental significance. There are only a few earlier allusions to Eros in Freud's writings, e.g. in 1910[26] and 1920[27] (though oddly enough Breuer had made one in the *Studien*[28]). And now he had recourse to the classical studies of his youth in support of his present conception of Eros. He quoted Plato's phantasy,[29] one probably derived from Indian sources, of the first human being as androgenous, one who later became separated into man and woman; the longing for union between them was really a longing for reunion. It is interesting that in one of his love letters nearly forty years before Freud had quoted this idea of Plato's to his betrothed to illustrate the intensity of his longing for union with her.[30] If we are to follow Plato's, and Freud's, thought in its entirety we must conclude that the ultimate reunion it betokened could only be with the mother, from whom one had unfortunately been separated at the beginning of life.

Another classical allusion Freud quoted in a subsequent paper, "Analysis Terminable and Interminable," was the passage in which Empedocles enunciated the two fundamental principles, not only of living beings but of the whole universe, as being φιλία νεῖκος , Love and Strife.[31] Except that Freud extended the latter into a death instinct, they are identical with his two opposing principles.

Although Freud first announced as purely tentative the ideas we have just been considering, a private train of thought, so to speak, that amused him but of the validity of which he was far from convinced—within a couple of years, in his book *The Ego and the Id,* he came to accept them fully, and as time went on with increasingly complete conviction. I remember that when, in my writings[32] and in correspondence I expressed some scepticism concerning his conclusions he wrote regretting my dilatoriness in accepting them and hoping I should soon do so; for himself he could no longer see his way without them, they had become indispensable to him.[33]

As was mentioned above, however, the new theories met with a very mixed reception among analysts, and that in spite of Freud's high prestige.[f] A few, including Alexander,[g] Eitingon and Ferenczi, accepted them at once. Others who wished to do so sought for further arguments in support. What seemed a promising direction for this purpose was the theory of physics in which there seemed to be some resemblances to Freud's hypotheses. Freud himself hinted as much in suggesting a possible relationship between the binding function of Eros and chemical affinity.[34] Alexander was the first to do this.[35] The aim was to establish a relationship between Fechner's principle of stability, which Freud had identified with his Nirvana principle and ultimately with the death instinct, and the second law of thermodynamics. This sinister law, the bogey of all optimists, can strictly speaking be expressed only in mathematical language, such as a quantity of heat divided by a temperature; the law of entropy states that *in a self-contained system* this number increases with time. This is true, however, only of a hypothetical closed system such as is never met with in nature, least of all in living beings where, as the eminent physicist Schrödinger has insisted, by taking in energy from without they actually acquire a negative entropy.[36] The more popular apprehension of it, however, is the conception that certain physical processes, being irreversible, must infallibly be reduced to terms of heat. The idea of the universe running down, therefore, easily suggested that the tendency to death implied in the death instinct was only a particular aspect of the general physical law. Bernfeld and Feitelberg dealt with this theme at length,[37] without coming to any very definite conclusions, and Lichtenstein fully accepted the identity in question.[38] From the physical side, however, two English writers, Kapp[39] and Penrose,[40] published dev-

---

[f] The most comprehensive discussion of the conceptions of the constancy principle, repetition-compulsion and death instinct is to be found in J. C. Flugel's posthumously published book: *Studies in Feeling and Desire* (London: G. Duckworth, 1955), Chapter IV.
[g] Alexander's opinion changed later.

astating criticisms of the confusions in these authors' works, which must finally dispose of the idea that there could be any relationship between entropy and the death instinct.

Nor was the attempt to obtain support from the realm of biology any more successful, in spite of Freud's endeavor to arrange his philosophical speculations in a biological framework. The thorough discussion of this theme by Brun, whose biological knowledge must command respect, is a complete demonstration of this.[41] No biological observation can be found to support the idea of a death instinct, one which contradicts all biological principles. Nacht has recently insisted on the essential distinction between the *conditions* of existence which—more or less mechanically—ultimately lead to the change we call death and, on the other hand, an active *force*, as Freud thought, more or less deliberately aiming at death.[42] Brun could not even find any reason for postulating a *primary* aggressive instinct, and regarded all the manifestations of aggression as secondary reactions to various situations (hunger, thwarting and so on).

So far as I know, the only analysts, e.g. Melanie Klein, Karl Menninger and Hermann Nunberg, who still employ the term "death instinct" do so in a purely clinical sense which is remote from Freud's original theory. Any clinical applications he made of it were postulated after devising the theory, not before. Thus we have the purely psychological observations of the infant's aggressive and cannibalistic phantasies, followed later by murderous ones, but one cannot infer from them any active will on the part of the cells of the body to lead that body to death. The very phrase "death wishes," i.e. murderous wishes, unavoidable in psychoanalytic work, seems to have wrought much confusion here through the mere play on the word "death." The fact that in rare cases of melancholia such wishes may, through complicated mechanisms of identification, etc., result in suicide is again no proof that they arose from a primary wish for self-destruction on the part of the body; the clinical evidence points clearly in the opposite direction.

It is quite essential to distinguish between the hypothetical aspects of the death instinct theory and the clinical observations that have become secondarily associated with it. Edward Bibring has put this point well in the following statement. "Instincts of life and death are not psychologically perceptible as such; they are biological instincts whose existence is required by hypothesis alone. That being so, it follows that, strictly speaking, the theory of the primal instincts is a concept which ought only to be adduced in a theoretical context and not in discussion of a clinical or empirical nature. In them, the idea of aggressive and destructive instincts will suffice to account for all the facts before us." [43]

The hard thinking in the book under consideration makes the train of thought by no means easy to follow, and several analysts, including myself, have attempted to present it in simpler language. The clearest presentation of it is the impartial one given by Bibring, to which the reader may be referred.[44] Freud's views on this subject have often been considerably misinterpreted. Perhaps the oddest example is that of a Dutch philosopher who tried recently to express Freud's philosophical conclusions as follows: "Freud's polarity may be reduced to a vital and a supravital instinct, which aims at development during mundane life, but beyond this at perfection in the supra-mundane life." [45] I can easily imagine Freud's comment on this rendering of his supposed outlook on life.

If so little objective support is to be found for Freud's culminating theory of a death instinct, one is bound to consider the possibility of subjective contributions to its inception, doubtless in connection with the theme of death itself. It is a theme that has assuredly occupied the mind of man from the beginning of time. Primitive man, as we know from anthropological studies, regarded himself as potentially immortal. Death, even from internal disease, could only be due to the action of some malign enemy, a concept that has lasted into historical times in the guise of the mythological figures of Atropos, Charon, Erebus, etc., and later the inexorable Reaper with the scythe. The same primitive faith in natural immortality was thus preserved by the belief that only a malign enemy could bring life to an end; otherwise it would continue for ever. It might be argued that the hypothetical death instinct subserves in effect the same function as those more anthropomorphic entities. The only difference is that in the former case the enemy is believed to be within. Whether this is to be regarded as an introjection of the external beings—all doubtless parental imagos—or whether the latter were projections of a real internal enemy, the death instinct, is a nice question. Our narcissism makes it very hard to admit that our vital processes have their own inherent limitation, that their strength is only enough to last a certain time, one which varies greatly with different species of animal. When it is exhausted, or has proved not equal to some strain put on it, we die without the need for any agency to slay us. Freud himself raised this very question of potential immortality, and discussed it at some length without being able to come to any satisfactory conclusion. Weismann had suggested that unicellular creatures are inherently immortal and that death appeared for the first time among the metazoa. Some experimental work indicating that the former can live for an apparently indefinite time in favorable circumstances did not, however, in Freud's opinion, exclude the possibility that nevertheless a death instinct might be concealed in them.

Now, in Freud's personality there were several features of note in his attitude toward the topic of death. In the world of reality he was an unusually courageous man who faced misfortune, suffering danger and ultimately death itself with unflinching fortitude. But in phantasy there were other elements. As far back as we know anything of his life he seems to have been prepossessed by thoughts about death, more so than any other great man I can think of except perhaps Sir Thomas Browne and Montaigne. Even in the early years of our acquaintance he had the disconcerting habit of parting with the words "Goodbye; you may never see me again." There were the repeated attacks of what he called *Todesangst* (dread of death). He hated growing old, even as early as his forties, and as he did so the thoughts of death became increasingly clamorous. He once said he thought of it every day of his life, which is certainly unusual. On the other hand there was a still more curious longing for death. After his fainting attack in Munich in 1912 his first remark after regaining consciousness was: "How sweet it must be to die." He groaned at the thought that he might have to live as long as his half-brother or his father. Yet whenever there was any real risk to his life he welcomed the respite of overcoming it. He often said that his chief fear was the haunting thought that he might die before his mother. This he explained by the reflection that such news would be terribly painful to her, but it would seem also to imply a separation from her. When it came about that she died first, he did not mourn but felt a deep sense of relief at the thought that now he could die in peace (and be reunited?). Altogether his attitude was a rich and complex one with many aspects. He more than once ascribed it, no doubt quite correctly, to the lasting influence of his death wishes in infancy.

(Some writers have suggested current events, particularly the death of his daughter, the onset of his cancer and the death of his favorite grandson, as sources for Freud's renewed interest in the subject of death at this time.[46] But it is definitely established that *Beyond the Pleasure Principle* was written several months before the first of these and four years before the other two.)

Thus Freud always had a double attitude or phantasy about death, which one may well interpret as dread of a terrible father alternating with desire for reunion with a loved mother.

In the light of all these considerations I think it fair to suggest that in forming an opinion about the validity of Freud's theory of a death instinct we are justified in taking into account possible subjective sources in addition to the arguments he adduced in his writings.

Super-ego and Id

The second group of ideas that Freud expounded about this time, two years later than those just discussed, is of a very different order. They were derived directly from clinical experience with the minimum of speculative superstructure, and so were amenable to the tests of comparative investigation. Nor were they as revolutionary in thought as the ideas surrounding that of the death instinct; they had indeed been adumbrated on several previous occasions, and the conclusions reached were in a direct line with Freud's main work. For these reasons they were more easily accepted by other analysts, and they now constitute an essential and valuable part of general psychoanalytic investigation, that into the psychology of the ego. This starting point provided by Freud has stimulated a vast number of studies in the thirty years that have since elapsed, resulting in an important addition to our knowledge of mental functioning.[47]

The ideas in question were most fully expounded in a book published in 1932 entitled *The Ego and the Id*.[48] They were more popularly expounded and somewhat expanded ten years later in a chapter of Freud's *New Introductory Lectures on Psycho-Analysis*.[49] The curious title *The Ego and the Id* needs a little explanation. We decided for linguistic reasons to use the Latin *Id*[h] to translate the German *Es* (= It), an impersonal term which Freud now employed to designate the non-personal part of the mind, that distinct from the ego or self. It is a term that had been extensively employed by Nietzsche and recently popularized by Groddeck. It comes much

[h] Weismann's use of this term to indicate the determinants of heredity —nowadays called "genes"—seems to be obsolete, so that there is no risk of confusion.

more naturally in German, where it accords with such phrases as "It dreamed to me" where we should say "I dreamed."

The Id is the primordial reservoir of energy, not differentiated energy but energy derived, according to Freud, from the two primary Life and Death Instincts. At all events it is essentially instinctual. It is completely unorganized, thus differing from the ego of which organization is the hall mark. It has all the negative features which Freud had previously described as characteristic of what he called the Primary System,[50] absence of negation or of contradictions, and so on.

This conception of the Id was both more comprehensive and more fruitful than the early one of the Unconscious, which in some respects it tended in practice to replace. It is broader, and the reasons Freud gave for this extension are very instructive. Originally his conception of the unconscious had made it synonymous with what was repressed; indeed it was through his discovery of the latter that he had arrived at his concept of the unconscious. For some time now, however, Freud had been realizing that the unconscious contained more than what was repressed. Apart from the hypothetical question of the state of the primary impulses before the forces of repression had been brought to bear on them, the most convincing reason for surmising the presence of other contents in the unconscious besides the repressed material was a purely clinical experience. When a patient manifests the easily recognized signs of resistance he is in most cases aware of his repugnance and recalcitrancy, but situations occur, and not infrequently, in which he is quite unaware of it; in other words, an unconscious resistance must be operative. The repressed impulses themselves are of course striving to reach consciousness to obtain expression, so that any resistances must emanate from the ego itself. The unavoidable conclusion follows that the ego is not limited to what the subject consciously calls his self, but is continued below the threshold of consciousness; part of the ego is conscious, part unconscious. And the latter part is not merely preconscious; it is unconscious in the fullest sense, since much work is needed to make it conscious.

This appreciation of the greater depth of the ego enabled Freud to give a more accurate account than previously of its nature. He had been accustomed to saying simply that the kernel of the ego was the accumulation of perceptions received from the outer world. He adhered to this statement, but amplified it by saying that the ego was that part of the Id which had become modified by those perceptions. Among the most important of these are the perceptions, and of course affects, to do with the human environment, typically the parents. Freud described at length the nature of the imprints derived from such sources, but added that less significant ones could be added later from identification with other figures in life. At times there may be important differences between the various identifications, leading to considerable disharmony in the ego. Freud would explain in this way the cases of so-called multiple personality.

In his amoeba analogy Freud had previously spoken of a primary narcissism of the ego, from which libido may stream toward the outer world and again be withdrawn from it; the latter process he called secondary narcissism. Freud now suggested that even the earliest narcissism of the ego was secondary and brought about in this same way, the process with which we were familiar in studying later life. The libido of the Id is directed from the start toward outer objects with the aim of obtaining gratification. When this fails it is re-directed toward the ego, but this time it no longer has a true sexual goal; it is "desexualized." Freud suggested that this was the essential step in the mysterious and important process called sublimation. Incidentally he remarked that inasmuch as the sexual goal had been given up, the processes of narcissism and sublimation no longer served the aims of Eros, in fact were opposed to these and therefore came under the domination of the death instinct. This was a further complication in his instinct theory.

Freud had ten years before expounded the conception of an *Ego Ideal*, an agency in the mind which criticized the deficiencies of the actual self and spurred it to attain stricter standards in the moral or aesthetic sphere. He now re-christened this the *Super-ego*,[1] but at the same time gave it a considerably wider connotation. In the first place he gave cogent reasons for concluding that like the ego itself an important part of the super-ego is unconscious. This unconscious part is far harsher in its condemnations than any stings of conscience on a higher level. It is closely connected with a profound sense of guilt, if it is not actually identical with this. Its activity can be eased by suffering or punishment, a fact that results in a patho-

---

[1] Hugo Munsterberg, incidentally one of Freud's strongest opponents, had used this term, or rather its German equivalent *überich*, so long ago as 1907, though he had given it a connotation more akin to Freud's Id.[51] I do not know whether Freud had come across it; it is not likely.

logical "need for punishment" found in many neurotics. Freud remarked that it was the study of the psychotic symptom of "delusion of observation" which first made him appreciate the action of this internal censuring agency.[52]

On the other hand Freud corrected a former view of his about the testing of reality being also a function of this censuring capacity of the ego ideal. He now maintained it was a function of the ego itself, which indeed comes into being through that very contact with outer reality. Freud here harked back to the view he had expressed nearly thirty years before.[53]

The moral agency which we call conscience is a derivative of the super-ego, as is the ego ideal. Although Freud did not propose it, it would be more convenient to reserve the latter term for our conscious ideals in a positive sense, the super-ego, or at least its unconscious part, being more concerned with the negative function of condemning. From this point of view it would be correct to say that man is both more moral and also more immoral (repressed impulses!) than he knows. Appreciation of this might deprive the unconscious of the bad name it has enjoyed for so long. The conscience itself is, according to Freud, a function of the tension existing between the ego and the super-ego, and its sensitiveness a measure of the degree of that tension.

Attention may be called at this point to a truly remarkable correspondence between Freud's conception of the super-ego and Nietzsche's exposition of the origin of the "bad conscience," which deserves to be quoted. "All instincts which do not find a vent without *turn inwards*[1]—this is what I mean by the growing 'internalisation' of man: consequently we have the first growth in man of what subsequently was called his soul. The whole inner world burst apart when man's external outlet became *obstructed*. These terrible bulwarks, with which the social organisation protected itself against the old instincts of freedom—punishments belong pre-eminently to these bulwarks—brought it about that all those instincts of wild, free, prowling man became turned backwards, *against man himself*. Enmity, cruelty, the delight in persecution, in surprises, change, destruction—the turning all these instincts against their own possessors: this was the origin of the 'bad conscience.' It was man who, lacking external enemies and obstacles, and imprisoned as he was in the

[1] Italicized in the original.

oppressive narrowness and monotony of custom, in his own impatience lacerated, persecuted, gnawed, frightened, and ill-treated himself; it was this animal in the hands of the tamer which beat itself against the bars of its cage; it was this being who, pining and yearning for that desert home of which it had been deprived, was compelled to create out of its own self an adventure, a torture-chamber, a hazardous and perilous desert; it was this fool, this homesick and desperate prisoner, who invented the 'bad conscience.' But thereby he introduced that most grave and sinister illness from which mankind has not yet recovered, the suffering of man from the disease called man as the result of a violent breaking from his animal past, the result, as it were, of a spasmodic plunge into a new environment and new conditions of existence, the result of a declaration of war against the old instincts, which up to that time had been the staple of his power, his joy, his formidableness." [54]

Nietzsche here depicts the process in phylogenetic terms, to which Freud would have fully subscribed and which he adumbrated in *Totem and Taboo*, but in the present book Freud dealt with it on a deep ontogenetic level, showing how the community of the enforced social life is represented in early childhood by the example of the parents. He would have maintained the continuity of the two sources, the inherited and the acquired, the nature of the process being identical with both.

Hitschmann had read a paper on this very book of Nietzsche's before the Vienna Society in April, 1908, and they had devoted two evenings to the discussion of Nietzsche.[k] It is unlikely that it left no impression on Freud's mind, though any such impression took many years to germinate.

What one has rather clumsily to call the unconscious sense of guilt[1] can be extremely severe and impose great suffering. The ego defends itself against such suffering, using for that purpose its most powerful weapon—repression. That is the chief reason why so much of the super-ego is unconscious. The mechanism is the reverse of the more familiar one in which the ego represses forbidden impulses at the behest of the super-ego; in the former case it has turned against its tyrannical mentor. This revolt may go so far as to produce an apparent absence of conscience, with unscrupulous behavior as a result. It is a paradox that persons most sensitive to the exhortations of

---

[k] I am obliged to Dr. Hartmann for drawing my attention to this passage.[55]
[1] It may be recalled that Freud gave a clear picture of this conception as early as 1907.[56]

conscience, or rather of the unconscious super-ego, may be those most able to indulge freely in antisocial conduct.

The same agency may lead to other undesirable results. There are patients, for instance, with whom successful analytic work results only in a worsening of their symptoms—what Freud called a negative therapeutic reaction. He was able to explain this extremely puzzling state of affairs, one not to be accounted for solely by the familiar obstacles of narcissism or castration fears, through his discovery that this type of patient was always burdened by an unusually powerful unconscious sense of guilt, one too painful to be allowed to enter consciousness. When such patients suffer consciously from a sense of inferiority—the celebrated "inferiority complex"—Freud was of the opinion that the guiltiness had been subsequently eroticized, so that the complex could be described as the erotic aspect of the sense of guilt.[57]

In spite of the basic contributions Freud made to the study of the origins of the super-ego it has proved more complex than was at first expected. When I reviewed the problems a few years later[58] Freud wrote to me: "All the obscurities and difficulties you describe really exist. But they are not to be removed even with the points of view you emphasize. They need completely fresh investigations, accumulated impressions and experiences, and I know how hard it is to obtain these. Your essay is a dark beginning in a complicated matter." [59] Two conclusions seemed to Freud to be definite. One was that the super-ego has a closer connection with the Id than the ego has. It originates rather in the inner world, the ego in the outer.[60] The other was that identification with the parents, particularly with the father, plays an important part in its genesis. This comes to expression especially at the time when the Oedipus complex is being resolved, so that Freud could assert that the super-ego is the heir of the Oedipus complex. He had a great deal to say about those identifications and the mechanism of them, and made the interesting point that the identifications were not so much with the actual egos of the parents as with their super-egos; the inheritance of tradition is in this way explained.[61] In discussing ambivalent attitudes toward parents he remarked that it was not all to be accounted for by the conflicts instituted by rivalry; one has also to bear in mind the matter of innate bisexuality.

This identification, however, is by no means the only source of the super-ego. The picture of a parent that is incorporated in the identification is commonly very distorted; the mildest parent may be represented by a harsh imago. The phantasy of the child which thus distorts the picture is a contribution of his own, and receives powerful additions from his sadistic impulses. Then there is the further likelihood that direct heredity may be important. Freud thought here in his Lamarckian fashion of the inherited influence of the experiences of previous generations.

9

Lay Analysis

SINCE THE TOPIC OF LAY ANALYSIS WAS THE FEATURE OF THE PSYCHO-
analytical movement that, with the possible exception of the Verlag,
most keenly engaged Freud's interest, and indeed emotions, during
the last phase of his life, it deserves a chapter to itself. It was associated with a central dilemma in the psychoanalytical movement,
one for which no solution has yet been found. It was Freud who
most clearly perceived the nature of that dilemma, and it will be
well to expound it before narrating the history of the problems it
gave rise to. Discounting the fact that psychoanalysis had originated
in the field of psychopathology, Freud recognized that the discoveries
he had made, and the theoretical basis established in respect of
them, had a very general and extremely wide bearing outside that
field. To him they constituted a foundation for a truly dynamic
psychology with all that this conclusion implies. Insofar as it signifies a more profound understanding of human nature, of the motives and emotions of mankind, it was inevitable that psychoanalysis
should be in a position to make valuable, and sometimes crucial,
contributions to all fields of human mentality, and that further researches would increase the value of such contributions to an extent
not easy to limit. To mention only a few of these: the study of anthropology, mythology and folklore; the historical evolution of mankind with the various divergent routes this has followed; the upbringing and education of children; the significance of artistic endeavor; the vast field of sociology with a more penetrating estimate
of the various social institutions, such as marriage, law, religion

and perhaps even government; possibly even the apparently insoluble problems of international relations. All these endless potentialities would be lost were psychoanalysis to end by being confined to a small section in the chapter on therapy in a textbook of psychiatry side by side with hypnotic suggestion, electrotherapy and so on. This he foresaw might well happen if psychoanalysis came to be regarded as nothing but a branch of medical practice.

It has sometimes been thought that Freud's crusade in favor of lay analysis sprang from resentment at the scurvy way in which he had for so many years been treated by the medical profession. In my opinion there is very little truth in this suggestion; what mainly influenced him was the wish for a broader outlook on psychoanalysis than could be expected from doctors alone. He certainly would have been more than grieved had doctors held aloof from his work, knowing as he did that the basis of research in it must always be the analysis of suffering people.

Freud further realized that, although practicing analysts could offer hints and suggestions in these diverse fields, the only permanently valuable contributions would have to be made by experts in them, experts who had also acquired a suitable knowledge of psychoanalysis by proceeding through the recognized training. An essential part of this training consists in the carrying out of psychoanalyses on those desiring to submit themselves to it. For we there encounter the basic fact around which all these problems revolve: namely, that no motive has yet been discovered, or is likely to be discovered in the future, making possible the investigation of the deepest layers of the mind other than that of personal *suffering*. That awesome fact irrevocably binds psychology, and all the sciences ancillary to it, to psychopathology. So an anthropologist, for example, desirous of applying psychoanalytic doctrines in his special field would first of all, at least for a time, have to become a psychotherapist. One might suppose that this was a very satisfactory solution to the whole matter, but unfortunately experience has unequivocally negated it. For in fact those coming from other fields to study psychoanalysis, whether from the fields of education, anthropology, art or literature, invariably wish to become practicing analysts for the rest of their lives, a decision which necessarily limits their usefulness in applying their newly acquired knowledge in their previous fields of work. Two motives, if we leave out of account any possible financial ones, are evident in such decisions: the greater attraction of interest in the new field; and the recognition that psychoanalytic insight into the deep layers of the mind is not something acquired once and for all at a given phase of study, but has to be refreshed and extended by continuous contact with the raw material of observation, i.e. the analysis of patients. Such a person is then termed a lay or non-medical psychoanalyst.

Accepting, if necessary, the limitation just mentioned, Freud nevertheless warmly welcomed the incursion into the therapeutic field of suitable people from walks of life other than the medical, and he proclaimed as a principle that in his opinion it was a matter of indifference whether intending candidates for psychoanalytic training held a medical qualification or not; nor did he even think that any kind of academic qualification was at all necessary for membership, as Jung had once urged.[1] Furthermore, he urged such candidates as asked his advice not to spend years of study in obtaining such a qualification but to proceed at once to psychoanalytic work. He envisaged a broader and better preliminary education for the novice in psychoanalysis. There should be a special college in which lectures would be given in the rudiments of anatomy, physiology and pathology, in biology, embryology and evolution, in mythology and the psychology of religion, and in the classics of literature.[2]

Freud stood apart from the hurly-burly of the outer world, and it was appropriate for him to take long views and conjure up visions of the distant future. But those of us in humbler stations of life were compelled to take shorter views and cope with more immediate contingencies. He had painted a seductive, and indeed grandiose, picture of a new and quite independent profession, and wanted to initiate it by opening the doors wide to lay analysts drawn from various sources. Much as one might be captivated by his vision, however, we had to take into account a number of considerations that would first have to be dealt with. To begin with, Freud firmly and rightly insisted that his lay analysts should not in fact be completely independent. Being untrained in all the matters that go to forming a medical diagnosis, they were incompetent to decide which patients were suitable for their treatment, and Freud laid down the invariable rule that lay analysts were never to function as consultants; the first person to examine the patient must be a doctor, who would then refer suitable cases to the analyst.[3] Plainly this implied cooperation with the medical profession and raised the question of how far, and under what conditions, this would be available. There were some countries, such as Austria, France and some of the United States, where the law forbade any therapeutic measures being carried out by anyone not possessing a medical qualification. There were many more where members of the medical profession were forbidden by law to collaborate with non-medical practitioners. Psychoanalysis, it is true, could claim to differ in essence from other forms of non-medical therapy, but to what extent would it be able to enforce this claim?

Then, if intending students of psychoanalysis were to be told that the study of medicine was irrelevant, would it not in time become irrelevant? How many of them would be quixotically inclined to spend tedious years of toil and expense in an unnecessary direction? That might lead to the majority of analysts being lay. In that event one might have to envisage the practice of psychoanalysis becoming increasingly divorced from the science of medicine, to its great practical and theoretical detriment. Moreover, its prospect of ever becoming recognized as a legitimate branch of science would be reduced perhaps to a vanishing point. Psychiatry in its broadest sense, i.e. the psychological aspects of medicine, is certainly its nearest link to the other branches of science, one more accessible than pure (academic) psychology.

With this background we may now follow the story of the events in Freud's lifetime bearing on this subject.

So far as I know the only non-medical analysts who practiced before the Great War were Hermine Hug-Hellmuth in Vienna and the Rev. Oskar Pfister in Zurich. There had been, it is true, from the very start non-medical members of the Vienna Society who never practiced, such as Max Graf and Hugo Heller, and some, such as Baron Alfred von Winterstein, who began to do so only at the outset of the war. Dr. Phil. Hug-Hellmuth conducted pedagogic analyses and contributed many useful analytic observations on children. She is remembered also for having devised the play technique for child analysis which Melanie Klein was to exploit so brilliantly after the war; incidentally, though it is generally forgotten, Freud himself had as long ago as 1904 given a broad hint of such possibilities.[4] Pfister's analyses were confined to adolescents troubled by moral conflicts, and he was able to supplement his analytic procedures by ethical advice and religious exhortations. Toward the latter part of the war Melanie Klein initiated her famous career by helping Ferenczi in his Budapest Clinic in the analytic treatment of children.

Toward the end of 1919 Bernfeld proposed to organize an association of lay persons interested in psychoanalysis which would be loosely affiliated to the Vienna Psycho-Analytical Society. Freud was so much in favor of the scheme that he decided to donate to it the sum of 11,000 Kronen ($2,200.00) he had just received from the von Freund fund.[5] Normally this would have been given to the *Verlag*, von Freund's foundation which meant so much to Freud himself; that he should be prepared to give preference to an undertaking in support of the laity is a measure of the importance he attached to that movement. For some reason, however, the whole plan was dropped. Six years later Ferenczi revived it and informed Freud that he intended to invite the next International Congress (Homburg, 1925) to institute under its auspices an outside body to be entitled "Friends of Psychoanalysis." Freud would have favored this also, but when the proposal was discussed before the Congress at a preliminary meeting of the "Committee" we unanimously condemned it, so it was not brought forward.[6] It assuredly would not have been accepted by the Congress.

In the first couple of years after the war a number of non-medical analysts began to practice in Vienna; Winterstein had already begun in 1914. Otto Rank was perhaps the first of them, though he half-apologetically told me then that he analyzed only children. The illusion was at that time prevalent that analyses of children were an easier affair than those of adults; that was the reason why when the New York Society in 1929 temporarily agreed to permit the practice of lay analysis they restricted it to child analysis, and even as late as 1938 this was the official view in the Hungarian Society. Rank was presently joined by Bernfeld and Reik, and in 1923 by Anna Freud; then later came Aichhorn, Kris, Wälder and others. At about the same time several began work in London also, notably J. C. Flugel, Barbara Low, Joan Riviere, Ella Sharpe, and before long James and Alix Strachey.

In Vienna most of those coming to be analyzed were Americans, and many of these set up in turn as lay analysts on their return to America. This was the beginning of a feud between American and European analysts which smouldered for many years and was finally healed only after the last war. In the parlous state of Austria at that time, when the most urgent necessities of life were hard to come by, it is not surprising that financial considerations impelled a few analysts, both lay and medical, to relax the standards generally thought desirable in professional work. I remember asking Rank, for instance, how he could bring himself to send back to America as a practicing analyst someone who had been with him barely six weeks, and he replied with a shrug of the shoulders "one must live." It should also be remembered that at that time "training" was entirely individual and unofficial, there being no standards imposed by an institute as in later years.

In 1925 Brill wrote an article for a New York newspaper expressing his disapproval of lay analysis, and in that autumn he announced to the New York Psychoanalytic Society his determination to break relations with Freud if the Viennese attitude toward America continued.

In the spring of 1926 a patient of Theodor Reik brought an action against him on the score of harmful treatment and invoked the Austrian law against quackery. Fortunately for Reik the patient was shown to be an unbalanced person whose evidence was untrustworthy. That and Freud's personal intervention with a high official decided the case in Reik's favor. But it was the occasion for Freud's hastily putting together in July a little book entitled *The Question of Lay Analysis*.[7] It was cast in the form of a dialogue between himself and a not unsympathetic listener modeled on the functionary just mentioned. The greater part of the book is a brilliant exposition to an outsider of what psychoanalysis is and does, and is one of the best examples of that expository art in which Freud always excelled. It is followed by a persuasive plea, doubtless the most persuasive that has ever been made, on behalf of a liberal attitude toward lay analysis; some of the arguments he adduced have already been indicated above. Freud's own description of the book—he was seldom complimentary to his own writings—was "shallow stuff with some cutting remarks, which because of my bad mood at present are rather bitter." [8] The bad mood in question came from his being more than usually plagued by his prosthesis so that he was even unable to speak. He told Eitingon of the capital the Vienna newspapers were making out of the Reik affair, and added: "The movement against lay analysis seems to be only an offshoot of the old resistance against analysis in general. Unfortunately many of our own members are so short-sighted, or so blinded by their professional interests, as to join in. I regard the whole movement as an expression of annoyance at the benevolent interest my seventieth birthday aroused in the outer world, and so feel partly responsible for it." [9]

Incidentally, the Reik case was not the last of its kind. A similar suit was brought against Mrs. Williams in Paris in 1951. The judge there, in true French fashion, remarked that a pretty defendant was an unfortunate choice for such a prosecution, and, partly perhaps on those grounds, she won. And as I write (1955) I hear that Dr. and Mrs. Werner Kemper have been arrested in Brazil on similar charges.

When I wrote to Freud on the publication of his booklet I said: "While you have left a few things unsaid, you have given a totally different perspective to the whole problem, a perspective which we must all feel to be of vast importance. The thing I think you have settled beyond all doubt is that it would be very injurious to our movement to forbid lay analysis. There will be lay analysts, and there must be because we need them. The necessity for training is of course obvious. The wider question of how far we should aim at making analysis an independent profession, having only certain links with the medical one, is extraordinarily interesting, and I find there is much to say about it. In all probability, however, it will not be settled by us, but by fate." [10] Freud replied: "I very much appreciate your last remarks on *Laien-analyse.*" Glad to know I have at least made some impression on you. I expected you to take the other side of the question. . . . You have justly guessed what my real intention is, but I saw no obligation to proclaim it to the public at this moment. To be sure fate will decide over the ultimate relation between psycho-analysis and medicine, but that does not imply that we should not try to influence fate, attempt to shape it by our own efforts." [11]

In the autumn of that year the New York Legislature passed a bill, on Brill's instigation according to Ferenczi,[12] declaring lay analysis to be illegal, and the American Medical Association also issued a warning to its members against any cooperation with such practitioners.

Foreseeing that the topic was going to be one of major interest at the next Congress, to be held in Innsbruck in September, 1927, Eitingon and I arranged for a preliminary discussion in the form of contributions to be published in the *International Journal* and the *Zeitschrift*, the official organs of the Association. Twenty-eight such contributions, including two final ones by Freud and Eitingon respectively, were published in the form of a literary symposium.[13] My own geographical position enabled me to appreciate the motives of the extreme camps on either side, and I also had the advantage of belonging to a Society that in its conduct had shown itself—and still does—far more liberal toward lay analysis than any other; at that time 40 per cent of our members were non-medical. But we did not adopt Freud's extreme position of dissuading intending candidates from studying medicine. That was enough for Freud to consider me as much an opponent as if I were altogether opposed to lay analysis. Actually Ferenczi was the only person to share Freud's extreme position, and also his critical attitude toward me. Eitingon, the President of the Association, was distinctly pro-medical, more so than I was, and, as Freud more than once complained, "lukewarm" on the subject of lay analysis. Still he was more pliable than I was and could nearly always be depended on to act in accordance with Freud's wishes.

I had suggested that the problem should be discussed beforehand at the various branch Societies in the hope of reaching some sort of solution that would obviate unpleasant and wasteful arguments at the Congress itself. This did not at all please Freud. He wrote to Eitingon: "An investigation such as Jones proposes is naturally very repellent to me from the start. I should like the whole of the Association to take the standpoint I have presented, but that is something we shall certainly not achieve. Perhaps we shall split our former comradeship if we adhere to our demands. So what ought we to do? . . . If we simply give the branch Societies autonomy, i.e. the right to do what they like, that would for the time being avoid a break, but it would destroy the right we have hitherto enjoyed of freedom to emigrate wherever we wish, inasmuch as a Viennese lay member would then lose the right to take part in scientific meetings in, for instance, America or Holland. To bring about a unitary agreement calls for an authority that is not at our disposal. Perhaps some kind of diplomatic shift is the most expedient—not that I should find it sympathetic—of a kind that would avoid any binding decision and content ourselves with a general statement in principle in favor of lay analysis." [14] Ferenczi's lay group in America wanted to join the International Association, and Freud regarded it as a test case.[15] Eitingon, however, was loth to accept them, and in fact did not do so. Freud sent Eitingon for his approval the supplement he had written to his booklet, and told him to omit some sharp remarks about the Americans if he found them not politic or dangerous; they might seize the excuse to secede.[16] When I met Eitingon in The Hague that summer he showed me the paper; we agreed it would be wiser to omit three sentences when printing it, and this was done. A few months later Freud reproached me with having advocated his publishing it with the intention of making bad blood with the Americans.[17] Such a complete travesty of my reconciling aims was evidence of Freud's suspicion that I was opposed to lay analysis. He could never understand midway positions, such as mine was and still is.

In May of that year the New York Society passed a resolution condemning lay analysis outright, a precipitate action which did not improve the atmosphere for the coming general discussion. I wrote to Brill vehemently begging him to do something at the eleventh hour to diminish the bad impression that had been produced in Europe, but it was too late.

As a result of the symposium Eitingon formulated a resolution to be laid before the coming Congress. Ferenczi, who had just returned from America, visited him in Berlin where they had a warm discussion. Concessions were made on both sides, which as usual pleased neither. Freud had been so disappointed at the negative reception his manifesto had received the year before that he tried, though only temporarily, to dissociate himself from the whole matter, and could not even bring himself to read Eitingon's resolution.[18]

At the preliminary meeting of the International Training Commission[a] Eitingon's resolution which laid stress on the desirability of candidates acquiring a medical qualification was accepted, but another one was postponed which suggested that the home country be *notified* when a candidate elected to train abroad. It was these "foreign" candidates, as they were called, that were causing the friction between Vienna and New York, so at the Business Meeting of the Congress I proposed that in such cases the training committees of the two countries concerned should first come to an agreement about the suitability of each particular candidate. This led at once to a very heated discussion, often with several speakers talking at once. When finally a resolution by Rado was adopted, in which the International Training Commission was instructed to draw up obligatory regulations, there was a storm of protest from the minority, from the Americans, the British and the Dutch, all of whom had voted against the resolution. In the ensuing discussion I remarked that the history of my country had taught us that force was not the most successful method to employ with Americans. Ferenczi later reported to Freud this obvious warning of mine as a threat on my part to withdraw the American groups, though it is hard to know how I was supposed to have the power to do this; at all events it confirmed Freud in his opinion that I was opposed to him in the dispute. Things looked distinctly unpleasant at the meeting when suddenly above the hubbub a girlish voice rang out with the words:

[a] See Chapter 3, p. 112.

"Meine Herren, ich glaube wir thun ein Unrecht." [b] It was this intervention of Anna Freud's which saved the situation. She pointed out that we were legislating for America on an occasion when there were only three Americans present and that we should not take advantage of this minimal representation. It was an historic moment in the dispute between the two continents, and it meant that for the time being the crisis was over.

In a recent book on American characteristics, the author Geoffrey Gorer, a distinguished sociologist, singled out as the most prominent one the American's tendency to reject authority, and more particularly any authority, such as that of foreign-born parents, emanating from Europe.[19] He could have found ample confirmatory evidence in the records of the International Psycho-Analytical Association in the years from 1925 to 1939.

In 1928 there was a sharp passage between New York and Vienna over the case of a lay psychotherapist who had been considered a "wild analyst," Freud's term for someone who pretends to practice psychoanalysis without troubling to learn how to do so. He came to Vienna and Freud referred him to the Psycho-Analytical Institute there. He went through some training, and on his return to New York inserted in the newspapers blatant advertisements claiming that he had studied with Freud, Adler and Jung, so was specially qualified. The New York analysts were indignant at this behavior, which they felt was likely to bring further discredit on themselves; as it was, they were in bad enough odor at that time. They protested to Vienna at the support they had given to such a man. Freud merely shrugged his shoulders, considered that they were making a mountain out of a molehill, and remarked: "Anyhow the man knows more about psychoanalysis than before he came to Vienna." Ferenczi shared his attitude, while I was more inclined to sympathize with the Americans—the more so because in London we were having trouble enough with the less reputable "practitioners" of psychoanalysis.

Freud was always unsympathetic to such complaints from across the Atlantic, and I think a main reason for it was this: Perhaps nowhere in the world has the medical profession been held in higher esteem than in pre-war Austria. A University title, Docent or Professor, was the passport to almost any rank of society. The Viennese were proud of their distinguished physicians and surgeons who were visited by students from all over the world, and they delighted to

[b] "Gentlemen, I think we are committing an injustice."

honor them by naming streets after them or in other ways. Freud never understood that the status of the medical profession could be quite different in other countries, and he imagined, for instance, that doctors holding university titles were respected as much abroad as in Austria. He had little notion of the hard fight they had fifty years ago in America, where all kinds of unqualified practitioners enjoyed at least as much esteem as physicians and often enough much more. He would never admit, therefore, that the opposition of American analysts to lay analysis was to a considerable extent a part of the struggle of various learned professions in America to secure respect and recognition for expert knowledge and the training needed to acquire it. The situation was, it is true, complicated by the circumstance that "wild," i.e. unqualified, psychoanalysts were by no means confined to the laity, but Americans felt that the conduct of undesirable medical colleagues was at least subject to more control and supervision than was that of members of the laity.

In January of the following year the group of lay analysts Ferenczi had organized during his stay in New York voluntarily dissolved. Nothing much else happened in that year (1928). In the spring Freud commented to Ferenczi that "the internal development of psychoanalysis is everywhere[c] proceeding contrary to my intentions away from lay analysis and becoming a pure medical specialty, and I regard this as fateful for the future of analysis. Really you are the only one of whom I can feel sure as unreservedly sharing my point of view." [20] And a month later he wrote: "You are right when you say that Eitingon has not his heart in the matter; he forced himself into a friendly attitude out of consideration to Anna and me. As usual he was here for my birthday and I used the opportunity to paint to him the gloomy future of analysis if it does not succeed in creating an abode for itself outside of medicine." [21] To Eitingon he described his position very aptly as that of a "Commander-in-Chief without an army." [22]

In March, 1929, Freud wrote to Eitingon: "Lehrman writes from Paris saying he has spoken with Jones, who seems quite bent on protecting America; that doesn't sound very hopeful. Jones intends to pay me a visit in June. I wonder if we should not propose to him that the theme be excluded from the Congress[d] and then in the next interval arrange a friendly separation with the Americans. I

[c] This was certainly not true of England, where we were constantly recruiting lay analysts.
[d] Oxford, 1929.

have no desire to give way in the lay question, and there is no means of bridging the gulf." [23]

In the middle of April, 1929, the newly organized Committee met in Paris to discuss the situation and prepare for the coming Congress in Oxford. Freud empowered Eitingon and Ferenczi to suggest that a friendly separation be arranged between the American and the European Societies, and he added that in his opinion the opposition to lay analysis was "the last mask of the resistance against psychoanalysis, and the most dangerous of all." [24] At the meeting van Ophuijsen and myself were opposed not only to this solution, but also to the more extreme one advocated by the other three members of the Committee, according to which the rules for admission of candidates for training should be compulsorily uniform for all countries. Whereupon Freud threatened that I should hear some straight talking when I came to visit him that June;[25] I have no recollection, however, that when I did so his reception of me was any less friendly than usual. Brill's visit to Freud, shortly after my own, did more to reassure him. Brill had almost equally strong European and American affiliations, and he did not always find it easy to reconcile them. On his visits to Freud, to whom he was devoted, he would be genuinely persuaded that American recalcitrancy was deplorable and would undertake to convince his colleagues on his return. Back in New York, however, he would soon resume his adoption of their attitude, which was really his own. On this occasion he was in a specially sunny mood and promised Freud to do all he could to diminish friction at the coming Congress. He had not attended a Congress for eighteen years, and his presence there was undoubtedly most helpful in smoothing matters.

In accordance with the instructions of the Innsbruck Congress Eitingon had appointed a Committee to work out a scheme that would, if possible, secure the agreement of the various branch Societies. He did not proceed very tactfully in this. There was criticism of his choosing only Berlin members—Karen Horney, Müller-Braunschweig and Rado—and still more when they proceeded to issue a circular to the branch Societies consisting of questions to which *answers* were appended. They were meant, it is true, merely as suggestions for discussion, but some groups were so incensed at the apparent forestalling of their discussions that they ignored the circular. At the Oxford Congress, therefore, this Committee had simply to register their failure, and a fresh one was appointed of eleven members drawn from all over the world with myself as Chairman. Everyone seemed satisfied with this decision, negative though it was, and Eitingon told Freud he was convinced that we should have no further difficulties over the lay analysis question.[26]

Brill carried out his promise to do his best to influence his colleagues in New York to modify their previous unyielding attitude, and in December Freud heard that the New York Society had altered their statutes in a way that now admitted the possibility of having lay members.[27] He was also pleased to hear from me that lay analysts were working in an official capacity at the London Clinic.[28]

At the Wiesbaden Congress, three years later, the second Committee presented a comprehensive report, which was received with applause and unanimously accepted. This contained the proviso that the rules for selection of candidates, including lay candidates, should be left to the discretion of each individual Society. Further: "The members of the Committee are unanimously of opinion that before any foreign candidate is accepted for training approval of his Home Training Committee be obtained. Harmony can only be obtained through adherence to this positive rule." [29] So my aim of safeguarding the integrity of the International Association was achieved, but at the cost of postponing to an uncertain future the persuading of those analysts who still objected to training lay analysts. The decision was of course a great disappointment for Freud, who had hoped to see their conversion in his lifetime, but I am sure any such hope would have been greatly diminished had matters been pushed to the extreme step of separation.

To complete the story I will relate a subsequent episode for which this time I had to take the blame. At the Lucerne Congress in 1934 a resolution proposed by Eitingon was carried enabling the Central Executive to grant "direct membership" in the International Association to those who had had to leave their own Society and country for political reasons. At that time this applied only to late members of the German Society. Without membership they had not the privileges of subscribing to the official organs and attending the scientific meetings of any other Society—not to speak of the moral isolation of having no contact with their colleagues. With a somewhat heavy heart I felt obliged to act on this and so issued membership—on the lines of the "Nansen passport" the League of Nations was just then issuing to refugees who had been deprived of their passports and so were stateless—to a number of analysts, including some lay analysts, who were emigrating to America. This was resented there as foreign interference with American institutions, and at the following Congress, in Paris in 1938, we were faced with a most formidable document from America. This announced that the American Psychoanalytic Association, which comprised all the branch Societies there, would be willing to consider "affiliation" to the International Association on three conditions: that the International Training Commission, which they maintained was a superfluous institution that interfered with internal affairs in America, be abolished; that the "free floating membership" be withdrawn from analysts settling in America; and that the International Association should meet for scientific purposes only and be deprived of all its administrative functions. Since the Americans had appointed a special committee to discuss these matters with us, and thus lessened the appearance of a final ultimatum, we decided to do likewise. It is gratifying to report that it proved unnecessary for these committees to act, since the advent of the Second World War altered the whole situation. When this was over, little was left of the psychoanalytical movement on the continent of Europe, and the Americans, now constituting the large majority of analysts in the world, have not only lost their former apprehension of the International Association, but have cordially cooperated with it to an extent that had never previously been possible. Our unity was therefore saved once more, but again at the cost of further postponing the still unsolved problem of the status of lay analysts.

In the late nineteen-thirties a report was widely current in the United States—oddly enough, it was said to emanate from European analysts settled in America—to the effect that Freud had radically changed the views he had expressed so definitely in his brochure on lay analysis, and that now in his opinion the practice of psychoanalysis should be strictly confined in all countries to members of the medical profession. Here is his answer[e] to an inquiry asking him if there was any truth in the rumor.

"July 5, 1938

"Dear Mr Schnier:

"I cannot imagine how that silly rumour of my having changed my views about the problem of Lay-Analysis may have originated.

[e] In English.

The fact is, I have never repudiated these views and I insist on them even more intensely than before, in the face of the obvious American tendency to turn psycho-analysis into a mere housemaid of Psychiatry.

"Sincerely yours
"Sigm. Freud"

10

Biology

FREUD WAS ONCE INVITED, IN 1913, TO STATE, WITHIN THE COMPASS OF a larger essay, what interest he thought psychoanalysis might have for biologists,[1] and it is worth while considering his answer to the request. The main theme on which he concentrated was the contributions psychoanalysis had made to the study of sexual development in man, a theme of evident biological import. He compared the autonomous life sexuality appears to lead in man, with its relative independence from the personality, with the independence of the immortal germ plasm from the somatic body. He further commented on the way in which human sexuality transcends the simple aim of propagating the species, and how it extends far beyond the genital organs themselves. Then he remarked on the difficulty of correlating the biological distinction between male and female with any comparable distinction in psychology. There seemed to be here no distinction in the nature of the instinct in the two sexes. All that could be found was a distinction between active and passive *aims*, and this applies to both sexes; he also mentioned the importance of bisexuality in mankind. He agreed that the contrast he had drawn between the ego and the sexual impulses corresponded roughly with the biological distinction between the instincts of self-preservation and those of preservation of the species.

Freud then pointed out that much of his work was based on his conception of a drive (*Trieb*), which he maintained was transitional between psychology and biology. He further insisted on the genetic nature of his work, which was in line with the developmental studies in biology. Stress was laid on the important phenomenon of regression, one which has many parallels in the bodily sphere. Finally there was a hint that the biological law "Ontogeny is a repetition of phylogeny" might well prove to be true of mental processes also.

The historian is justified in making more extensive claims for Freud's contribution to biology than he allowed himself to make. In the first place all additions to psychological knowledge may properly be called contributions to biology, since this branch of science is concerned with every aspect of life. But Freud also made a number of important contributions to biology in the more usual sense of the word.

The chief one was a contribution to the general theory of evolution. Even in his early neurological days Freud was well aware of the bearing of his work on this theory. The first paper he ever published went far to settle what was then a burning controversial question: namely, whether the nervous system of the higher animals contained elements *different in kind* from those of the lower animals or whether any apparent differences were only of degree.[2] His demonstration that the Reissner cells in the spinal cord of the Petromyzon fish represent the posterior ganglion cells of the higher vertebrates before their evolutionary departure from the spinal cord was a piece of biological research that has not often been equaled in brilliance by a medical student. His researches in his twenties in the field of human anatomy are of the same stamp.[3] His foreshadowing of the fundamental neurone theory, i.e. the discontinuity of neuronic fibrils, and his comparative work on the origins of cranial nerves and their ganglia as an extension of his studies of spinal ganglia, are of a purely evolutionary nature. Even his technical method, of tracing these origins by embryological investigations, was exquisitely genetic in character.

But there are far broader aspects of Freud's work in its relation to evolution than these more narrowly technical studies betray. When the doctrine of evolution came to be universally accepted by men of science in the second half of the nineteenth century it naturally caused much perturbation among those who still held to the religious view of man's unique place in nature and the special divine creation of mankind for lofty spiritual purposes. Their attempt to assimilate the new knowledge resulted, after some bitter controversy, in an interesting compromise. Even if for some inscrutable reason the Deity had chosen to bring man on the scene by a complicated evolutionary process lasting some thousands of millions of years instead of creating him on a particular day, as had previously been believed, this need only be true of his body. There must surely have been a moment when the Deity decided to add the higher mental attributes, notably the soul, to man, and thus fulfill His purpose of fundamentally distinguishing him from all other animals. Even Darwin's brave attempt, in his book *The Expression of the Emotions in Man and Animals,* was unable to fill this lacuna in the theory. Freud, however, whose main interest was in genetic development, was able to show that a great many of these higher attributes, including even the religious instinct itself, had passed through a lowlier evolution before attaining to their lofty heights, and that their existence could be accounted for without the necessity of invoking any supernatural intervention; even such an exquisitely human feature as the sense of self, the ego, Freud was able to derive, through the influence on it of the outer world, from the impersonal primordial group of impulses he designated as the Id. By so doing he closed the still remaining gap in the doctrine of human evolution, and thus rendered superfluous the idea that through such intervention man had a peculiar and unique relation to the Divinity. It was for this reason that I bestowed on Freud the title of the Darwin of the Mind.

Comparative morphology, to which Freud had in his youth made the contributions mentioned above, is a valuable and essential part of biology. But so is physiology, which studies the functions and use of the organs investigated by anatomy. Freud had strangely eschewed this branch of study in his laboratory days,[4] but his subsequent work in psychology, which had just these aims, more than made up for his previous reluctance. Before Freud, academic psychology had concentrated on what might be called the morphology of the mind, its constituents and their relation to one another. As Brun has well remarked, "It was Freud who first laid bare the true effective causes of human behavior; he did so by making instinctual behavior the central object of his investigations. In this way he was the first to create a biological psychology. Since Freud the functional terms of motive, aim, purpose, intention, meaning, have become an integral part of psychology. He introduced dynamic and economic concepts which are essentially biological in nature."[5]

Moreover, it has been shown that the particular mental mechanisms of displacement, regression, transference and so on, the study, and often the discovery, of which constituted a main part of Freud's contribution to psychology, find their counterpart in many aspects of animal behavior, even in animals so far apart from man as the insects. This was first pointed out by Brun,[6] and has been extensively confirmed by other biologists. Freud had thus in his purely psychological studies lighted on biological laws of the widest validity.

It is rather more difficult to assess the value to biology of Freud's conclusions about the nature of instincts.[a] The distinction he drew as early as 1905 between the source of an instinct and its aim has proved valuable in many respects. Ten years later he wrote an important essay entitled "Instincts and their Vicissitudes." [7] He had previously suggested that what distinguishes the various instincts from one another and endows them with specific qualities is their relation to their somatic sources and to their aims. "The source of an instinct is a process of excitation occurring in an organ, and the immediate aim of the instinct lies in the removal of this organic stimulus." [8] His definition of an instinct had been "the psychical representative of an endosomatic, continuously flowing, source of stimulation, as contrasted with a 'stimulus' (*Reiz*) which is set up by *single* excitations coming from *without*."

Freud associated the allaying of instinctual stimulation with Fechner's Stability Principle, whereby the reducing of tension to a minimum is a fundamental tendency of the mind. In 1920 Freud pursued this train of thought to its extreme by postulating a "death instinct" abolishing all the tension of life. As we have seen, however, it has not been found possible to find any confirmation in biology for this latter conclusion.[b]

The greater part of Freud's work was concerned with the various consequences of conflicts between different instincts. He described these in great detail: compromise-formation, reaction-formations, aim-inhibited activities, deflection (including sublimation), the turning of an instinct on to the self instead of the outer world, reversal into its opposite and so on. Most of these mechanisms have been confirmed by experimental work in biology, although Freud never took into account the work done in that sphere. His conclusion that an inhibited impulse retains its energy is in conformity with Sher-

[a] I would call attention here to a lively and stimulating essay on Freud's contributions to the theory of instincts by the well-known entomologist W. M. Wheeler, entitled "On Instincts," *Journal of Abnormal Psychology*, XV (1920), 295; (1921), 318.

[b] See p. 277.

rington's observation that the same holds good even with the simplest reflexes. In spinal dogs,[c] for instance, when the scratching impulse (essentially of libidinal nature) is abolished by the administration of a painful stimulus it resumes its activity as soon as the latter has ceased; Sherrington termed this an "after-discharge." [9]

Freud answered the question of which kind of instinct is victorious in the case of such conflicts by the statement that the social instincts are unless the more primary ones (sexual and self-preservative) are especially urgent. Exactly the same law has been found to be true in biological experiments.[10] Biologists use the term "collisions" for what in psychology are termed "conflicts," and they have formulated a law to the effect that the more recently acquired instincts are victorious when in collision with the primordial ones unless the situation is urgently critical.

An immense number of valuable observations have been collected in the sphere of natural history on the various forms of instinctual behavior, and both biologists and psychologists (notably McDougall) have compiled lists of them, e.g. maternal instinct, hunting instinct and so on. Freud never drew on these observations for analogies, illustrations or parallels to his own clinical work; the only exception I can call to mind is an allusion to the habits of eels and birds of breeding in their ancestral homes. There would appear to be two reasons for this rather curious omission on his part. One was his almost obsessional determination to confine himself to two sets of instincts only. These sets several times differed in kind, but they were invariably two in number. Then again Freud seems to have followed his ancestral traditions in feeling aloof from the animal world, an attitude that may be illustrated by the saying: "If a Jew says he enjoys fox hunting he is lying." It was only toward the end of his life that he got on to speaking terms with a dog; then, it is true, he established a close relationship of a human kind. One result of his observations here was a firm assertion that among the higher animals there is a distinction between ego and id, as in man, and he even suggested the presence of a super-ego in those animals who have a long period of helplessness in their youth. Freud seems never to have paid much attention to the zoological aspects of natural history, confining his interest to the botanical ones. He certainly could have found ample material to reinforce his conviction about the essentially conservative nature of instincts. Furthermore, observations in the field of natural history would have been useful

[c] I.e. dogs whose spinal cord has been severed from the brain.

in confirming or perhaps refuting his more debatable conclusions about the tendency of instincts to reinstate earlier conditions. This gap has been admirably filled by Brun in his numerous contributions.[11]   Freud would have been especially pleased at Brun's conclusion that instincts, through their action in reducing excitation, act as a regulating mechanism in the sense of Fechner's principle of stability by which Freud set so much store.

The classification of instincts at which Freud finally arrived was that substantially accepted by psychoanalysts today: a division into libidinal and aggressive instincts (the latter of which Freud derived from his hypothetical death instinct). Whether the latter are primary, in the sense of acting spontaneously, or secondary, i.e. reactive to various frustrating situations, is still a controversial question; Brunswick has recently called attention to the relative neglect of the defensive aspects of the aggressive impulses.[12] What Freud always found a baffling problem was the connection between love and hate. In his fullest discussion of this obscure matter he observed that if it could be shown that one of these is convertible into the other we should be driven back on to a monist conception of primary undifferentiated mental energy, a conception that was anathema to him.[13] He ingeniously evaded this unpleasant contingency by using the concept of desexualized libido in place of the undifferentiated energy.

Of one thing Freud was quite sure in this field: namely, that he could find no evidence of any instinct impelling man toward higher moral, ethical or spiritual aims, an idea which he termed a "benevolent illusion."[14] "The present development of human beings requires, as it seems to me, no different explanation from that of animals. What appears in a minority of human individuals as an untiring impulse towards further perfection can easily be understood as a result of the instinctual repression upon which is based all that is most precious in human civilization."[15]

Heredity

Before the precision of Mendelism founded the science of genetics early in this century the subject of heredity was wreathed in nebulous assumption, nowhere more so than in the field of medicine and particularly in that of psychiatry. In his early days, for instance, Freud asserted that syphilis in a parent, usually the father, affected the offspring in such a way as to predispose to neurosis,[16] and as far as I know he never abandoned this belief. In discussing problems of etiology he always allowed for heredity as one of the important elements. This he would call "congenital predisposition," but he was always aware of the difficulty of defining it more specifically. The only step he took in this direction was to specify it as "sexual constitution." This idea suggests the possibility of inborn variations in the relative sensitiveness of the several erotogenic zones, but Freud did not pursue the matter very far. His observation that hysterical symptoms in a woman often went with a corresponding perversion in her brother, this being the positive of her negative manifestation, is also suggestive and would deserve more systematic investigation.

The possibility of the inheritance of specific mental processes interested Freud, but he usually expressed himself cautiously when discussing it. Thus in a discussion at the Vienna Psycho-Analytical Society in 1911 he is reported as saying: "As for the possibility of a phylogenetically acquired memory content (Zurich school) which could explain the similarity between the constructions of a neurosis and those of ancient cultures one should bear in mind another possibility. It could be a matter of identical psychical conditions which must then lead to identical results. These special conditions would bring about the regression.[d] Thus the magical system of primitive peoples, by which the world is governed, corresponds with the omnipotence of thoughts in the obsessional neurosis. Certain associational activities can be shown to underlie all forms of magic, and when they operate in any human being he is bound to produce the same superstitions as did his ancestors. The inference of a phylogenetic inborn store of memories is not justified so long as we have the possibility of explaining these things through an analysis of the psychical situations. What remains over after this analysis of the psychical phenomena of regression could then be conceived of as a phylogenetic memory." [17] Again on a similar occasion four years later there occurs the definite statement: "I have never taken the view that phantasies are inherited as such." [18]

On the other hand Freud was convinced that certain primordial phantasies, notably those of coitus and castration, were transmitted through inheritance in some form or other, particularly as a predisposition to being aroused by suitable situations. In his discussion of the Schreber case in 1911 Freud wrote: "We shall soon have to extend a conclusion that we psycho-analysts have long maintained and

[d] I.e. to the ancient forms.

add to its individual ontogenetic content an anthropological phylogenetic one. We have stated that in dreams and in neuroses we find once more the child with all the peculiar features of its mode of thought and feeling. Now we may add: 'also savage, primitive man as he is revealed in the light of archaeology and ethnology.' " [19] A still clearer statement occurs in the *Introductory Lectures* in 1916. "The phylogenetic aspect is to some extent obscured in man by the circumstance that what is fundamentally inherited is nevertheless individually acquired anew, probably because the same conditions that originally induced its acquisition still prevail and exert their influence upon each individual. I would say: where they originally created a new response they now stimulate a predisposition." [20]

Followers of Jung have put forward the claim that Freud derived from him the idea that mental images may be inborn and inherited. Neither of them can assert the priority to such an elementary notion, but, as Edward Glover has demonstrated at length, there is a world of difference between Freud's view of the inheritance of highly specific and limited mental processes, all to do with concrete ideas or situations, and Jung's wide-ranging views of an inherited collective unconscious replete with the most complicated, abstract and spiritually-minded archetypes.[21]

In the last years of his life Freud became bolder, or less cautious, in this respect as in some others. In his book on Moses he gave reasons for thinking that more than mental dispositions must be inherited from the past. "In fact it [the material] seems to me convincing enough to allow me to venture further and assert that the archaic heritage of mankind includes not only dispositions, but also ideational contents, memory-traces of the experiences of former generations." [22] The implications of the word "experiences" here lead us to the next theme.

Transmission of Acquired Characteristics

Freud has told us that learning of Darwin's work on evolution had been a main motive in deciding his choice of a scientific career. By this he evidently meant the general theory of evolution,[e] which Darwin had made acceptable through his detailed investigations, and above all by the disclosure of the means by which it is brought

---

[e] In one passage he referred simply to "Darwin's theory of descent which broke down the barrier between human and other animals" (just as every theory of evolution did).[23]

about. It is the latter that constitutes the essence of what is called Darwinism, though to the popular mind the word is often taken to be identical with the doctrine of evolution itself. This doctrine had been promulgated in the eighteenth century by Darwin's grandfather, Erasmus Darwin, by the Frenchmen Buffon, Cuvier, Lamarck, St. Hilaire, and many others; indeed its origin can be traced back to Greek times.

Now comes an extraordinary part of the story, which provides us with a baffling problem in the study of the development of Freud's ideas, and also in that of his personality. Without much success I have searched Freud's writings, correspondence and memories of his conversation for allusions to Darwinism, although they would have been very much in place in his writings on man's early development; I refer, of course, to the doctrine of Natural Selection as the means whereby evolution has been brought about.ᶠ A stranger might almost suppose that Freud was ignorant of the doctrine, which is assuredly out of the question. With his omnivorous reading he must have read such a classic as *On the Origin of Species* and probably Darwin's other writings. The only book of his he actually possessed was *The Descent of Man*, though in the *Studies in Hysteria* he twice referred to Darwin's *The Expression of the Emotions in Man and Animals*,[26] and we know from his references to them that he had read the neo-Darwinian books by Weismann, Haeckel and others, which appeared in the eighteen-nineties and carried Darwin's theory to more exclusive lengths than Darwin himself had ventured to do.

Before Darwin, the only serious explanation of evolution that had any vogue was Lamarck's doctrine of the inheritance of acquired characteristics. Stated briefly, this maintains that some unusual experience or some effort on an animal's part would modify its body in such a way as to transmit that modification to its offspring; these in turn would make a further effort—the giraffe stretching his neck to reach higher is the familiar example—and the total results would be cumulative in the successive generations. This doctrine has been completely discredited for more than half a century. In support of this statement I will quote a passage from Julian Huxley, than whom there is no higher authority. "With the knowledge that has

---

ᶠ We may quote as an exception a casual remark that perhaps the origin of a difference between sexes came about "following Darwin's train of thought." [24] And the very same words had occurred in the Project when he was discussing the function of impermeable neurones.[25]

been amassed since Darwin's time it is no longer possible to believe that evolution is brought about through the so-called inheritance of acquired characters—the direct effect of use or disuse of organs or of changes in the environment. . . . All the theories lumped together under the heads of biogenesis and Lamarckism are invalidated. . . . They are no longer consistent with the facts. Indeed, in the light of modern discoveries, they no longer deserve to be called scientific theories, but can be seen as speculations without due basis of reality, or old superstitions disguised in modern dress. They were natural enough in their time, when we were still ignorant of the mechanism of heredity; but they have now only an historical interest." [27]

In spite of innumerable similar strictures Freud remained from the beginning to the end of his life what one must call an obstinate adherent of this discredited Lamarckism. Over and over again he implied or explicitly stated his firm belief in it. I will quote only two examples, from the earliest and the last phases of his career respectively. The first one dates from 1893. The context is the dilemma facing society in the absence of convenient and trustworthy contraceptives; the "actual neuroses" that result from the sexual practices to which people are in consequence driven Freud called the "incurable neuroses," they being not amenable to psychological treatment. "In the absence of such a solution society seems doomed to fall a victim to incurable neuroses which reduce the enjoyment of life to a minimum, destroy the marriage relation and through the action of heredity bring ruin on the whole coming generation." [28]

I take the other example from the last book Freud wrote, *Moses and Monotheism*, 1939.[29] In it he suggests that the excessive consciousness of guilt that haunts Jewish history and religion, and which by way of reaction spurred them to create high ethical ideals, was inherited from the unconscious memory of their forefathers having in an act of rebellion slain the father of their race, Moses. This, he said, was a powerful reinforcement of a universal process. The guilty reactions following the numerous prehistoric acts of parricide had been inherited—they constituted in fact the "original sin" of the theologians—and they were reanimated afresh in every generation through the occurrence of similar situations of jealousy. Now this implies that the conscious attitudes of primitive man made such a profound impression on him as to reverberate throughout his body, producing, perhaps via Darwin's "gemmules," a corresponding impression on his seminiferous tubules so that when—perhaps years later—they produced spermatozoa each of these had been modified in such a way as to create, when united with an ovum, a child who bore within him the memory of his father's experience. Yet Freud must have been familiar with the overwhelming evidence Weismann, among others, had brought forward showing that the germ cells are totally immune to the influence of any changes in the soma. For some reason he chose to ignore it.

Early in the war, during Freud's visit to Pápa in Hungary, he discussed with Ferenczi the project of writing a work together on the relation of Lamarckism to psychoanalysis. Other preoccupations intervened, but at the end of 1916, when the vanishing of his practice gave Freud plenty of leisure, he revived the idea and asked Ferenczi to confirm their arrangement.[30] He ordered books on the subject from the University library and said he could at once see a number of promising ideas the truth of which he was already convinced of. Ferenczi agreed, though without enthusiasm, so Freud promptly sent him an outline,[g] saying at the same time that he was busy reading Lamarck's *Philosophie Zoologique*.[31] The plan was that each should read various books and make notes; then they would each write a sketch and they would come together to compare.[32] Freud said he shared the views of the psycho-Lamarckians like Pauly, and anyhow it might be worth while to leave a visiting card for biologists.[33] Then his practice improved and he postponed the work till the summer.[34] When the time came he said he was not inclined to do any work in the holidays and would prefer to leave the whole theme to Ferenczi;[35] his interest was evidently waning. It stayed in his mind, however, and in October he asked Abraham whether he had told him of the project: "Its essential content is that the omnipotence of thoughts was once a reality." [36] On hearing from Abraham that he had not, Freud wrote to him as follows: "Our intention is to base Lamarck's ideas completely on our own theories and to show that his concept of 'need,' which creates and modifies organs, is nothing else than the power unconscious ideas have over the body of which we see the remains in hysteria—in short, the 'omnipotence of thoughts.' Fitness[h] would then be really explained psychoanalytically; it would be the completion of psychoanalysis. Two great principles of change (of progress) would emerge: one through adaptation of one's own body, the later one through alteration of the outer world (autoplastic and heteroplastic)." [37] In other words, Freud equated Lamarck's "need" on an animal's part with Schopenhauer's

[g] Unfortunately not preserved.
[h] *Zweckmässigkeit.*

will to power, the psychoanalytical omnipotence of thoughts; and this enabled the animal to bring about the adaptations, either of its own body, or of the environment, that would procure satisfaction of the "need."

Freud must have felt he was conceiving a great biological vision at this point, but some inner doubt about trespassing too far into foreign fields evidently checked him, since a little later he wrote to Ferenczi that he could not decide to proceed with the Lamarck work and that probably neither of them would write it. So nothing more came of it.

Nevertheless, as was mentioned above, Freud never gave up a jot of his belief in the inheritance of acquired characters. How immovable he was in the matter I discovered during a talk I had with him in the last year of his life over a sentence I wished him to alter in the Moses book in which he expressed the Lamarckian view in universal terms. I told him he had of course the right to hold any opinion he liked in his own field of psychology, even if it ran counter to all biological principles, but begged him to omit the passage where he applied it to the whole field of biological evolution, since no responsible biologist regarded it as tenable any longer. All he would say was that they were all wrong and the passage must stay. And he documented this recalcitrance in the book with the following words: "This state of affairs is made more difficult, it is true, by the present attitude of biological science, which rejects the idea of acquired qualities being transmitted to descendants. I admit, in all modesty, that in spite of this I cannot picture biological development proceeding without taking this factor into account." [38]

It is not easy to account for the fixity with which Freud held this opinion and the determination with which he ignored all the biological evidence to the contrary. We have seen that he associated it with the omnipotence of thoughts, the discovery of which must have impressed him greatly; it almost looks as if he himself shared that illusion when it came to Lamarckism. But he had held Lamarckian views many years before he came across the concept of omnipotence in 1908.[39] He had of course been profoundly impressed by the way in which strong emotional experiences can be incorporated in such a fashion as to alter a personality permanently, but still this is not the same as affecting the offspring of that person. Was an ineffaceable mark left on his mind when he learned as a child that God visits the iniquity of the fathers upon the children, to the third and fourth generation? For, according to Freud, it was, above all, guilt and fear that were transmitted in this fateful manner.

Whatever we may think of his explanation of it, however, there can be no doubt that Freud's general conclusions about mental heredity are of fundamental significance. And if further evidence should appear in favor of the inheritance of a few elemental images, it is more than likely that it might be explicable on pure Darwinian lines, i.e. via Natural Selection. There comes to my mind in this connection an apposite passage from a recent writer on science: "It is never wise to deny to men of genius the use of any methods to which their intuition may guide them; they can usually be relied upon to do the right thing, even though through the unfamiliarity of the procedure they may give the wrong reason for doing so." [40]

All in all we may say that Freud's contributions to biology, though incidental to his work rather than deliberate, will prove to be increasingly valuable.

11

CHAPTER

Anthropology

FREUD WAS ALL HIS LIFE ENGROSSED WITH THE GREAT PROBLEM OF HOW man came to be man, probably more than with any other problem. His interest in the early history of mankind, together with the contributions he made to that study, therefore deserves a chapter of its own.

He displayed but little interest in the future of mankind, and only occasionally expressed a few speculations about it. There were very definite reasons for this attitude. He was greatly impressed by the complexity of the human mind, and consequently by the difficulty of making any trustworthy predictions. Even in his own field of work, when he might be certain that particular factors in the past were important, or essential, causes of various psychological manifestations—neurotic or otherwise—in the present, he held that it would have been impossible to predict from a knowledge of them at the time what their effects would be; an unknown shift in the strength of the forces concerned could have produced different effects. There were two features that distinguished his field of work from that of exact sciences, where such prediction is commonly possible. One was that there was no way of isolating individual factors and excluding unknown ones, as one often can in, for instance, experimental physics. The other was that we have as yet no means of making any sort of quantitative measurement of the forces concerned and can make only very approximate guesses, of a largely subjective nature, about their relative strength.

Freud was primarily a discoverer, and his interest always turned to problems that offered some promising opening for investigation. Where none was visible, as with the problems of the future, his interest soon waned; it was a waste of time and thought to speculate about the unknown.

As for the present, Freud took an average interest in what was going on in the world around him, but he felt he had no great direct concern with it except where it affected his own work, on which he therefore concentrated as being the most useful occupation in which he could employ his talents.

Since all he had learned about the human mind had come from tracing its past development he had to think that this would probably always prove to be the main source of our knowledge. He did not agree with Jung and others that there were in the mind "progressive" tendencies of a teleological nature that drew men on in particular directions. They are urged on by the forces already in them, forces which, originating in early life, are compounded of inborn tendencies and external influences. The drama of life Freud saw as a never-ending conflict between the impulse to find freshly available forms of satisfaction of the primary instincts and the constant tendency to revert to older forms even when these had proved less successful. Man is thus always impelled forward by the past and yet drawn back toward it.

All this, therefore, necessarily directed Freud's interests toward the past, whether of the individual or of mankind as a whole. It was the only possible way of understanding something about the present, and possibly also about the future. He said once that only inferior people take no interest in the past. From the beginning of his psychological investigations he was given to linking his unraveling of individual development with studies of the historical past. Thus, among many allusions in his letters to Fliess to the connection between these two themes, we note after a passage describing the difficulties in his daily work (1899): "For relaxation I am reading Burckhardt's *History of Greek Civilisation*, which is providing me with unexpected parallels. My predilection for the prehistoric in all its human forms remains the same." [1]

This was one important element, probably the essential one, in Freud's interest: intellectual curiosity about how things came to be what they are. Beyond this, however, the mere contemplation of past times was a source of great pleasure, and here we touch on the element of phantasy. It is now familiar knowledge that a special interest in a distant past is commonly a substitute for the longing to return to one's own halcyon days of infancy long ago, and when we reflect on Freud's happy years in Freiberg and the truly hard times that followed them in Vienna we shall find it understandable if this observation was valid for Freud also. I quoted earlier a passage from one of his letters in which he actually brought the two themes together: "Strange secret yearnings rise in me—perhaps from my ancestral heritage—for the East and the Mediterranean and for a life of quite another kind: wishes from late childhood never to be fulfilled."[a] He was steeped in classical literature and history, the principal subject of his school days and one in which we know he excelled, and fifty years later he was to write that those glimpses of the engulfed world of ancient culture had proved "an unsurpassable comfort" to him in the storm and stress of life.[2]

Yet Freud's attitude was very far from being simply one of contemplation, however absorbing. What seemed most to engage his interest was the possibility of reconstructing from the relics of the ancient world something that would bring it to light and, at least in imagination, make it live again. Resuscitation is here the key word, as it was in his daily work where he was constantly reconstructing the past from the relics in front of him in the shape of his patients' symptoms. This also must have been the source of his intense pleasure in the remarkable collection of antiquities he made in the course of his long life. This hobby, the only one he ever indulged in, began at least as early as 1896 when he could ill afford such luxuries.[3] Later on his waiting room, consulting room and study were all filled almost to overflowing with beautiful, rare and interesting objects. Egyptian, Etruscan, Greek and Roman pieces predominated, but there were others from farther afield. Large glass cabinets were replete with vases, statuettes and iridescent wine goblets interspersed with Roman lamps. The desk at which he wrote was crowded with his favorite statuettes and similar objects which present a rather puzzling appearance in the well-known etching by Max Pollak depicting him seated there. On either side of the open door between his study and consulting room stood Egyptian stone reliefs. Facing him as he sat by the side of the analytical couch were two specially beautiful objects, a bronze head of Buddha and a Chinese bowl he had acquired on his visit to America in 1909. Over the couch hung an etching of the great temple of Abu Simbel, and next to it a plaster copy of the marble relief of the famous Gradiva.

It is gratifying to know that this collection is now charmingly

* See Chapter 3, p. 84.

housed in London, in the very room in which Freud died; his beloved objects from antiquity must have done something to console his last hours. He attached very special value to those pieces in his collection that had been perfectly preserved. They were beings that had lived for centuries, or else come back from the dead, without suffering any impairment of their integrity.

Suzanne Bernfeld in an essay on Freud's interest in archaeology has suggested that what I have called "resuscitation" should more properly be called "resurrection," since she would explain his interest as an outcome of early teachings by his Catholic nurse on this subject; in support of her view she quotes the way in which the date of Easter played a part in Freud's life.[4] Even if we suppose that the nurse had threatened the two-year-old youngster that he would "burn in hell" if he was naughty this seems to me a very shaky foundation for such a far-reaching interpretation as thoughts about death and a future life, in the existence of which, by the way, Freud never believed. On the other hand it may be true that interest in preservation of a precious past could serve to allay any unconscious fears of destruction. So, all in all, it is likely that Freud's profound interest in the past sprang from diverse deep sources in his personality. As is well known, a man's hobbies are often a clue to central elements in his being.

Freud's interest in the past far transcended any pleasure he derived from collecting antiquities. His thought and imagination constantly played with the actual life of the past and the nature of human beings who lived hundreds of thousands of years ago. Nor was this interest so remote from Freud's daily life as it might perhaps appear. For that consisted also in a constant process of resuscitation, a bringing to light submerged memories and impulses of the past which had somehow preserved their form and even their life despite their seemingly final disappearance from all ken. The analogy is indeed so close that Freud himself could not refrain from commenting on it, sometimes openly and sometimes indirectly.

An early example of this archaeological simile occurs in the introduction to the well-known Dora analysis, written in January, 1901. "In face of the incompleteness of my analytic results[b] I had no choice but to follow the example of those discoverers whose good fortune it is to bring to the light of day after their long burial the priceless though mutilated relics of antiquity. I have restored what is

[b] I.e. in this particular case, which was treated for only three months.

missing, taking the best models known to me from other analyses; but, like a conscientious archaeologist, I have not omitted to mention in each case where the authentic parts end and my constructions begin." [5] Later on, in the description of the case, there is an even more striking example of how closely mythological and psychopathological stories were associated in Freud's mind. "When Dora stayed with the K.'s she used to share a bedroom with Frau K., and the husband used to be quartered elsewhere. She had been the wife's confidante and adviser in all the difficulties of her married life. There was nothing they had not talked about. Medea had been quite content that Creusa should make friends with her two children." [6]

Nor should one forget that even earlier Freud's first thought on discovering in himself the wish to kill his father and marry his mother was that now he understood the profound effect the Oedipus story had had in Ancient Greece—and of course in later generations. [7]

In the discussion of conscious childhood memories he added to the second edition of *The Psychopathology of Everyday Life* (1907), Freud pointed out that most of them were really "screen memories," and that in this respect they show "a remarkable analogy with the childhood memories of nations which are embodied in their sagas and myths." [8] Two years later, in the chapter he wrote for Rank's *The Myth of the Birth of the Hero*, he expressed himself more confidently: "It is in these consciously recollected memories from the years of childhood that we find the key to the understanding of myths." [9] It was a theme he expounded more fully in the following year in his study of Leonardo, [10] and again in his *Scientia* essay "The Claims of Psycho-analysis to Scientific Interest" (1913). [11]

Freud would, moreover, draw in the course of his analytic treatments various parallels from mythology to illustrate the theme that was being discussed at the moment. An idea that lent itself specially well to such a line of thought was the contrast between the fate of psychical material exposed to the wear and tear of daily life in consciousness as compared with its intact and unaltered preservation in the unconscious. Thus in his account of another analysis, in 1909, he wrote: "I then made some short observations upon the psychological differences between the conscious and the unconscious, and upon the fact that everything conscious was subject to a process of wearing-away, while what was unconscious was relatively unchangeable; and I illustrated my remarks by pointing to the antique objects standing about in my room. They were in fact, I said, only objects found in a tomb, and their burial had been their preservation: the destruction of Pompeii was only beginning now that it had been dug up." [12]

Allusions from antiquity are strewn about throughout Freud's writings, so alive and immediate was his familiarity with them. He used them in the investigation of analytical problems, particularly of literary material; his study of the three caskets theme in the *Merchant of Venice* is a striking instance.[13] Freud penetrated also into the inner significance of myths, legends and fairy tales. Myths he likened to "secular dreams," i.e. daydreams that occupy the imagination of peoples over generations.[14] The same mechanisms as those he had elucidated in individual dream life—condensation, displacement, symbolism and so on—are operative also in these secular dreams, so that one has technical methods at one's disposal for ascertaining their original meaning, now disguised. Abraham, Rank, Riklin and many others have since made extensive use of Freud's methods in studying these products of the human imagination.

Myths and rituals had in the past been read in terms of very recondite mental pursuits which were fancied to be the chief preoccupation of early man. An engrossing interest in the forms of clouds, the rounds of the moon, the movement of the sun, and even purely linguistic exercises had at times been supposed to prepossess the thoughts of early man almost to the exclusion of more mundane matters. From the nature of his work Freud's outlook was entirely humanistic, and he interpreted cosmic and other myths as projections of motives, often in very disguised forms, which are near to the heart of human beings. Thus, for example, he regarded the curious stories about the relations between Uranus, Cronos and Zeus not in terms of fears about the sun being swallowed, but as representing the inevitable conflicts between successive generations. That Zeus should castrate his father was not astonishing to someone who had discovered the same wish in every male patient. The topics of birth, love and death Freud therefore placed, or replaced, at the center of human preoccupations in every age. It was a humanization of mythology.

Beyond mythology lies the vaster problem of religion, which will be considered separately. We may now leave the fields of archaeology and mythology for that of social anthropology, one in which much common ground is to be found between the findings of psychoanalysts and those of anthropologists.

Freud must have been gratified, if not astonished, when he came to recognize that most of the strangely archaic modes of thought he had come across in his analyses of patients could be closely paralleled by the beliefs and customs of savages. It was a piece of insight that seems to have dawned on him relatively late in life, and even then—as was often so with Freud—only slowly.

The first allusion to savages is apparently a fleeting passage in *Three Contributions to the Theory of Sexuality* (1905) where he made a suggestive reference, though one of uncertain validity, to savages as "hapless children of the moment," indicating that they are less influenced by personal memories than we are.[15]

It was in the essays published separately in the years 1912-13, and then together in his well-known book *Totem and Taboo*,[16] that Freud first concerned himself at all extensively with savage customs and beliefs. His theme throughout was the close parallelism between certain mental processes he had revealed in the unconscious of both neurotics and children with those recorded by field anthropologists.

Naturally any attempt to compare children with savages can only be made with great qualification. It would be more accurate to say that of the two types of mental functioning—which may for the moment be called the rational and the irrational—the more primitive of the two can be detected in greater measure among children than among adults, and the same seems to be true when comparing savages with civilized peoples. In both cases the more primitive mode of thinking has later been to a certain extent superseded.

The first chapter, on the "Horror of Incest," went at once to the heart of the matter. Anthropologists have found it hard enough to discover any clue that could lead them through the tangled jungle of savage beliefs with its daunting complexity and ramifications. They generally agree that only one theme in them approximates to universality: the dread of incest, and consequently the fierce measures taken to prevent it.[17] These precautions, or prohibitions, are extraordinarily complicated and apply not merely to literal incest, but to relations and situations even remotely associated with it. It is as if the underlying fear was so intense that anything that *might* remind the people of it had also to be avoided. This extension of prohibition is evidently of the same order as the radiations in phobias, so familiar to medical psychologists, from the original focus of danger to widening circles of association, a feature not always understood by anthropologists.[c]

Freud's first comment on the horror of incest was in a letter to Fliess (May 31, 1897) where he attributed it to its antisocial effect in binding the family too closely together and thus separating it from the general community.[18] But only five months later (October 15) he had found the true explanation in the repressed desires of infancy.[19]

Freud now fully agreed with Frazer that such strict laws are made only for crimes toward which a strong temptation exists, and it was easy for him to correlate the repressed, and therefore apparently non-existent, incestuous wishes among savages with precisely the same situation among our own children. He thus established at once a vital connection between psychoanalytic and anthropological data.

There is no doubt that here Freud was on solid ground, and that he made an important contribution to anthropology by illuminating and making intelligible one of the most important of its problems. But he went further, and in a direction less easy to confirm directly from anthropological data. His clinical researches had shown him that the dread of incest and the necessity to take elaborate precautions against it were inseparably bound up with the male head of the family—normally the father, but in matrilineal societies the uncle who acts for him. Hostility to the father, with the corresponding wish to kill or castrate him, is the active counterpart of the forbidden incest longings; they constitute the two halves of the Oedipus complex. Freud suggested that the totemic worship so often accompanying the practice of exogamy was an example of the same taboo, the totem representing the father, or ancestor, who must be preserved and not injured. The totemic feasts where this rule was periodically broken in an orgy he explained as a temporary "return of the repressed," a bursting through under certain specific social conditions of the original hostile impulses against the totem, i.e. father. Cannibalism and the slaughter of the old are not hard to postulate in primitive man and can be observed still among living savages.

[c] Thus I read recently that a prohibition against a son having sexual relations with his father's second wife could have nothing to do with the theme of incest because there was no blood relationship!

McClellan, who first described, in 1865, the primitive religion known as Totemism, considered that the worship of totems, with the corresponding taboos, was linked with exogamy, the practice that forbade sexual relations between members of the same clan, i.e. those who possessed the same totem. The association between the two is certainly frequent, though later writers have doubted its being invariable. However, Freud accepted the more general belief and was able to give a unitary explanation for the two groups. The two basic laws of Totemic religion simply represent the repression of the Oedipus complex, i.e. the corresponding impulses toward incest and father-murder. Incidentally, he was able to show that the prohibition against son-mother incest was more powerful than that against father-daughter incest, as is still so at the present day, and that the precautions taken to avoid it are probably more ancient than those affecting the latter.

Freud then proceeded to investigate the vast problem of taboo in general, one which has immense ramifications; a summary of this work has already been given.[20] The main conclusion that emerged from it was that primitive peoples have a more intense capacity for ambivalent emotions than have civilized ones, who seem to have made more progress in reconciling the conflicting impulses of love and hate. In this they resemble neurotics, though the repression, i.e. taboo, is here more concerned with sexual impulses than with the antisocial hostile ones.

Then came the study of animism and magic, where Freud traced several stages in development. The central feature here is the omnipotence of thoughts, a phenomenon Freud first encountered among obsessional neurotics and only later recognized to be a never-failing feature of the unconscious. The belief that one's wishes have the power to affect reality is still active enough and underlies all our superstitious practices. Under the name of "wish-fulfillment" it has achieved general popularity.

It has often been said that Freud labeled his *Totem and Taboo* work a "just-so story." It is true that he quoted this joke from an English anthropologist, ascribing it to an American one, Kroeber (misprinted Kroeger), who had cited it; it actually came from R. R. Marett.[21]

Five years after *Totem and Taboo* Freud returned to the field of anthropology in an essay entitled "The Taboo of Virginity." [22] He had been struck by the curious contrast between the customary attitude among civilized men of treasuring virginity in their bride, as if she had always belonged to them and to no one else, and the husband's careful avoidance of performing the act of defloration in so many primitive tribes. Here someone else is either employed to perform it or is granted the privilege of doing so; we seem to have retained a relic of the latter in our custom of the best man claiming the first kiss after a wedding, even before the husband. Freud found the answer to the paradox through his investigation of neurotics, whose emotional reactions are more accessible. An account of it was given earlier,[23] and it may rank as a contribution to both sociology and anthropology.

It is impossible to consider here all the detailed suggestions Freud threw out in the field of social anthropology, but it is incontrovertible that his study of the unconscious is of immense value for the understanding of the innumerable customs, beliefs and rituals of primitive peoples, particularly those that impress the more civilized mind by their apparent irrationality.

In his investigation of the unconscious mind, particularly of childhood, Freud must from the beginning have been impressed by its archaic and primitive nature. Yet not until the middle of his second period, in 1913, did he pursue the suggestive correlation between it and the mentality of early man. He confined himself to pointing out the many parallels between the phantasies he had uncovered and those embodied in folklore beliefs and Greek myths, reaching, therefore, no farther back than a few thousand years. Primitive man had to wait for further reflection.

There is one curious exception to what I have just said. As early as 1897, at a time when he was becoming familiar with the significance of anal erotism, he mentioned in a letter to his friend Fliess a suggestion he was often to repeat later in his writings. It was that early man's adoption of an upright gait must have been fateful in certain respects for his future development. He called Fliess's attention to two points. One was an alteration in the sense of smell: "Upright carriage was adopted, the nose was raised from the ground, and at the same time a number of what had formerly been interesting sensations connected with the earth became repellent—by a process of which I am still ignorant." The other point was that this event initiated a hereditary change in disposition which Freud called an "organic repression." It was, he thought, the basis for much else.[24]

The next extension of this idea was that it accounted for much of neurosis. In discussing the case of the Rat Man, in 1909, he asked "whether the atrophy of the sense of smell (which was an inevitable result of man's assumption of an erect posture) and the consequent organic repression of his pleasure in smell may not have had a considerable share in the origin of his susceptibility to nervous disease. This would afford us some explanation of why, with the advance of civilization, it is precisely the sexual life that must fall a victim to repression. For we have long known the intimate connection in the animal organization between the sexual instinct and the function of the olfactory organ." [25] The further points here are the idea of atrophy and its bearing on the genesis of neuroses, with a hint of this on sexual life in general.

Three years later, in "Contributions to the Psychology of Love," Freud amplified this last idea of the incompatibility of the coprophilic impulses with our aesthetic sense since raising the organ of smell from the level of the earth, and even suggested that conflicts of this order might in the end imperil the continuance of the human race.[26] So very much might really be the result of man's unfortunate advance toward his present posture.

Freud's last pronouncement on the subject, in 1930, was in many ways the most emphatic of all. The assumption of the upright gait resulted not only in the relative abrogation of the pleasure in smell, but made the genital organs more visible and vulnerable: hence the beginning of shame. "Thus the upright posture of man was the start of his fateful cultural development." [27] It was the resulting impossibility of ever attaining full sexual gratification that compelled man to seek other than sexual outlets for his libido, leading to all the cultural developments that are summed up by the word sublimation.[28]

There is no doubt that Freud was correct in calling attention to the profound influence that the unfortunate proximity of the excremental organs to the sexual ones has had in our mental life. The close association between the ideas of sex and dirt seems almost indissoluble. It is, however, much harder to substantiate his ideas about the assumption of an upright posture and its connection with the sense of smell. Man is no longer thought to have had an arboreal ancestry with a rather sudden descent to the ground, as was at one time thought; the pre-hominoids, e.g. Plesianthropus, Pithecanthropus and Sinanthropus, were more probably shambling but erect creatures. Nor is he unique among the primates in adopting an upright posture; the gorilla, for instance, is quite at home in it. In other words, it looks as if man's ancestors adopted this posture very early in their history, more than many millions of years ago, long before there could be any trace of cultural development.

Nor is there any evidence of a deterioration in the sense of smell in that lengthy period. It could hardly ever have been so important to man's ancestors as it doubtless is to predatory animals like wolves and their ungulate prey. Nor is it obvious why, even if that sense had deteriorated, this should have resulted in repulsion, of a change from pleasure into disgust. The historical evolution of disgust is, it is true, rather obscure, but there is much contemporary evidence alone to suggest that it is not likely to have been an ancient attitude. The latrines surrounding native encampments and the indifference with which even civilized beings can on occasion endure the foulest conditions may be instanced here. Considerable changes in the response to unpleasant odors have taken place in recent epochs, e.g. the nineteenth century, so that it is more likely that aesthetic repulsion has been evolved within the confines of civilization in the past few thousand years. It may well prove, therefore, that Freud's far-reaching speculation about the importance of an upright posture is not well founded.

In his later years Freud published another far-reaching speculation on the early history of mankind, one concerning the important problem of the mastery of fire. He mentioned it first in a footnote to *Civilization and its Discontents* (1930),[29] and later devoted a special paper to it.[30] It was based on the assumption, generally accepted, that man first used fire for his domestic purposes by carrying away a brand from a spontaneous fire long before he acquired the art of kindling it for himself; there are natives still living in this stage of imperfect knowledge. Freud postulated that man's first impulse was to urinate on a fire he encountered, and that this symbolized a homosexual act, the rising flame being a well-known phallic symbol; he did not mention that the act might also represent a murderous conflict between two males. It was only after man renounced this instinctual pleasure that he was rewarded by getting control of the burning material. The later paper expounded this startling idea more fully by arguments that need an analytically trained mind to follow in their entirety; it is largely based on a fascinating analysis of the Prometheus myth. Written at the age of seventy-six, this brilliant little paper displays Freud's imaginative powers still at their best; one is struck also by his retentive memory of recondite classical data.

As was mentioned above, it was in the years immediately preceding the First World War that Freud began to turn his attention seriously to the theme of primitive man, and to ask whether his findings about the archaic layers of the mind he had uncovered could not provide some clues to earlier stages in man's development.

It was in 1911, when Freud was reading Frazer's *Golden Bough* and other works, that his interest was seriously directed toward the topic of prehistory. In 1911, at the conclusion of his Schreber analysis, he made the following pregnant remarks: "I am of opinion that the time will soon be ripe for us to extend a principle, the truth of which has long been recognized by psycho-analysts, and to complete what has hitherto had only an individual and ontogenetic application by adding its anthropological and phylogenetically conceived counterpart. 'In dreams and in neuroses,' so our principle has run, 'we come once more upon the *child* and the peculiarities that characterize his modes of thought and his emotional life.' 'And we come upon the *savage* too,' thus we may complete our proposition, 'upon *primitive man*, as he stands revealed to us in the light of the researches of archaeology and of ethnology.' " [31]

Two years later, in his general exposition in *Scientia*,[32] Freud made a similar definite pronouncement. "In recent years it has been realized in psycho-analytic work that the sentence 'Ontogeny is a recapitulation of phylogeny' must be applicable also to mental life." [33] The statement Freud quotes here from Haeckel, though no longer held in its original crude presentation, still retains much validity. He ventured to assert that in the study of the early history of societies "the psycho-analytic mode of thought acts like a new instrument of research." The example he used to illustrate this was the primitive belief in omnipotence.

All this raises at once the difficult problem of the mode of inheritance. Freud at first approached this cautiously. In his *Introductory Lectures* (1917) he compared the stages of libidinal development in the infant with that in lowly animals and remarked that the activities of the former had to be acquired afresh. But, he added, the conditions in which they arise had operated in the lower animals in a creative fashion, while with the human infant they are merely evocative—plainly implying thereby the presence of a particular predisposition.[34] He soon specified this, however, by mentioning as an example of inheritance the Oedipus complex, including the fear of being castrated or devoured by the father and, moreover, the repression of the complex.[35] In his later terminology this applied also in some part to the super-ego itself.[36] Finally Freud gave it as his opinion that not only specific predispositions could be inherited, but definite mental contents—the memory traces of prehistoric events as well as particular symbols.[37]

As has been mentioned more than once in this volume, Freud conceived of this transmission of inheritance throughout in Lamarckian terms, as the inheritance of strong impressions made on an individual.

In his book *Totem and Taboo* Freud had propounded repression of the Oedipus complex as the explanation of totemic worship and of exogamy. To it he traced the beginnings of community life in primitive man with all the fateful consequences of this. He was therefore drawn to speculate on the origin of this all-important repression. In reflecting on the possible events of perhaps fifty or a hundred thousand years ago one can only replace the missing historical data with more or less plausible speculation. All Freud had to help him was the analogy of infantile development, one he once described vividly by saying that in the few years of infancy the child has to evolve from the stone age to modern civilization.[38] Following hints from those biologists who postulated struggles over the females by the older males in possession and the growing young ones, he drew a picture of the former as incorporated in an "old man of the horde" being killed and then eaten by his sons. The difficulty of then living together without making some renunciation led to remorse, repressions and inhibitions, a reaction which was subsequently incorporated as a conscience and inherited by future generations. Naturally Freud visualized these happenings as recurring again and again over many thousands of years, but the picture he drew of these gruesome events was so vivid that many anthropologists accused him of dating the whole genesis of culture from a single event—a gross misunderstanding. Freud did, it is true, talk of impressions being burned into the brains of the participants and then passed on to their descendants in a Lamarckian fashion. It is easy to criticize this, but there is no reason to suppose that the chain of events could not be described perfectly well in the more plausible terms of natural selection.

What made this hypothesis seem tenable to Freud was his experience of its exact counterpart in the infantile mind. There one finds the identical impulses of murder, cannibalism and incest he postulated in primitive man, and it is not straining one's imagination to perceive that with uninhibited creatures the transformation of wishes into deeds would be a very simple matter. It is two centuries since Diderot surmised that if a little boy were left to himself and possessed the violence of a man he would strangle his father and sleep with his mother! Furthermore, there is enough cannibalism left in the world at present, including the custom of slaying and devouring the elderly, to make Freud's suggestion far from fanciful.

He found some further support in Robertson Smith's work on sacrifice.[39] The totemic feasts where, amid orgies and excesses, the totem animal is killed and eaten evidently constitute a violation of the customary taboos. They appear therefore to represent a ceremonial repetition of the original crimes, so long repressed, and to possess a valuable social significance. There still exist many relics of such ceremonies; indeed it had not been left to Freud to point out the connection between them and the theophagy of the Holy Mass, the central ritual of Christianity.

Freud did not hesitate to formulate the conclusion that "the beginnings of religion, morality, social life and art meet in the Oedipus complex," [40] a conclusion which it will take mankind a long time to assimilate.

Freud saw the essential difference between human development and that of the lower animals in the helplessness of the human infant with its lengthy phase of immaturity. The dangers in the outer world to which it is exposed during this phase make it exceptionally dependent on its protectors, particularly the mother, and forge exceptionally intense emotional bonds between them. Doubtless connected with this feature is the curious one, unique among animals, of human sexual life undergoing a double instead of a continuous development; it sets in after birth and then again at puberty.[41]

Freud never published a speculation without first submitting it to very considerable self-criticism. I may mention one which failed to pass that censorship. At a time when he was considerably attracted by Ferenczi's proneness to bold, or even wild, guesses he allowed himself to indulge in a highly speculative phantasy which illustrates his eagerness to discover an historical basis for various phases in human development, and also his interest in the comparative study of the different psychoneuroses. I will quote the passage in full from a letter of 1915.[42]

"In preparing next session's lectures on the transference neuroses I am troubled by phantasies which are hardly suitable for public expression. So listen:

"There is a series of chronological starting points in patients which runs thus:

"Anxiety hysteria—conversion hysteria—obsessional neurosis—dementia praecox—paranoia—melancholia—mania.

"Their libidinal predispositions run in general in the opposite direction: that is to say, the fixation lies with the former set in very late stages of development, with the latter in very early ones. That statement, however, is not faultless.

"On the other hand this series seems to repeat phylogenetically an historical origin. What are now neuroses were once phases in human conditions.

"With the appearance of privations in the glacial period men became apprehensive: they had every reason for transforming libido into anxiety.

"Having learned that propagation was now the enemy of self-preservation and must be restricted they became—still in the time before speech—hysterical.

"After they developed speech and intelligence in the hard school of the glacial period they formed primal hordes under the two prohibitions of the primal father, their love life having to remain egoistic and aggressive. Compulsion, as in the obsessional neurosis, struggled against any return to the former state. The neuroses that followed belong to the new epoch and were acquired by the sons.

"To begin with they were forced to relinquish all sexual objects, or else they were robbed of all libido by being castrated: dementia praecox.

"They then learned to organize themselves on a homosexual basis, being driven out by the father. The struggle against that signifies paranoia. Finally they overpowered the father so as to effect an identification with him, triumphed over him and mourned him: mania—melancholia.

"Your priority in all this is evident."

Ferenczi received this enthusiastically,[43] but omitted to give Freud the detailed criticism he had asked for, and Freud wisely dropped the whole train of thought.

Freud had correctly predicted that *Totem and Taboo* would meet with the same fate as *The Interpretation of Dreams*. For many years his contributions to anthropology were contemptuously, and often angrily, rejected by the great majority of anthropologists in all countries. I remember, for example, that when I read what I thought was a conciliatory and persuasive paper on "Psycho-Analysis and Anthropology" [44] before the Royal Anthropological Institute some thirty years ago vehement protests were made, notably by Edward Clodd, against its being published in the official Proceedings. It was followed by a controversy between A. M. Hocart, the distinguished anthropologist, and myself.[45]

One of the few grudging acknowledgments of Freud's ideas is to be found in a contribution by Professor Wunderle to a *Festschrift* offered to Pater Schmidt. He admitted that "within strictly defined limits even Freud's psychoanalysis might be helpful to ethnology. For unfortunately [*sic*] sexual psychology must play a great role among savage peoples." [46]

There would be no point in detailing here the denunciations of Freud's anthropological suggestions; a bibliography of them has been compiled by Weinreich.[47] One or two examples may serve. Thus Vetter called Freud's answer to the problem of incest taboos "the preposterous guess under the name of *Totem and Taboo* in which he postulates enough clever nonsense to make the reader finish it as a fairy tale for its sheer paltry and imagination. But even a gullible sophomore used to believing outright his textbooks and the editorials in *The Times* baulks at this account." [48] In Radin's opinion "For so keen a thinker as Freud his *Totem and Taboo* is really a woeful performance." [49] The famous anthropologist Edward Westermarck repeatedly expressed his detestation at the doctrines, dealing always with conscious motivation.[50] "What father would threaten to castrate his little son because he embraces and kisses his mother?" "There is no reason whatsoever to attribute the frictions between father and son to sexual jealousy." And so on.

There is no doubt that this condemnation was essentially directed against Freud's concept of the primal crime in the Oedipus situation. The horror aroused by what was considered to be a monstrous and improbable suggestion had the unfortunate result that Freud's many other contributions to social anthropology were almost entirely ignored for thirty or forty years. Kroeber, perhaps the most distinguished of American ethnologists, was thought to have delivered the *coup de grace* to the concept of a primal crime by listing ten objections to it, but they contained little more than expressions of disbelief.[51] He maintained the same condemnation **twenty years** later, adding: "The reason why Freud's hypothesis might long before this have proved fertile in the realm of cultural understanding instead of being mainly rejected or ignored as a brilliant phantasy was that he stated a timeless psychological explanation as if it were also an historical one." [52] Freud had in fact believed that the gruesome deeds had really happened. The Austrian Pater Schmidt, always an opponent of psychoanalysis, delivered in extreme language a diatribe at an international gathering,[53] and Goldenweiser explained that "the failings and exaggerations of Freud's system are largely due to the fact that it is not rooted in systematic and comprehensive exploration of the mind," [54] a truly original suggestion. But a little later he grudgingly admitted that "It seems hardly fair to doubt that psychoanalysis will ultimately [!] furnish a satisfactory psychological explanation of this 'horror of incest.' " [55] In most anthropological circles, however, there was a pained silence. In Lowie's standard work, for instance, Freud is only mentioned once, and then on a very minor matter.[56] Nor do I find the criticisms in Steiner's recent and much praised book on *Taboo* very helpful, though it has a more respectful note than many such works.[57]

For a long time the only anthropologist who supported Freud was Géza Róheim, who had the advantage of field experience as well as psychoanalytical training.[58] But during the past few years, particularly since the end of the Second World War, there have been many signs of Freud's work being given a more sympathetic hearing among anthropologists. Margaret Mead has discussed at length the common links between social anthropology and the new psychiatry, which is largely based on Freud's work.[59] Kluckhohn, one of the leading American anthropologists, wrote not long ago: "The facts uncovered in my own field work and that of my collaborators have forced me to the conclusion that Freud and other psychoanalysts have depicted with astonishing correctness many central themes in motivational life which are universal. The styles of expression of these themes and much of the manifest content are culturally determined, but the underlying psychologic drama transcends cultural difference." [60] Furthermore, in a recent personal letter he wrote: "I am convinced that the essential universality of the Oedipus complex and of sibling rivalry are now established by the anthropological record." [61] On this side of the Atlantic an important addition to Freud's theory of the primal crime has been published by F. D. Klingender.[62] Fully accepting Freud's account he then suggests that it might be correlated in time with changes in the feeding habits of primeval man during and after the last Ice Age. It does seem highly probable that change from small family groups to larger communities, perhaps forced on man by economic reasons, represented a crucial turning point in his evolution.

In the latest and most authoritative study of early man, Carleton Coon, in a section entitled "Oedipus Goes to School," gives an account of man's early history which corresponds closely to that propounded by Freud nearly half a century before, though he does not mention Freud's name.[63] He discusses how the original "Oedipus behavior" gradually passed, via a homosexual stage, into the guilt of the Oedipus complex.

There is therefore ground for thinking that Freud's contribution to anthropology will no longer be ignored and will lead to fruitful cooperation between workers in what at first sight appear to be very different fields.

12

CHAPTER

Sociology

BEFORE CONSIDERING FREUD'S PUBLISHED CONTRIBUTIONS TO SOCIOLOGY
it will be well to give some account, however imperfect, of what is
known about his personal attitude toward his fellow-beings. There is
little doubt that it was one which had in important ways been influenced by the distressing experiences of his childhood and adolescence. The misery of poverty is never easy to bear; to a proud
and sensitive boy it must have been a truly grievous affliction. He had
to overcome the shock of the contrast between the esteem with
which he was regarded in his own family, with the high hopes built
on him, and the lowly position in which he found himself in the
outer world. Possibly he was over-sensitive to the slights from better
off companions; he certainly took every care later on to ensure that
his children did not suffer in the same way. In a passage written in
old age, which doubtless refers to his own experience, he said: "Anyone who has lived through the misery of poverty in his youth, and
has endured the indifference and arrogance of those who have possessions, should be exempt from any suspicion of having no understanding of or goodwill toward the endeavors made to combat the
economic inequality of men and all that it leads to." [1]

Some letters, as yet unpublished, dating from Freud's puberty,
suggest that his first response to this state of affairs was a somewhat
arrogant and defiant assertion of superiority. He wrote as if belonging to an aristocracy of intellect and education enabled him to feel
disdain for the mass of people. In early manhood this disdain had
vanished, and the disparaging attitude had become couched in

moral in place of intellectual terms. A year after being engaged he wrote to his betrothed an illuminating letter which was quoted earlier.[2] In it he maintained that the more civilized or refined one is the more does one devote oneself to avoiding pain rather than seeking pleasure. He came to think that this was characteristic of civilization altogether, so that its inevitable effect was to diminish the amount of enjoyment in life.

In a manuscript accompanying a letter to Fliess dated May 31, 1897, he laid down the formula: "Civilization consists in progressive renunciation. Contrariwise the superman."[3] This is a theme that plays a central part in his later writings on sociology. It probably dates from early life when he was impelled by deep inner motives to renounce personal (sexual) pleasure, and compelled for economic reasons to renounce other enjoyments, with the compensation of achieving thereby intellectual development and interests.

In his mature years there was a curious contrast between Freud's personal attitude toward individual people and his impersonal judgment of them in mass. The former was an expression of the optimistic and benevolent qualities in his personality. Unless he had good reasons to the contrary beforehand he would meet a newcomer with the friendly expectation of his being an agreeable and decent person; in this he was of course sometimes disappointed. But when he spoke of people in general he would enunciate much harsher judgments; with rare exceptions they were riff-raff with little good in them.[4] He was not far off when he described himself to Pfister as "a cheerful pessimist" in this respect.[5]

In later years Freud more than once spoke of his interest having returned via the circuitous path of medicine and psychopathology to his earliest love, philosophy. By that I believe he meant to use the word in its earliest sense of general knowledge and wisdom rather than in its more restricted modern academic and technical sense, one which does not seem ever to have interested him much. This last point is borne out by a remark in his *Autobiography*: "Even when I have moved away from observation I have carefully avoided any contact with philosophy proper. This avoidance has been greatly facilitated by constitutional incapacity."[6] In a postscript to that book, written when he was seventy-nine years old, he phrased the same thought thus: "My interest, after making a lifelong detour through the natural sciences, medicine and psychotherapy, returned to the cultural problems which had fascinated me long before, when I was a youth scarcely old enough to think."[7]

Presumably he meant by the words "cultural problems" the meaning and origin of civilization, the conditions of communal life, and the relation of man to society.

Freud has been reproached, quite unjustifiably, with neglecting the social aspects of his patients' lives. Even as early as 1905, in the first analytical case history he published, he wrote: "It follows from the nature of the facts which form the material of psycho-analysis that we are obliged to pay as much attention in our case histories to the purely human and social circumstances of our patients as to the somatic data and the symptoms of the disorder." [8] His conclusions were, it is true, founded on the psychology of the individual, but it was Freud more than anyone else who taught us that every aspect of that individual is really a social one. And, as Freud's later writings show, one can be profoundly interested in sociological problems without having to take part in the turmoil of political warfare.

We now come to Freud's published contributions in this field. His first sociological paper, in 1908, was that entitled "Civilized Sexual Morality and Modern Nervousness." [9] It was a trenchant criticism of our present sexual arrangements and of the idea that monogamy could ever be a cure for their defects. He was evidently in favor of revolutionary changes in this sphere, although he did not consider it within his province to specify the details. His main misgiving was lest the social restrictions in the sexual sphere, which had previously released so much energy for the purposes of civilization, were now reaching their limits in this direction and actually thwarting those purposes through the amount of neurotic incapacity they produce. A few years later (in 1912) he even thought it possible that further restrictions might ultimately endanger the very existence of the human race,[10] a gloomy possibility he again envisaged in later years in his correspondence with Einstein.[11]

On March 10, 1909, Adler read a paper before the Vienna Psycho-Analytical Society on "The Psychology of Marxism," and the Minutes of the Society, which will shortly be published, contain an account of the discussion that followed. Freud had not much to say on the theme of the paper itself, but he remarked that listening to it had stimulated a train of thought about the origins of civilization. There were two elements in this: the gradual widening of human consciousness and the constant increase in repression; "our civilization consists in an ever increasing subjection of our instincts to repression." The contradiction of the two elements is only an apparent one. The widening of consciousness, i.e. of interests and capacities, was won at the expense of the more primitive impulses that were being repressed. This was a conclusion that Freud never abandoned.

In the same discussion he threw out a suggestion that he developed later in another form. At that time he was still occupied with the unraveling of the various sexual impulses and their fate; he had not yet found a way of studying the other part of the mind, one which many years later was to lead to his psychology of the ego. Here, proceeding on the analogy of his own discoveries through psychopathology, he expressed the opinion that the best access to the psychology of the ego might be through investigating the disorders of society.

The book *Totem and Taboo*, 1914, which has already been discussed more than once in this biography, might well be considered, with its investigation into the origins of community life, as much a sociological study as an anthropological one. Then, in his essay "On Narcissism," published in the same year, he extended his consideration of this exquisitely individualistic phenomenon to matters of social import.[12] Thus he pointed out that the mental institution he termed the "ego ideal" had far more than a personal significance. It could become the common ideal of a family, a class, a nation. It contains a homosexual as well as a narcissistic component, and when there is disappointment at the non-realization of the ideal this homosexual libido is converted into (or provokes) a sense of guilt or social anxiety; here the original dread of parental disapproval is turned into dread of public opinion. These extremely condensed statements Freud expanded at length later, but they are mentioned here to show that the train of thought behind them had occupied Freud earlier than is sometimes supposed.

In Freud's middle years and to some extent later, the central idea in his conception of society was the difficulty the average man experienced in carrying out without hardship the renunciations demanded of him, and his clamor for external help in this task. In "The Future Prospects of Psychoanalytic Therapy," which he read before the 1910 Congress, he made the forcible remark: "You cannot exaggerate the extent of man's inner instability and his consequent craving for authority." [13] But it was after the World War, in Freud's last period, that he devoted himself more wholeheartedly to the "cultural problems" that had fascinated him as a youth.

In *Beyond the Pleasure Principle,* written in 1919, which inaugurated his remodeling of psychoanalytical theory, we may note an expression of disbelief in the existence of any impulse in mankind toward perfectibility.[14] What appears as such can be explained on purely psychological grounds without the aid of philosophy.

In his book on *Group Psychology and the Analysis of the Ego,* published in 1921, Freud expounded two main ideas, corresponding respectively with the two parts of its title. He first discussed very fully the nature of the bonds that unite members of a group, both a temporary group such as a crowd and a more lasting institution such as a church, army, or nation. He did not think that they could be explained as simply emanating from common interests in a utilitarian sense, and held that there must be more complex emotional factors in play. Nor did he think that the sense of security given by belonging to a group, with the fear of diverging from its other members, could afford the sole explanation. He described at some length the generally recognized differences in the behavior of an individual in his personal life and when functioning as a member of a group. Its features in the latter case: its irrationality, intolerance, illogical type of thinking, and its deterioration in moral standards and behavior, strongly suggest a reversion to some more primitive level.

It is plain that something in the mysterious bond limits the freedom of thought and judgment of the individual. At this point the analogy of hypnotism attracted Freud's attention, and after discussing the problem of suggestion in general he came to the conclusion that the emotional factor operating with groups must ultimately be of the same nature as with this: namely, aim-inhibited libido, just as it is in the earliest example of group formation—the family. He then showed how all the peculiar features of group psychology could be understood as an extension to the group of the original family situation. The most original part of Freud's contribution, however, was the stress he laid on the important part played by a leader (or an ideological concept replacing him). The bonds uniting the members of a group, and their identification with one another, depend essentially on their common bond with the leader.

The exposition is strewn, as always in Freud's writings, with stimulating ideas. Thus, remarking that he had long held social anxiety—i.e., fear of public opinion—to be the essence of conscience, he maintained that the demand for equality (that characteristic feature of our present post-war age) is the root of our social conscience and sense of duty. The passion for social justice generally associated with the demand for equality and equal treatment arises from a reaction to envy, and its beginnings can be plainly seen in the nursery in the attitude of one child to the others in relation to parental love.

Freud went further in his analysis, however, and compared the psychology of groups not only to that of the family, but also to that of the primeval horde whose existence he had postulated in *Totem and Taboo*. There the same agencies of conscience, sense of guilt, fear and libidinal bonds between the members, were also at work.

Incidentally, Freud disagreed with the usual belief that panic dissolves the bonds uniting a group, and he reversed the order of events. It is true that where there are weak bonds and an alarming danger appears, such as a fire in a theatre, the danger itself is the provocative cause of the disorderly and selfish turmoil. But in more organized groups, such as of soldiers in battle, a relatively slight danger, less than had often been withstood on other occasions, may be followed by panic if the discipline and sense of comradeship has previously been weakened. He gave as an example of this the breakdown of the German Army at the end of the First World War, when their belief in their common cause and in their leaders had been undermined by the course of events.

Freud was of the opinion that women were on the whole opponents of the cultural process, or rather of its demands on men. These compel men to withdraw from women much of the love and attention they would otherwise devote to them and the family.

The second half of the book was taken up with the new ideas about the psychology of the ego which Freud was to expound more fully a couple of years later in *The Ego and the Id*. In the present connection the important point was his insistence that the ideal put forward by the leader must have a close correspondence with the ego ideal of his followers. The oscillating relations between the ego and the ego ideal, which are brought about by the restrictions this forces on the ego, account for the various instabilities and changes to be observed in the life of the groups.

Some ten years later Freud, in *Civilization and its Discontents*,[15] gave the fullest account of his views in the field of sociology, one which, as he said elsewhere, "can be nothing other than applied psychology." [16] The book is easier to read with enjoyment than to summarize. Writing in a conversational fashion, Freud followed his thoughts in various directions, leaving pearls of wisdom as he went, and even when the considerations brought forward are not very original they are expressed in his inimitable style.

The book begins with the widest possible problem: man's relation to the universe. His friend Romain Rolland had described to him a mystical emotion of identification with the universe, which Freud called an "oceanic" feeling. Freud could not, however, bring himself to believe that this was a primary constituent of the mind, and he traced it back to the earliest stage of infancy, to a time when no distinction is made between the self and the outer world. He then raised the question of the purpose of life, one which obsesses many people. In his opinion the question has, strictly speaking, no meaning, being founded on unjustifiable premises; as he pointed out, it is one that is seldom raised in respect to the animal world. So he turned to the more modest question of what human behavior reveals as its aim. This seemed to him to be indisputably the search for happiness, but it is plain that he was using the term very broadly to include not only happiness in its narrower sense but also bliss, pleasure, peace of mind and contentedness—the satisfaction of all desires. Life is dominated by the pleasure-pain principle. In its most intense form this occurs only as a temporary episode; any continuation of the pleasure principle is experienced only as a mild contentedness. Human happiness, therefore, does not seem to be the purpose of the universe, and the possibilities of unhappiness lie more readily at hand. These have three sources: bodily suffering, dangers from the outer world, and disturbances in our relations with our fellow man—perhaps the most painful of all. There follows a detailed account of the various methods man has used to achieve happiness and avoid unhappiness; it is an interesting exposition, with many wise comments, but contains little really new.

Freud then passed to the topic of social relations, the very beginning of civilization. This came about through the discovery that a number of men who were placing limits on their own gratifications were stronger than a single man, however strong, who had been accustomed to gratifying his impulses unrestrainedly. "The strength of this united body is then opposed as 'Right' against the strength of any individual, which is condemned as 'brute force.' The substitution of the power of a united number for the power of a single man is the decisive step towards civilization. The essence of it lies in the circumstance that the members of the community have restricted their possibilities of gratification, whereas the individual recognized no such restrictions. The first requisite of a culture, therefore, is justice—that is, the assurance that a law once made will not be broken in favor of any individual." [17]

This situation inevitably led to a never-ending conflict between the claims of the individual for freedom to obtain personal gratification and the demands of society which are so often opposed to them. Freud then discussed the question, so vital for the future of civilization, of whether this conflict is irreconcilable or not. In this connection he put forward an impressive list of the restrictions imposed on man's sexual life: prohibition of auto-erotism, pre-genital impulses, incest and perversions; confinement to one sex and ultimately to one mate. Phylogenetically he laid special stress on the early repression of anal-erotism, with the consequent gain in the cleanliness and order which are such important constituents of society. "The sexual life of man is seriously disabled; it sometimes makes the impression of being a function in process of becoming atrophied." [18] These restrictions exact a heavy toll in the form of widespread neuroses with their suffering and the consequent reduction in the cultural energy available.

Why could a civilized community not consist of pairs of happy individuals linked to others merely by common interests? Why need it in addition draw on energy derived from aim-inhibited libido? Freud found a clue to the answer by considering the precept "Thou shalt love thy neighbor as thyself," one not only impracticable but in many ways undesirable. This high demand on the part of society comes about because of the strong instinct of aggressive cruelty in man, one which there is no need to go back as far as Genghis Khan to confirm. "Civilized society is perpetually menaced with disintegration through this primary hostility of men towards each other. . . . Culture has to call up every possible reinforcement in order to erect barriers against the aggressive instincts of men." [19] This tendency to aggression, which Freud maintained was the most powerful obstacle to culture, is "an innate, independent, instinctual disposition in man." [20]

The most characteristic way of dealing with this matter of aggression is to internalize it into a part of the self called the super-ego or conscience. This then exercises the same propensity to harsh aggressiveness against the ego that the ego would have liked to exercise against others. The tension between the two constitutes what is called the sense of guilt. A sense of guilt begins, not from an inborn sense of sin, but from the fear of losing love. In adult life this may be called "social anxiety," fear of public opinion. Many people are prepared to do "wicked" things so long as they are sure they will not be found out, but when the super-ego is firmly established then fear of its disapproval becomes stronger than fear of other people's disapproval. Mere renunciation of a forbidden act no longer absolves the conscience, as saints well know, because the wish still persists. On the contrary, privation, and, even more, misfortune intensifies the sense of guilt because it is felt to be a deserved punishment ("sackcloth and ashes" was the ancient answer to misfortune). At this point Freud put forward the novel idea that the sense of guilt is *specifically* the response to repressed aggressiveness. Since it is to a large extent unconscious its manifest expression is a feeling of uneasiness, of general discontent or unhappiness.

The main point of the book may be expressed in Freud's words as his "intention to represent the sense of guilt as the most important problem in the evolution of culture, and to convey that the price of progress in civilization is paid by forfeiting happiness through the heightening of the sense of guilt." [21]

Freud's contributions to sociology met with a much friendlier reception than his contributions to anthropology. As early as December 28, 1920, The American Sociological Society held a special "Round Table" conference under the title of "Sociological Significance of Psychoanalytic Psychology." Six papers were read.[22] A few years later the distinguished anthropologist W.H.R. Rivers, said that "if Freud's views hold good of the social mind they provide an ample explanation for the failure of those who have sought to learn the springs of social conduct by means of direct enquiry." [23]

It is naturally of interest to inquire into any hints Freud may have given about the future of civilization, and his views on the remedies that have been suggested for its deficiencies.

With all his knowledge of the complexity of human nature Freud could not fail to evince some scepticism about the utopian prospects of the panaceas that are offered us, notably the two chief ones: religion and communism. He had a good deal to say on the subject of ethics,[a]—"a therapeutic effort which deals predominantly with the point which is easily seen to be the sorest in any scheme of civiliza· tion." [25] But in its endeavors to heighten the standards of the social super-ego it often aims beyond what is feasible. "The command to

[a] Roger Money-Kyrle has made an important contribution to the objective evaluation of ethical standards.[24]

love our neighbors as ourselves is the strongest defense there is against human aggressiveness, and it is a superlative example of the unpsychological attitude of the cultural super-ego. The command is impossible to fulfill; such an enormous inflation of love can only lower its value and not remedy the evil. . . . What an overwhelming obstacle to civilization aggression must be if the defense against it can cause as much misery as aggression itself." [26] On the way ethics is often linked with religion, and with its promise of compensation in a better future life beyond the grave, Freud caustically remarked: "I should imagine that so long as virtue is not rewarded in this life ethics will preach in vain." He added: "I think it unquestionable that an actual change in men's attitude to property would be of more help in this direction than any ethical commands; but among the Socialists this proposal is obscured by new idealistic expectations disregarding human nature, which detract from its value in actual practice." Freud always took the view that illusions could have at the best merely alleviatory effects, and that often they resulted in as much harm as good. He would assuredly have subscribed to the dictum attributed to Socrates: "Seek out truth first, for only through knowing what is good can you do what is good."

His attitude toward the modern ideology of Marxism was hardly more encouraging. His humanism made him dislike the violence and cruelty apparently inseparable from it, and his realistic sense made him profoundly distrust its idealism. Both were well expressed in the remark he made to me quoted earlier.[b] Again, at the time of Mussolini's rise to power he was accused of being neither black nor red, neither Fascist nor Socialist; to which he replied: "No, one should be flesh coloured." [27] Imre Hermann has recently raised the question of why Freud was a revolutionary in the field of psychology, but an anti-revolutionary in the political field, and he answered it by the contention that Freud's attitude to politics derived from John Stuart Mill, some of whose writings Freud had translated when he was a medical student.[28] It is true that there was much in common in the outlook of the two men, but Freud was not wont to take over unthinkingly the views of someone else. And Hermann's premise is incorrect. Freud was quite as revolutionary in the field of sociology as in that of psychology—it would be hard to think of anyone more profoundly so—but just for that reason he was distrustful of simple, and to his mind superficial, solutions.

There is at least one sentence in Engels' writings with which

[b] See p. 16.

Freud would have been in complete agreement: "Mutual tolerance of the grown males, freedom from jealousy, was the first condition for the formation of large and permanent groups." [29] But Freud, knowing the indirect as well as the manifest expressions of that jealousy would have been more sceptical than Engels about the extent to which it has been overcome.

Since Freud and Marx have left a deeper imprint on our age than anyone else it is not surprising that endeavors have been made to compare or amalgamate their respective doctrines, e.g. those by Bartlett,[30] Eastman,[31] Jekels,[32] Jurinetz,[33] Kornilov,[34] Krische,[35] Marcuse,[36] Osborn,[37] Parkes,[38] Wilhelm Reich,[39] Sapir,[40] Pater Schmidt[41] and others. A full dress debate was held on the matter in Berlin in 1928 at the *Verein sozialistischer Aerzte*. There was widespread agreement, supported particularly by Bernfeld and Simmel, that psychoanalysis and Marxism were not only compatible but mutually complementary, though a few voices were raised criticizing Freud's supposedly non-materialistic outlook.[42] We are not concerned here with the success or failure of these endeavors, and I will content myself with quoting a summary of the comparison by Bertrand Russell: "Nor does it seem probable that impulses of cruelty can be traced, without residues, to economic causes. So long as they exist, every system which gives some men power over others—as every system must—will be liable to become a cause of suffering. It follows that, even when we are only considering large communities, the exclusively economic view is an over-simplification, and a more psychological outlook is essential to political wisdom." [43]

Freud publicly stated his attitude toward Marxist Socialism more than once. In *The Future of an Illusion*, 1927, he opened one chapter with the words: "At first we were tempted to see the essence of culture in the existing material resources and in the arrangements for their distribution. But with the discovery that every culture is based on compulsory labor and instinctual renunciation, and that it therefore inevitably evokes opposition from those affected by these demands, it became clear that the resources themselves, the means of acquiring them, and the arrangements for their distribution could not be its essential or unique characteristic; for they are threatened by the rebelliousness and destructive passions of the members of the culture: the coercive measures, and others that are intended to reconcile men to it and to recompense them for their sacrifices. And these last may be described as the psychical sphere of culture." [44]

In *Civilization and its Discontents,* 1930, he wrote: "The Communists believe they have found a way of delivering us from this evil. Man is whole-heartedly good and friendly to his neighbor, they say, but the system of private property has corrupted his nature. . . . If private property were abolished, all valuables held in common and all allowed to share in the enjoyment of them, ill-will and enmity would disappear from men. . . . I cannot inquire into whether the abolition of private property is advantageous and expedient. But I am able to recognize that this theory is founded on an untenable illusion. By abolishing private property one deprives the human love of aggression of one of its instruments, a strong one undoubtedly, but assuredly not the strongest. To do this in no way alters the individual differences in power and influence which are turned by aggressiveness to its own use, nor does it change the nature of the instinct in any way. This instinct did not arise as the result of property; it reigned almost supreme in primitive times when possessions were still extremely scanty; it shows itself already in the nursery when possessions have hardly grown out of their original form." [45] In his *New Introductory Lectures on Psycho-Analysis,* three years later, Freud devoted several pages to the topic, and the reader may be referred to them.[46] They follow on similar lines. And in his last book, *Moses and Monotheism,* there occurs the following sentence, which seems very representative of his convictions. "What profanation of the grandiose multiformity of human life we commit if we recognize as sole motives those springing from material needs." [47]

In 1937 R. L. Worrall took him to task for his implication that Marxism attributes social changes solely to economic forces, and informed him that Marx and Engels had admitted that their analysis of the part played by economic factors did not exclude the operation of psychological ones; he omitted to add, however, that in practice this admission has proved to be a matter of lip service only. Here is an extract from the modest letter Freud wrote in reply: "I know that my comments on Marxism are no evidence either of a thorough knowledge or of a correct understanding of the writings of Marx and Engels. I have since learned—rather to my satisfaction—that neither of them has denied the influence of ideas and super-ego factors. That invalidates the main contrast between Marxism and psychoanalysis which I had believed to exist. As to the 'dialectic' I am no clearer, even after your letter." [48]

Freud's tolerant objectivity was not reciprocated on the other side of the Iron Curtain. In the latest edition (1955) of the *Short*

Philosophic Dictionary, the authoritative statement of the Party line in Russia, "Freudism" is defined as "a reactionary idealistic trend widespread in bourgeois psychological science . . . now in the service of imperialism which utilizes these 'teachings' for the purpose of justifying and developing the basest and most repellent instinctual tendencies."

On the prospects of abolishing war Freud had an interesting discussion with Einstein, at the request of the League of Nations, and he came to a less pessimistic conclusion than might perhaps have been expected. The experience of the First World War had finally quenched any military ardor he may himself have felt in earlier years. "War is in the crassest opposition to the psychical attitude imposed on us by the cultural process, and for that reason we are bound to rebel against it; we simply cannot put up with it any longer. This is not merely an intellectual and emotional repudiation, we pacifists have a constitutional intolerance of war, an idiosyncrasy magnified, as it were, to the highest degree. It seems, indeed, as if the lowering of aesthetic standards in war plays a scarcely smaller part in our rebellion than do its cruelties.

"And how long shall we have to wait before the rest of mankind become pacifists too? There is no telling. But it may not be Utopian to hope that these two factors, the cultural attitude and the justified dread of the consequences of a future war, may result in a measurable time in putting an end to the waging of war." [49]

That was written the year before Hitler's advent to power. Freud lived to see the outbreak of another World War, but assuredly the experience of it would only have increased his abhorrence.

On the question of whether an extended knowledge of psychoanalysis could further a more satisfactory organization of society Freud was characteristically cautious. "If the evolution of civilization has such a far-reaching similarity with the development of an individual, and if the same methods are employed in both, would not the diagnosis be justified that many systems of civilization have become 'neurotic' under the pressure of the civilizing trends? To analytic dissection of these neuroses therapeutic recommendations might follow which could claim a practical interest. I would not say that such an attempt to apply psychoanalysis to civilized society would be fanciful or doomed to fruitlessness. But . . . in spite of all these difficulties we may expect that one day someone will venture on this research into the pathology of civilized communities." [50] No one has yet taken up just this task, but a British psychiatrist, Alex Comfort, has made the laudable endeavor to initiate a psychiatric approach to the problems of government and the personality of leaders.[51] Freud himself had suggested that more care should be devoted than hitherto to "the education of an upper stratum of men of independent minds, not open to intimidation and eager in the pursuit of truth." [52] He repeatedly expressed the opinion that much of our lack of freedom in thinking proceeds from the restrictions imposed by our education in the fields of religion and sexuality.[53]

Thomas Mann, whose standing as a thinker should carry weight, was a good deal more hopeful about the future value to society of psychoanalytical knowledge. Discussing Freud's work he wrote: "And no less firmly do I hold that we shall one day recognize in Freud's life-work the cornerstone for the building of a new anthropology and therewith of a new structure, to which many stones are being brought today, which shall be the future dwelling of a wiser and freer humanity. This physician-psychologist will, I make no doubt at all, be honored as the pathfinder toward a humanism of the future, which we dimly divine and which will have experienced much that the earlier humanism knew not of. It will be a humanism standing in a different relation to the powers of the lower world, the unconscious, the id: a relation bolder, freer, blither, productive of a riper art than any possible in our neurotic, fear-ridden, hate-ridden world. . . . Call this, if you choose, a poet's utopia, but it is after all not unthinkable that the resolution of our great fear and our great hate, their conversion into a different relation to the unconscious which shall be more the artist's, more ironic and yet not necessarily irreverent, may one day be due to the healing effect of this very science." [54] On another occasion he said of psychoanalysis: "It is, in my sincere conviction, one of the great foundation stones of a structure of the future which shall be the dwelling-place of a free and conscious humanity." [55]

In a thoughtful book recently published Herbert Marcuse gives more solid reasons than Thomas Mann for the hope that a more mature civilization than ours may develop. Distinguishing carefully between what he calls the basic or primary repressions, perhaps inherited, and the "surplus" repressions brought about by social influences, he points out that much of the former were instituted at a time when the struggle for bare survival prevailed, and that in an age of greater prosperity and security it could be expected that they would be gradually modified. Then the restraints of society would also be considerably relaxed, though absolute freedom could never be attained; freedom would be reserved for the sphere of art.[56]

About the future of society Freud always wrote in a vein of tempered optimism. In *Civilization and its Discontents* (1930) he wrote: "We may expect that in the course of time changes will be carried out in our civilization so that it becomes more satisfying to our needs and no longer open to the reproaches we have made against it. But perhaps we shall also accustom ourselves to the idea that there are certain difficulties inherent in the very nature of culture which will not yield to any efforts at reform." [57]

Writing at the height of the economic disasters that had overtaken the civilized world at that time, he ended the book with the hopeful words: "And now it may be expected that the other of the two 'heavenly forces,' eternal Eros, will put forth his strength so as to maintain himself alongside of his equally immortal adversary." Four years later, however (when Hitler had seized power), Freud in revising the book added this sentence: "But who can predict his success and the final outcome?"

13

Religion

THIS CRITICAL TOPIC, FREUD AND RELIGION, HAS BEEN THE OCCASION OF many books and a spate of essays. It has evoked more controversy and condemnation than any other of his writings except perhaps those on sexuality. We may consider separately Freud's personal attitude toward religion and the contributions he made toward the understanding of certain aspects of it.

Upbringing is usually an important factor in determining later attitudes toward religion, though it is far from being the only one. We know two things about Freud's. First, he had a Catholic Nannie until he was two and a half years old, and she used to take him to her church services. On his return he would imitate what he had seen for the benefit of the family. Even if this was greeted with mild amusement he may well have detected something of his parents' lack of enthusiasm for the Nannie's beliefs. My own opinion about such behavior is that its significance was theatrical rather than theological. The Nannie also told him about hell fire, and presumably threatened him with it if he was not obedient. But, as I know from my own similar experience, a young child takes such threats as applying to his personal life in the near future, rather than to a hypothetical existence beyond the grave which he is not yet in a position to comprehend.

Much has been made of this Nannie by writers who are eager to discover a neurotic origin for Freud's negative attitude toward religion. It is of course easy enough to weave conjectures and speculations on a theme of this sort, but I am not aware of any evidence that might justify one in attributing any lasting influence to the Nannie's theological beliefs, and in any event the contact ceased at the age of two and a half. It has even been suggested that his attitude to religion derived from the circumstance of his losing her at that age. It was only when he was forty-six that Freud learned from his mother the reason for the Nannie's disappearance—her being detected in theft. Yet we have been asked to believe that this precocious two-year-old himself divined that it was the result of her sinning against the ethics of her religion and deduced from this that Christianity was a hypocritical mockery. There is no limit to the fantastic whimsies writers will invent to further some adverse criticism of Freud.

Much more important must have been the attitude of his parents. While it is likely that both of these continued throughout their lives to pay lip service to a belief in the Deity, it is certain that in practice they were very freethinking people, and in such matters it is practice that counts most. Whatever may have been their custom previously, after coming to Vienna they dispensed with the Jewish dietary observances and with most of the customary rituals; the only exception I know of was the festival meal of Seder on the eve of Passover.¹ Jakob Freud was, it is true, fond of reading the *Torah*, a book of Jewish philosophy rather than of religion; it was no doubt an indication of his interest in trying to unravel the knotty problems of life. On the whole, therefore, we may say that, unquestionably Jewish as the family was, Freud was brought up in an almost entirely secular home atmosphere. He was of course obliged to attend occasional lessons in the synagogue during his school days; the memory of this seems to have faded in later years, otherwise he would not have been uncertain of the name of the most prominent object there—the Menorah.

On the other hand Freud was very conversant with the Bible and was always ready to quote from either Testament. He had begun to read the Old Testament at the age of seven. At first he must have been attracted by the illustrations, since the volume in question was the remarkable edition by Ludwig Philippson containing some five hundred woodcuts. The text is accompanied by a learned commentary far transcending the literal context and consisting of numerous passages on early history and comparative religion.² In all probability it was these more general aspects rather than the theological ones to which Freud paid most attention. We may assume that he was also impressed by the ethical teaching, particularly that on the theme of justice, which was always prominent in his thinking.

To this early knowledge of comparative religion must be added that which Freud acquired later in his cultural studies of the Roman, Greek, Egyptian and other Eastern religions of antiquity. He does not appear to have extended these studies far into the religions of India and China, though he had a passing acquaintance with these also. Altogether, therefore, Freud possessed an unusually comprehensive knowledge of various religious beliefs.

We have no reason to suppose that Freud passed through the religious phases so frequent in adolescence; he told me once that he had never believed in a supernatural world. Thus he went through his life from beginning to end as a natural atheist: that is to say, one who saw no reason for believing in the existence of any supernatural Being and who felt no emotional need for such a belief. The world of nature seemed all-embracing, and he could find no evidence of anything outside it. Religious people would presumably account for this state of affairs by concluding that Freud was unfortunately devoid of what they call a religious sense. Those of a similar way of thinking to himself, however, would find his attitude a natural one, needing no explanation. On the contrary, what they would consider calls for explanation is the superfluous invention of another imaginary, and perhaps illusory, world beyond the one we know. That assuredly was Freud's own view, and it accounts for his lifelong wonderment at the religious beliefs of other people and his ceaseless inquiry into the reason for them. It will be noted that this attitude long antedated his psychological investigations, which therefore in no way accounted for it.

Almost inevitably this interest was essentially devoted to the source of the Jewish and Christian religions, the two nearest to him. His attitude toward the former was that the rituals and observances that constitute such a large part of the religion were an antiquated nuisance; of its ethical teaching, however, he thought very highly. If people must believe in supernatural Beings it was preferable that they should believe in a single one. Many people do not find this preference so axiomatic. A sceptical friend of mine once remarked that the only argument he knew in its favor was a purely arithmetical one: monotheism was nearer the truth because one is nearer to zero than three or five. The reason Freud gave for his preference was as follows: "The race that first succeeded in thus concentrating the divine qualities (into a single figure) was not a little proud of this advance. It had revealed the father nucleus which had always lain hidden behind every divine figure; fundamentally it was a return to the historical beginnings of the idea of God. Now that God was a single person, man's relations to him could recover the intimacy and intensity of the child's relation to the father."

There can be no doubt that the attraction of monotheism must have deep roots in the unconscious, and that it lends itself to further psychological investigation. Barag has made a promising start in this direction by correlating it with the motives impelling toward repudiation of a mother fixation, one which culminated in Jesus' repellent remark to his mother "Woman, what have I to do with thee?" [3] It would then serve a similar function to that of the numerous puberty rites.

Roman Catholicism, with its Archangels and countless saints, with its syncretic absorption of so many pagan beliefs, therefore appeared to Freud as a regression rather than an advance on Judaism. As a Jew he was bound to feel prejudiced against Christianity in general, the religion that had inflicted such untold suffering on his people through the centuries. Nevertheless in practice he was tolerant enough, as his letters to Pfister encouraging him to make use of the Christian faith in his psychoanalytic work manifest. He said in one letter, "In itself psychoanalysis is neither religious nor the opposite, but an impartial instrument which can serve the clergy as well as the laity when it is used only to free suffering people." [4]

The central figure of Christianity, Jesus, was, in Freud's eyes, so clouded over with sayings and mythical beliefs evidently derived from earlier religious sources in the East as to be too indistinct to visualize clearly. He might have been one of the many wandering Jewish preachers of that time. Once in a conversation on the topic Freud remarked to me that Jesus could even have been "an ordinary deluded creature." But Paul seemed a far more definite and formidable person. He was more obviously an historical figure, the true Founder of Christian theology and in an important sense of the Christian religion itself. He wrote once to Pfister: "I liked very much your [essay on] Paul.[5] Paul with his truly Jewish character has always appealed to me." [6]

In his *Psychopathology of Everyday Life*, 1904, Freud gave an early expression to his naturalistic outlook on religion and allied topics. "I believe in fact that a great part of the mythological view of the world, which reaches far into the most modern religions, is *nothing other than psychological processes projected into the outer world*.* The obscure apprehending of the psychical factors and relationships of the unconscious is mirrored—it is hard to put it otherwise; one has to use here the analogy with paranoia—in the construction of *a supersensible reality*, which science has to retranslate into the *psychology of the unconscious*. One could venture in this manner to resolve the myths of Paradise, the Fall of Man, of God, of Good and Evil, of Immortality and so on, thus transforming *Metaphysics* into *Metapsychology*." [7]

For the time being Freud did nothing further in undertaking this ambitious task, but in January, 1907, he published a very original paper entitled "Obsessive Acts and Religious Practices." [8] Nor even then was this a spontaneous act; he had been invited to contribute something to the first number of the newly founded *Zeitschrift für Religionspsychologie*. Pointing out the sense of compulsion accompanying the various ritual acts in religious observances (praying, kneeling, etc.) with that accompanying the private ritual acts of the obsessional neurosis, he expounded the part played by fear and the sense of guilt if the acts are omitted. They are designed to ward off certain temptations, often unconscious ones, together with the punishments that yielding to them may bring. In the neurosis these are essentially sexual temptations, whereas religious observances are more concerned with aggressive and antisocial ones—with conduct in general. He summed up the contrast by saying that the obsessional neurosis may be regarded as a pathological counterpart to religion, an individual religiosity, while, from this point of view at least, religion might be called a universal obsessional neurosis.

Early in 1909 Hugo Heller read a paper before the Vienna Society on "The History of the Devil." [9] Freud spoke at length on the extraordinarily composite elements in the figure, whose temptations were extensively used in the Middle Ages as an attempted justification for forbidden indulgences. He connected the later transformation of the figure into a purely evil demon with the increased repression associated with the Reformation, and remarked on the part played in this by the guilt and fear aroused by the wave of syphilitic infection that was then sweeping over Europe.

In his study of Leonardo da Vinci, 1910, Freud stated unequivocally his conclusions about the source of religious beliefs, which in a succinct fashion express what was undoubtedly his main contribu-

* In italics in the original.

tion to the psychology of religion. "Psycho-analysis has made us aware of the intimate connection between the father complex and the belief in God, and has taught us that the personal God is *psychologically*[b] nothing other than a magnified father; it shows us every day how young people can lose their religious faith as soon as the father's authority collapses. We thus recognize the root of religious need as lying in the parental complex." [10]

It was, however, in the summer of 1911 that Freud began seriously to investigate the sources of primitive religion, studies which were incorporated in his well-known work *Totem and Taboo* two years later. I have given earlier a full account of the history and contents of this book, and the motives impelling Freud at that time.[11] The only subsequent allusion I have found in this connection is a humorous passage in a letter of September 10, 1911, written to Binswanger from the Dolomites (then called the South Tyrol): "The large number of Gods here in Tyrol, where they are more numerous than were until recently the pilgrims, has influenced me in the direction of religious-psychological studies, of which something may perhaps sometime see the light of day. After the publication I shall surely not be allowed in the Tyrol again." [12]

From various statements of Freud's it is plain that he envisaged his study as primarily one into the origins of religion. As it turned out, it proved to be equally one into the origin of civilization itself, since Freud traced religion, civilization, law, morality, and the very beginnings of community life to man's reactions to his conflict over the primordial Oedipus complex. This fundamental conclusion he adhered to in all his later thought, and in his subsequent writings had little of importance to add to it.

In a preface to a book by Reik on the psychology of religion,[13] 1919, Freud expounded as follows what he called "an unexpectedly precise conclusion: namely that God the Father once walked upon earth in bodily form and exercised his sovereignty as chieftain of the primal human horde until his sons united to slay him. It emerged further that this crime of liberation and the reactions to it had as their result the appearance of the first social ties, the basic moral restrictions and the oldest form of religion—totemism. But the later religions too have the same content, and on the one hand they are concerned with obliterating the traces of that crime or with expiating it by bringing forward other solutions of the struggle between

* Not italicized in the original.

father and sons, while on the other hand they cannot avoid repeating once more the elimination of the father." [14]

Freud postulated in his *Group Psychology*, 1921, a general identification of all members of a group with one another based on their sharing a common ideal in the form of a leader. In the postscript to the book he commented on the way in which the Catholic Church has transcended this formula. "Every Christian loves Christ as his ideal and feels himself united with all other Christians by the tie of identification.* But the Church requires more of him. He has also to identify himself with Christ and love all other Christians as Christ loved them. At both points, therefore, the Church requires that the position of the libido which is given by group formation should be supplemented. Identification has to be added where object-choice has taken place, and object-love where there is identification. This addition evidently goes beyond the constitution of the group. One can be a good Christian and yet be far from the idea of putting oneself in Christ's place, and of having like him an all-embracing love for mankind. One need not think oneself capable, weak mortal that one is, of the Saviour's largeness of soul and strength of love. But this further development in the distribution of libido in the group is probably the factor upon which Christianity bases its claims to have reached a higher ethical level." [15]

In his book on *The Ego and the Id*, 1923, Freud when dealing with the topic of the ego ideal remarked that it is a substitute for the early longing for a loved father and as such contains the kernel out of which all religions are constituted. Religion, morality and social feeling were originally one.[16] In the same year he published his study entitled "A Seventeenth Century Demonological Neurosis." [17] Its interest is mainly clinical; it showed how readily in earlier centuries repressed impulses could be projected on to imaginary demons where today they are internalized as bodily suffering. The analysis of this particular story confirmed Freud's views about the importance of conflicting emotions concerning the father in the genesis of religious ideas—or, as in this case, of delusions. He accepted the historical view that originally God and the Devil were one figure, which later split into two with opposing attributes. More than a quarter of a century before he had told Fliess about his interest in the medieval belief in Satanic possession.[18]

Then, in 1927, came Freud's much disputed work, *The Future*

* "We are all brothers in Christ."

of an Illusion, in which he dealt with the nature and future of religion rather than with its origin. Freud has often been accused of having in this book maintained that religious beliefs are untrue, illusory in the sense of their being non-existent. And this in spite of his care to explain exactly in what sense he was using the term "illusion," distinguishing it from error. "An illusion is not the same as an error, it is indeed not necessarily an error. . . . We call a belief an illusion when wish-fulfillment is a prominent factor in its motivation." [19] He gives the example of a poor girl indulging in the illusion that a prince will come and fetch her home. "It is possible; some such cases have occurred." Here there are no rational grounds for her cherishing this as a *belief,* any more than there are any for religious beliefs; it is a hope derived from certain wishes or needs. Having himself dealt in other ways with the needs and wishes that impel people to hold religious beliefs, Freud saw no reason for accepting them. He was simply an unbeliever.

In considering the human needs that lead people to construct their religious beliefs he had formerly laid all the stress on the necessity of coming to terms with their complicated emotions concerning the child's relations to its father. Here he added another factor complementing this: namely, the helplessness of mankind in face of the manifold dangers with which he has to cope—from the outer world, from within himself, and from his relations to his fellow man. He had told Ferenczi[20] and Jung[21] that he had suddenly appreciated on the last night of 1909 the vast importance of this idea. A few months later he expounded it in his book on Leonardo,[22] after which we hear nothing of it for another seventeen years. Both factors originate in early childhood and are to a large extent a continuation of that psychological situation. Freud showed clearly how the two are intimately connected.

"Man's helplessness remains, and with it his father-longing and the gods. The gods retain their threefold task: they must exorcise the terrors of nature, they must reconcile one to the cruelty of fate, particularly as shown by death, and they must make amends for the sufferings and privations that the communal life of culture has imposed on man." [23] Our increased knowledge of the laws of nature had weakened the first demand, the promise of immortality was an attempt to deal with the other two, but nowadays the principal business of religion was in its alliance with ethics in the endeavor to regulate the relations between men. Here its great value has been in strengthening the demands of society on those who have failed to internalize the rules of ethics; those who have succeeded in doing so are in less need of supernatural sanctions for their behavior. It is, however, in many ways disadvantageous, and leads to rigidity when these sanctions are extended from their primal aims—against murder, incest, etc.—to the detailed regulation of life.

Then came the important question of the future of religion. Could mankind ever find it possible to endure the hardships of life without having to have recourse to the consolations of religion? No one had revealed the enormous power of the emotions over reason more decisively than Freud, and yet here he put in an interesting plea for the latter. He admitted that he himself might now be indulging in an illusion, but nevertheless he ventured to express the opinion, and evidently the hope, that it might in some distant future be possible for mankind to face life without the help of religion. Two considerations weighed with him in this judgment. One was that if childhood and youth were no longer subject to the teachings of religion, "conditioned" to its beliefs, so to speak, and also liberated from some of the sexual restrictions society imposes on them, the intelligence thus freed might well prove to be far more effective than heretofore. The other consideration was the thought that religion, like the earlier mythologies, might turn out to be nothing more than a (necessary) phase in human evolution, one that might perhaps be likened to its adolescence. Here the analogy with individual development lies near. Every child has, in its education to reality, gradually to learn to distinguish between the ideas and wishes of its phantasies and the facts of the outer world, and, moreover, to learn to do without the protection of its parents. Perhaps the same might be true of mankind as a whole. Years before, in "The Claims of Psycho-Analysis to Scientific Interest," he had expressed his adherence to this evolutionary conception. "Parallel with the human progress in the mastery of the world has gone a development in his *Weltanschauung* which has more and more diverged from the original belief in omnipotence, and has mounted from the animistic phase through the religious to the scientific one." [24]

Freud even went so far as to assert that "in the long run nothing can withstand reason and experience, and the contradiction religion offers to both is only too palpable." [25] Nor would he admit that other avenues to knowledge, such as mysticism and religious intuition or faith, deserved to be placed on the same level as science, using this term in its broadest sense of knowledge acquired through verifiable experience. He replied to some of the criticisms made against science, such as that its results are never absolute, and concluded: "Finally an attempt has been made to discredit radically scientific endeavor on the ground that, bound as it is to the conditions of our own organization, it can yield nothing but subjective results, while the real nature of things outside us remains inaccessible to us. But this is to disregard several factors of decisive importance for the understanding of scientific work. Firstly, our organization, i.e., our mental apparatus, has been developed actually in the attempt to explore the outer world, and therefore it must have realized in its structure a certain measure of appropriateness; secondly, it itself is a constituent part of that world which we are to investigate, and which readily admits of such investigation; thirdly, the task of science is fully circumscribed if we confine it to showing how the world must appear to us in consequence of the particular character of our organization; fourthly, the ultimate findings of science, just because of the way in which they are attained, are conditioned not only by our organization but also by that which has affected this organization; and, finally, the problem of the nature of the world irrespective of our perceptive apparatus is an empty abstraction without practical interest.

"No, science is no illusion. But it would be an illusion to suppose that we could get anywhere else what it cannot give us." [26]

In his *Civilization and its Discontents*, three years later, Freud was a good deal more outspoken about his opinion of religion. The second section opens thus: "In my *Future of an Illusion* I was concerned much less with the deepest sources of religious feeling than with what the ordinary man understands by his religion,[d] that system of doctrines and pledges which on the one hand explains the riddle of this world to him with an enviable completeness, and on the other assures him that a solicitous Providence is watching over him and will make up to him in a future existence for any shortcomings in this life. The ordinary man cannot imagine this Providence in any other form but that of a greatly exalted Father, for only such a one could understand the needs of the sons of men, or be softened by their prayers and placated by the signs of their remorse. The whole thing is so patently infantile, so incongruous with reality, that to one whose attitude to humanity is friendly it is painful to think that the great majority of mortals will never be able to rise above this view of life. It is even more humiliating to discover what a large number of those alive today, who must see

[d] He added later that this is the only religion that ought to bear the name.

that this religion is not tenable, yet try to defend it inch by inch, as if with a series of pitiable rearguard actions." [27]

Equally outspoken is a later passage in the book: "At such cost— by the forcible imposition of mental infantilism and inducing a mass-delusion—religion succeeds in saving many people from individual neuroses. But little more. There are, as we have said, many paths by which the happiness attainable for man can be reached, but none which is certain to take him to it. Nor can religion keep her promises either. When the faithful find themselves reduced in the end to speaking of God's 'inscrutable decree,' they thereby avow that all that is left to them in their sufferings is unconditional submission as a last-remaining consolation and source of happiness. And if a man is willing to come to this, he could probably have arrived there by a shorter road." [28]

In his interesting chapter on *Weltanschauung* in his *New Introductory Lectures*, 1933, Freud raised the question as to whether there was a world outlook peculiar to psychoanalysis, and answered it with a decided negative. Psychoanalysis could have no other approach than that of science in general. He then embarked on an energetic defense of the scientific outlook on life. Its chief opponent Freud saw as religion, and he sharply contrasted the pre-suppositions and aims of the two. He vehemently denied the claim of religion to be concerned with a different sphere of truth, one science has no right to invade, and he insisted that religious beliefs were just as much a legitimate object of psychological investigation as any other mental phenomena.

"The final judgment of science on the religious *Weltanschauung*, then, runs as follows. While the different religions wrangle with one another about which of them is in possession of the truth, in our view the truth of religion may be altogether disregarded. Religion is an attempt to get control over the sensory world, in which we are placed, by means of the wish-world, which we have developed within as a result of biological and psychological necessities. But it cannot achieve its end. Its doctrines carry with them the stamp of the times in which they originated, the ignorant childhood days of the human race. Its consolations deserve no trust. Experience teaches us that the world is not a nursery. The ethical commands, to which religion seeks to lend its weight, require some other foundation instead, since human society cannot do without them, and it is dangerous to link up obedience to them with religious belief. If one attempts to assign to religion its place in man's evolution, it seems not so much to be a lasting acquisition as a parallel to the neurosis which the civilized individual must pass through on his way from childhood to maturity." [29]

H. B. Acton has called attention to some remarkable similarities between Freud's studies of religion and some suggestions—much cruder, it is true—which the philosopher Ludwig Feuerbach had put forward fifteen years before Freud was born. He writes: "There is the suggestion that the ravings of insane people and the beliefs of savages may provide clues that help us to understand the workings of more civilized and normal minds; there is the idea of the satisfaction in imagination of essential desires of which the individual is unconscious; there is the association of this process with dreaming; and there is the governing principle that when someone comes to know himself more fully he will be less obsessed with the thoughts of an imaginary world and will be able to deal more adequately with the real one. Feuerbach's observation (*Werke* VI. 107) that theology is pathology hidden from itself is most significant in the light of later theories". He further quoted Feuerbach's dictum (*Werke* VI. 169): "Religion is the dream of waking consciousness; dreaming is the key to the mysteries of religion." [30]

As mentioned earlier, "Freud and Religion" has become a favorite theme among essayists and writers of books, and, as might be expected, their judgment is mostly adverse. A. J. Storfer compiled a bibliography of the immediate responses to *The Future of an Illusion*.[31] There appear to have been three main criticisms of Freud's attitude.

The first was that he had no right to intrude into a field of thought not his own, a familiar objection raised on other occasions, e.g. art and anthropology. Beyond it lies the assertion that science in general has nothing to do with religion, the two possessing quite different sources of knowledge. In particular psychology should keep its hands off religion—a claim often opposed from William James onward—and this in spite of the undeniable fact that religious beliefs, emotions and attitudes are part of the mind of man. On this "criticism" Freud calmly commented: "Contradiction is not always refutation." [32]

The second was that Freud confined himself to the beliefs of the common man and ignored the rarer and more profound types of religious emotion experienced by mystics and saints. Freud himself admitted this lacuna in his exposition, justifying it by remarking that he was concerned primarily with what religion signified to humanity in general.[e] But in a later publication, *Moses and Monotheism*, he remedied this omission by discussing the question of how it is that religious emotion attains a greater sublimity, profundity and majesty than any other human emotion. He accounted for this by pointing out that it represents a re-emergence, after a long period of latency, from the very depths of the unconscious characterized by just those extremes of feeling that are inaccessible except in religious transformation.

The third criticism was that Freud was supposed to assert that religion had no other sources than those emanating from infancy to which he had called attention. Gervais, for instance, has recently excoriated this supposed assertion in a specially contemptuous fashion.[33] There is some misunderstanding here. Freud was of course in no position, nor is anyone else, to assert that religious beliefs have no correspondence with any supernatural reality. However much a belief in God may be influenced by the child's attitude toward its father, there may still happen to be a God as well. All he asserted was that such beliefs could be fully accounted for by the psychological and historical factors he had investigated, so that he personally could see no reason for adding to them an external supernatural one.

A collection could be made of the quaint misstatements one comes across in the reviews of Freud's writings on religion. I will mention only two examples. Gervais quotes a statement that Freud's attitude towards religion came from his having lived in a Protestant environment (in Vienna!).[34] Then it has been suggested that the super-ego is an introjection of God.[35]

Unexpectedly enough, one of the few writers to reflect seriously on Freud's contributions was a clergyman, the Reverend R. S. Lee, Vicar of the University Church in Oxford. He listened sympathetically to the view that religious behavior (and many beliefs) is a derivative of the more primitive instincts, chiefly the sexual one, and that wishes are the real source of the belief in God and in an afterlife, though he maintained that Christ's resurrection was a confirmation of the latter. He agreed further that psychoanalysis can cleanse Christianity of its non-Christian elements, and that in general the result of applying psychoanalysis to the understanding of religious beliefs is likely to cause some profound modifications in religious thought and practice.[36]

[e] See the passage quoted on p. 358.

In a later book, consisting of the Burroughs Memorial Lectures, he wrote: "I have found Freudian psychology by far the most illuminating. . . . I shall simply apply Freud's conceptions, in the belief that the result will show how valuable they are in illuminating the role of worship in the functioning of the human personality and its development." [37]

Another sympathetically written book, by the Reverend W. G. Cole, may also be mentioned. Like the last, it is written from a Christian point of view. It deals mainly with the historical changes that have taken place in the theological attitude toward sexual problems.[38]

On the other hand an extremely adverse criticism of all Freud's views on religion has just appeared in a book by another clergyman.[39] Dr. Philp comes to the remarkable conclusion that Freud contributed nothing whatsoever to our understanding of the psychology of religion. His sweeping condemnation reads like an echo of a fellow dignitary's summing up of On the Origin of Species as "a jungle of fanciful assumption."

Freud's final contribution to the subject of religion comes in the last book he ever wrote: Moses and Monotheism, 1939.[40] Written when he was over eighty, it represented his last creative effort. Some account was given earlier of the unusual conditions under which it was written,[f] which no doubt explains the curiously irregular arrangement of the book. When Freud said in 1938 that he had written it two years ago he could only have been referring to the rewriting in the summer of 1936, since the book had been written two years earlier still. We shall presently discuss the probable motive impelling Freud to write this remarkable work.

There are two main themes in the book: a study of the origins of the Jewish, and to some extent also of the Christian, religion; this is followed by a consideration of the significance of religion in general.

The first part raises the question of the racial origin of Moses. Other workers who had noticed that he bore an Egyptian name had merely said "very odd" and passed on; doubtless deterred by awe of Biblical tradition, they had not even allowed the obvious thought to enter their minds that the reason why Moses bore an Egyptian name was simply that he *was* an Egyptian. Freud, whose mind was not inhibited by any such influence, drew this direct deduction and confirmed it by a pretty analysis of the birth story. To anyone who has

[f] Chapters 5 and 6, pp. 194-95, 216, 225.

made a study of the extensive exposure myths[41] the conclusion that the Egyptian Princess was the real mother is very convincing; it confirms that drawn by many cynical readers, including that well-known Viennese character *"der kleine* Moritz." ᵍ

In the second part Freud examined the questions why a nobly born Egyptian should have thrown in his lot with a crowd of uncultivated immigrants, and in what sense it could be said that he gave them their religion. It had previously been surmised by many writers that the Jewish religion had been derived from the monotheistic proclamations of Akhenaten, with the noteworthy omission of the sun worship in these, and it was also thought that the practice of circumcision probably came from Egypt. Freud then made the original suggestion that Moses was faced, after the counter-revolution following Akhenaten's death, with the painful choice of becoming either a renegade or an exile. Being a man of exceptionally powerful character, and sincerely convinced of the truth and loftiness of Akhenaten's conceptions, he made the doughty decision, on being rejected by his Egyptian compatriots, of choosing, and in a sense creating, a people *of his own* who should carry on the religious beliefs so important to him. Freud made the further suggestion that the retinue accompanying the great nobleman Moses later became the Levites, thus accounting for the Egyptian names some of them bore; they formed an influential and pro-Moses minority in the new people.

Incidentally, we get here an answer to the well-known Oxford couplet about the Jews. One of their many unique features is their belief that God chose them, whereas elsewhere we only hear of peoples choosing one or another God; and it seems likely that this peculiar belief has greatly favored their survival as a separate entity. Freud translated it into its original terms: namely, the curious occurrence that Moses, their leader and creator, *chose* them. His aim was to make them the equals, if not the superiors, of the best of the Egyptians. So he taught them the purest of all religions, stamped them with the custom of circumcision, and boldly led them forth from their bondage. Moses experienced many rebellions against his authority, and Freud accepted the conclusion Ernst Sellin had drawn from Old Testament studies that one of these rebellions brought about a lethal end. This great murder was fateful in history. It begot a strong reaction of guilt and remorse, denial that monotheism had come from Moses—it having preceded him in the time of imagi-

ᵍ In his comment, "says she."

nary patriarchs—and the hope that the sin would some day be undone, i.e., the belief in a Messiah (and, incidentally, thus the Christian religion).

Here Freud encountered the historical conclusions of the higher critics who discard the Biblical story of Moses having lived in Egypt and maintain that he was a Midianite priest of a local volcanic God, Jahve, at Kadesh. The resolution he offered of this antinomy was that in the legendary figure of Moses two actual men are condensed: that of the Egyptian leader who forced his religion and laws on the Jews and was murdered in the wilderness, and that of a sweet-tempered priest, the son-in-law of Jethro, who lived a couple of generations later. Neither of these figures were, strictly speaking, Jews—though the Midianites were reckoned as distant kinsmen—so that Freud need not bear all the obloquy of depriving the Jews of their great national hero. Within a century of Moses' tragic end a compromise was reached between his religion and the Jahvistic one, between the Jews who had sojourned in Egypt and those they rejoined after leaving that country. At first the religion of Jahve predominated, being better suited to the lust of conquest with which the Jews were then animated than the pure religion of Aton, that of truth and justice. But this was never entirely forgotten, and in time it emerged more and more, being voiced ever anew by the great prophets until it won recognition. The bloodthirsty Jahve of the early Old Testament fell into the background: "The shadow of the God whose place he had taken became stronger than himself."

Freud summed up with this formula in which his love of dualism had free play: "To the well-known duality of that history—*two peoples* who fuse together to form one nation, *two kingdoms* into which this nation divides, *two names* for the Deity in the source of the Bible—we add two new ones; the founding of *two* religions, the first one ousted by the second and yet reappearing victorious, *two* founders of religions, who are both called by the name of Moses and whose personalities we have to separate from each other. And all these dualities are necessary consequences of the first: one section of the people passed through what may properly be termed a traumatic experience which the other was spared." [42]

There follows a description of the Jewish characteristics, notably their self-confidence and tenacity, and their preference for intellectual pursuits. Most nations feel themselves superior to others, but with the chosen people it was anchored in their religion and therefore more firmly based. They would scarcely have survived without the

Mosaic religion. The flaw in this religion, however, was that it gave expression to only one half of the ambivalency inherent in a powerful reaction of guilt, the sense of sin, which Freud suggested was in part a continuation of the remorse at having murdered the Great Father, Moses. The misfortunes they suffered were a welcome excuse for God's severity. "They deserved nothing better than to be punished by Him, because they did not observe the laws; the need for satisfying this feeling of guilt was insatiable, made them render their religious precepts ever more and more strict, more exacting, but also more petty." [43] This moral masochism led to a falling away from the pure conceptions of Moses, to the reinstatement of the ceremonial he had so eschewed, and to degeneration into the never-ending reaction-formations of obsessional neurosis.

The flaw just mentioned was subsequently remedied—also by a great Jew, Paul. Freud suggested that the belief in the Messiah, reiterated by all the prophets, may have originated in the wish that the murdered Father-Moses would return. When Jesus, whose ethical precepts surpassed even the heights attained by former prophets, had in turn been murdered, Paul, the creator of Christian theology, was seized by an inspiration of genius. Accepting Jesus as the Messiah, he correctly traced back the prevailing sense of guilt to its primeval source; he called it "original sin," a mortal (i.e., murderous) sin against God the Father. "The unmentionable crime was replaced by the fault of the somewhat shadowy conception of original sin." [44] In place of the murder wish itself, however, stood the phantasy of expiation, welcomed in the form of a gospel of salvation. "A Son of God, innocent himself, had sacrificed himself—and had thereby taken over the guilt of the world. It had to be a Son, since the sin had been the murder of the Father. . . . The Mosaic religion had been a Father religion; Christianity became a Son religion. The old God, the Father, took second place; Christ, the Son, stood in his place, just as in those dark times every son had longed to do. . . . From now on Jewish religion was, so to speak, a fossil." [45]

Hinting at the degeneration that later assailed Christianity, through its political syncretism, into ceremonial ritualism and almost into polytheism, Freud likened it to a renewed victory of the priests of Amon over the pure beliefs in Aton.

Freud then discussed the various sources of anti-Semitism, of which the one that is relevant here is the Jewish refusal to accept the Messiah, thus cutting themselves off from the expiation, or salvation, He offered. In the figure of Jesus the Jews were guilty of yet another murder of God, and the Christian reproach would run: "You won't *admit* that you murdered God (the archetype of God, the primeval Father and his reincarnations). It is true, we did the same thing, but we *admitted* it, and since then we have been purified." [46]

Passing from consideration of these two religions Freud went on to draw some conclusions about the development of religion in general. Here he quoted those he had made years before in his book *Totem and Taboo*. The chief point he added was the stress he now laid on the importance of latency periods, with a later "return of the repressed," to account for the special profundity of religious feeling. *The Future of an Illusion* had been criticized for seeming to ignore this feature of religion, but now Freud amply repaired any such omission. He agreed that no mere listing of the psychological elements that go to build up a religion could be regarded as adequate unless account could be given also of this unique profundity. The particular feature he offered as an explanation was the existence of a latency period, both in the individual and in the race, followed by the emergence of emotions from the unconscious. "To all matters concerning the creation of a religion pertains something majestic, which has not so far been covered by our explanations. Some other element should have part in it; one that has few analogies and nothing quite like it; something unique and commensurate with that which has grown out of it. . . . It must first have suffered the fate of repression, the state of being unconscious, before it could produce such mighty effects on its return and force the masses under its spell, such as we have observed—with astonishment and hitherto without understanding—in religious tradition." [47] What re-emerges are the emotions which at the beginning were attached to the idea of the Father. "The first effect of the reunion with what men had long missed and yearned for was overwhelming, and exactly as the tradition of law-giving on Mount Sinai depicts it. There was admiration, awe and gratitude that the people had found favor in His eyes. . . . The conviction that His power was irresistible, the subjection to His will, could not have been more absolute with the helpless, intimidated son of the father of the (primal) horde than they were here; indeed they become fully comprehensible only by the transformation into the primitive and infantile *milieu*. Infantile feelings are far more intense and inexhaustibly deep than are those of adults; only religious ecstasy can bring back that intensity. Thus a transport of devotion to God is the first response to the return of the Great Father." [48]

Freud had always asserted the *psychological* truth in religion, i.e., that it was concerned with real unconscious conflicts present in everyone. In this book he laid special stress on the *historical* truth in religion, i.e., that it was concerned with the unconscious memory of actual happenings; it was a thesis he had hinted at twenty years before.[h] About these happenings there can be little doubt: fathers, gods and kings have been slain innumerable times in the tragic history of mankind.

We cannot refrain from wondering how, when nearing his end, Freud came to be so engrossed in the topics described above, and to devote to them all his intellectual interest during the last five years of his life. To answer such questions we have to hark back to the earliest riddles of life that perplexed him, the great enigmas which Joubert epitomized in the words *"Je, d'où, où, pour, comment?"* The first must have concerned his personal identity and the problem of his birth, as with every child, but in more mature years this had taken the wider form of interest in the nature and origin of man in general. And to these questions his researches enabled him to give profound answers in his important studies of anthropology, prehistory and religion.

The personal origin of this intellectual curiosity about the nature of mankind could not avoid having a more restricted problem at its core. The bitter experiences of anti-Semitism were hardly needed to awaken in Freud such questions as "how did I come to be a Jew?; what exactly is a Jew?; how did Jews come to be what they are?" Indeed, Freud's deep conviction of his Jewishness, and his wholehearted acceptance of that fact, must inevitably have forced such questions on someone burning as he did with intellectual curiosity and throughout concerned with the problems of mankind rather than those of a material nature. We know how greatly he admired the great Semitic leaders of the past, from Hannibal onward, and how gladly in his early years he would have been willing to sacrifice his life to emulate their heroic deeds on behalf of their people.

The leader who kindled his imagination above all others was inevitably Moses, the great man who did more than anyone to build the Jewish nation, to create the religion that has ever since borne his name, and, in Freud's opinion, even to stamp on the Jewish people some of their most prominent and valuable character traits. I well remember how completely absorbed he had been years before in

[h] See p. 354.

his endeavor to decipher the character of Moses as displayed in the famous statue he wrote about, and the hours of deep thought he would devote to the faintest detail that might provide a clue.[49] The question over which Freud had then cudgelled his brains was this. Was Moses on descending from Sinai unable to control his anger, as the Bible related, or could he attain the heights of self-control which Freud maintained Michelangelo had depicted? We know that this preoccupation coincided with the time when he was suppressing his own indignation at the way his Swiss followers had suddenly repudiated his work, and that merely confirms what his intense preoccupation alone would have taught us: namely, that he had emotional reasons for identifying himself with his mighty predecessor.[1]

We should bear this background in mind when we ask what brought the figure of Moses so much to the forefront of Freud's mind in the years 1933-36. I do not find this question hard to answer. The reason that just then narrowed Freud's interest in mankind in general and its religions to the more specific question of the Jews and their religion could only have been the unparalleled persecution of his people that was getting under way in Nazi Germany, with the likelihood of this spreading to his native country. Like so many other Jews of that time who simply wished to live at peace with their fellow men without parading any of their particular differences from them, Freud was once more forced to wonder what it was in his people that evoked such horrible reactions, and how they had become what they were.

Such reflections, together with his knowledge of their sojourn in Egypt and the origin of monotheism in that land, inevitably led to the founder of his nation and the creator of its religion. It could not have taken Freud long to decipher the obviously disguised bulrush story of Moses' birth, which confirmed his suspicion aroused by the noble Egyptian name. What perhaps made Freud more alert to this discovery was his predilection for thinking that people often were not what they seemed to be (Shakespeare and others!), which in its turn is suggestive of his own "family romance." [50]

When the book appeared various wild guesses were circulated concerning Freud's motives for writing it. One malicious one was that he was venting his secret hatred of the Jews by depriving them

---

[1] I have idly wondered if Freud's little brother Julius's Jewish name could have been Moses, in which case Freud's identification with it would have the profound meaning of a reaction to hatred like Napoleon's with his brother Joseph. Unfortunately the Nazis destroyed all the relevant records.

of their cherished leader, although the Biblical critics had long done that in their conclusion that Moses was a Midianite. In fact, friends suggested to Freud that the publication might cause hurt feelings in certain orthodox quarters, but he modestly, and rightly as it turned out, maintained that nothing he could write on the subject of Moses would change anyone else's preconceived opinions. Then a more charitable suggestion was offered that, holding—as indeed he did—a main cause of anti-Semitism to be resentment against the strict code of morals imposed first by the Jews and then by the Christians, Freud hoped to soften this by asserting that it was not a Jew but an Egyptian who should bear the onus. I need hardly say that all such calculations were very foreign to Freud's nature. A desire to get at the simple truth as best he might dominated all other motives. Then, the coming to certain conclusions always expressed itself in their being written down and, whenever possible, published for the consideration of whoever might be interested. But he could never have hoped that his elucidating the causes of anti-Semitism would have much effect in checking it.

As critics have been quick to point out, there are weak links in the chain of reasoning just summarized. The weakest of all, however, they have overlooked:[j] Freud's theory of the unconscious transmission of historical events. This could certainly not have happened in the simple way he suggested, by the direct inheritance of traumatic impressions along Lamarckian lines. Probably he was influenced here by his experience in the analysis of individuals: the retention of such impressions in the unconscious and their later emergence after a period of latency. Nevertheless there are alternative possibilities, e.g., along Darwinian lines, which would preserve the essence of his conclusions.

As was perhaps to have been expected, the Jewish Biblical experts who have commented on Freud's book have unanimously rejected his conclusions and preferred to adhere to the traditional story of Moses. One of them, T. W. Rosmarin, devoted a booklet to criticism of it, filled with vituperative indignation.[52] Her main criticisms were, first that Freud was reckless and impudent to intrude into a field reserved for specialist scholars. No one had the right to express opinions on Biblical topics until he had first acquired a knowledge not only of Hebrew and Egyptian but of many of the neighboring languages of the Near East as well. On this count Freud

[j] With the exception of A. A. Roback.[51]

was certainly guilty, but it was a sin of which millions of other people have also been guilty without being ruthlessly condemned for it. Rosmarin's remark that Freud "was only a little better posted on ancient Near East history and the Bible than the average educated lay person" [53] is certainly untrue, though he cited only a small part of his very wide reading. Her second charge was that he was throughout animated in his writing by bitter hatred of the Jews, and it was this that made him resolve to strike a blow at them by depriving them of their famous leader. How remote this malevolent charge is from the truth there is no need for me to stress.

Another, more formidable, critic was Abraham Shalom Yahuda, a famous Biblical scholar. He published in Hebrew a long review of Freud's book,[54] and I am obliged to Harold Feldman and David Silver for furnishing me with a translation of it. He totally rejected Freud's hypotheses, and finished his review with the words: "It seems to me that in these words we hear the voice of one of the most fanatical Christians in his hatred of Israel and not the voice of a Freud who hated and despised such fanaticism with all his heart and strength." So apparently Freud, after having wholeheartedly despised such fanaticism, had now come to share it.

Insofar as any personal or national bias is to be detected or inferred in Freud's book, someone like myself, not emotionally involved in religious disputes, would come to an exactly opposite conclusion to that expressed by these critics. Assuming that the idea of monotheism originated with Akhenaten, who certainly enunciated it most vividly, and that he proclaimed in association with it the loftiest conceptions of ethics and justice, the fact remains that his fellow countrymen immediately and decisively rejected the teaching; they were apparently unworthy of it. In his laudation of Jewish spirituality Freud was manifestly proud of the religious and ethical genius of his own people who were able to accept that teaching and to rise to sublime heights far transcending the endeavors of the Egyptians or anyone else. That in turn the Jews produced a great religious teacher whom non-Jews elevated to the rank of a Deity was a counterpart that did not impress Freud; he regarded their belief as illusory and a departure from the pure monotheistic faith of his ancestors.

A more respectful, though still adverse, review was written by Professor Baron, who concluded that Freud's theory was "a magnificent castle in the air." [55] The most sympathetic one, however, came from the Rabbi Stephen Wise. He wrote as follows: "As a psychoanalytical treatise on the origin and development of religion it is of the first importance, and it will live. . . . Even where there is most doubt and deepest incertitude, a radiant mind still lights up the grandiose genesis of faith, though he sees only its exodus." [56]

There were four main features in Freud's reconstruction of the Moses legend, and it will be convenient to consider the criticisms of each in turn.

1. *Moses was an Egyptian.*

The evidently mythological story of his birth, or reputed adoption, certainly makes this probable enough. What is not altogether easy to understand is the enormous emotional importance to Jews of Moses' ultimate origin. The Biblical story itself tells us that the Princess, a daughter of Pharaoh, adopted the baby, named him and brought him up as her own son, i.e., as an Egyptian prince. There is a legend that he became an Egyptian priest.[57] Other accounts even refer to Moses as the heir to the Egyptian throne,[58] and there is the story of his having been an Egyptian general who conquered Ethiopia.[59] The Jewish descent of Moses, according to Max Weber, the great Biblical scholar, is "a late and artificial construct." [60] So, whatever may have been his inheritance, he was to all intents and purposes a highly placed Egyptian who later cast in his lot with a body of Jews, led and inspired them.

2. *Moses acquired a belief in monotheism in Egypt and converted the Jews to it.*

Here we touch on the extremely complicated question of the origin of monotheism. What makes it particularly obscure is the assuredly gradual evolution of the idea, and the slow passage of tribal gods into universal Deities. The idea that Jewish monotheism was derived from Egypt was first propounded by Brugsch in the eighteen-seventies, and it was supported by the great Egyptologist Flinders Petrie, who regarded Akhenaten as the prototype of Moses.[61] So the notion did not start with Freud; he may have first read of it in Petrie's books.

In all probability the idea of a one and only God was preceded by that of an omnipotent Being to whom all other Gods were subordinate, and this idea is more likely to have been reached in powerful Empires, such as those in Egypt, Greece and Rome, whether a subordinate pantheon was retained or not. Akhenaten's extraordinary, and premature, feat in the Egypt of the fourteenth century B.C. was beyond doubt a further stage in this development.

Two criticisms have been leveled against Freud's suggestion that Moses' monotheism derived from that of the Pharaoh Akhenaten. One is that this Pharaoh's monotheism was by no means as pure as Freud, following Breasted and other writers, believed. Akhenaten seems, for example, to have regarded *himself* as divine, being either a son of Aton or even identified with this universal ruler. Then he allowed Aton to become fused with the local sun god of Heliopolis, Re, though it is very possible that he considered Re's emblem of a solar disc with its rays as being simply a visible manifestation of Aton's power and mode of functioning. One cannot deny, however, the lofty spirituality and ethics of Akhenaten's teaching as displayed in his hymns, some of which Freud quoted. Freud fully discussed both the resemblances and the differences between the ideal of this great religious reformer and that which the Hebrew prophets finally succeeded in establishing in the Mosaic religion.

The other criticism is a chronological one. The date of the Exodus from Egypt is extremely disputed, but hardly any authority would put it nearer to Akhenaten's reign than a century or two. So if Moses derived his ideas from him it could only have been indirectly through those who still cherished them—a prospect which Freud, though unwillingly, took into account.

Freud called attention to the error—he stigmatized it as "a particularly clumsy invention"—of supposing that the rite of circumcision was peculiar to the Jews. According to Herodotus, the Syrians and Phoenicians had borrowed the custom from the Egyptians, among whom it had long been practiced, and other authorities besides Freud have suggested that the Jews had done the same.[62] This he naturally associated with the religious rites introduced by Moses. Since the Biblical story is so misleading about the uniqueness of the Jewish custom, its account of Moses himself being uncircumcised may also be a tendentious distortion; a passage in the Talmud actually says that Moses was born circumcised.[63]

The lofty ethical teaching of the prophets, and the more merciful conception of the Supreme Being, did not emerge in Jewish history until some centuries after the time of Moses. It had evidently had a hard fight in supplanting the earlier belief in the bloodthirsty demon Yahweh, with whom one could only bargain or offer sacrificial propitiations. Freud suggested that the nobler conception had originated with Moses, the later religion thus fully deserving the title Mosaic, and had through those centuries been nursed by a few faithful adherents to his teaching; the original Levites are generally supposed to have been personal followers of Moses,[64] and Freud suggested that they had accompanied him when he left Egypt. During that long period it combatted the cruder worship of Yahweh, and with the help of the inspired prophets it overcame this. It is a thesis hard either to prove or to disprove, but it certainly stirs the imagination.

3. Moses was slain in a tumult.

It seems inherently likely enough that Moses should have shared the fate of Savanarola, of so many martyrs and fanatical preachers. The image we have of him, well depicted in Michelangelo's famous statue, is that of a choleric and overbearing man, who did not brook opposition easily. He commanded the Jews, with dire denunciations, to renounce many of their favorite enjoyments and indulgences. Little wonder that we read a good deal about what the Bible euphemistically calls the "mutterings of the people" and of at least one open rebellion, Korah's being the most notable. Moses's father-in-law is said to have persuaded him to depute some of his dictatorial powers, but we are nevertheless told of his slaying three thousand men who worshipped the golden calf and ordering a man to be stoned to death for gathering sticks on the Sabbath.

In 1922 Ernst Sellin, one of the most distinguished Hebrew and Arabic scholars, startled the theological world by announcing that, through re-interpretation of some passages in Hosea, he had found some evidence pointing to the murder of Moses.[65] This was immediately rejected by all Jewish scholars, who fortified their rejection by maintaining that Sellin subsequently—some say ten years later and some seven—withdrew his suggestion and apologized for having made it. Yahuda, another great scholar, told Freud this when he visited him in 1938,[k] and Freud could only shrug his shoulders and say "It might be true all the same." It was Sellin's suggestion that made Freud decide to write his book; it fitted so well with his views on the importance of parricide.

There is a curious postscript to this story. I have made all possible endeavors to find out the truth about Sellin's supposed withdrawal, and have been given a number of different references to it, in his writings, in his addresses before Congresses and so on. All of them proved to be false. On the contrary, in a book Sellin published thir-

[k] See p. 234.

teen years later he not only adhered to his opinion, but stated that he had found "further confirmation" of it in a number of allusions to the murder, which he listed, in the writings of other prophets.[66] In spite of all that, however, there appears to be a certain basis for the rumor. A friend of Sellin's, Professor Rust of Berlin, has been good enough to answer my inquiries, and he informs me that on one occasion Sellin, when hard pressed in private talk, was willing to admit that he might have been mistaken in his interpretation of the passage in Hosea which had been the starting point of his theory.

Sellin's hypothesis could be supported by numerous suggestive passages in the *Torah* and other apocryphal literature hinting mysteriously at various legends concerning the death of Moses, but it would be impertinent to discuss them here.[67]

4. The tradition of the murder of Moses led to a lasting unconscious sense of guilt among the Jewish people.

This, according to Freud, reinforced the universal inherited sense of guilt dating from the parricides of primitive man, which are constantly reanimated by individual infantile experiences. It is from its very nature the most hypothetical and least demontrable part of Freud's whole Moses theory, but it is characteristic of his whole train of thought. From it he deduced far-reaching inferences concerning the differing reactions to guilt about parricide among Jews and Gentiles, and the different religious solutions they found.

Although we have found occasion to criticize Freud's Lamarckian assumptions on the transmission of the effects of experiences[1] this by no means disposes of his theory of the importance of an inherited sense of guilt or the importance of transmission by tradition. There are alternative presentations possible that would preserve the essence of his conclusions.

Freud first thought of his Moses theory as an interesting historical romance, but the more he reflected on it the more probable did it seem. He did not conceal the hypothetical elements in it, so difficult to substantiate, but we can hardly fail to regard it as a brilliant example of his imaginative intuition, and Freud's intuition was more often right than wrong.

[1] See pp. 309-13.

14

Occultism

FREUD'S ATTITUDE TOWARD OCCULTISM IS OF PECULIAR INTEREST TO HIS
biographer, since it illustrates better than any other theme the explanation of his genius which was put forward in an earlier volume.[1] In it we find throughout an exquisite oscillation between
scepticism and credulity so striking that it is possible to quote just as
many pieces of evidence in support of his doubt concerning occult
beliefs as of his adherence to them.

It is only fair to the reader to state at the outset that this chapter
would be written differently according to the views on the subject
held by the writer. One who accepts the evidence in support of
telepathy and clairvoyance as conclusive would only praise Freud's
open-mindedness on the subject and also his inclination to adopt
a positive attitude toward the conclusions drawn from it, as one
more example of his far-sightedness and willingness to contemplate
the improbable. On the other hand one who, like the present writer,
is sceptical concerning that evidence, and more inclined to regard the
conclusions drawn from it as relics of a more primitive type of thinking, must be more critical of Freud's attitude. To him it may prove
to be only one more example of the remarkable fact that highly developed critical powers may co-exist in the same person with an unexpected fund of credulity.

Before giving a chronological account of Freud's experiences and
utterances in this field it is desirable to say something about the
problems involved. The central one, though presenting itself in
endlessly varied guises, is whether thoughts or spiritual beings can

exist in space with no ascertainable connection with a corporeal body. To most of those who have undergone a biological, and particularly a neurological, training the evidence to the contrary seems overwhelming, and this judgment may be justly called a prejudice. Now, as Freud himself pointed out, prejudices may be fully justified in many circumstances and may be useful in saving one from wasting time, but they may also be unfortunate hindrances to an advance in knowledge, as has so often happened in the history of science, and it may be extremely hard to discriminate between the useful and the harmful ones; there is commonly no objective criterion to guide us.[2] There may well be irrational elements dictating the prejudice in question, but it is assuredly easier to point to powerful irrational agencies that have always operated in the opposite direction.

From the dawn of history until quite recent times man has believed firmly in the existence and activity of discarnate beings. We need only allude to the fantastic beliefs of savages in every part of the world and in every degree of social development. After the advent of Christianity the Classical and Teutonic mythologies were rationalized in a religious sense, with a multitude of saints to replace the twilight gods, but the uneducated people were still left with their fairies, gnomes, vampires and bogies. Then there was always the haunting of ghosts and the rappings of poltergeists, beliefs in whom still persist.

The decay of religious beliefs in the past hundred years has been accompanied by a change in dealings with the supernatural. Beginning perhaps with the performances of the Fox sisters in America, there has burgeoned an immense number of soothsayers or "mediums" earning a living by professing supernatural powers, notably of prevision and prediction of the future, communication with spirits of dear departed ones, "second sight," telepathy, levitation, palmistry, astrology, clairvoyance, and so on. In many cases this spiritism, euphemistically labeled "spiritualism," has assumed the guise of a formal religion. The vogue of such mediums has shown a certain periodicity. Thus it reached special heights in 1860 (the Daniel Home period), in 1880 (leading to the formation of the Society for Psychical Research), in 1900 (the period of the great physicists), and again at the present day. At the end of the last century an impressive list of men of science may be quoted as having, after careful investigation, subscribed to the truth of many of the mediums' claims: T. H. Flournoy, Lombroso, Richet, and Schrenk-Notzing on the Continent; William James and others in America; Sir William Barrett, Sir William Crookes, Sir Arthur Conan Doyle, Sir Oliver Lodge, F. W. H. Myers and Sir George Stokes in England. Some of these were highly distinguished exponents of the physical sciences and so thoroughly conversant with scientific modes of thought. Nevertheless in every single case the mediums who had produced the evidence that convinced these gentlemen of the truth of their claims have been exposed as tricksters who played on the vein of credulity present in the distinguished investigators.

It has been shown conclusively that no critical or sceptical capacity, however highly developed, has proved competent to investigate the alleged phenomena in question unless a knowledge of experimental science has been reinforced by a technical knowledge of what in the world of entertainment are called "magical devices." These professional "magicians" know how to perform feats which not only defy explanation but which appear to provide indubitable proof of supernatural powers, and yet when they reveal how they do them give only demonstrative proof of how any audience can be deceived by their extraordinary skill. Recently, for instance, an American "magician" by the name of J. K. Rinn has published an account of his sixty years of experience in the unmasking of the most famous mediums, just those who had deceived the distinguished men whose names were listed above.[3] Moreover he describes in detail a number of performances of his own in which quite astounding, and apparently absolutely impossible, feats were performed of which no explanation seemed conceivable except on the basis of his possessing both supernormal and supernatural powers. He then explains the complicated devices by means of which he had carried out the feats and completely deceived his audiences. He gives very convincing reasons in support of the thesis mentioned above, that no one is qualified to investigate these alleged phenomena unless he is equipped with an expert knowledge of the devices in question.

It was partly the unmasking of so many mediums, and partly a curious shame to which I shall presently allude at avowing beliefs in the occult, that have invested the subject with an air of the disreputable in orthodox scientific circles. The very word "psychical research" became suspect, so students of the subject looked for more respectable terms. "Parapsychic" and "paranormal" were tried and found wanting. Then came "parapsychology," "extra-sensory perception," a very descriptive term; at present "psi phenomena" seems to be the vogue.

Freud was always very sceptical about the spiritistic performance of mediums, although he often thought they might possess special telepathic powers. He expressed this well in his *Future of an Illusion*, 1927. "If all the arguments that are put forward for the authenticity of religious doctrines originate in the past, it is natural to look round and see whether the present, better able to judge in these matters, cannot also furnish such evidence. The whole of the religious system would become infinitely more credible if one could succeed in this way in removing the element of doubt from a single part of it. It is at this point that the activity of the spiritualists comes in; they are convinced of the immortality of the individual soul, and they would demonstrate to us that this one article of religious teaching is free from doubt. Unfortunately they have not succeeded in disproving the fact that the appearances and utterances of their spirits are merely the productions of their own mental activity. They have called up the spirits of the greatest of men, of the most eminent thinkers, but all their utterances and all the information they have received from them have been so foolish and so desperately insignificant that one could find nothing else to believe in but the capacity of the spirits for adapting themselves to the circle of people that had evoked them." [4]

Apart, however, from the assistance of mediums there is a vast range of what are called superstitious beliefs from which few people are completely free. The group that concerns us here is that to do with threats or warnings of misfortune, ultimately of death—either of oneself or of a loved one. These are the familiar premonitions, intuitions, omens and the like. There is a corresponding group, of amulets, charms, mascots and talismans, the function of which is to ward off such misfortune. Freud showed convincingly in the section on superstition in his *Psychopathology of Everyday Life* that such beliefs come about through the projection into the outer world of thoughts, fears and wishes, which have undergone repression; not recognizing their presence in his unconscious, and yet feeling signs of their presence, the subject concludes that they are operative in the outer world. It is highly significant that the majority of them can be traced to repressed death wishes, originally against some loved person.

Such beliefs operate in the most primitive level of the mind, that of animistic magic and belief in the omnipotence of thoughts. There is everywhere plentiful evidence of this level of pre-scientific mental functioning. It is a level of the mind the strength of which it is hard to overestimate, and with only the rarest of people has it been completely superseded by a more objective contact with reality.

With most people two regular features may be observed in connection with occult beliefs. When they encounter such happenings as inexplicable sounds in a haunted house or an intuitional premonition of misfortune there is commonly a critical reaction of doubt about their external reality and at the same time an indication of shame at the possibility of accepting it. Both features are to be explained from the knowledge in some part of the mind that the beliefs are of subjective origin and have to do with ideas of which they are ashamed and which are therefore in a state of repression. The extent to which a given superstitious belief is accepted by the mind is usually one of degree, and it is often very hard to ascertain to what extent the person "really" gives credence to it. It is a common experience to get the reply when someone is questioned on the point: "No, I don't really believe it, but all the same it is very odd." Acceptance and rejection are both operative.

Freud was no exception in this respect, and he would himself have not found it easy at times to say whether he accepted a given belief of this order or not. I shall do my best to present the data at our disposal in a manner that should enable the reader to form some opinion of his degree of acceptance in the various instances.

The first example we have of the kind, although from its nature in all probability not an isolated one, was his telling his betrothed how as a boy he had chosen the number 17 in a lottery that purported to reveal one's character, and the word that came out was "constancy." Now, lo and behold, that was the very number of the day of the month when he got engaged. To take this literally would mean that the lottery had foretold the quality of his future engagement, though there were other qualities in it quite as prominent as constancy. I feel sure that had Freud been asked about this he would have denied any such belief, and yet the fact remains that the number had been present in his mind for at least ten years and that he mentioned it, if only in jest, as *perhaps* having some significance, whereas an unbeliever in the occult such as myself would never have thought of connecting such a banal incident with a serious situation, nor have looked for such reassurances of his own or the lady's constancy. It is after all a psychological fact that he mentioned the matter, and it was Freud who taught us not to disregard psychological facts, even of apparently unwitting utterances.

The first examples we have of a telepathic nature were also in connection with his future wife. A month after becoming engaged he accidentally broke the engagement ring she had given him.[5] At the moment he thought nothing of it, but soon some mysterious doubts assailed him and he wrote to ask her on her honor whether she had been less fond of him "at eleven o'clock last Thursday." He said it was a good opportunity to put an end to a superstition, but there again one notes that there was a superstition that had to be dealt with. More striking was his reaction to some experiences probably during the first part of his stay in Paris. He related in the 1910 edition of his *Psychopathology of Everyday Life* how he often heard his name being called, unmistakably in her voice.[6] He was specially lonely at the time and was also finding it hard to understand the foreign speech. As is well known, this belongs to the banal type of hallucination that lonely tourists so often experience when abroad, the incomprehensible words of the natives being "assimilated" through the mechanism of wish-fulfillment into more familiar and welcome expressions. But Freud had to make a note of the exact time of each of these occurrences and then write to inquire what was happening to his beloved at that precise moment, actions which clearly postulate a belief in the *possibility* of messages being transmitted in space through hundreds of miles.

At this point some general remarks about the status of telepathy will be in place. There is no doubt that it is by far the most "respectable" element in the field of occultism, and therefore the one that has gained the widest acceptance. In Freud's opinion it probably represented the kernel of truth in that field, one which the myth-making tendencies of mankind had enveloped in a cocoon of phantastic beliefs. This idea of a "kernel of truth" specially fascinated Freud and cooperated with more personal motives in his unconscious to incline him toward accepting a belief in telepathy. He had more than once had the experience of discovering such a kernel in the complicated beliefs of mankind, beliefs often contemptuously dismissed as superstitious; that dreams really had a meaning was the most important example. So he felt intuitively that telepathy might be the kernel of truth in this obscure field.

Yet, as he himself remarked, to accept telepathy was a step of great consequence. It would mean admitting the essential claim of the occultists that mental processes can be independent of the human body. As he pointed out: *"Dans ces cas pareils, ce n'est que le premier pas qui coûte."* [7] It opens the door to endless possibilities, perhaps far more than a mere kernel. In the years before the Great War, I had several talks with Freud on occultism and kindred topics. He was fond, especially after midnight, of regaling me with strange or uncanny experiences with patients, characteristically about misfortunes or deaths supervening many years after a wish or prediction. He had a particular relish for such stories and was evidently impressed by their more mysterious aspects. When I would protest at some of the taller stories Freud was wont to reply with his favorite quotation: "There are more things in heaven and earth than are dreamed of in your philosophy." Some of the incidents sounded like mere coincidences, others like the obscure workings of unconscious motives. When they were concerned with clairvoyant visions of episodes at a distance, or visitations from departed spirits, I ventured to reprove him for his inclination to accept occult beliefs on flimsy evidence. His reply was: "I don't like it at all myself,[a] but there is some truth in it," both sides of his nature coming to expression in a short sentence. I then asked him where such beliefs could halt: if one could believe in mental processes floating in the air, one could go on to a belief in angels. He closed the discussion at this point (about three in the morning!) with the remark: "Quite so, even *der liebe Gott.*" This was said in a jocular tone as if agreeing with my *reductio ad absurdum* and with a quizzical look as if he were pleased at shocking me. But there was something searching also in the glance, and I went away not entirely happy lest there be some more serious undertone as well.

Freud would never admit that a belief in telepathy would be as destructive of scientific canons as might appear. The explanation of it he tentatively offered was as follows. He drew an interesting, though not fundamental, distinction between thought-transference and telepathy. The former was perhaps the simpler. In it a verbal message gets transformed into a wave or ray of quite unknown nature, much as it does in a telephonic or wireless message, and then on reception reconverted into mental terms. Telepathy itself predisposed a special sensitiveness, based on a close emotional bond, between two people of such a nature that if anything untoward (*nota bene*: not fortunate) happened to one of them the news of it would immediately be perceived by the other; as we shall see, Freud fancied several times that this happened between him and his eldest son

[a] *Ich mag das alles nicht.*

during the war. It was not explained how such a message was sent in case of a fatal accident; it was as if the accident itself was perceived without a verbal message.

After this digression on the general nature of telepathy and its significance we may now resume the chronological story of Freud's contacts with occult matters.

Freud has himself recorded several instances of magical actions unconsciously carried out with the aim of averting disaster. The first one was in 1905 when his eldest daughter was in danger of her life after a severe operation.[8] Freud was very far from being clumsy and was in fact so dexterous that he was never known to break by accident any of the delicate and precious objects in the collection that filled his rooms. On this occasion, however, he found himself skillfully aiming a blow with his slipper at a little marble Venus which it smashed. It was a sacrificial offering to preserve his child's life. In that connection he related two other unconsciously performed magical acts of the same kind: the breaking of the marble cover of an inkwell so as to induce his sister to present him with a worthier object,[9] and the breaking of a beautiful Egyptian figurine he had just bought, the purpose being to sacrifice it instead of a friendship he valued and which was in some danger.[10] This feature of Freud's mentality persisted through his life. As late as 1925 we hear of his losing his spectacles and case in the woods at a time when he was expecting his daughter Anna's arrival. There had just been a train accident, and by that sacrifice he was insuring against a repetition during her journey.[11]

The counterpart to these apotropaeic acts to ward off evil is the belief in the sinister significance of omens. I quoted earlier an incident where Freud, meeting someone who resembled him so closely as to give him the uncanny impression of seeing his "double," immediately thought that it might be an omen of his death.[12]

Then we have the extraordinary story of how extensively Freud accepted his friend Fliess's "biological" doctrine of the fateful influence of the portentous numbers 28 and 23; we have just seen that Freud's interest in mystic numbers long antedated Fliess's influence. Insofar as calculations based on them were thought to predict the future the doctrine may fairly be said to appertain to the occult. Even when Freud had emancipated himself after years of severe struggle from the influence of his old friend, indeed after a painful quarrel had parted them forever, he retained something of the

former beliefs.[b] In his correspondence there are many current allusions to the mysterious numbers. If he tells Ferenczi that an attack
of migraine came on 23 plus 2 days after his birthday, or reproaches Jung that he has had no letter from him even 28-3 days
from the last, we are bound to conclude that such pointless remarks,
half-jocular as they doubtless were, indicated some lingering belief
in the significance of such numbers.

In 1908 Freud described before the Vienna Psycho-Analytical Society three cases which could have been interpreted as indicating the
operation of thought transference. Analysis of them, however, disclosed more natural explanations and excluded the idea of telepathy.[13] Here also, as in the last instance, Freud's scepticism and
critical powers overcame any temptation there might have been to
believe in clairvoyance or telepathy.

In his *Gradiva* book, 1907, Freud gave a striking personal example
of how hard it is to become completely free from the irrational beliefs of childhood, and also of the shame one feels on the occasions
when they suddenly recur in circumstances that for a moment compel the old belief. "Consider now the fact that belief in spirits, ap-
paritions and returning souls, which finds so much support in the
religions to which, at least as children, we have all clung, has by no
means entirely vanished among all educated people, and that many
otherwise reasonable people find interest in spiritism compatible
with the demands of reason. Even someone who has grown to be
dispassionate and incredulous may perceive with shame how easily,
when moved and bewildered by some emotion, he may turn back
for a moment to a belief in spirits." He then related an experience
of his own; on encountering the sister of a dead patient, whom she
closely resembled, he was so taken aback that for a moment he
said to himself: "so after all it is true that the dead may return."
This was instantly followed by a feeling of shame at his momentary
weakness.[14]

Soon after this Freud came under the influence of two men, his
two chief friends at that time, who were both much more favorably
inclined toward occult beliefs than he ever became. They were Jung
and Ferenczi, the former coming a little earlier in time. Jung was
steeped in various occult interests and, as is well known, has remained so. On one of his first visits to Vienna, on March 25, 1909,
he regaled Freud one evening with astonishing stories of his experiences, and also displayed his powers as a poltergeist by making vari-

[b] Freud himself said so in a letter to J. Popper-Lynkeus, August 4, 1916.

ous articles in the room rattle on the furniture. Freud admitted having been very much impressed by this feat and tried to imitate it after Jung's departure. He then found, however, obvious physical reasons for any faint noises to be observed, and he remarked that his credulousness had vanished together with the magic of Jung's personality. He wrote at once to warn his friend to keep a cool head in the matter.[15]

Ferenczi's belief in the occult was also certainly stronger than Freud's. His interest in the subject had arisen quite independently, as is shown by the fact that the first paper he ever wrote (1899) dealt with it;[16] in this respect he resembled Jung. There is little doubt that his enthusiasm influenced Freud very much in this field, but his influence was not always in the same direction. There were times when Ferenczi's excessive credulity provoked a critical reaction on Freud's part and made him more cautious than he might otherwise have been. Nevertheless the cooperation between the two men was very close. A good deal of their correspondence over the years is taken up with discussions of various aspects of the subject. Contact between them on the matter began very early, in the first year of their acquaintance, and there is reason to suppose that it was first broached on Ferenczi's side.

I had eagerly looked forward to reading Freud's letters to Ferenczi on their return from America in 1909, hoping they would contain some interesting exchange of impressions over that famous visit. There was not much, however, and what little there was I have related in a previous volume.[17] Freud's letters to Ferenczi are almost entirely taken up with an animated discussion of an experience they had had in Berlin on the homeward journey. They had visited a soothsayer there whom Ferenczi knew of, presumably through a brother who lived in Berlin. This lady, Frau Seidler, claimed to have the gift of reading letters while blindfolded, one of the simplest tricks known to mediums. Freud saw through this trick, but both he and Ferenczi were inclined to think that she had telepathic powers and had read Ferenczi's thoughts concerning him, e.g., that Freud was dissatisfied with his environment, that he was a *savant*, and other such fairly obvious ideas. So they decided to put the matter to another test. Freud sceptically remarked that it would have been useless to ask her about the future, since "that is always reforming itself afresh, and even the Almighty doesn't know beforehand." [18] He had been very shaken by the woman's guessing that the letter they showed her (one from him to Ferenczi) had come from Vienna, until he remembered afterward that the word was written in the letter where she had doubtless read it. After reflecting on the experience for some days Freud wrote a long letter to Ferenczi giving his conclusions. There was in his opinion no other explanation possible than that the woman possessed a "physiological gift" whereby she could perceive someone else's thoughts, though often with many distortions produced during the passage from one brain to another. He denied that this implied accepting a belief in occultism. "Certainly not; it's only a question of thought transference. If this is demonstrated one has to believe in it. It is not a psychical phenomenon, but a purely somatic one—one, it is true, of the first rank in importance. . . . I am afraid you have begun to discover something big, but there will be great difficulties in the way of making use of it." Freud mentioned the matter to Heller, the publisher, who had had some experience himself with Frau Seidler, but in the meantime he swore Ferenczi to absolute silence.

Ferenczi sent several letters to his brother in Berlin, who took them to the clairvoyante. Nothing very much came of it, but Ferenczi was impressed by the woman saying that the writer of one letter, a painter, was someone who "stirred something in a pot with his hands." Freud found this a curious description of a painter.

Ferenczi then visited a soothsayer in Budapest called Frau Jelinek who had often functioned as a medium in theosophical circles. Her communications, however, were too banal to make much impression on him.[19]

Some months later he sent Freud a number of notes he had made of occasions in which a homosexual masochistic patient of his had begun the analytical hour with a few words which reminded Ferenczi of thoughts he himself had had in the previous twenty-four hours. They were matters which a sceptic would dismiss as coincidences or perhaps connect with thoughts Ferenczi could have previously expressed to the patient. The patient's associations to them, which Ferenczi unfortunately omitted to give, were purely personal and had no reference to the analyst.[20] Freud, however, was deeply impressed by the data and said emphatically that they put an end to any possible remaining doubt about the reality of thought transference. Henceforward the new knowledge was to be taken for granted.[21]

Then Freud communicated in a somewhat sceptical tone the following data. In Munich there was a "Court Astrologist," Frau Arnold, frequented by Bavarian royalty, who predicted the future from astrological data. A patient of Freud's who had consulted her gave her the birthday of his only sister's husband, and she promptly produced a good description of him. She predicted that in July (it was then January) he would suffer a poisoning from either oysters or crabs. This didn't happen when the time came, but actually the man had suffered a poisoning from lobsters in the *previous* July. So she had projected the past into the future. Freud's criticism that this was the worst imaginable blunder for a prophet to commit did not impress the patient "because he was so very pleased at the prospect." In April of the following year the lady predicted, from studying the dates of the patient's birthday and that of his sister, that there would be a death in their family that October or November— presumably of the disliked brother-in-law. The only coincidence in this was that the patient arranged to begin treatment with Freud that October and admitted he was counting on the death of his brother-in-law in the middle of November. So it looked as if the soothsayer had read the patient's evil thoughts. Freud gave Ferenczi her address so that he could consult her.[22] He published the case itself more than twenty years later.[23]

Ferenczi continued to send Freud examples of telepathy from his homosexual patient and then came out with the portentous discovery that he himself was "an excellent soothsayer[c] or thought reader." Conducting experiments with the same patient he had found that the latter could make approximate guesses of the thought in his analyst's mind. This would make a revolutionary difference to the technique of psychoanalysis.[24] At this point I would remark that a couple of years later he conducted similar experiments with me. He used his powers of suggestion to the full and almost tearfully begged me to perceive the significance of the resemblance between my associations and his unspoken thoughts, however remote the connection might be. His eagerness was so touching that at times I would yield out of politeness, but being pretty tough-minded in such matters I am afraid I was on the whole a disappointment to my friend, though he did not easily give up hopes of converting me.

He now announced to Freud, jestingly but a little proudly, his intention of presenting himself in Vienna as the "Court Astrologist of Psychoanalysts," and, more seriously, of publishing his data and conclusions. Freud was of course alive to the implications of this. Association with such a suspect topic could only add to the odium that already invested the "unscientific" subject of psychoanalysis.

[c] *Wahrsager.*

But he was never the man to flinch from asserting a truth, however unpopular. He told his friend he had no wish to interfere with his freedom of action, but suggested a delay of a couple of years. Then, in 1913, he would publish in the *Jahrbuch* whatever Ferenczi might care to write on the topic.[25]

That month (December, 1910) Freud was in Munich to meet Bleuler and Jung. He had intended to visit the astrologer mentioned above, but could only recollect the name of her street and not her own name. This he called a sign of his "weakness." From this remark one infers that he felt somewhat ashamed of the expedition, but perhaps it also signified a stirring of his critical powers. It was by no means the only time that Freud had made use of an unconscious parapraxis to interfere with his investigation of occultism.[d]

On this occasion he had a long talk with Jung about Ferenczi's findings; he was not surprised to hear that Jung had long been fully convinced of the reality of telepathy and had carried out most convincing experiments himself. Jung professed himself willing to cooperate with Ferenczi in the matter. The two exchanged a few letters on it, but for some reason the cooperation came to nothing.

At the beginning of the new year Freud sent Ferenczi the best example of telepathy he had yet come across. It was the case, which will be related presently, of the woman who was to bear twins at the age of thirty-two.[26]

Ferenczi was now getting venturesome. Seeing a soldier in a tramcar he made a guess at his name and as they got out asked him "Are you Herr Kohn"? The astonished man answered in the affirmative. Freud found the story "uncannily beautiful," but could not attribute it to telepathy because the man could hardly be expected to carry a visual picture of his name about with him. He said afterward, however, that he was impressed by Ferenczi's argument that a man's name was a sensitive area and thus could more easily be communicated to a stranger.[27] He added, "Jung writes to me that we must conquer the field of occultism and asks for my agreeing to his leading a crusade into the field of mysticism. I can see that you two are not to be held back. At least go forward in collaboration with each other; it is a dangerous expedition and I cannot accompany you."[28]

Ferenczi himself now began to wonder whether the plan of such an "expedition" was not premature, and Freud supported him. Ad-

[d] See pp. 401-402.

mitting that the matter could have grave or at least momentous consequences for the psychoanalytical movement, even fateful consequences if they proved to be on a wrong track, he asked Freud to invite Jung to meet him in Vienna and discuss the whole question.[29]

A month later Jung sprang a surprise by telling Freud of some astonishing astrological discoveries which he felt sure, and correctly so, would strike Freud as unbelievable.[30] It was a field in which Freud was a complete unbeliever.

Little more is heard of the topic for another year, when Ferenczi's interest was reawakened by the excitement in Germany caused by the wonderful performances of a horse in Elberfeld: "the clever Hans," who could add, substract, draw circles, etc. This he felt sure showed that telepathy was a primitive endowment in animals, of which only rudiments can be traced in men because of the development of consciousness. He now proposed to take a week away from his work in order to see this horse for himself and also pay another visit to the Berlin soothsayer. Then he would write a brochure on the subject for Freud's *Schriften zur angewandten Seelenkunde* (*Writings on Applied Psychology*).[31] He sent Freud an account of the four chapters this would contain and urged early publication lest his ideas be forestalled by someone else. Freud was now very pleased and promised to publish the number as soon as he could. He urged Ferenczi to take a fortnight away from his work instead of a week, to study the literature thoroughly, and to write the brochure as soon as he possibly could. He suggested as a title "The Unconscious and Thought-Transference." [32]

Freud himself did not think that the performances of the clever horse indicated the operation of telepathy; the native intelligence of animals accorded well enough with our ideas of the unconscious.[33]

Soon after, however, a new kind of proof of thought-transference appeared. Freud related that, not having heard from Ferenczi for several days, he had sat down to write and ask the reason. He inferred from this resolution that it must have coincided with Ferenczi's writing a letter—a telepathic message to this effect presumably reaching him from Budapest—and delayed writing so that their letters should not cross. And it turned out that he was right, as indeed often happens in such conjunctures.[34]

Ferenczi seems to have been deterred from his plan of writing a **brochure** on the subject by discovering the immense amount of lit-**erature** he would have to wade through. On November 19 of the following year, 1913, he addressed the Vienna Society on the topic and evoked intense interest there. But the soothsayer he had brought with him, a "Professor" Alexander Roth, was a dismal failure, so the meeting was rather a fiasco. Four days after that Freud arranged a séance at his home with the same man. It took place in the presence of his family and three other analysts, Rank, Sachs and Hitschmann. The medium who was to produce the mysterious phenomena was a woman whom Roth pressed hard in his questioning. Anna Freud recalled the episode very clearly and a letter of hers to me contains the following passage: "I remember that both my father and I were taken aback by the rough way in which the poor woman was urged, forced and hustled to produce results." To Ferenczi's keen disappointment, however, the result of the séance was completely negative, and Freud refused to give Roth the testimonial he expected.[35] Ferenczi had unwisely already given him one, and the man now went about boasting of his success among psycho analysts. Freud reproved Ferenczi rather sternly for his credulity over a man of whom Freud had received the worst impression. He said that if the man's swindling tricks were publicly exposed it would mean he would have to disavow Ferenczi, and he begged him to buy back from him the testimonial he had so hastily given.[36] Ferenczi could not see his way to doing this, but he decided in the circumstances to give up any idea of publication at least for the time being. He never did write anything on the subject.

On the occasion of the death of Emmanuel, Freud's half-brother, in November, 1914, Ferenczi expressed the opinion that it confirmed a prediction of Jung's that a great misfortune would happen to Freud in 1914. Freud thought this nonsensical and added: "You seem to be more caught up in occultism than I supposed. Wasn't the war itself enough of a misfortune. If it lasts long enough and somehow leads to my death then my own superstition about the numbers,[e] of which you know, would come true." [37]

I have mentioned earlier Freud's dream on July 8, 1915 about his son's death;[38] it was one of many such he had during the war, but this one was so vivid that he awaited news from the Russian front with anxiety. A postcard sent three days later mentioned a skin wound that had already healed. Freud then inquired about the exact date of this, but his question was ignored. He admitted that such messages could not be expected to distinguish between slight wounds and fatal ones, and expressed the opinion that the part of

[e] I.e. that he would die in 1918.

the brain working in this curious fashion was much more sensitive at night.[39] If we take that literally it can only mean that his brain had the capacity of perceiving incidents 300 miles away or that a wounded hero was able to transmit a message over the same distance. Either method certainly transcends known methods of communication. Ferenczi in his comment on the episode claimed not only that telepathy and clairvoyance fall within the realm of science but that the capacity to predict the future by such methods did also.[40] Martin Freud's own comment on this incident I have recorded earlier.[41]

Freud's ambivalent attitude, however, is well illustrated by the story. Besides his superstitious anxiety when waiting for news from the front there was also a critical attitude toward the occult possibility implied. The dream took place in a night after he had been reading Putnam's book on *Human Motives*, and he had been annoyed at Putnam's exordium to him to adopt a more favorable attitude toward religious beliefs. So, in his opinion, one meaning of the dream was a defiant challenge to occult powers to test whether they could be as destructive as he often feared.[42]

Ever since 1900 Freud had cherished what he called a superstitious belief that he was destined to die at the age of sixty-one or sixty-two, i.e. in 1917 or 1918. It seems to have been a pretty firm conviction, since he referred to it over and again in his correspondence. When 1917 passed without anything lethal happening, there only remained 1918, i.e. at the age of sixty-two, and for some reason February was regarded as the fatal month, perhaps because its number is 2. When this date was also safely passed he drily remarked to Ferenczi: "That shows what little trust one can place in the supernatural." The origin of this curious superstition he had revealed to Jung in the early days of their friendship. It appears that in the autumn of 1899 two events had coincided, one highly important, the other banal. The former was the publication of his great work, *The Interpretation of Dreams*, when he was forty-three years old; (the publication date of 1900 is incorrect). The other was his being given a new telephone number, 14362. Some months later at the time of the break with his numerological friend Fliess the numbers suddenly came together and acquired significance; 43 being common to both, there was left 61 and 62. Freud equated the superstitious belief with the thought that with *The Interpretation of Dreams* his life's work was done, so that nothing more need be expected of him and he could die in peace. But at the time it was doubtless a pleasant thought that a good many years would still be left before that final issue.[43]

The occasion of his relating this explanation was a discussion between him and Jung of "the things between heaven and earth that one cannot understand." He quoted, for instance, a mysterious experience he had had on his visit to Greece in 1904. On the way he had been struck by the frequency with which the number 61, or else 60 in connection with 1 or 2, pursued him with all objects that bore a number, railway tickets and so on. He carefully noted every instance, and on getting to Athens was relieved to find he was to be given a room on the first floor where such a number was unlikely. But he did not escape. The number of his room here was 31, half of 62. From then on there was a change, and for the next five or six years he was haunted by coming across the new number 31 wherever he went. In general, he added, he was inclined to explain such obsessions as the result partly of a heightened attention motivated from the unconscious and partly of the undeniably existing compliance on the part of chance, which plays the same part in the formation of delusions as somatic compliance does in that of hysterical symptoms.

A couple of years after the war Freud's interest in the topic of telepathy revived. His mind had been reflecting on the deepest problems of life and death and on the possibility of immortality (in protozoa or in the germ plasm), themes which can readily pass over into the problems of occultism. Furthermore Stekel had recently dealt at length with the topic in a book[44] which Freud quoted in his paper on "Dreams and Telepathy."[45] To Eitingon, who had sent him some books on occultism, he remarked: "The thought of that sour apple makes me shudder,[f] but there is no way of avoiding biting into it."[46] He would confess his doubts more readily to Eitingon and me, who were not very sympathetic on the matter, than to Ferenczi. He confessed to Eitingon a little later that there were two themes that always perplexed him to distraction:[g] the Bacon-Shakespeare controversy and occultism.[47] This was in reply to Eitingon's sending him from Paris a book Richet had recently published.[48]

In the summer of 1921 Freud was invited to act as co-Editor of three different periodicals devoted to the study of occultism; one of the invitations was from Hereward Carrington of New York.[49] Freud

[f] *Mir graut.*
[g] *bringen mich immer aus der Fassung.*

refused all three. Carrington afterward related that in his reply
Freud had stated: "If I had my life to live over again I should devote myself to psychical research rather than to psychoanalysis."
George Lawton, to whom he later told this, wrote at once to Freud
saying that although he believed Freud might have been interested
in psychical research as a field for the application of psychoanalytical
theories he found it hard to believe that he had made the statement
credited to him. Freud's answer dated December 20, 1929, was: "I
deplore the fact that you yourself did not read my letter to Carrington. You would have easily convinced yourself that I said nothing
to justify his assertion. I gladly confirm the fact that you have correctly judged my relationship to psychical research." [h] [50]

But Freud was wrong in his denial. In the eight years that had
passed he had blotted out the memory of that very astonishing and
unexpected passage. Dr. Nandor Fodor kindly procured from Mr.
Carrington a photostat of Freud's letter, and the passage in question
certainly occurs in it.

That was also the summer when Freud read to the "Committee"
his paper on "Psycho-Analysis and Telepathy" which was published
after his death.[51] He half-suggested reading it again before the next
Congress, the Berlin one of 1922, but Eitingon and I dissuaded
him. He was not to be held back altogether, however, and in 1922
he published his more cautiously worded "Dreams and Telepathy." [52]

Freud seems to have remained in two minds about publishing the
former paper, since a couple of years later he wrote to us as follows:
"The strongest literary impression of this month came to me from
a Report on Telepathy Experiments with Professor Murray (Proceedings of the Society for Psychical Research. Dec. 24). I confess
that the impression made by these reports was so strong that I am
ready to give up my opposition to the existence of thought-transference, although I naturally cannot make the least contribution to
explaining it. I should even be prepared to lend the support of psychoanalysis to the matter of telepathy. Eitingon took with him the
manuscript of the private essay in which I indicated such analytical
reinforcement of the telepathic hypothesis. I should decide today to
send that essay into the world, and should not flinch from the
scandal it would inevitably evoke. But there is the insuperable
obstacle of the limitation of medical discretion, which would be seriously impaired by publishing data from the life stories of two of my

[h] I am obliged to Mr. Lawton for calling my attention to this.

patients. It is the very sensation this publication would cause that imposes reserve as a duty; distortions are not permissible, nor would any sort of weakening help. If fate brings about the death of the two people whose predictions did not come true before my own death, the obstacle would vanish." [53] A month later he wrote to us: "Ferenczi was here recently on a Sunday. The three of us[1] carried out experiments with thought-transference. They were remarkably good, particularly those in which I played the medium and then analyzed my associations. The matter is becoming urgent for us." [54] On the other hand, on the day this letter was written I had sent a circular one in which the following passage occurred: "I cannot share Ferenczi's optimism about telepathy being used as objective proof of the contentions of psycho-analysis. On the contrary, in England at least, a great part of the opposition to psycho-analysis (see my review of McBride's book in Vol. VI of the *Journal*) is based on the imaginary idea that psycho-analysis operates with agents ('the psyche') which are supposed to be independent of the body. The prejudice against telepathy is also so strong that any mixture of the two subjects could have only one effect, that of delaying the assimilation of psycho-analysis. As the latter aim is the one nearest to Professor's heart, I find it comprehensible that he should personally defer any interest he may have in telepathy and I can only welcome his decision. At the same time, this is a sacrifice we cannot expect from all other psycho-analysts, but we can reasonably hope that anyone wishing to write on telepathy will make it clear that he does so independently of psycho-analysis and does not wish to infer that the truth of one stands or falls by the truth of the other. This would be simple act of justice to those psycho-analysts who, like myself, are far from convinced of the truth of telepathy, and who cannot therefore welcome the possibility of their convictions about psycho-analysis becoming involved with something else with which they do not agree. I should take up the same standpoint against any entanglement with any variety of philosophy, politics, etc."

My letter apparently had some effect, for when Ferenczi in that same week told Freud he would like to give an account of his telepathic experiments to the next Congress, the Homburg one of 1925, Freud wrote back: "I advise against. Don't do it. Your experiences and experiments are certainly not any more striking or free from doubt than those that have been incorporated in the literature, which so far have not received credence. The only new thing in

[1] Anna Freud was the third.

your lecture would be the personal element and the personal influence that must radiate from it. By it you would be throwing a bomb into the psychoanalytical house which would be certain to explode. Surely we agree in not wanting to hasten this perhaps unavoidable disturbance in our development." [55]

My apprehension proved to be fully justified. At the end of the year we published the fourth volume of Freud's *Collected Papers*, which of course contained a translation of his paper "Dreams and Telepathy." At the same time he published in the *Gesammelte Schriften* then being prepared a special section entitled "The Occult Significance of Dreams" in which he pretty plainly indicated his acceptance of telepathy.[56] In a circular letter I wrote: "This month's 'Psyche' has a leading article entitled 'The Conversion of Freud,' and also a second one on the subject containing the following passage: 'A few years ago the analysis of dreams must have seemed to many adherents of the Viennese school to be developing into a not altogether inexact science. . . . But today the wild men are once more not far from the fold—for if Telepathy be accepted the possibility of a definite oneiric aetiology recedes some decades, if not centuries, into the future.' Much wilder articles to the same effect have appeared in the popular Press. The so-called conversion has encouraged the mysticists, who also say that Freud's life instinct no longer differs from Bergson's *élan vital*, and it has been hailed by opponents who say their opinion has always been that psychoanalysis is a branch of occultism. So once more my predictions have unfortunately been verified and we have one more resistance to face." [57]

In the circular letter following this Freud wrote: "Our friend Jones seems to me to be too unhappy about the sensation that my conversion to telepathy has made in English periodicals. He will recollect how near to such a conversion I came in the communication I had the occasion to make during our Harz travels. Considerations of external policy since that time held me back long enough, but finally one must show one's colors and need bother about the scandal this time as little as on earlier, perhaps still more important occasions." [58] Whereupon I sent him a letter which illustrates how little of the supposed ogre Freud was and how frankly one could speak to him. "You are doubtless right, as usual, when you say that I am too much oppressed by the telepathy matter, for in time we shall overcome the resistance it evokes just as we do all others. But you are lucky to live in a country where 'Christian Science' together with all forms of so-called 'psychical research' mingled with hocus-pocus and palmistry do not prevail as they do here to heighten opposition to all psychology. Two books were written here recently trying to discredit psycho-analysis on this ground alone. You also forget sometimes in what a special position you are personally. When many things pass under the name of psycho-analysis our answer to inquirers is "psycho-analysis is Freud," so now the statement that psycho-analysis leads logically to telepathy, etc., is more difficult to meet. In your private political opinions you might be a Bolshevist, but you would not help the spread of psycho-analysis by announcing it. So when 'considerations of external policy' kept you silent before I do not know how the situation should have changed in this respect. Your first communication on the subject in *Imago*ʲ seemed to me to cover the ground adequately, to defend the dream theory from having to be altered even if telepathy were proved, so the second one seemed to me only irrelevant and harmful. At all events it gave me a new and unexpected experience in life, that of reading a paper of yours without a thrill of pleasure and agreement." [59]

In answer to this outburst of mine Freud wrote: "I am extremely sorry that my utterance about telepathy should have plunged you into fresh difficulties. But it is really hard not to offend English susceptibilities. . . . I have no prospect of pacifying public opinion in England, but I should like at least to explain to you my apparent inconsistency in the matter of telepathy. You remember how I had already at the time of our Harz travels expressed a favorable prejudice towards telepathy. But there seemed no need to do so publicly, my own conviction was not very strong, and the diplomatic consideration of guarding psychoanalysis from any approach to occultism easily gained the upper hand. Now the revising of *The Interpretation of Dreams* for the Collected Edition was a spur to reconsider the problem of telepathy. Moreover my own experiences through tests I made with Ferenczi and my daughter won such a convincing force for me that the diplomatic considerations on the other side had to give way. I was once more faced with a case where on a reduced scale I had to repeat the great experiment of my life: namely, to proclaim a conviction without taking into account any echo from the outer world. So then it was unavoidable. When anyone adduces my fall into sin, just answer him calmly that conversion to telepathy is my private affair like my Jewish-

ʲ "Dreams and Telepathy."

ness, my passion for smoking and many other things, and that the theme of telepathy is in essence alien to psychoanalysis." [60] There was no more to be said.

Toward the end of the year Freud asked Eitingon for the manuscript of the "Harz" essay,[61] perhaps with the idea of publishing it at last. Eitingon assured him he had brought it back personally, but apparently it got mislaid. It was found among Freud's papers after his death.

Our crossing swords on the occasion of Freud's last pronouncement on telepathy, the chapter in his *New Introductory Lectures*, at the end of 1932, was a much milder affair and not worth narrating.

The remaining piece of information we have dates from the last year of Freud's life. Nandor Fodor had sent him the manuscript of a book he had written: *Haunted People: the Story of the Poltergeist down the Centuries*. Here is Freud's reply.

"22. XI. 1938.
"20 Maresfield Gardens.
"London. N.W.3.

"Dear Sir:

"Perhaps you cannot imagine how vexatious the reading of such documents of experiments, precautions, evidence of witnesses and so on is for a reader to whom to start with the acceptance of supernormal happenings does not mean much, especially when they are concerned with such stupid tricks of a so-called Poltergeist.

"I have held out, however, and have been richly rewarded.

"The way you deflect your interest from the question of whether the phenomena observed are real or have been falsified and turn it to the psychological study of the medium, including the investigation of his previous history, seems to me to be the right steps to take in the planning of research which will lead to some explanation of the occurrences in question. It is greatly to be regretted that the International Institute for Psychical Research was not willing to follow you in this direction. Furthermore I regard as very probable the result you come to with the particular case. Naturally it would be desirable to confirm it through a real analysis of the person, but that evidently is not feasible.

"Your manuscript is ready for you to fetch.

"With many thanks for sending me the interesting material,

"yours truly
"Sigm. Freud"

A couple of days later Dr. Fodor called on Freud, who encouraged him to proceed with his investigations. Many of these have subsequently been published.[62]

Freud had been made a Corresponding Member of the Society for Psychical Research in London in 1911. I do not know whether this came about through the influence of T. W. Mitchell, a British psychoanalyst who became President of that Society in 1922, or from the memory of the expositions of Freud's work that had appeared in the Society's *Proceedings* many years before.[63] In 1915 he was made an Honorary Fellow of the American Society for Psychical Research, and in December, 1923 he received a similar honor from the Greek Society for Psychical Research. They were presumably expressions of hope that psychoanalysis would prove able to throw light on the obscure problems of occultism.

Let us now turn from these personal data to Freud's published writings on the subject. They give us, as was to be expected, a very different picture. Freud always showed the utmost caution in publishing opinions which he could not buttress by direct evidence, and in occult matters he had very little. Again, a publication is a much more responsible thing than a private letter or talk, one in which the author's critical powers are more evidently called for.

The first paper Freud wrote on the subject was found after his death and published two years later.[64] It bears the title "A Premonitory Dream Fulfilled," and is dated November 10, 1899, six days after the appearance of *The Interpretation of Dreams*. It is such a neat little analysis that one is surprised Freud decided not to publish it; the most likely reason is that of professional discretion. He gave, however, an abbreviated account of it in the second edition (1907) of his *Psychopathology of Everyday Life*.[65] Freud's meticulous analysis of the episode he related, that of an unlikely meeting which had been foreshadowed in a dream, demonstrated a perfectly natural explanation of what at first sight seemed a convincing proof of prophetic or clairvoyant powers.

In the first edition of his *Psychopathology of Everyday Life* (1904), Freud discussed the nature of superstition.[66] He showed very clearly how a quite unconscious mental process can be projected into the outer world and an intention ascribed to some agency there which really corresponds with the unconscious process in question. The inner, and unknown, thought comes to consciousness as a belief in some external action. He himself at that time emphatically disclaimed any belief that external circumstances, totally independent of his own mental life, could reveal to him any secrets about the future (obviously excluding here ordinary scientific prediction). He went further and maintained that various unconscious processes are mirrored in the beliefs of mythology and religion in the existence of an extra-sensory and supernatural world. By retranslating such beliefs, including those in good and evil, in God, immortality and so on, into their original form as unconscious mental processes, what was metaphysics becomes metapsychology.

In the third edition of this book (1910, the year Ferenczi and he were very occupied with the theme) Freud added to this section another on more truly occult problems: presentiments, prophetic dreams, telepathy, expressions of supernatural influences, etc.[67] He raised the question whether there were real sources of superstition of this nature, and said he was far from being inclined to dismiss the possibility of them out of hand; they called for thorough investigation. And even if still more extraordinary "spiritistic" phenomena could be demonstrated we should be prepared to accept them and to make any necessary modification of the existing natural laws "without deviating from our faith in the universal connections of the world." The only personal experience he related was of the time when he was living in Paris in 1886 and frequently heard his name called in the voice of his betrothed.[k]

On the other hand the examples he gave of apparently occult occurrences he was able to explain analytically on a purely naturalistic basis.

After this we do not find the theme mentioned again in Freud's writings until the years 1919-21, in which he wrote three papers on it. The first of them, called simply "The Uncanny," appeared in *Imago* just after the war (1919).[68] It was written in May, or rather rewritten; [69] so there must have been an earlier draft. It was a very thorough study, some thirty pages long, one that contains a great number of stimulating ideas. Freud considered the essay as being a contribution to aesthetics, using that word in its broad sense of "the psychology of feeling." He remarked that he himself had for long not experienced the feeling of uncanniness. This was doubtless true, if he meant intense fear, but he had at times experienced milder forms of the same feeling of the kind to which the word "queer" might be applied.

He isolated the peculiar nature of this particular feeling, a sense

ᵏ See p. 380.

of dread with creeping horror, from other kinds of fear, and called attention to the curious fact of the close relation between it and its exact opposite, ideas of familiarity and safety. This ambiguity comes to open expression in the German words *heimlich* and *un-heimlich*,[1] which in some contexts are quite interchangeable. The thesis was put forward that the contrast between the uncanny and the once familiar could for the most part be explained by repression of the latter. This he illustrated by a fascinating analysis of the Sandman in E. T. A. Hoffmann's *Tales*. Situations that indirectly stir repressed fears of castration or death are the most characteristic stimuli to the sense of uncanniness.

There are many varieties of this situation. Uncanniness may, for instance, be aroused when events give one the feeling of being haunted by inexplicable recurrences. Without mentioning that the example was taken from his own life,[m] Freud cited the case of a man's being pursued by the number 62, which turns out to be not only the number of his hotel room but of his railway ticket, the street number he wants and so on. As he said, "a superstitious person" will then begin to read some uncanny significance into the haunting, such as a presage of the age at which he will die; we know that Freud cherished this particular superstition for nearly twenty years—until the date in question had passed. He brought such observations, rather unnecessarily one might think, into association with the "repetition-compulsion" which he was expounding in the same year as a general principle of life.[n]

Among the many related topics discussed in this essay was that of the significance of a belief in one's "double," the *Doppelgänger* motif which plays such a large part in primitive thinking and from which Freud himself was not entirely free. He suggested that it had originated as a magical preservative against the fear of extinction, and that it was one source of the belief in an immortal soul.

Freud had shown in his book *Totem and Taboo* that the animistic stage through which mankind must, however imperfectly, have passed in his early stages of development recurs in the mental life of the young child, and so has to be once more "surmounted" before an adequate grasp of reality is achieved. This surmounting, however, is more often incomplete than is commonly thought, and there exists a tendency to revert to it in various circumstances. Situations

[1] Familiar and uncanny.
[m] See p. 391.
[n] See Chapter 8.

which revive this mode of thought, with its accompanying belief in magical powers, arouse the feeling of uncanniness. This feeling, therefore, can arise from two kinds of situation: those stimulating deeply repressed complexes of infancy, and those stimulating animistic attitudes that have been incompletely surmounted in the course of development. Naturally these two often coincide, since they both relate to the same period of life. Furthermore, the animistic attitude characteristically relates to ideas that have been deeply repressed, the belief that one's murderous wishes can be omnipotently effective being a typical example. The dread of something terrifyingly mysterious and malevolent proceeding from a demonic or supernatural agency, such as the appearance of a ghost at midnight, is always the result of projection into the outer world of unconscious repressed wishes.

The last part of the essay was devoted to a valuable discussion of the relation of imagination to reality, in which Freud broached the interesting topic of the aesthetic and emotional influence of fiction. Freud was led to this train of thought by appreciating that his conclusion about the sense of uncanniness being aroused by the recurrence of something repressed is not reversible; often such a recurrence has not this effect. On the whole the uncanniness resulting from the revival of repressed complexes operates in fiction as in actual life. But there is a great difference between fiction and real life in the class of case where it is a question of the surmounting of animistic beliefs. In fiction the effect altogether depends on whether the writer is avowedly moving in an unreal world, as happens in most fairy tales, or whether he pretends he is describing a world of physical reality; it is only in the latter case that we get a sense of the uncanny. In real life, on the other hand, those of us who have only partially surmounted infantile animism always get a sense of uncanniness when something happens to arouse the ancient beliefs. Freud had given earlier a personal example of a situation which suddenly wrung from him the exclamation, "So, after all, it is true that the dead may return." °

This essay, apart from the scientific value of its content, is of special interest for the student of Freud's personality. It might have been composed by any rationalist with sufficient psychological penetration, and it displays Freud's critical powers in this obscure field in what might be called a pure culture. There is throughout no hint that there might be any "kernel of truth" in the occult experiences

° See p. 383.

he is discussing. One has almost the impression that here Freud is laying bare to himself the deep psychological origin of his own superstitious tendencies. And yet only two years later there was a pronounced swing once more in the opposite direction, and we find Freud again more than hovering on the brink of reinstating his occult beliefs. Perhaps this curious reversion may be correlated with the remarkable release of his imagination, or phantasy, that led him to propound hypotheses on the deepest problems of mankind: the nature of death and the conflicts between love and hate, between the constructive and the destructive tendencies in life.

The next paper, "Psycho-Analysis and Telepathy," [70] was for the reasons mentioned earlier never published in Freud's lifetime and made its first appearance in 1941. It was written in Bad Gastein in August, 1921, and read before a meeting of the "Committee" [p] in the Harz in September. Perhaps the immediate stimulus came from his having received just before the three invitations mentioned above to cooperate in periodicals devoted to occultism. He had refused these, but evidently felt the need to counterbalance the refusal by stating, at least to a confidential audience, a more sympathetic attitude toward the subject.

He first listed a number of arguments showing how natural and promising an alliance between analysts and occultists should be, but then he raised some doubts about this conclusion. The aims of the two, after all, were not the same. Most occultists were searching only for confirmation of what they already believed, ultimately with a religious tendency. On the other hand, "analysts are fundamentally incorrigible mechanists and materialists, even when they have no intention of depriving emotional and intellectual processes of any still unknown peculiarities." Moreover there was no doubt that analysts investigating occult phenomena would soon be in a position to confirm the reality of many of them, whereupon occultists would utter a cry of jubilation and at once claim the authority of science for any fantastic explanation they might harbor. He then related two cases of the kind which had made a considerable impression on him, adding, however, that his own attitude towards them was "unwilling and ambivalent." The former feature he at once illustrated by telling us he had intended to relate three cases that had made an impression on him, but that when he left Vienna for his summer holiday he "forgot" to take with him the notes of the third case and could not

[p] Mistakenly called the Central Executive of the International Association in the *Gesammelte Werke.*

now reproduce all the details from memory; he had packed some unimportant papers in place of the notes in question. This he interpreted, no doubt quite correctly, as a symptom of his inner resistance against the topic. The third case was the "Forsyth" one which he published in full some years later.[71]

He had told Ferenczi some nine years previously about the two cases in question.[q] The first case he related, at considerably greater length than when he published it later,[72] was that of a young man he had analyzed a few years before the war. He had consulted a soothsayer in Munich, the Frau Arnold who was mentioned earlier,[r] to see what she would predict about the future of a hated brother-in-law. Freud of course completely discounted the complicated astrological reckoning by which the soothsayer asserted she obtained her information, but he could suggest no other explanation of the occurrence than a thought transference between the two.

The second case was one on which Freud set even greater store; it appears in two other of Freud's writings besides this one.[73] As with the former case, it was a question of a prediction that did not come true, but which seemed to indicate the reading of the patient's secret wishes. A woman whose husband was sterile consulted a soothsayer in Paris who assured her she would bear two children when she was thirty-two, i.e. in five years' time. She told Freud the story in analysis sixteen years later, and he discovered that her mother had in fact borne two children at that age. Unfortunately there was no way at that distance of time of being sure that she had not inserted the actual number herself after a banal prediction about begetting children. If that were not so then the soothsayer must have divined her secret wish to be as lucky as her mother.

Freud suggested that the same process might be the reason for some successes in drawing conclusions from handwriting, and he quoted the case of a patient who consulted the Viennese graphologist Rafael Schermann on two critical occasions and whose conclusions both times coincided with intense wishes of the patient's. When Freud published this case later he mentioned only one of the two predictions.[74]

Naturally we listened with great interest to this exposition of Freud's. Ferenczi was already completely sure of the reality of telepathy and found the cases and arguments entirely convincing.

[q] See p. 386.
[r] See p. 386.

Eitingon, Rank and Sachs were also somewhat impressed, but Abraham and I remained sceptical.

The next paper was written a couple of months after this Harz meeting in September. It was entitled "Dreams and Telepathy" and appeared in the March number of *Imago*, 1922. It contains the statement that it was read before the Vienna Psycho-Analytical Society, which was doubtless Freud's intention. After it was in the press, however, Freud changed his mind and let Abraham, then on a visit to Vienna, read another paper there instead.

After making some general remarks and suggestions which we have already noted, such as that telepathy may be the true kernel of occultism, Freud commented on the fact that none of the intuitions about distant events he had often experienced in his own life had come true, and, furthermore, that in his long years of practice he had never come across a real telepathy dream in any of his patients. He instanced two vivid premonitions from his own life, one the dream mentioned earlier about his son having been killed in the war, the other a dream that his sister-in-law in England had died. He was able to interpret both in a naturalistic fashion, but nevertheless they both cost him weeks of anxious waiting before news arrived that both dream victims were safe, and it is this latter feature on which we are justified in laying some stress.

The material he had to offer in this paper concerned two dreams described to him by correspondents whom he had never met. The first of these was a man's dream that his second wife had borne him twins. It took place a few hours after his daughter, at a distance, had in fact given birth to twins a few weeks before she had expected to be brought to bed. Freud's interpretation of the dream was that the man, differing from his second wife in being very fond of children, was expressing the repressed wish that his daughter could replace her, but he raised the question whether the stimulus to the dream could have been a telepathic message from the daughter. The man himself was more interested in this occult possibility than in giving associations to the dream, and Freud made the pregnant remark: "I foresee that it will always be so when psycho-analysis and occultism encounter each other. The former has, so to speak, all our instinctive prepossessions against it; the latter is met half-way by powerful and mysterious sympathies." But he himself was not inclined to evade the problem. "On the contrary, I maintain that it would be a great satisfaction to me if I could convince myself and others on unimpeachable evidence of the existence of telepathic processes." [75]

In commenting on this case Freud insisted that telepathy had nothing to do with dreams as such, but there are instances where only the analysis of a dream discloses a telepathic message that might otherwise have been overlooked. In that event it is used in the making of a dream in the same way as any other stimulus from without, such as a noise from the street.[76] "But it is undeniable that telepathy is favoured by the state of sleep." [77]

The second dream came from a woman, aged thirty-seven, living in Breslau. It was a recurrent and painful dream, which Freud interpreted as signifying an incestuous wish for a child. It had nothing to do with telepathy, but the same person, who throughout her life had been subject to various hallucinations and premonitions, related an episode in which she heard her brother calling out "Mother, Mother." At that moment, far away in the war, he was writing a card home, soon after which he died. There were no confirmatory details available, and it is not easy to see why Freud related the story, similar to so many in the literature.

Freud commented on the important fact that "by far the greatest number of telepathic premonitions are concerned with the theme of death. In the analysis of patients we can invariably show that these proceed from subjective death wishes that have been repressed." [78]

In spite of the statements quoted above, Freud ended the paper by saying he would be sorry if he had given the impression of being secretly favorable to the belief in the reality of telepathy. "For I really wanted to be strictly impartial. I have every reason for being so, since I have no opinion on the matter; I know nothing about it."

In 1925, when Freud was revising The Interpretation of Dreams for its incorporation in the Gesammelte Schriften, he wrote several sections called "Some Additional Notes Upon Dream-Interpretation as a Whole," one of which bore the title "The Occult Significance of Dreams." [79] He presumably intended to insert it in the next edition of the former book, but for some reason he did not. In it he definitely expressed his disbelief in any prophetic power of dreams, or indeed of any other mental states. "The notion that there is any mental power, apart from acute calculation, which can foresee future events in detail is on the one hand too much in contradiction to all the expectations and presuppositions of science, and on the other hand corresponds too closely to certain ancient and familiar human desires which criticism must reject as unjustifiable pretensions. I am therefore of the opinion that after one has taken into account the untrustworthiness, credulity and unconvincingness of most of these reports, together with the possibility of falsifications of memory facilitated by emotional causes and the inevitability of a few lucky shots, it may be expected that the spectre of prophetic dreams will disappear into nothing."

Many people would make the same remarks about telepathy, but here Freud moved in the opposite direction. He wrote: "I have often had an impression, in the course of experiments in my private circle, that strongly emotionally colored recollections can be successfully transferred without much difficulty. . . . On the basis of much experience I am inclined to draw the conclusion that thought-transference of this kind comes about particularly easily at the moment at which an idea emerges from the unconscious, or, in theoretical terms, as it passes over from the 'primary process' to the 'secondary process.'"

Freud again insisted, however, that there was no connection between telepathy and the formation of dreams beyond the likelihood that telepathic messages reach a sleeper more readily than a waking person. Then such material is treated in the construction of dreams just like any other.

Seven years later, in 1932, Freud was writing his *New Introductory Lectures*, and he entitled one of them "Dreams and Occultism." [80] It begins with a very persuasive account of the prejudices against occult beliefs, though he omitted to mention the most important consideration of all—the relation of such beliefs to primitive animism. He proclaimed that he had no convictions in the matter, but again suggested that telepathy might be the kernel of truth that had become surrounded by fantastic occult beliefs. Though it contained no ideas that had not previously been mentioned in his writings, it is perhaps the most attractive presentation of Freud's thoughts on the subject. On the connection with dreams themselves he had little to say and the only example he quoted was that of the man whose daughter had twins, one he had related at much greater length previously. So most of the lecture is devoted to other evidence.

There followed accounts of three cases previously described: the woman who was to bear two children when she was thirty-two, the student whose brother-in-law was to be poisoned from eating crabs, and the young man who frequented the graphologist. The only new case related was the one the notes of which he had forgotten to bring to the Harz meeting. After relating the first of these he added: "If we had to deal with only *one* case like that of my patient we should turn away from it with a shrug of the shoulders. It would not occur to anyone to base a belief which has such far-reaching implications on an isolated observation. But I can assure you that this is not the only case in my experience. I have collected a whole set of such prophecies, and I have the impression that in every instance the fortune-teller has only given expression to the thoughts, and particularly to the secret wishes, of his clients; so that we are justified in analyzing such prophecies as if they were the subjective productions, phantasies or dreams of the people concerned. Naturally not all such cases have equal evidential value, not in all cases is it equally possible to rule out more rational explanations; but taking all the evidence together there remains a heavy weight of probability in favor of the reality of thought transference." [81]

The new case was one with a play on the words Foresight, Forsyte, Forsyth, and it turned on whether a jealous patient had guessed that Dr. Forsyth had visited Freud just before he himself arrived. He had produced the word Foresight, a name his sweetheart had given him, and that was the starting point. Many would consider the case the most tenuous of those related. At all events there are so many alternative explanations to telepathy that it is not surprising Freud forgot to lay it before us at our Harz meeting. Furthermore, he had made his notes only some considerable time after the episode, and there is no guarantee against some unconscious touching up of the story. One minor error I can myself correct. Freud said I had been in Vienna a month before Forsyth's visit. In fact it was the same week, for I dined with Forsyth in Zurich when I was returning from Vienna and he on his way there.

From the foregoing material it is as easy to select quotations illustrating Freud's critical scepticism as it is to select passages illustrating the very opposite. The wish to believe fought hard with the warning to disbelieve. They represented two fundamental features in his personality, both indispensable to his achievements. But here he was truly wracked; little wonder he bewailed that the topic "perplexed him to distraction."

Freud was right in his prediction that analysts would be found who would adopt a belief in telepathy; it has even been suggested that use might be made of the process in the course of psychoanalytic treatment! [82] I recall an incident in this connection that happened to me years ago. A lady who consulted me explained that she could not leave her home a hundred miles away for long, and suggested that I devote an hour a day to analyzing her in her absence. When I expressed my regret that her plan was not feasible she gave a sigh and said "No, I suppose you haven't yet got that far in your work." But I should have been more than grieved had I known that at just that time my old friend Ferenczi believed he was being successfully psychoanalyzed by messages transmitted telepathically across the Atlantic from an ex-patient of his—a woman Freud called "Ferenczi's evil genius." How right Freud was when he wrote about telepathy: *"Ce n'est que le premier pas qui coûte. Das weitere findet sich."* *

---

* "It is only the first step that counts. The rest follows."

15

CHAPTER

Art

BOTH ERNST KRIS AND FREUD'S ARTIST SON ERNST COUNSELED ME NOT TO write this chapter, giving as their reason that since Freud had little aesthetic appreciation there could be nothing worthwhile to say on the subject. With all respect to these authorities, however, I find it needful to make a few points of a clarifying nature. Artists have justly reproached Freud with misunderstanding their aims: justly, because of the imperfection of Freud's exposition. I think it should be possible to smooth out this misunderstanding on both sides.

For some reason that is not at all obvious the exponents of one of the five recognized branches of art, namely painters, have largely appropriated the terms "art" and "artist" as pertaining only to their domain, though occasionally sculptors are also allowed to use them. This is a reversal of the attitude that obtained in Ancient Greece where the term artist was reserved for poets and musicians; painters, sculptors and architects were regarded as mere craftsmen, an attitude derived from the contempt then felt for any manual occupation. In the present chapter, however, we shall follow the current restrictive use of the term.

To begin with it is easy to make two quite definite statements about Freud's attitude to art. He had consistently a high and unstinted admiration for "artists" of whatever kind; this was occasionally tinged with a trace of envy for their superior gifts. Then his enjoyment and appreciation (whether strictly aesthetic or not) of the arts were in this descending order: poetry first, then sculpture and architecture, then painting, and music hardly at all (with a very few exceptions).

Now artists, i.e. painters, have been considerably incensed by what Freud wrote about them. This was most incisively expressed by the distinguished art critic and painter Roger Fry, whose criticisms we shall follow. An initial misunderstanding in such criticisms arises from the fact that when Freud wrote on the subject he had predominantly in mind creative writers, and what he had to say was more intelligible in this field than in that of painting.

The particular passage that roused Roger Fry's ire should be quoted in full. It appears in the *Introductory Lectures* and runs as follows: "Before you leave today I should like to direct your attention for a moment to a side of phantasy-life of very general interest. There is in fact a path from phantasy back again to reality, and that is—art. The artist has also an introverted disposition and has not far to go to become a neurotic. He is one who is urged on by instinctual needs which are too clamorous. He longs to attain to honor, power, riches, fame, and the love of women; but he lacks the means of achieving these gratifications. So, like any other with an unsatisfied longing, he turns away from reality and transfers all his interest, and all his Libido too, to the creation of his wishes in the life of phantasy, from which the way might readily lead to neurosis. There must be many factors in combination to prevent this becoming the whole outcome of his development; it is well known how often artists in particular suffer from partial inhibition of their capacities through neurosis. Probably their constitution is endowed with a powerful capacity for sublimation and with a certain flexibility in the repression determining the conflict. But the way back to reality is found by the artist thus: He is not the only one who has a life of phantasy; the intermediate world of phantasy is sanctioned by general human consent, and every hungry soul looks to it for comfort and consolation. But to those who are not artists the gratification that can be drawn from the springs of phantasy is very limited; their inexorable repressions prevent the enjoyment of all but the meagre daydreams which can become conscious. A true artist has more at his disposal. First of all he understands how to elaborate his daydreams, so that they lose that personal note which grates upon strange ears and become enjoyable to others; he knows too how to modify them sufficiently so that their origin in prohibited sources is not easily detected. Further, he possesses the mysterious ability to mould his particular material until it expresses the ideas of his phantasy faithfully; and then he knows how to attach to this reflection of his phantasy-life so strong a stream of pleasure that, for a time at least, the repressions are out-balanced and dispelled by it. When he can do all this, he opens out to others the way back to the comfort and consolation of their own unconscious sources of pleasure, and so reaps their gratitude and admiration; then he has won —through his phantasy—what before he could only win in phantasy: honor, power, and the love of women." [1]

Fry had two very pertinent criticisms to make of the account Freud here gave of his views.[2] The first was that the aims consciously motivating the artist listed in Freud's rather unhappily phrased closing words are valid only for very second-rate artists, what Fry calls "impure" artists, whose interest in art itself seems to be subordinate to quite other mundane wishes. That an artist is influenced, especially in the early stages of his development, by thoughts of an actual or imaginary audience is probably true, but, as Hanns Sachs has forcibly pointed out, by the time he approaches maturity the conception of an audience has become extensively internalized, fused with his super-ego, and this then attains a far greater value to him than any recognition that may be bestowed by the outer world.[3] The relative indifference to external appraisement, illustrated, for example, by such artists as Cézanne, reached its apogee in the anonymous religious artists of the Middle Ages, most strikingly perhaps in the creators of the Byzantine mosaics of Ravenna.

That brings us to Fry's second criticism: the undue stress Freud laid on the role of phantasy to the neglect of more strictly aesthetic features in a work of art. For our purposes we may define the latter as consisting in an intense emotional, but super-sensual, delight in apprehending and subsequently rendering certain significant and orderly relations of form. Worringer defined "the essence of form" by the two words *Gesetzmässigkeit* and *Notwendigkeit* (the regular order of law and the inevitability of necessity).[4] In painting, this corresponds with what in creative writing appears as preoccupation with inevitable sequences of cause and effect, of which tragedy is the supreme example. Fry, and with him a whole school of writers on art, maintained not only that the special kind of delight just mentioned is an essential constituent of art, but that it comprises the whole of true art. The emotional elements of aesthetic pleasure Fry related to (1) the rhythm of line, (2) a sense of mass, (3) a sense of space, (4) light and shade, (5) color. The central feature is the unity of geometrical balance and of successive relations.[5] Most pictures, Fry conceded rather regretfully, contained in addition some ideational content which through various associations was calculated to stir particular emotions; but he held that such emotions detracted from the purely aesthetic pleasure of the work of art and could be regarded as baits designed to attract the attention of the laity who were not concerned primarily with art itself, though the baits might lure them toward that sacred arcana.

This word "bait" is interesting, since Freud himself also uses it. For him it is the mysterious "artistic gift"—not necessarily identified with aesthetic appreciation in the strict sense—which serves as a bait to arouse the spectator's interest and lead him emphatically to enjoy the disguised gratification the artist is presenting of various unconscious wishes. It is what Freud called the "preliminary pleasure" (*Vorlust*) which leads on to the "final pleasure" (*Endlust*) of complete gratification. He called "the perceptual pleasure of formal beauty" an "incitement premium" to lure the observer into further depths.[6] This conception of two stages in the attaining of gratification was expounded by Freud in various spheres, notably in analyzing the technique and significance of wit, and its obvious prototype is found in the field of sexual desire. In the present connection, however, one notes that it is applied in the contrary sense to that of the artist's; to Freud, aesthetic appreciation is preliminary to the gratification of some unconscious phantasy, while for the artist emotional interest is preliminary to the aesthetic enjoyment. Both could claim to be right: the artist knows how often interest in the manifest content of a picture may lead the observer on to some appreciation of its aesthetic features, while Freud would go further and maintain that these features themselves are a bait to a response to the unconscious content.

One can of course arbitrarily assert, as Fry does, that art is nothing else than aesthetic appreciation (which is a different thing from saying that this is an *essential* part of art). It then becomes a matter of words. We may note, however, that artistic endeavors confined to this element, e.g. cubism, become increasingly arid in quality and correspondingly limited in their appeal. And when Fry insists that "the accumulated and inherited artistic treasure of mankind is made up almost entirely of those works in which formal design is the predominant consideration," [7] one may rejoin that they are never devoid of content, so that it remains an open question whether they owe their immortality to the one or to the other—or, most probably, to both. Even in the most recondite productions of Picasso or of Henry Moore it is usually possible to divine some unconscious imagery that is symbolized in the outlines.

It may very well be true that the artist's *conscious* interest is devoted, perhaps exclusively, to the aesthetic element. Freud remarked once in a letter to me describing an evening he had spent with an artist: "Meaning is but little to these men; all they care for is line, shape, agreement of contours. They are given up to the *Lustprinzip*." [8] Fry also insisted on the artist's *conscious* indifference to the content of what he is painting: "Rembrandt expressed his profoundest feelings just as well when he painted a carcass hanging up in a butcher's shop as when he painted the Crucifixion or his mistress." [9] Apropos Rembrandt, and proceeding by free association, I may mention that Freud told me once that Rembrandt was his favorite painter. I surmise, however, that what interested him was not the composition of a carcass, but the astounding penetration into character that Rembrandt displayed in his portraiture.

Evidently there is much in common between the artistic discovery of certain significant relationships in form and a scientific discovery of an orderly relationship constituting a new natural law. Fry distinguished the former by its peculiar emotional quality, one akin to the delight in the perception of beauty; in fact he wrote: "This emotion about forms which I will call the "passion for pure beauty." [10] He agreed with Freud [11] that this originates in the sexual instinct,[12] although it has become remote from it in the course of development. The aesthetic sense for beauty did not differ from the world of phantasy in its origin, but Fry rightly insisted that their function had become different when fully developed. He pointed out, further, that this aesthetic passion may be present even when the object depicted is actually ugly as judged by ordinary standards; if there is a purposeful order in the variety then there need not be any sensuous or perceptive beauty.[13]

Many tomes have been written on this baffling topic of beauty, the most penetrating analytic study of it I know of is that by Hanns Sachs.[14] I will only observe here that psychologically it appears to be closely associated with the sense of security and the desire for perfection. It has been suggested that the very starting point of an artistic creative impulse is this search for beauty, "the impulse to find some possibilities of rest in the bewildering phantasmagoria of the outer world." [15]

It is time to return to Freud. There is plenty of evidence to show that Freud had a keen sense of simple beauty, notably in the sphere of nature, and also that he had some capacity for aesthetic appreciation, but it is certain that he never cultivated this in any discriminating fashion, except perhaps to some extent in the field of literature. After all, no one could have spent his vacation for a dozen years wandering through the galleries of Italy, and gazing intently at its wonderful architecture and artistic collections, without being actuated, at least in some measure, by aesthetic feeling. His attention to this aspect of his enjoyment was evidently stimulated by his friend Fliess, who also gave him a book by Hehn on Italian art.[16] Just before starting on a tour of Northern Italy Freud wrote to him: "I am hoping this time to plunge somewhat more deeply into Italian art. Your point of view is dawning on me, which looks, not for what is of cultural-historical interest but for absolute beauty clothed in ideas and composition and in the fundamental pleasing sensations of space and color." [17] Four years later he wrote to his wife from Rome: "Today I have again seen the most magnificent things in the Vatican galleries from which one goes away as if intoxicated." [18] He could attain a still intenser degree of intoxication from the contemplation of nature. Writing to Jung from Ammerwald a few weeks before their journey to America he said: "Yesterday afternoon I dragged my tired bones up a mountainside, where nature with the simplest stage properties—with gleaming rocks, fields red with Alpine roses, a patch of snow, a waterfall, the whole against a background of green—achieved such a magnificent effect that I lost all sense of personality. You could have made a diagnosis of dementia praecox." [19]

Freud was quite aware that his aesthetic sense had remained in a simple primitive form and had never been cultivated like that of a connoisseur of art. He was deterred by the action of a stronger instinct in him, that of curiosity. When, as often happened, he was deeply moved by a work of art he could not rest until he had made every effort to find out what had moved him, and also what had moved the artist to produce that particular work.[20] This intense preoccupation swept aside any interest in what he would call the mere technique of art, that which to most artists constitutes the whole of their art. In other words, his scientific impulse easily predominated over any artistic one. He recognized a relationship between the two and gave much thought to it. His famous essay on Leonardo is largely devoted to the comparison and contrast between the two, also to the conflict that can arise between them as it did with Leonardo and Goethe.[21]

As we shall presently see, Freud was much more concerned with literary than with pictorial or sculptural art; it is significant that in his writings on Leonardo and Michelangelo he did not directly discuss the theme of aesthetic appreciation. As to the psychology of artists, the essence of what he had to say is contained in the passage quoted earlier: "Artists are endowed with a powerful capacity for sublimation and with a certain flexibility in their repressions." He felt sure that the source of their creative impulse must lie in some important unconscious phantasy. Beyond this he was singularly modest when touching on the psychology of art or of the artist. He gives the impression of having flinched from the problem as if he were deterred from approaching nearer by his enormous respect for artists and for some mysterious magic of genius. He certainly felt that any solution of the riddles they present was far beyond him, and that they were perhaps altogether insoluble. Other analysts, possibly less inhibited in this respect than Freud, have passed beyond the barriers he declared were final.

It is not always clear whether when Freud spoke of the inaccessible secret of the artist he had in mind his particular powers of sublimation that transform his personal unconscious phantasy into the universal field of great art or, on the other hand, the special technique which we have seen to be that of aesthetic appreciation. At all events it is desirable to quote a few of his dicta on the matter. In his book on Leonardo (1910) he wrote: "Since the gifts and abilities of the artist are closely bound up with the capacity for sublimation we have to admit that also the nature of artistic achievement is inaccessible to us psychoanalytically." [22] In the exposition of his work he wrote three years later for *Scientia* he stated: "Whence it is that the artist derives his creative capacity is not a question for psychology," [23] a negative statement with which few psychologists would be content. In his *Autobiography* there is the equally definite dictum: "It [psychoanalysis] can do nothing toward elucidating the nature of the artistic gift, nor can it explain the means by which the artist works—artistic technique." [24] And as late as 1928, at the beginning of his essay on Dostoevsky, he stated quite firmly: "Unfortunately analysis has to lay down its arms before the problem of the creative writer." [25] We may conclude with a more general remark of Freud's, dating from the previous year: "As we have long known, art offers substitutive gratifications for the oldest cultural renunciations, still the ones always most deeply felt, and for that reason it serves as nothing else to reconcile men to the sacrifices made on behalf of culture." [26]

A word may be said about the effect of psychoanalysis on artistic inspiration. Artists have often displayed concern, not to say apprehension, on this subject. It has shown itself in two opposite, and indeed contradictory, ways. On the one hand they have warned analysts against attempting to penetrate into their secrets. They have confidently asserted, and in doing so have been able to quote in their support the passages of Freud's mentioned above, that the sources of aesthetic feeling lie so deep that they must forever remain beyond the power of psychoanalysis to reach them or throw light on their nature; analysts would therefore be only wasting their time. On the other hand, however, they have vehemently counseled that no artist be analyzed lest the inspiration of his art be destroyed, though they have never explained why only this particular capacity should run such a terrible risk.

In discussing this matter we should adhere to the distinction drawn earlier between the two components of artistic capacity: the inspiration derived from some unconscious phantasy, and the gift of aesthetic appreciation. There are therefore two alleged dangers, and the purist in art deals with them somewhat differently. By discounting or even denying the importance of the phantasy component, with which indeed he is not consciously concerned, he can view with some complacency the idea of its being analyzed; to do so would not in any way impair what he regards as the real nature of art—aesthetic appreciation. It is this which is the final untouchable.

They are right in maintaining that the source of artistic appreciation lies deeper than any unconscious phantasy, and that it is more remote from our instinctual life than any other human interest, with the possible exception of pure mathematics; in other words, it represents the acme of desexualization. Remoteness, however, need not connote impenetrability. When one considers the material used in the five arts—paint, clay, stone, words and sounds—any psychologist must conclude that the passionate interest in bringing an orderliness out of chaos must signify at the same time an extraordinary sublimation of the most primitive infantile enjoyments and the most extreme denial of them. In psychoanalytical terms that passionate concentration represents a fixation on a stage of "preliminary pleasure" (*Vorlust*).

Only actual experience can answer the question posed above of the effect of psychoanalysis on artistic inspiration, and fortunately it has already done so in no uncertain fashion. Many artists, both first-rate and second-rate, have now been analyzed, and the results have been unequivocal. When the artistic impulse is genuine the greater freedom achieved through analysis has heightened the artistic capacity, but when the wish to become an artist is impelled by purely neurotic and irrelevant motives the analysis clarifies the situation. Freud himself expressed this same conclusion very succinctly in a letter written toward the end of his life to a violinist who asked him the same question we have been discussing, and I append his answer. She was Miss Maria Thoman, since deceased, the daughter of Stephan Thoman, a well-known pianist and professor at the Academy of Music in Budapest.[a]

"27. 6. 1934

"*Sehr geehrtes Fräulein,*

"It is not out of the question that an analysis results in its being impossible to continue an artistic activity. Then, however, it is not the fault of the analysis; it would have happened in any case and it is only an advantage to learn that in good time. When, on the other hand, the artistic impulse is stronger than the internal resistances analysis will heighten, not diminish, the capacity for achievement."

"With best wishes

"Freud"

[a] I am indebted to Otto Fleischmann for this material.

16
CHAPTER

Literature

AT THE OUTSET I WISH TO DISCLAIM ANY INTENTION OF DISCUSSING THE vast theme of Freud's influence on literature in general, a task far beyond my powers. I may call attention to a few of the many essays and books that have already dealt with this topic,[1] but we still await a comprehensive study of it. It is plain that Freud's work afforded a powerful stimulus to the understanding of psychological motivation, but a writer's task is concerned with depicting the complex ramification of such motives rather than with any exposition of unconscious processes themselves.

Here I propose to confine myself to three themes: Freud's own contributions to our understanding of creative activity and the study of certain literary productions; some account of his interest in literature; and a note on his contacts with literary personages.

Freud had assuredly more reason to be heard when he wrote about literary production than in other fields of art, since he was himself a distinguished master of prose style. The bestowal of the Goethe prize on him was a recognition of this feature of his work. In the numerous passages in which he discussed the nature of artistic capacity he usually had in mind not the painter but the poet (*Dichter*).[a] When Havelock Ellis and other critics assert that Freud was an artist rather than a scientist the statement is plainly intended not so much as praise of his artistry, though this was evident enough, as a means of discounting his scientific work; Goethe's scientific

---

[a] The German word *Dichter* means both a poet and what we simply call a writer.

work met with similar criticisms. We may, however, be pretty sure that had Freud's destiny not taken him along the path it did his creative faculties would have found a literary expression. He is said to have told someone that as a young man he had thought of becoming a novelist. The only slight contemporary allusion to such an idea is in a letter to Martha Bernays (April 1, 1884). "Here's a surprise for you. Over and again—I don't know how!! many stories have come into my mind, and one of them—a tale in an oriental guise—has recently taken a pretty definite shape. You will be astonished to hear that I am becoming aware of literary stirrings when previously I could not have imagined anything further from my mind. Shall I write the thing down, or would it embarrass you to read it? If I do so it will be only for you, but it will not be very beautiful. Also I have very little time just now. Still I believe that if the train of thought comes back it will really get done by itself. In that event I will write it, and you will chuckle to yourself without saying a word about it to anyone."

His interest in words and style certainly began early. Even in school his teachers commented on his peculiarly idiomatic manner of writing.[2] He was also specially interested in the subject of speech itself and had made unexpected discoveries concerning its significance. There was his first book of all, *On Aphasia*,[3] the discussion on speech in the Project for a Scientific Psychology,[4] and above all the importance he attached to the use of words as a criterion separating the preconscious from the unconscious mind. He wrote several papers on the structure of words.[5]

A certain similarity between his psychological investigations and the divinations of creative writers was often in Freud's mind. In the *Studies in Hysteria*, 1895, he wrote a little apologetically: "I was trained to employ local diagnoses and electro-prognosis, and it still strikes me as strange that the case histories I write should read like short stories and that, as one might say, they lack the serious stamp of science. . . . The fact is that local diagnosis and electrical reactions lead nowhere in the study of hysteria, whereas a detailed description of mental processes such as we are accustomed to find in the works of imaginative writers enables me, with the use of a few psychological formulas, to obtain at least some kind of insight into the course of that affection." [6]

He evidently felt an affinity between himself and the imaginative writers, though he admired, and perhaps somewhat envied, the facility with which they could reach a piece of insight that had cost him much labor to achieve. They were wonderful people. "One may heave a sigh at the thought that it is vouchsafed to a few, with hardly an effort, to salve from the whirlpool of their emotions the deepest truths, to which we others have to force our way, ceaselessly groping amid torturing uncertainties." [7]

Twenty years before writing that passage Freud had written similar words in his *Gradiva* book. "Imaginative writers are valuable colleagues and their testimony is to be rated very highly, because they have a way of knowing many of the things between heaven and earth which are not dreamed of in our philosophy. In the knowledge of the human heart they are far ahead of us common folk, because they draw on sources that we have not yet made accessible to science." [8] In that context he breaks a lance for the importance of medical psychology as an approach to the understanding of both the normal mind and severe mental disturbances, asserting here the common ground between it and the best literary productions. "Wilhelm Jensen has given us an absolutely correct study in psychiatry. . . . Perhaps in the judgment of the majority we are doing him a disservice when we declare his work to be a study in psychiatry. A writer should, so it is said, avoid any contact with psychiatry and should leave to doctors the portrayal of morbid mental states. In reality no true writer has ever heeded this precept. The portrayal of the psychic life of human beings is, of course, his most special domain; he has always been the forerunner of science, and thus of scientific psychology too. For the borderline between normal and what are called morbid mental states is to some extent a purely conventional one; furthermore it is so fluid that probably every one of us oversteps it many times in the course of a day. On the other hand, psychiatry would be making a mistake were it to try to confine itself permanently to the study of those severe and melancholy affections that result from coarse disturbances of the delicate psychic apparatus. It has no less interest in the minor and adjustable deviations from the normal which at present we cannot trace further than disturbances in the play of psychical forces; indeed, it is only through these that it can understand mental health as well as the manifestations of serious illness. Therefore the writer can no more shun the psychiatrist than the psychiatrist the writer, and the poetic treatment of a psychiatric theme may be perfectly correct without any loss in beauty." [9]

It is worth recalling in this connection that the first, and almost the only, person to appreciate the significance of Freud's earliest contribution to psychopathology, the *Studies in Hysteria*, was a writer, Alfred von Berger.[10]

In many passages of his writings Freud expressed his unstinted admiration for the achievements of creative writers. They, like all artists, possessed some mysterious gift which he could admire from a distance, but the secret of which he could not divine. This remark, already quoted, is typical of many: "Unfortunately psychoanalysis has to lay down its arms before the problem of the imaginative writer." [11]

Nevertheless he had something to say about the nature of artistic, and particularly of literary, production. He made two essential points. In the only paper he ever wrote specifically devoted to the topic, in 1908—"Creative Writers and Daydreaming"—he discovered links between the creative writer and the ordinary person in the connection between the play of childhood and the phantasies of later life, these being far more secretive than the former.[12] He established the formula that some current stimulus stirs a long-forgotten unsatisfied longing of early childhood and then creates the wish that in the future this longing should still achieve gratification. The way in which the poet or writer transforms the unconscious infantile wish into a work of art is his "most private secret," the true *Ars poetica*. The methods he uses enable the reader to respond to the gratification of these unconscious wishes in a way that would be otherwise impossible.

The second point was his distinction between preliminary pleasure and final pleasure, expounded three years later in his paper "Formulations on the Two Principles of Mental Functioning." [13] It was the former of these that he identified as the mysterious artistic technique.

All he had to say about the artist's nature was that he must possess an unusual capacity for sublimation and a certain lack of rigidity in the repressions concerned with unconscious conflicts.[14] He also remarked that "a (sexually) abstinent artist is not easily possible, whereas an abstinent young scholar is certainly no rarity." [15]

Freud perceived the social function of art in its compensatory effect in relation to the various inevitable dissatisfactions of life. The artist finds an indirect path from phantasy to reality. "But this he can attain only because other men feel the same dissatisfaction as he does with the renunciations demanded by reality, and because this dissatisfaction, resulting from the replacement of the pleasure principle by the reality principle, is itself a part of reality." [16] There is a similar passage, written sixteen years later: "Art, as we have long recognized, offers substitutive gratifications for the oldest, and therefore most deeply felt, renunciations imposed by civilization, and is thus the most effective appeaser for their victims." [17]

Perhaps the pithiest account Freud wrote of his views on imaginative creation was a passage in his *Autobiography* where he was describing the past development of his ideas. "The realm of imagination was evidently a sanctuary made during the painful transition from the pleasure principle to the reality principle in order to provide a substitute for the gratification of instincts which had to be given up in real life. The artist, like the neurotic, had withdrawn from an unsatisfying reality into this world of imagination; but, unlike the neurotic, he knew how to find a way back from it and once more to get a firm foothold in reality. His creations, works of art, were the imaginary gratifications of unconscious wishes, just as dreams are; and like them they were in the nature of compromises, since they too were compelled to avoid any open conflict with the forces of repression. But they differed from the asocial, narcissistic products of dreaming in that they were calculated to arouse interest in other people and were able to evoke and to gratify the same unconscious wishes in them too. Besides this, they made use of the perceptual pleasure of formal beauty as what I have called an 'incitement premium.' What psychoanalysis was able to do was to take the interrelations between the impressions of the artist's life, his chance experiences, and his works, and from them to construct his constitution and the impulses at work in it—that is to say, that part of him which he shared with all men." [18]

It is not easy to make any definite statements about Freud's ability as a literary critic. His many remarks on literary works indicate that it must have been of a high order, but he could not have cultivated in any special fashion the more technical aspects of criticism. Throughout his writings and correspondence, and in the Minutes of the Vienna Psycho-Analytical Society,[19] there are scattered numerous comments on literary themes and productions which would well bear collecting in a separate study; a typical example is quoted elsewhere where he discussed the position of historical truth in historical novels, reaching a definite but far from dogmatic conclusion.[b] In this connection an interesting letter, which we owe to Dr. Kurt Eissler's researches, may be reproduced.[20] In 1907 a Viennese publisher, Hugo

[b] See page 459.

Heller, invited a number of distinguished people to submit their choice of ten "good books." He published in a little brochure thirty-two replies, including those from Peter Altenberg, Hermann Bahr, August Forel, Ernst Mach, Thomas Masaryk, Arthur Schnitzler and Jakob Wassermann.[21] Here is Freud's; he had evidently found the request a stimulating one.

"You ask me to name 'ten good books' without vouchsafing any explanation, and so leave it to me not only to select the books but also to interpret the request. Accustomed as I am to heed minute signs I must adhere to the wording in which you couch your enigmatic request. You did not say 'the ten most magnificent works of world literature'—to which I should have had to reply, as would so many others, Homer, the tragedies of Sophocles, Goethe's *Faust*, Shakespeare's *Hamlet*, *Macbeth* and so on.

"Neither did you say the 'ten most important' books, which would have necessitated including such scientific achievements as those of Copernicus, the book on belief in witches by the old physician Johann Weier, Darwin's *Descent of Man*, and others. Nor did you even ask for my 'favorite books,' among which I should not have forgotten Milton's *Paradise Lost* and Heine's *Lazarus*. I think therefore that special significance attaches to your word 'good,' and that it carries the same implication as when we speak of 'good' friends, books to which a man owes some of his knowledge of life and his *Weltanschauung*; books which one has enjoyed and gladly recommends to others, but which do not evoke awe or dwarf one by their great stature.

"I shall name for you ten such 'good' books as they occur to me without much reflecting.

Multatuli, *Briefe und Werke*
Kipling, *Jungle Book*
Anatole France, *Sur la pierre blanche*
Zola, *Fécondité*
Merejkowsky, *Leonardo da Vinci*
Gottfried Keller, *Leute von Seldwyla*
Conrad Ferdinand Meyer, *Huttens letzte Tage*[c]
Macaulay, *Essays*
Gomperz, *Griechische Denker*
Mark Twain, *Sketches*

"I do not know what you intend to do with this list. It seems very

[c] Freud twice quoted a line from this book.[22]

odd to me, and I cannot quite leave it without comment. I do not want to discuss the problem of why I chose just these and not other equally 'good' books, but should like to throw some light on the relation between the author and his work. That relation is not in all cases so close as, for instance, in Kipling's *Jungle Book*. In most of them I could as well have given preference to another work by the same author; thus I might have chosen Zola's *Docteur Pascal*, and so on. The same man who has given us one good book has often given us several. With Multatuli I felt unable to discriminate in favor of the private letters against the love letters or the other way round, so I put down 'Letters and Works.'

"Literary productions of purely poetic value were excluded from the list, probably because your request for good books did not seem to be directed to such works; for in the case of C. F. Meyer's *Hutten* I must place its 'goodness' far above its beauty, edification above aesthetic enjoyment.

"Your request to name ten good books touches on something about which immeasurely much might be said. And so I conclude in order not to become more loquacious."

The first example we have of a psychoanalytic study of a literary production, one Freud himself never published, occurs in the correspondence with his friend Fliess. He there devoted a couple of pages to an analytic interpretation of the motives in a story, *Die Richterin*, by Conrad Ferdinand Meyer.[23] It was Fliess who introduced him to this author, and that was doubtless the reason why there are so many more allusions to him in the correspondence than to the other, far superior, Swiss author, Gottfried Keller. He unraveled the source of the author's phantasy from which the story must have proceeded, and commented: "Thus in every single feature it is identical with the revenge-and-exoneration romances which my hysterics compose about their mothers if they are boys." An essential point in the delineation of the phantasy is his account of what he called the "family romance" of being a foster child, born of superior and unknown parents. The interest of this theme will appear later in this chapter. Freud had first encountered it with paranoics, then in hysterics, and only later did he recognize it to be a common feature in normal child development.[24]

The first published example was no less than Freud's well-known interpretation of *Hamlet*, where he elucidated the old mystery by resolving the tragedy into a variant of the Oedipus situation.[25] He

424   The Life and Work of Sigmund Freud

had conveyed his conclusions to Fliess a couple of years before this, at the same time as his discovery of the Oedipus complex in himself.[26]

This epoch-making contribution appeared modestly as a footnote to *The Interpretation of Dreams*.[27] Ten years later I was able to fortify his conclusions from a large amount of comparative material which was ultimately expanded into a book.[28] Since then many psychoanalytical studies have appeared on various aspects of the tragedy, and J. I. M. Stewart (alias Michael Innes) has composed a brilliant play in which a doctor conducts with great penetration a posthumous psychoanalysis of Hamlet's character.[29]

Freud's path-finding contribution had momentous consequences. It was the first time it had been shown possible to correlate the manifest motivation of a great literary production with the unconscious motives it presupposes, to supply in this way a valuable criterion for the psychological integrity of such works throughout its various layers, and furthermore to throw light on the personality of the author by elucidating the deepest sources of his inspiration. It would transcend the bounds of this Biography even to enumerate the many studies that owe their ultimate stimulus to Freud's famous footnote.

Freud's next contribution to the study of imaginative composition dates from 1906, although it was never made public until 1942, after Freud's death. It was a little paper entitled "Psychopathic Characters on the Stage." [30] It has already been summarized,[31] and it is only necessary here to recall that it was concerned with the conditions under which certain forms of art, particularly drama, affect an audience and how they achieve their purpose. In this connection David Siever's detailed study of the extraordinary influence Freud's work has had on the American drama from 1912 onward deserves special mention.[32] Freud had as early as 1907 given an example of how useful actors could find the carrying out of unconscious "symptomatic actions," [33] and Adolf Deutsch has devoted a study to this interesting theme.[34]

In the following year Freud published the delightful little book generally called the *Gradiva*,[35] a very delicate analysis of a story by the North German writer, W. Jensen.[d] Here, as with Shakespeare, Freud was able to confirm in detail the correctness of the author's motivation by correlating its conscious with its unconscious aspects.

[d] In Volume II I had confounded him with the well-known Danish writer of the same name.

The book is one of the best examples of Freud's mastery of beautiful prose.

A year later Freud wrote a paper, his only one specifically devoted to the study of the artistic temperament and mode of creating.[36] This essentially dealt with the phantasy life of artists and its relation to forgotten childhood phantasies.

In 1913 Freud returned to his favorite, Shakespeare, with another of his delicate analyses in an essay entitled "The Theme of the Three Caskets." [37] It is written in an entrancing style that would alone ensure his rank as a literary artist. It began by unexpectedly placing side by side the choice Bassanio has to make in *The Merchant of Venice* with the question King Lear puts to his three daughters. Then by examining the mythological sources of these ideas he was able to trace the underlying motif to contemplation of the three grand themes connected with womanhood: birth, love and death. He further made plain that Shakespeare's intuition must have unconsciously divined the deepest meaning and so was able to hint at it in his presentation.

Two years later Freud attempted to unravel two other plays of Shakespeare's, but this time with less conspicuous success. He was considering a class of persons whom he labeled "Exceptions" because they claim special exemption from the rule that society demands a certain standard of conduct from its members. He could trace this to their belief that an injury had been unfairly inflicted on them in their infancy. Freud suggested that Richard III, at least as delineated by Shakespeare, belonged to this class, and he commented on the skill with which the dramatist wins some degree of sympathy for the "hero" or "villain" by adumbrating the inner meaning of his behavior rather than by bluntly insisting on it. It need hardly be said that Shakespeare's distorted picture of the king was derived from Tudor propagandist material, but here Freud was concerned with the dramatic rather than the historical presentation.

In another section of the same essay, entitled "Those Wrecked by Success," Freud tackled the problem of *Macbeth*, one which had long baffled him.[38] He felt intuitively that the Macbeths' failure to produce a male heir was a secret motivation of the tragedy, but he could not reconcile this with the time sequence given by Shakespeare, and he made another suggestion. It was that Macbeth and his wife, both of whom reverse their characters in the course of the drama, were, psychologically speaking, one and the same person: an example of the mythological "decomposition" which Shakespeare sometimes adopted. He was more successful in the same essay in his investigation of the character of Rebecca West in Ibsen's *Rosmersholm*. Here he carefully dissected the three layers of guilt affecting her and showed the relation between them.

The study of Goethe which Freud published in 1917 had little to do with literature, since it was confined to investigating the significance of a solitary memory Goethe had recorded from his childhood.[39] On the other hand, twenty years before that he had made some interesting analytical comments on the genesis of Goethe's *Werther*.[40]

In 1919 Freud published a little note calling attention to a penetrating passage in E. T. A. Hoffmann's *Die Elixiere des Teufels* (*The Devil's Elixir*) on the censorship separating consciousness from the unconscious.[41]

His last contribution to the psychology of literature appeared much later, in 1928.[42] This time the author studied was Dostoevsky, whose gifts Freud held in the highest esteem. He said of him: "As a creative writer he has his place not far behind Shakespeare. *The Brothers Karamasov* is the greatest novel that has ever been written, and the episode of the Grand Inquisitor one of the highest achievements of the world's literature, one scarcely to be overestimated." On the other hand Freud thought far less of him as a man and was evidently disappointed that someone who seemed destined to lead mankind toward better things ended up as nothing but a docile reactionary.

The analysis itself, which was carried out in conjunction with one of a brilliant short story by Stefan Zweig,[e] was, in the nature of things, not very original, since the theme of father-murder lay so near the surface. Freud remarked it was no chance that the three masterpieces of all time treat of this same theme: Sophocles' *Oedipus Rex*, Shakespeare's *Hamlet*, and Dostoevsky's *Brothers Karamasov*. He had many interesting things to say about Dostoevsky's personality, his hystero-epileptic attacks, his passion for gaming, and so on, but perhaps the most noteworthy part of the essay consists in Freud's remarks on all the different kinds of virtue, which he exemplified in the variety displayed by Dostoevsky.

Theodor Reik wrote a detailed criticism of this essay,[43] and in an answering letter to him Freud agreed with many of the points he made.[44] He added: "You are right in supposing that really I don't

* *Drei Meister* (Three Masters).

like Dostoevsky in spite of all my admiration for his intensity and superiority. That is because my patience with pathological natures is drained away in actual analyses. In art and in life I am intolerant of them. That is a personal characteristic of my own, which needn't hold good with other people."

Although Freud had very little leisure time, hardly any except in his vacations, he was all through his life a wide and deep reader. What made this possible was the extraordinary speed with which he could read and assimilate, together with a very retentive memory. He was fond of quoting snatches of poetry, usually with striking aptness, though he was often not word perfect in doing so. He was familiar from youth with the Latin, Greek and German classics, and he read a good many of those in English, French, Italian and Spanish. His published writings are replete with casual allusions to them. There is no doubt that, from the humanistic point of view, Freud would rank as a highly cultivated and well-educated man.[45] His incidental remark that Milton's *Paradise Lost* was one of his favorite books in itself places him in this company.

Of French authors Freud chiefly admired Anatole France, his favorite of all, Flaubert for his imaginative insight, and Emile Zola for his realism.

He was usually complaisant about reading books recommended to him, but I remember one occasion when I failed. I wanted him to read some of Browning's poems expressing his love for Italy, but Freud waved them aside with the remark "we have our own enthusiasts."

In later years, and especially when suffering, Freud turned a good deal to lighter reading. He liked Dorothy Sayers' detective stories, and I can remember his enjoying James Hilton's *Lost Horizons* and *Good-bye, Mr. Chips*, Kipling's *Jungle Book*, V. Sackville-West's *The Edwardians*; he had always been fond of Arnold Bennett, Galsworthy and Mark Twain, whom he had once heard give a lecture or reading in Vienna. On reading Harold Nicolson's *Public Faces* he was greatly amused by the motto it contains from W. H. Auden: "Private faces in public places are wiser and nicer than public faces in private places."

The chief writers whom Freud knew personally were Hermann Hesse, Thomas Mann, Romain Rolland, Lou Andreas-Salomé, Arthur Schnitzler, Arnold Zweig and Stefan Zweig. Of these he thought most highly of Mann, Schnitzler and Arnold Zweig. He carried on a correspondence with these and other writers, all of which has been placed at my disposal. The most valuable of these letters are those between Freud and Arnold Zweig, and they will probably be published in the near future.

The three great men in whose personality Freud seems to have taken the most interest, and with whom he perhaps partly identified himself, were Leonardo da Vinci, Moses and Shakespeare. Now it can hardly be chance that with each of these questions of identity arose in one form or other, evidently disguised variants of the theme to which Freud gave the name "Family Romance"—a theme with which he had been familiar since the beginning of his psychological work. Leonardo was separated from his own mother in early life and brought up by a step-mother, and Freud attributed certain features in the St. Anne, Virgin and Child picture in the Louvre to Leonardo's confusion between the two women, the Virgin and her mother being equally youthful and their figures melting into each other as if they were really the same person. We are familiar with Freud's view that Moses was not what he had always been believed to be, a Jew, but was actually a noble Egyptian. We shall see that he was obsessed with a similar idea about Shakespeare.

I am suggesting that something in Freud's mentality led him to take a special interest in people not being what they seemed to be. That was true not only with important figures, but also with common mortals. I recollect how pleased he seemed to be on our first encounter when he discovered I was not an Englishman, as one would expect from my record, but a Welshman.

The Shakespeare story goes back a long way. In his student days he had heard his great teacher Meynert proclaim his conviction that Bacon was the real author of Shakespeare's plays, on which he had sagely commented: "If that were so then Bacon would have been the most powerful brain the world has ever produced, whereas it seems to me that there is more need to share Shakespeare's achievement among several rivals than to burden another important man with it." [46] His scepticism was strengthened later when he heard that one of the founders of the Baconian idea was a Miss Bacon, of Boston, which suggested a personal reason for the cult. Nevertheless his interest persisted, and a few years before the First World War he pressed me to make a thorough study of the methods of interpretation employed by the Baconians, contrasting them with psychoanalytic methods. Then the matter would be disproved and his mind would be at rest. Needless to say, I had many reasons for not wanting to undertake such a task.

But was Shakespeare really an Englishman, and was his name what it appeared to be, comparable with Brakespeare and so on? He was taken with a suggestion by an Italian, Gentilli, that perhaps it was simply a corruption of Jacques Pierre; and indeed Shakespeare's features appeared more Latin than English. That was in the days when physical anthropologists tended to confound nations with primitive races and to make far-reaching inferences from skull measurements.

In 1913 he was interested to hear of my dining with Durning-Lawrence, whose Baconianism was so intense that he attributed to Bacon not only his own writings, but all those by Shakespeare, Spenser and Marlowe as well.

After that I remember nothing more on the subject until some ten years later when Freud read a book by an author with the unfortunate name of Looney, who maintained that the Shakespearean plays had been written by Edward de Vere, the seventeenth Earl of Oxford.[47] This at once made a deep impression on Freud. So after all Shakespeare, if not a Frenchman, was at least of Norman descent.

At the time of Freud's seventieth birthday, in 1926, Eitingon, Ferenczi and I spent the evening of May 5 with him and he expounded the de Vere theory to us at length. I remember my astonishment at the enthusiasm he could display on the subject at two in the morning. A year later he read Looney's book again, and this time was practically convinced of his conclusions. The year after, 1928, he begged me to make a thorough investigation of the subject, from which quite new psychoanalytic conclusions about the author's personality might be learned.[48]   I went over the material and sent him a critical letter, with which he strongly disagreed; [49] he was evidently disappointed at my cool reception of the new thesis.

In his letter of address accepting the Goethe prize in 1930 Freud expressed his belief that the Earl of Oxford, the hereditary Lord Great Chamberlain of England, was more likely to have written the famous plays than the uneducated son of a Stratford bourgeois.[50] In the same year his belief was further strengthened by the appearance of a book by Rendall which maintained that a study of the Sonnets showed that the real Shakespeare was the Earl of Oxford.[51] Writing to Dr. Flatter, a Shakespearean scholar with whom he had had some correspondence, Freud remarked: "I am indeed almost convinced that none but this aristocrat was our Shakespeare." [52]

In 1935 when Freud was revising his *Autobiography* he added the following footnote to the passage in which he had associated the writing of *Hamlet* with the death of Shakespeare's father. "This is an inference which I expressly wish to withdraw. I no longer believe that the actor William Shakespeare from Stratford was the author of the works so long attributed to him. Since the publication of Th. Looney's *Shakespeare Identified* I am almost convinced that in fact behind that pen name Edward de Vere, Earl of Oxford, lies concealed." [53] And he repeated the same conviction in the last essay he wrote, in the final year of his life—*An Outline of Psychoanalysis.*[54]

The hare that Looney started has by no means come to rest, and a bevy of earls have since appeared on the scene. Books have been written to prove that not the Earl of Oxford but the Earl of Derby or again the Earl of Rutland wrote Shakespeare's plays, and besides them the Earl of Pembroke, the Earl of Montgomery and the Earl of Southampton were all somehow implicated. And a recent plebeian attempt by Calvin Hoffman to prove that not a peer of the realm but the playwright Marlowe was the true author of Shakepeare's works was castigated in the most devastating criticism that even the *Times Literary Supplement* could ever have published.[55] But I do not know that Freud ever took stock of any of these inferior rivals.

Before he heard of the Looney book on the Earl of Oxford Freud had come to no definite conclusion about the possibility of Bacon having written the plays; the alternative Oxford idea must have come as a relief. He told Eitingon that there were two themes that "always perplexed him to distraction": the Bacon-Shakespeare controversy and the question of telepathy.[56] A psychoanalyst cannot refrain from asking if there could be any inner connection between these two ideas thus freely associated. Perhaps the phrase "things are not what they seem" may meet the case. With both there seems to be a wish that a certain part of reality could be changed.

From all this discussion about identity it may well be surmised that we are concerned with some derivative of the Family Romance phantasy in Freud. He had indeed mentioned himself a rather similar conscious phantasy from his youth: the wish that he had been Emmanuel's son and thus had an easier path in life.[57] What is interesting, however, is not that Freud's personality should have contained similar elements to those of lesser mortals, but that they should have been able to disturb his mind in such a remote fashion.

The following list of literary celebrities with whom Freud was in contact does not pretend to completeness. Count Coudenhove-Kalergi, Havelock Ellis, Gerhardt Hauptmann, Richard Beer V. Hofmann, Thomas Mann, Romain Rolland, Arthur Schnitzler, H. G. Wells, Franz Werfel, Arnold Zweig, Stefan Zweig. Most of these he knew personally, some intimately. In the preceding chapters there have been many allusions to them.

17

CHAPTER

Retrospect

MY PUBLISHERS HAVE URGED ME TO WRITE A CHAPTER ASSESSING FREUD'S influence on the world. With all respect to them I cannot think that they could have formed a very proper estimate of the size of such a task. This is not the only reason why I shrink from it, but it is itself a good one. Freud's name must have been mentioned many millions of times in newspapers, novels and other books, not to speak of the more technical fields ranging from medicine to pure psychology, from education to religion. It would need a corps of research workers to collect, correlate and coordinate this vast material. It is evidently beyond the powers of any individual.

There are two further difficulties to be overcome, one in the province of the historian, the other in that of the psychoanalyst. When we consider the "climate of opinion" which W. H. Auden said Freud has created we are faced with the problem of isolating Freud's contribution to it from the numerous other agencies that have been at work in the past half century. An obvious example of this is the greater freedom and frankness in the sphere of sexuality that has undoubtedly made its appearance in this period. While it is likely that Freud's doctrines have been a powerful factor in bringing this about it is certain that many others, political, sociological and economic, have cooperated, so it would need a very nice weighing of all the evidence before Freud's contribution could be justly assessed. The same is true of many other changes, in the fields of education, psychiatry and so on.

The psychoanalyst's difficulty in forming an estimate is a little harder to describe, but none the less real. What chiefly impresses him is the shallowness of so much of what passes as acceptance of Freud's ideas, and the superficiality with which they are treated. They are so often bandied about lightly as a form of lip service that one cannot help suspecting that much of the so-called acceptance is really a subtle form of rejection, a protection against assimilation of their profound import. Were this not so one might have looked for far-reaching changes in many departments of life where one is persuaded that the application of Freud's ideas could only exert a beneficial influence, or at least some organized support for research into further development of them.

In spite of these serious reservations, however, it may be worthwhile to offer a few general remarks. It will be understood that they are based on purely personal impressions and not on any systematic investigation, not even of the popular questionnaire variety. And when I list my impressions of various effects of Freud's influence I do not for a moment forget that few of them can be ascribed to his work alone; for the most part they have been brought about by other social and economic factors cooperating with it.

Psychiatry

A striking example of this combination is the vast extension of the field of psychiatry, in its broadest sense, that has come about during the past half century, and here I think it is fair to rank Freud's influence, direct and indirect, as a predominant factor. Those whose memories go back to the beginning of this century will recall how neuroses were regarded by the medical profession, with exceedingly few exceptions, as simply unintelligible nuisances. They were either "imaginary" complaints, i.e. in some mysterious sense really non-existent, or else they could be attributed to some minor physical deficiency and thus cease to be psychoneuroses. As a result it would not be unfair to say that the medical profession stood helpless in face of them.

Now Freud's work made a radical difference in this attitude, and in more respects than one. Taking these previously "non-existing" conditions seriously, he showed that they were extremely complicated structures, the investigation of which was full of human interest. Psychoneuroses were not diseases in the ordinary sense of the word, but the expression, one among many, of the difficulties certain people were finding in trying to solve various universal human conflicts—"human" meaning here both biological and social. Nor were neurotics a race apart, but simply persons whose attempted solution of their difficulties takes a clinical form resulting in what are called symptoms. Once this approximation between the neurotic and the normal had been made, it became easier to recognize that no one was entirely free from neurotic reactions; it was only a matter of degree. The medical profession became more willing to make the diagnosis of psychoneurosis, and it is not rare nowadays to read statements from general practitioners who assert that more than half of the symptoms for which they are consulted are of psychological origin—an enormous change from only a few years ago. All this would probably not have happened to the same extent had not Freud, in elucidating the nature of psychoneuroses, also devised a method of treatment which can usually alleviate and often cure the sufferings of the patient.

This wider recognition of the nature of neurosis has meant that a great many conditions and traits of behavior are as a result seen in a quite different light. Minor eccentricities which were formerly labeled as quirks or whimsies are appreciated as being of neurotic origin, whether they call for treatment or not. More important is the recognition that social situations producing unhappiness in a degree that makes life not worth living—sometimes literally so—are also of this nature. There are the countless examples of a person being unhappy in one marriage after another—and not only from the common complaints of impotence or frigidity—from the bickering and quarrels with relatives or friends, the inhibitions and feelings of inadequacy in daily work—in short, an immense variety of difficulties for which the sufferer would previously not have thought of consulting a psychiatrist. The application of this knowledge to the technique of industry, one with which the name of Millais Culpin is especially connected, would alone call for a long exposition.

Two other important effects have resulted from the changes just indicated. Further advances in psychopathology along the lines Freud laid down have produced extensive evidence of the far-reaching influence of mental factors in the causation of bodily disturbances, and a new field called psychosomatic medicine is being created. It is generally accepted now that such agencies play a considerable part in the aetiology of serious bodily disorders, notably duodenal ulcer, arterial hypertension and perhaps even coronary thrombosis.

The other effect concerns the subject of insanity. The greater freedom people feel in admitting that they are suffering from psychological difficulties has extended to those more gravely afflicted, and there is quite evident a pronounced change in the public attitude toward mental disorder. There is less fear engendered at the thought of it, a greater willingness to contemplate it and a more humane outlook in dealing with it. Freud had shown that the unintelligible jumble that makes up a good part of insane manifestations not only becomes comprehensible after the elucidation his methods have made possible, but is actually derived from the same ultimate sources as produce the other order of difficulties in the neurotic and the normal. To be mad, therefore, no longer signifies being entirely "alienated" from the rest of mankind. It has even proved possible by modifying some of Freud's therapeutic technique to bring about cures in certain forms of insanity. What was nothing but gloom, horror and despair has been invested with elements of cheerfulness and hopefulness where they were once conspicuously absent.

Education

Freud's influence in the field of education is equally unmistakable, even if it is often not explicitly acknowledged. His demonstration that children have far greater difficulties in their early development than had been supposed inevitably brought more sympathy, tolerance and understanding for their vagaries in this stage of life. There are grounds for thinking that the child has in the first three or four years of life to recapitulate in a modified fashion some twenty or fifty thousand years of mental evolution. In this perspective it is not surprising that hardly any pass through them unscathed, and that they are always accompanied by neurotic manifestations. Freud uncovered a whole world of phantasy in these early years with its terrible fears, conflicts over hostile and sexual impulses, and the remarkable combination of helplessness with omnipotent wishes. It is therefore no longer believed that punishment is a panacea when a small child exhibits continual tantrums, refuses to eat or persists in bed-wetting. The labeling of such behavior as "naughtiness" is being replaced by the recognition of a problem. All this knowledge has brought the psychiatrist, or medical psychologist, into an entirely new field, one previously reserved for pedagogues and clergy. The whole range of child guidance clinics that have sprung up over the world in the past thirty years are a witness to this revolutionary extension of the psychiatrist's province.

Another result of Freud's work is the gradual understanding that most of the troublesome behavior, anxieties, inhibitions in learning and other difficulties so frequent during school years are indications of imperfect success in surmounting the conflicts of early childhood. The assistance that every new generation imperatively needs from the older one is seen to be even more important than was previously known, but unfortunately also more difficult to render. Incidentally, that the transition from a primary to a secondary school, which used to take place at the age of fourteen, has been advanced a couple of years is the result of Freud's observation that mental puberty distinctly antedates physical puberty.

Psychology

Freud would undoubtedly have ranked his contributions to the science of psychology, the understanding of human nature, as the most important he had to offer. The methods of investigation he devised may be compared with the value the discovery of the microscope had for gross anatomy in founding the new subject of histology. In both cases a hitherto invisible world was revealed. The concept of dynamism, with the light it threw on motivation and causation, replaced the previous descriptive accounts of data, or rather added to and explained them. I shall not attempt to summarize here what Professor McDougall called the "greatest contributions to psychology since Aristotle," but I should like to call special attention to one very unexpected feature of them; the essential significance of psychopathology for normal psychology. Freud viewed mental development as a combination of two factors: a ceaseless search for the endless possible ways in which various fundamental biological drives may achieve satisfaction; and the complicated "reaction-formations" that serve as defenses against the ever-present dread of these drives in their primitive form. Psychopathology is much nearer to the sources of both these sets than is normal psychology; they are magnified under the lens of pathology. Moreover, the changes and disguises the primitive drives undergo are much simpler, and therefore easier to disentangle, with psychopathological manifestations than with the more obscure, i.e. more distorted, expressions of the so-called normal. It sounds paradoxical to maintain that psychology would most profitably be based on psychopathology, but it remains true that so far it is the latter that provides the most promising avenue of approach to the intricate secrets of the normal mind.

And the paradox disappears when one remembers that these two branches are merely two aspects of the same problems and are fundamentally identical.

Philosophy

It has always been true that any advance in psychological knowledge is reflected in a clearer appreciation of philosophical problems, so it is not surprising to learn that Freud's work has had a number of repercussions in this most august field of thought. His investigation of the unconscious has thrown new light on two of the most debated questions of philosophy: the problem of free will and the relativity of ethics. With both, some justification has been found for each of the fiercely contested sides of the dispute, and a possibility of reconciliation proffered.

In the examples investigated of apparent free will, sometimes called uncaused volition, it has been possible to detect in the unconscious the motive determining the conscious decision or selection, thus supporting the determinist position. But since this is unknown to the subject he is justified in claiming his act as spontaneous and emanating solely from his ego, the more so since in fact it does commonly proceed from unconscious parts of the ego

The same source of information similarly illuminates the difficult problem of whether there is an absolute and objective standard accessible to research in ethics or whether all standards observed are purely relative to racial factors, social situations and individual constitutions. What seems to speak so convincingly for the former view is, as Kant insisted, that in moral crises the voice of conscience may assert "This is right" with such an incontrovertible air of final authority that it is hard not to believe in its representing a basic law of the universe. Yet even here Freud was able to penetrate into the obscure problems of the origin and status of conscience, together with the sense of morality, and to show good reason for supposing that it has an entirely naturalistic basis. His work on the Oedipal genesis of the super-ego is being taken more and more into account by philosophers,[1] nor should one forget his suggestions concerning a probable prehistoric, phylogenetic background.

Anthropology, Sociology, Religion, Art, Literature

Separate chapters in this volume have been devoted to these topics, so that nothing further needs to be added here.

Criminology

In this field Freud's contributions have already borne considerable fruit. The central importance of the individual's responses to his family upbringing is generally recognized. Not that this matter is so simple as is sometimes supposed. It is clear, for instance, that with juvenile delinquency the ego ideal often gets attached to the attitude of rebelliousness, so that conformity with the customary moral standards is regarded with contempt, and this may happen even where the family influences would appear, without deeper investigation, to be favorable enough.

More startling was Freud's discovery of what an important factor in criminology the deep-seated "need for punishment" could be. In order to assuage a primordial and unbearable sense of guilt, of which the subject may be quite unaware, criminal actions may be undertaken in circumstances where detection and punishment are easy to expect. What percentage of criminal acts is dictated by this curious motive is as yet unknown, but it is likely to be greater than might be expected. The old saying that the murderer always leaves his visiting card is based on a similar piece of insight.

More readily understandable are the numerous cases where unsatisfied sexual impulses urge the person to commit acts which in his unconscious adequately symbolize either that impulse itself or one inherently connected with it. In kleptomania, for example, the object abstracted may have a variety of unconscious meanings, and the obsessive act represent a medley of related sexual and hostile motives.

Even the administration of the law, though to a much less extent its formulation, show perceptible signs of influence radiating from Freud's insight. It is quite common nowadays for various sexual perversions to be recognized as neuroses rather than vices, and the person charged in court simply recommended to seek psychological treatment. It would be hard to find instances of this a quarter of a century ago. It is in consequence reasonable to hope that this more humane attitude may extend to certain other forms of criminal misdemeanor, and that purely legalistic criteria be tempered by some knowledge of the complexities of human motivation.

Social Life

Divagations in behavior from the accepted code of sexual morals do not provoke now the strength of reprobation that they did fifty, or even thirty, years ago, and assuredly the freedom with which sexual topics can now be discussed socially is far greater than then. Many factors, economic, political and social, have contributed to bring about these changes, so that it is peculiarly difficult to isolate among them the influence of Freud's work. One must, however, suppose it to have been very considerable and to have been exercised both directly and indirectly.[2] Even the knowledge that sexual habits may have a bearing on matters of health seems to be fairly widespread, so that doctors' inquiries into this sphere do not give the offence they would have previously.

More unequivocal examples of Freud's influence on society are not hard to find. To no one else can be ascribed the knowledge, common among educated people, that dreams have a meaning, and one of considerable personal significance. People are becoming more cautious about relating their dreams in the casual way they used to. With such people there is, of course, little technical knowledge about the methods of interpretation of dreams, but nevertheless episodes and emotions occurring in them are often taken more seriously and provoke some measure of reflection.

Similar remarks might be made about the mistakes in daily life, the forgettings, mislayings, slips of the tongue and pen and so on. Such occurrences are no longer always passed by as "accidental," and often enough an approximately correct interpretation of them is made with disquieting consequences. But this has the advantage of inculcating some recognition of the complexities of the human soul and tolerance for the discovery that none of us is made in one piece.

Most important, however, is the increasing sense people have of being moved by obscure forces within themselves which they are unable to define. Few thinking people nowadays would claim a complete knowledge of themselves or that what they are consciously aware of comprises the whole of their mentality. And this recognition, with all its formidable consequences for the future of social organization, we owe above all to Freud.

In his book *Group Psychology* and elsewhere Freud threw a good deal of light on the complex problems of social cohesion and social behavior. The parallels he drew between group and individual motivation were more than analogies. They point to a profound genetic connection, and in consequence it has become increasingly hard for sociologists to pursue their investigations of institutions on a social basis alone. If, for instance, we are ever to come nearer to the apparently insoluble problem of the most suitable form of Government, it can only be through taking seriously into account the comparison between the relations of governed to governors and that of children to parents, and also those between children themselves.

The necessity for power and force in restrained measure and, on the other hand, the almost invariable abuse of such power provide problems the solution of which would benefit the world enormously. There is a psychological approach available, the investigation of the particular type of person who seeks power. The motivation here will probably turn out to be more complex than might appear and to be connected with mysterious inner needs which impel toward that particular expression. Such considerations have also an obvious bearing on the overridingly important matter of international relations if these are ever to be lifted above their present childish level of fear, suspicion and enmity.

At a deeper level still, and probably underlying all the others, is the basic problem of sexual relations between persons of opposite sexes as well as those between persons of the same sex. It is on our ability to find solutions for it that our whole community life depends. Much advance has undoubtedly been made in the past twenty thousand years, and yet much more remains to be accomplished. Every form of marriage relationship so far attempted, for instance, has been accompanied by serious disadvantages. Polygamy, monogamy, easy divorce: none provides a satisfactory solution. If one is ever to be found it can only be based on Freud's discovery that the sexual attitudes and peculiarities of the adult are derived from variations in the sexual development during childhood, including the relationship between child and parent.

When we consider the breath-taking achievements of man in art and in science we must judge that no limits are foreseeable to his power to attain happiness and security. But this vision is offset by one as somber as that is glowing. In it are three main strands. The advances in medical science, which are now bound to continue rapidly, combined with the increase in general prosperity, have diminished the natural selection of quality. They have also brought about such an enormous increase in quantity of population that the time cannot be far distant when the resources of the earth to sustain it will be seriously strained. Moreover, greed and lack of foresight have not only failed to nourish those resources, ultimately the soil and the minerals of the earth's crust, but are ruining them at a truly alarming pace. Still graver is the consideration that man's destructive powers have been so fortified by the recently acquired knowledge of new weapons that it is now within his reach to achieve devastation beside which the efforts of an Attila, a Timurlane or a Genghis Khan are but the puny gestures of an infant. It is now no longer massacre that is threatened, but the possible extinction of all life on this planet. There needs only a madman in the seat of authority of the kind we have just witnessed to set this holocaust ablaze, nor can we be sure that someone less mad may not bring it about.

Amid the turmoil of conflicting ideas in which we live, in the spheres of art, of science, and above all of politics where statesmen of towering importance can display in their savagery, fear and unreasonableness all the worst features of an undisciplined nursery, there seems to be one proposition commanding nearly universal assent. *The control man has secured over nature has far outrun his control over himself.* Man's unhappiness and the threats of doom overhanging him proceed from this unassailable truth. Man's chief enemy and danger is his own unruly nature and the dark forces pent up within him.

If our race is lucky enough to survive for another thousand years the name of Sigmund Freud will be remembered as that of the man who first ascertained the origin and nature of those forces, and pointed the way to achieving some measure of control over them.

Appendix A

Miscellaneous Extracts from Correspondence

1. To ALBERT MORDELL. MAY 21, 1920.
   (*One of the many encouraging letters to young authors.*)

"Dear Mr. Mordell:

"I have indeed read your book[1] with great interest and am glad you were able to do for the English-American literature something similar to what Rank did for the German in his book on the Incest Motive. I should also like to tell you not to take so hard the attacks and unfavorable criticisms. At present there is nothing else to be expected, and besides one good criticism by Havelock Ellis outweighs a couple of dozen bad ones. I hope you will continue your literary studies and often give us pleasure with their results.

"*Mit herzlichem Gruss und Hochachtung*

"*Ihr*

"Freud"

2. To LOU ANDREAS-SALOMÉ. October 20, 1921.
   (*L. A.-S. had accepted an invitation to stay with the Freuds. The revolution had cut off the considerable income she had formerly derived from Russia.*)

Verehrteste Frau:

". . . I am touching on one point to do with your journey without any fear of misinterpretation. If the severing of connection with your fatherland has impaired your freedom in traveling please let me send you from Hamburg some money for the journey. My son-in-law there takes care of what marks I hold; my practice has made me relatively rich in good foreign currency (American, English, Swiss). And I should like to get some pleasure out of my new wealth."

3. To ARTHUR SCHNITZLER. May 14, 1922.

(*I am abstracting with his approval one of the Freud letters which Schnitzler's son has published.*)[2]

"*Verehrter Herr Doktor:*

"Now you too have reached the age of sixty, while I, six years older, am approaching the end of life and may soon expect to see the close of the fifth act of this pretty incomprehensible and not always amusing comedy.

"Had I still retained any belief in the 'omnipotence of thoughts' I should not let pass this opportunity of sending you the strongest and warmest good wishes for the future years you may expect. I leave this foolish performance to the countless numbers of your contemporaries who will have you in mind on May 15.

"But I shall make a confession to you which I will ask you to be good enough to keep to yourself and not share it with any friends. I have plagued myself over the question how it comes about that in all these years I have never sought your company and enjoyed a conversation with you (assuming that it would not have been unwelcome to you).

"The answer is this much too intimate confession. I think I have avoided you from a kind of awe of meeting my 'double.' * Not that I am in general easily inclined to identify myself with anyone else or that I had any wish to overlook the difference in our gifts that divides me from you, but whenever I get deeply interested in your beautiful creations I always seem to find behind their poetic sheen the same presuppositions, interests and conclusions as those familiar to me as my own. Your determinism and your scepticism—what people call pessimism—your deep grasp of the truths of the unconscious and of the biological nature of man, the way you take to pieces the social conventions of our society, and the extent to which your thoughts are preoccupied with the polarity of love and death; all that moves me with an uncanny feeling of familiarity. So the impression has been borne in on me that you know through intui-

* *Doppelgängerscheu.*

tion—really from a delicate self-observation—everything that I have discovered in other people by laborious work. Indeed I believe that fundamentally you are an explorer of the depths, as honestly impartial and unperturbed as ever anyone was, and that had you not been so your artistic gifts, your mastery of language and your creativeness would have had free play and made you into something more pleasing to the multitude. It is natural to me to prefer the investigator. But forgive me for drifting into psychoanalysis; I simply can't do anything else. I know, however, that psychoanalysis is not the means of making oneself popular.

> *"In herzlicher Ergebenheit*
> *"Ihr Freud"*

4. To Lou Andreas-Salomé. August 5, 1923.
"Liebste Lou:

"I have been horrified to learn from a good source that you are analyzing for ten hours a day. Naturally I regard it as a badly concealed attempt at suicide. That astonishes me very much, since so far as I know you have very little neurotic feelings of guilt. I conjure you to cease this by raising your fees in some correspondence with the cascading fall of the mark. The chorus of fairies who surrounded your cradle apparently omitted to bestow on you the gift of reckoning. Please do not wave aside my warning."

5. To Lou Andreas-Salomé. May 13, 1924.
Liebste Lou:

"I have seldom admired your tact so much as in your last letter. There is someone who, instead of working on properly into old age and then dying without any preliminaries, goes and acquires a horrible disease in middle life, has to be treated and operated on, has to live with discomforts and affect those around him with them, and then goes on crawling around for an indefinite time as an invalid; in *Erewhon*—I hope you know Samuel Butler's brilliant phantasy—such a person would inevitably be punished and locked up. And yet you manage to praise me for having borne my suffering so wonderfully. Even that is not true; I have stood the foul realities pretty well, but I don't bear well the thought of the possibilities in front of me, and I can't get used to the idea of an existence on sufferance."

6. To MARIE BONAPARTE. April 7, 1926.
"Meine liebe Prinzessin:

"In what you say about Laforgue and the trauma of weaning I have once more admired your judgment. Naturally what is concealed behind it is the denial of the castration complex. Rank, from whom this tendency dates, had openly admitted it in the book he wrote with Ferenczi. The main objection to the theory is clinical experience which shows the castration complex in a tangible form, but not the other."

7. To MARIE BONAPARTE. April 16, 1926.
"Meine liebe Prinzessin:

"I am not surprised that the phrase 'the eternal suckling' has somewhat impressed you. There is indeed something in it. Oral erotism is the first erotic manifestation, just as the nipple is the first sexual object; the libido is led along definite paths from these first positions into the new organizations. But the question that interests us is not the *genetic* one, but the *dynamic* one. Even if the idea of losing the genital organ has a normal prototype, it is only with castration that the danger of loss becomes pathogenic: since only the penis carries the colossal narcissistic cathexis that corresponds with the importance of propagation. Furthermore, as you very rightly emphasize, all the cultural associations are related to the genitals, not to the oral location. Abraham has expounded at length the character traits, preferences, antipathies and peculiarities that may be left over from the oral phase. Generally symptoms also come about through regression to this phase, which provide an excuse for the exaggerations of our friends."

8. To FRANZ ALEXANDER. May 17, 1926.
(*A reassurance after sending a previous letter containing some criticism.*)

"Lieber Herr Doktor:

"It is unnecessary to assure you that your letter gave me great pleasure. Perhaps equally unnecessary to repeat that all of us count you as one of our strongest hopes for the future. But, after all, not quite unnecessary, since it probably does a young man good when from time to time he hears a friendly word from an old man. It is only the end part of your letter that I do not quite approve;

it sounds too resigned and too unassuming. I never intended to dispirit you. I do not believe that you and other colleagues will have to content yourselves with the working out and making a synthesis of our present analytical knowledge. You cannot divine what greater tasks may lie before you, and as you resolve them may you recall some friendly thoughts of me."

9. To Franz Alexander. July 23, 1926.
"Lieber Herr Doktor:

"I read through the manuscript of your book at one sitting the day it came, and enjoyed it very much. It is good to know that there is someone who can do such work, in whose head my abstractions gain life and will grow further.

"I find it much harder than you know to accept the modifications the material must undergo when someone else treats it—probably because my own train of thought proceeds so obsessively. So you must take the comments I shall make on your first lectures as expressions of this narcissistic narrowmindedness and not as contradictions of your work. I had not begun with the new concept of the super-ego, but with a presentation of the conditions impelling to its formation. It is clear that this is the dark part of the super-ego conception, and that further progress has to start there. That the sub-dividing of the super-ego into an ego and pure id components gives the explanation I do not find a compelling or satisfying answer. Your dramatic or personifying presentation could be in part replaced by uncovering the economic necessity and then come later as a sort of 'secondary elaboration.' You bring out very well the complementary conditioning of punishment and gratification. That is evidently your main interest; from my approbation you will guess correctly that I had myself already followed this path of generalizing. I halted then because the proof with the conversion hysteria was wanting. Have you found it? Your formula for distinguishing the three mechanisms is fascinating: simultaneous gratification together; simultaneous gratification separately; gratification of one before the other. I hope to find in a later lecture that this sequence corresponds with a gradual weakening in the synthetic power of the ego; that is to say a further diffusion of the instincts." [b]

[b] *Zunahme der Triebentmischung.*

10. To Marie Bonaparte. September 13, 1926.

(*In answer to a question concerning the translating of the Schreber case history.*)

"*Meine liebe Prinzessin:*

"I had asked a pupil in Dresden[c]—who later fell in the war—to procure for me information about Schreber, which I naturally made no use of in my paper. I learned from him that Schreber was fifty-three years old when the disorder broke out, in the male menopause, so to speak. Furthermore, that my guess was correct about his having lost an older brother by death. Evidently it was from him that the transference to Flechsig took place. Then that after being discharged he lived at home contentedly for a number of years until his wife fell ill of a severe apoplexy. After that he felt insecure and again entered the hospital. There was no later information, but it may be guessed that the motive for his illness was the turning away from his wife and his dissatisfaction over her not bearing any children. With the apoplexy feelings of guilt and of temptation returned."

11. To Marie Bonaparte. March 19, 1928.

"*Meine liebe* Marie:

"You are right: one is in danger of overestimating the frequency of an irreligious attitude among intellectuals. I get convinced of that just now on observing the reactions to my 'Illusion.'[d] That comes from the most varied drinks being offered under the name of 'religion,' with a minimal percentage of alcohol—really nonalcoholic; but they still get drunk on it. The old drinkers were after all a respectable body, but to get tipsy on pomerit (apple-juice) is really ridiculous."

12. To Franz Alexander. May 13, 1928.

"*Lieber Herr Doktor:*

"I can only thank you half-heartedly for your friendly birthday congratulations, i.e. absolve you, since I had begged all my friends to take no further notice of the day.

"I have read your criticism of the draft on the subject of training. They are practical questions which as a rule I keep back from answering. But it seems to me that your counter-proposal does not take into account important practical considerations. I am afraid that

[c] A. Stegmann.
[d] *The Future of an Illusion*, 1927.

renouncing any preliminary choice (of candidates) would threaten us with an excess of work that would often be useless. There is no assurance that the analysis would bring about the necessary character changes, and in any event it presupposes years of effort; you could hardly expect that to be agreed on in Vienna, for example, where almost all the training analyses are carried out gratis. Moreover, one ought to demand guarantees from the candidates which are not necessary with patients, since regular analytic work has deleterious effects on one's psyche just as work with Roentgen rays has on one's tissues; it needs to be countered by steady hard work. Finally, since rejection by an analytical society[e] possesses neither legal nor practical powers, I am afraid that just the candidates who fail would, insisting on their long analysis, turn into wild analysts."

13. To Lou Andreas-Salomé. July 28, 1929.
"*Liebste* Lou:

"You will with your usual acuteness have guessed why I have been so long in answering your letter. Anna has already told you that I am writing something, and today I have written the last sentence, which—so far as is possible here without a library—finishes the work.[3] It deals with civilization, consciousness of guilt, happiness and similar lofty matters, and it strikes me, without doubt rightly so, as very superfluous, in contradistinction from earlier works, in which there was always a creative impulse. But what else should I do? I can't spend the whole day in smoking and playing cards, I can no longer walk far, and the most of what there is to read does not interest me any more. So I wrote, and the time passed that way quite pleasantly. In writing this work I have discovered afresh the most banal truths.

"Thomas Mann's essay is certainly an honor.[4] It gives me the impression that he had an essay on romanticism ready to hand when he was requested to write something about me, so he furnished the essay at the beginning and at the end with a veneer of psychoanalysis (as the cabinet maker would say); the body is of a different substance. However, when Mann says something it is always pertinent.

"What you have to say concerning the analysis of my productions interests me to the full and finds me with no opinion about it. I only know that I have given myself a loathsome amount of trouble, so that the rest was obvious. It should have been done much

[e] I.e. if the results of the training analysis are unsatisfactory.

better. I only took notice of the topic, not of myself. My worst attributes, among them a certain indifference toward the world, have assuredly had the same share in the end result as my good ones, e.g. a defiant courage about truth. But in the depths of my being I remain convinced that my dear fellow-creatures are—with individual exceptions—good for nothing.[*]

"I should have greatly enjoyed continuing this talk with you in our idyllic beautiful and peaceful Schneewincelchan if I could only have invited you here. But there is no room in the house, and not an attic to let in Berchtesgaden. We have had all possible visitors, including my three sons in turn, two of whom found at last some accommodation at a considerable distance. Ernst and Lux have taken advantage of Anna's absence and are staying with us. Anna, according to her telegraphic reports, is having a rather hard time in Oxford; by this evening she will have given her paper and after that will feel easier. She describes the accommodation there with the words 'more tradition than comfort.' You know that the English once they had created the conception of comfort have not been willing to have anything more to do with the thing itself.

. . .

"Ihr alter

"Freud"

14. To Marie Bonaparte. January 15, 1930.

"You know that with psychoses of that kind we can do nothing through analysis. Above all a normal ego is wanting with which one can enter into contact. We know that the mechanisms of the psychoses are in essence no different from those of the neuroses, but we do not have at our disposal the quantitative stimulation necessary for changing them. The hope of the future here lies in organic chemistry or the access to it through endocrinology. This future is still far distant, but one should study analytically every case of psychosis because this knowledge will one day guide the chemical therapy."

15. To A. A. Roback. February 20, 1930.
"Dear Dr. Roback.

"I hasten to acknowledge the receipt of your book 'Jewish Influence, etc.' and to thank you for it. I have not delayed in reading the reprint you sent with it and have also looked through the book.

[*] *Gesindel.*

"I cannot avoid confessing a certain disappointment. In the book you honor me highly, mention my name together with the greatest names of our people (which far transcends my ambition), and so on; in the chapter of the doctrine of Lapses you express disbelief concerning just that part of psychoanalysis that has most readily found general recognition. How then are you likely to judge our other less attractive discoveries? My impression is that if your objections to the conception of lapses are justified I have very little claim to be named beside Bergson and Einstein among the intellectual sovereigns. . . .

"I have not yet fully read your section on psychoanalysis. I fear to find there incorrect statements that I shall regret. In many of your statements I do not recognize myself: for example, no one has before now reproached me with having mystical leanings; in the question of hypnosis I took sides against Charcot, though not entirely with Bernheim."

16. To A. A. Roback. March 24, 1930.
"Dear Dr. Roback,

"I got your letter today together with a small library of your writings, and do not want to postpone thanking you until I have read them. I also feel impelled to put an end to a situation which is a very unusual one for me. For more than thirty years I have let people talk and write about myself and my doctrines whatever they like and contradict them only in quite exceptional instances (e.g. in the 'History of the Psycho-Analytical Movement'). I also know very well that nothing I might say would be of any use, since people feel the need to express themselves thus and not otherwise. And now I am finding myself involved with you in an exchange of criticisms and counter-criticisms, although I cannot deny you too the right to say things about me as freely and as incorrectly as you please. I know that my exceptional behavior comes from your having touched on the Jewish side, which so easily evokes an echo in me. My sympathy was aroused by it, and I was sorry to find a discrepancy between the high position you are prepared to grant me and your knowledge of my person or your understanding of my work. No offence, I hope. I will not do it again.

"I am glad to hear that you yourself take criticism well. I shall give you the opportunity of doing so, through two remarks concerning myself and psychoanalysis.

"You write that you have said nothing unpleasant about me that is not already known. But where did you get your knowledge of me? From Wittels' biography, a truly murky source.

"In my opinion one may ask of a critical spirit that he submits the credibility of his authorities to some examination. The book by Wittels was written after many years of estrangement from me and my circle and under the hostile influence of Stekel; consequently it is overrich in errors of fact as well as erroneous views. When he broke with Stekel a little while later and applied to be accepted in our Society he promised to disavow the book in some way, to stop its publication or to correct the offensive parts in it. I have not bothered to find out whether, or in what way, he has kept his promise. According to him I am extraordinarily revengeful. Whoever has enough respect for everything that is in print is welcome to believe that. A truly critical person would probably not commit himself to a judgment merely because he has read it in a book, when he knows nothing of the author or how the book came to be written.

"Here is the second critical remark. I infer from your arguments against many parts of the psychoanalytical theory that you personally have had very little opportunity to form a sound judgment; that you have never yourself carried out an analysis, never learned how to, and never passed through the irreplaceable discipline of a personal analysis. You are certainly not the only one—in America or Europe —who with such an imperfect preliminary education condemns analysis in public. On the contrary, most of our opponents are in the same situation, just like an anatomist who criticizes histology without looking through a microscope. And I admit that you are not one of the malicious or quite stupid ones. But you will perhaps understand it when we confess that the objections of this inexperienced and ingenuous person make for the most part no impression on us.

"When you replace 'mystical' by 'speculative leanings'—the two things are not the same, and psychoanalysis is an empirically based doctrine—I am willing to agree. When you give your youth as an excuse for this mistake it gives me the opportunity of admitting a mistake I made about you; I had assumed, from the air of great certitude in all your statements, that you must be a dignified old gentleman. In your interest I am glad to be wrong. I had overlooked what the effect must be of a conjuncture of American-democratic outlook and Jewish 'Chuzpah.' " [g]

[g] Impudence.

17. To Richard Flatter. March 30, 1930.

"Dear Dr. Flatter:

"Many thanks for the copy of your translation of *King Lear* you kindly sent me. It gave me the occasion to read that powerful work once more.

"As to your question whether we are justified in regarding Lear as a case of hysteria I should like to say that one has scarcely the right to expect a poet to present us with clinically perfect examples of mental illness. It should be enough if our instinctive reaction is nowhere upset, and if what may be called our popular psychiatry allows us to follow in all his vagaries the person who is depicted as abnormal.

"This is so in the case of Lear. We are not shocked to see that in his mortification he loses his contact with reality, nor that, clinging to the trauma, he indulges in phantasies of vengeance; nor that, in the extravagance of his passion, he storms and rages—although such behavior would disrupt the character of a consistent psychosis. I am not sure, though, whether such psychoses, mixed of affective clinging to the trauma and psychotic turning away from it, do not occur in real life often enough.

"His quieting down and his normal response when he realizes he is safe in Cordelia's protection do not seem to me to justify a diagnosis of hysteria.

"Sincerely yours
"Freud"

18. To Lou Andreas-Salomé. April 3, 1931.

Liebe Lou:

"From the new number of the *Psychoanalytische Bewegung* I gather that not long ago you must have reached the age of seventy.

"You get no recognition for this discreetness.

"Somewhere or other there must be a limit to dignity and a thought for friendship; otherwise it runs the risk of being confounded with haughtiness. Perhaps I should have been glad of the chance of saying to you on your birthday how greatly I esteem and love you.

"Hearty Greetings from what is left of

"your
"Freud"

19. To Lou ANDREAS-SALOMÉ. May, 1931.

(*L. A.-S. had written an essay on her relations with Freud and psychoanalysis. It appeared years later in her posthumously published autobiography.*)

"*Liebe* Lou:

"I am writing to you again before I get your reply, because now I have had time to read through your essay.

"It certainly has not often happened to me that I admire a psychoanalytical essay instead of criticizing it, but I have to this time. It is the most beautiful thing of yours I have ever read, an involuntary proof of your superiority over all of us—in accord with the heights from which you descended to us. It is a true synthesis, not the nonsensical efforts (confined to therapy) of our opponents, but a true scientific one in which one can have confidence and where you transform back again into a living organism the collection of nerves, tendons and blood vessels into which the analytic knife has turned the body. Could we only magnify in a plastic way what you have sketched with your fine brush we should perhaps be able to grasp the final truths.

"Not everything you deal with was clear to me at once, and not all of it equally worth knowing. But, despite what some people say, I am no artist; I could never have depicted the effects of light and color, only hard outlines."

20. To EDOARDO WEISS. April 24, 1932.

"What you relate about your occult experiences interested me very much, but also made me a little anxious. My point of view is not that of arrogant rejection *a limine*. Let me explain it more exactly. When I watch a conjuror's performance who charms pigeons out of a hat I am quite unable to understand how he does it. But it doesn't perturb me, because there is no claim of supernatural powers connected with it. Now I think that so long as these mediums work in the dark, in conditions which restrict so greatly the observer's capacity for judgment, they do not deserve any more confidence being placed in them than the conjurors. Nor do they turn out anything useful, and over and over again they are detected as cheats. In all probability your medium is no better. I am, it is true, prepared to believe that behind all so-called occult phenomena lies something new and very important: the fact of thought-transference, i.e. the transferring of psychical processes through space to other people. I know of proofs of this from observations made in daylight and am thinking of expressing my opinion publicly about it. Naturally it would be unfavorable for the part you play as the pioneer of psychoanalysis in Italy were you to proclaim yourself at the same time a partisan of occultism."

21. To MARIE BONAPARTE. April 30, 1932.
"*Meine liebe* Marie:

"The questions in your letter provide the analyst with a very interesting theoretical problem. Has psychoanalysis any reason for discountenancing incestuous relations between mother and son? And if so, what are they? They evidently cannot be the usual ones of simple taboo.

"It is very curious—but perhaps easily to be understood—that just the most powerful prohibitions of mankind are those that are hardest to justify. That is because the justifications are prehistoric, taking their root in man's past.

"The situation with incest is just the same as with cannibalism. There are of course real grounds in modern life against slaying a man in order to devour him, but no grounds whatever against eating human flesh instead of animal flesh. Still most of us would find it quite impossible.

"Incest is not so remote, and indeed happens often enough. We can readily see that if generally practiced it would be just as harmful socially today as in ancient times. This social harm is the kernel which has undergone an apotheosis after being adorned by a taboo. In individual exceptional cases incest would even today be harmless, although, it is true, it would still be unsocial as abrogating one of those sexual restrictions necessary to the maintenance of civilization.

"For a particular case there is also the following consideration to be borne in mind. It might be possible for someone who has escaped the influence of the phylogenetic repressions to allow himself incest without any harm, but one could never be sure of that. These inheritances are often stronger than we are prone to estimate; then the trespass is followed by feelings of guilt against which one is quite helpless."

22. To EDOARDO WEISS. May 8, 1932.
"I want to remove a misunderstanding. A psychoanalyst's refraining from taking part publicly in occult studies is a purely practical

measure, and only a temporary one, not at all an expression of principle. Contemptuous rejection of these studies without any experience of them would really be to imitate the pitiful example of our opponents. In this matter I think just the same as you. Furthermore that to take flight, in a cowardly fashion and behind the shelter of disdain, from the allegedly 'supernatural' shows very little confidence in the trustworthiness of our scientific *Weltanschauung*.

"The medium business, however, is a disagreeable chapter. The unquestionable deceptions on the part of mediums, the simpleminded and tricky nature of their performances, the difficulties of testing them in the peculiar conditions obtaining, the obvious impossibility of many of their claims; all that calls for the utmost caution. There must surely be better ways of showing what is real in the occult. The techniques used up till now are too reminiscent of the traveling and currency restrictions which do not work any better."

23. To A. A. ROBACK. June 11, 1932.

(*In reference to a statement of Adler's that Freud used to consult him about his patients.*)

"Thank you for the explanations in your letter. The account Adler gave you is a distorted aspersion, which cannot surprise anyone who knew him. It can only relate to a single case: a cousin of his whom he brought to me for treatment and whose hystero-epileptic attacks only increased during the analysis. When I gave up treating her it was only natural that I discussed the case with him. That is what he calls 'appealing to him.' He astonished me even then by his opinion that the treatment had been very successful!"

24. To RICHARD FLATTER. September 20, 1932.[h]
"Dear Dr. Flatter:
"Thank you for sending me your translations of the *Sonnets*. I confess my amazement at seeing them translated in such a fashion. Some of them read as if they were originals. And I know how difficult it is to render such brief poems adequately.

"What you say in your letter about the appreciation of the *Sonnets* seems to me obsolete, by which I mean that there can no longer be any doubt concerning their serious nature and their value as self-confessions. This is, I think, to be accounted for by the fact

[h] This and the previously quoted letter to Dr. Flatter were published in the *Shakespeare Quarterly*, II, No. 4, October 1951.

that they were published without the author's cooperation and passed on after his death to a public for whom they had not been intended.

"The contents have been used to ascertain the poet's identity, which is still doubtful. There lies in front of me a book by Gerald H. Rendall: *Shakespeare's Sonnets and Edward de Vere*, 1930. It puts forward the thesis that those poems were addressed to the Earl of Southampton and written by the Earl of Oxford. I am indeed almost convinced that none other than this aristocrat was our Shakespeare. In the light of that conception the *Sonnets* become much more understandable.

"Yours very sincerely,

"Freud"

25. To EDOARDO WEISS. September 22, 1932.
"Lieber Herr Doktor:

"You are quite right again. I greatly regret the way I keep getting taken in by these reporters. One feels oneself obliged to make a few polite remarks, and ought to reckon every time with their being misused. I can at least assure you that each of them takes me in only once."

26. To MARIE BONAPARTE. February 19, 1934.
"Meine liebe Marie:

"Again warm thanks for repeating your invitation. It is naturally invaluable to know that a beautiful spot exists where one would be welcome until a new home could be found. But it is assuredly understandable that I am in no hurry to leave the old home, especially since I have four bodily troubles that would make so much harder any change of domicile. So everything turns on whether we feel compelled to flee from Vienna. It is hard to judge that; no one can be sure about it, for the future is unpredictable. Only one thing seems clear to me. The decision is not urgent; we shall have weeks, probably months, to think it over.

"If the Nazis come here and make one stateless, as they have in Germany, then of course we shall have to leave. I am rather inclined to believe, however, that we shall get a fascism of an Austrian kind, which with all its discomforts would be much easier to endure, so that one could stay. That there is a risk of personal danger, as Ruth and Mark are never tired of telling me, I can hardly believe. I am pretty well unknown in Austria; the best informed only know that any ill-treatment of me would provoke a great stir abroad."

27. To James S. H. Bransom. March 25, 1934.

"Dear Mr. Bransom:

"I have been eagerly studying your study of Lear and have come to the following conclusions. You are right; the last small section of the book discloses the secret meaning of the tragedy, the repressed incestuous claims on the daughter's love. In the beginnings of the human family, we assume, all females belonged to the father; the daughters were his sexual objects no less than their mothers. Enough of that attitude has been retained in actual life of the present day; in the unconscious these ancient wishes remain in all their force. A poet may dimly perceive them more strongly than other people and try to find expression for them. Shakespeare showed us in *Hamlet* how sensitive he was to another of these repressed attitudes, the Oedipus complex.

"Your supposition illuminates the riddle of Cordelia as well as that of Lear. The elder sisters have already overcome the fateful love for the father and become hostile to him; to speak analytically, they are resentful at the disappointment in their early love. Cordelia still clings to him; her love for him is her holy secret. When asked to reveal it publicly she has to refuse defiantly and remain dumb. I have seen just that behavior in many cases.

"I have already taken the liberty of hinting to you my belief in the identity of Shakespeare with Edward de Vere, the seventeenth Earl of Oxford. Let us see if this assumption contributes anything to the understanding of the tragedy. Oxford really had three grown-up daughters (other children had died young, including the only son): Elizabeth, born 1575, Bridget 1584 and Susan 1587. I will call your attention to a striking change Shakespeare made in his material. In all the accounts of the sources the daughters are unmarried at the time of the love test and got married only later.[5] In Shakespeare the two elder are married at that time (Goneril already pregnant), and Cordelia still single. When we date the composition of Lear—surely with right—in the poet's late years then we have a striking agreement. Elizabeth married Lord Derby in 1595; Bridget married Lord Norris in 1599. Since Oxford died in 1604 and Susan, our Cordelia, married Lord Pembroke only in 1605, she was single throughout her father's lifetime. We have, of course, to take it that Lear was composed after 1599, naturally before 1604.[6]

"The other, decisive change the poet made in his material was, as is well known, that he depicted Lear as insane, and he did so of his own initiative without any support from the sources. We may perhaps understand that if we consider the analogy of the 'absurd' in dreams. This signifies a forceful rejection of the content of the dream, as much as to say 'it would be nonsensical to believe such a thing.' Shakespeare could have done the same if his sexual desires for the daughters came too near to his consciousness: meaning 'only a madman would have such desires.' Lear had to be mad just because the True Chronicle History had stressed his excessive love for his daughters. Is it not curious, by the way, that in the play that deals with the father's relations to his three daughters there is no mention whatever of the mother, and after all there must have been one. This is one of the traits that gives the tragedy a rather harsh note of inhumanity. If Shakespeare was Lord Oxford the figure of the father who gave all he had to his children must have had for him a special compensatory attraction, since Edward de Vere was the exact opposite, an inadequate father who never did his duty by his children. A squanderer of his inheritance and a miserable manager of his affairs, oppressed by debts, he could not maintain his family, did not live with them, and left the education and care of his three daughters to their grandfather, Lord Burleigh. His marriage with Ann Cecil turned out very unhappily. If he was Shakespeare he had himself experienced Othello's torments.

"When one compares the date of Oxford's death (1604) with the dates of publication and the state of the text one surmises that the poet did not finish one play after another but for a long period worked at several together, so that several of them were not finished when he died. They were then somehow completed by his friends and colleagues and arranged for performance and publication. (Lord Derby, his first son-in-law—to be equated with Albany in Lear and Horatio in Hamlet—is the name of a favorite cousin of Oxford's, Horatio de Vere).

"In an early essay 'The Theme of the Three Caskets' (1913) I gave another interpretation of the Lear story, which only appears to contradict yours. What I tried to establish there was the mythological content of the material, to which the connection between father and daughter was originally alien. With the insertion of this feature the saga gains a psychological interest which puts the earlier one in the background; I hope to show that in Shakespeare's Lear the old meaning shimmers at times through the new one.

> "Mit ergebenen Grüssen
> "Ihr Freud"

28. To ARNOLD ZWEIG. May 11, 1934.

(*Commenting on Arnold Zweig's plan of writing a book on Nietzsche's illness.*)

"It seems that we touch here on the problem of poetic license versus historical reality. I know that in that matter I am rather conservative. Where there is an unbridgeable gap in history or biography a writer may step in and try to guess how things were. An uninhabited country he may well settle with the creatures of his imagination. Even if the happenings are known but are far removed and alien to common knowledge he can disregard them. Thus it is no valid criticism of Shakespeare that about the year 1000 Macbeth was a just and benevolent King of Scotland. On the other hand he should respect reality where it is established and has become common property. Bernard Shaw, who makes his Caesar gape at a stony Sphinx as if he were a Cook's tourist, and forget to take leave of Cleopatra when he sails from Egypt, shows what a clown he is who puts jesting above everything else. The historical Caesar got her to come to Rome after her Caesarion was born, where she remained until she took flight after his murder. Writers, it is true, do not often keep to these rules; Schiller does not in *Don Carlos*, nor Goethe in *Egmont* or *Götz von Berlichingen*, etc. But it is mostly not for the better when they disregard them.

"Now when it is a question of a person of our time with such a living influence as has Friedrich Nietzsche, a picture of his being and his destiny should have the same aim as a portrait, i.e., however the conception be elaborated the main point should be the resemblance. And since the subject cannot sit for the artist one has first to collect so much material about him that all that remains is to complete it with a penetrating understanding. Otherwise what happens is the same as with the devoted son and the Hungarian painter: 'Poor Father; how greatly you have changed.' Then just think, what are we to do with an imaginary Friedrich Nietzsche? Whether there exists enough material for such a portrait you should know. Podach's book seems to have made you confident about that. But with Friedrich Nietzsche there is something that goes beyond what is usual. There is also an illness, and that is harder to explicate and reconstruct; that is to say, there are no doubt psychical processes in a certain sequence, but not always psychical motives generating them, and one can go very much astray in trying to unravel these. Anyhow a non-expert has not much interest in the details of an illness.

"I cannot say whether these are my true reasons against your plan. Perhaps they have something to do with the way in which you compare me to him. In my youth he signified a nobility to which I could not attain. A friend of mine, Dr. Paneth, had got to know him in the Engadine[1] and he used to write to me a lot about him. Later on also my attitude toward him was about the same as you described in 'Die Bilanz.' To turn to this book: I have read it and find it very painful. I hope that writing it did you good as a safety valve to discharge your feelings, for I am almost choking with pent-up rancor and fury.[j] I naturally do not believe half of what you write about me. But, all the same, my friend Yvette has a song in her repertoire: '*Ça fait toujours plaisir.*' "

29. To BARON KARL FERDINAND TINTY. (Chicago), July 10, 1934.
"*Sehr geehrter Herr* Baron:

"I was glad to learn from your letter that your interesting plan of making Schellaburg into an international intellectual center has come so near completion.

"When some years ago you offered me your castle to make it into the headquarters of the psychoanalytical movement I had to decline, on the one hand because of our lack of means, and on the other hand because the demands both of therapy and of training tie us to a large city. A quite different possibility would be the employment of psychoanalysis in the framework of your institution. Perhaps that could be arranged, and it would be advantageous for us. But I am no longer the person to decide such matters. My age and impaired health have put me in the background. The persons to whom you should apply when your plan has got far enough are Dr. A. A. Brill, 1 West 70th St., N.Y., President of the American Psychoanalytical Association, and Dr. Ernest Jones, 81, Harley Street, London. President of the whole International Psycho-Analytical Association—both close friends of mine. I hope to hear from both of them about the further developments.

"*Mit den besten Wünschen*
"*Ihr ergebener*
"Freud"

[1] Probably in 1885.
[j] Of course, over the Nazi regime.

30. To Lou Andreas-Salomé. May 16, 1935.
"Liebe Lou:

"When one lives long enough (such as 79) one at last gets a letter and even a picture from you, whatever the latter may look like. I enclose one of myself for you. What an amount of good-naturedness and humor is needed to endure the gruesomeness of growing old. The garden outside and the flowers in the room are beautiful, but the spring is, as we say in Vienna, a mockery.[k] I am finally learning how to freeze. My doctor gives me sugar water to drink against my subnormal temperature which makes one feel miserable.

"Don't expect to hear anything sensible from me. I don't know if I can still write anything creative. I hardly get to it, so occupied am I in looking after my health. This is evidently like the Sibylline books: the less that remains of them, the more precious do they become. Naturally I am more and more dependent on Anna's care of me, just as Mephistopheles once remarked:

'At the end we depend on the creatures we made.'

"At all events it was very wise to have made her. I wish very much I could tell you personally how near to my heart your well-being is.

"Ihr alter
"Freud"

31. To A. A. Roback. October 19, 1936.
"Geehrter Herr Doktor:

"I got today your book on Persetz, which is assured of my interest and for which I thank you. I am less grateful for the news in your letter a few days earlier concerning your plan for celebrating my eightieth birthday. I wonder that you did not get into contact with me before sending out the invitations; that would have been the proper and usual thing to do, unless you wanted to give in to your negative impulses.

"You give a list of the people you have invited to express themselves on the subject of psychoanalysis. Among these are a few who have a right to be heard. All the others either (a) have no connection with analysis, or (b) understand nothing of it, as can easily be demonstrated, or (c) are declared enemies to it. What would emerge in these circumstances could only be thoroughly useless and

[k] *Fopperei.*

disagreeable. I myself naturally am not thinking of participating in any way in the symposium. I can only hope that you yourself will be obliged to drop the matter by most of those invited refusing. I know definitely of one who will not answer: that is Sante de Sanctis, who died in February.

"Nor can your phantasy that I should preside over a Congress to celebrate the jubilee of psychoanalysis be fulfilled. Above all because there is no prospect of such a celebration. Psychoanalysis was born in 1895 or 1900 or in between. When it is fifty years old I shall not be here any more. I do not know what ignorant journalist has been imagining this fairy tale.

"With an expression of my regret that such an accomplished man should be willing to let himself into such an undignified undertaking I greet you as

"*Ihr ergebener*
"Freud"

32. To THOMAS MANN. November 29, 1936.
"*Verehrter Freund:*

"The beneficent personal impressions of your last visit to Vienna keep recurring in my memory. Not long ago I finished reading your new volume of the Joseph story[1] with the sad thought that this great experience is now over, and that I shall probably not be able to read the continuation.

"The impressions of this story, combined with the thoughts about the *gelebte Vita* you expressed in your lecture and the mythological prototype, have led me to develop a set of ideas which give me an occasion for conversing with you, as if you were sitting in my room opposite me, without my expecting either a polite response or any detailed consideration of what I have to say. I myself do not take the idea very seriously, but I find it has a certain charm, rather like what the crack of the whip had for the old postilions.

"Is there an historical person for whom the life of Joseph was a mythical pattern, so that the phantasy of Joseph may be divined as the secret dynamic motor through his whole life? I think Napoleon was such a person.

"(a) He was a Corsican, the second son in a crowd of brothers and sisters. His eldest brother was called Joseph, and this circumstance— in the way the accidental and the inevitable get combined in life— was fateful for him. In a Corsican family the privilege of the eldest

[1] Part of the tetralogy: *Joseph und seine Brüder.*

is surrounded with a quite specially sacred arcana. (I believe Alphonse Daudet once depicted this in a novel. In *Nabab?* Or am I mistaken? Perhaps in some other book, or was it Balzac?) Through this Corsican custom a normal human relation becomes exaggerated. The eldest brother is the natural rival, and the younger cherishes toward him an elemental unfathomably deep enmity, for which in later years the expressions death wish, murderous intention, would apply. To push Joseph aside, to take his place, to become Joseph himself, must have been the little Napoleon's strongest emotion. It is curious, and one often observes it, that just those excessive infantile impulses tend to change round into their opposite. The hated rival becomes a loved being. So it was with Napoleon. We infer that he must have at first hated Joseph with a burning hate, but we hear that later on he loved him above all other human beings and could hardly take amiss anything from that worthless and unreliable person. The original hatred, therefore, had been over-compensated, but the early aggression only lay in wait to be transferred to other objects. Hundreds of thousands of strangers had to pay the penalty of this little fiend having spared his first enemy.

"(b) In another layer of his mind the young Napoleon's tender feelings were bound up with his mother, and he was concerned to replace his dead father in caring for the younger brothers and sisters. As soon as he became a General it was recommended that he marry a young widow, older than himself, who had charm and influence. A good deal could be said against her, but probably what was decisive for him was the fact that she was called Josephine. Thanks to this name he could transfer to her some of the tender emotions he felt for the eldest brother. She did not love him, treated him badly, betrayed him, but he, the despot who was otherwise cynically cool toward women, clung to her passionately and forgave her everything; he could not be angry with her.

"(c) The love for Josephine B. was an obsessive one on account of the name, but naturally it was not an identification with Joseph. This came to the strongest expression in his famous expedition to Egypt. Where else should one go to if one is Joseph and wants to appear great in front of his brothers? If one were to examine more closely the political justification for this undertaking of the young General one would probably find them to be only rationalizations of a phantastic idea. This campaign, by the way, brought about the reawakening of Egypt.

"(d) The aim that had driven Napoleon to Egypt was realized in his later years in Europe. He took care of his brothers by making them Princes and Kings. The useless Jerome was perhaps his Benjamin. And then he became disloyal to his myth; he allowed realistic considerations to make him decide to put aside the beloved Josephine. With that began his descent; from then onward the great destroyer worked toward his own destruction. The hazardous and not well prepared campaign against Russia brought about his downfall. It was like a self-punishment for his disloyalty to Josephine, for the regression from his love to his original enmity toward Joseph. Nevertheless, even here, against Napoleon's intention, fate repeated another part of the Joseph story. It was Joseph's dream, that sun, moon and stars should bow down before him, that led him on till he was cast into a pit.

> "Herzlich
> "Ihr
> "Freud"

33. To Marie Bonaparte. May 27, 1937.
"Meine liebe Marie:

"I will try to answer your question [about aggression]. The whole topic has not yet been treated carefully, and what I had to say about it in earlier writings was so premature and casual as hardly to deserve consideration.

" 'Sublimation' is a concept that contains a judgment of value. Actually it signifies the application to another field in which socially more valuable achievements are possible. One must then admit that similar deviations from the goal of destruction and exploitation to other achievements are demonstrable on an extensive scale for the instinct of destruction. All activities that rearrange or effect changes are to a certain extent destructive and thus redirect a portion of the instinct from its original destructive goal. Even the sexual instinct, as we know, cannot act without some measure of aggression. Therefore in the regular combination of the two instincts there is a partial sublimation of the destructive instinct.

"One may regard finally curiosity, the impulse to investigate, as a complete sublimation of the aggressive or destructive instinct. Altogether in the life of the intellect the instinct attains a high significance as the motor of all discrimination, denial and condemnation.

"The turning inward of the aggressive impulse is naturally the counterpart of turning outward of the libido when it passes over from the ego to objects. One could imagine a pretty schematic idea of all libido being at the beginning of life directed inward and all aggression outward, and that this gradually changes in the course of life. But perhaps that is not correct.

"The repression of aggression is the hardest part to understand. As is well known, it is easy to establish the presence of 'latent' aggression, but whether it is then latent through repression or in some other way is not clear. What usually happens is that this aggression is latent or repressed through some counter-compensation, i.e. through an erotic cathexis. And with that one approaches the theme of ambivalency, which is still very puzzling.

"Forgive me for the lecture.

"Cordially

"yours

"Freud"

34. To Marie Bonaparte. June 17, 1937.

". . . Please do not overestimate my remarks about the destructive instinct. They were only tossed off and should be carefully thought over if you propose to use them publicly. Also there is so little new in them."

35. To Marie Bonaparte. August 13, 1937.

Meine liebe Marie:

"I can answer you without any delay, since I have little to do. Moses II was finished yesterday, and one forgets one's little troubles best in the friendly exchange of thoughts.

". . . Immortality evidently means to a writer the being loved by many unknown people. Now I know I shall not mourn your death, for you will long survive me. And I hope you will soon console yourself over my death and let me go on living in your friendly recollections—the only kind of limited immortality I recognize.

"The moment one inquires about the sense or value of life one is sick, since objectively neither of them has any existence. In doing so one is only admitting a surplus of unsatisfied libido, and then something else must happen, a sort of fermenting, for it to lead to grief and depression. These explanations of mine are certainly not on a grand scale, perhaps because I am too pessimistic. There is going through my head an advertisement which I think is the boldest and most successful American one I know of. 'Why live, when you can be buried for ten dollars?' "

36. To Karl Weissmann. March 21, 1938.
"Sehr geehrter Herr:

"Good news is always welcome, and in times like these specially cheering. I have heard with the greatest interest of your activities on behalf of psychoanalysis in conjunction with Dr. Pereira da Silva, and with great regret of the untimely death of Professor Porto-Carrero.

"I can read Spanish easily, but the resemblance between it and your language only confuses me. I have often tried without success to read something in Portuguese, nor did I manage any better with your book.

"I hope that your study of psychoanalysis will give you ever increasing satisfaction as you deepen your knowledge. And I send you my warmest wishes for your success."

> *"Ihr sehr ergebener*
> "Freud"

37. To Marie Bonaparte. August 21, 1938.
"Meine liebe Marie:

"I have just read the manuscript of your paper on 'Time' and am having it copied. From the part on the unconscious onward it gets better, more important and full of content. We have already talked about our agreement over the final conclusions. The work does you honor.

"My first impression is that a second section might follow, taking up the theme with analytic methods. I will make a modest suggestion in this direction. There is an area whose frontiers belong both to the outer world and to the ego: our perceptual superficies. So it might be that the idea of time is connected with the work of the system W.-Bw.[m] Kant would then be in the right if we replace his old-fashioned 'a priori' by our more modern introspection of the psychical apparatus. It should be the same with space, causality, etc." [n]

38. To Arnold Zweig. December 13, 1938.

(*On hearing of a severe motor accident.*)

"Lieber Meister Arnold:

"Eitingon had sent me a full account, but it is a very different thing seeing your own handwriting. The good news on which I had

[m] Perceptual consciousness.
[n] A little later Freud tried to picture the development of the sense of time in terms of Planck's quantum theory.

counted becomes the easier to believe. The nonsense and unreasonableness of fate! Why need one be reminded of the uncertainty of life when one is anyhow convinced of it? I was also very concerned about your son, who was driving the car. I thought it was Adam, since I had not heard anything about him. I was glad to hear that he was blameless. May the devil not forget that drunken officer when he is choosing from the English.

"There is no news from here. Everything would be all right were it not for this and that and t'other. I am still waiting for a second sequestrum which should come away like the first one.

"Please thank your dear wife for what she added.

"And now specially warm wishes for your speedy recovery.

"Ihr *alter*

"Freud"

Appendix B
Surgical Notes

IN THE SIXTEEN YEARS DURING WHICH PROFESSOR PICHLER ATTENDED Freud he kept regular notes of the case, every visit being recorded and the details entered with an admirable exactitude. For months at a time there would be daily interviews, so hard was it to relieve the discomfort in the wound. The notes were made in a variation of the Gabelsberger system of stenography invented by Pichler's father and so were unintelligible to other people. After his death there was only one person who could decipher them, his old secretary. The indefatigable Max Schur, to whom Pichler had left his notes on his death, sought her out and persuaded her to undertake the laborious task of transcribing them: this in spite of the difficulty that all the medical expressions were indicated only by abbreviations. Even so the notes occupy fifty-three foolscap sheets of close type. They give an unforgettable picture of the long drawn out distress, or even agony, through which Freud passed in those years.

Dr. Lajos Levy has been good enough to translate these notes into English, and Dr. Schur has checked the translation from his personal knowledge of the details. I have made a small selection of them, mainly for their medical interest, and append them here. But they can give little idea of the day-to-day struggle, by the countless manipulations and applications, to procure some relief for the continual discomfort and pain.

Extract of Case History[a]

9/26/23 Consultation with laryngologist Hajek who operated on a papillary prolifering leukoplakia at right anterior palatinal arch last spring, excision far into healthy tissue. (Histolog. carcinoma.) Now recurrence at anterior edge of operation-site, at posterior end of superior processus alveolaris, in form of crateriform ulcer extending over large part of buccal mucous membrane and small part of tongue and mandible. I constructed prosthesis, then undertook on special request clearance of submandibular and cervical glands and ligature of carotis externa and, shortly afterward, resection of maxilla including anterior part of ramus ascendens mandibulae. Soft palate preserved, with posterior edge within area of scar in palatinal arch. Wound in soft tissue covered with Thiersch-graft.

11/12/23 Operation of recurrence at posterior border with removal of most of right soft palate and of processus pterygoideus. Thiersch-graft.

End of Dec., 1923 Prosthesis finished. X-ray irradiations during 1923 and 1924. Since then repeated alteration of prosthesis, finally provided with springs.

11/19/25 Operation of impacted Lower Left 5 with small cyst.

1929 Patient had new prosthesis constructed by Professor Schroeder in Berlin, with drift for upper teeth, still in use now.

10/10/30 Excision of small papillary leukoplakia in operation area, Thiersch-graft.

2/7/31 Removal of new warty papilloma by diathermy.

4/23/31 Another excision and Thiersch-graft.

Sept., 1931 New attempt to have prosthesis constructed by Dr. Kazanijan from Boston. Subsequently several more prostheses.

3/7/32 Other small operations of the same kind: 7/29, 8/16, 10/6, 12/8/32, 5/16 and 9/5/33 excisions and coagulations of small papilloma. (Histolog. negative.)

[a] Summary report sent to Exner by Pichler on Freud's departure for London.

1/12/34   Cauterization with caustic potash.

3/23–7/11/34   165 radium mgh. Contact-irradiations at distance of ca. 4-8 mm and 1 mm brass filter. Has to be abandoned since patient felt that irradiations caused migraine and severe disturbances of general condition.

9/24–12/6/34   125 mgh. radium. Had to be abandoned again.

3/23/35   Destruction of small papillomata by diathermy.

4/30/35   Destruction of small papillomata by diathermy.

8/19/ and 10/11/35   Destruction of brown dry keratosis by diathermy.

3/10/36   Destruction of papilloma by diathermy.

7/14/36   Excision of more elevated nodule by diathermy (histolog. findings cancer) therefore

7/18/36   deepening of wound, resection of some bone substance and thorough coagulation.

12/12/36   Coagulation of very suspect ulcer.

4/22/37   Biopsy excision of warty proliferation at site of former operation at inner wall of ramus ascendens mandibulae; evipan narcosis. (Histolog. negative.)

1/22/38   Excision of ulcerous and simultaneously raised place and thorough coagulation of focus. (Histolog. findings positive.)

2/19/38   Excision of suspect wart at site of last operation. (Histolog. negative.)

6/2/38   Last examination. In one place keratosis in form of recurrent brown crust. In several places slight papillary formations, non-suspicious according to previous experience.

Pichler Notes

1923—9/26   Consultation with Dr. Hajek. In spring he performed an excision at the right anterior arch of the palate because of a proliferative papillary leukoplakia. It had been planned as an explorative measure, but was extended far beyond the diseased parts. The histological findings were positive. After the operation no complaints. Now, in the last weeks, pains and progressive lockjaw. There is a crater-shaped typical ulcer at the posterior part of the Tub. maxillaris with slight infiltration into the palato-glossal fold continuing into the buccal mucous membrane and over the margin of the mandible. The palate itself is reduced in size by the previous operation and scarred. The surface of the hard palate at its posterior part has some protrusions. Only one submaxillary lymphatic gland is palpable, immediately behind the exterior maxillary artery. Patient makes the condition that he should not be attended as a colleague, but pay a fee.

Project: partial resection of the maxilla with block-anaes-thesia and removal of a splinter of the mandible (Resectio anguli interni). Experiment on corpse demonstrates that it is possible to weaken the mandible from the buccal side by multiple piercings and by cutting with fissure-burrs until a splinter together with the coronary process up to the Incisura can be split off and the whole piece including the upper jaw bone be removed.

9/27 Cleaning of teeth. Exploration of teeth.

10/4 Operation at the Sanatorium Auersperg. Assistant: Dr. Bleich-steiner. Pantopon 0,03, Scop. 0,003, Di. 0,02, ⅔ cc. of this solution to start and 1½ cc. later; block-anaesthesia with ½% novocain into Cerv. and Lingu. nerves, angular incision. Typical clearance of the submaxillary glands and ligature of the art. carotis ext. peripherally to the artery thyreoidea sup. Two jugular and some submaxillary glands are enlarged and at cross section a little suspicious (no malignant cells on histological examination).

10/11 Operation at the Sanatorium Auersperg. Assistants: Dr. Hofer and Dr. Bleichsteiner. 1½ cc. of above mentioned solution; excellent success of block-anaesthesia: 3rd branch by oblique path, 2nd branch by Payr's method, local anesthesis of palate and lip faultless. Cut through the middle of the upper lip, then around the nose till half height. After that, broad cut around the buccal mucous membrane till Upper Right 7, exposing the Fossa canina by raspatory and separating the mucous membrane and the buccal gum at Upper Right 7-3. Then division of the masseter muscle above at the os zygomaticum, to

10/11/23—*continued*

enable it to be turned down later, to cover with it the gap at the mandible and to stitch it up to the margin of the cut palate. Then opened the jaws by Heister, detaching the sinew of the m. temporalis from the Proc. coron., extraction of Upper Right 7 and from the alveola of Lower Left 7 to the Incis. setting some bore-holes obliquely from upper outside to lower inside at the mandible, linking them partly by sawing with Sudeck fraise and partly chiseled through. Then chiseled off the crista zygomatica high above, cutting around tumor from Upper Right 3 which has been extracted too, through the soft palate, the superior parts of the tonsils and the lingual mucous membrane of the mandible, chiseling through the fossa canina, the proc. pter. at its root and at the hard palate, and finally pulling forward the tumor and severing the nervus pterygoideus internus. At this point, the whole piece broke up into 3 fragments: Proc. cor., upper jaw and the tumor. At the wound side of the latter no macroscopically observable diseased tissue. No strong bleeding. Suturing the mucous membrane of the palate below to the Masseter muscle, further below to a 2 cm. broad flap which has been isolated from the buccal mucous membrane (below up to the gum), disregarding the papilla Stenoni to create at least one unstrained bridge of mucous membrane from the palate arch over to the angulus int. Insertion of the prosthesis, the wound margin of the soft palate being drawn sidewise with two sutures below the prosthesis. Maxillary sinuses polypous but otherwise normal, mucous membrane only partly removed. Tamponed [Packed], above the tampon the deep gap between the upper and lower jaw, which partly goes into the soft palate below the mucous membrane, filled up by a Stents-clod of which anterior margin lies under the wound-surface of the cheek-flap. Thiersch-graft of this Stents-clod from the left upper arm. Skin suture. The prosthesis in addition to the clasps fastened also to Upper Left 1-4. Patient sleeps during the greater part of the operation. Nervus alv. inf. and lingualis may not have been injured. Perhaps the only mistake not to have removed more of the M. pter. int. Afterward pulse good, 64. Caffeine, calcium, digitalis-injection. Drip-enema.

10/12   Very slight reaction. Condition good, slept well. Pat. cannot speak. Thirst. Drip-enema.

10/13   After feeding by nasal tube, patient, who felt very weak, improved very much. Evening sudden rise of temperature to 39 [102.2°], with sensation of weakness. Camphora, Digitalis. After 2 or 3 hours decrease of temperature to normal. Objectively everything all right.

11/7   Since day before yesterday increasing pain. Seems to originate from region of Proc. pt. where small irregular ulcer is visible after sloughing off necrotic tissue. Some ex-cochleation at this point. Some pus oozing from one spot. No sequestrum to be seen. Upper clod tested and prosthesis taken for vulcanisation.

11/9   UL 4 bites heavily on Proc. alv. Chiseling improves entry and removal of prosthesis. Bite satisfactory on the right but pushes upper prosthesis backward and spoils contact with neck of teeth. If tied on above, bite too high. Therefore polishing of both 3 right side and removal of UR 5-4 from prosthesis.

11/10   Again increased pain. Decreasing size of prosthesis at the point of the suspicious lesion; improvement. Stents-cast with upper prosthesis to supply it with teeth.

11/12   Received Stoerck's pathological report, visited patient, informed him, induced him to decide to be operated on the same day.

P.M.   Operation in Sanatorium Auersperg. Assistants: Dr. Hofer and Dr. Hertzka. After pantopon scopolamine, block-anaesthesia: Payr and 3rd branch into Foramen ovale. Incision at cheek-scar toward fissura oris and speculum suffices for access. Cut through soft palate ca 1½ cm from free margin, from here around tumor up to palate bone and proc. pter. Chiseling off and extracting the latter by severing the soft tissue-connections. Probably transection of nervus and arteria alv. inf. Heavy bleeding but not from major blood-vessel. After inspection of specimen, margins of which appear healthy, removal of additional piece at inferior and lingual border; kept for biopsy. Following this, insertion of a Stents-clod with Thiersch-graft, covered by prosthesis. Both sheets of soft palate sutured to each other, one of sutures joined to prosthesis. Finally, suturing of rhombic defect in the buccal mucous membrane along opposite diagonal.

11/14   Suture between soft palate and prosthesis came off, Stents-clod slipped into mouth causing great trouble. Clod shredded and removed with probable damage to Thiersch-graft.

11/19 Calls on patient on 15th, 16th, 17th. On 19th violent pain, no fever. On 17th patient underwent a Steinach-operation[b] for "rejuvenation," hoping for possible effect on cancer-predisposition. Investigation of specimens by Sternberg show only granulation tissue on two particles of the specimen, carcinoma on one side of third particle.

11/27 Lower prosthesis adjusted with black guttapercha on lower left. No pain; bite still somewhat high. Cannot understand why bite too high after having taken impressions twice. Anyway, clasp LL 4 not far enough lingually.

11/28 Bite still somewhat high but not troublesome, can remain. Lower prosthesis with clasp-supplement taken for vulcanization. Cast of upper clod with wax-extension, should be vulcanized and simultaneously extended upward and to posterior pharyngeal wall. More guttapercha added to top of upper plate and inserted with packing for enlargement of antrum.

12/10 Since prosthesis tied now only to UL 1 with some support from clasp UR 2, these teeth sensitive through overstrain. UL 1 shows movement toward lingual side since prosthesis tends to drop in this direction. Have to counteract this by occlusion on lower right; if necessary all front teeth will have to be connected by wire-gallery and used for support. Some additional guttapercha added to top of clod to provide extension into the antrum. All teeth tied, last molar extracted to lower bite. Otherwise all right. Swallowing and speech very good.

12/20 Prosthesis fits now almost perfectly, no sagging backward. Prosthesis treatment can be considered completed. Patient manages to-day to remove and re-insert all parts of prosthesis. Decision for prophylactic x-ray therapy. Consultation with Holzknecht who comes to my consulting room to examine the patient. Decides for irradiation partly with, partly without prosthesis and begins with first session immediately to-day.

1924—2/7 New prosthesis with gallery-clasp for front teeth and hook-closure, otherwise as before. Fits tighter than prosthesis No. 1, weighs less. Speech better right away. Removal and insertion easier than with No. 1.

[b] Ligation of the spermatic duct.

2/11   Insertion of prosthesis 2 with closure of hinge-clasp repaired and closing-hooklet removed backward. Patient feels pressure on left upper part, speech worse.

2/12   Everything all right on left upper part. Speech much worse, perhaps hinge-clasp too loose. Tightened, some polishing on lower left.

2/26   Altered prosthesis fits rather well, but speech is very bad. Considerable improvement after further addition of guttapercha to back of clod.

2/28   This time clod fitted badly on lower part, not having clicked into groove on back. Has to be remoulded completely and palate-plate pressed upward and backward during insertion. Fits well after insertion but speech quite nasal.

3/6   Pain left on upper and lower part. Correction of pressure points. Otherwise, pain seems to originate chiefly from soft palate which is jammed at its cut edge ca. 2 mm in front of the uvula between posterior sharp margin of palate plate and the quasi obturating back part of the left half palate extending to guttapercha clod. Soreness caused by jamming. Rounding off posterior margin of plate, correction of pressure point. Guttapercha-supplement and clod which became separated, united again. General swelling of mucous membrane, caused possibly by "flu."

3/12   All kinds of unpleasant sensations; speech worse. Cannot find the reason. Have given more play to soft palate, especially on nasal side.

3/14   Consultation with Docent Stern[e] who finds hardly any sign of rhinolaly. Gutzmann's test a—j shows almost no difference whether nose occluded or open. Substantial subjective improvement, speech relieved since last chiseling. Some more chiseling. Now rather difficult to insert prosthesis so that it clicks into channel. Patient will have to exercise it by biting on piece of wood with upper and lower right molars.

4/10   Prosthesis taken for mending of countersunk holes. Prosthesis 1 is very poor substitute by now, has to be tied on as best possible. Repaired prosthesis 2 reinserted.

[e] A speech specialist.

5/27 Speech worse, obviously nasal, all the more so since last modification. Supply of guttapercha at the point of uvula-channel seems to improve it. Lockjaw much improved. Also swallowing of fluids, which has been much more troublesome, seems improved.

7/1 Closure when drinking cold water worse again, therefore attempt to supply more guttapercha. Closure improved. But greatest discomfort from pressure and strain on right side for which cause cannot be found. Perhaps due to sinus trouble which is treated by Neumann. Advice to remove prosthesis more frequently to improve condition if possible.

9/30 New prosthesis 2 excellent for three days. Since then worse, coinciding with heavy cold, possibly some general swelling, no other findings. Inside prosthesis no fluids, hardly any uncleanness.

10/6 Tension entirely gone but the disagreeable fact remains that prosthesis drops on both sides, on the left some more than on the right, creating discomfort. Only remedy would be springs which I should like to avoid as long as possible. Instead attempt to correct hold of hinge-splint by supplying Kerr at front.

12/23 Pain improved but mastication and drinking worse, fluids regurgitating through nose since plate fits more loosely again. Fastening of screw by 1½ turns seems insufficient. Unless patient gets used to it, only remedy to increase supply of guttapercha on top of plate again so as to produce better adhesion. May try to fit some sort of padded bands or riders to prevent slipping of hinge-clasp toward necks of teeth. Treatment with silver nitrate of upper and lower necks of teeth repeated.

1925—2/10 Coryza improved. Some discomfort due to wobbling of prosthesis. Since tightening of screws helps only temporarily and hinge-clasp continues to mount toward neck of teeth, plan to fit knobs. First a platinum band is affixed to UR 2 with small platinum-pin, a screwed gold peg to UL 4, with corresponding holes drilled into hinge-clasp. If necessary, perhaps teeth UR 3-1/UL 1-3 to be altered similarly. Prosthesis 2 to receive the same new hinge-clasp.

3/10 UL 2-3 pulps extracted and roots filled.

3/12 UL 3 screw cemented in. Fits very well now but speech completely nasal. Therefore prosthesis inserted with guttapercha. UR 1 and perhaps UL 2 to be devitalized and then prosthesis finally adjusted to palate.

4/24 Prosthesis 3 very good for one day, then very bad again due to "hanging down of teeth right above." Seems to have come about through twisting of the knob at closure and might be remedied by tightening of screw. Screw fixed in this position with cement. Prosthesis 2 with new gold-gallery fits into place after some difficulties, but interferes with bite now considerably, has to be adjusted further.

7/5 Several good days, then very bad again. What is worst is the depressing hopelessness about the inability to do anything. Has slept eleven hours. No objective evidence except slight gingivitis, especially at lingual side of UR 2 and at papilla between UR 2-1, where gum is extraordinarily hyper-sensitive. Evidently the matter is mainly "nervous." Ablation of papilla and part of free gingivamargin by electrocautery. Orthoform and later massage.

9/9 At the incision-margin of the hard palate, toward the center of the hole leading to the nose, a circular, flat, ragged protuberance has appeared, with the mucous membrane in the vicinity perhaps more papillary than before. Area appears somewhat suspect, might mean recurrence. Worst of all is catarrh of nasal mucous membrane. Even before his operation patient suffered once or twice yearly from purulent discharges from sphenoidal and ethmoidal sinuses; was not much disturbed by these otherwise.

11/19 For five days now some sensitiveness left below; since last night swelling and pain, no sleep during night. On 17th attempt to arrest inflammation by irradiation. But Holzknecht considers operation unavoidable.
Operation in my consulting room. o. 7 Modiscop and three times 2 cc. 4% novocain mandibular and buccal. Opening of gum distally at LL 3 where it adheres strongly to bone affected by inflammatory process. Moderate quantity of pus evacuated. Curetting of granuloma of moderate size with exposure of crown of LL 5 incrusted by tartar. Further exposure of this through chiseling away of bone, finally easy extraction with elevator since

11/19/25—*continued*

tooth fairly loose. Root found to be short, enormously thickened
by cement-deposits. Cyst-sac and granuloma extirpated fully.
Packing.

1926—11/10   Fitting of new prosthesis 4. Impossible to insert as a
whole. Fits quite well when inserted but speech gets indistinct.
Bite in oral cavity rather difficult. Discussed trouble caused by
unending tiresome sinus catarrhs with secretion which Laufer
used to treat successfully by irrigation.

1927—6/9   Since last time patient saw Dr. Wolf twice because of
paradental abscess of UL 4. Great improvement after curettage.
Since apex can be reached with scaler, and since patient is on
point of leaving Vienna, tooth is extracted with fingers, white
guttapercha substituted for it on duplicate prosthesis. Right
above further reduction of pressure-point, removal of old guttapercha.

6/27   Bad state after two days' relief with use of prosthesis 3. Again,
one excellent day. Upper part a bit loose. Guttapercha bolster
renewed. At point outside, where lacuna of mucous membrane
was situated, blunt excision of piece (preserved); mucous membrane here at least 5 mm thick, covered toward lumen with resistant thin skin (perhaps epithelium extending over from
Thiersch-graft).

7/4   Exactly the same as before; only one tolerable day after using
old prosthesis for 1-2 days with manifold discomfort. Patient
suggests removal of extension which protrudes into antrum.
After casting for eventual restoration of status quo extension
removed.

10/4   Prosthesis 4 supplied with guttapercha and vulcanized, fitted
with steel-spring holders with ricochet-channel above and below.

10/18   After several alterations of springs in interval, to-day severe
pain, general discomfort, pressure as if springs were too strong.
Objectively noticeable that springs fail now to keep posterior
part right above in place, being either too weak altogether or
having working point too far frontal.

11/4   Springs of prosthesis 4 lengthened again and soldered at one
point. Gold clasp of prosthesis 3 corrected further; should be
tried for a longer period, may adjust itself through shrinkage of

bed. New lower prosthesis is made from cast of old one. Fits well. Prosthesis 4 continues to produce "swellings" and disturbs hearing. Perhaps owing to obturation of tube.

1928—3/6 Right spring much better but not altogether comfortable. Prosthesis 5 with casted clod cannot be inserted fully and elevates bite. Stents-clod to be reduced all over by ½ cm and piece provided with vertical springs running in tubes.

3/8 Prosthesis 5 tried with vertical spring tucked into two telescope-tubes. Impossible to insert owing to lockjaw. Has to be shifted more lingually.

4/2 Tubed spring removed from prosthesis 5, on right side teeth partly removed, partly shifted more lingually, former type of spring resorted to again but further lingually. New guttapercha supplied with resultant great improvement of speech. To be used for several hours.

4/16 Everything bad. Pain at back, where swelling, sensitiveness and redness is found at posterior pharyngeal wall. Removal of guttapercha backward on upper part, some supply further below; right spring exchanged for heavy gold spring.

4/24 Prosthesis 5 cannot be used, too thick and large. Part of clod removed and replaced by shellac. Still too large. Pressure point on prosthesis 4 reduced.

5/7 Prosthesis 4 now caused pressure right below and spring interfered badly with tongue. Pressure points corrected and spring bent more outward. Prosthesis 5 handed over. It is vulcanized in one piece, hollow and closed with stopper, weighs 75 grams without springs.

1929—11/23 Patient arrives with Dr. Weinmann who attends him now, cleans prosthesis, etc., and with prosthesis made by Schroeder in Berlin. Upper teeth are joined to form compact bridge; soldered distally to this are oblique slanting slides of wide range on to which prosthesis is slipped. Prosthesis leaves left posterior half of palate uncovered, closes merely as sort of obturator. Actual clod of prosthesis seems of smaller dimensions. At present functions rather well, was still better in beginning; now variable. Only objection is risk that all pillars of upper bridge may loosen simultaneously some time and then the catastrophe would be great. Patient calls since Weinmann, and

11/23/29—*continued*

apparently also Schroeder, regard one spot as suspicious. This is an area which was marked down for some reason several years ago where mucous membrane of nose encroaches downward on palate. Nothing pathological. Perhaps swelling due to present bad coryza.

1930—10/3 Small leukoplakia behind prosthesis at palate and one place at Thiersch-graft near arch of palate where decubitus occurred; here a papillary change of surface in area of ca. 1 cm. which is suspect of precancerous proliferation of epithelium. Advice: excision and Thiersch on prosthesis. Since prosthesis not fully adjacent here, preliminary supplement of Kerr or guttapercha. One week's observation in case of spontaneous receding.

10/14 Operation: application of cedenta on prosthesis corresponding to changed area. Excision. Subjacent tissue soft and perfectly normal. Surprisingly little scar tissue. After excision more cedenta applied to fill hole completely and prosthesis pasted with several Thiersch-flaps. Diathermy-destruction of leukoplakia at edge of soft and hard palate left, near middle end of small wartlike nodule closely behind posterior margin of prosthesis left above in area of foramen palatinum. (Assistant Berg[a] and Weinmann.)

10/17 Yesterday patient had severe pain and bad night, took two veramon and pantopon, stomach upset, vomited, looks badly. Better to-day. Have resisted his wish to remove prosthesis till now but wants it so much that I decided in favor of it. Thiersch-flaps come out together with prosthesis. Hope that wound inoculated with epithelium by now. Cedenta-mass reduced and prosthesis reinserted.

10/18 Histological findings: small tissue piece covered over histologically with epithelium, slightly cornified in places which is prolifering to a certain depth in area described. Papillae of epithelium very deep and coarse, demarcated sharply everywhere from the substratum. This consists on the surface of rather loose connective tissue, in certain parts with chronic inflammatory infiltration; the deeper layers consist of tauter connective tissue undergoing hyaline degeneration, here without inflammatory infiltrations. No sign of malignancy. Excrescence in area of for-

[a] Pichler's private assistant.

mer transplantation may be due to big and coarse papillae of epithelium. Also hyaline degeneration of submucosa may have been subsidiary cause. (Report sent to Dr. Schur.)

10/23 Patient has had small broncho-pneumonia. One day fever but weakened by it and complains of pain when opening mouth which improved to-day. Supply on prosthesis removed. Wound looks all right. No obvious epithelium visible. Only orthoform prescribed.

1931—2/3 Dr. Weinmann gone abroad for one week. In the meantime patient wants to know from me: 1) why prosthesis functions so badly (rough, difficult speech, hard to understand) and 2) what wart-like protuberance at operation-site signifies. Supply of guttapercha improves condition for the moment. Protuberance is doubtless a papilloma, to be removed by electro-coagulation. Some doubts whether operation by knife would not be preferable since a suture from anterior to posterior might be established. Papilloma seems accreted with masseter or proc. pterygoideus. Lifts when contracted.

2/7 Operation: Assistant Dr. Bleichsteiner, Dr. Schur and Dr. Weinmann present. Cutting around with diathermy-knife at low current-intensity, then extirpation and coagulation of base consisting of entirely hard, infringed, tough connecting tissue; after that again thorough excochleation and again coagulation of margins. Spraying with orthoform and insertion of prosthesis.

2/13 Pain with prosthesis inserted was intolerable. Have to urge patient to tolerate prosthesis nevertheless since removal would increase later troubles. Agrees finally.

4/14 Area of diathermy epithelized for some time. But new appearance of a tumor further frontally corresponding to the scar fold protruding into mouth. Tumor is soft, irregular, partly dark colored, no longer wholly villous or velvety, has wrinkles and folds and can be shifted on underlying base. Supposedly grown fast and much. Considerable lockjaw, ca. 15 mm. Since aftereffects of diathermy operation are reported to have lasted throughout these two months, advise excision and Thiersch-graft. Guttapercha supplied to prosthesis. Patient to celebrate his seventy-fifth birthday soon, has bad coryza. Would like postponement. I advise against such long postponement. I believe soft tumor still precancerous but am against waiting (in view of fast growth,

4/14/31—*continued*

which I have not pointed out to patient). Asked whether tumor could be left alone and malignancy risked, I advised against it. Asked whether radium or x-ray could be tried, I advise consultation with Holzknecht. The latter in sanatorium at present after operation on hand. Discussion with Dr. Schur over the telephone.

4/17   Dr. Schur expresses wish to call for consultation Dr. Rigaud, famous radiologist, director of Curie Institute, Paris. Of course, agree readily, decision to await arrival. No change. Since hollow prosthesis is tapped and difficult to close, fluids enter and increase weight unnecessarily. Propose to prepare duplicate which could serve eventually also for insertion of radium.

4/20   From Paris advice against radium so long as malignancy of tumor uncertain. Therefore this plan abandoned and another consultation with Holzknecht arranged. H. insists on excision including surrounding, slightly modified Thiersch-surface.

4/23   Operation at Sanatorium Auersperg. Assistants: Berg, Weinmann, present Dr. Schur and Dr. Ruth Mack-Brunswick. ½ cc ephetonin, eucodal-scopolamine and locally 1%. Excision of Thiersch area in wide circumference of place with altered appearance including place where last papillae were excised, almost to bone of mandible but without removing periosteum. Afterward excision of greater part of scar-cord. Prosthesis inserted with cedenta under considerable pressure, Thiersch-graft of big flap from upper arm. Fairly severe bleeding from artery. Three ligatures. Effect of scopolamine good. Everything tolerated. Since patient moves mandible restlessly after operation, capistrum head bandage applied. Pneumovit injection. Advised Dr. Schur to try hormone treatment in view of favorable effect of vasoligature after first operation. Evening: Some drowsiness as during operation. Temporary confusion. Pulse good. Fluids can be drunk without difficulty.

4/26   Patient had 2 severe attacks of pain, otherwise feels much better, no fever. Capistrum unchanged. Histological report Erdheim. (No malignancy.)

9/8   During August, treated by Professor Kazanijan from Boston, partly in my consulting room. Prof. Kazanijan reduced and narrowed existing prosthesis considerably and finally made three prostheses. One of hard rubber, two with back part of soft rubber. These have doubtless the great advantage that they cannot lever at front teeth. Patient speaks much better with soft-rubber prosthesis but cannot smoke with it at all and bites his tongue. At right margin on tongue which has not recovered full sensitivity yet a suspect ulcer has developed. It decreased in size since this prosthesis has been used less, therefore excision abandoned.

1932—1/9   This time not better. Prosthesis 2 tried once again. Very uncomfortable but no pressure in precisely those places where pressure worst with prosthesis 3. Targesin. Some papillary hypertrophies at fold which protrudes right below.

1/27   Again swollen and worse. Also papilla seems more enlarged again after temporary diminution. Resection-prosthesis cannot be tolerated for more than ten minutes, therefore reduction of soft rubber not feasible.

3/7   Operation: ½ cc modiscop and ¾% tutocaine locally. After local infiltration, posterior margin, otherwise visible in mirror only, is easily discernible; clear indication where to cut. Now cut around modified area of "mucous membrane" deep into healthy part with resulting extraction of wedge of ca. 1 cm thickness. Further, excision of remaining scar by scissors and attempt a suture. Successful only frontally. Attempt has to be abandoned below and above because of lack of movability and impossibility of undermining. Several sutures with silk and steel wire, packed with iodoform-gauze. Prosthesis fitted experimentally, insertion easy, removed again.

6/23   Increasing discomfort, not improved by rinsings. Investigation for sensitive places reveals one at buccal edge of residual antrum where epithelium lacks clear borders, appears somewhat modified and perhaps more papillary. Separated from this, close under the edge of antrum, two round white elevated papillomata, size of millet-seed, very sensitive to touch. Attempt at cauterization with Kerkhoff-paste causes immediate severe pain but leaves no special sensations.

7/18   Little discomfort until day before yesterday. Now speech disturbed again, sensations of swelling and tension. The two cauterized spots at orifice of antrum less sensitive. But swelling be-

7/18/32—continued

hind slope of existing velum still highly sensitive even though somewhat decreased. Some additional cauterization with Kerkhoff-paste. Immediate severe pain. Orthoform ointment.

7/29 Cauterized area and margin between soft palate, Thiersch-graft and nasal mucous membrane looks normal now. But there is a white place with the appearance of an hyperkeratous wart at the outer edge of the antrum within area of the antral mucous membrane, appr. size of hemp seed, sensitive to pressure. After psicoaine surface-anaesthesia and injection, painless destruction with diathermy (grade 4). In case procedure has to be repeated, still weaker current would be indicated.

8/10 In area where soft palate adjoins defect, a new granulating protuberance of pepper-corn size is to be seen. Discomfort, especially when speaking. This small area cauterized with Kerkhoff—otherwise with camillosan.

8/16 Another warty thickened overhanging edge at outer edge of antrum. Destroyed with diathermy (grade 3); coagulated piece scales off easily from hard base. Further, some superficial diathermy at nasal-palatal border.

10/4 Now somewhat larger area of 1.5:1 cm is sensitive with distinct papillary structure, the whole situated at outer and above all posterior area of residual antrum. Removal seems absolutely necessary.

10/6 After 1 allonal and 1 titran and after infiltration in palate, attempt at subbasal anaesthesia of ramus III. Excision of 2 cushions, at first under and inside residual antrum (piece No. 1) and then directly at inferior posterior edge including small piece of nasal mucous membrane. This includes removal of whole thickness of old scar. In second place some bone exposed with intention to remove clip. Base of processor pteryoideus. Intention not carried out since bone without doubt healthy. After this both places slightly diathermized and bridge between them cut with linear 3 mm broad diathermy cut to provide for scar from right to left. Third remaining red cushion at outer edge thoroughly destroyed with diathermy only. Some iodoform-gauze on bone in upper wound-hole, otherwise only orthoform and prosthesis.

11/10 Histological report Erdheim: Specially noticeable this time is widespread inflammation which covers the whole of the mucous membrane and is the consequence of excessive smoking. There is every evidence that the inflammation develops first and that the typical leukoplakia appears as its sequel. Further, both pieces contain places where the leukoplakia shows intensified proliferation of the epithelium, i.e. a precancerous stage; both pieces contain also places where stratifying globules begin to develop. But there is no serious growth into the depth; the underlying connective tissue is callous, scarred and enough has been removed to ensure the radical removal of the local proliferation of epithelium.

11/18 Patient has had very disagreeable severe influenza with otitis dextra with paracentesis, the latter surprisingly painless. Diathermy wounds healed with smooth scars. There is one slightly sensitive place at outer edge of residual antrum with minimal leukoplakia appearance; a second place far back below on protruding fold shows severe papillary modification, almost no sensitivity. Both places should be subjected to diathermy before long.

12/8 After infiltration surroundings of small tumor at palatinal arch delineated with diathermy-cuts, including adjacent piece of leukoplakia in downward direction. Further, cutting out of piece and coagulation of base, the latter restricted to area below warty thickening. Orthoform. Prescription: Perhydrol mouth wash to counteract tendency to formation of leukoplakia.

1933—2/15 Again complaints about "swellings," certain pressure when inserting prosthesis, etc. Rhinologist does not hold nasal catarrh responsible. Nothing to be seen apart from prosthesis being coated rather thickly with dried nasal secrete, partly encrusted which may cause pain. After swabbing one place with perhydrol, an evident leukoplakia shows distinct white discoloration. Swabbing repeated and patient instructed to resume the interrupted rinsings with hyperoxyd mouth wash. All frontal teeth painted with iod-iodzinc. LR 3 filled provisionally.

4/6 "There has never been a worse week." Pressure, interference with speech. Nothing visible apart from some inflammation of nasal mucous membrane, no sensitiveness. This behind former ulcer area, corresponding to corner of prosthesis. Reduction there.

5/16   Patient complains of severe pain since yesterday. Place lingual right below appears swollen and irritated. Reduction of prosthesis there. Other place not sensitive but coagulated with diathermy after novocain injection. Orthoform, oxygen treatment of upper gum.

9/5   Diathermy of a strip where epithelium is thickened and very sensitive to pressure, from lingual surface across former scar-cord into overlaying groove. Further puncturing of single sensitive and thickly palpable point at outer edge of antrum. Orthoform.

9/15   Patient felt very ill subsequent to small operation, angina pectoris with coronary infarct.[e] Subsequent to this pneumonia of right lower lobe. All right again now.

1934—1/12   Pain, if anything, worse. No visible evidence except for greater tendency to bleed in sensitive place; probably once more beginning of papillary modification of surface epithelium. Since patient is not supposed to go out, attempt at superficial cauterization with Kerkhoff (original); causes violent pain; preliminary surface anaesthesia therefore preferable next time.

1/16   Worse; pain, pressure; insufficient relief with orthoform. At the point of last cauterization a wound with moderate sensitivity. The most painful spot further below on posterior declivity of fold which adjoins prosthesis outside. Small thickened place visible and palpable there since no compression at edge of prosthesis. Surface appears slightly papillary but same color as Thiersch-graft. Area painted with contralgin, prosthesis reduced there and lower part of modified surface cauterized with Kerkhoff; this time little pain. Probably again exactly same papilloma-formation as on former occasion.

1/23   Consultation with Eisler[f] and Schur. Increasing pain. Both cauterized areas already much smaller, but still eroded and already flattened. Small wart on upper lip near corner of mouth, very hard and pointed, appearance of epithelioma incipiens, to be irradiated. Painful area to be irradicated with small doses in patient's home.

2/24   Patient has been irradiated by Eisler, feels no relief from pain. But last reduction of prosthesis, perhaps also retaining at night

[e] Actually "coronary insufficiency."
[f] Radiologist.

has improved pressure and lockjaw. Further reduction at highest convexity. In fold quite near lower edge of prosthesis new small area with papillary increase.

3/6 Pain said not to be better. Several sensitive places, especially above, area of normal mucous membrane covered with hard dry scraps of mucus and orthoform which are difficult to remove. The previously cauterized areas show irregular surface covering, in parts leukopl. white; only frontally below, where edge of prosthesis irritates scar-cord, distinct papillary raised area. Eisler suggests radium not x-ray for treatment of wart on lip.

3/19 Consultation with Fuhs,[g] Eisler, Schur. Decision to use old duplicate prosthesis for insertion of 50 mg radium at point of papillary proliferation. Cast of old prosthesis made, reduced in size.

3/23 50 mg radium inserted for 1 hour. All metal parts coated with lacquer and wax.

4/23 Insertion of 50 mg radium for 1 hour 12 min.

6/21 Check-up. Ulcer not healed, on the contrary bigger and more marked. Edge thickened papillary, especially mesial. Opening of mouth improved, perhaps through reduction of prosthesis. Pain not better. Prosthesis reduced further. Radium-prosthesis fitted.

6/27 Insertion of 50 mg radium for ½ hour avoiding direct contact. Condition to-day rather better than before. By agreement with Professor Fuhs to be repeated three to four times at intervals of several days.

7/6 Patient had epistaxis right side and violent attack of migraine preceded by scotoma, ascribed to radium. Probably wrongly, since bleeding originated in septum frontale. Advice: to carry out the four irradiations, to lengthen intervals, possibly slightly but not too much; if milder treatment decided on, to distribute the 100 mg planned for four sessions over five instead. Holder might profitably be shifted further forward by increasing cut-out place for it in prosthesis ca. 4 mm in forward direction.

7/30 Patient reacts each time with pain, swellings, tiredness and anginal attacks. Therefore decision to postpone another week.

[g] Radium specialist.

8/9   Had another very bad day: migraine, heart trouble, bad speech and severe local discomfort. Objectively: whole former swelling subsided and smooth. One spot, 3-4 mm in diameter, discolored brown, probably consisting of papillae, distinctly sensitive to pressure, raised somewhat above surroundings. Perhaps residue of former, perhaps new papillary swelling. Otherwise whole mucous membrane much improved, smooth and clean. Prosthesis reduced slightly at this place. Wait and see!

8/30   Yesterday exceedingly bad day. To-day better. Place marked exactly on radium-prosthesis. Brown spot gone completely. Some reduction at edge.

9/24   Failure when trying to insert radium-prosthesis plus black guttapercha after generous reduction of clod. Prosthesis together with lower one is too big for mouth. Horizontal groove for holder is replaced by vertical one which, therefore, extends further upward and downward. This achieves additional distance of ¾ cm and enlargement of field. 1 mm brass, all metal coated with wax. Recently very slight bleedings from mouth and nose. Wart on lower lip dropped off spontaneously. Dr. Schloss's[h] action based on conviction that radium with its minimal dosage of secondary importance, construction of new prosthesis of first importance. 50 mg radium for twenty-four minutes.

10/16   Papilloma vaguely visible but distinctly sensitive. Condition varied but lockjaw troublesome and pain and pressure persist. There seems no possibility for patient to come to my consulting room again. Another old prosthesis tried with guttapercha, still much too large, interferes with bite even without lower prosthesis which cannot be inserted. Insisted on further radium treatment against opposition.

11/16   50 mg radium inserted. This time much further backward than before since several distinct warty nodules have developed there whereas manifestations in old area have diminished further still. Radium should be applied soon again still further backward.

11/22   Check-up. Reaction said to be stronger than before. On day following treatment scintillating migraine as before and swellings. Old area locks all right but the two warty nodules promi-

[a] Radium specialist.

nent as before. Discussion with Dr. Schur: to try radium first, yet with awareness that diathermy would be preferable in this place. Advice to begin hormone treatment with androstin.

1935—3/20 General condition good but severe pressure-pain. Palpation shows sensitivity especially at edge of antrum and there mostly on area frontally outside, sharply circumscribed, of appr. 1 cm circumference, composed of very large coarse papillary groupings; this spot is fielded, circular, very slightly raised, slightly resistant and, of course, not movable on base of scar tissue. Conspicuous quality is its coarse spotting up to 1½ mm in diameter while all papillomata or warts till now were composed always of very small elements of quite equal size. This area is suspect and will have to be removed with diathermy unless it clears up spontaneously in the very near future. Patient not told yet. The two warts above the edge of prosthesis are definitely smaller though, perhaps more protruding, almost pedunculated but slightly hard.

3/23 Infiltration of area with 1½ cc novocaine without admixture of adrenalin and thorough coagulation of modified area; coagulated tissue lifted out of it with pincers. No manifestation of pain. Insufflation with orthoform and insertion of prosthesis after reduction of latter by 1-2 mm at this point.

4/30 Electro-coagulation of both nodules probably including base and surroundings. Several small pieces scratched out with sharp spoon and preserved.

5/5 Patient had sudden violent pain when inserting prosthesis, therefore further reduction. Two places, one with the small papilloma-remnants mentioned before, the other higher above with dry brown slough adhering. The latter very hard to touch, only partly removable with hydrogen-hyperoxyd. Seems epithelium similar to black crusts of labial epithelioma.

5/6[1] Patient reports great difficulty in inserting prosthesis. In the morning after cleaning insertion impossible. Yesterday still inserted with pain. To-day impossible, very upset, etc. Visit in consulting room. Apparent that rider right above slightly twisted which prevents prosthesis from slipping into place. An old non-fitting resection-proshtesis can be inserted. Imperfect insertion

---

[1] Seventy-ninth birthday!

5/6/35—*continued*

causes violent pain. Attempt to achieve insertion by reassurance, etc. fails. Decision to construct new prosthesis. Kerr-cast for new rider.

7/9 Two very bad days, then better after giving up ointment. Naturally, this has increased again the adherent slough. Cannot be removed fully with hydrogenhyperoxyd; probably has hyper-keratosis as base.

8/19 Eschar not removable, sharply bordered; slightly larger, more elevated, pressure on it probably responsible for discomfort. Keratosis almost certain. Tiny spot further backward, pin-point in size, shows similar condition. Formerly slough could be removed with care and patience, now tiny wart remains. Decision to electro-coagulate wart. In presence of Dr. Popper[j] injection 4% novocaine into base. ca. 1 cm³ into three puncture-points. Cut around with diathermy needle. Puncture close to tumor. Lifted out with sharp spoon, proliferation of tumor into ca. 2-3 mm depth revealed. Circumference ca. 8-10 mm. Base coagulated, covered with phenol-camphora gauze, powdered with orthoform, prosthesis inserted. (1 cm³ novocaine without adrenalin).

8/26 Report Erdheim:[k] "No cancer present but papillomata of this kind are precursors of cancer unless removed."

10/11 Excision of oviform papilloma, dark brown as before, with diathermy needle, excochleated, base coagulated. 4% novocaine without admixture.

1936—1/16 Operation: local injection of novocaine without adrenalin. Anaesthesis good except for one place backward above, then encircling by series of closely spaced diathermic needle punctures, then excochleation and thorough fulguration of base.

2/11 Dr. Schur and Miss Anna complain of crusts, almost impossible to remove. In fact, rather small and not too many. If really not removable, cauterization with trichloracetic acid or superficial coagulation would be indicated. Scarlet-red ointment to be tried to relieve discomfort. At alveolar crest near UR 5 new white warty typical leukoplakia.

[j] Substituting for Dr. Schur, who was vacationing.
[k] Pathologist.

2/18 Crusts not worse thanks to plenty of eurecin ointment but not wholly removable. Probably based on small dry keratoses, same as before last operation. Removal to be tried with trichloracetic acid. X-ray picture to be taken of leukoplakia in area of UR 5 to keep bone under observation. Instead of orthoform tentative painting with pantocaine, and eucerin ointment with admixture of 2% pantocaine to avoid possible irritating effect of orthoform.

2/20 Two places with brown crusts closely anterior to last operation defect cauterized with trichloracetic acid without visible white discoloration. Perhaps not enough. Upper leukoplakia at inner edge of antrum tested for pressure from prosthesis. Placed exactly where groove has been made in prosthesis to ease insertion. Not happy about it, should be removed some time.

7/13 Crusts reappeared. Trichloracetic acid in two places. Besides, there is now at posterior part of former leukoplakia on alveolar crest right above a circular ulcer bordered by kind of capsule; looks very suspicious since marginated circularly like node growing from depth. But node, as well as borders, not hard and hardly raised.

7/14 Submucous infiltration of described area at edge of alveolar crest backwards quite near to root of soft palate. 4% novocaine without adrenalin. Encircling into healthy tissue with diathermic needle punctures, then attempt to extirpate; violent pain relieved only by injection into node through wound. Probably corresponding to point near canalis sphenopalat. Then cutting out with knife and scissors since tissues not sufficiently softened by diathermy. Ad Erdheim. Then fulgurizing of borders and posterior part of focus. Anterior base is of smooth bone, not modified by disease.

7/16 Telephone message that examination shows epithelial carcinoma. (Report Erdheim.)

7/17 Examined slides with Erdheim in *Jubilaeumsspital*. They show carcinoma sharply bordered linearly by surrounding epithelium, itself, of course, strongly modified but not carcinomatous which forms overhanging wall; not extending far into depth and bordered underneath by scarred connective tissue. In other places of piece, not visible in present slides, carcinomatous tissue extended with some papillae into level of separating surface.

7/17/36—*continued*

Therefore decision to coagulate base only. For this purpose in Sanatorium Auersperg provision for nitrous oxide narcosis in case conduction-anaesthesia not successful.

7/18   Pantocaine after preceding thorough mouth cleaning and removal of brown crusts which come off easily now. Attempt at conduction-anaesthesia at foramen pterygoideum from outside. Not very successful. Isolation of formerly fulgurated soft tissue until bone exposed, then coagulation of base, with many interruptions because of pain. Then nitrous oxide narcosis, at first very successful, so that bone can be removed with Luer from edge of palate and also from medial wall of antrum. Further, very thorough fulguration of surroundings causing state of excitation and complaints of very violent pain. Afterward insertion of prosthesis and slight stuffing with iodoform gauze between prosthesis and operation area. Afterward coramine.

12/7   Daughter notices two small pits in lowest part of cheek which retain food remnants and are sensitive. Probably merely effect of shrinking. Above them hard nodule covered by mucous membrane. Higher above frontally small strongly protruding wart and frontally next to this flatter wart.

12/11   To-day small pit has unmistakable cancer appearance, walled margin. Diameter of infiltration hardly more than 6 mm. To be coagulated tomorrow. Strange that place which appeared unsuspicious on 12.7 leaves hardly any doubt of the clinical diagnosis to-day.

12/12   Coagulation of ulcer. Novocaine injection with good effect in posterior part where tissue has loose appearance, less good frontally. Infiltration impossible above where bone lies immediately under mucous membrane, but unnecessary since anaesthesia has set in. First outer walls encircled with line of electric needle pricks, then piece of center excochleated, seems of nonsuspicious consistency, finally base coagulated. Patient has no pain to start with; says towards end that he cannot stand any more, though I cannot think why. [!]

12/18   Lockjaw very disagreeable and apparently difficulty with swallowing; only fluids can be taken and cleaning is hardly possible. Short wave treatment, carried out as before in patient's home gives some relief of pain and discomfort.

12/28   Some very bad days. After visit Dr. Berg orthoform-rods with effect of achieving wide opening of mouth so that prosthesis can be removed. Operation area bordered below by highly raised margin. Some hard keratoses which have caused pain.

1937—4/19   Dr. Schur has noticed for several days soft almost pedunculate movable wart grown from area of old pit after last operation. Macroscopic very suspicious appearance because of dentritic structure. Probably recurrence coming from depth after last operation. Decision to remove for examination, because of violent pain during last operation arrived at decision to do it in evipan-narcosis. If operation reveals that growth comes from depth, i.e. from bone, then ramus ascendens will have to be resected after microscopic examination.

4/22   Trial excision in evipan-narcosis. Cut around with needle, grasped with hooklet and separated from base partly with knife since it resists loosening with sharp spoon. Base of wound consists of hard connective tissue, no softer place where spoon can enter, as anticipated. Surroundings and base electro-coagulated and insufflated with orthoform. No bandage. Upper prosthesis inserted, patient to insert lower one after waking up. Specimen to Chiari.[1]

1938—1/17   Lockjaw, if anything, worse. Suspicious place rather more convex. Inflammation of surroundings receded. Observe some more days

1/22   Operation Sanatorium Auersperg. After some difficulties a handle for the diathermy apparatus has been found, long enough to reach tumor from left. Evipan. Encircling of piece of tumor with diathermy needle. Failure to secure it with sharp spoon since tissue hard, scarred, adheres tightly to base. No instrument present for cutting at base, squeezing out of pulpy masses. After excision with scissors (ad Chiari), diathermy coagulation of this place and all other modified areas; thoroughly, but smallness of burner which had to be used leaves doubt whether everywhere. Both warts destroyed by needle. Then atheroma in left submandibular area encircled and cut out with scissors without causing injury. Complete suture after one ligature. Orthoform powder on mouth wound. Prosthesis, which broke shortly

[1] Pathologist.

1/22/38—*continued*

before operation, repaired meanwhile, inserted. Lower prosthesis reduced slightly to ease removal and insertion.

2/19   Excision of suspect wart in area of last operation. (Histologically negative.)

6/2   Last examination before departure to England. Keratosis in one place, in form of recurrent brown crust. Several places not quite all right but not suspicious according to previous experience.

9/7   Examination in London. Dr. Exner had been ready to remove quick-growing cancer anteriorly to last operation site, in area of protruding skin-fold which had developed into unmistakable tumor, when he and Dr. Schur noticed second very suspicious place behind and over last operation-site, near to passage into maxilla. This place definitely sensitive to pressure and immovable towards ramus ascendens as ascertained in examination immediately after journey to London. Therefore decision to operate tomorrow and, if necessary, to exarticulate upper part of ramus ascendens, so as to remove suspicious bone and danger of increasing lockjaw.

9/8   Operation by Prof. Pichler, at London Clinic. Narcosis first evipan, continued with nitrogenoxydul via nasal tube. Lip divided and cut continued along nose to enable good access for once. Then excision of cheek tumor with diathermy needle and, finally, of wholly modified tissue backward above over anterior edge of ramus ascendens. Excision of large pieces of very hard tough tissue. Macroscopically no appearance of cancer but of callous scar. Removed until needle meets soft healthy muscle, though perhaps not everywhere reliably in modified tissue. Finally, fixed anterior edge of ramus ascendens is exposed and coagulated to extent of 1½ cm. When impression gained that everything removed, prosthesis inserted, wound cavity insufflated with orthoform, and tamponed with 5% iodoform-gauze.

9/17   Report on excision from cheek: no definite cancer, microscopically precancerous stage. Posterior pieces so far not examined owing to some error.

1939—2/11   Dr. Schur reports that end of December a fairly large sequestrum was discharged followed by temporary improvement. Then again pain and a node and ulcer which Schur considers carcinomatous. Since patient cannot be subjected to another operation, radium seems indicated. Asks for report on previous dosage.

2/15 Advice to coagulate additional to radium. Report on doses applied earlier.

2/20 Dr. Schur reports on impending visits by Drs. Trotter and Lacassagne, the latter to give the radium treatment in Paris; asks whether I would come to Paris, if necessary. Answer: slides sent and ready to come but do not think necessary since coagulation can be done in Paris.

2/28 Letter Dr. Schur: x-ray negative, biopsy suspect (Dr. Exner), examination by Drs. Trotter and Lacassagne from Paris. Dr. Trotter wants to wait further week. Dr. Lacassagne wants another surgical opinion in case of another biopsy.

5/15 Exner: recurrence high above in antrum. Operation not indicated any more. Radium has been applied by way of prosthesis for two hours daily, no ill effects, no headaches; additional to this deep x-ray irradiations. Tumor receded but metastases.

5/29/46 Letter Dr. Exner: Further applications of radium in small doses, two hours daily, besides deep x-ray irradiations. Metastases and extension of disease into eye-socket. Death on 9/23/39 after being unconscious for twenty-four hours.

Short Title Index

References to letters which Freud wrote in English are marked with an asterisk.

Reference Notes

CHAPTER 1

REUNION

1 *Eit.*, Oct. 12, 1919.
2 *M.B.*, Oct. 21, 1925.
3 *Loc. cit.*
4 *E.J.*, Dec. 11, 1919.
5 *E.J.*, March, 1920.
6 *Fer.*, March 15, 1920.
7 *Fer.*, Nov. 28, 1920.
8 *Eit.*, Feb. 20, 1920.
9 *Eit.*, Dec. 2, 1919.
10 *Eit.*, Jan. 21, 1920.
11 *Eit.*, May 16, 1920.
12 *Eit.*, April 1, 1920.
13 *Fer.*, April 24, 1920.
14 *E.J.*, Dec. 23, 1919.
15 *Eit.*, Oct. 12, 1919.
16 *Fer.*, April 20, 1919.
17 *E.J.*, Dec. 8, 1919.
18 *E.J.*, July 28, 1919.
19 *E.J.*, April 4, 1919.
20 *Fer.*, April 20, 1919.
21 *Eit.*, May 9, 1919.
22 *E.J.*, May 28, 1919.
23 Letter to Freud from *Fer.*, Dec. 26, 1918.
24 *Fer.*, Jan. 1, 1919.
25 *Fer.*, July 10, 1919.
26 *Ab.*, May 18, 1919.
27 *Eit.*, Nov. 19, 1919.
28 A. E. Hoche, "Mögliche Ziele der Traumforschung," *Archiv für Psychiatrie und Nervenkrankheiten*, LXI (1919), 451.
29 Ernst Kretschmer, "Zur Kritik des Unbewussten," *Zeitschrift für die gesamte Neurologie und Psychiatrie*, XLVI (1919), 268-387.
30 Letter to Freud from Hanns Sachs, Feb. 26, 1919.
31 Letter to Freud from *Fer.*, April 29, 1919.
32 Letter to Freud from *Fer.*, May 30, 1920.
33 *Ab.*, June 3, 1919.
34 *Fer.*, April 12, 1919.
35 *Eit.*, Oct. 28, 1919.
36 *Ab.*, Jan. 6, 1920.
37 *Eit.*, Nov. 19, 1919.
38 *Eit.*, Jan. 21, 1920.
39 *Fer.*, May 12, 1920.
40 *Fer.*, Jan. 29, 1920.
41 *Eit.*, Feb. 3, 1920.
42 Schiller, *Die Piccolomini*, Act I, Scene 4.
43 Goethe, *Egmont*, Act V, Scene 3.
44 *Fer.*, Feb. 4, 1920.
45 *E.J.*, Feb. 12, 1920.

[46] *Ab.*, July 4, 1920.

[47] *Fer.*, Oct. 31, 1920.

[48] Havelock Ellis, "Psychoanalysis in Relation to Sex," *Journal of Mental Science*, LXIII (Oct., 1917), 537-55.

[49] *Eit.*, Feb. 15, 1920.

[50] **E.J.*, Feb. 12, 1920.

[51] *S.E.*, XVII, 211-15.

[52] K. R. Eissler, "Malingering." In George Wilbur and Warner Muensterberger (eds.), *Psychoanalysis and Culture* (New York: International Universities Press, 1951), pp. 218-53.

[53] Julius Wagner-Jauregg, *Lebenserinnerungen* (1950), p. 70.

[54] *Fer.*, Oct. 11, 1920.

[55] *Ab.*, Oct. 31, 1920.

[56] J. Wagner-Jauregg, *op. cit.*, p. 72.

[57] *Fer.*, May 14, 1920.

[58] *Eit.*, July 18, 1920.

[59] *Eit.*, Aug. 3, 1920.

[60] *Fer.*, May 8, 1921.

[61] *Loc. cit.*

[62] Letter to Freud from *Ab.*, Aug. 3, 1919.

[63] *Ab.*, July 4, 1920.

[64] *S.E.*, XVIII, 4-5.

[65] Karl Abraham, *Selected Papers on Psychoanalysis* (New York: Basic Books, 1953), p. 338.

[66] Sandor Ferenczi, *Further Contributions to the Theory and Technique of Psychoanalysis* (New York: Basic Books, 1952), p. 198.

[67] *The Lancet*, Sept. 30, 1939, p. 765.

[68] **E.J.*, Oct. 4, 1920.

[69] *Pf.*, Dec. 25, 1920.

[70] Letter to Edward Bernays, Oct. 2, 1920.

[71] Letter to Edward Bernays, Dec. 19, 1920.

[72] *Fer.*, Nov. 28, 1920.

[73] *Pf.*, Dec. 25, 1920.

[74] Letter to Freud from *E.J.*, Dec. 7, 1920.

[75] *Fer.*, March 17, 1919.

[76] See *Vol. II*, 116.

[77] *Eit.*, Jan. 4, 1920.

[78] *E.J.*, May 31, 1921.

[79] Letter to Freud from *E.J.*, April 25, 1919.

[80] **E.J.*, Dec. 11, 1919.

[81] **E.J.*, Jan. 26, 1920.

[82] **E.J.*, Oct. 21, 1920.

[83] *G.W.*, II/III, 513-626; *S.E.* IV, 509-610.

[84] *G.W.*, IX, 122-94; *S.E.*, XIII, 100-61.

[85] *G.W.*, X, 264-303; *S.E.*, XIV.

[86] *Gyógyaszat*, XIII (1919), 192; *S.E.*, XVII, 171-73.

[87] *Revista de Psicoanalisis*, March, 1955.

[88] *Fer.*, Jan. 6, 1919.

[89] *Fer.*, Jan. 24, 1919.

[90] See *Vol. II*, 308. It was published in the *I.Z.*, V (1919), 151-72.

[91] *G.W.*, XIII, 3-69; *S.E.*, XVIII, 1-64.

[92] *Fer.*, March 17, 1919.

[93] *Fer.*, March 31, 1919.

[94] *Fer.*, May 12, 1919.

[95] *Fer.*, July 10, 1919.

[96] *Fer.*, May 12, 1919.

[97] I, V (1919), 297-324; *G.W.*, XII, 229-68; *S.E.*, XVII, 219-56.

[98] *E.J.*, July 28, 1919.

[99] See *Vol. II*, 278.

[100] *E.J.*, March 8, 1920.

[101] *I.Z.*, VI (1920), 1-24.

[102] *Eit.*, May 27, 1920.

[103] *Eit.*, July 18, 1920.

[104] *Eit.*, Feb. 8, 1920.

[105] *Ab.*, Nov. 28, 1920.

[106] *Eit.*, Oct. 31, 1920.

[107] F. Wittels, *Sigmund Freud: His Personality, His Teaching and His School* (New York: Dodd, Mead, 1924).

[108] *E.J.*, July 14, 1923.
[109] See *Vol. I*, 50, 78-79, 84.
[110] *M.*, Aug. 16, 1882.
[111] See *Vol. II*, 194.
[112] *G.W.*, XIII, 73-161; *S.E.*, XVIII, 69-143.
[113] *Fer.*, May 12, 1919.
[114] *Fer.*, Feb. 8, 1920.
[115] *Eit.*, Feb. 8, 1920.

[116] *Ab.*, May 14, 1920.
[117] **E.J.*, Aug. 2, 1920.
[118] *Fer.*, Aug. 20, 1920.
[119] *Fer.*, July 19, 1921.
[120] *Ab.*, Nov. 28, 1920.
[121] *Eit.*, Feb. 17, 1921.
[122] *Eit.*, March 27, 1921.
[123] Letter to Freud from *Ab.*, Aug. 8, 1921.

CHAPTER 2

DISUNION

[1] *L.*, Feb. 11, 1921.
[2] *E.J.*, March 23, 1922.
[3] Jan. 7, 1922.
[4] Letter to Freud from *E.J.*, April 10, 1922.
[5] **E.J.*, April 16, 1922.
[6] **E.J.*, May 17, 1922.
[7] *L.*, July 3, 1922.
[8] *V.*, Nov. 26, 1922.
[9] *L.*, Dec. 4, 1922.
[10] (New York: Nervous and Mental Disease Pub. Co., 1925).
[11] *Fer.*, Aug. 24, 1922.
[12] "Recollecting, Repeating, and Working Through." See Vol. II, 236-37.
[13] *Fer.*, April 4, 1925.
[14] *Ab.*, March 4, 1924.
[15] Letter to Freud from *Fer.*, Jan. 30, 1924.
[16] *Fer.*, Feb. 4, 1924.
[17] *Fer.*, Jan. 22, 1924.
[18] *Fer.*, Feb. 4, 1924.
[19] (New York: Robert Brunner, 1952).
[20] O. Rank, *"Zum Verständnis der Libidoentwicklung im Heilungsvorgang,"* I.Z., IX (1923), 435-71.
[21] *Fer.*, March 24, 1924.
[22] *Fer.*, Feb. 4, 1924.
[23] *Fer.*, March 26, 1924.
[24] Letter to Freud from *Ab.*, Feb. 21, 1924.
[25] *Ab.*, Feb. 25, 1924.

[26] Letter to Freud from Hanns Sachs, Feb. 20, 1924.
[27] Letter to Freud from Hanns Sachs, March 1, 1924.
[28] Letter to Freud from Hanns Sachs, March 10, 1924.
[29] *Ab.*, March 3, 1924.
[30] *Fer.*, Sept. 4, 1924.
[31] Letter to Freud from *Fer.* March 18, 1924.
[32] *Fer.*, March 20, 1924.
[33] *Fer.*, March 20, 1924.
[34] *Ab.*, March 31, 1924.
[35] *Fer.*, March 26, 1924.
[36] *Ab.*, Oct. 27, 1925.
[37] *Ab.*, April 28, 1924.
[38] *Ab.*, May 4, 1924.
[39] *Fer.*, March 26, 1924.
[40] *Fer.*, Feb. 4, 1924.
[41] Letters to Freud from *Fer.*, Feb 14 and March 24, 1924.
[42] Letter to Freud from *Fer.*, Aug 3, 1924.
[43] *Fer.*, Aug. 8, 1924.
[44] *Fer.*, Aug. 29, 1924.
[45] *Eit.*, Aug. 27, 1924.
[46] *Fer.*, Aug. 27, 1924.
[47] *Fer.*, Sept. 6, 1924.
[48] *Fer.*, Sept. 9, 1924.
[49] *Fer.*, Oct. 12, 1924.
[50] Letter to Freud from *Fer.*, Sept 21, 1924.
[51] *Eit.*, Sept. 27, 1924.
[52] *Eit.*, Oct. 26, 1924.
[53] *Fer.*, Oct. 26, 1924.

⁵⁴ E.J., Nov. 5, 1924.
⁵⁵ Eit., Nov. 9, 1924.
⁵⁶ E.J., Nov. 5, 1924.
⁵⁷ Letter to Freud from E.J., Nov. 11, 1924.
⁵⁸ E.J., Nov. 16, 1924.
⁵⁹ Letter to Freud from E.J., March 6, 1924.
⁶⁰ Fer., Dec. 21, 1924.
⁶¹ Eit., Dec. 29, 1924.
⁶² Fer., Dec. 21, 1924.
⁶³ Letter to Joan Riviere, Dec. 29, 1924.
⁶⁴ E.g., Fer., March 15, 1924.
⁶⁵ E.J., Jan. 6, 1925.
⁶⁶ Be., Nov. 26, 1924.
⁶⁷ V., March 15 and April 16, 1925.

⁶⁸ V., June 14, 1925.
⁶⁹ Letters to Freud from Fer., Sept. 16, 1925; Ab., Sept. 8, 1925; E.J., Sept. 19, 1925.
⁷⁰ Eit., Aug. 7, 1925; V., Sept. 11, 1925.
⁷¹ V., Nov. 15, 1925.
⁷² Fer., April 23, 1926.
⁷³ Eit., April 13, 1926.
⁷⁴ Otto Rank, Technik der Psychoanalyse (Leipzig: F. Deuticke, 1926).
⁷⁵ "From the History of an Infantile Neurosis." See Vol. II, 273-78.
⁷⁶ I.Z., XIII (1927), 1-9.
⁷⁷ Eit., June 7, 1926.
⁷⁸ G.W., XVI, 60; S.E., XXIII.

CHAPTER 3

PROGRESS AND MISFORTUNE

¹ V., June 11, 1921.
² E.J., June 9, 1921.
³ Pf., July 29, 1921.
⁴ Fer., Oct. 13, 1921.
⁵ Pf., Feb. 4, 1921.
⁶ E.J., Aug. 18, 1921.
⁷ Fer., May 8, 1921.
⁸ "Postscript to my Paper on the Moses of Michelangelo," G.W., XIV, 321-22; S.E., XIII, 237-38.
⁹ E.J., Aug. 18, 1921.
¹⁰ Eit., Aug. 29, 1921.
¹¹ Eit., Sept. 5, 1921.
¹² L., Feb. 1, 1921; V., April 1, 1921.
¹³ E.J., March 18, 1921.
¹⁴ E.J., Sept. 5, 1921.
¹⁵ Communication from Professor Hans Kelsen.
¹⁶ Eit., July 31, 1921.
¹⁷ Fer., Aug. 18, 1921.
¹⁸ "Psychoanalysis and Telepathy," G.W., XVII, 27-44; S.E., XVIII. 177-93.

¹⁹ G.W., XIII, 165; S.E., XVIII, 197-220; I., VIII (1920), 1-22.
²⁰ "Some Neurotic Mechanisms in Jealousy, Paranoia and Homosexuality," G.W., XIII, 195; S.E., XVIII, 223-32.
²¹ E.J., Jan. 28, 1921.
²² E.J., Oct. 2, 1921.
²³ Fer., Nov. 6, 1921.
²⁴ Letter to Freud from Pf., Oct. 24, 1921.
²⁵ Letter to Ludwig Binswanger, Nov. 3, 1921.
²⁶ L., Feb. 11, 1922.
²⁷ "The Madonna's Conception through the Ear," Essays in Applied Psycho-Analysis (London: International Psycho-Analytic Press, 1923).
²⁸ L., May 1, 1922.
²⁹ *E.J., March 23, 1922.
³⁰ Eit., March 21, 1922.
³¹ Fer., March 30, 1922.
³² Pf. April 6, 1922.
³³ *E.J., April 7, 1923.

34 Communicated by Dr. Herbert I. Kupper.

35 *Neue Rundschau*, LXVI, 1955.

36 *E.J.*, May 12, 1922.

37 *L.*, Jan. 11, 1922.

38 *L.*, Dec. 4, 1922.

39 *V.*, June 21, 1921.

40 *I.Z.*, VIII (1922), 234.

41 Edward Hitschmann, "Zehn Jahre Wiener Psychoanalytisches Ambulatorium," *I.Z.*, XVIII (1932), 265.

42 *Eit.*, June 27, 1922.

43 *Eit.*, Aug. 2, 1922.

44 *E.J.*, Aug. 24, 1922.

45 *G.W.*, XIII, 237-89; *S.E.*, XIX.

46 *Selected Papers on Psychoanalysis* (New York: Basic Books, 1953).

47 *Thalassa: Theory of Genitality* (Albany: The Psychoanalytic Quarterly, 1938).

48 *V.*, Nov. 15, 1922.

49 *Eit.*, Nov. 13, 1922.

50 *Pf.*, Dec. 25, 1922.

51 *Neue Freie Presse*, Sept. 20, 1923.

52 *G.W.*, XIII, 301-14; *S.E.*, XIX.

53 *Ab.*, March 30, 1922; *V.*, Aug. 1, 1922.

54 See *Vol. II*, 260.

55 Letter to Felix Deutsch, Aug. 8, 1923.

56 *Fer.*, June 20, 1923.

57 Communication from Robert Hollitscher.

58 *M.B.*, Nov. 2, 1925.

59 *Fer.*, July 18, 1923.

60 Letter to Ludwig Binswanger, Oct. 15, 1926.

61 *Fer.*, Aug. 6, 1924.

62 Letter to Joan Riviere, July 2, 1923.

63 *V.*, May 1, 1923.

64 *Eit.*, Sept. 26, 1923.

65 *Eit.*, Sept. 11, 1923.

66 *E.J.*, Sept. 26, 1923.

67 Letter from Abraham to Felix Deutsch, Jan. 18, 1925.

68 *V.*, Feb. 28, 1923.

69 *V.*, March 18, 1923.

70 *Le Temps*, Aug. 14, 1923.

71 *V.*, Feb. 1, 1923.

72 *V.*, March 15, 1923.

73 *V.*, Feb. 28, 1923.

74 *Fer.*, April 17, 1923.

75 *L.*, June 15, 1923.

76 *Fer.*, Aug. 6, 1925.

77 Letter to Freud from *E.J.*, May 1, 1923.

78 *Fer.*, July 21, 1922.

79 Letter to Freud from *Fer.*, April 15, 1923.

80 *G.W.*, XIII, 317-53; *C.P.*, IV, 436-72.

81 *Eit.*, Nov. 13, 1922.

82 *G.S.*, XI, 201-23; *G.W.*, XIII, 211; *S.E.*, XVIII, 235-59.

83 *G.W.*, XII, 309-12; *S.E.*, XVIII, 263-65.

84 *G.W.*, XIII, 357; *S.E.*, XIX.

85 *G.W.*, XIII, 293-98; *S.E.*, XIX.

86 *Ab.*, March 4, 1924.

87 *Eit.*, April 3, 1924.

88 *Ab.*, Jan. 4, 1924.

89 *Eit.*, March 22, 1924.

90 *Fer.*, Feb. 2, 1924.

91 *Ab.*, May 4, 1924.

92 *Fer.*, May 28, 1924.

93 *Fer.*, May 13, 1924.

94 *S.Z.*, May 11, 1924.

95 Communication from Yvette Guilbert's niece, Eva Rosenfeld.

96 Communicated by Rudolf von Urbanstchitsch.

97 *Ab.*, June 6, 1924.

98 *Ab.*, July 4, 1924.

99 *Fer.*, Sept. 13, 1924.

100 *Fer.*, May 28, 1924.

101 *Ab.*, June 4, 1924.

102 *Ab.*, Aug. 22, 1924.

103 Letter to Freud from *Ab.*, Oct. 15, 1924.

104 Letter to Freud from *E.J.*, Aug. 12, 1924.

[105] V., Feb. 15, 1925.

[106] E.J., Sept. 25, 1924.

[107] Letter to Freud from E.J., Aug. 12, 1924.

[108] *E.J., Oct. 23, 1924.

[109] V., Nov. 15, 1925.

[110] E.J., July 16, 1924.

[111] *E.J., Sept. 25, 1924.

[112] E.J., Nov. 16, 1924.

[113] Eit., Oct. 7, 1924.

[114] Ab., Nov. 23, 1924.

[115] V., Oct. 20, 1925.

[116] V., Dec. 15, 1924.

[117] Ab., Oct. 17, 1924.

[118] Fer., Oct. 12, 1924.

[119] G.W., XIII, 387-91; S.E., XIX.

[120] G.W., XIII, 363-68; S.E., XIX.

[121] Letter to Freud from Ab., May 25, 1924.

[122] G.W., XIII, 371-83; S.E., XIX.

[123] Fer., Jan. 21, 1924.

[124] G.W., XIII, 395-402; S.E., XIX.

[125] Fer., March 20, 1924.

[126] Letter to Freud from Fer., March 24, 1924.

[127] Fer., March 26, 1924.

[128] E.J., Oct. 23, 1924.

[129] G.S., XI, 183; S.E., XIX.

[130] Letter to Freud from Fer., July 15, 1924.

[131] Letter to Freud from Ab., Feb. 6, 1925.

[132] Ab., Feb. 11, 1925.

[133] Letter to Freud from Ab., April 5, 1925.

[134] Fer., Feb. 7, 1925.

[135] Ab., March 20, 1925.

[136] Ab., May 10, 1925.

[137] Letter to Freud from E.J., May 15, 1925.

[138] G.W., XIV, 33-96; S.E., XX.

[139] Letter to Freud from E.J., July 31, 1925.

[140] Letter to Prof. Levi-Bianchini, June 16, 1925.

[141] V., June 14, 1925.

[142] Ab., July 1, 1925.

[143] G.W., XIV, 562-63; S.E., XIX.

[144] Ab., July 9, 1925.

[145] Time, July 24, 1925.

[146] E.g. The New York Times, July 30, 1925.

[147] Eit., Aug. 7, 1925.

[148] Letter to Freud from Fer., Aug. 10, 1925.

[149] Fer., Aug. 14, 1925.

[150] G.W., IV, 187; S.E., VI.

[151] Eit., Sept. 30, 1925.

[152] G.W., XIV, 19-30; S.E., XIX.

[153] Letter to Freud from Fer., Sept. 16, 1925.

[154] F. Alexander: "Einige unkritische Gedanken zu Ferenczis Genitaltheorie," I.Z., XI (Oct., 1925), 444.

[155] Fer., Oct. 18, 1925.

[156] Eit., Nov. 1, 1925.

[157] Eit., Dec. 13, 1925.

[158] Fer., Dec. 1, 1925.

[159] Fer., Dec. 1, 1925.

[160] V., Jan. 13, 1925.

[161] V., April 16, 1925.

[162] Ab., April 5, 1925.

[163] Eit., Dec. 13, 1925.

[164] Dr. Freud, An Analysis and a Warning (New York: Hellman, Williams, 1947).

[165] V., Feb. 15, 1925.

[166] Letter to Freud from Ab., June 7, 1925.

[167] Ab., June 9, 1925.

[168] Ab., Aug. 10, 1925.

[169] Time, Oct. 27, 1925.

[170] Ab., Nov. 5, 1925.

[171] Letter to Freud from Ab., Oct. 19, 1925.

[172] V., Oct. 20, 1925.

[173] Fer., Dec. 1 and Dec. 12, 1925.

[174] E.J., Dec. 30, 1925.

[175] Letter to Freud from Ab., Feb. 26, 1925.

[176] Ab., Oct. 17, 1924.

[177] Eit., Oct. 13, 1924.

[178] Letter to Freud from E.J., Feb. 17, 1925.

179 Letter from Eugen Bleuler, Feb. 17, 1925.
180 *Fer.*, Aug. 6, 1924.
181 *G.W.*, XIV, 99-110; *S.E.*, XIX.
182 *G.W.*, XIV, 3-8; *S.E.*, XIX.
183 *Ab.*, Nov. 28, 1924.
184 *G.W.*, XIV, 11-15; *S.E.*, XIX.
185 *G.W.*, XIV, 113-205; *S.E.*, XX.
186 *Ab.*, July 21, 1925.
187 Letter to Freud from *Fer.*, Aug. 10, 1925.

CHAPTER 4

FAME AND SUFFERING

1 Letter to Freud from *E.J.*, Jan. 18, 1926.
2 Letter to Rado, Jan. 28, 1926.
3 Letter to Freud from *E.J.*, Feb. 25, 1926.
4 Letter to Felix Deutsch, March 17, 1926.
5 *Fer.*, Feb. 24, 1926.
6 Letter to Freud from *Fer.*, Feb. 26, 1926.
7 *Fer.*, Feb. 27, 1926.
8 *E.J.*, March 7, 1926.
9 *M.B.*, April 7, 1926.
10 *Eit.*, March 19, 1926.
11 Marie Bonaparte, *Cinq Cahiers* (Privately printed, 1939), p. 67.
12 *M.B.*, June 4, 1926.
13 *M.B.*, April 27, 1926.
14 *V.*, Feb. 18, 1926.
15 *Wiener Medizinische Wochenschrift*, No. 18, 1926.
16 *M.B.*, May 10, 1926.
17 *Neue Freie Presse*, May 6, 1926.
18 *Op. cit.*
19 Communication from Sir Charles Webster.
20 *M.B.*, April 26, 1926.
21 *M.B.*, May 10, 1926.
22 Edward Hitschmann, "Sigmund Freud und seine Werke," *Mitteilungen von B'nai Brith*.
23 *Fer.*, March 3, 1926.
24 J. W. Drawbell, *Dorothy Thompson's English Journey* (London: Collins, 1942), p. 179. It is repeated in the same words in his *All Change Here* (London: Hutchinson, 1943), p. 92.
25 George Sylvester Viereck, *Glimpses of the Great* (London: Duckworth, 1930), pp. 28 ff.
26 *Eit.*, June 7, 1926.
27 *V.*, July 19, 1926.
28 *Eit.*, June 21, 1926.
29 *M.B.*, Aug. 18, 1926.
30 *V.*, Nov. 23, 1926.
31 *Fer.*, Sept. 19, 1926.
32 Letter to Max Marcuse, Sept. 26, 1926.
33 *Eit.*, Sept. 30, 1926.
34 *L.*, Jan. 18, 1926.
35 Letter to Freud from *E.J.*, July 30, 1926.
36 *E.J.*, Aug. 30, 1926.
37 *Fer.*, Oct. 23, 1926.
38 *Fer.*, Dec. 13, 1926.
39 *Loc. cit.*
40 *V.*, Nov. 23, 1926.
41 Letter to Ludwig Binswanger, Dec. 4, 1926.
42 *V.*, Jan. 15, 1927.
43 *Fer.*, Jan. 2, 1927.
44 *M.B.*, Jan. 11, 1927.
45 *G.W.*, XIV, 113-205; *S.E.*, XX.
46 *V.*, Feb. 18, 1926.
47 *G.W.*, XIV, 299; *S.E.*, XX.
48 *G.W.*, XIV, 306.
49 *M.B.*, June 26, 1926.
50 *G.W.*, XIV, 207; *S.E.*, XX.
51 *Fer.*, July 4, 1926.
52 *M.B.*, June 26, 1926.
53 *Fer.*, July 29, 1926.
54 *Eit.*, July 31, 1926.
55 (New York: W. W. Norton, 1935).

56 Letter to Freud from E.J., Feb. 21, 1927.

57 M.B., Jan. 19, 1927.

58 Letter to Freud from Fer., June 30, 1927.

59 Eit., June 30, 1927.

60 Fer., Aug. 2, 1927.

61 Letter to Freud from Fer., Oct. 2, 1927.

62 Fer., Oct. 25, 1927.

63 Eit., Aug. 26, 1927.

64 Fer., Aug. 22, 1927.

65 Letters to Freud from Fer., July 13 and 16, 1927.

66 Letter to Freud from E.J., July 18, 1927.

67 Letter to Freud from Fer., Jan. 14, 1926.

68 Eit., March 30, 1927.

69 Eit., April 1 and July 15, 1927.

70 Letter to Freud from Eit., July 15, 1927.

71 Fer., June 9, 1927.

72 Eit., March 22, 1927.

73 Eit., June 30, 1927.

74 Fer., Aug. 8, 1927.

75 M.B., Aug. 5, 1927.

76 M.B., Aug. 5, 1927.

77 Fer., Aug. 2, 1927.

78 I.J., VIII (1927), 339-87.

79 E.J., Oct. 9, 1927.

80 V., Nov. 20, 1927.

81 See Vol. II, 366.

82 Eit., June 30, 1927.

83 G.W., XIV, 321-22; S.E., XIII, 237.

84 G.W., XIV, 311-17; S.E., XXI.

85 Eit., Aug. 8, 1927.

86 M.B., Aug. 5, 1927.

87 Sexual Aberrations (New York: Liveright, 1952).

88 Fer., Aug. 8, 1927.

89 G.W., XIV, 383-89; S.E., XXI.

90 Eit., loc. cit.

91 Eit., Aug. 14, 1927.

92 G.W., XIV, 325-80; S.E., XXI.

93 H. L. Philp, Freud and Religious Belief (New York: Pitman, 1956); B. A. Farrell, "Psychological Theory and the Belief in God," I.J., XXXVI (1955), 187-204; Heinrich Racker, "On Freud's Position towards Religion," American Imago, XIII (1956), 97-121.

94 Letter to Freud from Eit., May 26, 1927.

95 Letter to Freud from Eit., Oct. 27, 1927.

96 Eit., Oct. 10, 1927.

97 Fer., Oct. 23, 1927.

98 E.J., Dec. 1, 1927.

99 M.B., Jan. 16, 1928.

100 Letter to Freud from Fer., Feb. 8, 1928.

101 M.B., loc. cit.

102 Eit., March 17 and April 8, 1928.

103 *E.J., Feb. 18, 1928.

104 Eit., April 1, 1928.

105 Eit., April 22, 1928.

106 E.J., May 3, 1928.

107 Gilbert Robin, "Freud en Personne," Nouvelles Littéraires, May 19, 1928.

108 Der Tag, June 10, 1928.

109 M.B., June 18, 1928.

110 Eit., Aug. 31, 1929.

111 M.B., March 19, 1928.

112 Fer., April 24, 1928.

113 E.J., July 1, 1928.

114 Fer., Nov. 17, 1928.

115 M.B., July 28, 1928.

116 Ernst Kris, Psychoanalytic Explorations in Art (New York: International Universities Press, 1952), Chap. VI.

117 G.W., XIV, 291; S.E., XXI.

118 G.W., XIV, 399; S.E., XXI.

119 Eit., Oct. 3 and 10, 1926.

120 Jolan Neufeld, Dostojewski, A Psycho-Analytical Sketch (Leipzig: Internationaler psychoanalytischer Verlag, 1923).

121 Eit., Jan. 27, 1929.

122 M.B., March 6, 1929.

⁵ See *Vol. I*, 164, 166, 175.
⁶ A.Z., March 21, 1938.
⁷ E.J., April 28, 1938.
⁸ Letter to Ernst Freud, May 12, 1938.
⁹ Communicated by F. R. Bienenfeld.
¹⁰ Communication from Robert A. Kann.
¹¹ See *Vol. II*, 14.
¹² M.B., June 8, 1938.
¹³ M.B., June 8, 1938.
¹⁴ *The Lancet*, June 11, 1938.
¹⁵ *British Medical Journal*, June 11, 1938, p. 1273.
¹⁶ Eit., June 6, 1938.
¹⁷ Communicated by Dr. Indra to Dr. Bienenfeld.
¹⁸ *Vol. I*, 178, 293 ff.
¹⁹ M.B., Oct. 4, 1938.
²⁰ M.B., Nov. 23, 1938.
²¹ Letters from Simmel, June 9, Sept. 28, 1938.
²² A.Z., June 28, 1938.
²³ Salvador Dali, *The Secret Life of Salvador Dali* (New York: Dial Press, 1942), pp. 24, 184.
²⁴ *Vol. I*, 169.
²⁵ A. Koestler, *The Invisible Writing* (New York: Macmillan, 1954), pp. 409-10. "Un Rencontre avec Freud," *Preuves*, IV (1954), 56.
²⁶ M.B., Oct. 10, 1938.
²⁷ Jacob Meitlis, "The Last Days of Sigmund Freud," *Jewish Frontier*, XVIII (Sept., 1951), 20.
²⁸ M.B., Nov. 17, 1938.
²⁹ M.B., Jan. 29, 1939.
³⁰ M.B., Aug. 20, 1938.
³¹ G.W., XVII, 67; S.E., XXIII.
³² M.B., Sept. 4, 1938.
³³ G.W., XVII, 59; S.E., XXIII.
³⁴ "Ein Wort zum Antisemitismus," *Die Zukunft* (*Ein Neues Deutschland: Ein Neues Europa*), No. 7 (Nov. 25, 1938), 2.
³⁵ Koestler, *op. cit.*, p. 410.
³⁶ Eit., March 5, 1939.
³⁷ M.B., March 20, 1939.
³⁸ M.B., May 18, 1939.
³⁹ M.B., June 16, 1939.

CHAPTER 7

CLINICAL CONTRIBUTIONS

¹ G.W., XIII, 301-14; S.E., XIX.
² *Vol. II*, 240.
³ "The Subtleties of a Parapraxis," G.W., XVI, 37; S.E., XXII.
⁴ G.W., XVI, 57-99; S.E., XXIII.
⁵ G.W., XVI, 43-56; S.E., XXIII.
⁶ G.W., XIII, 195-207; S.E., XVIII, 223.
⁷ *Vol. II*, 268-73.
⁸ G.W., XIII, 387-91; S.E., XIX.
⁹ G.W., XIII, 363-68; S.E., XIX.
¹⁰ G.W., XIV, 99; S.E., XIX.
¹¹ G.W., XIV, 11-15; S.E., XIX.
¹² G.W., XIV, 113-205; S.E., XX.
¹³ Rank, *The Trauma of Birth* (New York: Robert Brunner, 1952).
¹⁴ C.P., IV, 201.
¹⁵ G.W., XI, 414; S.E., XVI.
¹⁶ *Origins*, p. 93; G.W., I, 338; S.E., III.
¹⁷ W. Stekel, *Nervose angstzustande und ihre behandlung* (Berlin: Urban and Schwarzenberg, 1908).
¹⁸ G.W., II/III, 406n; S.E., V, 400n.
¹⁹ "Contributions to the Psychology of Love," G.W., VIII, 65; S.E., XI.
²⁰ G.W., XI; S.E., XV, XVI.
²¹ G.W., XIII, 237-89; S.E., XIX.
²² G.W., XIV, 194 ff.; S.E., XX. See also G.W., VII, 350; S.E.,

X, 116 and Max Stern, "Anxiety, Trauma and Shock," *The Psychoanalytic Quarterly*, XX (1951), 179-203.

23 G.W., XIV, 180; S.E., XX.

24 G.W., XIV, 155; S.E., XX.

25 G.W., XIV, 120; 137-38.

26 G.W., XIV, 172; S.E., XX.

27 G.W., XV, 101; S.E., XXII.

28 See *Vol. II*, 328-31.

29 See a fruitful development of this theme by Thomas Szasz, "The Ego, The Body and Pain," *Journal of the American Psychoanalytic Association*, III (1955), 177, and "What is Pain?," *Archives of Neurology and Psychiatry*, LXXIV (1955), 174.

30 G.W., XV; S.E., XXII.

31 G.W., XVII, 67-138; S.E., XXIII.

32 *Vol. II*, 308-309.

33 *Vol. II*, 278-81.

34 G.W., XII, 305; S.E., XVIII, 266.

35 Max Marcuse, ed., *Handworter-buch der Sexualwissenschaft* (Bonn: Marcus and Weber, 1923). G.S., XI, 201-25; S.E., XVIII.

36 G.W., XIII, 293; S.E., XIX.

37 G.W., VIII, 452. S.E., XII.

38 G.W., XIII, 371; S.E., XIX.

39 G.W., X, 220; S.E., XIV.

40 G.W., VII, 135; S.E., IX.

41 G.W., XIII, 395; S.E., XIX.

42 G.W., XIV, 19-36; S.E., XIX.

43 G.W., XIV, 311-17; S.E., XXI.

44 "Leonardo da Vinci: A Psychosexual Study of Infantile Reminiscence," G.W., VIII, 128-211; S.E., XI.

45 G.W., XIV, 509; S.E., XXI.

46 G.W., XIV, 517; S.E., XXI.

47 Ernest Jones, *Papers on Psycho-Analysis*, 5th ed. (London: Baillière, Tindall and Cox, 1948), Chaps. XXV, XXVI, XXVII.

48 G.W., XV; S.E., XXII.

49 See *Vol. I*, 263-67.

50 Manes Sperber, *Preuves*, IV (Dec., 1954) 20.

CHAPTER 8

METAPSYCHOLOGY

1 *Origins*, p. 157n.

2 *Vol. II*, 185.

3 G.W., XIII, 3-69; S.E., XVIII, 1-64

4 G.W., X, 230-31; S.E., XIV.

5 G.W., XIII, 60; S.E., XVIII, 55-56.

6 G.W., XIII, 372-73; S.E., XIX.

7 L. S. Penrose, "Freud's Theory of Instinct and Other Psycho-Biological Theories," *I.J.*, XII (1931), 92.

8 *Vol. I*, 343.

9 G.W., I, 162; S.E., II, 105.

10 G.W., V, 144; S.E., VII, 242.

11 G.W., XIII, 34; S.E., XVIII, 33.

12 M. Dorer, *Historische Grundlagen der Psychoanalyse* (Leipzig: Meiner, 1932), p. 109.

13 H. Lichtenstein, "Zur Phänomenologie des Wiederholungszwangs und des Todestriebes," *I.*, XXI (1935), 466-80.

14 R. Brun, "Ueber Freuds Hypothese vom Todestrieb," *Psyche*, 1953, 81-111.

15 G.W., XVI, 93; S.E., XXIII.

16 G.W., XIII, 60, 278; S.E., XVIII, 56, XIX.

17 G.W., XIII, 42; S.E., XVIII, 40.

18 G.W., XIII, 69; S.E., XVIII, 63.

19 Johann Falk, *Goethe; Portrayed from Personal Intercourse* (1833), p. 76.

20 G.W., XV, 144-45; S.E., XXII.

21 G.W., XVI, 22; S.E., XXII.

22 W. Stekel, "Beitrage zur Traumdentung," *Jahrbuch der Psychoanalyse*, I, (1909), 489.

23 Paul Federn, *Ego Psychology and the Psychoses* (New York: Basic Books, 1952).

24 G.W., XIV, 469; S.E., XXI. See also G.W., XV, 110; S.E., XXII.

25 Sabina Spielrein, "Die Destruktion als Ursache des Werdens," *Jahrbuch der Psychoanalyse*, IV (1912), 89.

26 G.W., VIII, 136; S.E., XI.

27 G.W., V, 32; S.E., VII, 134.

28 Breuer and Freud, *Studien über Hysterie* (Vienna: Deuticke, 1895), p. 216.

29 See M. Nachmansohn, "Freuds Libidotheorie verglichen mit Eroslehre Platos," *I.Z.*, III (1915), 65-83, a paper Freud quoted (G.W., XIII, 99; S.E., XVIII, 91).

30 M., Aug. 28, 1883.

31 G.W., XVI, 92; S.E., XXIII.

32 Ernest Jones, "Psycho-Analysis and the Instincts," *British Journal of Psychology*, XXVI (1935), 272-88.

33 A sentence from G.W., XIV, 479; S.E., XXI.

34 G.W., XIV, 63.

35 F. Alexander, "Metapsychologische Betrachtungen," *I.Z.*, VI (1921), 270-85.

36 E. Schrödinger, *Science and Humanism* (Cambridge: Cambridge University Press, 1951).

37 S. Bernfeld and S. Feitelberg, "Der Entropiesatz und der Todestrieb," *I.*, XVII (1930), 137-206.

38 Op. cit.

39 R. Kapp, "Comments on Bernfeld and Feitelberg's The Principle of Entropy and the Death Instinct," *I.J.*, XII (1931), 82-86.

40 L. S. Penrose, *op. cit.*

41 R. Brun, *op. cit.*

42 Sacha Nacht, "Instinct de mort ou instinct de vie?" *Revue française de psychanalyse*, XX (1956), 405.

43 Edward Bibring, *I.J.*, XXII (1941), 118.

44 Ibid., "Zur Entwicklung und Problematik der Triebtheorie," *I.*, XXII (1935), 147-76; *J.*, XXII (1941), 102-31.

45 E.A.D.E. Carp, *Psychopathologische Opsporingen* (1951), p. 253.

46 E.g. Rudolf Eckstein, "A Biographical Comment on Freud's Dual Instinct Theory," *American Imago*, VI (1949), 213.

47 See especially Heinz Hartmann, "Ichpsychologie und Anpassungsprobleme," *I.Z.*, XXVI (1941), 175; and Hartmann, Kris and Loewenstein, "Some Comments on the Formation of Psychic Structure," *Psychoanalytic Study of the Child*, II (New York: International Universities Press, 1946).

48 G.W., XIII, 237-89; S.E., XIX.

49 G.W., XV; S.E., XXII.

50 See Vol. II, 313, 323-24.

51 Hugo Munsterberg, *Philosophie der Werte: Grundzüge einer Weltanschauung* (1908), p. 448.

52 G.W., XV, 64-65; S.E., XXII.

53 See Vol. I, 389.

54 F. Nietzsche, *The Genealogy of Morals* (1910), pp. 100-101.

55 Vol. II, 343.

56 G.W., VII, 135; S.E., IX.

[57] G.W., XV, 91; S.E., XXII.
[58] Ernest Jones, "The Origin and Structure of the Superego," I.J., VII (1926), 303-11.

[59] E.J., Nov. 20, 1926.
[60] G.W., XIII, 264, 278; S.E., XIX.
[61] G.W., XV, 73; S.E., XXII.

CHAPTER 9

LAY ANALYSIS

[1] Jg., Oct. 31, 1910.
[2] G.W., XIV, 288; S.E., XX.
[3] G.W., XIV, 274.
[4] G.W., IV, 220-21; S.E., VI.
[5] Fer., Jan. 21, 1920.
[6] Letter to Freud from Fer., Sept. 16, 1925.
[7] G.W., XIV, 209 ff.; S.E., XX.
[8] Fer., July 6, 1926.
[9] Eit., July 19, 1926.
[10] Letter to Freud from E.J., Sept. 23, 1926.
[11] E.J., Sept. 27, 1926.
[12] Letter to Freud from Fer., Sept. 17, 1926.
[13] I.J., VIII (1927), 174 ff.
[14] Eit., March 22, 1927.
[15] Eit., May 31, 1927.
[16] Eit., June 30, 1927.

[17] E.J., Sept. 23, 1927.
[18] Fer., July 16, 1927.
[19] Geoffrey Gorer, The American People: A Study in National Character (New York: W. W. Norton, 1948).
[20] Fer., April 22, 1928.
[21] Fer., May 13, 1928.
[22] Eit., April 3, 1928.
[23] Eit., March 27, 1929.
[24] Fer., April 27, 1929.
[25] Fer., May 11, 1929.
[26] Letter to Freud from Eit., Aug. 28, 1929.
[27] Letter to Freud from Frankwood Williams, Dec. 3, 1929.
[28] Letter to Freud from E.J., Oct. 14, 1929.
[29] I.J., XIV (1933), 157.

CHAPTER 10

BIOLOGY

[1] G.W., VIII, 407-11; S.E., XIII, 179-82.
[2] See Vol. I, 46-47.
[3] See Vol. I, 48 ff.
[4] See Vol. I, 52-54.
[5] R. Brun, "Biologie, Psychologie und Psychoanalyse," Wiener Zeitschrift für Nervenheilkunde und deren Grenzgebiete, IX (1954), 344.
[6] Idem., Biologische Parallelen zu Freuds Trieblehre (Leipzig: Internationaler Psychoanalytischer Verlag, 1926).
[7] See Vol. II, 316-20.

[8] G.W., V, 67; S.E., VII, 168.
[9] C. S. Sherrington, The Integrative Action of the Nervous System (1906), p. 230.
[10] R. Brun, Biologische Parallelen zu Freuds Trieblehre.
[11] E.g., R. Brun, op. cit.
[12] D. Brunswick, "A Revision of the Classification of Instincts or Drives," I.J., XXXV (1954), 224.
[13] G.W., XIII, 271-73; S.E., XIX
[14] G.W., XIII, 43; S.E., XVIII 42.
[15] G.W., XIII; S.E., XVIII.

16 Vol. II, 291-92.
17 Minutes, Nov. 8, 1911.
18 Minutes, March 17, 1915.
19 G.W., VIII, 319-20; S.E., XII.
20 G.W., XI, 368; S.E., XVI.
21 Edward Glover, Freud or Jung (London: Allen and Unwin, 1950).
22 G.W., XVI, 206; S.E., XXIII.
23 G.W., XIV, 109; S.E., XIX.
24 G.W., XIII, 61; S.E., XVIII, 56.
25 Origins, p. 365.
26 G.W., I, 147, 251; S.E., II, 91, 181.
27 Julian Huxley, Evolution in Action (New York: Harper, 1953) p. 40.

28 Anf., Manuscript B, Feb. 8, 1893, p. 81.
29 G.W., XVI, 200-201, 207 ff.; S.E., XXIII.
30 Fer., Dec. 22, 1916.
31 Fer., Jan. 1, 1917.
32 Fer., Jan. 4, 12, 1917.
33 Fer., Jan. 25, 1917.
34 Fer., March 2, 1917.
35 Fer., May 29, 1917.
36 Ab., Oct. 5, 1917.
37 Ab., Nov. 11, 1917.
38 G.W., XVI, 207; S.E., XXIII.
39 See Vol. II, 266.
40 W. P. D. Wightman, The Growth of Scientific Ideas (New Haven: Yale University Press, 1951), p. 94.

CHAPTER 11

ANTHROPOLOGY

1 Origins, p. 275.
2 G.W., X, 205; S.E., XIII, 241.
3 Vol. I, 330-31.
4 Suzanne Bernfeld, "Freud and Archaeology," The American Imago, VIII (June, 1951), 107.
5 G.W., V, 169; S.E., VII, 12.
6 G.W., V, 222; S.E., VII, 61.
7 Origins, p. 223.
8 G.W., IV, 56; S.E., VI.
9 G.W., VII, 228; S.E., IX.
10 "Leonardo da Vinci: A Psychosexual Study of Infantile Reminiscence," G.W., VIII, 151-52; S.E., XI.
11 G.W., VIII, 414-16; S.E., XIII, 184-87.
12 G.W., VII, 400; S.E., X, 176.
13 G.W., X, 24; S.E., XII.
14 G.W., VII, 222; S.E., IX.
15 G.W., V, 144; S.E., VII, 242.
16 Vol. II, 350-60.
17 See, for example, A. L. Kroeber, The Nature of Culture (Chicago: University of Chicago Press, 1952) p. 307.

18 Origins, p. 209-10.
19 Origins, p. 221.
20 Vol. II, 355-57.
21 S.E., XVIII, 122n, 128n.
22 G.W., XII, 159; S.E., XI.
23 Vol. II, 300-301.
24 Origins, pp. 186, 231.
25 G.W., VII, 462; S.E., X, 247-48.
26 G.W., VIII, 90-91; S.E., XI.
27 G.W., XIV, 459n; S.E., XXI.
28 G.W., XIV, 466n.
29 G.W., XIV, 449; S.E., XXI.
30 "The Acquisition and Control of Fire," G.W., XVI, 3-9; S.E., XXII.
31 G.W., VIII, 319-20; S.E., XII.
32 Vol. II, 216-17.
33 G.W., VIII, 413. S.E., XIII, 184.
34 G.W., XI, 368; S.E., XVI.
35 G.W., XII, 155, 208; XVI, 190; S.E., XVII, 119, 188.
36 G.W., XVI, 138; S.E., XXIII.
37 G.W., XVI, 86, 204-206; S.E., XXIII.

[38] G.W., XIV, 275; S.E., XX.

[39] W. Robertson Smith, *The Religion of the Semites* (New York: Meridian Books, 1956).

[40] G.W., IX, 188; S.E., XIII, 156.

[41] G.W., XII, 328; XIV, 186-87; S.E., XVII, 261; XX.

[42] *Fer.*, July 12, 1915.

[43] Letter to Freud from *Fer.*, July 15, 1915.

[44] Ernest Jones, *Essays in Applied Psycho-Analysis* (London: Hogarth, 1951), Vol. II, Chap. IV.

[45] *Man* (Jan., March and Dec., 1925).

[46] Georg Wunderle, "Ueber Wesen und Aufgabe der psychologischer Forschung unter den Primitiven," *F. W. Schmidt Festschrift* (1928), p. 770.

[47] Otto Weinrich, *Archiv für Religionswissenschaft*, XXVIII (1930), 344.

[48] George Vetter, "The Incest Taboos," *Journal of Abnormal Psychology*, XXIII (1928), 236-37.

[49] Paul Radin, "History of Ethnological Theories," *American Anthropologist*, XXXI (1929), 24.

[50] Edward Westermarck, *Three Essays on Sex and Marriage* (New York: Macmillan, 1934); *The Future of Marriage in Western Civilization* (New York: Macmillan, 1936); "Methods in Social Anthropology," *Proceedings of the Royal Anthropological Institute*, LXVI (1936), 234-35.

[51] A. L. Kroeber, "Totem and Taboo: An Ethnologic Psychoanalysis," *American Anthropologist*, XXII (Jan., 1920), 48-55.

[52] *Ibid.*, "Totem and Taboo in Retrospect," *American Journal of Sociology*, XLV (Nov., 1939), 446-51.

[53] Wilhelm Schmidt, "Ursprung und Arten der Exogamie und die Heiratsverbote," *Semaine Internat. d'Ethnologie Réligieuse* (Sept., 1929), 327-43.

[54] Alexander Goldenweiser: *History, Psychology and Culture* (New York: Alfred A. Knopf, 1933), p. 430.

[55] *Idem.*, *Anthropology* (New York: Alfred A. Knopf, 1937), p. 303n.

[56] Robert H. Lowie, *Primitive Society* (New York: Liveright, 1947).

[57] Franz Steiner, *Taboo* (New York: Philosophical Library, 1956).

[58] Among his many books may be mentioned *Psychoanalysis and Anthropology* (New York: International Universities Press, 1950).

[59] Margaret Mead, "Some Relationships between Social Anthropology and Psychiatry," in Franz Alexander (ed.), *Dynamic Psychiatry* (Chicago: University of Chicago Press, 1952).

[60] Clyde Kluckhohn, "The Influence of Psychiatry on Anthropology in America during the past One Hundred Years," Gregory Zilboorg and J. K. Hall (eds.), *One Hundred Years of American Psychiatry* (New York: Columbia University Press, 1944).

[61] *E.J.*, Dec. 5, 1955.

[62] F. D. Klingender, "Palaeolithic Religion and the Principle of Social Evolution," *British Journal of Sociology*, V (June, 1954), 138.

[63] Carleton Coon, *The Story of Man* (New York: Alfred A. Knopf, 1955), pp. 64-66.

CHAPTER 12

SOCIOLOGY

[1] G.W., XIV, 472n.; S.E., XXI.

[2] Vol. I, 190-91, 197.

[3] Anf., p. 223.

[4] See Letters to Pfister, Vol. II, 448 (March 17, 1910); 457 (Oct. 9, 1918).

[5] Vol. II, 98.

[6] G.W., XIV, 86; S.E., XX.

[7] G.W., XIV, 32; S.E., XX.

[8] G.W., 176; S.E., VII, 18.

[9] Vol. II, 292-94.

[10] G.W., VIII, 91; S.E., XI.

[11] G.W., XVI, 26; S.E., XXII.

[12] G.W., X, 169; S.E., XIV.

[13] G.W., VIII, 109; S.E., XI.

[14] G.W., XIII, 44; S.E., XVIII, 41.

[15] G.W., XIV, 421-506; S.E., XXI.

[16] G.W., XV, 194; S.E., XXIII.

[17] G.W., XIV, 455; S.E., XXI.

[18] G.W., XIV, 465; S.E., XXI.

[19] G.W., XIV, 471; S.E., XXI.

[20] G.W., XIV, 481; S.E., XXI.

[21] G.W., XIV, 493-94; S.E., XXI.

[22] American Journal of Sociology, XXVI (1920), 354, 519. A fuller account is given by E. W. Burgess: "The Influence of Sigmund Freud upon Sociology in the United States," American Journal of Sociology XLV (1939), 341-55

[23] W.H.R. Rivers, Psychology and Ethnology (New York: Harcourt Brace, 1926), p. 19.

[24] Roger Money-Kyrle, Psycho-Analysis and Politics (London: G. Duckworth, 1951).

[25] G.W., XIV, 503; S.E., XXI.

[26] G.W., XIV.

[27] Joan Riviere, Lancet, Sept. 20, 1939, p. 766.

[28] Published in Hungary. Personal Communication from Imre Hermann.

[29] Quoted in Reuben Osborn (pseudonym for Reuben Osbert), Friedrich Engels: The Origin of the Family: Private Property and the State (London: Victor Gollancz, 1940), p. 6.

[30] Francis H. Bartlett, Sigmund Freud: A Marxian Essay (London: Victor Gollancz, 1938).

[31] Max Eastman, Marxism: Is it Science? (New York: W. W. Norton, 1941).

[32] Ludwig Jekels, "Psychoanalysis and Dialectic," Psychoanalytic Review, XXVIII (1941), 228-53.

[33] Jurinetz: "Psychoanalyse und Marxismus," Unter dem Banner des Marxismus, I (1929), 93.

[34] K. N. Kornilov, "Psychology in the Light of Dialectical Materialism," in Carl Murchison (ed.), Psychologies of 1930 (Worcester: Clark University Press, 1930), pp. 243-78.

[35] Paul Krische, Marx und Freud: Neue Wege in der Weltanschauung und Ethik des Freidenkers (1922).

[36] Herbert Marcuse, Eros and Civilization (Boston: Beacon Press, 1955).

[37] R. Osborn, Freud and Marx (London: Victor Gollancz, 1937).

[38] H. B. Parkes, Marxism: An Autopsy (Boston: Houghton Mifflin, 1939).

[39] Wilhelm Reich, "Dialektischer

Materialismus und Psychoanalyse," *Unter dem Banner des Marxismus* (1929).

40 Sapir, "Freudismus, Soziologie, Psychologie," *Unter dem Banner des Marxismus* (1929-30).

41 Pater Schmidt, *Der Oedipus Komplex der Freudschen Psychoanalyse und die Ehegestaltung des Bolschevismus* (1929).

42 *Der Sozialistische Arzt*, II (1928) 2, 3. Abstracted in *I*, XIV (1928), 385.

43 Bertrand Russell, *The New Statesman and Nation*, March 15, 1937.

44 *G.W.*, XIV, 330-31; *S.E.*, XXI.

45 *G.W.*, XIV, 472-73; *S.E.*, XXI.

46 *G.W.*, XV, 191-97; *S.E.*, XXII.

47 *G.W.*, XVI, 154; *S.E.*, XXIII.

48 Letter to R. L. Worrall, Sept. 10, 1937.

49 *G.W.*, XVI, 267-87; *S.E.*, XXII.

50 *G.W.*, XIV, 504-505; *S.E.*, XXI.

51 Alex Comfort, *Authority and Delinquency in the Modern State* (London: Routledge and Kegan Paul, 1950).

52 *G.W.*, XVI, 24; *S.E.*, XXII.

53 E.g. *G.W.*, VII, 25, 27, 162; *S.E.*, IX.

54 Thomas Mann, *Essays of Three Decades* (New York: Alfred Knopf, 1947), p. 427.

55 *Idem.*, *Past Masters* (1933), p. 190.

56 Herbert Marcuse, *op. cit.*

57 *G.W.*, XIV, 475; *S.E.*, XXI.

CHAPTER 13

RELIGION

1 Communication from Judith Heller, née Bernays.

2 See Eva Rosenfeld, "Dream and Vision," *I.J.*, XXXVII (Jan., 1956), 97.

3 G. Barag, "The Question of Jewish Monotheism," *I.*, IV (1947), 8-25.

4 *Vol. II*, 440.

5 O. Pfister, "Die Entwicklung des Apostels Paulus," *I*, VI (1920), 243-90.

6 *Pf.*, May 9, 1920.

7 Sigmund Freud, *Zur Psychopathologie des Alltagslebens*, *G.W.*, IV, 287-88.

8 *Vol. II*, 339-40.

9 *Minutes*, Jan. 27, 1909.

10 *G.W.*, VIII, 195; *S.E.*, XI.

11 *Vol. II*, 350-60.

12 Ludwig Binswanger, *Erinnerungen an Sigmund Freud* (1956), p. 50.

13 Th. Reik, *Probleme der Religionspsychologie. Erster Teil: Das Ritual* (Leipzig: Internationaler Psychoanalytischer Verlag, 1919).

14 *G.W.*, XII, 328; *S.E.*, XVII, 262.

15 *G.W.*, XIII, 150-51; *S.E.*, XVIII, 134-35.

16 *G.W.*, XIII, 265; *S.E.*, XIX.

17 *G.W.*, XIII, 317-53; *S.E.*, XIX.

18 *Origins*, pp. 187-88.

19 *G.W.*, XIV, 353-54; *S.E.*, XXI.

20 *Fer.*, Jan. 1, 1910.

21 *Jg.*, Jan. 2, 1910.

22 *G.W.*, VIII, 195; *S.E.*, XI.

23 *G.W.*, XIV, 339; *S.E.*, XXI.

24 *G.W.*, VIII, 416; *S.E.*, XIII, 186.

25 *G.W.*, XIV, 378; *S.E.*, XXI.

26 *G.W.*, XIV, 380.

27 *G.W.*, XIV, 431; *S.E.*, XXI.

28 *G.W.*, XIV, 443.

29 G.W., XV, 181; S.E., XXII.

30 H. B. Acton, *The Illusion of the Epoch* (Toronto: Burns and MacEachern, 1955), pp. 120-22.

31 A. J. Storfer, "Einige Stimmen zu Sigm. Freuds' 'Zukunft einer Illusion,'" *I.*, XIV (1928), 377-82.

32 G.W., XVI, 240; S.E., XXIII.

33 T. W. Gervais, "Freud and the Culture-Psychologists," *British Journal of Psychology*, XLVI (Nov., 1955), 294 ff.

34 *Op. cit.*

35 F. V. White: *God and the Unconscious* (1952), p. 20.

36 R. S. Lee, *Freud and Christianity* (New York: A. A. Wyn, 1948).

37 *Idem.*, *Psychology and Worship* (London: Students Christian Movement Press, 1955), p. 12.

38 William Graham Cole, *Sex in Christianity and Psychoanalysis* (New York: Oxford University Press, 1955).

39 H. L. Philp, *Freud and Religious Belief*, (New York: Pitman, 1956).

40 G.W., XVI, 103-246; S.E., XXIII.

41 See G.W., VIII, 74-76; S.E., XI.

42 G.W., XVI, 154; S.E., XXIII.

43 G.W., XVI, 243.

44 G.W., XVI, 244.

45 G.W., XVI, 136, 138, 215.

46 G.W., XVI, 196.

47 G.W., XVI, 202.

48 G.W., XVI, 242.

49 Vol. II, 363-67.

50 Vol. II, 296-97.

51 A. A. Roback, *Psychorama: A Mental Outlook and Analysis* (Cambridge: Sci-Art, 1942), p. 141.

52 Trude Weiss Rosmarin, *The Hebrew Moses. An Answer to Sigmund Freud* (New York: Jewish Book Club, 1939).

53 *Op. cit.*, p. 37.

54 Abraham Shalom Yahuda, "Sigmund Freud on Moses and his Torah," *Aver V'Arav. Memorabilia and Impressions* (1946).

55 Salo W. Baron, *American Journal of Sociology* (1939), pp. 471-77.

56 Stephen S. Wise, *The Virginia Quarterly Review* (1939), pp. 623-66.

57 William Winwood Reade, *The Martyrdom of Man* (1872), p. 185.

58 Josephus Flavius, *The Antiquities of the Jews* (1803), Book II, Chap. IX, p. 56. *Biblical Antiquities*, Loeb edition (1935), pp. 279, 283, 293, 301.

59 Eusebius Pamphili, *Evangelicae praeparationis libri* (1857) IX, 432.

60 Max Weber, *Ancient Judaism* (Glencoe: Free Press, 1952), p. 122.

61 W. M. Flinders Petrie: *Religion and Conscience* (1898); *Researches in Sinai* (1906), p. 193; *Religious Life in Ancient Egypt* (1924), p. 95.

62 E.g. Max Weber, *op. cit.*, p. 92.

63 *Talmud, Sotah*, 12 A., p. 62.

46 Max Weber, *op. cit.*, p. 170.

65 Ernst Sellin: *Mose und seine Bedeutung fuer die israelitisch-juedische Religionsgeschichte* (1922).

66 Ernst Sellin, *Geschichte des israelitisch-jüdischen Volkes* (1935), pp. 76-78.

67 See, for instance, Meyer Abraham, "La Mort de Moïse," *Légendes juives aprocryphes sur la vie de Moïse* (1925). Louis

Ginzberg, *The Legends of the*   Rosenfeld, *Der Midrasch über*
Jews (1947), pp. 417-73. M.   *den Tod des Moses* (1899).

CHAPTER 14

OCCULTISM

[1] *Vol. II*, 427-34.
[2] G.W., XV, 34; S.E., XXII.
[3] J. K. Rinn, *Searchlight on Psychical Research* (London: Rider, 1954).
[4] G.W., XIV, 349-50; S.E., XXI.
[5] See *Vol. I*, 106-108.
[6] G.W., IV, 290; S.E., VI.
[7] G.W., XVII, 44; S.E., XVIII, 193.
[8] G.W., IV, 187; S.E., VI.
[9] G.W., IV, 185.
[10] G.W., IV, 188.
[11] *Fer.*, Aug. 14, 1925.
[12] *Vol. II*, 21.
[13] *Minutes*, March 4, 1908.
[14] G.W., VII, 99; S.E., IX.
[15] *Jg.*, April 16, 1909.
[16] G.W., I, 529-54; S.E., III.
[17] See *Vol. II*, correspondence with Ferenczi.
[18] *Fer.*, Oct. 6, 1909.
[19] Letter to Freud from *Fer.*, Nov. 20, 1909.
[20] Letter to Freud from *Fer.*, Aug. 17, 1910.
[21] *Fer.*, Aug. 20, 1910.
[22] *Fer.*, Nov. 15, 1910.
[23] G.W., XV, 46; S.E., XXII.
[24] Letter to Freud from *Fer.*, Nov. 22, 1910.
[25] *Fer.*, Dec. 3, 1910.
[26] G.W., XIII, 178; XV, 43; S.E., XVIII, 209; XXII.
[27] *Fer.*, May 14, 1911.
[28] *Fer.*, May 11, 1911.
[29] Letter to Freud from *Fer.*, May 13, 1911.
[30] *Jg.*, June 12, 1911.
[31] Letter to Freud from *Fer.*, June 5, 1912.

[32] *Fer.*, June 6, 1912.
[33] *Fer.*, July 20, 1912.
[34] *Fer.*, Oct. 17 and 20, 1912. Letter to Freud from *Fer.*, Oct. 21, 1912.
[35] *Fer.*, Nov. 23, 1913.
[36] *Fer.*, Nov. 27, 1913.
[37] *Fer.*, Nov. 25, 1914.
[38] *Vol. II*, 180.
[39] *Fer.*, July 21, 1915.
[40] Letter to Freud from *Fer.*, July 27, 1915.
[41] *Vol. II*, 180.
[42] *Fer.*, July 10, 1915.
[43] *Jg.*, April 16, 1909.
[44] Wilhelm Stekel, *Der Telepathische Traum* (1920).
[45] G.W., XIII, 168; S.E., XVIII, 199.
[46] *Eit.*, Feb. 4, 1921.
[47] *Eit.*, Nov. 13, 1922.
[48] Charles Richet, *Traité de Métapsychique* (1922).
[49] V., Aug. 1, 1921.
[50] George Lawton, *The Drama of Life after Death* (New York: Henry Holt, 1932), p. 562.
[51] G.W., XVII, 27-44; S.E., XVIII, 177-93.
[52] G.W., XIII, 165-91; S.E., XVIII, 197-220.
[53] V., Feb. 15, 1925.
[54] V., March 15, 1925.
[55] *Fer.*, March 20, 1925.
[56] G.S., III, 180 ff., especially 182, 183.
[57] L., Feb. 15, 1926.
[58] V., Feb. 18, 1926.
[59] Letter to Freud from E.J., Feb. 25, 1926.
[60] E.J., March 7, 1926.
[61] *Eit.*, Nov. 5, 1926.

⁶² Nandor Fodor, "The Poltergeist Psychoanalyzed," *The Psychiatric Quarterly*, April, 1948.

⁶³ See *Vol. II*, 27.

⁶⁴ G.W., XVII, 21-23; S.E., V. 623-25.

⁶⁵ G.W., IV, 291-92; S.E., VI.

⁶⁶ G.W., IV, 81-83.

⁶⁷ G.W., IV, 135-40.

⁶⁸ G.W., XII, 229-68; S.E., XVII, 219-56.

⁶⁹ *Fer.*, May 6, 1919.

⁷⁰ G.W., XVII, 27-44; S.E., XVIII, 177-93.

⁷¹ G.W., XV, 51; S.E., XXII.

⁷² G.W., XV, 46; S.E., XXII.

⁷³ G.S., III, 182-83; G.W., XV, 43-45; S.E., XXII.

⁷⁴ G.W., XV, 48-49; S.E., XXII.

⁷⁵ G.W., XIII, 173; S.E., XVIII, 204.

⁷⁶ G.W., XIII, 176-77; S.E., XVIII, 207.

⁷⁷ G.W., XIII, 190; S.E., XVIII, 219; G.W., XV, 39; S.E., XXII.

⁷⁸ G.W., XIII, 189; S.E., XVIII.

⁷⁹ G.S., III, 180; G.W., I, 569; S.E., XIX.

⁸⁰ G.W., XV, 32; S.E., XXII.

⁸¹ G.W., XV, 45.

⁸² See Helen Deutsch, "Okkulte Vorgänge während der Psychoanalyse," *I.*, XII (1926), 418, and "*Bulletin XVI*," Boston Society for Psychic Research, 1932, p. 87. George Devereux, *Psychoanalysis and the Occult* (New York: International Universities Press, 1953). Jan Ehrenewald, *New Dimensions of Deep Analysis* (London: Allen & Unwin, 1954). Nandor Fodor, *New Approaches to Dream Interpretation* (New York: Citadel, 1951), and "Through the Gate of Horn," *American Journal of Psychotherapy*, 1955, pp. 283-94. Emilio Servadio, "Sul meccanismo psichico delle allucinazioni telepatiche," *La Ricerca Psichica*, 1933, p. 577, and "Psychoanalyse und Telepathie," *I.*, XXI (1935), 489.

CHAPTER 15

ART

¹ G.W., XI, 390-91; S.E., XVI.

² Roger Fry, *The Artist and Psycho-Analysis* (London: Hogarth, 1924). Among the numerous writings on the present topic I would single out Hermann Hesse, "Künstler und Psychoanalyze," *Almanach der Psychoanalyse*, I (1926), 34-38, Richard Sterba, "The Problem of Art in Freud's Writings," *The Psychoanalytic Quarterly*, IX (1940), 256-68, Daniel E. Schneider, *The Psychoanalyst and the Artist* (New York: International Universities Press, 1954), and Louis Fraiberg,

"Freud's Writings on Art," *I.J.*, XXXVII (1956), 82-96.

³ Hanns Sachs, *The Creative Unconscious* (Cambridge: Sci-Art, 1950), pp. 57 ff.

⁴ W. R. Worringer, *Abstraction and Empathy* (New York: International Universities Press, 1953) p. 42.

⁵ Roger Fry, *Vision and Design* (1925), pp. 19, 21-22.

⁶ G.W., XIV, 90; S.E., XX.

⁷ Fry, *The Artist and Psycho-Analysis*, p. 9.

⁸ *E.J.*, Feb. 8, 1914.

⁹ Fry, *op. cit.*, p. 16.

10 Fry, *op. cit.*, p. 18.

11 G.W., V, 55*n.*; S.E., VII, 156 *n.* The note was added in 1915.

12 Fry. *op. cit.*

13 Fry, *Vision and Design*, p. 20.

14 Hanns Sachs, *op. cit.*, Part II.

15 Worringer, *op. cit.*, p. 45.

16 Victor Hehm, *Italien—Ansichten und Streiflichter* (1896).

17 *Anf.*, Aug. 18, 1897.

18 *M.*, Sept. 9, 1901.

19 *Jg.*, July 19, 1909.

20 G.W., X, 172-73; S.E., XIII, 211-12.

21 G.W., VIII, 128-211; S.E., XVII.

22 G.W., VIII, 209; S.E., XI.

23 G.W., VIII, 417; S.E., XIII, 187.

24 G.W., XIV, 91; S.E., XX.

25 G.W., XIV, 399; S.E., XXI.

26 G.W., XIV, 335; S.E., XXI.

CHAPTER 16

LITERATURE

1 Edmund Bergler, *The Writer and Psycho-Analysis* (New York: Doubleday, 1950). F. M. Cornford, "The Unconscious Element in Literature and Philosophy," Proceedings of the Classical Association, *I.J.*, IV (1922), 180. L. Edel, *The Psychological Novel* (1935). W. Empson, *The Seven Types of Ambiguity* (1931). Hermann Hesse, "Künstler und Psychoanalyse," *Almanach der Psychoanalyse*, (1926). M. Hodgart, "Psychology and Literary Criticism," *The Listener*, Sept. 11, 1952, p. 420. F. J. Hoffmann, *Freudianism and the Literary Mind* (Baton Rouge: Louisiana State University Press, 1945). R. Hoops, "Der Einfluss der Psychoanalyse auf die englische Literatur," *Anglitische Forschungen*, LXXXVIII (1934), reviewed by Kris. Ernst Kris, *Psychoanalytic Explorations in Art* (New York: International Universities Press, 1952) especially Chaps. X, XI. Ernst Kris, "Psychoanalysis and the Study of Creative Imagination," *Bulletin of the New York Academy of Medicine*, XXIX (April 1953), 334. Walter Lippmann, *Preface to Politics* (1913). Thomas Mann, *Freud, Goethe, Wagner* (New York: Alfred A. Knopf, 1937). Thomas Mann, *Freud und die Zukunft* (1936). W. Muschgg, *Psychoanalyse und Literaturwissenschaft* (1930). Herbert Read, "Psycho-Analysis and the Problem of Aesthetic Value," *I.J.*, XXXII (1951), 73. S. Selander, "The Influence of Psycho-Analysis in Modern Literature," *Dagens Nyheter*, Dec. 5 and 6, 1931 (abstracted in *Die Psychoanalytische Bewegung*, III). L. Trollope, "Freud and Literature," *Horizon*, 1947. Adalbert Wegeler, "Der Einfluss Freuds auf die Literatur," *Wort in der Zeit*, II (1950), 1-6.

2 *Vol. I*, 20.

3 *On Aphasia*, E. Stengel, Trans. (New York: International Universities Press, 1953).

4 *Vol. I*, 379 *ff.*

5 *Vol. II*, 310, 349.

6 G.W., I, 227; S.E., II, 160.

7 G.W., XIV, 495; S.E., XXI.

[8] G.W., VII, 33; S.E., IX.

[9] G.W., VII, 70; S.E., IX.

[10] Vol. I, 253.

[11] G.W., XIV, 399; S.E., XXI.

[12] G.W., VII, 213-23; S.E., IX.

[13] G.W., VIII, 230-38; S.E., XII.

[14] G.W., XI, 391; S.E., XVI.

[15] G.W., VII, 160; S.E., IX.

[16] G.W., VIII, 237; S.E., XII.

[17] G.W., XIV, 335; S.E., XXI.

[18] G.W., XIV, 90; S.E., XX.

[19] Notably those of May 5, 1909, Feb. 15, 1911 and Nov. 19, 1918.

[20] I.J., XXXII (1951), 319.

[21] Vom Lesen und von guten Büchern (1907). Freud's contribution was reprinted (with others) in the *Jahrbuch deutscher Bibliophilen und Literaturfreunde* (1931), 117.

[22] Origins, p. 279, and G.W., VII, 347; S.E., X, 113.

[23] Origins, pp. 256-57.

[24] Vol. II, 65.

[25] The Interpretation of Dreams, G.W., II/III, 271-72; S.E., IV, 264-66.

[26] Origins, p. 224.

[27] Die Traumdeutung (1900), p. 183. It was incorporated into the text in the fourth (1914) and subsequent editions.

[28] Ernest Jones, Hamlet and Oedipus (New York: Doubleday, 1954).

[29] Raynor Heppenstall and Michael Innes, *Three Tales of Hamlet* (Toronto: Longmans, 1950).

[30] S.E., VII, 303-10.

[31] Vol. II, 337-38.

[32] W. David Sievers, *Freud on Broadway. A History of Psychoanalysis and the American Drama* (New York: Hermitage House, 1955).

[33] G.W., IV, 227; S.E., VI.

[34] Adolf Deutsch, "Symptombandlungen auf der Bühne," I.Z., I (1913), 269.

[35] Vol. II, 340-43.

[36] Vol. II, 344-45.

[37] Vol. II, 361-62.

[38] Vol. II, 371-73.

[39] Vol. II, 374-75.

[40] Origins, p. 208.

[41] I.Z. V (1919), 308; S.E., XVII, 233n.

[42] G.W., XIV, 399-418; S.E., XXI.

[43] Theodor Reik, *Freud als Kulturkritiker* (Wien: Dr. Max Prager Verlag, 1930), pp. 46 ff.

[44] Op. cit., p. 63.

[45] Vol. I, 172-75.

[46] M., June 22, 1883.

[47] Thomas Looney, *Shakespeare Identified* (New York: Duell, Sloan & Pearce, 1920), Vol. II.

[48] E.J., March 11, 1928.

[49] E.J., May 3, 1928.

[50] G.W., XIV, 549; S.E., XXI.

[51] G. H. Rendall, *Shakespeare's Sonnets and Edward de Vere* (1930).

[52] Letter to Dr. Flatter, Sept. 20, 1932.

[53] G.W., XIV, 96; S.E., XX.

[54] G.W., XVII, 119; S.E., XXIII.

[55] Times Literary Supplement, Jan. 27, 1956.

[56] Eit., Nov. 13, 1922.

[57] Vol. I, 24.

CHAPTER 17

RETROSPECT

[1] Lawrence Friedman, "Psychoanalysis and the Foundation of Ethics," *The Journal of Philosophy*, Jan. 5, 1956, and nu-

merous papers in the *Journal of the Philosophy of Science.*

2 See Havelock Ellis, "Freud's Influence in the Changed Attitude towards Sex," *American Journal of Sociology;* XLV (Nov., 1939), 309.

APPENDIX A

1 Albert Mordell, *The Erotic Motive in Literature* (1919).

2 Henry Schnitzler, "Freud's Briefe au Arthur Schnitzler," *Die Neue Rundschau,* LXVI (1955).

3 "Das unbehagen in der Kultur," G.W., XIV, 419-506.

4 Thomas Mann, "Die Stellung Freuds in der Modernen Geistesgeschichte," reprinted in *Die Forderung des Tages: Reden und Aufsätze aus den Jahren* (Berlin: 1930).

5 Rudolf Fischer, *Quellen zu König Lear* (1914).

6 B. M. Ward, *The Seventeenth Earl of Oxford* (1928).

Index